海上交通与安全研究

郑中义 等著

大连海事大学出版社

ⓒ 郑中义 2019

图书在版编目(CIP)数据

海上交通与安全研究：英、汉／郑中义等著．—大连：大连海事大学出版社，2019.6
ISBN 978-7-5632-3806-4

Ⅰ.①海… Ⅱ.①郑… Ⅲ.①海上交通—交通运输安全—文集—英、汉 Ⅳ.①U698-53

中国版本图书馆 CIP 数据核字(2019)第 114980 号

大连海事大学出版社出版

地址：大连市凌海路1号　邮编：116026　电话：0411-84728394　传真：0411-84727996
http://www.dmupress.com　E-mail:cbs@dmupress.com

大连海大印刷有限公司印装　　　　大连海事大学出版社发行

2019 年 6 月第 1 版　　　　　　　　2019 年 6 月第 1 次印刷

幅面尺寸：184 mm×260 mm　　　　　印张：24.75

字数：571 千　　　　　　　　　　　印数：1~500 册

出版人：徐华东

责任编辑：张　华　　　　　　　　　责任校对：李继凯
封面设计：张爱妮　　　　　　　　　版式设计：张爱妮

ISBN 978-7-5632-3806-4　　　定价：75.00 元

前　言

　　本书共汇集了学术论文五十余篇,时间跨度大,反映了我们在海上交通与安全领域的学术研究的成果。其中的部分研究成果至今仍具有实际意义和一定的学术价值。

　　在自主驾驶船舶、自主航行船舶大力研发之际,本书出版了。作者认为,海上交通与安全必然是自主驾驶与自主航行船舶的核心内容之一。本书的出版发行或许能够对开发者们提供一些有益的帮助。

　　本书是自然资源部项目"北极航道开发与冰上丝绸之路建设研究"(CAMA201805)成果之一,也是交通运输部项目"北极通航战略规划研究"(2014-322-225-190)的成果之一。

　　为了本书的出版,曾仕豪、牟家奇、向琛、蒋成名、田序伟、屠强、张韬博、刘楷文做了大量工作,在此表示感谢。

作　者
2019 年 5 月

目 录

Vessel Trajectory Data Compression Based on Course Alteration Recognition …………… 1
A Measure of Similarity Between Trajectories of Vessels ……………………………… 11
A Cellular Automaton Model for Ship Traffic Flow in Waterways ……………………… 21
Marine Traffic Model Based on Cellular Automaton: Considering the Change of the Ship's
 Velocity Under the Influence of the Weather and Sea ………………………………… 38
基于 AIS 数据约束聚类的海上交通特征分析 ……………………………………………… 56
基于时空密度的船载 AIS 数据聚类分析方法研究 ………………………………………… 63
ISM 规则国内化 …………………………………………………………………………… 71
Study on the Domestication of ISM Code ………………………………………………… 77
中韩航线客货班轮公司 SMS 研究 ………………………………………………………… 83
基于正反馈修正 – 支持向量机的 PSC 选船模型 ………………………………………… 87
国际安全管理规则对海上安全影响分析 …………………………………………………… 93
ISM 规则 2010 年修正案实施有效性量化分析 …………………………………………… 97
国际海事规则制定中安全水平法的研究进展 ……………………………………………… 100
Uncertainty Analysis of the Estimated Risk in Formal Safety Assessment ……………… 105
A Practical Method for the Evaluation of Societal Risk in the Context of the International
 Maritime Organization's Safety Level Approach ……………………………………… 124
Uncertainty Analysis Method Based on Fuzzy Random Variables and Time Window
 Selection ………………………………………………………………………………… 138
Vessel Traffic Risk Assessment Based on Uncertainty Analysis in the Risk Matrix ……… 143
基于改进粒子群 – BP 神经网络算法的 PSC 选船模型 …………………………………… 157
港口国监控选船新模型研究 ………………………………………………………………… 163
基于突变机理的海上交通事故致因研究 …………………………………………………… 170
基于突变理论的海上交通安全系统演化 …………………………………………………… 176
Risk Mutability Analysis and Pre-control of Dynamical System ………………………… 182
船舶保安报警系统的设计 …………………………………………………………………… 188

基于熵与耗散理论的海上危险化学品运输系统 ················· 195
海上危化品运输系统安全管理博弈模型 ····················· 200
不确定条件下海上危化品运输安全演变机理 ·················· 208
港口船舶航行环境危险度的灰色评估数学模型 ················ 217
90年代海上交通定量研究成果的统计分析 ··················· 222
船舶安全配员研究 ··································· 226
受限航道中船舶的限速 ································ 232
大风浪船舶安全航行的研究综述 ·························· 239
Relation Between the Number of Observational Days and the Accuracy on the Estimation of
　　Marine Traffic Volume ··························· 244
大风浪中船舶安全性评估方法综述 ························ 250
安全管理体系运行有效性的评价 ·························· 256
大风浪中航行船舶风险体系分析 ·························· 262
恶劣天气条件下船舶开航安全性评估方法 ··················· 267
通航水域危险度评价模型 ······························ 272
Maritime Compulsory Salvage in China ···················· 280
干散货船在大风浪中的安全评价 ·························· 289
基于粗糙集的港口通航环境对航行安全的影响 ················ 295
我国海上战略通道数量及分布 ··························· 300
港口船舶事故致因的灰色关联分析模型 ····················· 307
船舶交通事故等级模糊划分的数学模型 ····················· 311
大风浪海损事故的灰色关联分析 ·························· 317
通航水域航行安全评价的研究 ··························· 323
港口交通事故与其环境要素关系研究 ······················ 329
港口交通事故与环境要素关系 ··························· 335
客滚船船龄与船舶事故关系研究 ·························· 341
海上搜救模拟中的可视化灾难再现模型研究 ·················· 346
浅议贝叶斯网络应用于海上交通事故致因分析的可行性 ·········· 350
船舶搁浅致因分析研究 ································ 356
参考文献 ··· 362

Vessel Trajectory Data Compression Based on Course Alteration Recognition*

Abstract: The vessel trajectory data from automatic identification system (AIS) is massive and contains much redundant information, which makes it difficult to use the data in research and applications. To solve the problem, a data compression algorithm for vessel trajectory was proposed based on vessel course alteration recognition. To recognize the vessel course alteration, the characteristics of trajectory during vessel course alteration were analyzed. It was found that the vessel course alteration on trajectory was similar to the corner on line, so the corner detection algorithm was referenced. Then the representative point of course alteration on trajectory was determined and kept. Other points on trajectories were deleted as redundant points, thus the data of vessel trajectory was compressed. In order to compare the performance of this algorithm with traditional compression algorithms, experiments were implemented base on actual trajectories of vessels from AIS. The results show that the data compression ratio of this algorithm is higher than traditional compression algorithms in vessel trajectory data compression. And this algorithm has a strong adaptability to different voyages of trajectories. The experiments demonstrate that the proposed algorithm is effective and promising for the study of maritime traffic based on AIS.

Keywords: Vessel trajectory; Data compression; Vessel course alteration recognition; Corner detection algorithm

0 INTRODUCTION

With the development of big data, knowledge mining and machine learning theory, it is research hotspot to use vessel trajectory data effectively for improving the safety and efficiency of maritime traffic [1-3]. Vessel trajectory, which is the route of a vessel and contains motion features, is the vital data source in maritime traffic study. With the improvement of maritime traffic monitoring systems, especially the automatic identification system (AIS), a large number of vessel trajectories are recorded. However, the information frequency of AIS is very high, so vast amounts of data and redundant information are produced, which makes the data from AIS is difficult to be used directly. Therefore it is necessary to compress the data of vessel trajectory from

---

* 本文发表在《Systems, Science and Technology》2016 年第 17 卷,作者齐乐、郑中义。

AIS. Moreover, in practical application, e. g., AIS data importing, analysis and display in electronic chart display and information system (ECDIS), the vessel trajectory data also needs to be compressed.

1 STATE OF THE ART

Trajectory is a kind of vector data. The traditional algorithms for vector data compression are choosing interval points algorithm, light bar algorithm, vertical distance algorithm, Douglas Peucker algorithm and offset angle algorithm[4,5]. Other algorithms mostly base on the five algorithms and are improved according to the practical application. At present, the study of vessel trajectory compression mainly concentrates on solving issues in practical application based on Douglas Peucker algorithm. However, Douglas Peucker algorithm and other traditional algorithms only consider the features of vector data, the vessel trajectory contains other features, e. g., steering, directly shipping etc., which can not be effectively dealt with by them. To solve the problem, a new trajectory data compression algorithm was proposed based on vessel course alteration recognition in this paper. By analyzing the characteristics of trajectory during vessel course alteration, it is found that corners on line are similar to the point on trajectory where vessel altered its course. So the course alteration recognition is achieved based on corner detection algorithm and characteristics of course alteration. Corner detection algorithm is widely used in computer vision[6-10], intelligent identification[11,12], retrieval, etc. Corner detection algorithm has many advantages, e. g., stronger adaptive performance, not affected by curve space scale, etc. [13-17] The algorithm suitable for image edge corner detection, object contour, etc. [18-23], but not suitable for course alteration recognition absolutely. So a improvement of corner algorithm is studied. Base on real vessel trajectory data from AIS, the new algorithm is compared with traditional compression algorithms through experiment. And the results show that the compression algorithm based on course alteration recognition has better performance.

The remainder of this paper is organized as follows. Section 3 describes the methodology of the data compression algorithm. Section 4 presents the experiments in which the performance of the algorithm is tested and compared with five traditional algorithms, and the results are analyzed and discussed. Conclusions are summarized in Section 5.

2 METHODOLOGY

(1) Vessel Course Alteration Extraction and Smooth

A vessel trajectory, trajectory A, in the Qiongzhou strait is shown in Figure 1. The coordinate of the i_{th} point of trajectory A is $(x_A(i), y_A(i))$. $x_A(i)$ is the longitude and $y_A(i)$ is the latitude. $i = 1, 2, \cdots, n$. Let θ_A stand for the course over ground of the vessel. $\theta_A(i)$ is the course from point $(x_A(i), y_A(i))$ to point $(x_A(i+1), y_A(i+1))$. Let the set $\theta_A = \{\theta_A(i) | 1, 2, \cdots, n-1\}$ stand for the course of the points on trajectory A. Let $\Delta\theta_A$ stand for the vessel course altera-

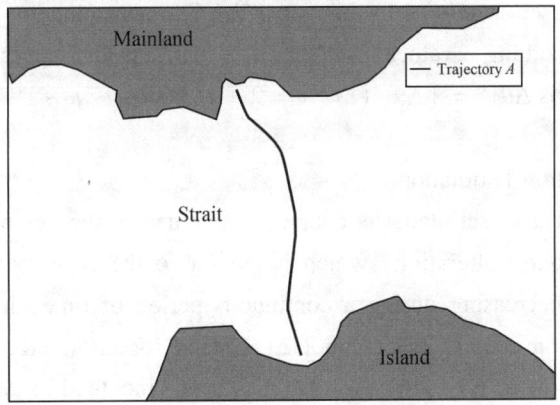

Figure 1　Trajectory A

tion. $\Delta\theta_A(i)$ is the course alteration from $\Delta\theta_A(i-1)$ to $\Delta\theta_A(i)$. If $\Delta\theta_A(i) > 0$, the vessel turned right on the point $(x_A(i), y_A(i))$. On the contrary, the vessel turned left on the point $(x_A(i+1), y_A(i+1))$. There is no course alteration information at the start and end points of trajectory. The course alteration of trajectory A can be expressed by the set $\Delta\theta_A = \{\Delta\theta_A(i) | i = 1, 2, \cdots, n-1\}$. The curve of course alteration, $\Delta\theta_A$, is shown in Figure 2.

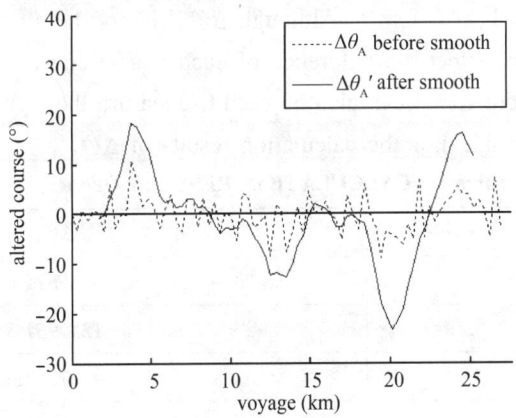

Figure 2　Curve smoothing of course alteration of trajectory A

In order to get the macroscopic changing of course alteration curve and remove local variation and noise which may be caused by equipment error, environmental influence, etc., $\Delta\theta_A$ should be smoothed before the next step. So the purpose of this step is to smooth the curve of $\Delta\theta_A$, Let symbol $\Delta\theta_A'$ stand for the smoothing result.

$$\Delta\theta_A'(i) = \Delta\theta_A(i) \otimes \varphi(i) \quad (1)$$

Where $\otimes$ stands for convolution and $\varphi(i)$ is a low passfilter function. There are many types of filters, like triangle filter, Hanning filter, Gauss filter, Butterworth filter, Chebyshev wave record, etc. According to the motion feature of vessels, the course alteration is a slow process. Therefore, the course alteration on each point is greatly influenced by the points which are near to it. But the points which are far away from the points have little influence to its course alteration. And the degree of the influence is declining along with the distance growing. The Gauss filter and triangle filter can be chosen as $\varphi(i)$. In this paper the Gaussian function is taken as an example. There are two main smoothing parameters in $\varphi(i)$, which are Gaussiansmoothing-scale $\sigma^{[24]}$ and $q^{[19,20]}$. And the result is $\Delta\theta_A' = \{\Delta\theta_A'(i) \mid i = 2+q, 3+q, \cdots, n-1-q\}$, as shown in Figure 2.

(2) Course Alteration Estimation

It is known that, if a vessel alters its course, the course of the vessel keeps on increasing or decreasing during the course alteration, which is similar to the corner on line. Therefore, if θ_A keeps on increasing or decreasing during a continuous period of time, it can be considered that there may be an alteration action. Let symbol $\Delta\Theta_A$ stand for the altered course of each action, which can be calculated from $\Delta\theta_A$. Because $\Delta\theta_A$ has been smoothed to get $\Delta\theta_A'$. Therefore, correspondingly, $\Delta\Theta_A'$ can be calculated from $\Delta\theta_A'$.

Let the set of $\Delta\theta_A'$ be divided into m subsets. If the values of two adjacent elements are of same sign, they should be assigned to a same subset. Each subset is a candidate of course alteration. Let the j_{th} subset be

$$\{\Delta\theta_A'(h), \Delta\theta_A'(h+1), \cdots, \Delta\theta_A'(h+k)\}, 2 \leq h \leq k \leq n-1-q$$

$$\Delta\Theta_A'(j) = \sum_{i=h}^{h+k} \Delta\theta_A'(i) \qquad (2)$$

$\Delta\Theta_A' = \{\Delta\Theta_A'(j) \mid j = 1, 2, \cdots, m\}$. Although $\Delta\Theta_A'$ is not the altered degree of each course alteration action, $\Delta\Theta_A'$ can reflect the deference of each course alteration, as $\Delta\theta_A'$ is the smoothing result of $\Delta\theta_A$. Therefore $\Delta\Theta_A'$ can also be used to measure the significance of altered degree of each course alteration. Table 1 is the calculation results of $\Delta\Theta_A'$.

Table 1 CALCULATION RESULTS OF $\Delta\Theta_A'$

j	$\Delta\Theta_A'$
1	$-0.8746°$
2	$124.9515°$
3	$-107.3235°$
4	$4.3802°$
5	$-164.5168°$
6	$90.4166°$

To determine the course alteration from the candidates, a threshold of $\Delta\Theta_A'$ is needed[25]. This threshold is used to remove the weak and insignificant course alteration from candidates. Let $\Delta\Theta_{A,threshold}'$ stand for the threshold. If $|\Delta\Theta_A'| > \Delta\Theta_{A,threshold}'$, there is a point where vessel altered course in the subset $\{(x_A(i), y_A(i)) \mid i = h, h+1, \cdots, h+k\}$. If the course alteration is too small, this subset is a straight line.

$$\pm \Delta\Theta_{A,threshold}' = mean(|\Delta\Theta_A'|) \pm K \cdot std(|\Delta\Theta_A'|), K \geq 0 \qquad (3)$$

Where $mean(|\Delta\Theta_A'|)$ is the mean of all elements of set $|\Delta\Theta_A'|$, $std(|\Delta\Theta_A'|)$ is the deviation of all elements of set $|\Theta_A|$, K is adjusting coefficient. The larger the value of K is, the less the number of course alteration is. The smaller the value of K is, the more the number of course alteration is. $K=0$, $\Delta\Theta_{A,threshold}' = 82.0772$. $j=2$, $j=3$, $j=5$ and $j=6$ are the four subsets which correspond four vessel course alterations.

(3) Course Alteration Point Determination and Data Compression

The purpose of this subsection is determining where the course alteration has taken place, which means determining the point on trajectory where vessel altered course. In corner detection algorithm, the determination of corner location is a difficult and import part. In different situation, the methods of the determination are always different. Similarly, the location of course alteration should be determined by considering the motion regularity of vessels, physical significance of the course alteration, the distribution characteristics of the coordinate points, etc. Therefore, an appropriate method is proposed in this subsection.

Because the course alteration on trajectory is a process, usually there are no less than a candidate points on trajectory for a course alteration. In order to compress the data volume, only one point is kept as the representative point of course alteration. All of the other points are deleted as the redundant points. Let the j_{th} subset be

$$\{(x_A(i), y_A(i)) \mid i = h, h+1, \cdots, h+k\} \quad |\Delta\Theta_A'(j)| > \Delta\Theta_{A,threshold}'$$

The method of locating the point where vessel altered course in this paper is to add $\Delta\theta_A'$ from $\Delta\theta_A'(h)$ to $\Delta\theta_A'(h+k)$ and choose i when the accumulative results is near to half of $\Delta\Theta_A'(j)$ as shown in Eq. (4).

$$I_j = \underset{h \leq i \leq h+k}{\operatorname{argmin}} \left[\left| \left| \sum_{l=h}^{i} \Delta\theta_A'(l) \right| - \frac{|\Delta\Theta_A'(j)|}{2} \right| \right] \quad (4)$$

Let (X_j, Y_j) be the course alteration point of j_{th} subset.

$$\begin{cases} X_j = x(I_j) \\ Y_j = y(I_j) \end{cases} \quad (5)$$

According to Eq. (4), the four course alteration points on trajectory A are recognized, as shown in Figure 3.

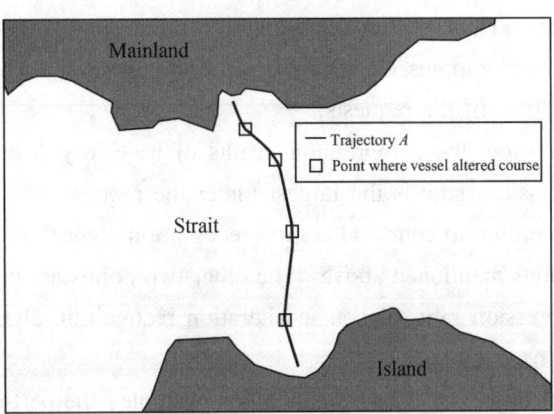

Figure 3 The points where vessel altered course on trajectory A

The origin and destination on trajectory A are known. With the four representative points a-

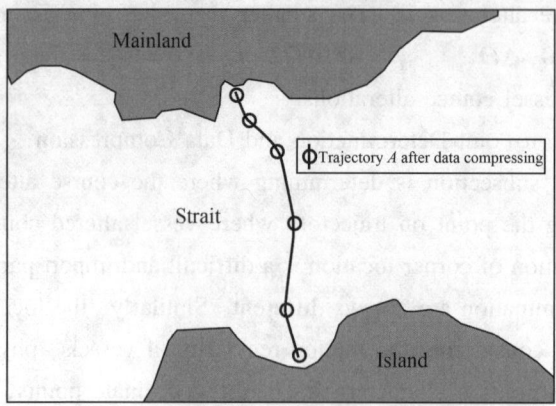

Figure 4   Trajectory A after data compressing

bove, the trajectory can be replaced by the six points and the lines which connect them one by one, as shown in Figure 4. All of the other points on trajectory A are deleted. Then, the data volume of trajectory A has been compressed.

3 RESULT ANALYSIS AND DISCUSSION

To compress the data volume, the characteristics of trajectory have been analyzed. First, the voyages of trajectories are always different. Therefore the algorithm must have a strong adaptation to deal with trajectories of different size. Secondly, the course of a vessel could alter a lot in a short local segment. Generally this is caused by the collision avoidance. This phenomenon is very important for the study of maritime traffic. Therefore the local points need to be kept after the data compression. Trajectory B is taken as example to test the algorithm proposed in this paper and five traditional algorithms, which are choosing interval points algorithm, light bar algorithm, vertical distance algorithm, Douglas Peucker algorithm and offset angle algorithm. As shown in Figure 5, seven segments in the trajectory corresponding seven course alterations. And the other parts of trajectory B are straight lines. Thus, seven representative points in the seven short local segments should be kept after the data compression according to each algorithm. The parameters in the algorithms need to be adjusted to fit the requests.

Figure 6 (a) ~ (f) show the compression results of trajectory B according to the six algorithms, when the compression radio is the largest under the requests above. Nine points are kept after the compression according to course alteration recognition algorithm. Seven of the nine points are the representative points mentioned above. The other two points are the start and end points. It is obvious that the compression ratio of course alteration recognition algorithm is higher than the other traditional algorithms.

By taking the vessel trajectory data from AIS for example, the performance of course alteration recognition algorithm and the traditional algorithms can be tested and compared. The number of raw trajectories is 1450, and the number of points on the trajectories is 622069. The samples and test results are shown in Table 2.

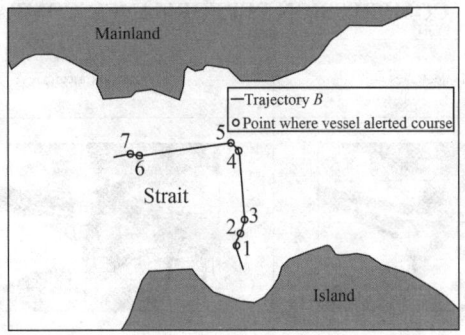

Figure 5　Trajectory *B*

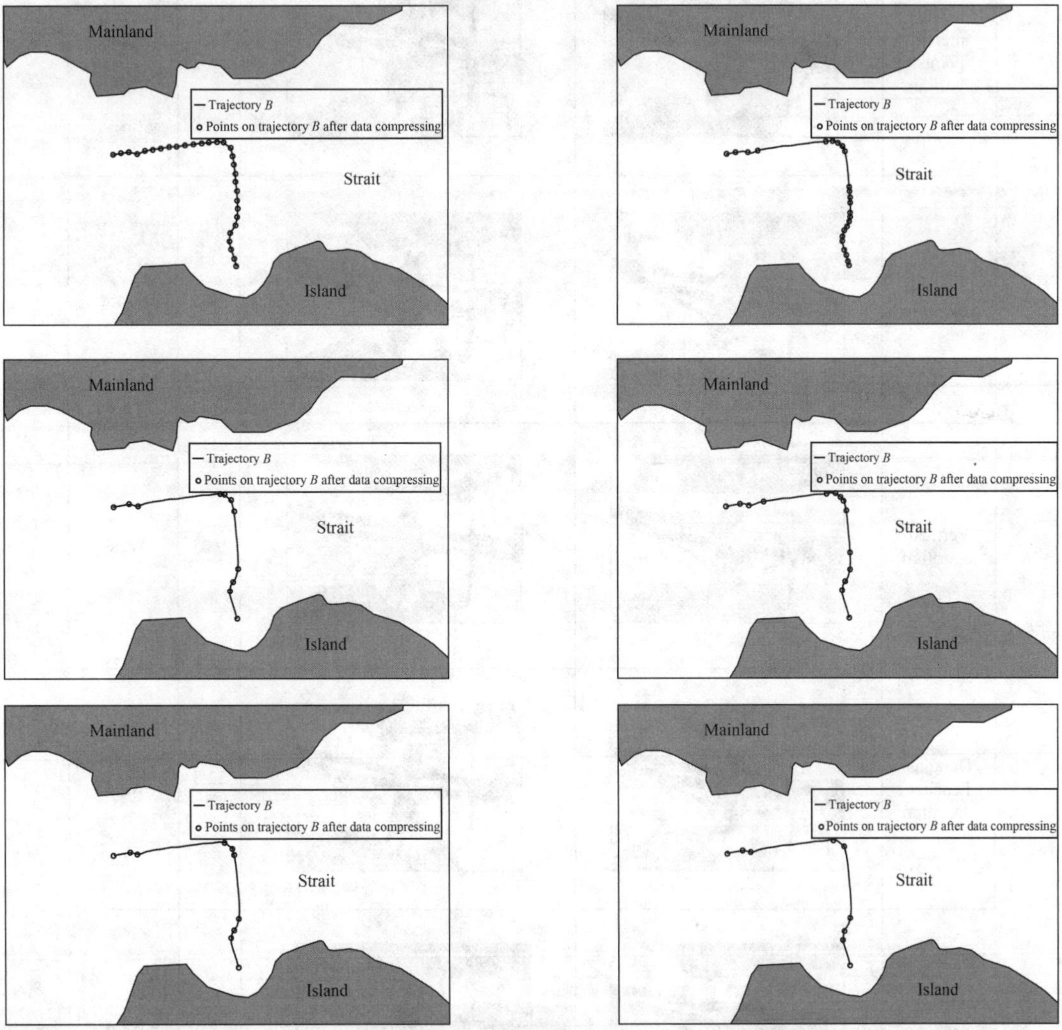

Figure 6　Compression results of trajectory *B* according to six algorithms

Table 2 COMPRESSION PERFORMANCE COMPARISON

Data compression algorithms	Trajectories	The points on trajectories	Compression ratio	Voyage changing adaptability
None (samples)			—	—
Choosing interval points algorithm			4.34	Strong
Light bar algorithm			3.93	Strong
Vertical algorithm			9.23	Weak
Douglas Peucker algorithm			12.35	Weak
Offset angle algorithm			20.53	Weak

The trajectories are the actual track lines of vessels, which are the fundamental information for the study of maritime traffic. Because the representative points must be kept as described above, the distortion of trajectories is very low after the compression according to each algorithm, as shown in Table 2. And it is hard to find the difference of performance between each algorithm by the trajectories maps. But the points on trajectories can reflect the difference of data volume and point distribution after compression. The compression ratio, voyage changing adaptability and computational complexity are compared and analyzed based on the experimental results.

Firstly, the six algorithms ordered by the compression ratio from high to low are course alteration recognition algorithm, offset angle algorithm, Douglas Peucker algorithm, vertical algorithm, choosing interval points algorithm, light bar algorithm. The light bar algorithm is sensitive to the local course alteration of curve. It is suitable for dealing with the vector curve, whose angular is obvious. But for the smooth vector curve, the compression ratio may be decreased. Therefore the light bar algorithm is not suitable for compressing the vessel trajectory. For the choosing interval points algorithm, the point which can be kept after the compression is irregular. Therefore, to make sure all of the points where vessels altered course are kept, the only way is to decrease the compression ratio. So the compression ratio of the choosing interval points algorithm is low too. The theories of vertical algorithm and Douglas Peucker algorithm are perfect and reasonable. The compression ratios are higher than the two algorithms above. The offset angle algorithm is sensitive to the course alteration of curve, which is similar to light bar algorithm. It is sensitive to the global changing. But vessel trajectory is a kind of smooth vector curve. Even so, this algorithm can compress the data better than other traditional algorithms. The course alteration recognition algorithm can track the process of course alteration. It is sensitive to both local and global course alteration of trajectory. This feature can decrease the points which must be kept. Therefore the ratio is increased. The compression ratio of the course alteration recognition algorithm is higher than the traditional algorithms.

Secondly, the vertical algorithm and Douglas Peucker algorithm are sensitive to distance. The compression ratio of them is related to the value of distance threshold. Thus, the two algorithms have weak adaptabilities to the voyage changing. But the other four algorithms, choosing interval points algorithm, light bar algorithm, offset angle algorithm and course alteration recognition algorithm are not sensitive to distance, so they have strong voyage changing adaptabilities.

Finally, the computational complexity of Douglas Peucker algorithm is higher than other five algorithms. The reason is that Douglas Peucker algorithm is a process of recursively calling disintegrating method, which leads to a high computational complexity. But the other five algorithms are implemented by traversing the data, so the computational complexities are low.

From above, the performance of course alteration recognition algorithm is better than the five traditional algorithms. It is suitable for compressing vessel trajectories. The points where vessels altered course can be kept with a high compression ratio and automatically adapt to the voyage changing. Besides, its computational complexity is low.

4　CONCLUSION

In this paper, a new data compression algorithm is proposed to compress the trajectory data of vessels. In this algorithm, the course alteration information was kept and the other information was deleted as redundancy. 1450 trajectories were taken as samples to test the performance of this algorithm and five traditional data compression algorithms. The test results were compared and analyzed. Although the compression ratio of course alteration recognition algorithm is 54.05, which is higher than the five traditional algorithms, the distortion of trajectories after compression is very low. Because the course alteration recognition algorithm is sensitive to both global and local course alteration of trajectory, it can adapt to different voyage of trajectory with high compression ratio. Besides, the course alteration recognition algorithm consumes little computational resource, for its low computational complexity. Therefore, this algorithm can delete redundant data of vessel trajectory from AIS efficiently, which can reduce the data storage spaces and computational resources to expand the availability of AIS data in the development of maritime intelligent traffic system. Further maritime traffic research based on this algorithm is required, e. g., microcosmic traffic flow, vessel domain, trajectory tracking, etc.

A Measure of Similarity Between Trajectories of Vessels*

Abstract: The measurement of similarity between trajectories of vessels is one of the kernel problems that must be addressed to promote the development of maritime intelligent traffic system (ITS). In this study, a new model of trajectory similarity measurement was established to improve the data processing efficiency in dynamic application and to reflect actual sailing behaviors of vessels. In this model, a feature point detection algorithm was proposed to extract feature points, reduce data storage space and save computational resources. A new synthesized distance algorithm was also created to measure the similarity between trajectories by using the extracted feature points. An experiment was conducted to measure the similarity between the real trajectories of vessels. The growth of these trajectories required measurements to be conducted under different voyages. The results show that the similarity measurement between the vessel trajectories is efficient and correct. Comparison of the synthesized distance with the sailing behaviors of vessels proves that results are consistent with actual situations. The experiment results demonstrate the promising application of the proposed model in studying vessel traffic and in supplying reliable data for the development of maritime ITS.

Keywords: Trajectories of vessels; Similarity measurement; Feature point; Synthesized distance

0 Introduction

Trajectory, which is the route of the movement of an object, contains significant spatial information that is necessary in studying the behaviors of vessels. With the development of information techniques, a growing amount of vessel movement information can be monitored, and voluminous records of historical trajectories can be stored[26]. Several new and efficient methods have been proposed to utilize big data in promoting the development of maritime intelligent traffic systems (ITS)[27-29]. Notably, similarity measurement between the trajectories of vessels is a fundamental issue that needs to be solved in these methods[1-3]. The raw trajectories of vessels usually include many redundant points, outliers, and other elements[30,31]. When the volume of trajectory data is large, similarity measurement requires the feature points to be extracted from trajectories[32-35]. Moreover, to study the traffic characteristics of vessels, the similarity measurement re-

---

* 本文发表在《Journal of Engineering Science and Technology Review》2016 年第 9 卷,作者齐乐、郑中义。

sult must be consistent with the actual motion of vessels[36-39]. The trajectory spatial distance describes the motion position information, and the trajectory shape shows the changes in the motion direction. Therefore, an efficient model is necessary to consider both factors to solve the aforementioned problem.

1 State of the Art

A trajectory can be mathematically expressed as a vector curve[11,14,15,20,40,41]. To detect feature points, one can use the characteristic point detection algorithms from the image compression and matching research fields. Several characteristic point detection algorithms have been proposed and widely used in computer vision[42-46], pattern recognition, intelligent identification[47], and retrieval[48]. Awrangjeb et al.[14] identified five main detection steps from these algorithms, namely, edge extraction and selection[49-51], smoothing[52-56], estimation, characteristic point detection, and coarse-to-fine characteristic point tracking. However, these algorithms cannot directly detect the feature points of trajectories because the calculated results must meet the requirements of the similarity measurement model that is proposed in this paper. Therefore, improvements are required.

Fu et al.[57] classified the algorithms for measuring vector curve similarity into two categories. First, global similarity measurement algorithms, such as Fourier descriptor algorithm[58], moment invariant algorithm[59], curvature scale space algorithm[60], shape context algorithm[61], curvature tree algorithm[62], normalized parametric polar transform algorithm[63], neural-network-based algorithm, and symbolic representation algorithm, can perform effectively in cases where the trajectories are complete. Second, part-to-part similarity measurement algorithms are applicable in cases where the trajectories have been transformed via rotation, translation, or scaling. These algorithms, which include Euclidean transform algorithms, similarity-invariant algorithms based on polyline approximation, energy function algorithm, and state-of-the-art algorithm[64], adopt the local curve features by identifying the corresponding sub-curves of the two curves. These algorithms can also be divided into 3D trajectory similarity measurement algorithm[65] and 2D trajectory similarity measurement algorithm depending on the objects under study.

However, the aforementioned methods do not simultaneously consider shape difference and spatialdistance, thereby preventing their measurement results from reflecting actual vessel sailing behaviors. However, some studies have synthesized these two factors. Trajectory data are generally enormous and dynamic in practical applications; thus, the static algorithm cannot solve such problems efficiently because a large amount of computational resources and huge storage space are required. Therefore, the feature-point detection algorithm was proposed to reduce the consumption of computational resources and storage space.

The rest of this paper is organized as follows. Section 3 describes the methodology of the similarity measurement model. Section 4 presents the experiments in which the performance of the model was tested, including their results, analysis, and discussion. Section 5 concludes the paper.

2 Methodology

The model includes two main steps. In the first step, the feature points are detected to denoise the trajectories of the raw vessels and extract the feature points. In the second step, the synthesized distance, shape difference, and spatial distance between trajectories are calculated. The similarity between trajectories is then determined by synthesizing the two calculated results.

The proposed model can significantly reduce the computing cost in dynamic applications by calculating only the increasing segment in each execution because the feature points and synthesized distance from the last execution are still valid.

2.1 Feature-point Detection

A trajectory comprises feature points and the lines that connect them. Feature points are not only very important parts of trajectories but are also vital factors in examining vessel sailing behaviors. By extracting feature points from a trajectory, the main feature information on the trajectory can be obtained and the data volume can be compressed.

The proposed feature-point detection algorithm utilizes the detection technology from the fields of image compression and matching. This algorithm removes the noise and local variation of a trajectory by filtering, smoothing, and judging the steering action via course alteration as well as by determining the corresponding feature point of each steering action. This algorithm is also relevant in dynamic applications because the extracted feature points can be reused when the trajectories are increased.

A in Figure 1 denotes the raw trajectory of a vessel. To alter a course macroscopically, curve smoothing must be performed to remove the local variation and noise that result from equipment failures and environmental influences. The course changing of the vessel, $\Delta\theta_A$, can then be achieved. To reflect vessel sailing behaviors, $\Delta\theta_A$ must be partitioned into several segments, with each segment being a candidate for course changing. $\Delta\theta_A'$ denotes the sum of altered courses in each segment. A threshold of $\Delta\theta_A'$ must be defined to obtain the strong and significant feature points of trajectory A, as well as to remove the weak and insignificant segments from the candidates. $\Delta\theta_{threshold\_A}$, which represents the threshold, is obtained from empirical results or calculated via the interval estimation method as follows:

$$\Delta\theta_{threshold\_A} = mean(\mid \Delta\theta_A' \mid) + std(\mid \Delta\theta_A' \mid) \quad (1)$$

where $mean(\mid \theta_A' \mid)$ denotes the mean of all elements in set θ_A' and $std(\mid \theta_A' \mid)$ denotes the standard deviation of all elements inset θ_A'. Figure 2 shows the curves of θ_A, θ_A', and $\pm \theta_{threshold\_A}$. The vessel has altered its course five times, and the five points of trajectory A can be determined. Using the origin and destination points, all feature points of trajectory A are extracted as shown in Figure 3.

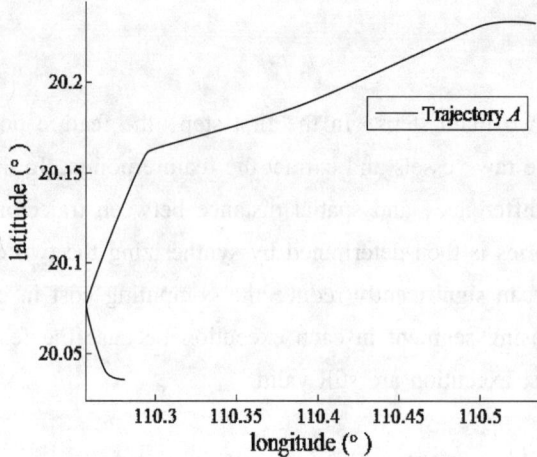

Figure 1　Trajectory A

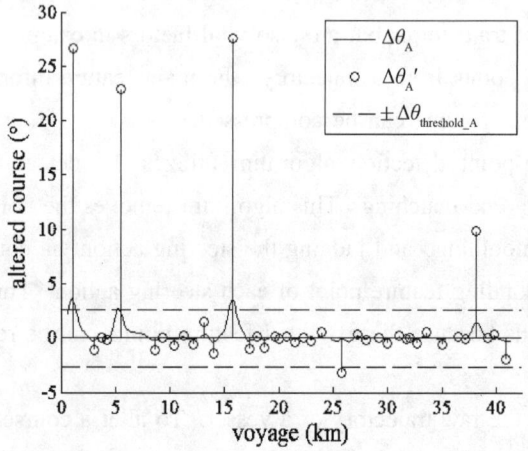

Figure 2　Curves of $\Delta\theta_A$, $\Delta\theta_A'$, and $\pm\Delta\theta_{threshold\_A}$

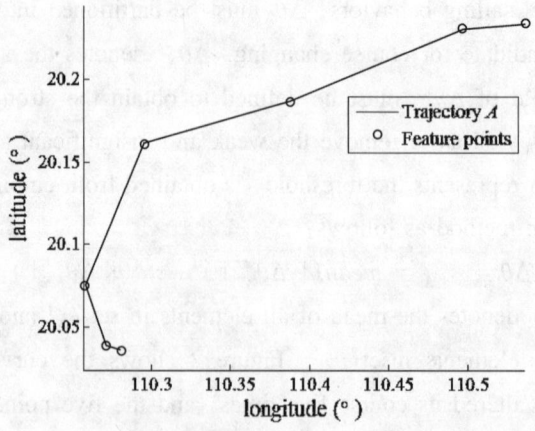

Figure 3　Feature points of trajectory A

2.2 Synthesized Distance Calculation

First, the shape difference must be quantized. In Figure 4, B denotes another trajectory that differs from trajectory A. Θ denotes the course when a vessel sails from one feature point to the next. (X_A, Y_A) denotes the feature points of trajectory A and can be computed as follows:

$$(X_A, Y_A) = \{(X_A(i), Y_A(i)) \mid i = 0, 1, \cdots, p+1\} \quad (2)$$

where $p+1$ denotes the number of feature points of trajectory A. The courses between the adjacent points in (X_A, Y_A) are computed as follows:

$$\Theta_A = \{\Theta_A(i) \mid i = 0, 1, \cdots, p\} \quad (3)$$

where $\Theta_A(i)$ denotes the course from $(X_A(i), Y_A(i))$ $(X_A(i+1), Y_A(i+1))$. (X_B, Y_B) denotes the feature points trajectory B and can be computed as follows:

$$(X_B, Y_B) = \{(X_B(i), Y_B(i)) \mid i = 0, 1, \cdots, p'+1\} \quad (4)$$

where $p'+1$ denotes the number of feature points of trajectory B.

$$\Theta_B = \{\Theta_B(i) \mid i = 0, 1, \cdots, p'\} \quad (5)$$

where $\Theta_B(i)$ denotes the course $(X_B(i+1), Y_B(i+1))$.

Let

$$s_A = \{s_A(i) \mid i = 0, 1, \cdots, p+1\} \quad (6)$$

where $s_A(i)$ denotes the voyage $(X_A(0), Y_A(0))$ to $(X_A(i), Y_A(i))$.

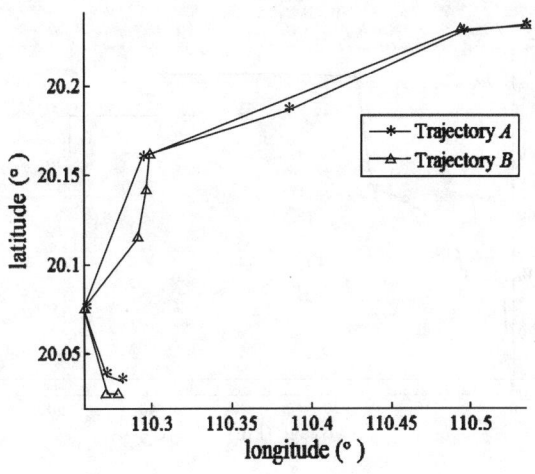

Figure 4 Trajectories A and B

Let

$$s_B = \{s_B(i) \mid i = 0, 1, \cdots, p'+1\} \quad (7)$$

where $s_B(i)$ denotes the voyage $(X_B(0), Y_B(0))$ to point $(X_B(i), Y_B(i))$.

$$i = f(s); \ if \ s(i) \leqslant s < s(i+1); i = 0, 1, \cdots \quad (8)$$

Let d represent the shape difference between trajectories. The shape difference between trajectories A and B can be calculated as follows [23]:

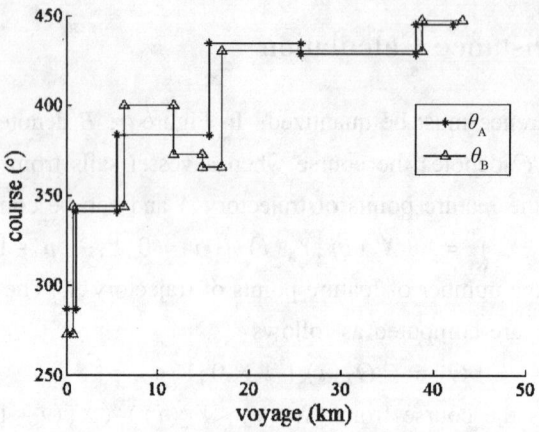

Figure 5 Curves of Θ_A and Θ_B

$$d_{AB}(s) = \int_0^s |\Theta_A(f(s')) - \Theta_B'(f(s'))| ds' \quad (9)$$

Figure 6 shows the curve of $d_{AB}(s)$, which is not affected by the distance between the two trajectories. Thus, the translation movement of the trajectories does not affect the results of (9). The spatial distance between a couple of points of the two trajectories describes the translation distance. Second, the distance between the representative points of trajectories A and B must be calculated. A couple of points of the two trajectories describe the translation distance.

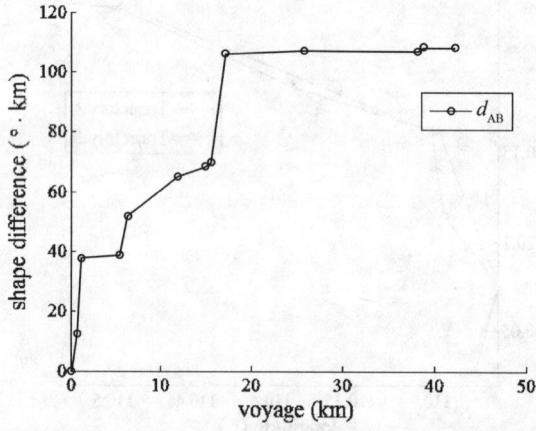

Figure 6 Shape difference between trajectories A and B

Second, the distance between the representative points of trajectories A and B must be calculated. A couple of points must be chosen from trajectories A and B. The latest point of a trajectory is selected as the representative point because of its importance and easy calculation. Let d' denote the distance between representative points. Suppose that trajectories B and A are historical and new trajectories, respectively. The voyage of trajectory A is growing. The latest point of a trajectory A for a specific moment is $(X_A'(s), Y_A'(s))$, where s denotes the voyage from the origin point to $(X_A'(s), Y_A'(s))$. The total voyage of vessel B must not be shorter than s to calculate the distance. Thereafter, the point $(X_B'(s), Y_B'(s))$ of trajectory B must be obtained, and the voyage from the origin point to this point is denoted by s. $(X_A'(s), Y_A'(s))$ and $(X_B'(s), Y_B'(s))$ are the representative points at the moment. The distance between the representative points of trajectories A and B is $d_{AB}'(s)$, which also denotes the spatial distance between trajectories A and B.

Third, the shape difference and spatial distance must be synthesized. Suppose that n voyages have been recorded during the growth of trajectory A, which is expressed as $\{S_i | i = 1, 2, \cdots, n\}$. $S_i < S_{i+1}$, $i = 1, 2, \cdots, n$. Therefore, the shape differences between trajectories A and B are expressed as follows:

$$\{d_{AB}(S_i) \mid i = 1, 2, \cdots, n\} \tag{10}$$

The spatial distances between trajectories A and B are denoted as follows:

$$\{d_{AB}'(S_i) \mid i = 1, 2, \cdots, n\}. \tag{11}$$

Let D_{AB} denote the synthesized distances, which can be calculated as follows:

$$D_{AB}(S_i) = K_d \cdot \frac{d_{AB}(S_i)}{\text{Max}D} + (1 - K_d) \frac{d_{AB}'(S_i)}{\text{Max}D'}; i = 1, 2, \cdots, n\ ; 0 \leqslant K_d \leqslant 1, \tag{12}$$

where $\text{Max}D$ is the largest spatial distance, $\text{Max}D'$ is the largest shape difference, and K_d is the adjusting coefficient of shape difference and spatial distance. A larger K_d results in greater influence of shape difference on synthesized distance and smaller influence of spatial distance on synthesized distance. When $K_d = 1$, the synthesized distance describes the shape difference. When $K_d = 0$, the synthesized distance is the spatial distance. A smaller D_{AB} leads to greater similarities between trajectories A and B.

$$d_{AB}(S_{i+1}) = d_{AB}(S_i) + \int_{S_i}^{S_{i+1}} |\Theta_A[f(s')] - \Theta_B'[f(s')]| ds', i = 1, 2, \cdots, n - 1. \tag{13}$$

Derived from (9) and (10), formula (13) indicates that if the last calculated result of shape difference is known, only the increased segment must be calculated to obtain the latest shape difference. The same characteristics are observed in calculating synthesized distance as shown in (12). Therefore, this algorithm can be used in dynamic applications.

3 Analysis and Discussion

The data for trajectory A are collected from a vessel with a growing voyage. Four historical trajectories, namely, a, b, c, and d, are known. The similarities between A and the fourtrajectories must be measured following the aforementioned steps. The average data compression ratio of the five trajectories is 39.23. Figure 7 shows the feature points of trajectories a, b, c, d, and A. a is the most similar trajectory to A, d is the most dissimilar trajectory to A, and b is more similar to trajectory A than to c.

$d_{Aa}(S)$, $d_{Ab}(S)$, $d_{Ac}(S)$, and $d_{Ad}(S)$ denote the shapedifferences of trajectory A from trajectories a, b, c, and d. S denotes the voyage. Figure 8 shows that if $S \leqslant 15$ km, the shape difference between trajectories A and the four trajectories are resemblant. By contrast, if $S > 15$ km and S continues to grow, the shape difference between trajectories A and the four trajectories become inconsistent. The results in Figure 8 are consistent with the shape features of trajectories in Figure 7.

Let $d_{Aa}'(S)$, $d_{Ab}'(S)$, $d_{Ac}'(S)$, and $d_{Ad}'(S)$ denote the spatial distances of trajectory A from the other four trajectories. Figure 9 shows that the spatial distances of A from c and d increase along with the growth of S. $d_{Ad}'(S)$ has a higher growth speed than $d_{Ac}'(S)$, but the spatial distances of A from a and b have not changed significantly. The results presented in Figure 9 are also consistent with the features of trajectories shown in Figure 7.

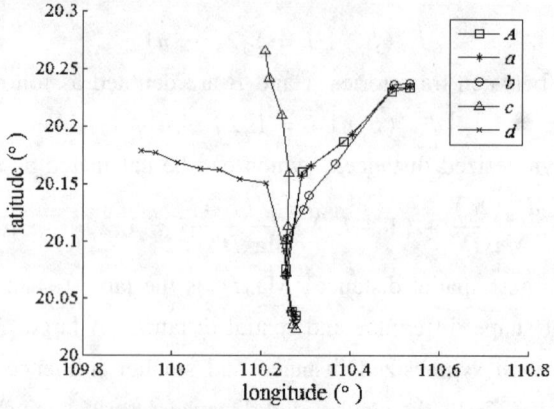

Figure 7 Trajectories A, a, b, c, and d

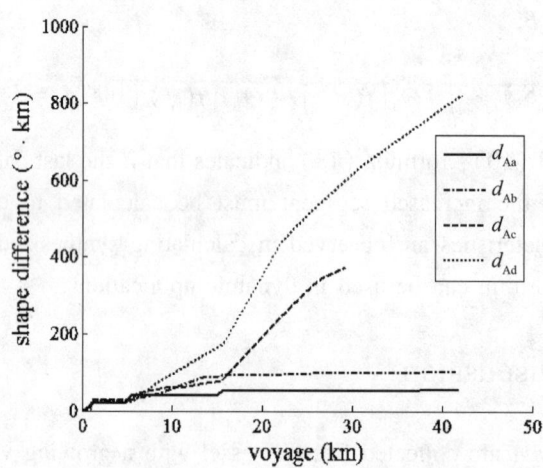

Figure 8 Shape differences between A and a, b, c, and d

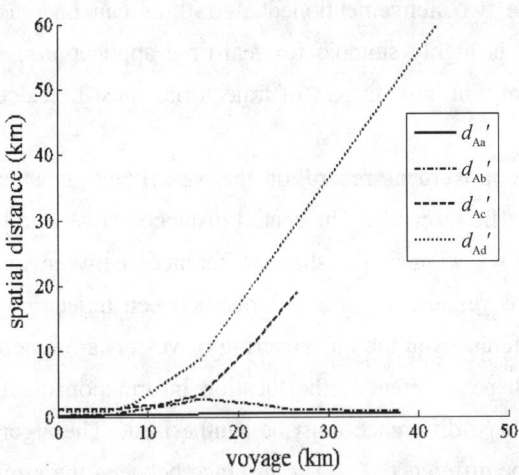

Figure 9 Spatial distances of A from a,b,c, and d

Table 1 Synthesized distances from trajectory A to trajectories a,b,c, and d

S (km) / Trajectories	5	10	15	20	25	30	35	40
a	0.0144	0.0226	0.0217	0.0297	0.0297	0.0303	0.0306	—
b	0.0142	0.0396	0.0650	0.0657	0.0603	0.0589	0.0582	—
c	0.0225	0.0447	0.0637	0.1700	0.2955	—	—	—
d	0.0182	0.0756	0.1482	0.3177	0.4771	0.6110	0.7362	0.8581

When the shape difference and spatial distance are known, the synthesized distance can be calculated according to formula (12). Let Max$D$ = 60 km and MaxD' = 1,000 km. Table 1 shows the calculated synthesized distance. When S = 5 km, d becomes the most similar trajectory to A. Trajectories a, c, and d are also very similar to trajectory A, but when $S \geqslant 10$ km, a becomes the most similar trajectory to A, while d remains the most dissimilar trajectory to A. The voyages of a, b, and c are shorter than 40 km; thus, some synthesized distances from A to these three trajectories cannot be calculated. The results in Table 1 are consistent with the features of trajectories in Figure 7, which means that the similarity measurement results are consistent with the vessel sailing behaviors.

The similarities between the trajectories are measured by extracting the feature points and synthesizing shape difference and spatial distance. The data volume has been extremely compressed in the experiment. All feature points that are needed in the next step of the model have been retained. The proposed algorithm almost represents a loss less compression algorithm for measuring the similarity between trajectories because the course changing information is not deleted. Furthermore, the synthesized distances between a trajectory and the other four trajectories are calculated. The synthesized distance between the two most similar trajectories is 0.0306, and the highest dissimilarity of 0.7362 is obtained when the voyage is 35 km.

The calculations of the two abovementioned algorithms can be reused in dynamic applications. The proposed model is highly suitable for real-time applications, such as traffic detection and monitoring, because only the growth part of trajectories must be calculated when the voyages of vessels are increased.

Trajectory denotes the movement record of the vessel and is among the most important sources of data for vessel traffic research. The spatial distance between trajectories denotes the spatial distribution of traffic flow, whereas the shape differences between trajectories result from the different sailing behaviors of vessels. If the similarity between trajectories is measured by spatial distance, the individual differences in the maneuvering of vessels are ignored. By contrast, if such similarity is measured by shape difference, the location information of vessels is ignored. Therefore, spatial distance and shape difference must be synthesized. The algorithm developed by Ping Xie is used to quantize shape difference[40]. The distance between the representative points of trajectories is calculated to measurethe spatial distance between trajectories for two reasons. First, such distance can be easily calculated. Second, such distance emphasizes the latest distance between vessels in real-time application. This distance can also be replaced by another type of distance, such as the maximum distance and mean distance between trajectories, when needed.

Some attribute parameters, such as time, acceleration, and speed, are not considered in the model because they do not represent the information of a trajectory. The attribute information must be quantized according to professional knowledge and the specific application situation. The quantization results can be added to formula (12) in an appropriate form. Some parameters in the model, such as K_d, can be changed to extend the applicability of this model.

4 Conclusions

This paper proposed a model for measuring the similarity between the trajectories of vessels. The detection algorithm from the image compression and matching fields was imported and improved to extract feature points from raw trajectories. A new synthesized distance algorithm was then proposed to measure the similarity between trajectories. The experiment results show that the data have been compressed at a very high compression ratio. However, the important information, which is needed in the model, has been retained. By considering the shape difference and the spatial distance between trajectories, the synthesized distances successfully reflect the different motion behaviors of vessels and the disparity of the spatial distribution of trajectories. By reusing the measurement results, the similarity can be measured quickly and correctly when the trajectories are growing. The proposed algorithm can compress the data efficiently in real time to save storage space and computing resources. The measurement results have significant potential to support marine traffic research. Further research based on this model is necessary, especially for trajectory clustering, matching, and prediction.

A Cellular Automaton Model for
Ship Traffic Flow in Waterways*

Abstract: With the development of marine traffic, waterways become congested and more complicated traffic phenomena in ship traffic flow are observed. It is important and necessary to build a ship traffic flow model based on cellular automata (CAs) to study the phenomena and improve marine transportation efficiency and safety. Spatial discretization rules for waterways and update rules for ship movement are two important issues that are very different from vehicle traffic. To solve these issues, a CA model for ship traffic flow, called a spatial-logical mapping (SLM) model, is presented. In this model, the spatial discretization rules are improved by adding a mapping rule. And the dynamic ship domain model is considered in the update rules to describe ships' interaction more exactly. Take the ship traffic flow in the Singapore Strait for example, some simulations were carried out and compared. The simulations show that the SLM model could avoid ship pseudo lane-change efficiently, which is caused by traditional spatial discretization rules. The ship velocity change in the SLM model is consistent with the measured data. At finally, from the fundamental diagram, the relationship between traffic ability and the lengths of ships is explored. The number of ships in the waterway declines when the proportion of large ships increases.

Keywords: Cellular automaton; Ship traffic flow; Waterway; Spatial-logical mapping model; Ship domain

1 Introduction

As one of the three main transportation forms, maritime transportation plays an important role in freight transportation, especially for international trade[66]. Recently, with the development of maritime transportation, ships are becoming larger and waterways are becoming narrower for ships. Some important waterways in the world are becoming very busy[67,68], and complicated phenomena are observed in those waterways. Such phenomena always have some relationship to traffic safety and efficiency, but this cannot be precisely explained by the macroscopic traffic flow model. Therefore, in order to improve traffic conditions, it is necessary to build a microcosmic

---

* 本文发表在《PHYSICA A-STATISTICAL MECHANICS AND ITS APPLICATIONS》2017 年第 471 卷,作者齐乐、郑中义、江龙晖。

traffic flow model to study these complicated phenomena. One of the best choices is the cellular automaton (CA) model, which is widely used in the study of vehicle traffic flow. A CA model can simulate complex phenomena in the real world using a set of simple rules[69-72]. CA micro simulations can be easily implemented using computers and have been successfully applied to the modeling of traffic flows[73-76]. In CA simulations, very simple models are capable of capturing the essential features of systems of extraordinary complexity[77-79]. Some heterogeneous CA models have been proposed recently[80-83], which can support the study of ship traffic, because different ships have different maximum velocities, types, sizes, etc. However, two important issues should be solved first. One is that in most cases there are no lanes for ships in waterways and the width of waterways always change, which makes it hard to achieve spatial discretization. The other is that the interactions among ships are different from those of vehicles due to the differences of traffic rules and movement characteristics between vehicles and ships.

To study ship traffic flow, some models have been proposed based on the CA model. In these models, issues like ship interactions in narrow water channels, and ship movements in narrow and busy shipping channels, etc. have been solved successfully. According to spatial discretization rules and update rules, ship CA models can be divided into two main types. In the first type, a waterway is imagined to be composed of one or two lanes without any bottleneck[66, 84]. Each lane is integrated and has no part missing. In this model, which is similar to the classic vehicle traffic flow models, the research results of vehicle traffic flow can be used directly. Then by considering the motion features of the ship, some complex phenomena in ship traffic flow can be simulated. This performs very well in studying ship traffic flow where there is no bottleneck in the waterway. In the second type, a waterway is imagined to be constituted of one or two lanes too. But there is bottleneck, and part of lane is reduced[85]. This model can simulate ship traffic perfectly, when there is an obstacle in the waterway and ships have to steer clear of it. The influence of the bottleneck on ship traffic flow can be studied and predicted, which is very helpful for ship traffic management.

However, it is known that the widths of waterways are always changing and sometimes this leads to a traffic bottleneck. First, because the bottleneck is not considered in the first model above, it cannot simulate the ship traffic flow in this situation. Second, when ships sail through the bottleneck, the direction of ships may not change much. And the ships tend to veer at a small angle, in order to avoid speed reduction. But in the second model, some ships have to steer and change lane because part of lane is reduced at the bottleneck. The ships slow down in this process. Therefore, the second model is not suitable to simulate the ship traffic flow in this situation either.

In addition, another novel model was presented recently[86]. In that model, the waterway was discretized to two-dimensional spatial cells. The velocity of ships was also divided into two directions. No lane was defined and the rules for lane-changes are not applicable anymore. Instead, the relative position between ships can be achieved and the movement of ships follows collision avoidance regulations. The shape of the waterway can be irregular and the course of ship can be any direction. The spatial discretization in this model is similar to the two-dimensional cellular automaton for pedestrian traffic simulation[87]. Traffic conflicts can be studied very well using this model. And the time a ship takes to sail through a complex traffic net can be calculated successfully. So it is more suitable to simulate ship traffic flow at intersections, in harbors, etc., where the ships' movements are more complex in two-dimensional planes than the one-directional traffic flows in waterways. As it is a two-dimensional cellular automaton, much of the research results on vehicle traffic models based on one-dimensional cellular automaton cannot be referenced. This model is more complex than the two models above and consumes more computing resources.

As mentioned above, the widths of waterways always change, and the models are not very applicable to simulate ship traffic flow under these conditions. Based on the advantages of the above research results and according to the motion features of ships, a novel cellular automaton model for ship traffic flow in waterway was proposed, called the spatial-logical mapping (SLM) model. This model contained a mapping rule with which the lanes for ships were redefined. Ship lane-changes were consistent with the actual situation at the bottleneck. In addition, the dynamic ship domain was considered in building update rules to define the safe gap between ships, which helped to describe ships' interactions more exactly.

The remainder of this paper is organized as follows: Section 2 describes the methodology of the SLM model. Section 3 presents simulation results and discusses the performance of the model. Section 4 summarizes the conclusions as well as the prospect of future research.

2 Methodology

In the CA model, the interactions among the particles, like vehicles, pedestrians, trains, ships, etc., are based on understandable behavioral rules rather than functions[79]. For the CA-based traffic flow model, the discrete space and time should be identified. First, time discretization can be determined empirically, balancing accuracy and computational resource consumption. Second, because a waterway is different from a road, in the SLM model, novel spatial discretization rules are proposed, which contain a mapping rule to solve the problems caused by changes in waterway width. Based on the discretized space and time, improved update rules are built. Next, the spatial discretization rules and update rules are introduced.

2.1 Spatial discretization rules

In ship traffic, variation in the waterway width is very common. If there is a bottleneck because part of a road lane is reduced, a vehicle needs to steer and change lanes to get through, as shown in Figure 1(a). However, there may be no lane-change and no steering action when a ship sails through a waterway where there is bottleneck caused by width narrowing, as shown in Figure 1(b). Therefore, the width variation of a waterway cannot be discretized by reducing or adding lanes as can be done on a road. But if there is no lane reduction or addition, the influence caused by the width variation may be ignored, which is unreasonable. To solve this problem, a mapping method is introduced next.

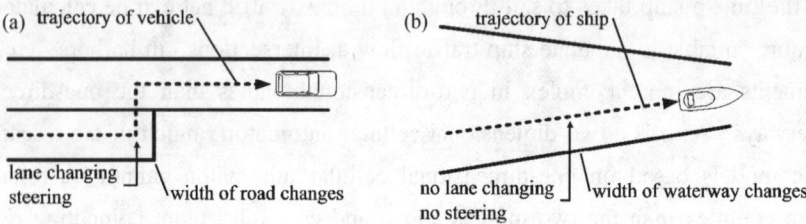

Figure 1 Comparison of vehicle and ship trajectories when the road and waterway widths change

First, the waterway should be discretized according its spatial distribution, as shown in Figure 2. The cells are spatial cells and the lanes are spatial lanes. Suppose the direction of ship traffic flow is from left to right. Let variable $S_{i,j}$ stand for the spatial cell, and l_i stand for the spatial lanes. i is the serial number of spatial lanes, and j is the numerical order of lane i. The four cells in Figure 2 are $S_{1,1}$, $S_{2,1}$, $S_{2,2}$ and $S_{3,1}$. The three spatial lanes are $l_1: S_{1,1}$, $l_2: S_{2,1} \rightarrow S_{2,2}$ and $l_3: S_{3,1}$.

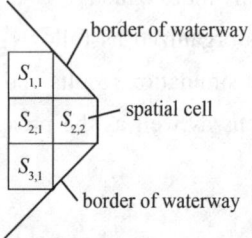

Figure 2 Schematic diagram for spatial discretization of a waterway whose width changes

Assume a ship sails through this waterway and the course does not change. As shown in Figure 3, the trajectory is a straight line. After discretization according to the spatial cells above, the discrete trajectory is $S_{3,1} \rightarrow S_{2,1} \rightarrow S_{2,2}$, which contains a lane-change. But the ship has not steered in actual fact, so this lane-change has no influence on the velocity of the ship. Therefore, this is a pseudo lane-change and will lead to a simulation error, because steering has a great influence on the velocities of ships according to the motion features of the ships.

To fix the simulation error above, let the spatial cell sequence, like $S_{3,1} \rightarrow S_{2,1} \rightarrow S_{2,2}$, be a lane, which contains the pseudo lane-change caused by the width variation of the waterway. The three lanes from Figure 3 are $S_{1,1} \rightarrow S_{2,1} \rightarrow S_{2,2}$, $S_{2,1} \rightarrow S_{2,2}$, $S_{3,1} \rightarrow S_{2,1} \rightarrow S_{2,2}$, as shown in Figure 4. The lengths of the three lanes are different. But that is reasonable, because the voyage of the ship sailing at the edge of the waterway is longer than that of the ship sailing at the center. The neighbors of each cell are known in same lane. The next step is to determine the neighbors in adjacent lanes.

In order to make the neighbors in adjacent lanes unchanged as much as possible, a new type of cell is needed, which is a null cell. No spatial cell corresponds to the null cell. It can be inserted anywhere in the lanes in Figure 4. The null cell has no influence on the voyage of any lanes.

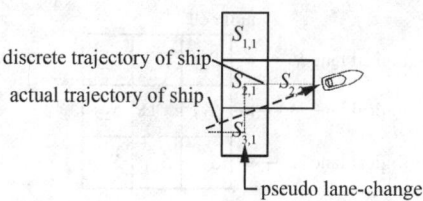

Figure 3　Pseudo lane – change phenomenon

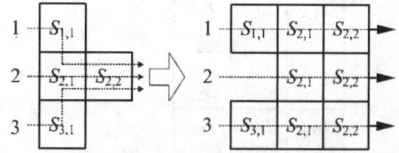

Figure 4　Logical lane determination from the spatial cells

But the cell can increase the cells number of each lane. Therefore, if a null cell is inserted into the lane $S_{2,1} \rightarrow S_{2,2}$, the cells numbers of the three lanes are same and the voyages of them are still unchanged. Then by arranging the three lanes, new cells for the waterway are created, as shown in Figure 5. The new lanes are logical lanes, represented symbolically by l_i'.

To describe the mapping rule, let $L_{m,n}$ stand for the logical cell in Figure 5. m is the serial number of a logical lane. n is the numerical order of lane m. As shown in Figure 6, there is a mapping relationship between the logical cells and the spatial cells. This mapping rule is called the SLM rule. Some important characteristics of the mapping rule are listed as follows:

(a) A spatial cell may correspond to one or more logical cells, but a logical cell can only correspond to one spatial cell or none.

(b) One or more logical cells that correspond to the same spatial cell can be occupied by one ship at a time. If a logical cell is occupied by a ship, the other logical cells that share the same spatial cell cannot be occupied by other ships. The logical cell that corresponds to a null cell cannot be occupied by any ship.

(c) The voyage from logical cells $L_{m,a}$ to $L_{m,b}$ in lane l_m' is calculated by the following equation:

$$\sum_{j=a+1}^{b} D_{m,j} \tag{1}$$

where $D_{m,j}$ is the length of a spatial cell. But if $L_{m,j}$ corresponds to a null cell, the value of $D_{m,j}$ is zero.

(d) The distance between two adjacent cells in different lanes depends on the spatial cells that they correspond to. If the two spatial cells belong to the same lane, the distance is zero.

In the following sections, the calculation of distance and the direction between two cells is based on the items above.

Take spatial cells of a waterway for example, as shown in Figure 7(a), the logical cells can be calculated using the SLM rule. The null cell distribution is shown in Figure 7(b). The lanes that are near to the center of waterway contain more null cells. According to Eq. (1), the voyage

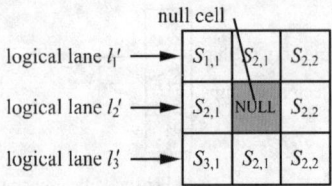

Figure 5   Null cell and logical lanes

$L_{1,1}$ $(S_{1,1})$	$L_{1,2}$ $(S_{2,1})$	$L_{1,3}$ $(S_{2,2})$
$L_{2,1}$ $(S_{2,1})$	$L_{2,2}$ (NULL)	$L_{2,3}$ $(S_{2,2})$
$L_{3,1}$ $(S_{3,1})$	$L_{3,2}$ $(S_{2,1})$	$L_{3,3}$ $(S_{2,2})$

Figure 6   The mapping relationship between spatial cells and logical cells

of each lane can be calculated from the starting point on the left. By connecting the cells that have the same voyage values, the voyage contour in the logical cells can be calculated, as shown in Figure 7(c). A voyage in lanes near the center of the waterway is shorter than that in lanes near the edge of waterway. This is consistent with the result in Figure 7(b). As shown in Figure 7(d), the spatial lanes in logical cells can also be gotten, because the spatial lane of each logical cell is known. When the width of the waterway is narrow, the spatial lane number becomes small, which is consistent with the spatial cells in Figure 7(a).

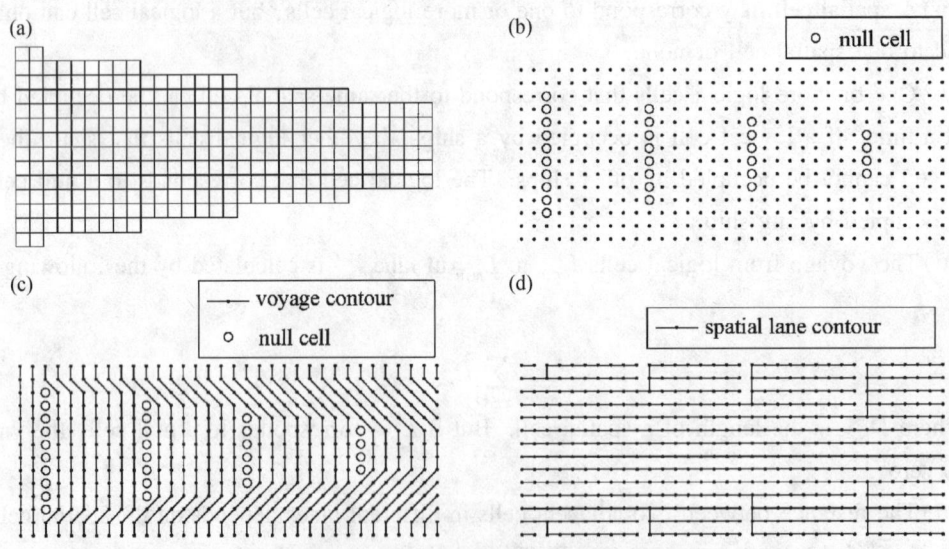

Figure 7   An example of spatial discretization under SLM rules

(a) the distribution of spatial cells; (b) the distribution of null cells in logical cells; (c) the voyage contour of logical cells; (d) the spatial lane contour of logical cells

2.2 Update rules

In order to avoid traffic collisions in navigable waterways, ships are required to maintain a safe zone between each other, which is known as the ship domain[88-93]. The domain is similar to the safety distance between two vehicles or two trains[94-97]. This phenomenon is very important for studying the motion behaviors of ships. The first ship domain model was developed by Fujii and Tanaka in 1971[88,90]. Since then, many ship domain models have been proposed. The latest research shows that the ship domain is dynamic[67,89,91-93]. Size, velocity, type, navigator skill, environmental conditions, waterway conditions, etc., are factors that influence the size of a ship domain.

In the study of ship traffic flow, Ship domain was used to define the safe distance between ships[84]. There are two advantages to consider the dynamic ship domain in this model. The first one is that the relationship between safe distances and sizes of ships has been considered in the dynamic ship domain. The ship traffic flow is heterogeneous traffic. The sizes of ships are different in traffic flow, which makes the safe distances between ships are different either. Therefore, the ship domain is very suitable to define the safe distance between ships in heterogeneous traffic flow model. The second advantage is that the dynamic factors, which are ship's velocity and environmental conditions, like wind, ocean current, tide, etc., have been considered in the dynamic ship domain. Different from the road traffic, the factors have greater influence to the safe distance between ships than vehicles, pedestrians, etc. Thus, by considering the dynamic ship domain, the safe distance between ships in this model is more exact than that in the model based on stationary parameters.

If the ship domain is known, the minimum safe distance between a ship and other ships around can be calculated. D_f is the minimum distance from a ship to its preceding ship. D_l is the minimum distance from a ship to its left ship. D_r is the minimum distance from a ship to its right ship. Parameters like the size, speed, and type of different ships vary, so the value of D_f, D_l and D_r are always different between ships at different times.

Similar to other CA-based traffic models, the SLM model is also a discrete traffic model. Each cell can accommodate at most one ship at a time. Each ship occupies a cell at a time. Unlike vehicle traffic, the domain of a ship may occupy several lanes, depending on the value of D_l and D_r. Other ships are not allowed to be inside of this domain at any time, nor are they allowed to sail through it. If a ship sails in a lane that overlaps with another ship's domain, the two ships have an anteroposterior relationship. In this situation, the lag ship has to follow the preceding ship and cannot overtake it without a lane-change.

When a ship wants to overtake the preceding ship, the first step is to check if there is enough space for the ship to change lanes safely. In vehicle traffic, this requirement can be decided by the merging gap acceptance and the time to collision (TTC), which also applies to ship traffic[47,98-101]. When the sailing environment does not meet the requirements for executing a lane-change, the ship has to decelerate and follow the preceding ship.

Ship traffic is heterogeneous. Mostly, the max velocity V_{max} of different ships varies. Influenced by the waves, wind, current, etc., ships may decelerate. Although the causes may different, the same phenomenon also happens in vehicle traffic[102]; this is called the randomization deceleration probability, represented by p in this model.

Based on the above, the update rules are described as follows.

(a) Safe distance: Safe distance is the distance to the preceding ship that ships must maintain so as to avoid being inside of the other ship's domain. Thus, due to the dynamic feature of ship domains, these safe distances are dynamic and different among ships, as follows:

$$gap_{safe,n} = 2v_n(t) + D_{f,n}(t) \qquad (2)$$

where $gap_{safe,n}$ denotes the safe distance of the nth ship, $v_n(t)$ denotes the velocity of the nth ship at t, and $D_{f,n}(t)$ denotes the minimum distance from the nth ship to its preceding ship.

(b) Acceleration: The space that ship n gives to its preceding ship is gap_n. If $gap_n > gap_{safe,n}$, for ship n, $v_n(t) \to \min(v_n(t)+1, V_{max})$. This reflects the behavior of ship operators seeking a faster speed.

(c) Deceleration: When the distance between the lag ship and the preceding ship is smaller than the required safe distance, $gap_n < gap_{safe,n}$, and the sailing environment does not meet the requirements for executing a lane-change, ship n should decelerate. Thus:

$$v_n(t) = \min[v_n'(t), gap_n - D_{f,n}(t)] \qquad (3)$$

where v_n' denotes the velocity of the preceding ship of n.

(d) Overtaking: If $gap_n < gap_{safe,n}$ and the sailing environment meets the requirements for executing a lane-change, ship n should change lanes and overtake the preceding ship. Unlike a vehicle, the ship making a lane-change has a great influence on velocity. The speed of the ship is reduced during a lane-change. Let $l_n(t)$ stand for the lane where ship is in at t. Let $l_n'(t)$ stand for the target lane. The distance between $l_n(t)$ and $l_n'(t)$ is $\Delta dl_n(t)$. According to ship-motion equations, a simplified equation for velocity change in this CA model can be calculated as follows:

$$v_j(t) = \frac{[v_j(t)]^2}{\sqrt{[v_j(t)]^2 + [\Delta dl_j(t)]^2}} \qquad (4)$$

(e) Random slowing: p is the random slowing probability for ships. A uniformly distributed random number between 0 and 1, p_n', is generated. If $p_n' < p$, then $v_n(t) \to \max[v_n(t)-1, 0]$. This reflects the deceleration of ships caused by factors described above.

(f) Velocity and location update: After the steps above, the velocity of ship n at $t+1$ can be calculated as $v_n(t+1) = v_n(t)$. The location of ship n is $x_n(t)$ at t. Then at $t+1$ the location of ship n is $x_n(t+1) = x_n(t) + v_n(t+1)$.

All of the rules above must be executed by following the characteristics of the mapping rules listed in Section 2.1.

3 Simulation results and discussion

As shown in Figure 8, two segments of the waterways in the Singapore Strait and Changshan

Channel were taken as examples to test the performance of the SLM model. The spatial distributions of the two waterways are similar. The widths of the two selected waterways both change. And there is a bottleneck at the narrowest part of each waterway. The spatial distribution characteristics of the two waterways are very common for ship traffic. By the simulation of ship traffic flow in the two waterways, the performance of the SLM model can be validated. The influences of waterway width changes on ship traffic flow were studied. The ship velocity changes in the simulations were compared with the measured data and analyzed. And the relationship between ship length and traffic capacity was researched.

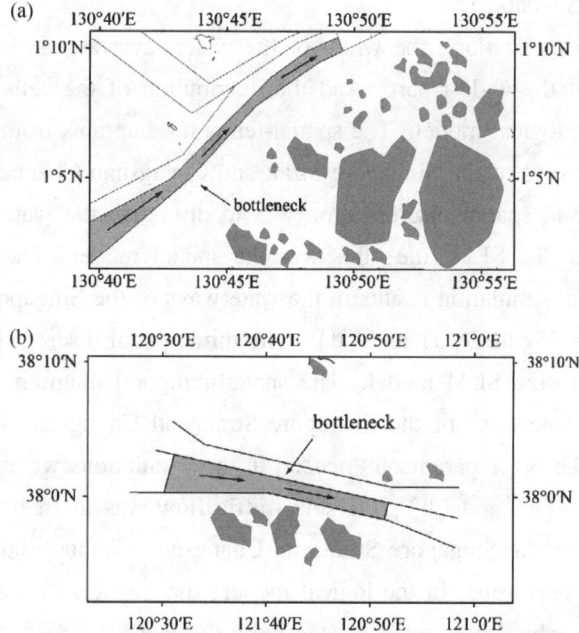

Figure 8　Segments of the waterways and a bottlenecks in: (a) the Singapore Strait, (b) the Changshan Channel, which were used to test the performance of SLM model

As the length and width information of the waterway in Figure 8 is known, the spatial cells can be achieved by spatial discretization. The widest part of the selected waterway in the Singapore Strait is about 2,100 m and the narrowest part is about 700 m. And the widest part of the selected waterway in the Changshan Channel is about 4,700 m and the narrowest part is about 2,200 m. Referencing the sizes and velocities of ships, the size of each spatial cell was 30 m × 30 m and time span was one minute, to balance the accuracy and computational resource consumption. Then according to the SLM rule, the logical cells and mapping relationship were derived from the spatial cells.

3.1　The influence of waterway width changes on ship traffic flow

To prove the ability of the SLM model to reflect the influences of waterway width changes on ship traffic flow, the simulation base on three different spatial discretization results of the Singapore Strait and Changshan Channel were executed, under open boundary conditions. Let L stand for the length of the waterway, q was the number of ships in the waterway, and k was the density of ships in the waterway.

The random slowing probability was $p = 0.10$. The average density of ships in the Singapore Strait was $k = 0.75$ ship/km and the average density of ships in the Changshan Channel was $k = 1.50$ ship/km. The length of the ship was a uniformly distributed random number from 60 to 350 m. And the maximum velocities of ships were normal distributed. The mean of ship velocity was $\mu_v = 21$ km/h and the variance was $\sigma_v = 6$ km/h, which was from the statistical result of Automatic Identification System (AIS) data.

In the first spatial discretization, the width of the waterway was considered to be invariable and equal to the length of the widest part. And the distribution of the cells was the same as the logical cells; this was the logical model. The spatial-temporal diagrams from the ship traffic simulation results in the waterways of the Singapore Strait and Changshan Channel are shown in Figure 9(a) and (b). The second spatial discretization was to discretize the waterway according to its spatial distribution without the SLM rule; this was the spatial model. The spatial-temporal diagrams from the ship traffic simulation results in the waterways of the Singapore Strait and Changshan Channel are shown in Figure 9(c) and (d). The third spatial discretization was to discretize the waterway according to the SLM model. The spatial-temporal diagrams from the ship traffic simulation results in the waterways of the Singapore Strait and Changshan Channel are shown in Figure 9(e) and (f). The other parameters needed in the simulations were same.

As shown in Figure 9(a) and (b), the ship traffic flow was in free-flow state. The width change of the waterways in the Singapore Strait and Changshan Channel did not form any bottleneck in the simulations. Therefore, in the logical model, the impacts of the width change of the waterways were ignored, which was not consistent with the facts.

As shown in Figure 9(c), synchronized flow and wide moving jam appeared in the ship traffic flow. From the spatial distribution of the waterway in Singapore Strait, there was a bottleneck in the simulation, which was caused by the narrowing down of the waterway at about 6,000 m. The influence of the bottleneck on ship traffic flow was the synchronized flow. However, a wide moving jam is found in the spatial-temporal diagram where the waterway width changes are not tremendous. The reason is that some of lanes were still reduced, and some ships had to change lanes in the waterway. The steering operation for the lane-change leaded to ships deceleration and caused traffic jams. But in fact, there were no designated lanes for ships; and ships always choose a straight course to avoid frequently steering, for safety and efficiency reasons. As mentioned in Section 2.1, the lane-changes in Figure 9(c) are pseudo. Therefore, the influence of width change in the waterway was enlarged in the spatial model. In Figure 9(d), a synchronized flow appeared which was caused by the narrowing down of the waterway at about 15,000 m. But the wide moving jam is not found. The reason is that the width change of the waterway after 15,000 m is very little. Therefore, nearly no pseudo lane-change had happened in this segment of the waterway. By comparing Figure 9(c) and (d), it can be found that the simulation results based on the spatial model are different, although the spatial distributions of the two waterways are similar for ship traffic. This was caused by the pseudo lane-change. Thus, the spatial model cannot be used to simulate the ship traffic flow exactly and reliably when the width of the waterway changes.

As shown in Figure 9(e) and (f), the synchronized flow can be found at about 6,000 and 15,000 m. In the other parts of the waterways, the traffic flows were in free-flow state. On one hand, different from the logical model, the influence of bottlenecks in waterways is reflected in the spatial-temporal diagram. On the other hand, the pseudo lane-change, which may lead to false traffic jams, disappeared. Compared with Figure 9(c), no wide moving jam is found in Figure 9(e). And without of the influence of pseudo lane-change, in Figure 9(f) the width of the synchronized flow is narrower than that in Figure 9(d).

Consequently, because of the spatial discretization rules, the SLM model can be used to simulate ship traffic in waterways, whose widths change, more correctly than the other two models. And the problems caused by pseudo lane-change were successfully solved. Thus, the simulation results based on SLM model are more exact and reliable than the spatial model.

3.2 Ship velocity changes in waterways

To study the velocity change of ships in the three models, as mentioned in Section 3.1, the simulations of ship traffic flows in the Singapore Strait and Changshan Channel based on each model were carried out. According to AIS, six hundred samples were randomly selected from the ships that sailed through the waterways in the Singapore Strait. And ten days of data from ships that sailed through the waterway of the Changshan Channel was achieved. The average velocity of the ships in the two waterways was used to assess the performance of the three models.

Let $V_i(x)$ stand for the velocity of the ith ship when its distance to the starting point in a waterway is x. The average velocity of ships at x is:

$$\bar{V}(x) = \frac{\sum_{i=1}^{Q} V_i(x)}{Q} \quad (5)$$

where Q is the total number of ships that sailed through the waterway. V is the average velocity of ships along the waterway.

In Figure 10, simulation results of the ship traffic flow in the waterway of the Singapore Strait are shown. The simulations based on the three models were carried out under open boundary conditions, $p = 0.10$, the ship arrival pattern and the other parameters were consistent with the facts. The spatial-temporal diagram of the simulation result base on the logical model is shown in Figure 10(a). It shows that the ship traffic flow was in free-flow state in the simulation. And there is no significant speed change as shown in Figure 10(d). This is similar to the simulation results in Figure 9(a) and (b). When the width of the waterway did not change much and the density of ships was not high, the ship traffic flow would be in free-flow state.

The spatial-temporal diagram of the simulation result base on the spatial model is shown in

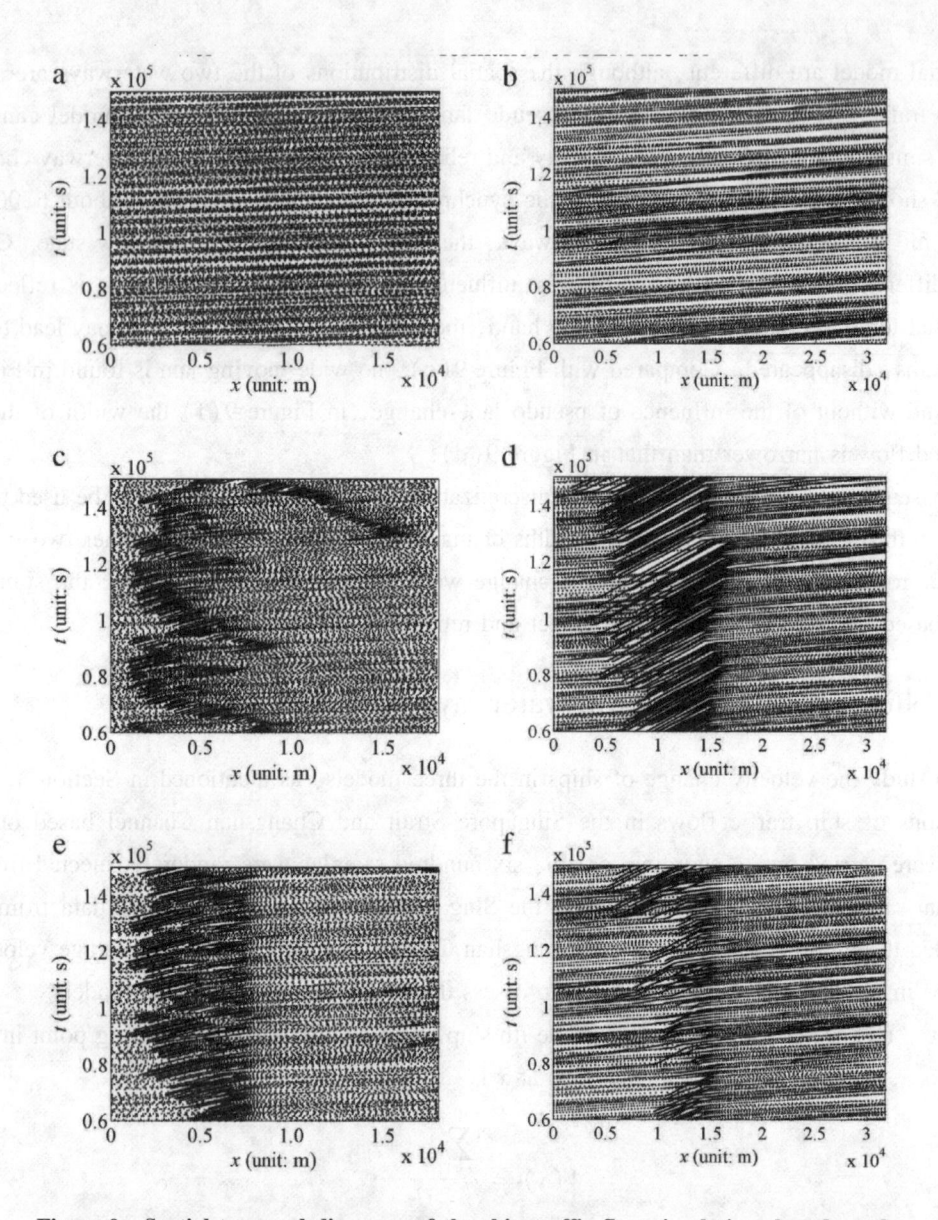

Figure 9 Spatial-temporal diagrams of the ship traffic flow simulations based on the three models, when $k = 0.75$ ship/km in the Singapore Strait and $k = 1.50$ ship/km in the Changshan Channel, $p = 0.10$. (a) The logical model, the Singapore Strait; (b) the logical model, the Changshan Channel; (c) the spatial model, the Singapore Strait; (d) the spatial model, the Changshan Channel; (e) the SLM model, the Singapore Strait; (f) the SLM model, the Changshan Channel

Figure 10(b). The phenomena of ship deceleration can be observed. Some of them occurred near the bottleneck. The others occurred after the bottleneck in the waterway. Because the arrival interval time of ships in the waterway was long and the ship density was low, no traffic jam was formed. But the average velocity of ships V was keeping slowdown from the starting point to the bottleneck as shown in Figure 10(d). And V reached to the minimum, about 13 km/h, at the bottleneck. After the bottleneck V raised to about 14 km/h and kept at this speed until to the terminal point. The spatial-temporal diagram of the simulation result base on the SLM model is shown in Figure 10(c). The ship traffic flow in this simulation was similar to free-flow. Only little phenomena of ship deceleration can be observed near the bottleneck. As shown in Figure 10 (d), the value of velocity and the velocity changes in SLM model is consistent with the measured data. The influence of waterway width changes on the velocities of ships can be reflected correctly. But in the logical model, the velocities of ships nearly unchanged and was little higher than the measured data. The logical model cannot be used to simulate the deceleration of ships caused by the narrowing down of the waterway. In the spatial model, the impact of false deceleration, cased by pseudo lane-change, on ship traffic was enhanced, which leaded to a lower curve of V than the measured data.

In Figure 11, the simulation results of the ship traffic in the waterway of the Changshan Channel are shown. The simulations based on the three models were carried out under open boundary conditions, $p = 0.10$, the ship arrival pattern and the other parameters were consistent with the facts. The spatial-temporal diagram of the simulation result base on the logical model is shown in Figure 11(a). Similar to the Figure 10(a), it shows that the ship traffic flow was in free-flow state in the simulation too. The spatial-temporal diagram of the simulation result base on the spatial model is shown in Figure 11(b). Different from Figure 10(b), it shows that nearly all of the deceleration occurs at the bottleneck and before the bottleneck. After the bottleneck, the average velocity of ship raised to the initial velocity slowly. The reason is that the width of the waterway after the bottleneck changed little; and little false deceleration occurred, cased by the pseudo lane-change, which is consistent with the analysis results of Section 3.1. The spatial-temporal diagram of the simulation result base on the SLM model is shown in Figure 11(c). The phenomena of ships' deceleration only can be observed near the bottleneck. And the other part of the ship traffic flow is similar to free-flow. As shown in Figure 10(d), the curve of the velocity change based on SLM is the most similar curve to the measured data.

From Figures 10 and 11, in the logical model, the influence of the waterway width changes on velocity cannot be simulated. Although the ships' deceleration at the bottleneck was simulated based the spatial model, the effect of the waterway width changes was enlarged. This made the simulation results were inaccuracy. But the value and change trend of the ships' velocities are consistent with the measured data in the simulation based on SLM model. Therefore, the SLM model can be used to simulate the changes of ships' velocities more exactly than the other two models.

3.3 Relationship between ships' lengths and traffic capacity

It is known that the sizes of ships in waterway are always different, which makes the safe distances between ships are different. Therefore, it is necessary to study the influence of the ships sizes on traffic flow. Based on the distribution of ships lengths in Singapore Strait, the ships, whose lengths are over 200 m, are supposed to be the large ships. Let P_L stand for the proportion of the

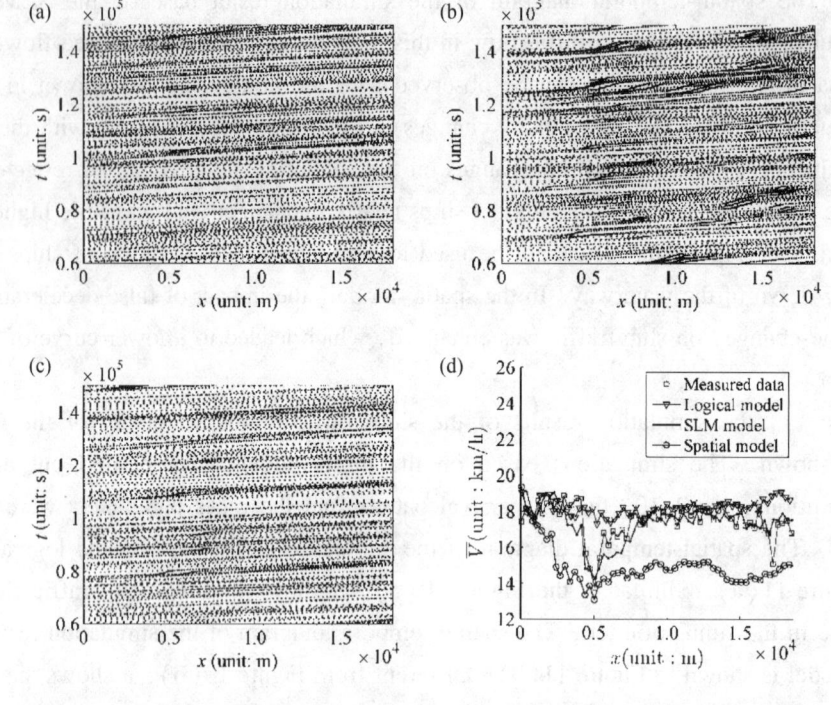

Figure 10 Simulation results of the ship traffic flow in the waterway of the Singapore Strait based on the three models, when $p = 0.10$, the ship arrival pattern and the other parameters were consistent with the facts. (a) The logical model; (b) the spatial model; (c) the SLM model; (d) the curves of the ships average velocity along the waterway, $V(x)$, from the simulation results based on the three models and the measured data

large ships, and P_S stand for those under 200 m. $P_L + P_S = 1$. To analyze the relation ship between the ship length and the traffic flow. The simulations of the ship traffic flow in the waterway of the Singapore Strait base on SLM model were executed when $P_L = 0$, $P_L = 0.25$, $P_L = 0.50$, $P_L = 0.75$ and $P_L = 1$, under periodic boundary conditions, $p = 0.10$, $k = 0.75$ ship/km. The other parameters were same as Section 3.1. The simulation results are shown in Figure 12. In Figure 12(a) only the synchronized flow is found near the bottleneck. The reason is that all of the ships in the waterways were small ships; the average safe distance between ships was very small. Only near to the bottleneck, the ship density was high enough to make the distance between ships smaller than the safe distance. Then the interaction between ships can lead to the ships deceleration. When P_L became larger the average safe distance between ships became larger too. The synchronized flow became wider and the minimum of V became smaller, as shown in Figure 12(b), (c) and (f). When $P_L = 0.75$, the wide moving jam appeared in the ship traffic flow, as shown in Figure 12(d). Not only the ships near bottleneck but also the ships in the whole waterway decelerated, as shown in Figure 12(f). When $P_L = 1$, the phenomena of wide moving jam was more obvious, as shown in Figure 12(e); the velocity of ships was further reduced, as shown in Figure 12(f). In summary, with the increase in the proportion of large ships, more traffic jams appeared

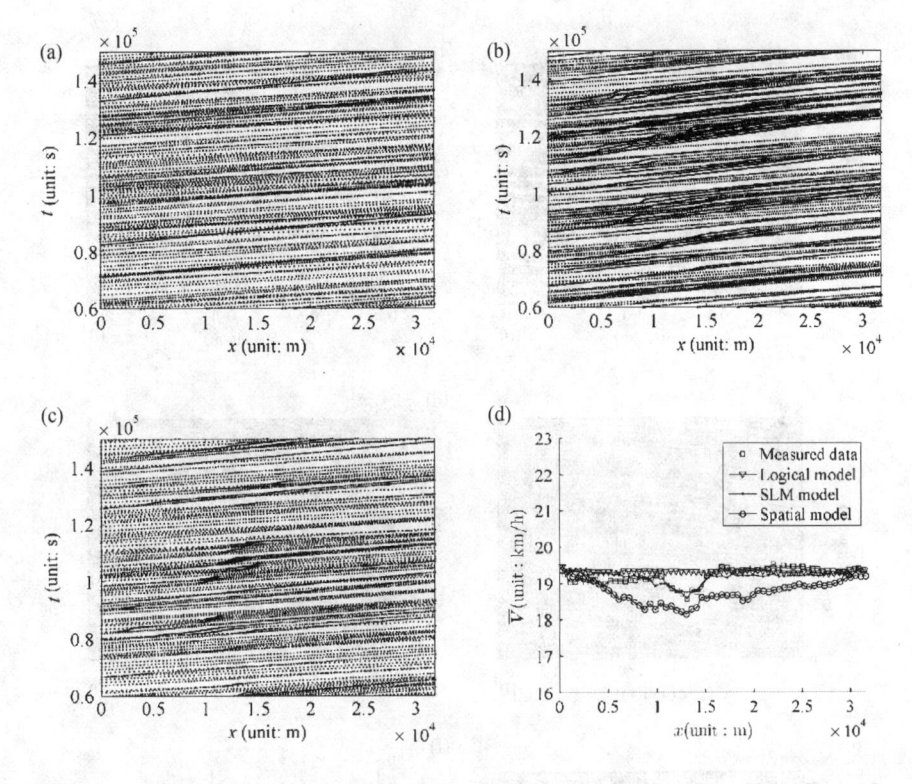

Figure 11 Simulation results of the ship traffic flow in the waterway of the Changshan Channel based on the three models, when $p = 0.10$, the ship arrival pattern and the other parameters were consistent with the facts. (a) The logical model; (b) the spatial model; (c) the SLM model; (d) the curves of the ships' average velocity along the waterway, $V(x)$, from the simulation results based on the three models and the measured data

and the average velocity of ships slowed down.

To study the traffic capacity of the waterway, the simulations of the ship traffic in the waterway of the Singapore Strait based on the SLM model were executed under periodic boundary conditions and different ship density. The other parameters were same as the simulations in Section 3.2. Figure 13 presents the fundamental diagrams. It is known that the difference in the lengths of ships is more significant than that for vehicles, so it is necessary to study the influences that ships' lengths have on traffic flow in the SLM model. One of the important applications of the CA model is the assessment of the traffic capacity. Therefore, the relationship between the length distribution of ships and the traffic capacity of a waterway was studied. The fundamental diagram is shown in Figure 13, when $0 \leqslant P_L < 0.25$, $0.25 \leqslant P_L < 0.50$, $0.50 \leqslant P_L < 0.75$ and $0.75 \leqslant P_L \leqslant 1$. The number of ships in the waterway declines when the proportion of large ships increases. And with the development of high-speed large-scale vessels, this relationship should be considered in traffic capacity assessment based on an SLM model.

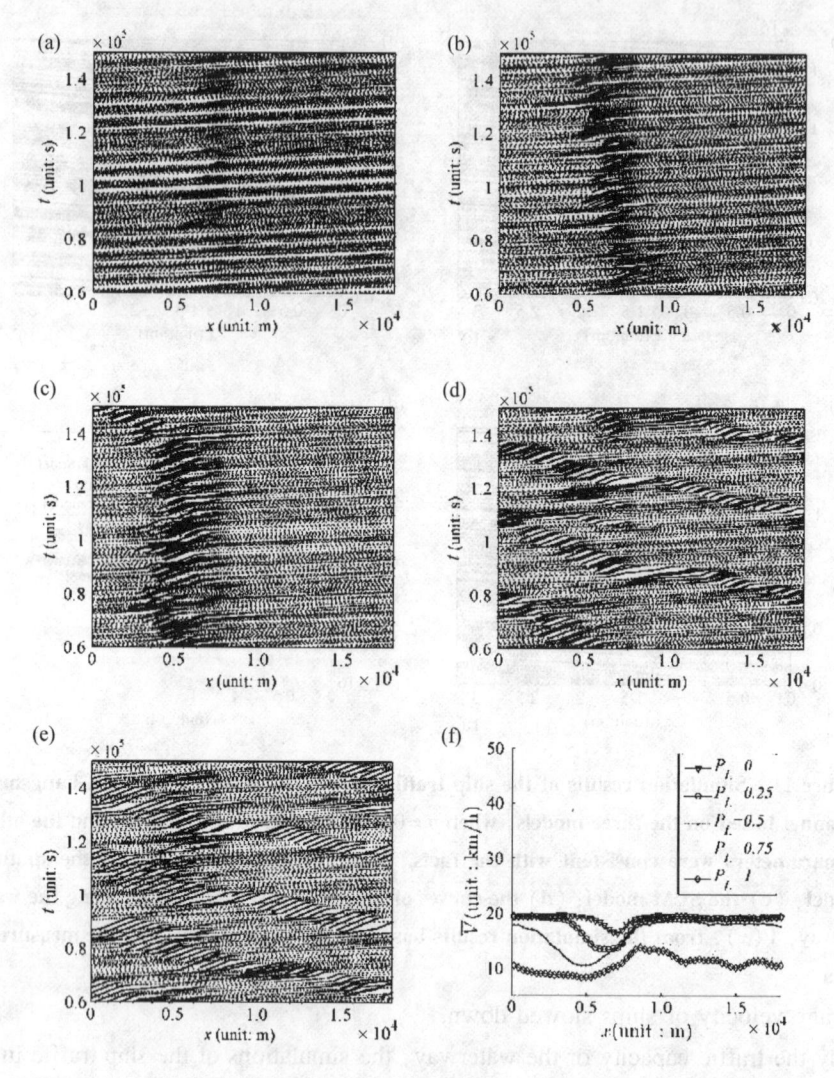

Figure 12 Simulation results of the ship traffic flow in the waterway of the Singapore Strait based on the SLM model, when $p = 0.10, k = 0.75$ ship/km and the proportion of large ships is: (a) $P_L = 0$; (b) $P_L = 0.25$; (c) $P_L = 0.50$; (d) $P_L = 0.75$; (e) $P_L = 1$. (f) The curves of the ships' average velocity along the waterway, $V(x)$, from the five simulation results and the measured data

4 Conclusions and prospects

A novel CA-based model, the SLM model, was proposed for ship traffic flow. This model contains a new spatial discretization rule, called the SLM rule, which is used to fix the pseudo lane-change problem. The update rules referenced the dynamic ship domain, which helped to describe ships' interaction more exactly. The simulation was executed and compared with other two typical CA models without the SLM rule. The results show that the SLM model can simulate ship

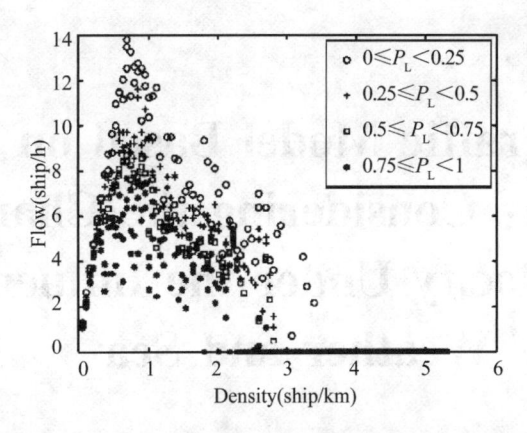

Figure 13 Fundamental diagram based on an SLM model when $p = 0.10$ and the proportion of large ships is different: $0 \leq P_L < 0.25$, $0.25 \leq P_L < 0.50$, $0.50 \leq P_L < 0.75$ and $0.75 \leq P_L \leq 1$

traffic more correctly when the width of the waterway changes. Based on the measured data of ships that sailed through the Singapore Strait, the velocity change along the waterway in the simulation was assessed, and it was proved that the SLM model can reflect the microchange of velocity in the waterway correctly. Besides, from the fundamental diagrams of different distributions of ships' lengths, the relationship between ships' lengths and traffic capacity was found. The number of ships in the waterway declines when the proportion of large ships increases. This is helpful in assessing the traffic capacity of waterways. The impact of high-speed large-scale vessels can be considered in the SLM model.

To study ship traffic flow based on CAs is imperative in order to improve marine transportation efficiency and safety. And more research results on ships behaviors, like intelligent automatic collision avoidance expert system for ships, ships arena model, etc., are required to be added to the CA model. But there are still some problems in achieving it. Thus, new algorithms need to be studied to fix these problems in the future. Then more complex phenomena in ship traffic can be explained, and the application of the CA model can be extended in marine transportation.

Marine Traffic Model Based on Cellular Automaton: Considering the Change of the Ship's Velocity Under the Influence of the Weather and Sea*

Abstract: It was found that the ships' velocity change, which is impacted by the weather and sea, e. g. , wind, sea wave, sea current, tide, etc. , is significant and must be considered in the marine traffic model. Therefore, a new marine traffic model based on cellular automaton (CA) was proposed in this paper. The characteristics of the ship's velocity change are taken into account in the model. First, the acceleration of a ship was divided into two components: regular component and random component. Second, the mathematical functions and statistical distribution parameters of the two components were confirmed by spectral analysis, curve fitting and auto-correlation analysis methods. Third, by combining the two components, the acceleration was regenerated in the update rules for ships' movement. To test the performance of the model, the ship traffic flows in the Dover Strait, the Changshan Channel and the Qiongzhou Strait were studied and simulated. The results show that the characteristics of ships' velocities in the simulations are consistent with the measured data by Automatic Identification System (AIS). Although the characteristics of the traffic flow in different areas are different, the velocities of ships can be simulated correctly. It proves that the velocities of ships under the influence of weather and sea can be simulated successfully using the proposed model.

Keywords: Ship traffic flow; Velocity change; Weather and sea; Cellular automaton

1 Introduction

Generally, different from a vehicle, a train or an airplane, the velocity of a ship is always slow. It always takes a long time for a ship to finish its trip. A ship may spend several hours to sail through a fairway. In a marine traffic study, the duration of a ship's movement is always longer than that of a vehicle, a bicycle, or a pedestrian in a road traffic study. Therefore, the impacts of the weather and sea on ships' velocities accumulate over time, which make the changes of ships' velocities significant and impossible to ignore. Figure 1 shows the velocity-time curves

---

* 本文发表在《PHYSICA A-STATISTICAL MECHANICS AND ITS APPLICATIONS》2017 年第 483 卷,作者齐乐、郑中义、江龙晖。

of ships that sailed southwestward in the Dover Strait for 3 days.

Recently, in some marine traffic models based on cellular automaton (CA), the velocity change under the influence of weather and sea was not considered[84]. In some other models, the velocity change was considered as a random event, i. e., the impacts of tide, sea current, and wind are formulated by random variables. And normal distributions are used to represent the impact of these parameters on speed[66, 86]. This approach is similar to the randomization probability in vehicle traffic models that is essential in simulating realistic traffic flow[74]. Using the randomization probability, the natural velocity fluctuations caused by human behavior or due to varying external conditions were taken into account in the vehicle traffic simulation. For a CA-based model, the randomization probability can reflect the likelihood of a driver speeding up or slowing down. Therefore, the randomization probability is always used to describe the stochastic driver acceleration-deceleration behavior[83, 103-109].

By importing the idea of randomization probability in marine traffic model, the random fluctuation of a ship's velocity can be simulated. In addition, the model can be used to simulate the marine traffic flow when the duration time is short and the accuracy requirement of ships velocities is not very strict. However, besides the random change of velocity, there are obviously regular changes of velocities in the marine traffic, as shown in Figure 1, which is different from the vehicle traffic. Therefore, to build a model that can be used to simulate the marine traffic with high velocity accuracy in a long duration of time, the characteristics of the regular change of velocity caused by the impacts of weather and sea cannot be ignored[110-117]. Some studies indicated that the changes of ships' velocities caused by the impacts of the natural condition may follow other rules and require a detailed study[86].

In the vehicle traffic study, the main impact of the weather on the traffic flow is the decrease of vehicles' velocities and traffic capacity in poor weather conditions, e. g., rainfall and snow. In rainfall conditions, because of the wet and slippery roads, a driver tends to slow down for safety. The study results show that the heavier the rain is, the slower the vehicles move. Under ice and snowfall conditions, not only do the vehicles' velocities decrease but also the start-up time is delayed[118-123]. First, compared with marine traffic, the impacts of weather on road traffic flow are not always significant and only occur under specific conditions. In contrast, in marine traffic, the velocity of a ship is impacted by the weather and sea all the time during the travel. Second, the characteristics of the velocity change caused by the impacts of weather are different between a vehicle and a ship. For the vehicle traffic, the research focus is on the decrease of the velocity, the delay of the start-up time, etc., which are negative factors for traffic efficiency. In contrast, for marine traffic, the ship velocity can decrease or increase, depending on the weather and sea conditions. Therefore, a new model is required that considers the unique characteristics of the changes of ships velocities under the influence of weather and sea.

As shown in Figure 1, the changes of ships' velocities exhibit regular changes and random fluctuations. Thus, the accelerations of the ships can be considered to be composed of a regular component and a random component. First, the regular component must be analyzed according to the spectral analysis method. The purpose of the spectral analysis is to determine the characteristics of the macro regularity of the velocity change, not the local features or outliers. In addition, the movement information of ships, achieved by the Automatic Identification System (AIS), is discrete[67, 68, 124, 125]. Therefore, the fast Fourier transform (FFT) method is referenced to study the regular component and confirm the form of the function for regular component[126]. Second, for the random component, the randomness of the acceleration must be estimated according to the auto-correlation function (ACF), and using the statistical method, the distribution of the random component can be determined[127]. Third, as the form, data and distribution of the two components are known, the coefficient of the functions for these components can be achieved by the curve fitting methods. To meet the requirements of the two components' characteristics above, the curve fitting method is improved. The curve fitting residual of the regular component, which is the random component, must be random sequence. This residual is added to the curve fitting method as a constraint condition. Last, the two components are combined to regenerate the acceleration, which is added to the ship's velocity in the update rules. In summary, based on the analysis of the velocity change characteristics and a comparison of different models, a CA-based model for marine traffic that considers the velocity change impacted by the weather and sea is proposed. In the simulations, based on this model, the accuracy of ships' velocities is improved.

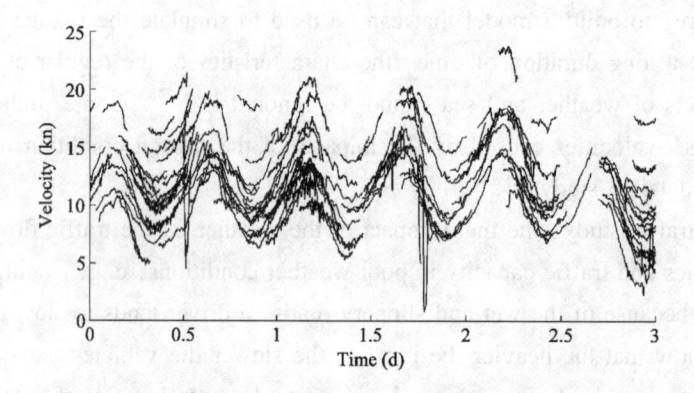

Figure 1 The velocity-time curves of the ships that sailed southwestward in the Dover Strait for 3 days

The remainder of this paper is organized as follows: Section 2 describes the methodology of the model. Section 3 presents simulation results and discusses the performance of the model. Section 4 summarizes the conclusions and the prospect of future research.

2 Methodology

As described in the previous section, the acceleration of a ship is composed of two components, regular and random components, as shown in Figure 2. a is the acceleration, a' is the regular component and a'' is the random component. In this section, the methods of obtaining the two components from ships' velocities are introduced, and the update rules for ship movement are built. In the update rules, the acceleration is regenerated and added to the ship's velocity.

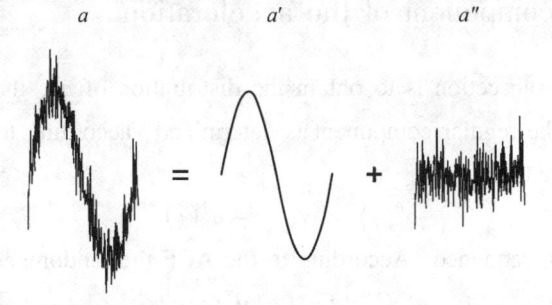

Figure 2 The schematic diagram of the relationships between the acceleration a, the regular component a' and the random component a''

Let $v_i(t)$ denote the velocity of vessel i at t in the specified area of study. The definition of the acceleration at time t in this model is

$$a_i(t) = \frac{v_i(t + \Delta t) - v_i(t)}{\Delta t} \quad (1)$$

where Δt is the sampling interval. Let n_t denote the total number of ships in the specified area at t. The average acceleration of ships in the specified area at t is

$$a(t) = \frac{\sum_{i=1}^{n_t} a_i(t)}{n_t} \quad (2)$$

As shown in Figure 2, $a(t)$ is composed of the regular component, $a'(t)$, and the random component, $a''(t)$.

$$a(t) = a'(t) + a''(t) \quad (3)$$

2.1 The regular component of the acceleration

The purpose of this subsection is to obtain the function of a', the regular component of the acceleration. The acceleration, a, needs to be analyzed by the FFT method as mentioned in Section 1. Next, the cycle of a' can be determined. Let T denote the cycle of a'. As shown in Figure 1, an obvious characteristic of a trigonometric function is found in the curves. Therefore, the form of the fitting function can be

$$a'(t) = \sum_{i=1}^{N} \left[A_i \cos(2\pi t \frac{i}{T}) + B_i \sin(2\pi t \frac{i}{T}) \right] \quad (4)$$

where N is the number of the subcomponents of a under different cycles. The length of each cycle is $\frac{T}{i}$, $i = 1, 2, \cdots, N$. The value of N is correlated with the random component and is discussed in the next subsection. A_i and B_i are the coefficients that must be determined using the curve fitting method.

2.2 The random component of the acceleration

The purpose of this subsection is to obtain the distribution of a'', the random component of the acceleration. When the regular component is determined, according to Eq. (3), the random component can be obtained by

$$a''(t) = a(t) - a'(t). \tag{5}$$

a'' must be a random sequence. According to the ACF the randomness of a'' can be judged.

$$C = f_{ACF}(a'', Lag), \tag{6}$$

where C is the auto-correlation of a'' when the time-lag is Lag.

First, when C is known, the double standard deviation of C can be calculated. Under normal distribution condition, a confidence interval of approximately 95% for the randomness could be determined, when the standard deviation is ± 1.96. If a stricter standard for the randomness of a'' is requested in the applications, the standard deviation can be increased to achieve a confidence interval with higher confidence. Second, Box-Ljung statistics Q can be achieved, which approximately obey the chi-square distribution. The smaller Q is, the more likely the value of C is zero. For the convenience of the testing, it can be converted to the probability value of the chi-square distribution. As long as the probability value is less than 0.05, the confidence level can be up to 95%.

If the requirements above have been met, then a'' could be considered as a random sequence, and a'' obeys the Generalized Gaussian distribution. Let G represent this distribution.

$$a'' = G \tag{7}$$

If a'' is not a random sequence, then the curve fitting result of a' does not meet the requirements in this model. More subcomponents must be classified into the regular component. Therefore, requirements above must be added to the curve fitting of a' as a constraint condition. In addition, the value of N should be changed as a coefficient to meet the constraint condition.

When a' is known, the value of a'' can be obtained by Eq. (5). The coefficients of the Generalized Gaussian function for a'' can be determined using the curve fitting method based on the statistical results of a''. Next, a'' can be regenerated in the traffic simulation, as shown in Eq. (8). $GR(t)$ is the generated value at t, which follows the Generalized Gaussian distribution.

$$a''(t) = GR(t) \tag{8}$$

2.3 Update rules

The purpose of this subsection is to build the update rules of the ship's movement. The changes of ships' velocities under the influence of the weather and sea are considered in the rules. At t, the regular and random components of a ship's acceleration can be calculated according to Eqs. (3), (4) and (8). Thus, the velocity change can be calculated, as shown in item (v) next.

To avoid traffic collisions in the marine traffic flow, a safe zone around a ship, which is known as the ship domain, must be maintained[88-93]. The ship domain is similar to the safety distance between a vehicle and its preceding vehicle[79, 85, 96, 128, 129]. When the ship domain is known, the minimum safe distance between a ship and other ships around can be calculated. Let d_f denote the minimum distance from a ship to the preceding ship. Let d_l denote the minimum distance from a ship to its left ship. d_r is the minimum distance from a ship to its right ship. d_l and d_r are used to judge whether there is enough lateral distance for a ship to overtake its preceding ship in the fairways. When the velocities, d_l, d_r and d_f of a ship and its surrounding ships are known, the requirements for executing an overtaking maneuver can be determined by referring to the multi-lanes traffic model[98, 99, 130-133]. When the sailing environment does not meet the requirements for executing a overtaking, the lag ship must decelerate and follow the preceding ship.

Let $v_j(t)$ denote the velocity of the jth ship at t. The update rules are described as follows.

(i) Safe distance: Safe distance is the distance from a ship to its preceding ship that must be maintained for safety, when the lateral distance between the jth ship and its preceding ship is less than d_l or d_r.

$$gap_{\text{safe},j}(t) = D_j(t) + d_{f,j}(t), \tag{9}$$

where $gap_{\text{safe},j}(t)$ denotes the safe distance from the jth ship to its preceding ship, $D_j(t)$ denotes the braking distance of the jth ship at t, and $d_{f,j}(t)$ denotes the minimum distance from the jth ship to its preceding ship.

(ii) Acceleration: Let $gap_j(t)$ denote the space that ship j gives to its preceding ship at t. If $gap_j(t) > gap_{\text{safe},j}(t)$, for ship j, $v_j(t) \to \min[v_j(t) + 1, V_{\max}]$. This reflects the behavior of ship operators seeking to travel at a higher velocity.

(iii) Deceleration: If $gap_j(t) < gap_{\text{safe},j}(t)$, and the conditions do not meet the requirements for executing an overtaking maneuver, ship j must decelerate and follow the preceding ship.

$$v_j(t) = \min[v_j', gap_j(t) - d_{f,j}(t)] \tag{10}$$

where $v_j'(t)$ denotes the velocity of the preceding ship of the jth ship.

(iv) Overtaking: If $gap_j(t) < gap_{\text{safe},j}(t)$ and the sailing environment meets the requirements for executing an overtaking maneuver, ship j should overtake the preceding ship. The lane-change in the overtaking maneuver has a obvious influence on the ship velocity, which cannot be ignored. According to the ship-motion equations, a simplified equation for velocity change in this CA-based model can be calculated by

$$v_j(t) = \frac{[v_j(t)]^2}{\sqrt{[v_j(t)]^2 + [\Delta dl_j(t)]^2}} \tag{11}$$

Where $\Delta dl_j(t)$ is the lateral movement distance during the overtaking.

(v) Velocity change caused by the impacts of weather and sea: If there is no acceleration, deceleration, or overtaking, then the main factor of influence on the ship velocity is the weather and sea. Let $a_j'(t)$ denote the regular acceleration, which can be calculated by Eq. (4). Let $a_j''(t)$ denote the random acceleration, which can be calculated by Eq. (8). The velocity of the ship is

$$v_j = v_j(t) + a_j'(t) \cdot \Delta t + a_j''(t) \cdot \Delta t \tag{12}$$

where Δt is the time span.

(vi) Velocity and location update: After the steps above, the velocity of ship j at $t+1$ can be updated as $v_j(t+1) = v_j(t)$. The location of ship j is $x_j(t)$ at t. Thus, at $t+1$ the location of ship j is $x_j(t+1) = x_j(t) + v_j(t+1)$.

Based on item (v), the changes of ships' velocities under the influence of weather and sea are reproduced.

3 Test and simulation results

The purpose of this section is to test the performance of the model proposed above. First, according to the contents of Sections 2.1 and 2.2, the velocities of ships that sailed through a specified area in the Dover Strait were studied. The regular and random components of the accelerations were determined. Next, according to the update rules in Section 2.3, the marine traffic simulation was performed. By comparing the results with the measured data by AIS, the accuracy of the velocities in the simulation was analyzed and evaluated. Second, more ship traffic flows in different areas were selected to test the reliable and universal of the model. By analyzing and comparing the simulation results, the applicability of the model for the traffic flows under different conditions is evaluated.

To study the impacts of the weather and sea on ships' velocity, the impacts from navigators should be excluded. Generally, the areas at sea are always wide and the ship density is low. Ships need not slow down or speed up during navigation frequently. In the tests, as the ships' densities are not very high, the impacts from navigators can be ignored. However, for the traffic flow in which the ships' density is very high, the changes of ships' velocities caused by the impacts of navigators should be recognized and excluded before obtaining the regular and random components of the acceleration.

3.1 Velocity change study and marine traffic simulation

A specified traffic flow in the Dover Strait was taken as an example to test the accuracy of the model. As shown in Figure 3, some of the ships' trajectories are shown. The direction of the traffic flow is roughly southwest. The width of the traffic flow is approximately 2.3 – 4.4 n mile. The length of the traffic flow is approximately 55.2 n mile.

According to AIS, the traffic data of ships for 3 consecutive days in the specified area was obtained. The sampling interval is 1 min. Generally, in the vehicle traffic study, the sampling interval is 1 s. However, the average velocity of ships is slower than that of the vehicles. In addition, the duration of time for marine traffic study is always longer than the vehicle traffic. Thus, the sampling interval for marine traffic should be longer than that for vehicle traffic. The curves of ships' velocities are shown in Figure 1. According to Eqs. (1) and (2), the average acceleration of ships, a, was calculated, as shown in Figure 4. From Figures 1 and 4, the trend of ships' ve-

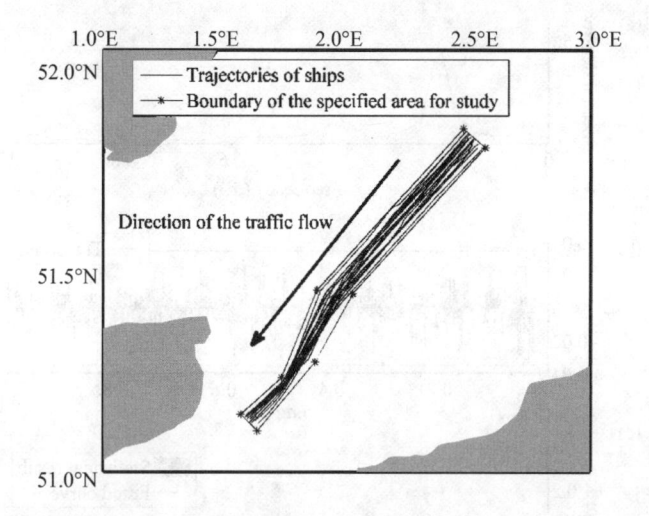

Figure 3 The schematic diagram of the relationships between the acceleration a, the regular component a' and the random component a''

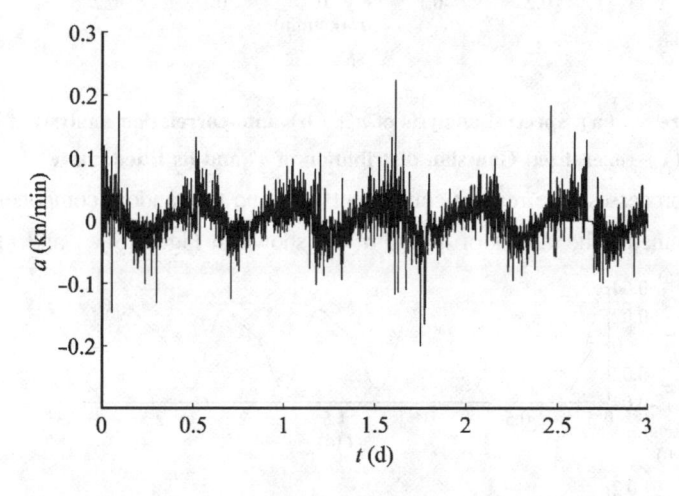

Figure 4 The average acceleration of the ships that sailed southwestward in the Dover Strait for 3 days

locities and accelerations curves are found to be periodic and wavy, despite the noisy interference.

When a is known, the next step is to determine a' and a''. By performing a Fast Fourier transform, the frequency distribution of a was achieved. The result is shown in Figure 5(a). There are two main periodic subcomponents. The frequency of the first one is approximately 1.94 times per day, which is approximately half the frequency of the second one, approximately 3.87 times per day. The cycle length of the regular components is approximately 12.4 h, which is consistent with the tidal cycle length. As the mathematical function form of a' is known, a' can be determined using the curve fitting method mentioned in Sections 2.1 and 2.2. In this model, the residual of a after the curve fitting, which is a'', must be a random sequence. By Eq. (6), the auto-correlation of a'', which is C, was calculated. The result is shown in Figure 5(b). The statistical result of a'' and the fitted curve are shown in Figure 5(c).

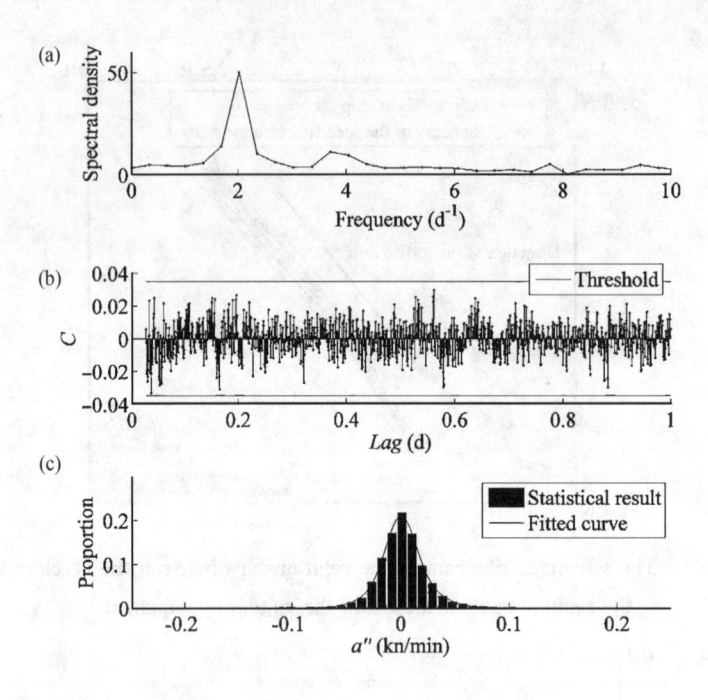

Figure 5 (a) **Spectral analysis of** a'; (b) **auto-correlation analysis of** a'';
(c) **generalized Gaussian distribution of** a'' **and its fitted curve**

After the above processes, the regular component, a', and the random component, a'', of the acceleration were determined. The curves of a' and a'' are shown in Figure 6(a) and (b), respectively.

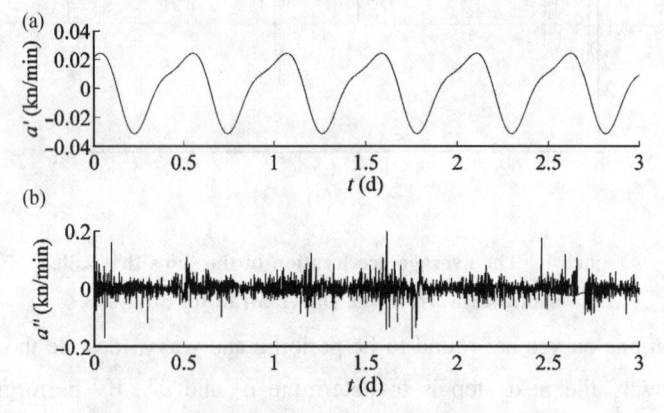

Figure 6 (a) **Curve of the regular component,** a';
(b) **curve of the random component,** a''

The coefficients of Eqs. (4) and (7) can be obtained using spectral analysis, curve fitting, autocorrelation analysis, statistics, etc. Therefore, in the marine traffic simulation, the acceleration of a ship, a_s, was regenerated according to Eq. (3). Let a_s' denote the random component of a_s. Let a_s'' denote the random component of a_s. Let a_m denote the actual acceleration from the measurement. Figure 7 shows the curves of a_s', a_s'', a_s and a_m within one cycle. By comparing Figure 7(c) and (d), the curve of the acceleration in the simulation is found to be very similar to the curve of the acceleration from the measurement.

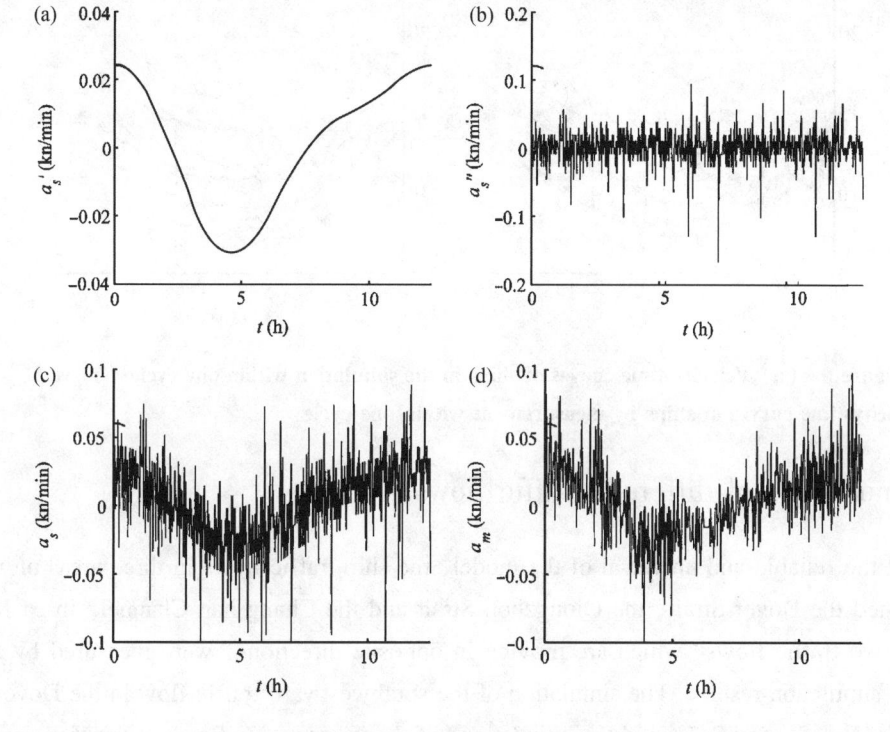

Figure 7 (a) Curve of the regular component in the simulation within one cycle; (b) curve of the random component in the simulation within one cycle; (c) acceleration determined by combining the regular and random components in the simulation within one cycle; (d) acceleration obtained by measurement within one cycle

According to the update rules in Section 2.3, the southwestward traffic flow in the specified area in Dover Strait was simulated under open boundary conditions. The arrival interval time and distribution of ship velocity were obtained from the statistical result of the measured data by AIS. The time span is 1 min, which is consistent with the sampling interval described above. The velocity-time curves of ships in the simulation within one cycle are shown in Figure 8(a). Figure 8(b) shows the velocity-time curves of ships by measurement within one cycle. First, the macroscopic trend of the velocity change in the simulation results is consistent with the actual measured result. In the period of 0 – 6.2 h, the velocities of ships are decreasing. In the period of 6.2 – 12.4 h, the velocities of ships are increasing. Second, the local fluctuation of velocity curves in Figure 8(a) is similar to that in Figure 8(b). The amplitude and frequency of these fluctuations are found to be very similar. Therefore, by comparing Figure 8(a) and (b), the characteristics of the velocity change in the simulation are consistent with the actual situation.

In summary, using the methods proposed in this paper, the regular and random components of ships' accelerations caused by the impacts of weather and sea were successfully determined. The accelerations of ships in the traffic flow were regenerated. In the marine traffic simulation, the regenerated accelerations were added to the ships' velocities to simulate the velocity change impacted by the weather and sea. The simulation results show that the characteristics of the ships' velocities changes have been simulated accurately when the ship density is not very high.

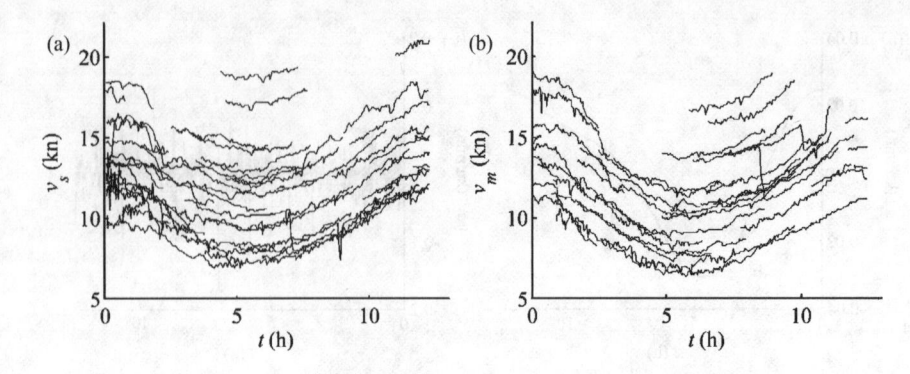

Figure 8 (a) Velocity-time curves of ships in the simulation within one cycle; (b) velocity-time curves of ships by measurement within one cycle

3.2 Simulations of different traffic flows

To test the reliable and universal of the model, the ship traffic flows in three areas on the sea were simulated the Dover Strait, the Qiongzhou Strait and the Changshan Channel. In each area, the data of two traffic flows, which are moving in opposite directions, were measured by AIS to validate the simulation results. The simulation of the southwestward traffic flow in the Dover Strait was introduced in Section 3.1, and the simulations of the other traffic flows in the three areas are introduced in this subsection. The spatial information of the traffic flows is shown in Table 1.

Table 1 Spatial information of the traffic flows

Location	Direction of the traffic flow	Width of the traffic flow (n mile)	Length of the traffic flow (n mile)
Dover Strait	Northeast	4.8 – 11.1	55.2
Qiongzhou Strait	East	1.3	14.1
Qiongzhou Strait	West	1.3	14.1
Changshan Channel	East	1.2 – 3.0	23.4
Changshan Channel	West	1.1 – 2.3	23.4

Figures 9, 12, 15, 18 and 21 show the traffic flows on maps. The direction, geographical location and region of each traffic flow are marked on the maps. Parts of the ships trajectories in the traffic flows are drawn.

According to Sections 2.1 and 2.2, the regular and random components of ship's accelerations were obtained in the simulation of the traffic flows above. Using Eq. (4), the regular components of ships' accelerations were reproduced, as shown in Figures 10(a), 13(a), 16(a), 19(a), and 22(a). The cycle length of the regular component of the northeastward traffic flows in the Dover Strait is approximately 12 – 13 h, which is similar to the southwestward traffic flow in the Dover Strait. However, the cycle lengths of the other four traffic flows are approximately 24 – 25 h. The shapes of the regular component curves are different for the traffic flows in different areas.

Using Eq. (8), the random components of the ships' accelerations were also reproduced, as shown in Figures 10(b), 13(b), 16(b), 19(b), and 22(b). In the Changshan Channel, the random components of the ships' accelerations are larger than those in the Dover Strait and the Qiongzhou Strait. However, the proportion of the random components with a large value is small. Therefore, the regular changes of the accelerations in the Changshan Channel are still obvious. The difference is that some great changes of accelerations will occur occasionally.

By combining the two components according to Eq. (3), the ships' accelerations of each traffic flow were regenerated, as shown in Figures 10(c), 13(c), 16(c), 19(c), and 22(c). The ships' accelerations of each traffic flow by measurement are shown in Figures 10(d), 13(d), 16(d), 19(d), and 22(d). By comparing the regenerated accelerations' curves with the actual measured accelerations' curves, it can be found that the former curves are consistent with the latter curves. Not only the macroscopical regular change but also the random fluctuation of the acceleration can be reproduced accurately. The methods of achieving the regular and random components are reasonable. Moreover, the method of combining the results of the two components to reproduce the acceleration is accurate and reliable. This model is suitable for simulating the ships' velocities of marine traffic flows in different areas, as described above.

The simulations were conducted based on the update rules in Section 2.3. In the simulations, the distributions of ship velocities and arrival interval times were consistent with those of the actual situation, which were achieved from the statistical results of the measured data by AIS. The other parameters in the simulations were the same as the simulation in Section 3.1. In the Dover Strait, the curves of the ships' velocities decrease and increase one time per cycle, which is approximately 12 – 13 h. In the Qiongzhou Strait, the curves of ships' velocities decrease and increase one time per cycle; however, the cycle length is approximately 24 – 25 h. In the Changshan Channel, the curves of ships' velocities decrease and increase two times per cycle, which is approximately 24 – 25 h. Therefore, the characteristics of the changes of the ships' velocities of different traffic flows are different. However, the simulation results are consistent with the measured data, as shown in Figures 11, 14, 17, 20 and 23. Although the position, width, length, direction of each traffic flow are different, the characteristics of the ships' velocities changes can be accurately simulated based on this model.

(1) Northeastward traffic flow in the Dover Strait;
(2) Eastward traffic flow in the Qiongzhou Strait;
(3) Westward traffic flow in the Qiongzhou Strait;
(4) Eastward traffic flow in the Changshan Channel;
(5) Westward traffic flow in the Changshan Channel.

In summary, the characteristics of ships' velocities changes in the traffic flows were simulated accurately, although the characteristics of each traffic flow are different. These results show that the model has a strong universality for marine traffic simulation when the ship density is not very high.

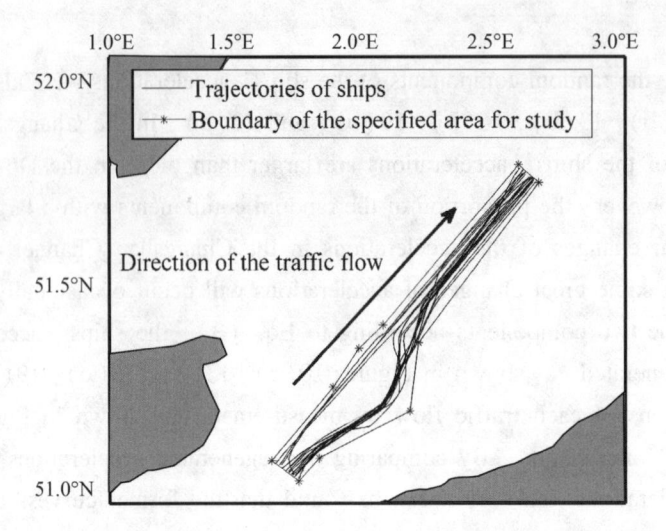

Figure 9 The map of the specified northeastward traffic flow in the Dover Strait

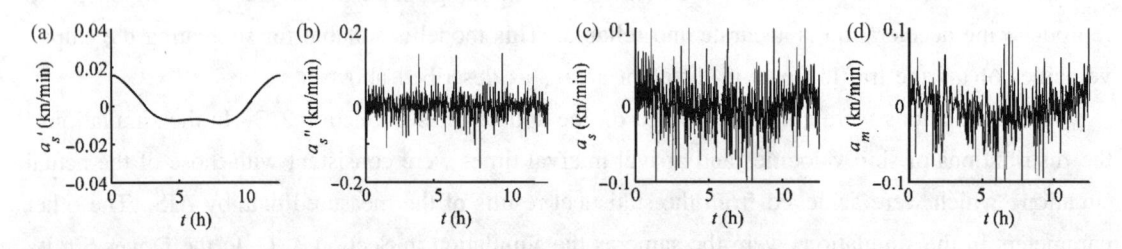

Figure 10 (a) Curve of the regular component in the simulation within one cycle; (b) curve of the random component in the simulation within one cycle; (c) acceleration determined by combining the regular and random components in the simulation within one cycle; (d) acceleration obtained by measurement within one cycle

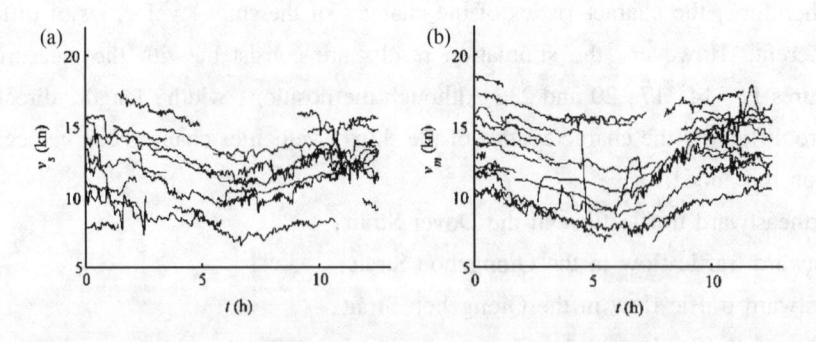

Figure 11 (a) Velocity-time curves of ships in the simulation within one cycle; (b) velocity-time curves of ships by measurement within one cycle

— 50 —

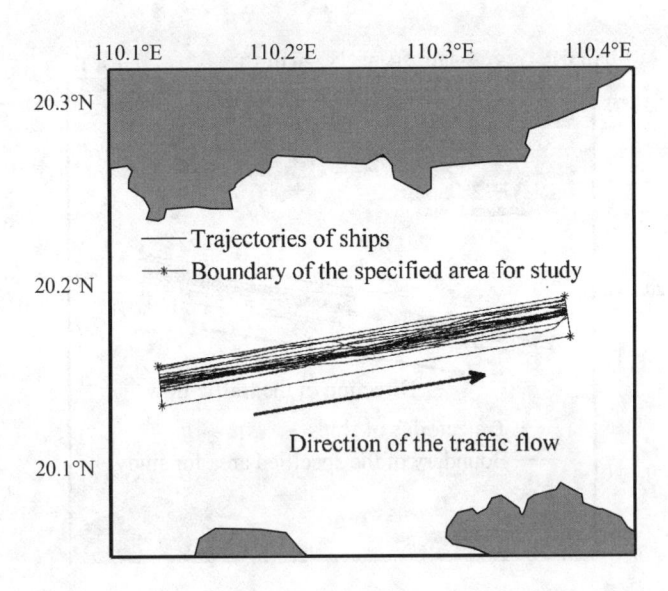

Figure 12　The map of the specified eastward traffic flow in the Qiongzhou Strait

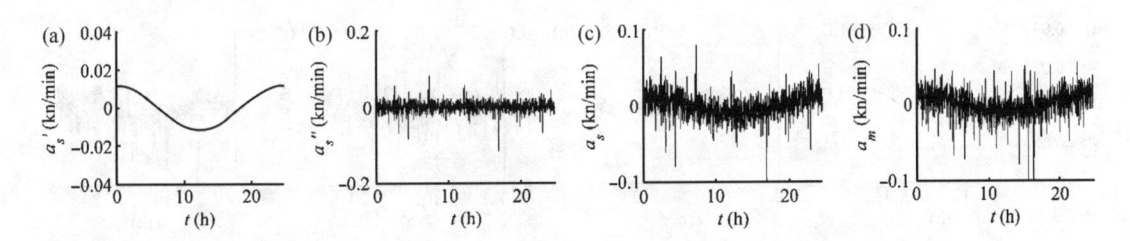

Figure 13　(a) Curve of the regular component in the simulation within one cycle; (b) curve of the random component in the simulation within one cycle; (c) acceleration determined by combining the regular and random components in the simulation within one cycle; (d) acceleration obtained by measurement within one cycle

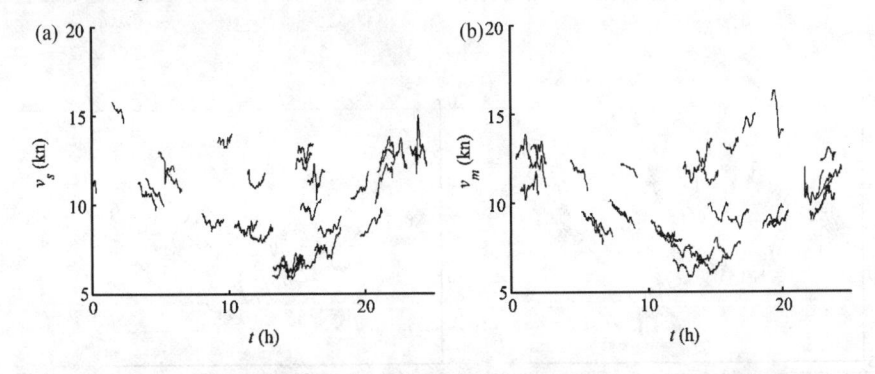

Figure 14　(a) Velocity-time curves of ships in the simulation within one cycle; (b) velocity-time curves of ships by measurement within one cycle

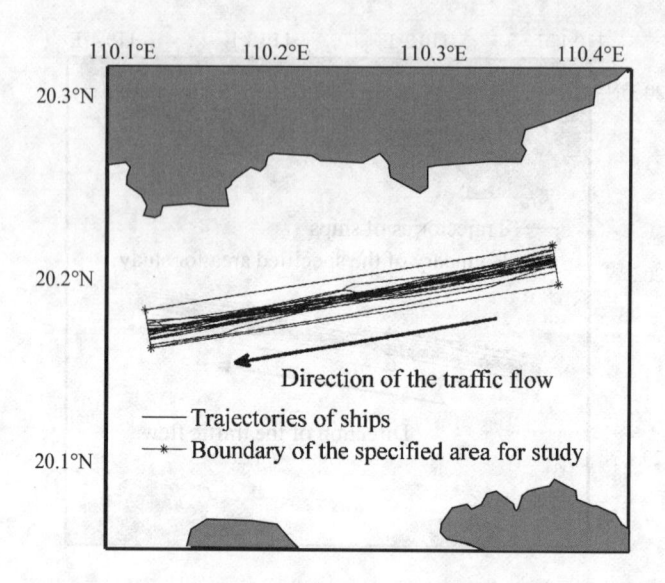

Figure 15 The map of the specified westward traffic flow in the Qiongzhou Strait

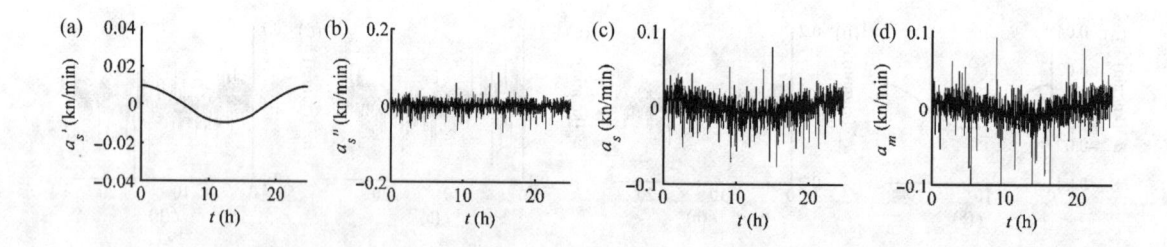

Figure 16 (a) Curve of the regular component in the simulation within one cycle; (b) curve of the random component in the simulation within one cycle; (c) acceleration determined by combining the regular and random components in the simulation within one cycle; (d) acceleration obtained by measurement within one cycle

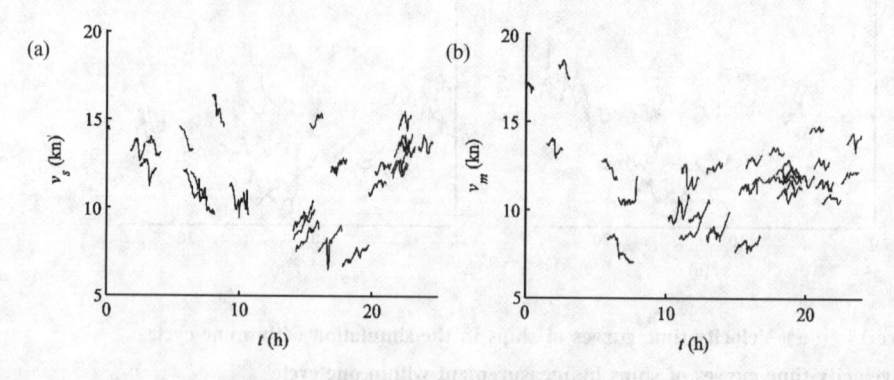

Figure 17 (a) Velocity-time curves of ships in the simulation within one cycle; (b) velocity-time curves of ships by measurement within one cycle

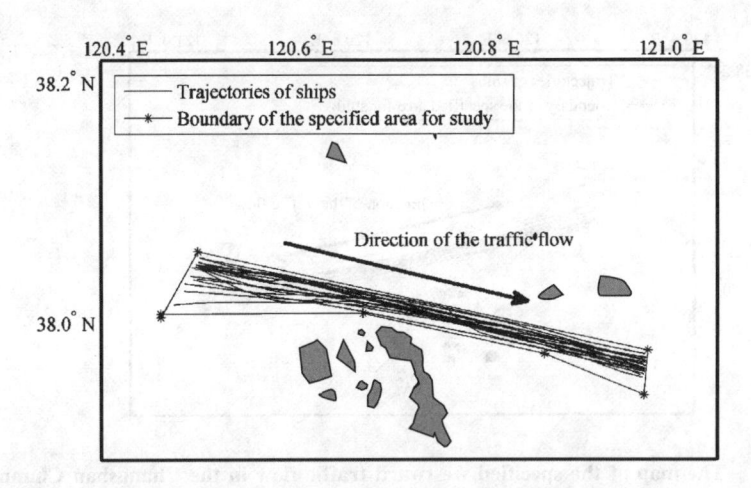

Figure 18 The map of the specified eastward traffic flow in the Changshan Channel

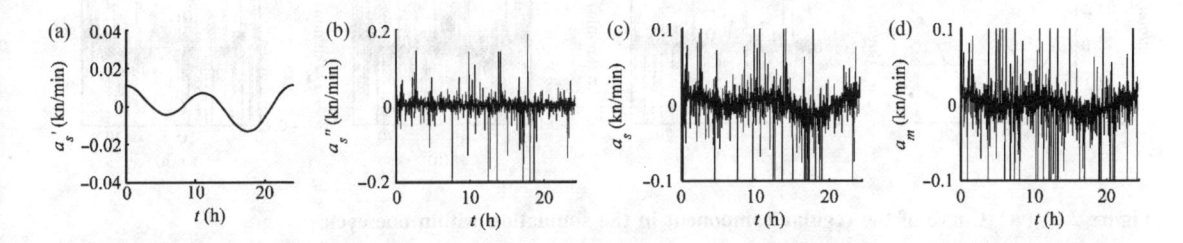

Figure 19 (a) Curve of the regular component in the simulation within one cycle; (b) curve of the random component in the simulation within one cycle; (c) acceleration determined by combining the regular and random components in the simulation within one cycle; (d) acceleration obtained by measurement within one cycle

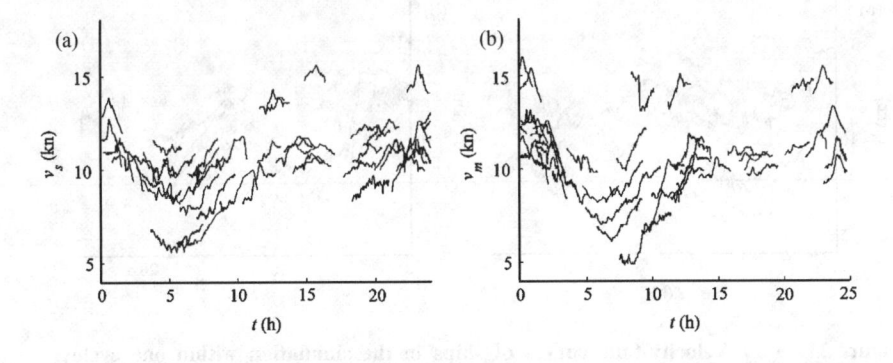

Figure 20 (a) Velocity-time curves of ships in the simulation within one cycle; (b) velocity-time curves of ships by measurement within one cycle

— 53 —

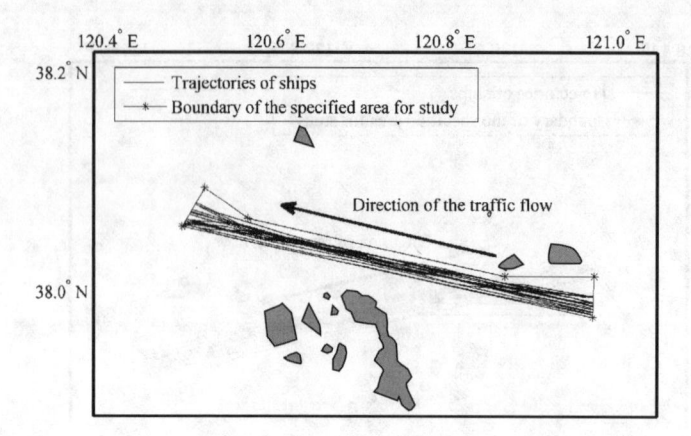

Figure 21 The map of the specified westward traffic flow in the Changshan Channel

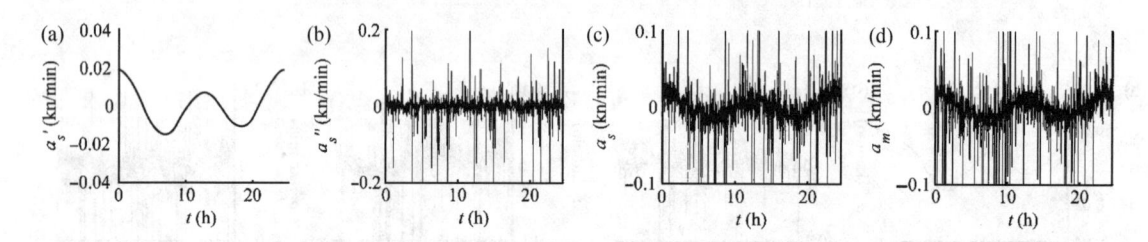

Figure 22 (a) Curve of the regular component in the simulation within one cycle; (b) curve of the random component in the simulation within one cycle; (c) acceleration determined by combining the regular and random components in the simulation within one cycle; (d) acceleration obtained by measurement within one cycle

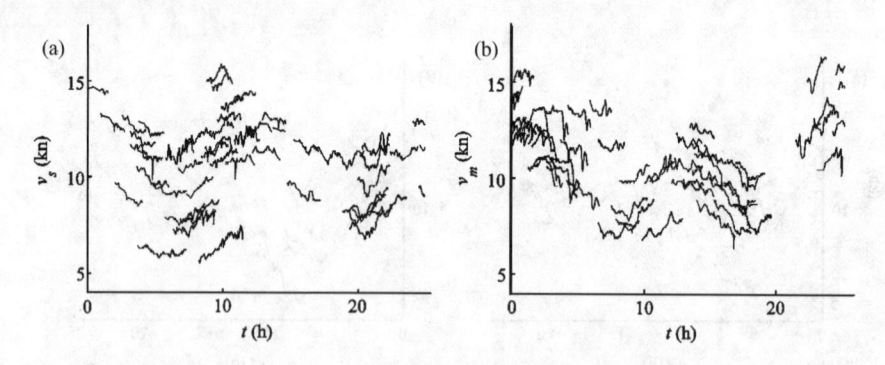

Figure 23 (a) Velocity-time curves of ships in the simulation within one cycle; (b) velocity-time curves of ships by measurement within one cycle

4 Conclusions and prospects

A new CA-based marine traffic model was proposed by considering the velocity change characteristics under the influence of the weather and sea. Based on this model, the simulation of southwestward traffic flow in the Dover Strait was conducted. The results show that the changes of ships' velocities in the simulation are consistent with the measured data. The characteristics of ships' velocities were accurately reproduced. Next, the simulations of the marine traffic flow in other areas, the Changshan Channel, the Qiongzhou Strait were conducted. Although the characteristics of ships' velocities changes were different in different traffic flows, the simulation results based on this model were found to be consistent with the actual situation. Therefore, this model has a strong universality in terms of marine traffic simulation when the ship density is not very high.

Because of the advantages mentioned above, higher accuracy, reliable information of ships' velocities in marine traffic study can be achieved. This method can be used to supply support for the ship route optimization, ship navigation, ship behavior study, marine traffic management, traffic flow prediction, etc. In the future, more studies need to be performed to improve the model for different professional applications.

基于 AIS 数据约束聚类的海上交通特征分析*

摘要：为识别船舶交通流，分析海上交通特征，根据海上交通工程理论和数据挖掘技术，考虑 AIS 数据点的多种属性约束，改进一种基于密度的聚类算法，从大量 AIS 数据中解析不同类型的船舶交通流，计算平均航向和航速，并选取浙沪交界复杂水域进行实例验证。聚类结果与实际相符，证实了算法的可行性和有效性。

关键词：DBSCAN 算法；船舶自动识别系统；聚类分析；海上交通特征

0 引言

近年来 AIS 数据挖掘方法和应用迅速发展。学者们主要基于 AIS 数据点[134-136]或轨迹线[137]，利用一定的数学模型和信息技术开展相关数据挖掘。数据点方法能充分利用 AIS 对象的多个属性开展定制化分析，轨迹线方法在分析船舶航路、航线上取得良好效果。通过挖掘历史 AIS 数据可以识别海上锚泊区、作业区、拥挤区等特殊区域[136]，识别船舶主要航路[138]，分析船舶领域和运动模式[139]，研究船舶密度和速度分布[140]，评估船舶会遇或碰撞风险[141]，推算到港概率或航迹趋势[142]，开展异常检测[143]，设计或审查定线制[144]，研究碳排放[145]等。

在海上交通特征分析方面，虽然出现很多研究成果甚至成熟的软件，但鲜见充分利用 AIS 数据对象的多种属性进行约束聚类分析的文献。本文采用 AIS 数据点方法，引入航速、航向和海上移动通信业务标识(Maritime Mobile Service Identify, MMSI)属性，改进 DBSCAN(Density-Based Spatial Clustering of Applications with Noise)算法，对大量船舶 AIS 数据进行约束聚类分析，辨识船舶航路，区分不同类型船舶的交通流，并计算平均航向和航速，为主管部门开展航路规划、实施船舶交通组织提供依据。

1 船舶 AIS 数据

AIS 是一种船舶导航设备，在航时最快 2 s、最慢 3 min 发送 1 次，内容包含船舶静态数据（船名、呼号、MMSI、船舶编号、船舶类型、船长、船宽等）、船舶动态数据（经度、纬度、船首向、航向、航速等）和船舶航次数据（载货、吃水、目的地、计划到达时间等）[146]。AIS 的强制配备和广泛应用，不仅提高了船舶航行安全和效率，而且为挖掘海上船舶交通特征提供了较好的素材。

定义 1 基于 AIS 数据的船舶运动点集为有限序列 $T = \{p_1, p_2, \cdots, p_n\}$，第 i 个船舶运动

---

* 本文发表在《船海工程》2018 年第 47 卷第 1 期，作者李永攀、刘正江、蔡垚、郑中义。

点 $p_i = \{time_i, mmsi_i, lon_i, lat_i, sog_i, cog_i\}$。其中，$time_i$ 为产生时间，$mmsi_i$ 为所属船舶的海上移动通信业务标识，lon_i 为经度，lat_i 为纬度，sog_i 为对地航速，cog_i 为对地航向。

MMSI 由 9 位数字组成：$M_1I_2D_3X_4X_5X_6X_7X_8X_9$。其中：$M_1I_2D_3$ 为水上识别国家代码，代表分配给某个国家或地区的水上识别代码，基本范围为 201～799，中国籍船舶的 $M_1I_2D_3$ 为 412、413 或 414，其他为国际船舶。X 则为 0～9 中的任意一个数字，由管理机构负责分配[147]。

2 改进 DBSCAN 算法

2.1 传统算法局限及改进思路

DBSCAN 算法是一种具有噪声、基于密度的聚类分析算法，可以将数据集分成若干簇，并有效地处理噪声点，过滤低密度区域。其基本思想是在含有噪声的数据空间中，通过不断扩展有足够高密度的区域来进行聚类，发现任意形状的高密度点集。由于 DBSCAN 算法提出较早，聚类效果、时间复杂度和算法复杂度的综合评价较高，在空间聚类算法领域得到了广泛的应用。学者们主要从提高聚类效率和效果、增加处理对象属性维度等两个方面改进 DBSCAN 算法。

对于船舶运动点 p_i，6 个属性均包含着丰富的交通特征信息。考虑到 MMSI 编码有一定的规律，沿同一航路行驶的船舶具有近似的速度和航向，本文通过引入 MMSI、航速、航向 3 个属性值改进 DBSCAN 聚类算法，即将 MMSI 满足指定类别、具有相似的航速和航向的船舶聚类。

定义 2 船舶 eps 邻域是以特定点为圆心，以 eps 为半径的圆内且满足一定条件的点集，即给定轨迹集 D，轨迹点 p 的邻域 $N(p) = \{q \in D \mid dist(p,q) < eps\ \&\&\ |p.sog - q.sog| < MaxSog\ \&\&\ |p.cog - q.cog| < MaxCog\ \&\&\ p.mmsi \in 指定类别\}$。其中，$dist(p,q)$ 指考虑地球曲度后的地理距离。注意到 359°与 1°实际只差 2°，$|p.cog - q.cog|$ 需经过必要的转换。

2.2 基于 AIS 数据改进 DBSCAN 算法

为解析航速相近、航向相似的（特殊）船舶流，改进 DBSCAN 算法进行 AIS 数据约束聚类时，约束条件是航速差小于 MaxSog，航向差小于 MaxCog 且同属于（指定的）船舶类别。改进后的算法（AIS - DBSCAN）伪代码如下。

输入：船舶 AIS 点集合 D，航向变化范围 MaxCog，航速变化范围 MaxSog，mmsi 类别 MC，邻域半径 eps 和最小邻域点数 MinPts；
输出：簇集，标记每个点的簇名。
AIS - DBSCAN（D, eps, MinPts, MaxCog, MaxSog, MC）
clustered = 0;
标记所有点为未分类点；
for(p ∈ D) do
  if(点 p 为未分类点) then

从 p 中解析出 mmsi；
邻域为 Q = QUERYNEIGHBOR(p,eps,MinPts,MaxCOG,MaxSOG,MC)，总数为 np；
if(np≥MinPts)then
标记 p 为核心点，p 及 Q 集合内点 label = clusterId；
EXPEND(Q,clustered,eps,MinPts)；
clustered + 1；
endif
else
标记 p 为噪声点；
endelse
endif
endfor
EXPEND(Q,clusterId,eps,MinPts)
while(Q 不为空)do
取出 Q 集合中的点 q，计算 q 的邻域 K = QUERYNEIGHBO(q,eps,MinPts,MaxCOG,MaxSOG,MC)，总数记作 nq；
If(nq1≥MinPts)then
for(k ∈ K)do
If(k 是未标记点或者是噪声点)then
标记点 k 的 label = clusterId；
endif
if(k 是未标记点)then
将 k 添加到 Q 集合中；
endif
endfor
endif
从 Q 中移除 q；
endwhile
QUERYNEIGHBOR(p,eps,MinPts,MaxCOG,Max − SOG,MC)
新建集合 Q；
for(q ∈ D)do
if(dist(p,q) < eps)then
if(p. mmsi ∈ MC&&|p. SOG − q. SOG| < MaxSOG&&|p. COG − q. COG| < MaxCOG)then
Q. add(q)；
endif
endif
endfor
returnQ；
算法 AIS − DBSCAN 调用 2 个函数 EXPEND 和 QUERYNEIGHBOR，和原 DBSCAN 具有

同样的复杂度 $O(n^2)$。

3 实例分析

3.1 数据抽取和预处理

实例选取舟山北部的浙沪交界水域,浙江沿海东航路、中航路、洋山港主航道、小型船舶和渔船习惯航路等在这里交汇,交通流密集,通航状态复杂。使用一款软件调取 2016 年 7 月—12 月的船舶流量线,如图 1 所示。

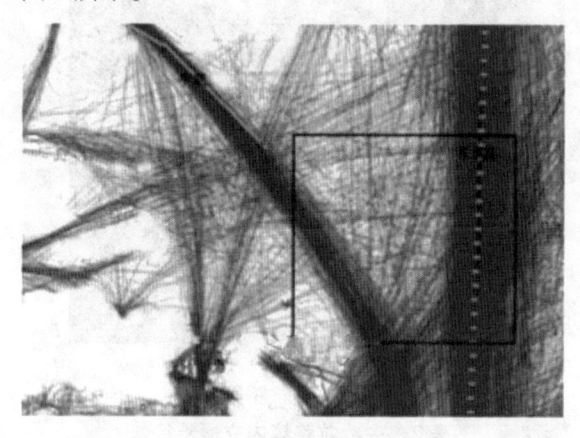

图 1 研究区域

东航路流量线最密集,中航路其次,洋山港主航道不明显。该图尽管能看出大致的船舶航路,但无法解析船舶 AIS 点集合的聚类特征,难以计算主要船舶流的航向、航速,无法识别国际船舶等重要船舶交通流。

以图 1 中 ABCD 围起的四边形为研究对象,提取 2017 年 1 月 1—10 日的 23 余万条船舶 AIS 数据。对数据进行预处理,去除速度小于 0.5 kn、属性值缺失、MMSI 不合规范的点,得到 221 695 条数据,格式如表 1 所示。

表 1 AIS 数据列表

时间	MMSI	经度	纬度	速度/kn	航向
2017-01-04 18:48:46	412321789	122.636 76°	30.509 687°	8.4	198.2°
2017-01-04 18:51:16	412321789	122.635 32°	30.503 660°	8.7	187.4°
2017-01-06 16:40:24	218426000	122.619 08°	30.457 288°	2.3	326.3°
2017-01-06 08:57:40	218426000	122.625 88°	30.450 780°	2.4	301.1°
…	…	…	…	…	…

3.2 聚类分析

使用 JAVA 语言编写并借助 WEKA 软件运行以上算法。根据日常经验,将速度差 MaxSog 设置为 2 kn,航向差 MaxCOG 设置为 5°。选取不同的 MMSI 类别,反复调整 eps、MinPts 参数,得到下述聚类结果。

3.2.1 主要航路聚类

当 MMSI 不加限制、eps 为 0.01、MinPts 为 300 时,聚类得到 7 个簇,可视化结果见图 2,各簇聚类数量和比例、平均航速与航向见表 2。

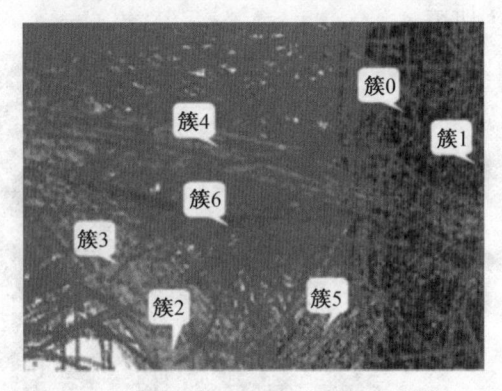

图 2　主要航路聚类

表 2　主要航路簇内交通特征

参数	簇号						
	0	1	2	3	4	5	6
数量/个	31 880	35 824	17 769	13 092	2 349	11 800	2 754
比例/%	27	31	15	11	2	10	2
平均速度/kn	9.6	9.1	8.1	9.5	9.7	9.1	12.7
平均航向/(°)	181	2	324	145	281	220	103

聚类得出了 7 条船舶密集交通流,其中 1 条(簇 5)目前航路指南中尚未明确。洋山港主航道出口船舶速度明显较大,说明洋山港主航道船舶多数满载进港,空载离港。东航路、中航路双向交通流交织,缺乏定线制规则和必要的交通组织,通航秩序较差。

3.2.2 国际船舶交通流聚类

当 MMSI 指定为国际船舶(201≤MID<412 或 415≤MID<799)、eps 为 0.01、MinPts 为 400 时,聚类得到 2 个不同的簇,可视化结果见图 3,各簇聚类数量和比例、平均航速与航向见表 3。

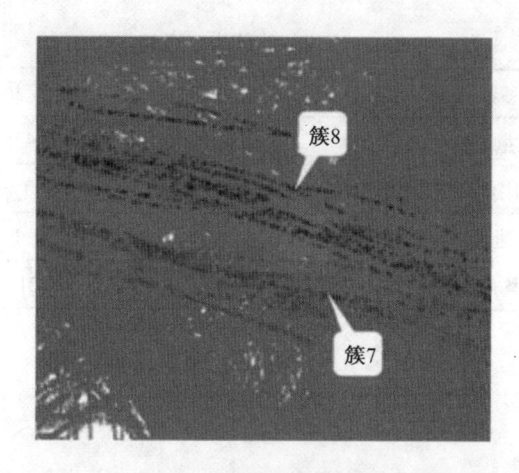

图3 国际船舶航路聚类

表3 国际船舶航路簇内交通特征

参数	簇号	
	7	8
数量/个	7 062	7 968
比例/%	47	53
平均速度/kn	13.9	10.6
平均航向/(°)	102	283

簇7平均航向181°,平均速度13.9 kn,占47%,为洋山港主航道出口船舶流;簇8平均航向283°,平均速度10.6 kn,占53%,为洋山港主航道进口船舶流。

簇7、簇8在平均航向、速度以及可视化轨迹上都与簇4、簇6类似,说明洋山港主航道进出口以国际船舶为主。进出口船舶交通流分界明显,通航秩序较好。

该簇和簇5在平均速度、航向以及位置都非常相似,可推断这是一条渔船习惯进出航路。

渔船航路聚类如图4所示,渔船航路簇内交通特征如表4所示。

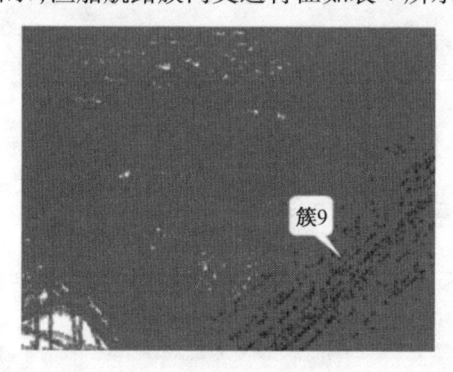

图4 渔船航路聚类

表4 渔船航路簇内交通特征

参数	簇9
数量/个	2 435
比例	100%
平均速度/kn	9.1
平均航向	221°

4 结论

改进DBSCAN算法,引入航速、航向和MMSI开展约束聚类,并结合实际AIS数据情况调整相关参数,成功识别出国际船舶和渔船航路,计算了簇内平均航速与航向,提取到总体数量少但主管部门监管任务重的特殊船舶的航行特征。所提方法突破了DBSCAN算法仅使用空间密度的局限,增加了多种属性约束,且可以根据语义需要随意调整,具有较大的灵活性。实例测试结果与监管经验相符,说明该方法可行和有效。

本文仅提取AIS动态数据开展研究,如何整合包含船舶类型、尺度等要素的AIS静态数据开展聚类分析,将是下一步研究方向。

基于时空密度的船载 AIS 数据聚类分析方法研究

*

摘要：船载 AIS 数据包含位置、时间和其他属性，属于典型的时空数据，对其开展时空聚类分析有助于挖掘海上交通特征。结合 AIS 数据的具体特征，提出时间切片化方法，有效约简 AIS 数据并处理报告间隔不等的问题。在 DBSCAN 算法基础上综合考虑时间和空间要素，提出船载 AIS 数据时空聚类算法，并对实际数据开展分析。该方法能更好顾及船舶交通流的时空耦合特征，识别隐含的时空模式，为主管机关开展船舶交通管理、优化通航秩序、保障航行安全等提供一种新途径。

关键词：交通运输工程；时空密度；聚类分析；DBSCAN 算法；船载 AIS

0 引言

船舶自动识别系统(Automatic Identification System, AIS)是一种船载设备，向岸基及周边船舶发送自身的静态、动态和航次数据。AIS 的强制配备和广泛应用，不仅提高了船舶航行安全和效率，且为开展相关数据挖掘、寻找海上交通规律、协助海上交通规划与管理提供了宝贵素材。

近年来船载 AIS 数据挖掘方法和应用迅速发展。学者们主要基于 AIS 数据点[148]或轨迹线[137]的经纬度、航向和航速等属性，利用一定数学模型和信息技术开展相关数据挖掘。通过挖掘 AIS 数据可识别海上锚泊区、作业区和拥挤区等特殊区域[148]、识别主要船舶航路[140]、分析船舶领域和运动模式[139]、研究船舶密度和速度分布[5]、评估船舶会遇或碰撞风险[141]、推算到港概率或航迹趋势[142]、开展异常检测、设计或审查定线制、评估碳排放等。

在海上交通特征方面：潘家财等分析 AIS 蕴含的航向、航速变化率，提出船舶会遇的时空数据挖掘算法[135, 141, 142]；唐存宝等研究了基于 AIS 的船舶航迹分布算法[149]；肖潇等提出基于 AIS 信息的船舶轨迹线聚类模型[137]；宁建强等提出一种基于海量船舶轨迹数据的细粒度网格海上交通密度计算方法[150]；刘涛等将船舶领域的概念引入 DBSCAN(Density-Based Spatial Clustering of Applications with Noise)算法并开展水上交通拥挤区域的聚类分析与识别[151]；丁兆颖等提出一种基于改进 DBSCAN 的面向海量船舶位置数据码头挖掘算法[152]；魏照坤等引入 AIS 数据运动轨迹特征，利用 DBSCAN 算法开展船舶运动模式识别与应用[153]；G. PALLOTTA 等基于船载 AIS 数据点提出无监督的航路辨识和异常检测模型[148]；LIUBO 等引入航

---

* 本文发表在《重庆交通大学学报》2018 年第 37 卷 10 期，作者李永攀、刘正江、郑中义。

向、航速的概念拓展 DBSCAN 算法,验证船舶是否遵守航路规定及查找异常情形[144]。

以上文献较少综合考虑时间和空间两方面对船载 AIS 数据进行时空聚类分析。然而船载 AIS 数据包含位置、时间和其他属性,属于典型时空数据,隐含着时空耦合特征和模式。笔者旨在开展 AIS 数据时空聚类分析、挖掘隐含的海上交通时空特征。

1 相关工作

时空数据是对现实世界中时空特征和过程的抽象概括。随着传感技术、计算机和大数据技术的发展,时空聚类成为海量时空数据分析的一个重要手段和前沿研究方向[154]。时空聚类是一个无须先验知识的非监督分类过程,依据一定相似性准则将时空实体划分成一系列子类,同一类内实体间的相似度尽可能大于不同类实体间的相似度[154]。

目前常见时空聚类分析算法大多从 DBSCAN 发展而来。DBSCAN 算法不提前设置簇数量,在含有噪声的数据空间中,通过不断扩展有足够高密度的区域来进行聚类,可发现任意形状的高密度簇集,并有效地处理噪声点,过滤低密度区域[155]。该算法提出较早,聚类效果、时间复杂度和算法复杂度的综合评价较高,在空间位置分析领域得到了广泛的应用,已经成为很多学者进一步完善的主要方法[156]。G-DBSCAN(General-DBSCAN) 算法除了空间属性外,还引入权重值考虑了其他非空间属性,认为 DBSCAN 只是一种特殊情况[157]。ST-DBSCAN(Spatio-Temporal-DBSCAN) 算法在 DBSCAN 算法的基础上,引入时间维和非空间属性,通过指定空间半径、时间窗口与密度阈值,计算、识别出核心对象和噪声对象,从而构建任意形状的时空邻近簇[158]。4D + SNN(a spatio-temporal density-based clustering approach with 4D similarity)算法在共享近邻方法基础上,综合考虑空间(2D)、时间(1D)和语义属性(1D),是 DBSCAN 算法的新发展[159]。

ST-DBSCAN 和 4D + SNN 算法属于综合时间、空间维度和其他属性的时空聚类分析,笔者借鉴上述算法理念,考虑船载 AIS 数据报告特征并加以时间切片化处理,在 DBSCAN 算法基础上提出船载 AIS 数据时空聚类算法。

2 AIS 数据约简

船载 AIS 设备分 A、B 两类,300 GT 以上船舶安装 A 级 AIS,航行时报告间隔 2 ~ 12 s,锚泊时报告间隔 3 min。其他小型船舶及渔船安装 B 级 AIS,移动速度不超过 2 kn 时报告间隔 3 min,锚泊时报告间隔 6 min,其他均小于 30 s[160]。

定义 1 基于 AIS 数据的船舶运动点集为三维时空域中的有限序列 $P = \{p_1, p_2, p_3, \cdots, p_n\}$。第 i 个船舶运动点 $p_i = (time, mmsi, lon, lat)$,经度 lon、纬度 lot 和时间 $time$ 构成三维时空域,属性 MMSI 为海上移动通信业务标识(Maritime Mobile Service Identity),可推断该船为国际船舶、国内船舶或渔船[147]。

船载 AIS 设备连续发送数据报告,但报告间隔不同[21]。在相同时间内,不同船舶报告 AIS 数据对象的数量可能相差十几倍。指定时间内 AIS 数据点数与船舶数不成一定比例,使得盲目指定时间距离开展时空聚类分析没有实际意义。为便于时空聚类分析,仅考虑速度大于 2 kn 的在航船载 AIS 数据点,并对其开展时间切片化约简,即每分钟只选取第一个报告点,去除该分钟内其他报告点。

定义2 AIS 数据时间切片化指对某船所有 AIS 数据点根据时间量度进行约简,即按时间先后排序,只保留每分钟内第一个报告点。

算法1 AIS 数据时间切片化

输入:某区域某时间段内的原始 AIS 数据集 $D1 = \{p_1, p_2, p_3, \cdots, p_n\}$。

输出:该区域该时间段内每艘船舶每分钟有且仅有第一个报告点的新数据集 D2。

步骤:

(1)去除速度小于 2 kn、属性值缺失和 MMSI 不合规范的点。

(2)将 D1 中所有数据 p_i 以 *mmsi* 为主要关键字、*time* 为次要关键字排序。

(3)将 *time* 的秒位设置成 0。

(4)去掉 MMSI、time 均相同的数据元素。

对于速度大于 2 kn 的在航船舶,不论装载 A 或 B 级 AIS 系统,报告间隔均小于 30 s,其 AIS 数据经算法 1 处理后每分钟内有且仅有第一个 AIS 报告点。比如,某船舶以 10 kn 速度航行,时间属性值分别为 12:31:02、12:31:13、12:31:21、12:31:32 的 4 条连续报告 AIS 数据经算法 1 处理后,变为 12:31(12:31:00,实际为 12:31:02)时间点数据,即只取第 1 条(12:31:02),后 3 条舍去,误差为 2 s,10.3 m。根据 AIS 报告间隔规律和实际数据抽样查证,正常情况下某分钟内第一条数据都在其前 30 s 内,且大部分都在前 20 s 内。由于沿海船舶平均速度较低,约 10 kn 左右,30 s 内仅航行百余米,故将某分钟的第一条数据看作整分时刻的数据所造成的误差在可接受范围之内。

3 AIS 数据时空聚类算法

作为 DBSACN 在时空域的拓展,将密度、邻域、噪声等在时空域进行新的定义。

定义3 任意一点的时空密度是以该点为圆心、邻域半径 E_{ps} 为半径、2 倍时间距离 t 为高的圆柱体内所包含的点的数量。如图 1 所示,p 点的时空密度为 7。

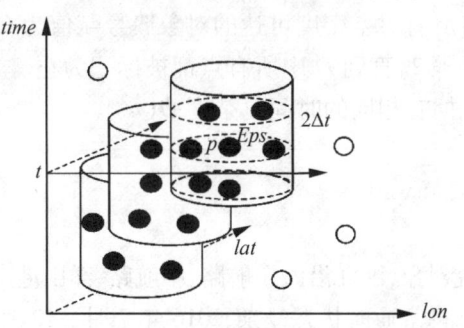

图1 船舶 AIS 数据的时空维度

定义4 任意一点的时空邻域是以该点为圆心、邻域半径 E_{ps} 为半径、2 倍时间距离 t 为高的圆柱体内所包含的点的集合,即 $N(p) = \{q \in D \mid dist(p,q) < E_{ps}, delta(p,q) < \Delta t\}$。其中: $dist(p,q) = \sqrt{(p.lon - q.lon)^2 + (p.lat - q.lat)^2}$,表示空间距离(在研究区域面积较小情况下,可不经过地理距离换算而直接使用欧拉距离); $delta(p,q) = |p.time - q.time|$ 表示时间

距离。

定义 5 若满足条件点 q 在点 p 的时空邻域内,且 p 是时空核心点,则称点 p 到点 q 时空直接密度可达。

定义 6 若有一组有序集 $Y = \{p_1, p_2, \cdots, p_n\}$（其中,$p_1 = p, p_n = q$）,对于任意的 $k(k < n)$ 都满足条件点 p_k 到点 p_{k+1} 时空直接密度可达,则称点 p 到点 q。

定义 7 若存在点 $o \in D$ 使得点 p 和点 q 均从点 o 时空密度可达,则称点 p 和点 q 时空密度连接。

定义 8 若集合 C 是数据库 D 的一个非空子集,点 $p \in C$ 时空密度到达的任一点 $q \in C$,且任意 $p \in C$、$q \in C$,p 和 q 是时空密度连接的,那么称集合 C 是一个时空簇。

定义 9 时空核心点是在指定邻域半径 E_{ps} 和时间距离 Δt 的时空邻域中含有大于最小邻域对象数 MinPts 的点。

定义 10 时空边界点是在时空域中自身不是时空核心点,但是与某一个或者几个时空核心点密度连接的点。

定义 11 时空噪声点是不属于任何时空簇的点。

在上述定义的基础上,基于船载 AIS 数据的时空密度聚类算法的步骤如下：

算法 2 船载 AIS 数据时空聚类算法

输入:数据点集 D、MinPts、E_{ps} 和 t。

输出:时空聚类簇。

步骤:

(1) 将数据集 D 中的所有对象指定为未标记状态。

(2) 读取一个未标记的对象 p,在 D 中寻找未标记的所有满足 $\text{dist}(p, q) < E_{ps}, \text{delta}(p, q) < t$ 的对象 q。

(3) 如果查找出的对象数大于等于 MinPts,则标记该对象为时空核心点,建立新的时空簇 C,簇号为 ClusterID;反之则标记为时空噪声点,并且转步骤 2。

(4) 将 p 时空邻域内所有对象加入 C,将其的簇号赋值为 ClusterID。从 C 中未被标记的对象开始逐一继续搜索,将所有时空密度可达的对象簇号赋值为 ClusterID。

(5) ClusterID +1,转步骤 2,直到 D 中所有点都被标记为止。

上述算法和 DBSCAN 拥有相同的时间复杂度 $O(n^2)$。

4 实例分析

以浙沪交界水域为研究对象,浙江沿海东航路、中航路、洋山港主航道、小型船舶和渔船习惯航路等在这里交汇,交通流密集,通航状态复杂,2016 年 7 月—12 月的船舶流量线如图 2 所示。在图 2 中 ABCD 四边形界限内提取 2017 年 1 月 5、10、15、20、25 日共 40 万余条船载 AIS 数据。

4.1 数据预处理

以 1 月 15 日 75 722 条数据为例,经算法 1 处理后,即对于同一艘船舶每分钟内仅保留第一条 AIS 数据,得到 20 850 条 AIS 数据,见表 1。

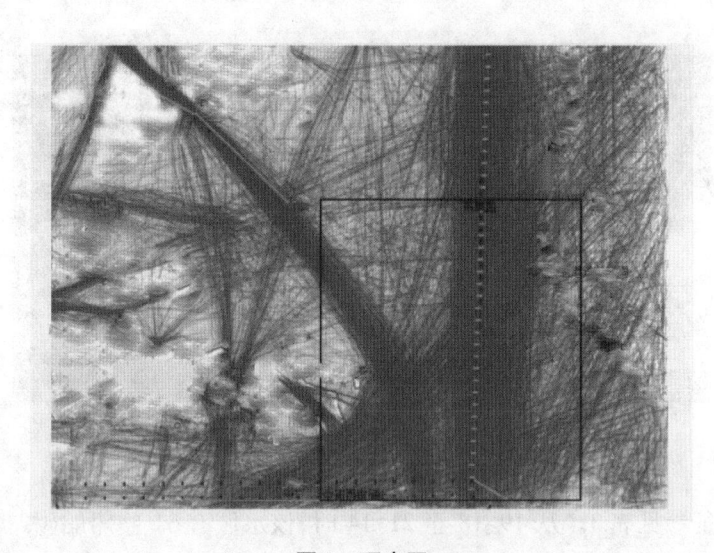

图 2　研究区

表 1　处理后的 AIS 数据列表

时刻	MMSI	经度	纬度
6:16	374176000	122.510 3°	30.511 65°
6:17	374176000	122.507 6°	30.511 81°
16:03	412205110	122.57 94°	30.368 62°
16:04	412205110	122.578 1°	30.370 59°
…	…	…	…

4.2　时空聚类分析

以上述 20 850 条 AIS 数据为基础,使用 JAVA 语言编写并借助 WEKA 软件运行船载 AIS 数据时空聚类算法。反复调整参数,当 $E_{ps}=0.9$ n mile、$t=3$ min、MinPts $=35$ 时,即对于任意一点 p,在以 p 为圆心、$E_{ps}=0.9$ n mile 为半径、分别向上向下延伸高度为 $t=3$ min 的圆柱体内至少有 MinPts $=35$ 个点,该圆柱体在三维时空域内不断游走,直至不再包含 35 个点,所有网进的点形成一个时空邻近簇。所选数据集形成 2 个时空簇,如图 3、表 2 所示。

表 2　聚类结果

时间	MMSI	经度	纬度	簇
20:50	412425318	122.656 2°	30.511 73°	cluster0
20:49	412425318	122.654 9°	30.510 25°	cluster0
17:25	412427363	122.545°	30.515 62°	cluster1
17:50	412427363	122.560 6°	30.503 11°	noise
…	…	…	…	…

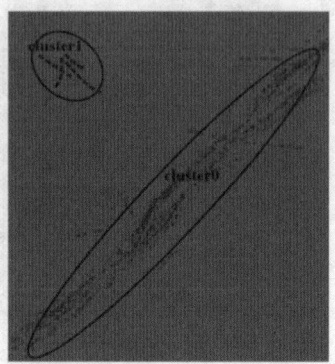

(a) 全部点集　　　　　　　　(b) 隐藏噪声点

图 3　聚类结果示意

聚类结果特征参见表 3。从 19:18 至 21:14 时,该水域有 31 艘船舶(根据 MMSI 编码规律分析[22],含 25 艘渔船,3 艘国际航行船舶,3 艘国内货船)的 1 725 个 AIS 数据点在图中位置集中出现,满足时空密度条件构成簇 0(cluster0)。从 17:15 至 17:30 时,该水域有 9 艘船舶(含 8 艘渔船,1 艘国际航行船舶)的 121 个 AIS 数据点在图中位置集中出现,满足时空密度条件构成簇 1(cluster1)。

由此可看出,当日 17:00、20:00 前后该水域渔船结伴而行、密集活动的情况较突出,东航路、中航路虽然 AIS 数据点密集,但由于商船之间独立性较强,并未发生 AIS 数据点在时空邻域内密集出现的情况。

表 3　聚类结果特征

簇号	AIS 点数	船舶数	时间跨度	空间跨度
cluster0	1 725	31	19:18—21:14	见图 3(b)
cluster1	121	9	17:15—17:30	见图 3(b)

4.3　聚类对比分析

按照 4.1、4.2 节所述方法对该月其他 4 天(为总结规律,不选择连续日期)的 AIS 数据开展时空聚类分析,参数 $E_{ps}=0.9$ n mile、$t=3$ min、MinPts = 30 或 35,最后形成 1 或 2 个簇,如图 4 所示。

当月 5 天的数据聚类结果对比如表 4 所示。

5 天 AIS 数据聚类形成多个不同的簇,各簇的点在空间分布上相对分散,但时间分布上呈现一定规律,18:00—19:00 时左右船舶在时空域上比较密集(占总簇数 60% 以上)。

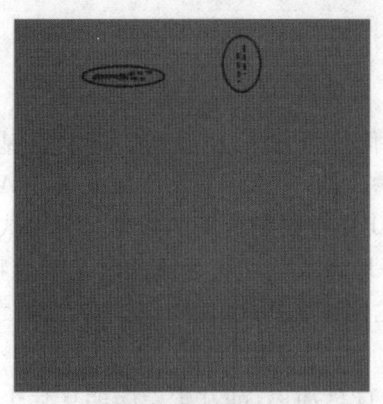

(a) 1月5日AIS数据　　　　　　(b) 1月10日AIS数据

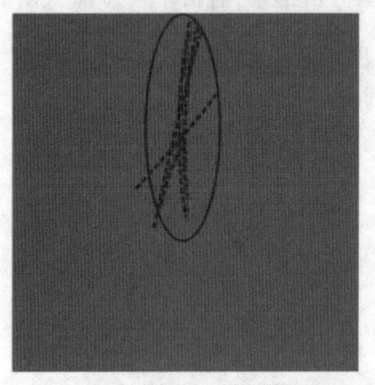

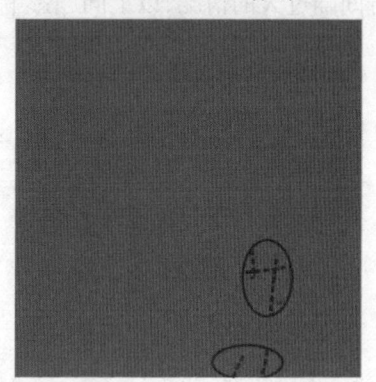

(c) 1月20日AIS数据　　　　　　(d) 1月25日AIS数据

图 4　聚类结果示意

表 4　聚类结果特征对比

日期	簇号	AIS 点数	船舶数	时间跨度	空间跨度
1月5日	2	43	7	02:00—02:06	见图4(a)
	3	42	10	18:24—18:30	见图4(a)
1月10日	4	53	7	01:27—01:34	见图4(b)
1月15日	0	1 725	31	19:18—21:14	见图3(b)
	1	121	9	17:15—17:30	见图3(b)
1月20日	5	303	11	18:57—19:29	见图4(c)
1月25日	6	67	7	18:36—18:44	见图4(d)
	7	30	5	18:51—18:55	见图4(d)

5 结语

通过分析船载 AIS 数据特征,提出时间切片化约简方法,在 DBSCAN 算法基础上引入时间和空间元素给出船载 AIS 数据时空聚类算法,并对浙沪交界复杂水域的船载 AIS 数据开展时空聚类分析,得出渔船结伴而行、18:00—19:00 左右船舶密集的常见交通模式。与其他船载 AIS 数据挖掘算法相比,笔者所提算法能更好地顾及船舶交通流的时空耦合特征,发现隐含的时空模式,为主管机关开展船舶交通管理、优化通航秩序、保障航行安全等提供了一种新途径。

该算法对参数较敏感,参数选择需较多专业背景知识,部分小型船舶存在不开启 AIS 或 AIS 数据报告间隔过大的情况,以上问题影响数据分析结果,有待下一步深入研究。

ISM 规则国内化*

摘要：对 ISM 规则国内化的可行性进行了研究。根据对国内航运公司及其船舶的大量调查，采用模糊推理理论和方法得到了合理的结果。在具体推理过程中，利用系统工程主成分分析确定了模糊推理所采用的指标体系；采用聚类分析方法确定了各因素的评价权重值；采用模糊推理理论建立了评价模型。研究得到的结果为 ISM 规则国内化提供了重要参考。

关键词：船舶；安全营运；防污染；管理规则；国内化

0 引言

1993 年 11 月，国际海事组织以 A.741(18) 号决议通过了《国际船舶安全营运和防止污染管理规则》(ISM 规则)，并由 SOLAS 1974 缔约国大会于 1994 年 6 月决定强制实施，使其成为强制性规则。该规则与 IMO 以往制定的规则明显不同[161]。第一，它既不是针对船舶或船舶设备等硬件的技术标准或要求，也不是针对船员的技术标准或要求，而是针对负责船舶营运公司的标准和要求，它把公司管理作为预防海上事故的重点。第二，该规则把安全系统工程原理和方法运用于海上安全和防污染管理，其核心是要求船公司建立、实施和保持安全管理体系。从这两方面讲，强制实施 ISM 规则是航运安全和防污染管理的一场革命。

我国国际航运公司实施 ISM 规则的实践证明，实施 ISM 规则给我国国际航运安全管理带来了深刻的变化。调查结果表明，实施 ISM 规则以来，各公司的安全管理工作日趋规范化，总体安全管理水平明显提高；各种记录越来越全；船舶与岸上公司最高管理层之间的联系渠道畅通，各类信息及时传递，公司对船舶的监控加强；工作人员的安全意识和责任感增强，观念从"要我安全"向"我要安全"转变；规章制度逐步健全，安全工作落到实处，逐渐步入良性循环的轨道；职责清晰，分工明确，推诿扯皮现象明显减少，办事效率明显提高；船舶和设备维修状况改善，维修费用降低；船岸应急反应有了明显的加强。与此同时，我国船舶的单船年度事故率、单船年度事故死亡率和单船年度事故损失率等都有了明显的下降。

当前，我国国内航线船公司的安全管理状况相对较差，主要表现在以下几个方面：

第一，主要依靠被动反应型的传统安全管理方法，安全管理跟着事故走；

第二，重效益轻安全；

第三，职能交叉，船岸衔接不畅；

第四，人员素质相对较差，管理力量薄弱；

第五，规章制度不健全；

---

* 本文发表在《大连海事大学学报》2002 年 2 月第 28 卷第 1 期，作者吴兆麟、郑中义、张宝晨。

第六,船况普遍较差;

第七,安全责任不到位。

在这样的情况下,能否借助 ISM 的原理和方法,加强国内航行船舶及船公司的管理,是一个重要的研究课题。

1 国内航行船舶应用 ISM 规则的调查和分析

尽管国内航行船舶的公司实际情况不同于那些国际公约强制要求实施 ISM 的国际航运公司,但二者之间存在许多共性。为了充分了解我国国内航行船舶的状况以及航运公司管理的实际情况,便于对国内航行船舶实施 ISM 规则的可行性进行研究,在全国范围内对从事国内航运的公司及其船舶进行了抽样调查,调查的主要内容包括:航运公司所有制形式、船舶种类构成、船舶航区构成、各种船舶平均船龄等 42 项内容。

1.1 国内航行船舶简况

本次抽样调查涉及了 344 家航运公司,其船舶总数为 6 803 艘,船舶总吨位达 300 万吨以上。该数据对于国内航行的船舶具有一定的代表性。从被调查船舶的航区构成来看,内河运输船舶所占的比例较大,为 76%;航行于遮蔽航区的船舶占 12%;从事沿岸航行的船舶占 11%;航行于近海航区的船舶占 1% 左右。尽管从数量上看主要代表内河船舶的情况,但它在船舶吨位上所占的比例较小。从被调查的船舶种类构成来看,涉及了杂货船、散货船、油船、客船、高速船、化学品船、气体运输船、移动式钻井装置、其他货船,船舶种类的调查范围比较广泛,其中其他货船所占的比例为 80%,油船约占 5%,客船约占 4%,散货船约占 2%。从各类船舶的平均船龄情况来看,气体运输船平均船龄为 17 年,油船平均船龄为 18 年,散货船平均船龄为 20 年,杂货船平均船龄为 15 年。

1.2 国内航行船公司状况

调查分析表明,尽管存在船龄老化、船况差和通航环境差等客观原因,但是比例不高,而由于"未健全安全管理机制"和"管理人员素质差"占有较大的比例。大多数航运公司虽然以文件形式规定了船长权力和义务以及对新上岗、转岗船员考核,但差距较大。尽管已有 81.7% 的航运公司建立了险情报告制度,但只有 1.2% 建立了全套的安全管理程序,有部分程序的占 60.5%,有防污应急计划的占 15.1%。可见大多数国内航运公司尚未健全安全管理机制,不能充分地保障船舶、人命财产安全和防止海洋污染。

调查显示,13.7% 的国内公司已经掌握 ISM 规则,65.2% 的国内航运公司熟悉 ISM 规则,这使 ISM 规则的国内化具有较好的基础。

2 ISM 规则国内化可行性定量分析的思路及模型

2.1 思路

在对调查数据进行分析的基础上,首先,从多因素中确定反映航运公司"规模"的因素,利用系统工程主成分分析方法确定反映航运公司"规模"的主要指标,建立定量分析的指标体系,这在一定程度上减少了指标数量,突出重点。其次,为了科学地反映各种船公司对实施 ISM 规则的表决情况,根据所确定的主要分析指标,利用聚类分析方法将所调查的航运公司分成若干类,以确定各类航运公司表决的权重值。再次,利用无量纲的聚类中心作为各类航运公司表决的权重,结合各类航运公司统计结果,得出客观的评价结果。

2.2 评价指标体系的建立

根据对各航运公司调查的 42 个指标,经征求专家意见,初步选取确定了 12 个指标,即:船舶艘数、船舶吨位、船长人数、轮机长人数、管理人员总数、自有船员人数、高级船员人数、公司领导人数、公司领导中有船上资历人数、安全与防污染部门数量、安全主管人数、大专以上人数。为了突出主要因素,去掉重复因素,进一步采取系统工程主成分分析方法并借助 MATLAB 工程计算软件,按照主成分分析法的计算步骤,对调查样本数据进行计算处理,经计算得出了相关矩阵 R 的特征值及占总体百分比,如表 1 所示。

如果按累计百分比为 90% 来选取主成分,根据表 1,则选取的反映航运公司规模大小的主要因素为:总吨位、船舶艘数、高级船员人数、自有船员人数、管理人员总数、轮机长人数和船长人数 7 个因素。

2.3 对调查样本的聚类分析

在选取反映航运公司规模的指标体系建立过程中,得到了 7 个因素,既突出了重要因素,同时也简化了聚类中所要考虑的指标数量,从而简化了对众多样本进行聚类所需的计算工作量。

在聚类分析过程中,首先应对原始数据进行处理,样本的不同指标一般有不同的量纲和数量级别,因此在比较时先对数据进行变换处理。

表1 各因素的特征值及占总体百分比

序号 i	主因素	特征值 λ_i	特征值占总体比例	累计百分比
1	总吨位	3.957 3	32.977 9	32.977 9%
2	船舶艘数	2.299 2	19.160 3	52.138 2%
3	高级船员人数	1.434 2	11.951 7	64.089 9%
4	自有船员数	1.135 3	9.460 9	73.550 8%
5	管理人员总数	0.948 1	7.901 2	81.452 0%
6	轮机长人数	0.650 0	5.670 5	87.122 5%
7	船长人数	0.539 8	4.498 4	91.620 9%
8	公司安全主管人数	0.471 9	3.932 6	95.553 5%
9	大专以上人数	0.387 4	3.228 4	98.781 9%
10	安全与防污染管理部门数	0.068 6	0.572 0	99.353 9%
11	有船上资历的领导人数	0.048 3	0.402 2	99.756 1%
12	公司领导人数	0.029 3	0.244 0	100%

设样本数为 n，变量数为 m，则原始观测数据表示为 x_{ij}（第 i 个样本的第 j 个指标变量），用矩阵 x 表示样本矩阵，则有

$$x = \begin{pmatrix} x_{11} & x_{12} & \cdots & x_{1m} \\ x_{21} & x_{22} & \cdots & x_{2m} \\ \vdots & \vdots & \ddots & \vdots \\ x_{n1} & x_{n2} & \cdots & x_{nm} \end{pmatrix}$$

对原始数据进行标准化处理，即

$$x_{ij}' = \frac{x_{ij} - \overline{x_j}}{s_j} \ (i = 1, 2, \cdots, n; j = 1, 2, \cdots, m)$$

其中

$$\overline{x_j} = \sum_{i=1}^{n} x_{ij}$$

$$s_j = \left[\frac{1}{n-1} \sum (x_{ij} - \overline{x_j}) \right]^{\frac{1}{2}} (j = 1, 2, \cdots, m)$$

如用 d_{ij} 表示第 i 个样本和第 j 个样本间的距离，则获得的方法有多种。本文采用明科夫斯基(Minkowski)距离，即

$$d_{ij}(q) = \left[\sum_{k=1}^{m} (x_{ij}' - x_{jk}')^q \right]^{\frac{1}{q}}$$

当 $d_{ij}(q)$ 的数值越大，表明 i 个样本和 j 个样本属于同类的可能性越小。

样本经标准化处理后，利用 MATLAB 工程计算软件进行聚类处理。在聚类中对样本具体分为几类应根据实际情况综合考虑，若对调查样本分类数量过多，则各类可能不具有集中代表性，也不利于简单化问题；相反若分类过少又会显得过于笼统，不能突出各类的重点和抓住

各类的代表性。经综合分析并结合本文所要解决的问题,将样本分为四类,即大、中、一般和小。并求得各类相对的聚类中心距离为:

$$d_i = (11.9823 \quad 5.1444 \quad 1.0000)(i = 1,2,3,4)$$

对其进行归一化处理后可视为各类表决的权重值,即:

$$w_i = (0.5794 \quad 0.2488 \quad 0.1235 \quad 0.0484)$$

对分别属于上述四类的航运公司就实施 ISM 规则的表态,即赞成、不赞成、弃权三种意见分别进行统计,并用矩阵形式表示如下:

赞成
$$V_1 = (64.28751\% \quad 80\% \quad 70.2381\% \quad 73.51598\%)$$

不赞成
$$V_2 = (21.42857\% \quad 12\% \quad 15.47619\% \quad 9.589041\%)$$

弃权
$$V_3 = (14.28571\% \quad 8\% \quad 14.28571\% \quad 16.89498\%)$$

国内航运公司对实施 ISM 规则的可行性评价集为 U_i,则

$$U_i = w_i \cdot (V_1' \quad V_2' \quad V_3') = (69.3761\% \quad 17.7757\% \quad 12.8433\%)$$

通过上述分析,较客观地反映出不同规模国内航运公司对实施 ISM 规则的评价,加权计算的结果表明,多数航运公司赞成实施 ISM 规则。

3 ISM 规则国内化的思路

第一,全面应用 ISM 规则的基本原理。

ISM 规则与 IMO 以往制定的规则明显不同,该规则的基本原理是把系统工程的思想、原理和方法运用于航运安全和防污染管理,核心是要求负责船舶营运的公司建立、实施和保持经船旗国主管机关认可的安全管理体系,在安全管理问题上时时处处要坚持系统论的观点。安全管理体系不是一个简单的文件体系,它涉及安全与防止污染管理有关的组织机构及其职责和职能分配、管理过程控制、资源支持等。按 ISM 规则的要求建立并在岸上和船上实施的安全管理体系有以下特点:

(1) 它是一个闭环的、动态的、自我调整和完善的管理系统;
(2) 它涉及船舶安全和防止污染的一切活动;
(3) 它把船舶安全和防止污染管理中的策划、组织、实施和检查、监控等活动要求集中、归纳、分解和转化为相应的文件化的目标、程序、方案和须知;
(4) 体系本身使所有体系文件受控。

由于 ISM 规则的特点,在将该规则国内化时,坚持和全面运用其基本原理将是十分重要的。

第二,制定《国内安全管理规则》(NSM 规则)。

由于不同水域航行的船舶,可能遭受的风险不同,对船员操作的要求也不同,因此对从事国内水上航运公司及其船舶没有必要完全按照 ISM 规则的要求进行规范,在全面遵守 ISM 规则原理的前提下,根据沿海及内河航行的特点,制定 NSM 规则,不仅便于操作,而且也有利于航运业的发展。

第三,深入调查研究,做好准备工作。

ISM 国内化一方面要弄清所有国内航运公司的情况,这包括人员情况、船舶情况、公司的安全管理和公司及其船舶目前的状况;另一方面要弄清作为推动和具体进行审核的主管机关和审核员队伍的准备情况等,所有这一切都需要做充分准备。

第四,对船公司主要人员进行培训。

实施 ISM 或者 NSM 的目的是保证水上人命财产安全和防止污染水域,虽然强制实施后由水上安全主管机关监督,但主要的实施者和遵守者是航运公司及其船上人员,因此在实施前对其进行培训,使其完全了解 ISM 或 NSM 的原理、运行机制等也是十分重要的。

第五,分步实施 NSM 审核发证制度。

在实施 NSM 审核发证制度时一定要区别对待各类公司。根据目前各类船舶的安全状况,对那些事故率高、危险较大的船舶,如客滚船、液化气船、散货船、油船、化学品船等,首先实施 NSM 规则。

另外,航运公司理解规则、建立体系和进行人员培训都需要一个较长的过程,要让所有国内航运公司的安全管理水平突然出现一个飞跃也是不现实的。针对我国不同水域航运船舶及其船公司的特点,在实施 NSM 规则时,可以先考虑在沿海航行船公司实施。因为从整体上沿海航行船公司的管理要好于内河航行船公司,而且其船况也相对较好,以后再逐步对内河航行船公司实施。

4 结束语

本文通过对国内航运船公司的抽样调查,利用系统工程主成分分析方法、聚类分析方法及模糊推理理论,对国内航运公司及其实施 ISM 或 NSM 的可行性进行了研究。得到的结果是客观的并具有重要的参考价值。本研究的特点归纳为:

(1)在对国内航运公司实施 ISM 的可行性研究时,采用了主成分分析方法确定评价指标体系。利用该种方法既简化了指标体系中指标的数量,又抓住了问题的所有主要方面,这在确定评价指标体系的方法上有所突破。

(2)在确定各主要因素的评价权重时,采用了聚类分析方法。根据所调查船公司所确定的主要指标,聚类成大、中、一般和小四类,以各类的聚类中心并经标准化后作为其评价的权重值。这样做避免了专家调查等方面所产生的偏差。

(3)本研究还提出了 ISM 规则国内化的思路。

Study on the Domestication of ISM Code

1 Introduction

In November 1993, the *International Management Code for the Safe Operation of Ships and for Pollution Prevention* (hereinafter referred to as the ISM Code) was accepted by 1974 SOLAS assembly on June 1994, and ISM Code becomes a compulsory code. This Code is different from other IMO codes or rules apparently. Firstly, it is not the technical standards or requirements for ship or ship's equipment, and is not for seafarers. It is the standards and requirements for the shipping companies. It emphasizes on the prevention from accidents by reinforcing the management of shipping companies. Secondly, the principle and method of Safety System Engineering is used in safety and pollution prevention management at sea. The core of this Code requires the shipping company to establish, enforce and maintenance a safety management system. On these two aspects, the enforcement of ISM Code is a of safety and pollution prevention management.

The practice in enforcement of ISM Code has proved that it caused great changes in safety management in international shipping companies. The result of investigation shows that the safety management in every shipping company has been being standardized gradually, and the safety level has been improved apparently. The records become whole and complete. The connection channel between ship and the top of safety management on shore has been become unblocked, every kind of information can be delivered timely, and the control of shipping company for her ships is reinforced. The consciousness and responsibility of the employees have been enhanced, the concept—I have been required safety turns to the concept—I must be safety gradually. The ruler system of safety management is being completed, the safety work is done where requires it be done beforehand, and it is going to a good cycle. The responsibility of employees is clear; the efficiency of employee's work is been improved apparently. The conditions of maintenance of ship and her equipment are improved and the fees and charges are lowered. The emergence reaction on shore and ship is also reinforced. At the same time, the accident rate, the losses of life and ships of a single ship in per year are reduced too.

Presently, the conditions of safety management in domestic shipping companies are worse than that in international companies, it shows as follows: First, the safety management depends on passive and traditional methods, and follows the accidents; Second, emphasis on beneficial and

---

* 本文发表在 2002 年大连国际海事技术交流会论文集(第一卷),作者吴兆麟、郑中义、张宝晨。

look down on safety; Third, function crossing and the connection channel between shore and ship is often blocked; Four, the quality of employees are relative lower than the requirement; Five, the regulation system is not perfect; Six, the condition of ship is generally worse than that engages in ocean going transportation; Seven, safety management is not in his position. Under these cases, it is an important research subject to use the principle and method of ISM Code to improve the safety management of domestic shipping companies and their ships.

2 The investigation and analysis of domestic shipping companies and their ships

Though the actual conditions in domestic shipping companies differ from that in the international shipping companies, there have many same characteristics. On the purpose of full understanding the conditions in the domestic shipping companies and their ships, and of research on the possibility for the companies to enforce ISM Code, the investigation has been done on these companies. The contents of investigation mainly include: the forms of ownership of the companies, the constitution of ship categories, the average age of ships, and so on total 42 items.

2.1 General conditions of ships sailing in domestic waters

The investigation involves in 344 companies, including 6,803 ships and the total gross tonnage (GT) more than 3,000 thousand. It can be thought a representative of these kinds of ships engaging in domestic transportation. On the view of sailing waters of investigated ships, the percent of ships that sail in inland waterway is 76%; sailing in protected waters is 12%; sailing along shore waters is 11%; sailing in coastal waters is 1%. Though the quality of investigated ships sailing in inland waters is higher, the percent of the total GT is lower. The categories formation of investigated ships involves in general ship, bulk carrier, oil tank, passenger, high-speed craft, chemical ship, gas carrier, movable drill equipment and other cargo ship. So the categories of investigated ships are wide-ranging, the percent of cargo ships is 80%, oil tanker is 5%, passenger is 4% and bulk carrier is 2%. On the view of average age of each category of ship, gas carrier is 17 years, oil tanker is 18 years, bulk carrier is 20 years and general cargo ship is 15 years.

2.2 The general conditions of domestic shipping companies

The investigation shows that though the ships engaging in domestic transportation exist some problems, such as the ship aging and bad conditions of ship etc. the percent is not very high. The percent of no establishment management system and the unqualified person in charging of safety management is high. Many companies determine the captains' authorities and responsibilities in documents and also about the seafarers, but the complete and requirement are far from the ISM Code. 81.7% percent of companies have established system of dangerous management, but only 1.2% percent of companies have established a whole procedure of safety management, 60.5% percent of companies have the procedure partially, and 15.1% percent of companies have emergence plan. So the conclusion is that many shipping companies have not complete system of safety management to protect life, property at sea and protect the marine environment.

The investigation also shows that 13.7% percent of companies have mastered ISM Code and 65.2% percent of companies are familiar with the Code. It is a good basis for domestic shipping companies to enforce ISM Code.

3 The method and model of quantitative analysis on possibility

3.1 Routing

On the basis of qualitative analysis on data of investigation, firstly, the factors of reflection the scope of companies are determined, and then the method of Principle Component Analysis is used to determine the main factors reflecting the scope of companies, and the main factors are used to establish the factor system. Using this method minimizes the number of factor and is outstanding to the focal point; secondly, in order to reflect the voting conditions of companies to enforce ISM Code, the method of cluster analysis is used to divide investigated companies into different cluster to determine the voting weights of different companies according to the main factors; thirdly, the value of no measure name of various cluster center regards as the weight of the company belongs to the cluster. Using this weight and connecting with the statistics result for various companies, the possibility of enforcement of ISM Code in domestic shipping companies is obtained.

3.2 The establishment of evaluation index system

Based on the asking for experts, 12 main factors are chosen initially from 42 factors to establish evaluation index system. There are: the number of ships, GT of ships, captains, engineers, safety management personnel, officers in seafarer, company leaders, leaders served on a board, departments of safety and pollution protection, persons in charging of safety, number of experienced education of junior college. For the purpose of outstanding the main factors, the related-matrix R, characteristic value and the percent of each factor possessing in all are obtained by having the aid of Principle Component Analysis and MATLAB engineering software. Details see Table 1.

If using 90% percent of total percentage choose the main factors, so the factors reflecting the scope are: numbers of GT, ships, officers, crew self-owning by company, persons in charging of safety management, engineers and captains.

Table 1 The characteristic-value and percent of each factor

No.	Main factors	λ_i	Ratio of λ_i	Total percent
1	Gross tonnage	3.9573	32.9779	32.9779%
2	Number of ships	2.2992	19.1603	52.1382%
3	Number of officers	1.4342	11.9517	64.0899%
4	Crew of self-owning	1.1353	9.4609	73.5508%
5	Numbers of safety management	0.9481	7.9012	81.4520%
6	Engineers	0.650	5.6705	87.1225%
7	Captains	0.5398	4.4984	91.6209%
8	Persons in charging of safety management	0.4719	3.9326	95.5535%
9	Numbers experienced education of junior college	0.3874	3.2284	98.7819%
10	Numbers of department of safety and pollution protection	0.0686	0.5720	99.3539%
11	Leaders served on a board	0.0483	0.4022	99.7561%
12	Leaders	0.0293	0.2440	100%

3.3 Cluster Analysis on investigated samples

For the sake of Principle Component Analysis, there are only seven main factors to be chosen, this procedure reduces the number of main factors in index system, so that it simplifies the workload of cluster calculation.

In the procedure of cluster analysis, the initial data should be standardized firstly, and then the standardized data clustered by using Minkowski distance.

While consideration of dividing samples into how many clusters, the actual conditions of the question should be considerate carefully. If the clusters are so many, that the cluster may does not present the samples, which belong to. Otherwise, if the clusters are less, the research will appear general and non-outstanding the main aspects, which are emphases on. Based on comprehensive analysis and incorporation the question in this paper, the samples are divided into four clusters.

The distances of every cluster center are:
$$d_i = (11.9823 \quad 5.1444 \quad 2.5534 \quad 1.0000), \quad i = 1,2,3,4$$

Standardizing the distances of every cluster center further more as:
$$w_i = (0.5794 \quad 0.2488 \quad 0.1235 \quad 0.0484)$$

The voting attitude of each company that belongs to every cluster is been statistic, and been expressed as matrix:

Approval:
$$V_1 = (64.28751\% \quad 70.2381\% \quad 73.51598\%)$$

non-approval:

$$V_2 = (21.42857\% \quad 15.47619\% \quad 9.589041\%)$$

Abstain:
$$V_3 = (14.28571\% \quad 8\% \quad 14.28571\% \quad 16.89498\%)$$

If U_i is the collection of possibility for domestic shipping company to enforce ISM Code, then
$$U_i = w_i \cdot (V_1' \quad V_2' \quad V_3') = (69.3761\% \quad 17.7757\% \quad 12.8483\%)$$

Through the analysis and evaluation above, the results are objective for different scope company to enforce ISM Code, results show majority of companies are approval to enforce the code.

4 The thought of enforcement of ISM Code in domestic companies

First, using the general principles of ISM Code. The safety management system is not a simple document system, it involves in the organization, assignation of functions and responsibilities, control of management procedure, and support of resource connecting with management of safety and pollution protection. According to the requirements of ISM Code, the safety management established and enforced on board and shore has following characteristics: (1) It is a management system of closed circle, self-adjustment and improvement; (2) It includes all the activities involving in safety and pollution protection; (3) It centralizes, sums, decomposes and transforms for the plan, organization, enforcement, inspection and control to relative targets, procedures, projects and instructions of document. (4) The system itself makes all the documents of the system controlled.

Second, mapping out "national safety management code" (NSM). The ships sailing in different waters experience different risks, and have different requirements for seafarers to handle them; therefore, it is not necessary for domestic ships to obey the requirements of all ISM Code. Under prerequisite of obeying the principles of ISM Code, the NSM Code is mapped out according to the different requirements of coastal waters and inland waterways.

Third, investigation and research on all cases, makes the works ready. Internalization of ISM Code shall possess the conditions of all domestic shipping companies, the conditions include: employees, ships and safety management; and possess the conditions of the authority and its persons and prepare enforcement the code. All there must be done before the enforcement.

Fourth, training persons in charging of safety management. The purpose of enforcement the ISM Code or NSM Code is to ensure the safety of life and property waterborne, and protect the environment from pollution, though the authority supervises the enforcement of the code after the code goes into force; the obeying party is domestic shipping company and its seafarer working on board, so that before the code goes into force, it is very important for the persons in charging of the company to be trained to be familiar with the principle and running mechanism of ISM or NSM code.

Fifth, the examining and verifying system is carried out step by step. The idea of treatment different domestic shipping company in a different way must be considered, when the examining and verifying system is carried out. According to the safety conditions of various category ships at present, the ships of higher rate of accident and more dangerous enforce NSM Code previously. Such as Ro/Ro ship, liquefied ship, bulk ship, oil tank and chemical carrier etc.

Moreover, shipping companies need a long time to understand the code and establish safety management system, and train their persons, and also it is not true that requires the safety management level of all domestic shipping companies to change suddenly. Being aim at the characteristic of domestic shipping companies and their ships sailing in different waters, the companies that engage in transportation of coastal water are enforced the code firstly. The reason is that the safety management, and the condition of the companies are better than that of inland waterways, and then is the companies engaging in inland waterway.

5 Conclusions

Based on the sample investigation on domestic shipping companies, the Principle Component Analysis method of SystemEngineering, Cluster Analysis method and Fuzzy Reasoning method are used to research on the possibility of enforcement for domestic shipping companies to enforce ISM Code or NSM Code in this paper. The result obtained is objective and is an important reference. The characteristics of this research are follows:

(1) When the possibility of domestic shipping companies to enforce ISM Code or NSM Code is researched on, the Principle Component Analysis is used to establish the evaluation index. The method reduces the number of index, and catches the main aspect of the question.

(2) The Cluster Analysis method is adopted to determine the weights of evaluation factors. According to the main factors, shipping companies are divided into four clusters, there are big, middle, general and small, and the value of every cluster center standardized is regarded as the weight of that company, which belongs to the cluster. This method avoids the deviation by the investigation on experts. It makes a breakthrough in the method of determining the weights of evaluation index.

(3) The research gives the train of thought for domestic shipping companies to enforce the Code.

In a word, this research studies on the possibility to enforce ISM Code in domestic shipping companies, and at the same time, we devote ourselves to bring forth new ideas in the specific procedure of evaluation method. If there were inappropriate in the paper, we would enjoy the experts and scholars to criticize and correct them.

中韩航线客货班轮公司 SMS 研究*

摘要：中韩航线各客货班轮公司在性质、规模、人员构成、管理水平等方面各不相同，各公司的安全管理体系(SMS)及其运行方式也存在较大差异。笔者对中国船东协会中韩客货班轮委员会 12 家成员公司的 SMS 进行了调研，归纳出中韩合资船公司 SMS 四种颇具代表性的运行模式，总结了船公司履行 ISM 规则时普遍存在的一些问题。结合 IMO 关于 ISM 规则的研究报告，提出了对策。

关键词：中韩航线 SMS 运行模式；责任主体；指定人员

0 引言

近年来，中韩两国间的贸易不断扩大，对海上运力的需求也不断增加。许多投资者看到了其中的商机，纷纷成立船公司、购买船舶投入营运。由于目前进入我国航运市场的门槛相对较低，致使进入中韩客货班轮运输的各船公司在性质、规模、人员构成、管理水平等方面各不相同，特别是公司的安全管理状况存在较大差别。某些公司的安全管理存在一定的隐患。为了全面了解中韩航线上各客货班轮公司安全管理体系(以下简称 SMS)的运行情况，规范市场秩序，交通运输部国际合作司专门立项研究该课题。笔者有幸参与该项目，因而对中韩航线上各客货班轮公司 SMS 的运行情况有了较为深入的了解。

1 现状

笔者于 2007 年 9 月至 10 月间调研了中国船东协会中韩客货班轮委员会的全部 12 家公司。这 12 家船公司全部为中韩合资公司，双方各占 50% 的股份。在中、韩两国都有办公场所。但各公司在经营、管理及分工方面各不相同。这 12 家公司的 SMS 运行模式可归纳为以下四种：

第一种情况，以威海威东公司为例，公司建立了本公司自己的 SMS，并且 SMS 在公司中韩两方都有专人负责运行，各种培训、检查、审核、文件和记录齐全。

第二种情况，有 6 家公司建立了自己的 SMS，并由公司的韩方负责，SMS 负责人和 DP 都由韩方人员担任，中方一般只负责公司经营方面的业务。

第三种情况，有 4 家公司期租中海国际船舶管理公司的船舶，并委托中海国际船舶管理公司负责 SMS 的运行，本公司没有自己的 SMS。

---

* 本文发表在 2008 船舶安全管理论文集，作者李猛、郑中义、李红喜。

第四种情况,有1家公司没有自己的SMS,其SMS委托韩国某管理公司运行。

2 存在的问题

2.1 安全责任不明确

这12家公司存在的普遍问题是明确了分工但没有明确安全责任主体,也就是说没有明确一旦出现事故,究竟由哪一方出面负责。这样容易产生的后果是,出事后相互推诿,不利于事故的处理。

这个问题不仅出现在中韩航线上,中外合资的船公司都存在类似问题。要解决好这个问题,必须事先在合同中明确安全管理责任主体。

2.2 某些公司的岸上人员不熟悉本公司的SMS

在调研中发现,有些公司的岸上人员,甚至是管理层的人员对本公司的SMS并不熟悉,他们认为SMS只是相关部门的职责,这种观点是不符合ISM规则的要求的。ISM规则虽然只是规定"公司应当保证与其安全管理体系有关的所有人员充分理解有关法规、规定、规则和指南。"(ISM CODE 6.7),但实际上,SMS几乎涉及公司的每一位主要员工,所以从这个角度来说,每位主要员工都与SMS有关,都应定期接受培训,都应熟悉公司的SMS。另外,安全管理不应只是公司某个部门或某些人的职责,而应是全体员工的共同职责,要在公司中形成一种人人懂安全,人人管安全的安全管理文化,这是实施ISM规则真正要达到的目的。

2.3 某些公司的指定人员(DP)不具备海上资历,或不是公司的主要领导

在12家公司中,只有1家公司的DP具备海上资历(委托管理SMS的除外后而这些DP在公司中也非主要领导。根据ISM规则,指定人员(DP)在SMS中应发挥重要作用。ISM规则中DP的职责是"为保证各船的安全营运,提供公司与船上之间的联系渠道,公司应当根据情况指定一名或数名能直接同最高管理层联系的岸上人员。指定人员的责任和权力应包括对各船的安全营运和防止污染方面进行监控,并确保按需要提供足够的资源和岸基支持。"由于DP职责中包括对船舶的安全和防污染方面进行监控,这项工作需要有航海相关专业知识和丰富的实践经验,因而要完成DP的职责,一定的海上资历是必需的。

根据国际海事组织专家的调查,现实中,关于DP的设置有两种截然不同的做法,一种是DP在公司中有重要地位,参与公司的决策,履行ISM规则的各种要求。另一种是由刚毕业的学生担任,其职责是保持公司DOC和SMC有效。尽管这两种做法从法律角度来说都符合ISM规则的要求,但显然第二种做法是形式上符合公约要求,第一种做法才是实质上符合公约的要求。

3 相关建议

3.1 必须明确安全管理责任主体

由于中韩航线客货班轮承担旅客运输,一旦出现人命事故,除了承担相应的经济损失外,还要面临国际舆论的压力。所以双方应在合同中明确安全管理的责任主体,即一旦出现事故,由哪一方出面负责善后工作。笔者建议谁管理,谁负责。即由负责 SMS 的一方为责任主体。

3.2 公司应建立自己的 SMS,且在中外双方都有专人负责,并加强 SMS 的宣传和培训工作

根据公约及相关法规的要求,船公司可以建立并运行自己的 SMS,也可以将安全管理委托给其他管理公司。但实践中,船公司建立自己的安全管理体系无论从节约经营成本还是从安全管理的角度来看,都是首选的。建立并运行自己的安全管理体系,可以节省委托管理的费用,更重要的是,建立和不断完善 SMS 的过程,就是使公司员工深刻理解 ISM 规则及 SMS 的过程,从而提高公司的安全管理水平。委托管理是有弊端的,有些管理公司管理十几条甚至几十条船,公司的负责人和 DP 甚至从没有见过他所负责的船舶,他们更多的工作是设法让受托公司的 DOC 和船舶的 SMC 证书保持有效。显然,这种做法是不合乎公约的实质的,因为公约的重点不是证书,而是它提供的安全管理的程序和做法。

建立了自己的 SMS 后,应在中外双方都有专人负责运行,而不是仅由外方或中方负责,要加强 SMS 的宣传和培训工作,这在前面已论述,这里不再重复。

3.3 公司的 DP 应由航海相关专业、具备一定海上资历的人员担任,且其地位应属于公司的领导层

根据 IMO 的研究报告[1],如图 1 所示,DP 在 SMS 运行中发挥着重要作用。无论从规则要求还是从 IMO 的报告中还可以看出,多数公司的 DP 在公司中的地位是属于领导层的。也只有这样,DP 才能有效地履行安全管理职责。

4 结论

中韩航线各客货班轮公司 SMS 运行的四种模式具有一定的代表性,其安全管理中存在的问题在其他航线上的合资船公司中也普遍存在,应引起有关部门的高度重视。ISM 规则不同于其他公约或规则之处在于它提供的不是技术标准,而是一种安全管理的程序或做法。ISM 规则实施十年来,其最大的成就是潜移默化地形成了一种安全管理文化,使人们的安全观念从"要我安全"跨越到"我要安全"。但在国内,ISM 规则还没有得到充分理解和认可,许多船公司履行 ISM 规则还只是停留在表面或流于形式,仅在证书和文件上下功夫。这和 ISM 规则的精神实质是相悖的。

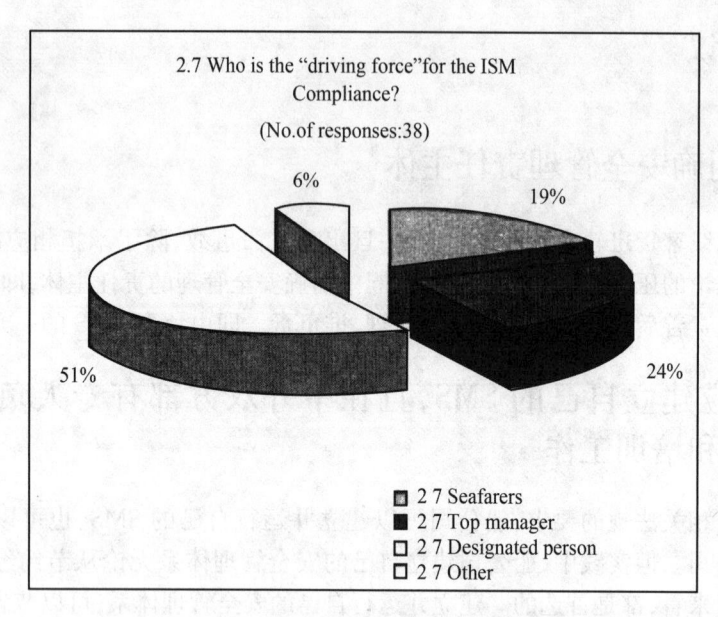

2.7 Who is the "driving force" for the ISM Compliance?
(No. of responses: 38)

- 2 7 Seafarers — 6%
- 2 7 Top manager — 19%
- 2 7 Designated person — 24%
- 2 7 Other — 51%

ISM规则实施"推动力"统计表

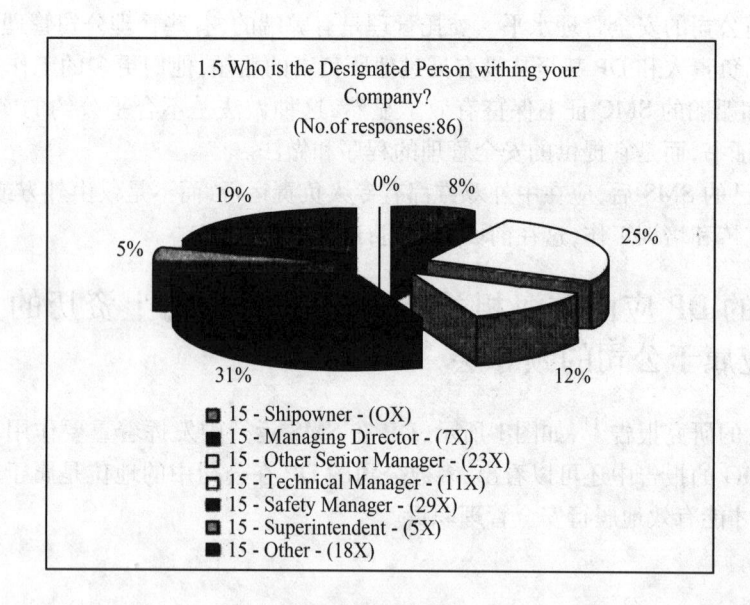

1.5 Who is the Designated Person withing your Company?
(No. of responses: 86)

- 15 - Shipowner - (0X) — 0%
- 15 - Managing Director - (7X) — 8%
- 15 - Other Senior Manager - (23X) — 25%
- 15 - Technical Manager - (11X) — 12%
- 15 - Safety Manager - (29X) — 31%
- 15 - Superintendent - (5X) — 5%
- 15 - Other - (18X) — 19%

图 1　IMO 的研究报告

基于正反馈修正－支持向量机的PSC选船模型[*]

摘要：为定量评估港口国监督目标船的风险值，提出基于正反馈修正－支持向量机的PSC选船模型.对东京备忘录"APCIS"信息系统的PSC检查历史记录进行正反馈修正，获得样本数据，并运用支持向量机模型对样本进行分类，得到了合理的结果.

关键词：正反馈修正；支持向量机(SVM)；PSC选船模型

0 引言

港口国监督在维护海上安全和防止海洋污染方面发挥了积极的作用。各港口国的检查资源有限，因此，对目标船进行一定的筛选就显得尤为重要。目前，国内外学者对PSC选船模型做了许多重要研究。其中，文献[162]运用层次分析法确定选船指标的权重，结合模糊综合评判法建立综合选船模型。文献[163]借鉴巴黎备忘录对船旗国分类模型，将"黑—灰—白"名单方法用来解决目标船舶风险值动态调整的问题。文献[164]采用BP神经网络和船舶安全检查专家选船经验相结合的方法，建立船旗国监督检查选船模型，对PSC选船提供参考。文献[165]在研究巴黎备忘录和东京备忘录选船体系的基础上，提出支持向量机(SVM)选船模型，提高了风险评估的准确率。

在考虑选船时所能获得的资料基础上，根据巴黎备忘录和东京备忘录的选船标准，建立选船指标体系，划分风险等级，并提出基于正反馈修正－支持向量机(EF-SVM)的PSC选船模型。该模型减少了人的主观性影响。

1 模型基本原理

1.1 正反馈修正模型原理

巴黎备忘录最早提出正反馈修正模型，用来解决船旗国风险值动态调整问题。其主要思想是引入"黑—灰"和"灰—白"两个界限和一个EF系数，根据船旗国3年时间间隔的检查和滞留统计数字将船旗国分为黑、灰、白3部分，并通过EF系数对船旗国风险值进行动态调整[166]。

"黑—灰"和"灰—白"界限公式分别为

---

[*] 本文发表在《大连海事大学学报》2014年5月第40卷第2期，作者孙墨林、郑中义。

$$U_{\text{black-grey}} = Np + 0.5 + z\sqrt{Np-(1-p)}$$
$$U_{\text{grey-white}} = Np - 0.5 - z\sqrt{Np-(1-p)}$$

其中:N 为检查次数;p 为允许的滞留界限,港口国监督委员会定为 $p=7\%$;$z=1.645$,表示此时统计学上可接受的概率为 95%;U 为"黑—灰"界限或"灰—白"界限。若某一船旗国的滞留数字大于"黑—灰"界限,则列入黑名单;滞留数字小于"灰—白"界限,则列入白名单;滞留数字介于"黑—灰"与"灰—白"界限之间,则列入灰名单。"黑—灰"和"灰—白"界限公式适用于检查时间间隔内接受超过 30 次检查的船旗国。黑、灰、白名单 EF 系数计算公式分别为

$$\begin{cases} p' = p + (EF_{\text{black}} - 1)Q \\ U' = Np' + 0.5 + z\sqrt{Np'(1-p')} \end{cases}$$

$$EF_{\text{grey}} = (U' - U_{\text{grey-white}})/(U_{\text{black-grey}} - U_{\text{grey-white}})$$

$$\begin{cases} p' = p + (EF_{\text{white}} - 0)Q \\ U' = Np' - 0.5 - z\sqrt{Np'(1-p')} \end{cases}$$

其中:U' 为滞留数。

1.2 支持向量机原理

SVM 的基本思想是通过事先选择好的某一个非线性变换,将输入向量映射到高维特征空间中,并在此构造一个最优分类超平面。

SVM 算法过程如下[167]:

训练向量为 $x_i \in \mathbf{R}^n$,$i=1,\cdots,l$,进行二分类,指标向量为 $y \in \mathbf{R}^l$,$y_i \in \{1,-1\}$,则 SVM 的分类问题就转换为求解一个二次规划问题:

$$\min_{\omega,b,\xi} \frac{1}{2}\boldsymbol{\omega}^{\text{T}}\boldsymbol{\omega} + C\sum_{i=1}^{l}\xi_i$$

$$\text{Subject to } y_i[\boldsymbol{\omega}^{\text{T}}\boldsymbol{\varphi}(x_i) + b] \geq 1 - \xi_i$$

$$\xi_i \geq 0, i=1,\cdots,l$$

其中:$\boldsymbol{\omega}$ 为权值向量;C 为惩罚参数;ξ_i 为松弛变量;$\boldsymbol{\varphi}$ 为低维到高维的非线性映射;b 为偏置。

通过引入核函数,并应用 Lagrange 乘子法求解二次规划问题的对偶问题,得到决策函数:

$$\text{sgn}[\boldsymbol{\omega}^{\text{T}}\boldsymbol{\varphi}(x) + b] = \text{sgn}\left[\sum_{i=1}^{l} y_i a_i K(x_i, y_i) + b\right]$$

其中:$K(x_i, y_j) = \boldsymbol{\varphi}(x_i)^{\text{T}}\boldsymbol{\varphi}(y_j)$;非负变量 a_i 为 Lagrange 乘子。

2 基于 EF-SVM 的 PSC 选船模型[168]

2.1 数据准备模块

(1)从东京备忘录"APCIS"信息系统中选取 80 条船舶信息作为样本,并人工划分出训练

样本和测试样本。

(2)对样本 7 个属性值所对应的分数进行计算,得出各样本在同一时间间隔内接受初始检查时的风险等级。

2.2 EF 算法模块

(1)适用于 EF 系数算法的属性,求"黑—灰—白"界限并进行正反馈修正,得到其 EF 系数。

(2)不适用于 EF 系数算法的属性,求其平均数或进行归一化处理。

2.3 SVM 算法模块

(1)在对 80 条样本数据预处理的基础上,通过 MATLAB LibSVM 工具箱中的 C-SVC 分类模型,进行模型训练和测试。

(2)选取最佳核函数,并通过遗传算法选择最佳的惩罚参数($-c$)和核函数参数($-g$)。

2.4 测试评价模块

通过对测试结果的分析,构建基于 EF-SVM 的 PSC 选船模型。模型的建立流程如图 1 所示。

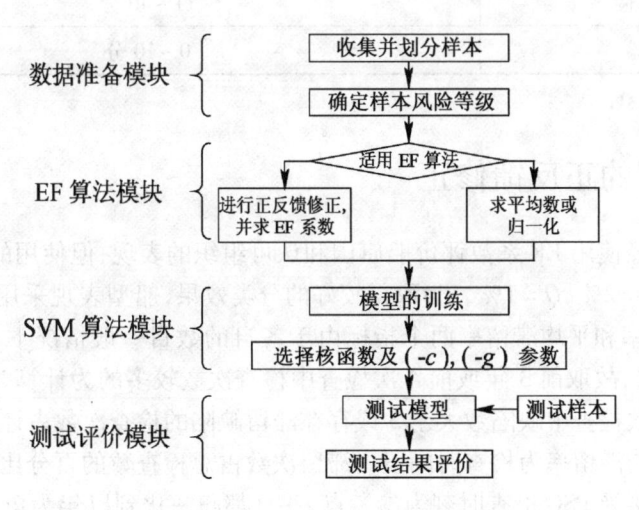

图 1 PSC 选船模型的建立流程

3 实例验证

3.1 收集样本数据

参考东京备忘录、巴黎备忘录的选船指标体系,结合"APCIS"信息系统中可获得的资料建立选船指标体系。指标体系包括船龄、船型表现、船旗国表现、认可组织表现、检查时间间隔、平均缺陷数和平均滞留数7个指标。巴黎备忘录和东京备忘录分别有各自划分风险等级的标准,如表1所示。东京备忘录的高风险等级区间为60分,极高风险等级区间为大于100分。通过对"APCIS"信息系统中船舶检查记录分析,极高风险船舶的分数集中在120分左右,分值分布的区间比高风险船舶小,并且样本数量比高风险船舶少很多,导致高风险和极高风险两个风险等级区分困难。若采用支持向量机对极高风险和高风险等级进行区分,极高风险等级的分类准确率小于20%。故在东京备忘录风险等级划分的基础上,将极高风险划入高风险等级,得到80条样本数据的风险等级。

表1　巴黎备忘录和东京备忘录的风险等级划分

风险等级	巴黎备忘录风险等级划分
高风险	≥5 分
低风险	符合低风险标准
中等风险	介于高风险与低风险之间
—	—
	东京备忘录风险等级划分
极高风险	>100 分
高风险	41~100 分
中等风险	11~40 分
低风险	0~10 分

3.2　样本数据的正反馈修正

东京备忘录已经使用 EF 系数评价船旗国和认可组织的表现,但使用的参数不同,分别为 $p=7\%$, $Q=3\%$ 和 $p=2\%$, $Q=1\%$。为取得较好的分类效果,船型表现采用和船旗国一样的 p 和 Q 值。平均缺陷率和平均滞留率两个指标由于各自的数目一般情况下小于30次,所以不适用于 EF 系数算法,故取前3年或前4次检查中检查次数较多的为计算时间段计算平均值。平均缺陷率采用每次检查中缺陷数大于5或存在滞留缺陷的检查次数占计算时间段内的总检查数的百分比。平均滞留率为检查时间段内滞留次数占总检查数的百分比。船龄因素和检查时间间隔因素均以接受 PSC 检查时刻为参考点,并且都归一化到以年为单位。对样本数据进行正反馈修正,确定训练和测试 EF-SVM 模型的样本数据。表2为部分样本数据。

表2 部分样本数据

船型表现	船旗国表现	认可组织表现	船舶年龄	检查时间间隔	平均缺陷数	平均滞留数
−1.35	−0.54	−1.64	4.00	0.41	0.00	0.00
−1.42	−1.26	−1.64	3.00	0.90	0.33	0.00
−0.84	−0.23	−1.69	7.00	0.73	0.00	0.00
−0.84	−1.69	−1.64	4.00	0.91	0.00	0.00
−0.46	−0.54	−1.64	11.00	0.04	0.67	0.00
1.59	−0.90	−1.75	5.00	0.21	0.25	0.25
−0.46	1.56	−1.64	14.00	0.26	0.17	0.00
1.59	−0.25	−1.75	15.00	1.31	0.50	0.00

3.3 获得基于EF-SVM模型的分类器

(1)采用MATLAB LibSVM中的C-SVM模型,通过40条样本数据对支持向量机进行训练,得到"modle"分类器。

(2)核函数的选择。通过MATLAB LibSVM中的($-t$)参数比较线性核函数、多项式核函数、径向基核函数和S型核函数的预测准确率。径向基核函数对应的分类准确率最高。

(3)最佳($-c$)和($-g$)参数的选择

将样本数据规范到$[-1,1]$,并通过SVM_GUI中的遗传算法模型对支持向量机的($-c$)和($-g$)参数进行优化,进化代数和种群数量分别取100和20,并通过训练样本的交叉验证,得出最佳的($-c$)和($-g$)参数。此时($-c$)和($-g$)参数分别为7.131 1和0.619 03。求取最佳($-c$)和($-g$)参数过程如图2所示。

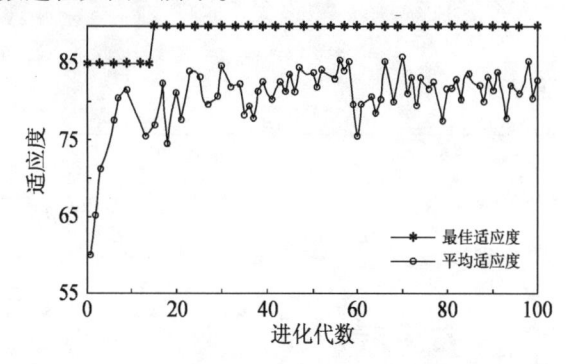

图2 最佳($-c$)和($-g$)参数求取过程

3.4 测试评价结果分析

在最佳($-c$)和($-g$)参数基础上,通过剩余的40条样本数据进行模型测试,得到测试数据的实际分类与预测分类比较(图3)。基于 EF-SVM 的 PSC 选船模型最终的分类准确率为 92.5%。40 个测试样本中共有三个样本点分类错误。高风险船没有分类错误,中等风险分别有 1 个样本被错分到了高风险和低风险船舶,低风险有一个样本点被错分到了中等风险目标船。

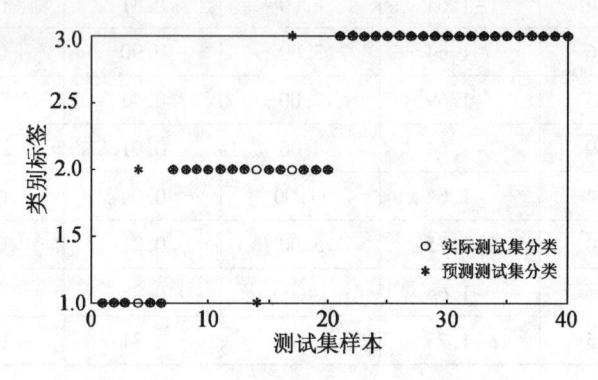

图 3 实际分类与预测分类比较

4 结语

在建立选船指标体系的基础上,引入 EF 系数,对选船指标进行正反馈修正,结合支持向量机模型,对目标船进行风险评估。基于正反馈修正 - 支持向量机模型进行 PSC 选船,减少了人的主观性影响,结果更具有客观性和普遍性,可为港口国进行 PSC 选船提供参考。

国际安全管理规则对海上安全影响分析*

摘要：在分析海上安全基本要素结构的基础上，系统分析国际安全管理规则对船旗国审核和港口国监督检查的影响，利用事故因果连锁理论，构建海上事故致因链，定性分析国际安全管理规则在减少事故及事故损失方面的作用。

关键词：国际安全管理规则；海上安全；事故致因链；定性分析

0 引言

《国际安全管理规则》(International Safety Management Code, 简称 ISM 规则) 自 2002 年 7 月全面实施，目前，针对 ISM 规则实施效果的评价，国内外学者已做了许多重要的研究。其中，国际海事组织为了对 ISM 规则的实施效果进行评价，专门成立专家组对船上、岸上、船公司和主管机关人员进行问卷调查，得出 ISM 规则对安全文化的建设有积极影响，并且一定程度上简化了行政过程[169]。其中，陈伟炯从船舶安全的控制模式出发，对"ISM 规则 + PSC"船舶安全控制模式的运作机制进行研究[170]。徐红明在陈伟炯研究的基础上，从船舶保险理赔额、散货船安全性、PSC 船舶滞留率及海难人为因素的角度，对 ISM 规则实施前后的船舶安全状况变化进行研究[171]。

1 海上安全控制模式

海上安全是由人(Man, 船员)、机(Machine, 船舶、货物)、环境(Environment, 运作环境)和管理(Management, 船舶公司、主管当局)四大要素构成的四面体结构，如图 1 所示。各要素之间相互影响，联系密切。为了保证海上安全，避免对海洋环境造成污染，IMO 借助各方关心的利益机制，运用船旗国、港口国的行政网对海上安全的基本要素结构"人—机—环境—管理"实施监督管理[170]。

《联合国海洋法公约》第 94 条和第 217 条明确阐述了船旗国对确保本国船舶履行国际公约具有首要责任[172]。船旗国对本国船舶的审核构成了海上安全控制模式中的第一道防线。然而，在实践中，船旗国仅凭借自身的力量很难保证本国船舶随时符合国际公约的要求。由于认可组织拥有较多技术专长人员，并且在全球范围拥有广泛的船舶检验机构，大多数船旗国授权认可组织代其履行和检查技术性国际海事公约的要求。虽然认可组织是非营利的专业机构，但其仍然存在商业利益，这不免会使认可组织"公正"的形象受到质疑[173]。当船旗国、认

---

* 本文发表在世界海运 2018 年第 8 期第 37 卷，作者孙墨林、郑中义、闫化然。

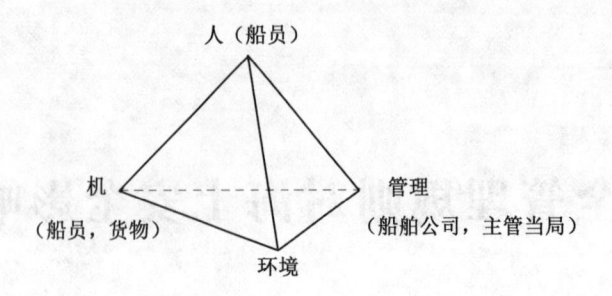

图 1　海上安全的基本要素结构

可组织均未能很好地履行自己的职责时,作为海上安全控制模式中的第二道防线——港口国监督(PSC)发挥了积极的作用。

2　国际安全管理规则的实施

2.1　国际安全管理规则概述

ISM 规则旨在提供船舶安全管理、安全营运和防止污染的国际标准[174],要求船公司建立、运行和保持符合其规定的 SMS(安全管理体系),确保人员、船舶、操作、应急、SMS 文件得以有效控制,确保履行相关公约、法规等强制性规定和考虑建议性要求。

ISM 规则作为 IMO 的第一个管理类标准,自 1998 年 7 月 1 日实施以来,经历了一系列的修正,最近的 ISM 修正案于 2010 年 7 月 1 日生效,该修正案对 ISM 规则中的 1.2、5.1.5、7、8.1、9.2 和 10.3 分别做了修改。中国于 1995 年 3 月正式开始实施 ISM 规则,并于 1998 年和 2000 年完成第一批和第二批船公司及船舶的审核发证工作[175]。

2.2　海上安全防线中 ISM 规则的检查

ISM 规则要求船旗国及其授权的认可组织对安全管理系统(SMS)文件及其执行情况进行审核,对符合 ISM 规则的船舶及其船舶管理公司分别签发安全管理证书和符合证明。未通过 SMS 审核的船舶和船舶管理公司,不得进入国际航运市场。港口国主管机关已将 ISM 规则符合性检查融入日常的 PSC 检查中,对 SMS 方面存在缺陷的外籍到港船舶,提出包括滞留在内的处理意见。若船舶在港口国监督检查中被滞留,则会在一定程度上降低其船旗国、认可组织和船舶管理公司在国际航运市场上的名誉。由于港口国主管机关在目标船选择时会考虑其 PSC 检查历史记录,导致有滞留记录的船舶对应的分值较高,使其频繁地被港口国主管机关检查,而每次检查都不可避免地会发现一些问题,而发现和遗留的缺陷增多,则又增加检查的频度,陷入恶性循环。海上安全控制模式的两道防线对船舶及其船舶管理公司的 SMS 审核及检查情况如图 2 所示。

3　ISM 规则对海上安全的影响

根据事故因果连锁理论,事故是由一连串因素以因果关系依次发生,如链式反应的结

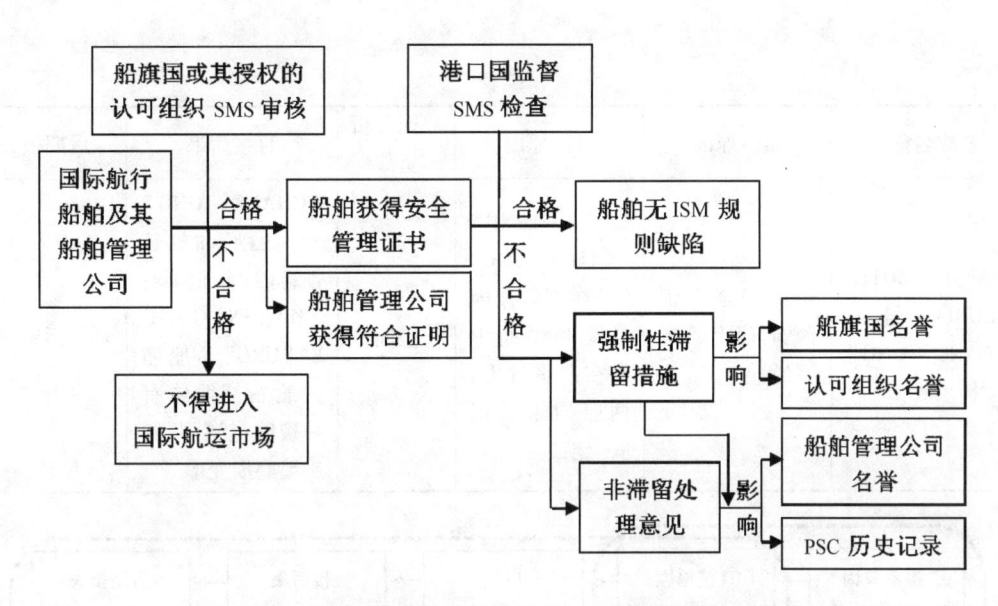

图 2 国际航行船舶及其船舶管理公司 SMS 审核及检查情况

果[176]。为了揭示 ISM 规则对海上安全的影响,对 ISM 规则在海上事故致因链中的影响进行定性分析。

3.1 海上事故致因链的构建

博德事故因果连锁理论认为,虽然人的不安全行为和物的不安全状态是导致事故发生的直接原因,但究其根本,只不过是事故发生前的表面现象,根本原因是管理存在缺陷。参考博德事故因果连锁理论,对 31 起海上事故案例的原因进行分析[177, 178],部分案例的事故原因汇总如表 1 所示。从 31 起海上事故原因中可以看出,导致事故发生的根本原因是船上的管理不当和船员技能不足等。根本原因的存在诱发了人为失误、主机故障等险情,进而导致了海上事故的发生。事故的发生会产生燃油泄漏并威胁船员的人命安全等直接后果,随着时间的推移,会造成环境污染和人命伤亡等后期损失。海上事故致因链如图 3 所示。

表 1 事故原因汇总表

事故名称	根本原因	直接原因	致因分析事故	直接后果	后期损失
"勤丰 128"号船撞桥事故	使用未经改正原海图	违规穿越大桥非通航孔	碰撞	舯桅断裂,驾驶台严重变形,金塘大桥两片梁板折断	船长、大副、二副和值班水手死亡
捕鱼船舶沉没事故	船员缺乏航海技能	操纵避让不当	沉没	触碰锚驳船锚钢丝,船上 24 人全部落水	11 名船员死亡

续表

事故名称	根本原因	直接原因	致因分析事故	直接后果	后期损失
"HANJIN GOTHENBURG"号与"CHANG TONG"号碰撞事故	船员安全意识薄弱,船上管理不当	"HANJIN GOTHENBURG"号在判断碰撞危险和局面中存在严重过失,两船均未采用安全航速	碰撞	"CHANG TONG"号5舱底油柜破损,燃油泄漏;"HANJIN GOTHENBURG"号船艏尖舱右侧船体有一裂缝;船首两侧胸墙磨损变形	环境污染

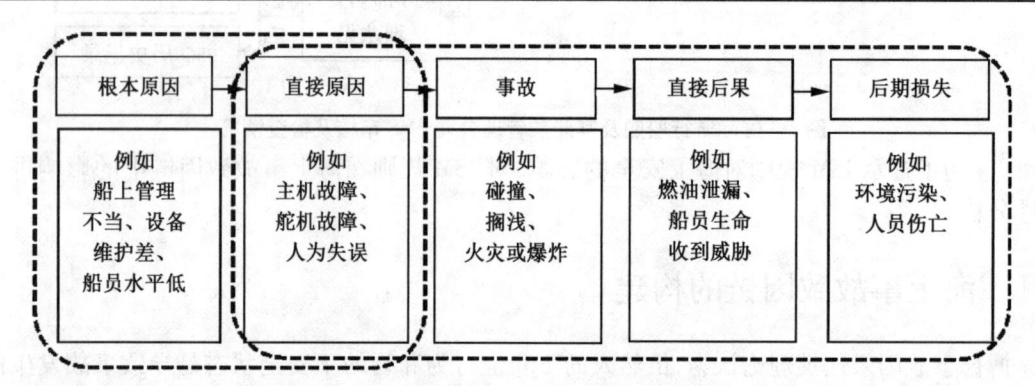

图3 海上事故致因链

3.2 ISM规则对海上事故及其损失的影响分析

ISM规则中的条款,既包括船舶"软件"方面的规定,也包括船舶设备"硬件"方面的管理要求。船舶"软件"方面的规定包括资源和人员标准、船上操作方案的制定和应急准备等,涉及事故致因链的全过程,若船舶满足ISM规则"软件"方面的规定,则会抑制事故致因链中各部分的转化,降低事故发生率和事故损失。船舶设备"硬件"方面的管理要求包括船舶和设备的维护要求等,在事故致因链中涉及"根本原因"向"直接原因"的转化,若ISM规则"硬件"管理要求在实际中有效地执行,则会大大减少险情的发生,进而减少海上事故的发生。

4 结语

船旗国及其授权的认可组织对ISM规则证书的审核和港口国监督对ISM规则缺陷的检查是确保ISM规则有效实施的两个途径。通过海上事故致因链的构建和定性分析,ISM规则作为海上安全基本要素结构中的管理因素,其对海上安全的影响,体现在抑制海上事故致因链中各部分的转化,进而减少海上事故的发生。

ISM 规则 2010 年修正案实施有效性量化分析*

摘要:在分析海上安全基本要素结构的基础上,定性分析 ISM 规则对海上安全的影响,基于 PSC 数据的相关分析,确定 ISM 规则实施效果的评价指标,并通过决策树 CHAID 算法,构建 ISM 规则实施有效性评价模型,进而对 ISM 规则 2010 年修正案的实施效果进行评价。

关键词:ISM 规则;海上安全;港口国监督

0 引言

ISM 规则作为 IMO 的第一个管理类标准,自 1998 年 7 月 1 日开始实施以来,经历了一系列的修正,最近的 ISM 规则修正案于 2010 年 7 月 1 日生效,该修正案对 ISM 规则中的 1.2、5.1.5、7、8.1、9.2 和 10.3 分别做了修改。ISM 规则 2010 年修正案实施效果的分析,对于研究 ISM 规则对海上安全的影响,以及 ISM 规则未来进一步的修正具有一定的参考价值。

1 构建 ISM 规则 2010 年修正案实施有效性量化评价模型

构建 ISM 规则 2010 年修正案实施有效性量化评价模型,主要包括以下两部分内容。

(1)在分析 ISM 规则对海上安全影响的基础上,以巴黎备忘录 PSC 数据为研究对象,通过相关分析,确定 ISM 规则实施效果的评价指标。

(2)基于 PSC 的滞留记录,通过决策树 CHAID 算法,构建 ISM 规则实施有效性评价模型,并对 ISM 规则 2010 年修正案的实施效果进行分析。

1.1 ISM 规则实施效果评价指标的筛选

ISM 规则作为海上安全基本要素结构中的管理因素,其对海上安全的影响,从 PSC 的角度来说,不但体现在 ISM 规则的缺陷状况,而且通过影响其他缺陷状况,进而对海上安全产生影响。为了定量评价 ISM 规则 2010 年修正案的实施效果,确定评价 ISM 规则对海上安全影响的指标很重要。

由于 ISM 规则于 2002 年起全面实施,以巴黎备忘录 2003 年—2012 年的 PSC 缺陷数据为研究对象,对 ISM 规则缺陷与其他 16 类缺陷进行相关分析。为了消除 PSC 检查中船舶艘数对相关分析的影响,分别计算各类缺陷的平均单船缺陷数,各类缺陷的平均单船缺陷数为各类

---

* 本文发表在《珠江水运》2014 年第 8 期,作者孙墨林、郑中义、闫化然。

缺陷数与检查艘数之比。利用 Pearson 相关系数来衡量其相关性。相关分析结果中可以看出，ISM 规则缺陷与危险货物、主动力和辅助设备和防污染三类缺陷呈显著相关，即 ISM 规则缺陷与这三类缺陷具有较高的相互关联性。故 ISM 规则、危险货物、主动力和辅助设备和防污染四类缺陷共同体现了由于 ISM 规则实施不当导致的海上风险。

1.2 ISM 规则 2010 年修正案实施有效性分析

1.2.1 变量的选取

由于各港口国对国际公约的认识程度不同，所以在执行 PSC 时发现的缺陷情况可能会有所不同，但滞留作为强制措施，涉及各方面的利益，各港口国较为谨慎，故取是否由于 ISM 规则实施不当导致的滞留，作为评价 ISM 规则实施效果的评价指标，即作为 CHAID 算法中的因变量。由于 ISM 规则实施不当导致的滞留包括至少存一个 ISM 规则、危险货物、主动力和辅助设备和防污染四类滞留缺陷的情况。

为了分析 ISM 规则 2010 年修正案的实施效果，选取滞留时间、船型、船龄和船舶总吨作为效果评价指标，即 CHAID 算法中的自变量。其中，滞留时间取 ISM 规则 2010 年修正案实施前后各 3 年；船型取《船检条例》中强制入级的五种船型，分别为客船、化学品船、滚装船、油船和液化气船，由于客船对应的滞留数较少，不适用决策树进行分析，故暂不考虑客船的滞留情况；船龄划为 1~4、5~8、9~12 和 13~ 等四段，在 CHAID 算法中对应的序号变量分别为 1、2、3 和 4；船舶总吨划为 0~2 500、2 501~5 000、5 001~10 000 和 10 001~ 等四段，在 CHAID 算法中对应的序号变量分别为 1、2、3 和 4。

1.2.2 CHAID 算法参数的选取

基于东京备忘录 2007.7.1—2013.7.1 的化学品船、滚装船、油船和液化气船的 744 条 PSC 滞留数据，通过 SPSS 软件建立 ISM 规则实施有效性评价模型。决策树 CHAID 算法中最大树深取默认值 3，为了能使决策树每一个分支都达到 3 层树深，父节点和子节点的最小个案数分别取 100 和 30；拆分节点的显著性水平取 0.06；决策树 CHAID 算法的分类结果如图 1 所示。

1.2.3 结果分析

从图 1 中可以看出，由于 ISM 规则实施不当导致的滞留数据在不同船龄段中的比例不同，船龄在 5~12 年的化学品船、滚装船、油船和液化气船由于 ISM 规则实施不当导致滞留百分比为 27.6%，与其他船龄段相比较少，随着 ISM 规则 2010 年修正案的实施，由于 ISM 规则实施不当导致的滞留百分比从 ISM 规则 2010 年修正案实施之前的 33.3% 减低到修正案实施之后的 19.7%，即 ISM 规则 2010 年修正案的实施减少了由于 ISM 规则实施不当所导致的滞留情况，也就是降低了由于 ISM 规则实施不当所导致的海上风险，体现出 ISM 规则 2010 年修正案的实施是有效的。同理，对于船龄在 13 年及以上的化学品船、滚装船、油船和液化气船，ISM 规则 2010 年修正案的实施也是有效的，并且由于 ISM 规则实施不当导致的滞留百分比下降幅度更大。对于船龄在 4 年以下的化学品船、滚装船、油船和液化气船，决策树子节点为吨位，而不是滞留时间，说明吨位对该段船龄滞留情况的划分更有效，ISM 规则 2010 年修正案的实施效果在该船龄段不明显。

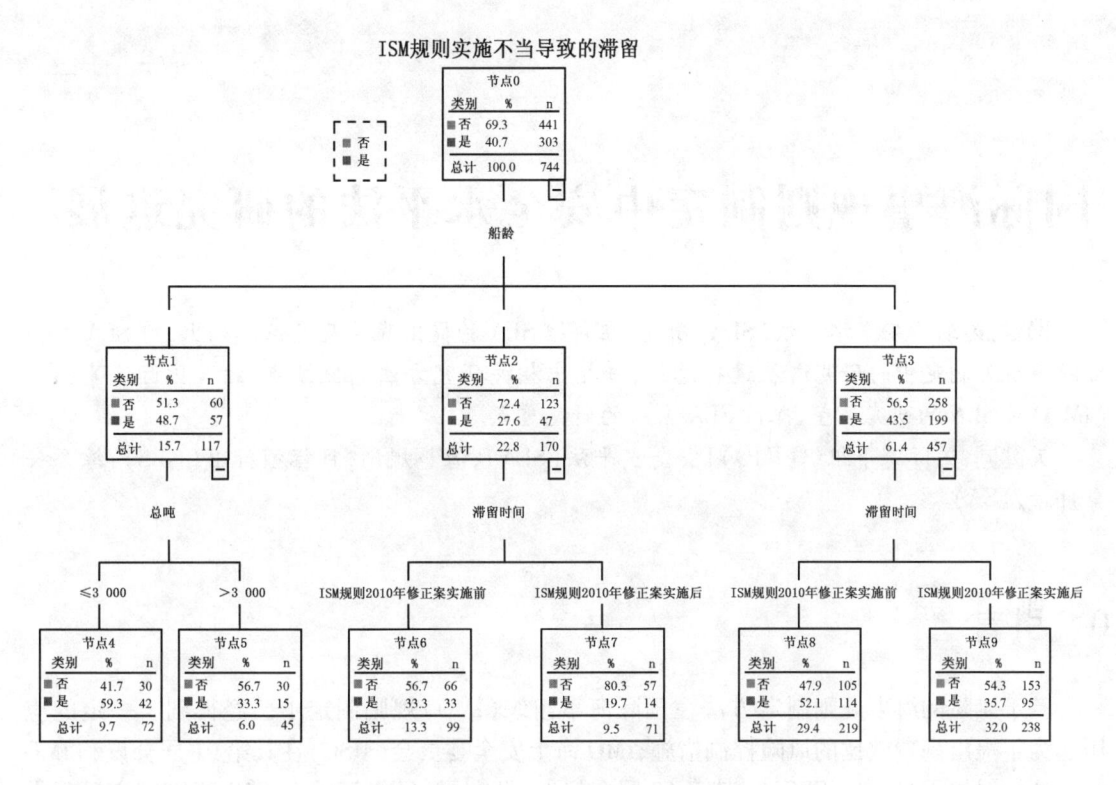

图 1 决策树 CHAID 算法的分类结果

2 结论

在确定 ISM 规则实施效果评价指标的基础上,通过决策树 CHAID 算法,定量评价 ISM 规则 2010 年修正案的实施有效性。ISM 规则 2010 年修正案的实施对于船龄在 5 年及以上的化学品船、滚装船、油船和液化气船的效果明显,降低了由于 ISM 规则实施不当所导致的风险。对于船龄在 4 年及以下的化学品船、滚装船、油船和液化气船,ISM 规则 2010 年修正案的实施效果不明显。

国际海事规则制定中安全水平法的研究进展*

摘要：为助力安全水平法(SLA)研究,在介绍SLA的提出背景及定位基础上,对SLA在国际海事规则制定中的研究进展进行总结,并指出相关研究方法的优缺点,结合国际海事组织(IMO)对SLA的研究展望,探讨SLA未来的研究重点。

关键词：国际海事组织(IMO);安全水平法(SLA);海事规则;目标型标准(GBS);综合安全评估(FSA)

0 引言

基于风险的海事规则制定方法在国际海事组织(IMO)规则制定中已经得到了一定的应用。为了提出高费效比的风险控制措施,IMO海上安全委员会(MSC)在其第91届会议和IMO海上环境保护委员会(MEPC)在其第65届会议上,批准了《经修订的在IMO规则制定过程中使用综合安全评估(FSA)指南》。基于该指南,IMO对《1974年国际海上人命安全公约》(SOLAS公约)的第Ⅱ章等内容进行了修订。为了在目标型标准(GBS)中利用基于风险的方法验证规则的符合性,IMO提出了安全水平法(SLA)的概念。

SLA是IMO在决策过程中基于风险方法的结构性应用,旨在通过评价现有规则的安全水平,来制定或修订国际规则。从SLA提出至今,IMO在导则的制定以及研究内容的梳理方面已经取得了一定的研究成果,但在实践方面的研究并不多。为助力SLA的研究进程,并为其跟踪和研究提供参考,本文在介绍SLA的提出背景及定位的基础上,从SLA安全目标的设立、功能要求的量化,以及规则符合性验证等3个方面,对SLA在国际海事规则制定中的研究进展进行综述,并结合IMO对SLA的研究展望探讨SLA未来的研究重点。

1 SLA提出的背景及定位

GBS是IMO规则结构化的一种框架,该框架包括目标、功能要求、符合认证、船舶规范、行业惯例和标准等5个结构层次。对于以何种方法制定GBS,IMO存在两种观点:一种观点支持运用"规范法",即根据多年的实践经验来制定标准;另一种观点则主张采用基于风险的方法来制定或修订标准,这种方法即为SLA。经过几届会议的讨论,针对积累了较多实践经验的散货船和油船,IMO决定采用"规范法"制定GBS,而对于实践经验匮乏的其他船型则采用SLA。根据分析SLA与GBS定位及其与FSA的关系如图1所示,可以进一步明确SLA的

---

* 本文发表在《水运管理》2017年第6期第39卷,作者孙墨林、郑中义。

区别和联系。

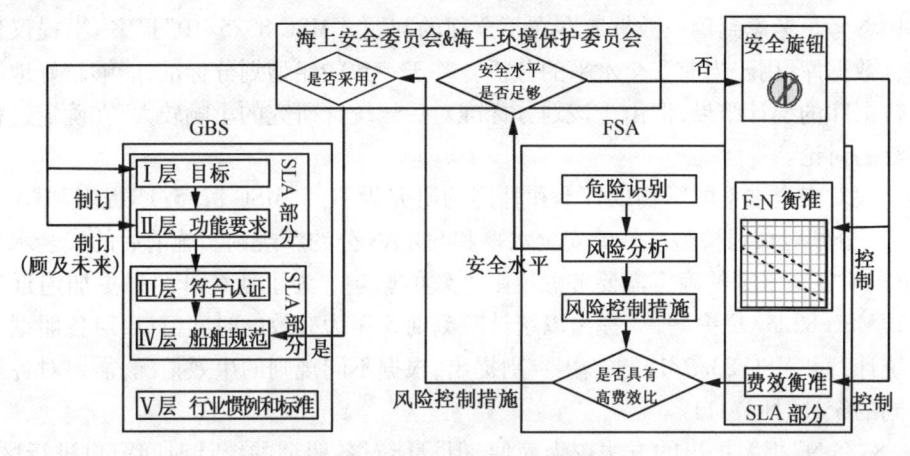

图1 SLA与GBS和FSA关系

SLA在GBS结构体系中的应用可以分为2个方面:(1)利用基于风险的方法制定安全目标及其对应的功能要求;(2)通过风险模型来验证海事规则对安全目标和功能要求的符合性。FSA可应用于基于风险的海事规则的制定,是SLA的重要工具,可为SLA提供安全水平评估和高费效比的风险控制措施等;反之,SLA也可用于控制FSA中的FN衡准、费效衡准等参数。

2 SLA安全目标的设立

设立合适的安全目标,需确定当前的安全水平及该安全水平的社会可容忍度。当前的安全水平可以细分为船舶安全、货物保护、环境保护、乘客安全、船员安全、社会相关问题(也称"第三方安全")等6个方面。

2.1 当前安全水平的确定

当前安全水平的确定主要有基于历史事故数据的统计方法和基于风险的方法2种。MSC对利用统计方法确定安全水平方面进行了初步的研究,包括当前安全水平的量化、船型的划分、规则生效对安全水平的影响等。在"MSC 82/5/1"提案[179]中,国际船级社协会(IACS)基于历史事故数据,对多种船型的事故率、船员及乘客的死亡率和溢油风险进行统计分析;波兰认为在货物保护水平量化方面可以简单量化为">船舶安全水平",这对IACS的研究起到了补充的作用;丹麦细化了IACS在船员安全方面的研究,将船员职业事故分为职业死亡事故、5%及以上永久伤害的职业事故和其他事故3类。

在确定当前安全水平的过程中,基于统计的方法简单易行,但对海上历史事故数据的完整性和准确性要求较高。由于海上严重事故的发生概率小、潜伏周期可能较长,并且存在漏报的现象,仅利用统计方法可能会高估当前的安全水平。

由于各数据库在船型划分方面不一致,导致各统计研究之间无法进行融合或比较。对此,在"MSC 83/5/3"提案[180]中,IACS提出了对各种船型建立统一的划分标准和先研究部分船型的划分问题的2种解决方案。波兰基于Lloyd's Register Fair play数据库中散货船的船型解释,估计出相对应的散货船数量,进而计算出散货船的事故率,为不同数据库统计结果的融合和比较提供参考。考虑到单一数据库存在不全面的问题,"MSC 83/5/10"提案[181]提议建立一个新的综合数据库,用于当前安全水平的分析。基于一致的船型划分标准,能够较好地融合和比较不同数据库的统计结果,但由于该划分标准对后续统计研究的影响较大,在确定过程中需要进行广泛的讨论。

规则生效对安全水平的影响以日本和韩国的研究为主。"MSC 82/5/1"提案和"MSC 82/5/7"提案[182]分别对加强检验计划的安全水平和SOLAS公约新规则实施前后的安全水平进行统计,指出当前安全水平的确定需要考虑规则生效的影响。为了使统计结果更加逼近当前的安全水平,"MSC 83/5/9"提案[183]提出以统计时刻前5年为有效的时间窗口,对各船型的安全水平进行统计;而"MSC 83/5/16"提案[184]则提出,根据不同规则的生效情况,需要对各船型分别划定不同的统计时间窗口。

"MSC 83/5/9"提案提出的方法较为简便,但没能对各船型的统计时间窗口进行区分,并且缺乏确定时间窗口长度的依据。"MSC 83/5/16"提案提出的方法能体现规则生效对安全水平的影响,但影响安全水平的因素众多,在确定最佳统计时间窗口时,需要综合考虑各个因素的影响。

针对基于风险的方法确定当前安全水平方面,SLA主要有2种观点:第一种观点以日本和挪威为代表,"MSC 81/6/3"提案[185]认为已完成的FSA研究可以为当前安全水平的确定提供参考,"MSC 82/5/1"提案进一步指出所有的FSA研究已足够确定当前的安全水平;第二种观点以希腊为代表,"MSC 81/6/16"提案[186]指出利用基于风险的方法确定当前的安全水平,仍需要进一步的基础研究,安全水平计算结果的可靠性对后续SLA的应用研究有很大的影响,甚至会导致不合理规则的产生。

以基于风险的方法来确定当前安全水平,能够全面地考虑影响安全的诸方面因素,在历史事故数据匮乏时,其相比于统计方法的优势更加明显。FSA作为基于风险的分析方法之一,能够为SLA安全目标的确定提供重要的参考依据,但考虑到安全水平计算结果的可靠性对SLA的影响较大,需要对FSA风险分析结果进行不确定性分析。

2.2 安全水平的社会可容忍度

目前,在安全水平的社会可容忍度方面,在SLA提案中没有直接的研究成果,但相关提案如"MSC 81/6/10"提案和"MSC 82/5/1"提案均指出,FSA中关于社会风险衡准的研究可以为SLA提供参考。社会风险衡准是用于评估社会风险可容忍度的标准,包括上下2条边界,分别代表最大可容忍度或可忽略的社会风险。在FSA应用研究中,客船、客滚船、油船、LNG船、集装箱船、杂货船和散货船等7种船型的社会风险衡准上边界汇总如图2所示。

FSA研究中社会风险衡准的确定均采用"MSC 72/16"提案[187]中提出的方法,即通过考虑不同船型运营的经济价值及其与国民生产总值的关系,确定一个平均可接受的潜在人命损失值(PLL)。高于该PLL一个量级以上的风险,被定义为不可容忍的社会风险;低于该PLL一个量级以上的风险,则被认为是可忽视的社会风险。

"MSC 72/16"提案中提出的方法以各船型运营的经济价值来表示其对社会的重要性,进而对各船型的社会风险衡准进行区分。由图2可以看出,客船的社会风险衡准上边界最高,这

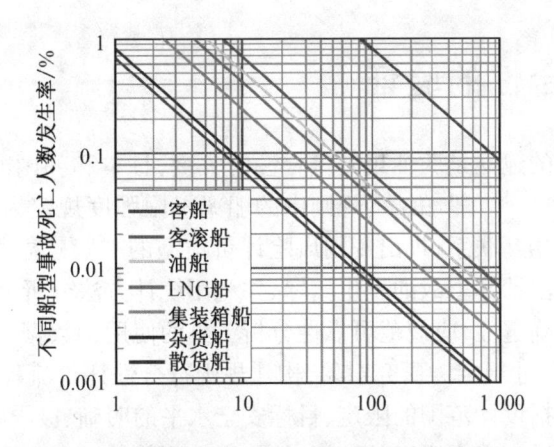

图2　7种不同船型的社会风险衡准上边界汇总

是由于客船运营的经济价值最高导致的。但需要注意的是,社会风险衡准是在FSA的研究中提出的,主要目的是为了评价风险控制措施制定的紧迫性;而在SLA研究中,社会风险衡准是为了度量当前安全水平的可容忍度,并为安全目标的设立提供参考,与"MSC 72/16"提案中的方法用途不一致,不可以直接借用,但可作为参照。

3　SLA功能要求的量化

IMOMSC第81、82、83届会议对SLA功能要求的量化和细分进行了理论研究。"MSC 81/6/14"提案[188]提出,失效概率可以作为功能要求的量化指标。基于该提议,在"MSC 82/5/1"提案中,波兰、希腊和日本均以散货船船体结构为研究对象,分别利用事故树模型、第一性原理模型以及事件树模型对失效概率的估算进行研究;印度和中国分别通过成功树模型和致因分析,对"船舶安全"中"消防安全"的实现路径和"人员安全"对应的失效模式进行细分。"MSC 83/5/16"提案进一步指出,"船舶安全"的功能要求不仅应包括技术层面,还应考虑人的因素。

功能要求的实践研究主要聚焦于"救生设备"功能细分网络结构的建立。"MSC 91/5/1"提案对首次功能要求进行实践研究,将"应急控制"功能细分为火灾和气体检测、预防油类泄漏、适用于紧急状况的医疗、救助、人员撤离以及灭火等6大功能,并对"人员撤离"功能的进一步细分进行举例。"DE57/7/2"提案[189]进一步将"人员撤离"的功能细分与GBS应用研究中"救生设备"的功能细分进行比较,指出二者在细分结果和用语方面均存在差异。为了将当前的海事规则与功能一一对应,"SSE 1/INF.5"提案[190]提出了基于风险的功能细分方法,即将功能所面临的主要危险进行功能细分。该方法能够对海事规则进行重组,但在重组规则的过程中,"SSE 1/8/2"提案[191]发现当前规则存在不协调的现象。"MSC 94/5/2"提案[192]进一步提出,应以简洁的语言对功能要求进行描述,指出所面临的危险,并进行量化,用于符合性的验证。

功能要求量化和细分的研究成果为其在海事规则制定或修订方面的进一步应用提供了支持。功能要求的细分是量化基础,为了降低人的主观性对功能要求细分的影响,需要对功能要求的细分过程进行规范,并保证功能要求对安全目标的实现具有充分性。

4 SLA 规则符合性的验证

规则风险评价模型的建立是验证规则符合性的关键,日本和韩国的研究具有一定的代表性。"MSC 85/5/3"提案[193]以船舶结构规则中的船梁极限强度规定为研究对象,利用风险的概念将规则与功能要求相互联系,提出规则风险评价模型的一般建立思路。该思路的核心是通过结构可靠性分析方法计算事故的发生概率,并利用统计方法分析事故后果。同时,为了降低可靠性分析结果的不确定性,应规范可靠性分析工具的使用和数据的输入。"MSC 90/INF. 8"提案[194]以船体结构尺寸规定为研究对象,构建规则符合性评价流程图,细化规则符合性的评价过程。评价过程包括设计范围的限定、目标安全水平的明确、极限状态方程和设计变量的使用、结构可靠性分析、设计安全水平的计算、结构安全评估等 6 个步骤。

"MSC 85/5/3"提案提出的风险评价模型建立思路和"MSC 90/INF. 8"提案建立的规则符合性评价过程,均为规则符合性验证的研究提供基础,但目前的研究对象较为单一,研究深度也较浅,而且尚未进行实践研究。

5 结论

IMO 提案对 SLA 安全目标的设立、功能要求的量化和规则符合性验证等 3 个方面均进行了一定的研究,但研究深度较浅。为了加快 SLA 的研究进程,结合 IMO 对 SLA 的研究展望,SLA 需要重点研究以下 3 个方面:(1)在安全目标的确定过程中,需要深入研究最佳统计时间窗口的确定、FSA 风险分析结果的不确定性分析和安全水平的社会可容忍度测量等。(2)需要规范功能细分网络结构的建立和功能要求量化模型的使用,从而保证功能要求对安全目标的实现具有充分性。(3)需要进一步探索能够将海事规则与功能要求相互联系的基于风险的方法,并积累海事规则符合性定量评价的实践经验。

Uncertainty Analysis of the Estimated Risk in Formal Safety Assessment*

Abstract: An uncertainty analysis is required to be carried out in formal safety assessment (FSA) by the International Maritime Organization. The purpose of this article is to introduce the uncertainty analysis technique into the FSA process. Based on the uncertainty identification of input parameters, probability and possibility distributions are used to model the aleatory and epistemic uncertainties, respectively. An approach which combines the Monte Carlo random sampling of probability distribution functions with the a-cuts for fuzzy calculus is proposed to propagate the uncertainties. One output of the FSA process is societal risk (SR), which can be evaluated in the two-dimensional frequency-fatality (FN) diagram. Thus, the confidence-level-based SR is presented to represent the uncertainty of SR in two dimensions. In addition, a method for time window selection is proposed to estimate the magnitude of uncertainties, which is an important aspect of modeling uncertainties. Finally, a case study is carried out on an FSA study on cruise ships. The results show that the uncertainty analysis of SR generates a two-dimensional area for a certain degree of confidence in the FN diagram rather than a single FN curve, which provides more information to authorities to produce effective risk control measures.

Keywords: uncertainty analysis; risk analysis; societal risk; time window; formal safety assessment

0 Introduction

Formal safety assessment (FSA), aimed at enhancing maritime safety, is a structured and systematic methodology. FSA comprises five steps: identification of hazards (step 1), risk analysis (step 2), risk control options (step 3), cost-benefit assessment (step 4) and recommendations for decision-making (step 5). The purpose of the risk analysis in step 2 is a detailed investigation of the causes and initiating events and consequences of the more important accident scenarios identified in step 1. The output from step 2 can be used to identify the high-risk areas so that the effort can be focused to produce effective risk control measures in step 3 of the FSA[195].

There are several methods that can be used to perform a risk analysis, and different types of

---

* 本文发表在《Sustainability-Open Access Journal》第 10 卷,作者孙墨林、郑中义、江龙晖。

risk (i.e. risks to people, the environment or property) can be addressed according to the scope of the FSA. Risk analysis methods comprise multivariate statistical techniques[196], event tree models[197], fault tree models[198], risk contribution tree models[199], risk matrixes[200], failure mode and effect analyses[201], fishbone diagrams[202] and Bayesian networks[203]. The scope of the FSA, types of hazards identified in step 1, and the level of data available will all influence which method works best for each specific application.

In most FSA application studies, the event tree model is used to perform the risk analysis and societal risk (SR) is often taken as the risk indicator[204, 205]. SR reflects the average risk, in terms of fatalities, experienced by a whole group of people exposed to an accident scenario. It is common to represent SR by the frequency-fatality (FN) curve in a two-dimensional FN diagram, which shows the relationship between the cumulative frequency of fatality events and the number of fatalities. The evaluation of the FN curve is carried out by assessing the cumulative frequency of fatality events and the number of fatalities at the same time[206].

In the context of FSA and the usage of risk analysis, concerns have been raised regarding the accuracy of the methodology, in particular with respect to the uncertainty of input parameters[207]. Without assessing the significance of the uncertainty in the risk analysis process, the reliability of the risk analysis cannot be examined, which may produce risk control measures in low effect or in vain[208, 209]. In fact, the uncertainty analysis is required to be carried out in the process of FSA by revised guidelines for FSA for use in the International Maritime Organization (IMO) rule-making process[195]. The IMO is the United Nations specialized agency with responsibility for the safety and security of shipping and the prevention of marine pollution by ships[210]. Although the existence of uncertainties in the FSA process is well recognized, there are few studies which quantitatively address the uncertainties[211]. The purpose of this article is to introduce the suitable uncertainty analysis technique into the process of FSA according to the characteristics of the event tree model, which is used to perform the risk analysis in most FSA application studies.

In general, uncertainty is considered to be of two different types: aleatory and epistemic uncertainties. The aleatory uncertainty arises from randomness due to inherent variability, and the epistemic uncertainty refers to imprecision due to a lack of knowledge or information[212, 213]. Both types of uncertainty are very common in the risk analysis process of FSA. For example, accident frequencies can often be considered as parameters with aleatory uncertainty due to inherent variability[214]. In addition, the number of fatalities of each accident scenario, which are obtained by expert elicitation procedures can be taken as parameters with epistemic uncertainty due to incorporating diffuse information by experts[215].

In the recent FSA application studies, both types of uncertainty are represented by means of probability distributions, which are built by the statistical analysis method of Poisson data and expert statements[211]. When sufficiently informative data are available, probability distributions are correctly used to represent the aleatory uncertainty. However, when the available information is very scarce, even if the elicitation of expert knowledge is used, a probabilistic representation of epistemic uncertainty may not be possible[216].

As a result of the limitations associated with a probabilistic representation of epistemic uncertainty, a number of alternative representation frameworks have been proposed. These include fuzzy set theory[217], possibility theory[218], interval analysis[219] and evidence theory[220]. In addition, several approaches have been proposed to propagate the two types of uncertainty, such as a possibilistic Monte Carlo approach[221], a possibilistic-scenario-based approach[222], and an evidence-theory-based hybrid approach[223]. Among them, possibility theory has received growing attention because of its representation power and its relative mathematical simplicity[224]. Therefore, possibility theory is used to characterize the epistemic uncertainty in this article. Correspondingly, the possibilistic Monte Carlo approach is selected to propagate aleatory and epistemic uncertainties in the risk analysis process of FSA.

The possibilistic Monte Carlo approach can be used to address the uncertainty of the cumulative frequency of fatality events calculated by the event tree model, which is one component of the FN curve. For the purpose of examining the reliability of the risk analysis, the uncertainty of the number of fatalities, which is the other component of the FN curve, should also be taken into consideration[225, 226]. In order to make it possible to do so, a confidence-level-based SR is proposed, which is represented by a two-dimensional area for a certain degree of confidence in the FN diagram rather than a single FN curve.

An important aspect of modeling uncertainties lies in the appropriate selection of the time window, which is used for the inclusion of data[227]. The traditional empirical approach can lead to either a too conservative or non-conservative estimates of the magnitude of uncertainties based on the arbitrary choice of the length of time window[211]. To reduce the subjectivity of the selection of time window, a method for time window selection is proposed by analyzing the uncertainty and the stability of statistical data.

The contributions of the present study are summarized as follows. First, since uncertainty studies of the risk analysis process of FSA are few, the uncertainty analysis technique is introduced, considering the aleatory and epistemic uncertainties of input parameters. Second, confidence-level-based SR is presented to represent the SR uncertainty in two dimensions so as to identify the high-risk areas in the two-dimensional FN diagram. Third, a method for time window selection is proposed to avoid either too conservative or non-conservative estimates of the magnitude of uncertainties, which is an important aspect of modeling uncertainties.

The remainder of the paper is structured as follows. In Section 2, the risk analysis process of FSA is described. Section 3 discusses the process of aleatory and epistemic uncertainty modeling, time window selection and the representation of SR uncertainty. In Section 4, the uncertainty propagation procedure in the event tree model is described. The case study is discussed and the validation of the proposed methods is made in Section 5. Findings and limitations are provided in the last section.

1 Risk Analysis Process of FSA

The risk analysis process of FSA is carried out by analyzing accident frequencies and accident consequences separately. Accident frequencies can be determined by means of statistical analysis on the historical accident data and accident consequences are often analyzed by the event tree model. When more information about the causes of accidents is provided, the determination of accident frequencies can be performed by the fault tree model, which can show the causal relationship between events which singly or in combination occur to cause the occurrence of a type of accident or unintended hazardous outcome[195]. If the available information about accident frequencies and accident consequences is very scarce, the risk matrix method will be adopted to perform a risk analysis[228]. A risk matrix displays the basic properties, "consequence" and "frequency" of an adverse risk factor and the aggregate notion of risk by means of a graph. As both the consequence and frequency in the risk matrix are measured by a category scale, applications of the risk matrix are limited in practice[229]. As mentioned in the introduction section, the event tree model is used to perform the risk analysis in most FSA application studies according to the level of data available.

The event tree model is an inductive logic and diagrammatic method for identifying the various possible outcomes of a given initial event. The frequency of each particular outcome can be considered as the product of an initial event frequency and the conditional probability of the subsequent events along the related branch. Based on these frequencies of outcomes, one can compute the cumulative frequency of outcomes by summing up all of the frequencies of particular outcomes[230]. The structure of the event tree model, in terms of its branches, is determined by input parameters, which are event frequencies and outcomes caused by a chain of events. Some event frequencies are estimated by sufficient statistical data, which can be statistically verified. The other event frequencies and all outcomes caused by a chain of events are obtained based on qualitative considerations and expert judgement because the available information is very scarce[231].

As mentioned in the introduction section, SR is often taken as the risk indicator in the risk analysis process of FSA. When dealing with SR, outcomes caused by a chain of events and frequencies of these outcomes in the event tree model refer specifically to the number of fatalities (N) and the exact frequencies of N fatalities. It is common to represent SR by the FN curve in the FN diagram, which shows the cumulative frequencies of events causing N or more fatalities on the vertical axis against the number of fatalities (N) on the horizontal axis. Based on the outcomes and their frequencies in the event tree model, the cumulative frequencies of events causing N or more fatalities can be calculated by adding all the exact frequencies of N or more fatalities and plotted in the form of an FN curve[232].

When the number of fatalities (N) is set to 0, there is no need to calculate the frequency of N fatalities because the abscissa of the FN curve starts at the non-zero value of fatalities on the horizontal axis and increases gradually[232]. In other words, the FN curve shows the relationship between the cumulative frequencies of events causing N or more fatalities and non-zero values of fatalities (N) in a two-dimensional diagram. In most FSA application studies, accident consequences are specified by expert judgement considering casualty reports, observation in model tests, as well as numerical investigations because of the uncertainty and the potentiality of the accident occurrence[211]. It should be noted that the focus of this article is on the uncertainty analysis of the estimated risk in FSA studies, which has been carried out. Thus, the event tree model and all its input parameters have already been provided and described in FSA application studies.

2 Handling Uncertainties in the Risk Analysis Process

2.1 Aleatory and Epistemic Uncertainty Modeling

When using the event tree model to perform the risk analysis in step 2 of the FSA, input parameters are event frequencies and outcomes caused by a chain of events. These input parameters can be categorized into two types in the uncertainty analysis. If the uncertainty of input parameters arises from randomness due to inherent variability, these input parameters can be categorized as input parameters with aleatory uncertainty, such as event frequencies estimated by sufficient statistical data[211]. When the uncertainty of the input parameters refers to imprecision due to a lack of knowledge or information, these input parameters can be categorized as input parameters with epistemic uncertainty, such as event frequencies and outcomes obtained by expert judgement[233].

Aleatory and epistemic uncertainties require different mathematical representations. Probability distributions are assigned to represent aleatory uncertainties when there is sufficient information for statistical analysis. In the situation that the available information is very scarce, even if one adopts the elicitation of expert knowledge to incorporate diffuse information, possibility distributions are used to model the epistemic uncertainty.

The probabilistic uncertainty modeling depends upon the selection of the probability distribution of input parameters, which can be propagated using the Monte Carlo technique along the related branch in the event tree model. Since beta distribution is a suitable model for the random behavior of percentages and proportions defined on the interval $[0, 1]$[234], it was selected as the probability distribution for event frequencies with aleatory uncertainty in this study. Beta distribution is parametrized by two shape parameters, denoted by α_1 and β_1. The mean (μ) of beta distribution can be expressed by[234]:

$$\mu = \frac{\alpha_1}{\alpha_1 + \beta_1} \tag{1}$$

In order to determine the two parameters of beta distribution, we adopt the assumption that the occurrence of events in the event tree model of FSA is Poisson-distributed[211]. Based on the Poisson distribution assumption, the confidence interval of the number of times an event occurs can be calculated by[235]:

$$\lambda_U = \frac{\chi^2_{1-\omega/2}(2n+2)}{2}$$
$$\lambda_L = \frac{\chi^2_{\omega/2}(2n)}{2} \tag{2}$$

where λ_U and λ_L are the upper boundary and lower boundary of the confidence interval for the mean value of a Poisson distribution, respectively; n is the number of times an event occurs in an interval, such as the number of marine accidents; ω is defined as the significance level of the statistics; $\chi^2_{1-\omega/2}(2n+2)$ is the $(1-\omega/2)$ th quantile of the chi-squared distribution with $(2n+2)$ degrees of freedom; $\chi^2_{\omega/2}(2n)$ is the $(\omega/2)$ th quantile of the chi-squared distribution with $(2n)$ degrees of freedom; and $\chi^2_{1-\omega/2}(2n+2)$ and $\chi^2_{\omega/2}(2n)$ can be found in the table of chi-squared distribution.

Then the mean value of event frequencies and the corresponding confidence interval can be estimated by:

$$\theta = n \cdot \frac{1}{S}$$
$$\theta_U = \lambda_U \cdot \frac{1}{S} \quad (3)$$
$$\theta_L = \lambda_L \cdot \frac{1}{S}$$

where θ is defined as the mean value of event frequencies; θ_U and θ_L are the upper boundary and lower boundary of the confidence interval of θ, respectively; and S is the product of the number of experiments and an interval of time, such as ship years. It should be noted that the assumption that the occurrence of events is Poisson-distributed does not conflict with the selection of beta distribution to model the aleatory uncertainty of event frequencies, because the objects modeled are different.

Then the two parameters of beta distribution can be determined when the mean value (θ) and bounds of the confidence interval (θ_U and θ_L) calculated by the Poisson distribution are regarded as the beta distribution's mean value (μ) and the bounds of the confidence interval under the same confidence level[211]. The confidence interval of the beta distribution, which is parametrized by ω, α_1 and β_1 can be obtained by the software @RISK[236]. In other words, under the constraints of Equation (1), the two parameters of beta distribution can be estimated roughly through the enumeration method to make the confidence interval of the beta distribution deviate slightly from the confidence interval calculated by the Poisson distribution under the same confidence level (ω).

For input parameters with epistemic uncertainty, we use symmetric triangular distributions to model the epistemic uncertainty. As described in Section 2, values for these input parameters are estimated by expert judgement as crisp values. According to the interpretation of uncertainty in these parameters, value ranges of these input parameters can also be estimated roughly. Based on the crisp values and their approximate ranges, symmetric triangular distributions can be formed by introducing an as small as possible uncertainty. When there are more interpretations of these input parameters, the selection of other possibilistic distributions is possible. Using different possibilistic distributions to model the epistemic uncertainty will lead to relatively small differences in uncertainty quantifications. The symmetric triangular distribution was parametrized by three parameters, denoted by lower limit α_2, upper limit β_2 and mode γ_2. Also, γ_2 equals the average value of α_2 and β_2. We used the crisp values of input parameters as the mode γ_2, which has a membership value of one. Then we assigned symmetric triangular distributions to input parameters with epistemic uncertainty according to the interpretation of uncertainty in these parameters.

2.2 A Method for Time Window Selection

Although the length of time window is an important factor for modeling the uncertainty of input parameters, it has received little empirical study. The time window can be taken as the time interval for which historical data are collected[237]. The longer the time window is, the more informative the data for statistical analysis, and the more accurate uncertainty modeling is. There are also indications that more recent statistics represent a more conclusive database than old statistics reflecting recent technical or operational developments, new requirements, or specific arrangements on ships being analyzed. To coordinate the contradiction described above, the uncertainty and the stability of statistical data are used as the two indexes to determine the optimal length of time window, over which the uncertainty of input parameters cannot be estimated too conservatively or non-conservatively.

When event frequencies are listed in time order, a time series can be built up. Through the uncertainty analysis of the time series, each individual value of a time series is no longer an exact value but an interval of possible values, which is defined as an uncertain time series. The confidence interval of each individual value of the time series under a certain level of confidence can be calculated according to Equations (2) and (3).

With respect to the stability of statistical data, the sliding window method is used to implement the segmentation of uncertain time series, which aggregates the relatively concentrative confidence interval. Each of the segments represents a level of event frequencies. The sliding window method takes the first point in time as the first segment and continues to expand until the value at a certain point in time goes beyond the confidence interval of a previous segment. This point in time is taken as the beginning of the next segment. The above process repeats until it comes to the end of the uncertain time series. When a segment only contains one point in time, this point in time should be placed into the adjacent segment which has a smaller difference with the value at this point in time according to the orderliness and the continuity of the time series. After the segmentation of the uncertain time series, the closest segmentation to the research date is taken as the optimal time window used for modeling the uncertainty of the input parameters.

Whether the value at a certain point in time goes beyond the confidence interval of a previous segment is the condition for the segmentation. According to the orderliness and the continuity of the time series, when the value at a certain point in time goes beyond the confidence interval of a previous segment under a certain level of confidence, it means that the value at a certain point in time changes a lot compared with the previous segment. In other words, the value at a certain point in time still changes aside from the random fluctuation of data and it is reasonable to consider this point in time as the beginning of the next segment under a certain level of confidence.

2.3 The Representation of Societal Risk Uncertainty

As described in the introductory section, SR is often taken as the risk indicator in most FSA application studies and it is common to represent SR by the FN curve. The evaluation of the FN curve can be carried out by assessing the cumulative frequency of events causing N or more fatalities, denoted by $F(N)$, and the number of fatalities, denoted by N, at the same time. In order to examine the reliability of the FN curve evaluation, confidence level based SR is put up to consider $F(N)$ and N as fuzzy variables and to represent the SR uncertainty in two dimensions in the FN diagram. Specifically, α-cuts of $F(N)$ and N are taken as the confidence interval in the process of quantifying the SR uncertainty according to the possibility theory.

In the possibility theory, for each set A contained in the universe of discourse U_c of the variable C, the α-cut of C is defined as A_α and it is possible to obtain the confidence level of the interval A_α by the possibility measure $\Pi(A)$ and the necessary measure $N(A)$ from the possibilistic distribution $\pi(c)$ of C, by[212]:

$$\Pi(A) = \max_{c \in A}\{\pi(c)\}$$
$$N(A) = 1 - \Pi(\bar{A}) \qquad \forall A \subseteq U_c \qquad (4)$$
$$N(A) \leq P\{c \in A\} \leq \Pi(A)$$

If we replace A with A_α, then we have:

$$N(A_\alpha) \leq P\{c \in A_\alpha\} \leq \Pi(A_\alpha) \qquad (5)$$

According to the definition of the possibility measure $\Pi(A)$ and the necessary measure $N(A)$, we get $N(A_\alpha) = 1 - \alpha$ and $\Pi(A_\alpha) = 1$. Through proper simplification, we thus have

$$P\{c \in A_\alpha\} \geq 1 - \alpha \qquad (6)$$

As can be seen from Equation (6), A_α can be taken as the confidence interval with a confidence degree of $(1 - \alpha)$. Thus, uncertainties of SR can be quantified as confidence intervals, α-cuts of $F(N)$ and N, on the vertical and horizontal orientation in the FN diagram, respectively. It should be noted that α-cuts of $F(N)$ and N can be plotted on the same FN diagram with the same degree of confidence.

3 Uncertainty Propagation Procedure

Let us consider the event tree model whose output is a function $f(x_1, x_2, \cdots, x_I, y_1, y_2, \cdots, y_J)$ of $(I+J)$ input variables, which are ordered in such a way that the first I variables are described by random variables $(X_1, X_2, \cdots, X_I)$ and the following J variables are characterized by fuzzy numbers $(Y_1, Y_2, \cdots, Y_J)$. The propagation of such mixed uncertainty information can be performed by the Monte Carlo technique combined with the α-cuts for fuzzy calculus[238]. The uncertainty propagation procedure is described as the following steps:

Step 1. Sample the r-th realization $(x_1^r, x_2^r, \ldots, x_I^r)$ of the random variables $(X_1, X_2, \cdots, X_I)$;

Step 2. Select a possibility value $\alpha \in [0: \Delta\alpha: 1]$ ($\Delta\alpha$ is the step size, e.g., 0.05) and the corresponding α-cuts $(\underline{y_1^\alpha}, \overline{y_1^\alpha}), (\underline{y_2^\alpha}, \overline{y_2^\alpha}), \cdots, (\underline{y_J^\alpha}, \overline{y_J^\alpha})$ of fuzzy numbers $(Y_1, Y_2, \cdots, Y_J)$;

Step 3. Compute the smallest and largest values of $f(x_1^r, x_2^r, \cdots, x_I^r, y_1^\alpha, y_2^\alpha, \cdots, y_J^\alpha, z_1, z_2, \cdots, z_K)$, denoted by $\underline{f_\alpha}$ and $\overline{f_\alpha}$, respectively, considering all values located within the α-cut interval for each fuzzy number.

Step 4. Return to step 2 and repeat for another α-cut. After having repeated steps 2 to 3 for all the α-cuts of interest, the fuzzy random realization π_r^f of $f(x_1, x_2, \cdots, x_I, y_1, y_2, \cdots, y_J, z_1, z_2, \ldots, z_K)$ is obtained as the collection of the values $\underline{f_\alpha}$ and $\overline{f_\alpha}$;

Step 5. Return to step 1 to generate a new realization of the random variable. An ensemble of realizations of fuzzy intervals $(\pi_1^f, \pi_2^f, \cdots, \pi_r^f)$ is obtained, where r is the number of realizations for random variables $(X_1, X_2, \cdots, X_I)$;

For each value of α, an imaginary horizontal line is drawn. This line crosses each of the individual fuzzy intervals $(\pi_1^f, \pi_2^f, \cdots, \pi_r^f)$ twice, and therefore $([\underline{f_\alpha^1} \quad \overline{f_\alpha^1}], [\underline{f_\alpha^2} \quad \overline{f_\alpha^2}], \cdots, [\underline{f_\alpha^r} \quad \overline{f_\alpha^r}])$ is obtained. The confidence interval of $f(x_1, x_2, \cdots, x_I, y_1, y_2, \cdots, y_J, z_1, z_2, \cdots, z_K)$ for the confidence value $(1-\alpha)$ can be determined by a $(\alpha/2)$ probability of getting lower and higher values of $(\underline{f_\alpha^1}, \underline{f_\alpha^2}, \cdots, \underline{f_\alpha^r})$ and $(\overline{f_\alpha^1}, \overline{f_\alpha^2}, \cdots, \overline{f_\alpha^r})$, respectively[239].

4 Case Study

The approaches for uncertainty modeling and propagation illustrated in Sections 3 and 4 have been applied to the risk analysis of cruises in the FSA report from the European Maritime Safety Agency[211] and the FSA proposal for cruise ships by Denmark[214] (hereafter both of the reports are called the FSA report for cruises).

4.1 The Event Tree Model

From the statistical analysis of the historical cruise accidents, it is noted that the risk level is dominated by collision, grounding and fire/explosion scenarios resulting in the loss of lives. Therefore, the event tree in the FSA report for cruises, which contains three types of cruise accidents is used and shown in Figure 1.

As can be seen from Figure 1, event frequencies and consequences are represented by notations. The input parameters of the event tree model include all the notations in Figure 1 except frequencies of fatalities (F1 to F49), which are calculated as the product of initial event frequency and conditional probability of the subsequent events along the related branch. As discussed in Section 2, input parameters are estimated based on the informative data available or on expert judgement, which are provided and described in the FSA report for cruises.

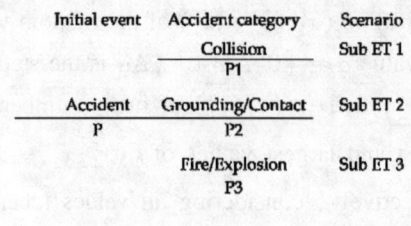

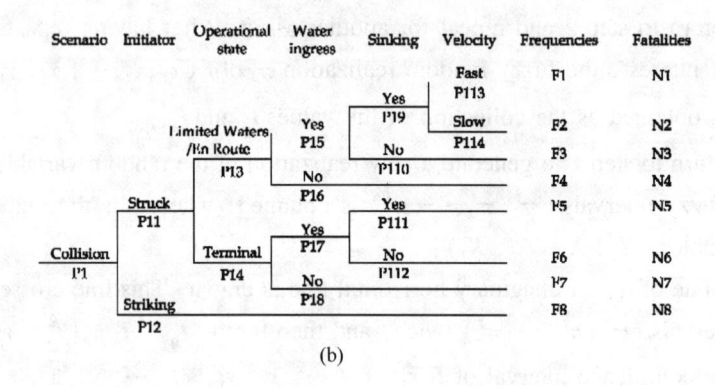

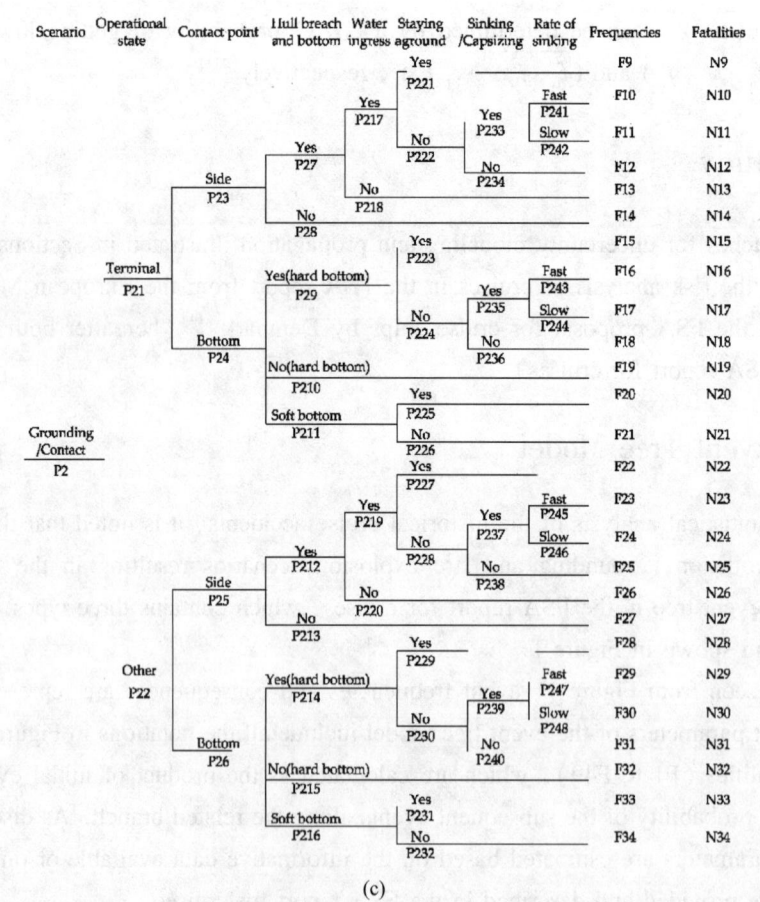

(a)

(b)

(c)

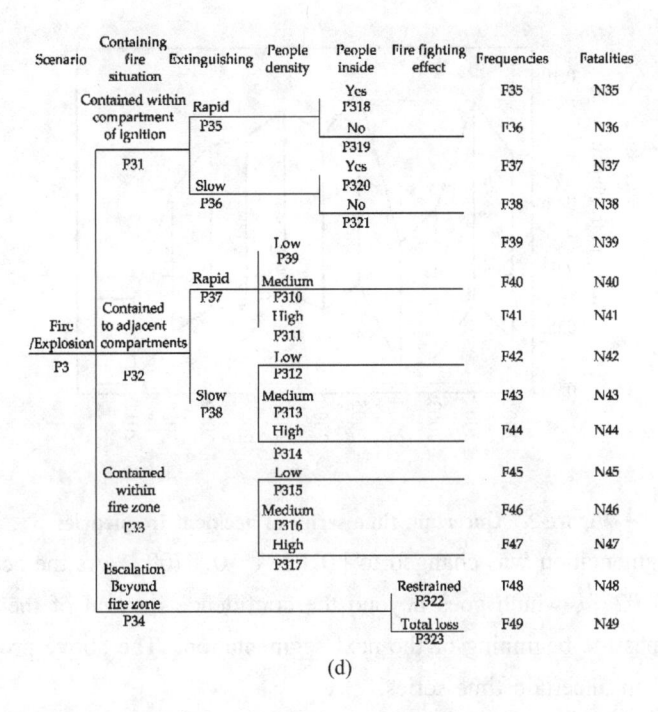

Scenario	Containing fire situation	Extinguishing	People density	People inside	Fire fighting effect	Frequencies	Fatalities
	Contained within compartment of ignition P31	Rapid P35		Yes P318		F35	N35
				No P319		F36	N36
		Slow P36		Yes P320		F37	N37
				No P321		F38	N38
Fire /Explosion P3	Contained to adjacent compartments P32	Rapid P37	Low P39			F39	N39
			Medium P310			F40	N40
			High P311			F41	N41
		Slow P38	Low P312			F42	N42
			Medium P313			F43	N43
			High P314			F44	N44
	Contained within fire zone P33		Low P315			F45	N45
			Medium P316			F46	N46
			High P317			F47	N47
	Escalation Beyond fire zone P34			Restrained P322		F48	N48
				Total loss P323		F49	N49

(d)

Figure 1 (a) **The overall event tree model for cruise accidents. Expanded tree details are shown for**: (b) **the collision scenario**, (c) **the grounding/contact scenario and** (d) **the fire/explosion scenario**

4.2 Time Window Selection

The method for time window selection is only applied to the sum of the number of collisions, that of grounding and that of fire/explosion. No similar analysis is carried out separately in this study because the number of accidents in each casualty type is relatively small. Applying the method to the casualty type separately will reduce statistical reliability.

The number of cruise accidents and cruise ships for each year 2001 to 2012 are provided in the FSA report for cruises. Therefore, the accident frequency for cruises for each year 2001 to 2012 and the corresponding confidence interval for the confidence value 0.9 can be calculated by Equation (2) and Equation (3). The accident frequencies and boundaries of the confidence interval are represented by short dashes and line segments in Figure 2, respectively. To represent the change of accident frequencies more vividly, the upper boundaries and lower boundaries of the confidence interval are connected with a line.

The sliding window method is used to implement the segmentation of uncertain time series of accident frequencies in Figure 2. Firstly, the year 2001 is taken as the first segmentation. According to Figure 2, the accident frequencies of the year 2001 and the year 2002 were 0.0382 and 0.0533, and the confidence interval of the first segmentation was [0.0166 0.0754]. Since the accident frequency of the year 2002 was in the confidence interval of the first segmentation, it was placed into the first segmentation. Based on Equation (2) and Equation (3), the confidence in-

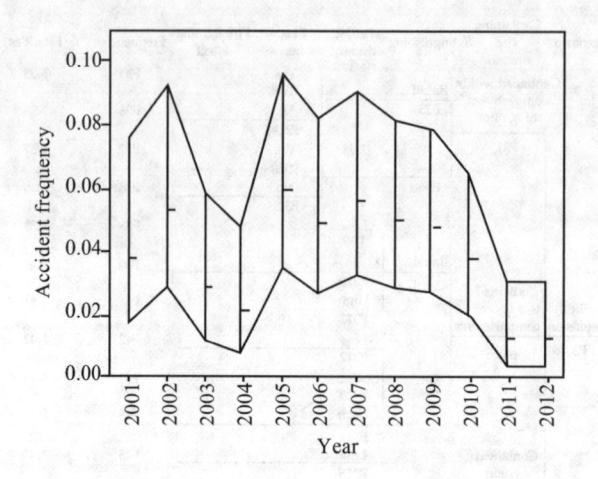

Figure 2 Uncertain time series of accident frequencies

terval of the first segmentation was changed to [0.0284 0.0709]. As the accident frequency of the year 2003 was 0.0278, which goes beyond the confidence interval of the first segmentation, the year 2003 becomes the beginning of the next segmentation. The above process repeats until it comes to the end of an uncertain time series.

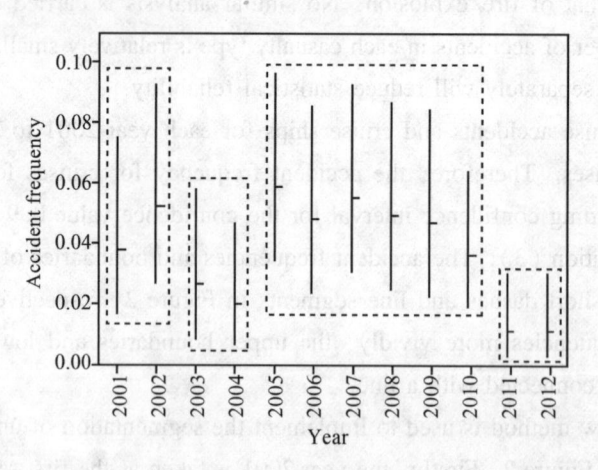

After the segmentation of uncertain time series, we find that there is a segment that only has the year 2010. According to Section 3.2, the year 2010 should be placed into the previous segment, which has a smaller difference than the accident frequency of the year 2010. Finally, four segments were determined, which were 2001 to 2002, 2003 to 2004, 2005 to 2010, and 2011 to 2012. As shown in Figure 3, each segment is represented by a rectangle. The closest segment to the research date, 2011 to 2012, was taken as the optimal time window used for modeling the uncertainty of accident frequencies.

Figure 3 The segmentation of uncertain time series

In order to verify its superiority, the method proposed was compared with the traditional empirical approach, which extends the length of time window as far as possible. When applying the traditional empirical approach, the most recent twelve years (2001 to 2012) were selected as the statistical time window. Then the accident frequency and its confidence interval for the confidence value 0.9 were calculated as 0.037 5 and [0.0314 0.0445] according to Equations (2) and (3). As can be seen in Figure 3, the most recent two years (2011 to 2012) were selected as the optimal statistical time window in this study. The corresponding accident frequency and its confidence interval for the same confidence value 0.9 were calculated as 0.011 7 and [0.0051 0.0231] based on Equations (2) and (3). The size of the confidence interval can be considered as the outcome of the uncertainty quantification. It should be noted that the more informative data there are for uncertainty modeling, the smaller the size of the confidence interval becomes, and the more the accurate uncertainty modeling is. Although more informative data are used to model the uncertainty of the accident frequency and the size of the confidence interval is slightly smaller, the traditional empirical approach does not take into account that the accident frequency continued to decline in the most recent six years (2007 to 2012), which can be seen in Figure 2. Thus, the time window obtained by the method proposed in this study is a more appropriate time interval for modeling the uncertainty of the accident frequency because recent developments in the ships being analyzed are reflected as much as possible while not enlarging the size of the confidence interval much.

4.3 Uncertainty Modeling of Input Parameters

All the input parameters in the event tree model can be categorized into two types in the uncertainty analysis based on the method used for estimating these input parameters. When there are sufficient statistical data to estimate them, input parameters can be categorized as input parameters with aleatory uncertainty. If input parameters are obtained by expert judgement, they can be considered as input parameters with epistemic uncertainty. As discussed in Section 3.1, the aleatory and epistemic uncertainties are modeled by probability distributions and possibility distributions, respectively. Although all the input parameters have uncertainties, only 65 input parameters are considered in the process of uncertainty modeling because they are in the related branches of the event tree, which correspond to non-zero values of fatalities.

There are 14 input parameters which are categorized as input parameters with aleatory uncertainty and one of them is the input parameter P11, which denotes the probability of a cruise ship struck when it is involved in a collision accident. According to the FSA report for cruises, 32 cruise ships were struck when 62 cruise ships were involved in collision accidents in the time window (2011 to 2012). Therefore, the value of P11 was estimated as 0.516. When the values given above were put into Equations (2) and (3), the confidence interval of P11 could be calculated as [0.376, 0.693] for the confidence value 0.9. Then α_1 and β_1 of the beta distribution could be roughly estimated at 11 and 10.3, respectively, using the software @risk to make the mean value of beta distribution equal to 0.516 andits confidence interval deviate slightly from [0.376, 0.693], according to Section 3.1. The same computations were performed to build the beta distributions of other input parameters with aleatory uncertainty. Table 1 reports the parameters of the beta distributions of input parameters with aleatory uncertainty.

Table 1 The parameters of beta distributions

Notations of Input Parameters	Parameters of Beta Distribution (α_1, β_1)
P1	(0.3, 218.5)
P11	(11, 10.3)
P14	(2.8, 1.5)
P2	(2.2, 413.6)
P21	(44, 32.4)
P24	(3.4, 39.1)
P25	(7, 7.3)
P29	(4, 1.5)
P212	(6.7, 1.5)
P214	(3.3, 1.3)
P217	(3.6, 3.3)
P224	(31.5, 31.1)
P230	(15, 3.8)
P3	(0.3, 218.5)

Explanations of input parameters can be found in the event tree in Figure 1.

With respect to input parameters with epistemic uncertainty, 51 input parameters were identified. P19 is one of the input parameters with epistemic uncertainty, which represents the probability of a cruise ship sinking when it is involved in collision accidents. The value of P19 is provided as 0.14 by expert judgement in the FSA report for cruises and it is set to the mode γ_2 of symmetric triangular distribution. Since γ_2 is equal to the average value of α_2 and β_2, the parameters of the symmetric triangular distribution of P19 are simply set as (0, 0.14, 0.28). The same processes of possibilistic uncertainty modeling were executed to build the symmetric triangular distribution of other input parameters with epistemic uncertainty. The parameters of the symmetric triangular distribution of input parameters with epistemic uncertainty are reported in Table 2.

Table 2 The parameters of symmetric triangular distribution

Notations of Input Parameters	Parameters of Symmetric Triangular Distribution (α_2, γ_2, β_2)
P19, P111	(0, 0.14, 0.28)
P113	(0, 0.18, 0.36)
P15	(0, 0.33, 0.66)
P17	(0, 0.071, 0.142)
P233, P237	(0, 0.087, 0.174)
P235, P239	(0, 0.083, 0.166)
P241, P243, P245, P247	(0, 0.18, 0.36)
P27	(0.62, 0.81, 1)
P219	(0.7, 0.85, 1)
P222	(0, 0.15, 0.3)
P228	(0, 0.33, 0.66)
P32	(0, 0.06, 0.12)
P33	(0, 0.03, 0.06)
P34	(0, 0.01, 0.02)
P37	(0.6, 0.8, 1)
P312, P315	(0, 0.4, 0.8)
P310, P313, P316	(0, 0.3, 0.6)
P311, P314, P317	(0, 0.3, 0.6)
P322	(0.6, 0.8, 1)
N1, N23, N29	(0.6, 0.8, 1)
N49	(0.05, 0.075, 0.1)
N2, N5, N10, N11, N16, N17, N24, N30	(0.025, 0.05, 0.075)
N47	(0.005, 0.025, 0.045)
N48	(0.00125, 0.005, 0.00875)
N44, N45, N46	(0.0005, 0.00125, 0.002)
N40, N41, N42, N43	(0, 0.0005, 0.001)

Explanations of input parameters can be found in the event tree in Figure 1. Parameters of symmetric triangular distributions of fatalities denotes the percentages of people on board died.

4.4 Uncertainty Propagation

Before the propagation of aleatory and epistemic uncertainties in the event tree model, the general method with crisp input parameters (hereafter called the general method) was processed as a comparison. According to the event tree model in the FSA report for cruises, the exact frequency of N fatalities per accident category can be obtained, which is shown in Table 3. In order to plot the FN curve of cruise ships, the cumulative frequencies $F(N)$ causing N or more fatalities needs to be derived by adding all the exact frequencies of N or more fatalities, which are also shown in Table 3.

Table 3 Frequency of N fatalities per accident category and the cumulative frequency $F(N)$ for cruise ships

N (Fatalities)	Collision (1/ship * year)	Grounding (1/ship * year)	Fire/Explosion (1/ship * year)	Total (1/ship * year)	$F(N)$ (1/ship * year)
3	—	—	4.92×10^{-5}	4.92×10^{-5}	3.04×10^{-4}
8	—	—	3.25×10^{-5}	3.25×10^{-5}	2.55×10^{-4}
34	—	—	1.06×10^{-5}	1.06×10^{-5}	2.22×10^{-4}
168	—	—	1.25×10^{-5}	1.25×10^{-5}	2.12×10^{-4}
337	2.13×10^{-5}	1.61×10^{-4}	—	1.82×10^{-4}	1.99×10^{-4}
505	—	—	2.65×10^{-6}	2.65×10^{-6}	1.74×10^{-5}
5384	3.17×10^{-6}	1.17×10^{-5}	—	1.47×10^{-5}	1.47×10^{-5}

After probability distributions and possibility distributions were assigned to the input parameters, the uncertainty propagation approach was applied to the event tree model. With respect to the input parameters with aleatory uncertainty (X_1, X_2, $\cdots$, X_I), the sampling realization size was set to 1000. For each of these realizations, 21 α-cut values ($\Delta\alpha = 0.05$) were set for the input parameters with epistemic uncertainty (Y_1, Y_2, $\cdots$, Y_J). The ensemble of fuzzy interval realizations ($\pi_1^f, \pi_2^f, \cdots, \pi_{1000}^f$) for scenarios where 80% of people on board died in the event tree is taken as an example to demonstrate the process of the uncertainty propagation, which is illustrated in Figure 4.

When α is set to 0.1 in Figure 4, an imaginary horizontal line can be drawn that crosses each of the individual fuzzy intervals ($\pi_1^f, \pi_2^f, \cdots, \pi_{1000}^f$) twice, and therefore ($[\underline{f_{0.1}^1}\ \overline{f_{0.1}^1}], [\underline{f_{0.1}^2}\ \overline{f_{0.1}^2}], \cdots, [\underline{f_{0.1}^{1000}}\ \overline{f_{0.1}^{1000}}]$) is obtained. Then the confidence interval of the cumulative frequencies $F(N)$ of scenarios where 80% of people on board died can be determined as $[8.36 \times 10^{-7}, 1.12 \times 10^{-4}]$, for the confidence value 0.9 when there is a 5% probability of respectively getting lower and higher values of ($\underline{f_{0.1}^1}, \underline{f_{0.1}^2}, \cdots, \underline{f_{0.1}^{1000}}$) and ($\overline{f_{0.1}^1}, \overline{f_{0.1}^2}, \cdots, \overline{f_{0.1}^{1000}}$). In addition, the confidence interval of the number of fatalities for scenarios where 80% of people on board died is calculated as [4173, 6595] for the confidence value 0.9 when 6730 people are assumed on board according to

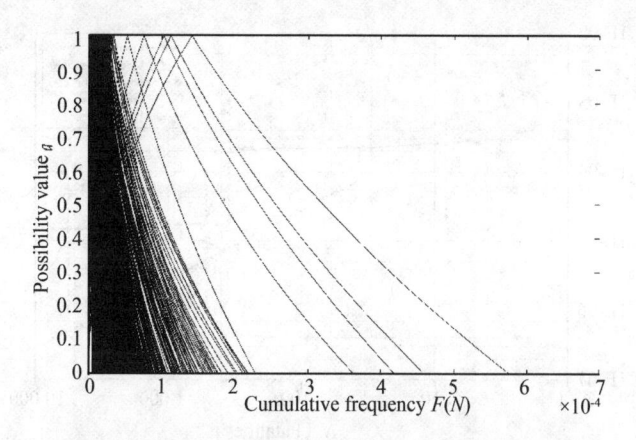

Figure 4 The ensemble of fuzzy interval realizations.

the FSA report for cruises.

The process for determining the overlapping areas of the rectangle, which represents two-dimensional uncertainty in the FN diagram, is depicted in Figures 5-7. Figure 5 represents the uncertainty of the cumulative frequencies $F(N)$, whereas Figure 6 represents the uncertainty of the cumulative frequencies $F(N)$ and the number of fatalities C. Figure 7 shows the final result of two-dimensional uncertainty in the FN diagram, in which confidence boundaries are denoted by dot dash lines. FN criteria are also plotted in Figures 5 to 7, which can be considered as reference FN curves. Based on the comparison with the FN criteria, the FN curve can be evaluated. The FN criteria include the upper criterion and the lower criterion, which are used and provided in the FSA report for cruises. If any part of the FN curve crosses the upper criterion, it indicates that the part of the FN curve is intolerable, which needs to be brought down by risk control measures. The FN curve derived from the general method with crisp input parameters is also shown in Figures 5 to 7, and is denoted by the solid line.

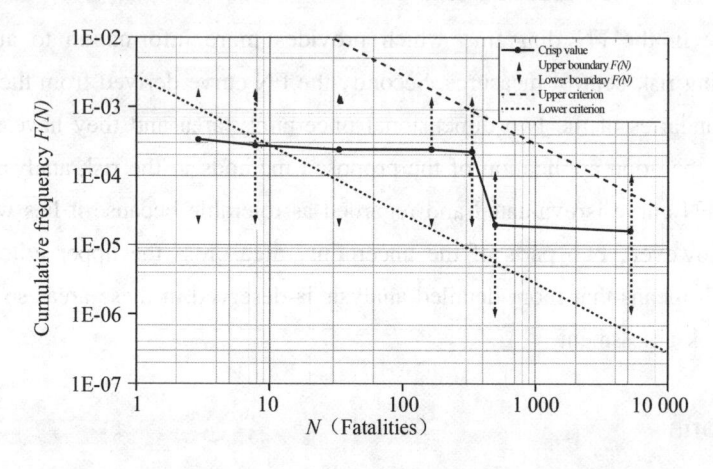

Figure 5 The uncertainty of the cumulative frequencies $F(N)$

The following observations can be drawn from Figure 7. First, the general method provides a single FN curve, whereas the proposed methods generate a two-dimensional area for a certain de-

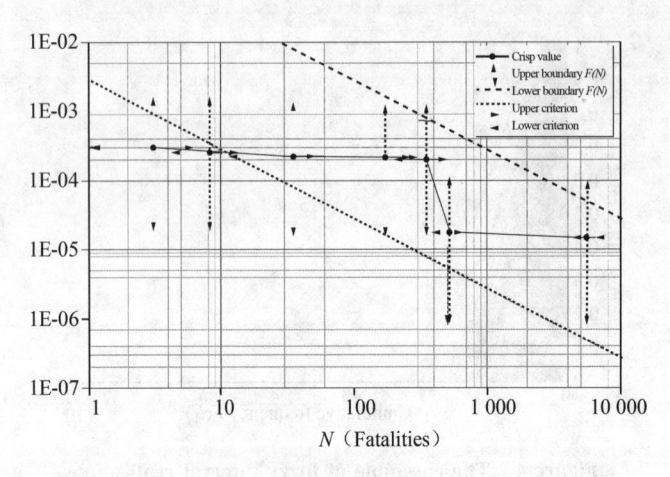

Figure 6 The uncertainty of the cumulative frequencies $F(N)$ and the number of fatalities C

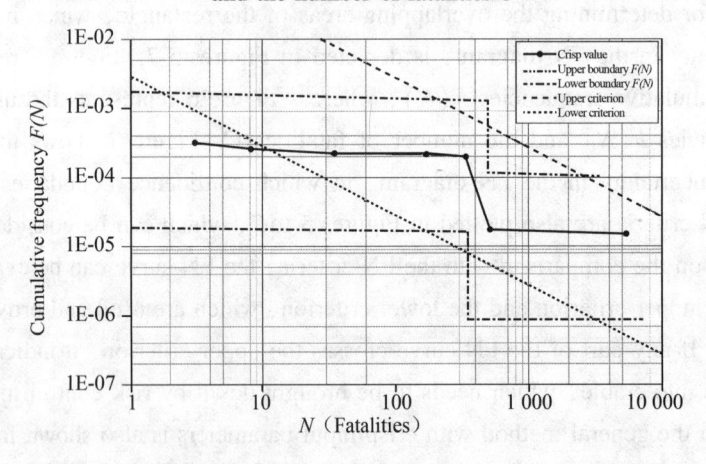

Figure 7 The two-dimensional uncertainty in the frequency-fatality (FN) diagram

gree of confidence in the FN diagram, which provides more information to authorities in the process of producing risk control measures. Second, the FN curve derived from the general method lies within the boundaries of the two-dimensional uncertainty area and they have similar variation trend. It indicates the good application of the proposed methods in the risk analysis process of the FSA. Third, the FN curve is evaluated and regarded as tolerable because it lies wholly below the upper criterion. However, two parts of the uncertainty area cross the upper criterion, as can be seen in Figure 7. It means that more detailed analysis is deserved in these areas so as to ensure the reliability of the risk assessment.

5 Conclusions

Uncertainty analysis has been conceived as a necessary step in the FSA process. In this article, uncertainty analysis technique was introduced considering the aleatory and epistemic uncertainties of the input parameters. In addition, confidence-level-based SR was proposed to represent the uncertainty of SR in two dimensions when identifying the high-risk areas in the two-dimensional FN diagram. Considering that accurate uncertainty modeling lies in the appropriate selection of the time window, a method for time window selection is proposed, which provides the theoretical foundation and reduces the subjectivity for determining the length of time window in the uncertainty modeling process. Finally, a case study was carried out on the FSA study on cruise ships. The proposed methods suit the risk analysis process of the FSA and can provide more information to authorities so that the effort can be focused to produce effective risk control measures.

A word of caution is in order with respect to the assumptions underlying the uncertainty analysis procedure. First of all, the uncertainty propagation method is developed by assuming independence among the probabilistic and possibilistic variables, and independence within the probabilistic variable set. Then dependence is introduced among the possibilistic variables, because the same confidence level in possibilistic variables is used to build the α-cuts. These assumptions are worth further investigation both from the theoretical and practical points of view.

A Practical Method for the Evaluation of Societal Risk in the Context of the International Maritime Organization's Safety Level Approach

Abstract: Safety Level Approach (SLA) is a structured application of risk-based methodologies for the International Maritime Organization's (IMO's) rule-making process. When the SLA is applied, safety goals have to be provided. In order to set appropriate levels for safety goals, it is necessary to measure the tolerance degree of the current safety level. Based on the consistency with individual risk criteria and the principle of continuous improvement, this paper proposes an approach to establish the societal risk criteria, which can be used for setting safety goals in the context of the IMO's SLA. Furthermore, by defining dynamic factors to express risk aversion, a method for tolerance measurement of the current societal risk is developed. Finally, a case study is carried out to the societal risk evaluation of cruises and Roll-On Roll-Off (RO-RO) passenger ships.

Keywords: Safety level approach; Societal risk; Frequency-Fatality (FN) diagram; Risk criteria

1 INTRODUCTION

The "Safety Level Approach" (SLA) has been proposed by the International Maritime Organization (IMO) to develop goal-based standards using a risk-based methodology[169]. SLA is the structured application of risk-based methodologies for the IMO rule-making process[240]. It is essentially an application process of risk analysis and risk management theory to maritime safety standard-setting and it will provide IMO with a basis for guiding work for continuous improvement.

There are five elements in the structure of the SLA. As a starting point for the application of SLA, safety levels should be incorporated into the first element named safety goals. In order to avoid sudden discontinuities in setting safety goals, it is necessary to measure the tolerance degree of the current safety level. It should be noted that in the context of IMO's SLA, the required safety level reflected in the goals should address as a minimum: safety of life at sea including occupational health, safety of the ship and prevention and control of pollution from the ship[240]. Only the safety goals for people on board are considered in this work.

Societal Risk (SR) is an expression of average risk, in terms of fatalities, experienced by a

---

* 本文发表在《The Journal of Navigation》2018 年第 71 卷,作者孙墨林、郑中义、江龙晖。

whole group of people exposed to an accident scenario. Usually SR is taken to be the risk of death and can be expressed as risk matrix, Frequency-Fatality (FN) diagrams, or the average number of fatalities per year which is typically known as Potential Loss of Life (PLL)[211]. A risk matrix displays the basic properties, "consequence" and "likelihood" of an adverse risk factor and the aggregate notion of risk by means of a graph. As both the consequence and likelihood in the risk matrix are measured by a category scale, applications of the risk matrix are limited in practice[229]. PLL is defined as the expected value of the number of fatalities per year, which can be taken as a one-dimensional measurement of SR. SR expressed by FN diagrams shows the relationship between the cumulative frequency of an accident and the number of fatalities in a two-dimensional diagram. PLL is a simpler format of SR than the FN diagram[195]. Since the two-dimensional graphical presentation of SR can be used to show "existing" and "upgraded" process performance and overcomes some statistical problems of one-dimensional measure of SR[241], the FN diagram is a more appropriate choice for the representation of SR in the context of IMO's SLA.

In the literature, different methods for establishing FN criteria have been proposed. The FN criteria can be taken as reference FN curves for SR assessment purposes. The mathematical formalism of the FN curve has been introduced[242], and improved continuously[243-245], which provide the basis for the determination of FN criteria. After theoretically analysing the relationship between SR and Individual Risk (IR)[246], FN criteria can be formulated to be fully consistent with IR criteria[247, 248]. Furthermore, based on the historical FN curves, FN criteria can also be established. For example, in Kaneko et al. (2015)[249], the FN criteria are developed by multiplying a parameter with the historical FN curve. In Zhang et al. (2015)[250], the bounds of the 95% confidence interval of the historical FN curve are taken as the FN criteria.

Although it is theoretically obvious that IR and SR calculations should lead to equal expected values, they might not always be consistent since the two risk indices are proposed based on distinct perspectives in practice[251]. Furthermore, it should be noted that serious accidents are very rare events which do not necessarily occur at regular intervals, so that FN criteria should not be based just on historical data, but also take the authority's point of view of how much risk is tolerable into consideration[252, 253].

An alternative way of establishing FN criteria which is widely used in Formal Safety Assessment (FSA) is based on the economic importance of the activity and calibrated against the average fatality rate per portion of Gross National Product (GNP)[252]. The FN criteria can be treated as guidelines that help encourage reduction of catastrophe risks[211], rather than as a basis for setting safety goals. In order to set appropriate levels for safety goals in the context of the IMO's SLA, new FN criteria need to be established.

In this article, a practical method for evaluating SR is proposed in the context of the IMO's SLA. The method consists of two steps. The first step is to establish new FN criteria which are fully consistent with revised IR criteria. The revised IR criteria can be obtained according to the principle of continuous improvement and calibrated with the current IR criteria. Based on the new FN criteria, by defining dynamic factors to express risk aversion, an approach to a numerical measure of the tolerance degree of FN curves is proposed in the second step. Finally, the method is verified by applying them to the SR evaluation of cruise ships and Roll-On Roll-Off Passenger (RoPax) ships.

The remainder of the paper is structured as follows. In Section 2, basic definitions of IR and SR criteria are described. Furthermore, principles and steps for establishing risk criteria are summarised. Section 3 discusses the modelling process for new FN criteria and dynamic factors for expressing risk aversion. In Section 4, a case study is carried out to the societal risk evaluation of cruises and RoPax ships. Findings and limitations are provided in the last section.

2 INDIVIDUAL RISK CRITERIA AND SOCIETAL RISK CRITERIA

2.1 Definition

Individual risk (IR) is defined as the risk of death, injury and ill health as experienced by an individual at a given location[195]. The purpose of IR criteria is to limit the risks to people on board the ship or to individuals who may be affected by shipping accidents. The current IR criteria in IMO are listed in Table 1[254].

Table 1　IR criteria

Bounds for IR criteria[a]	IR value
Maximum tolerable IR for crew members	10^{-3} annually
Maximum tolerable IR for passengers	10^{-4} annually
Maximum tolerable IR for public ashore	10^{-4} annually
Negligible IR for all people	10^{-6} annually

[a] Note that the names of bounds for IR criteria in this research are derived from IMO (2000).

The IR criteria in Table 1 are typically used as outer limits on a process that tries to make the risks as low as reasonably practicable in the context of FSA[211]. However, unlike IR, Societal Risk (SR) represents the risk to a group of people[195]. The purpose of SR criteria is to limit the risks from ships to society as a whole, and to local communities which may be affected by ship activities[254]. It has been discussed in the introduction that FN criteria can be used to evaluate SR. When plotted on log-log scales, the FN criteria are mostly depicted as straight lines. This way, the generated line is not based just on historical data, but also on the authority judgments and discretion[253]. The FN criteria[254] can be expressed as:

$$PLL_{upperbound} = \sum_{N=1}^{N_u} Nf_{upperbound-N} = F_{upperbound-1}\left[\frac{1}{N_u^{b-1}} + \sum_{N=1}^{N_u-1} \frac{(N+1)^b - N^b}{N^{b-1}(N+1)^b}\right]$$

$$PLL_{lowerbound} = \sum_{N=1}^{N_u} Nf_{lowerbound-N} = F_{lowerbound-1}\left[\frac{1}{N_u^{b-1}} + \sum_{N=1}^{N_u-1} \frac{(N+1)^b - N^b}{N^{b-1}(N+1)^b}\right]$$

(1)

where $PLL_{upperbound}$ (or $PLL_{lowerbound}$) is the maximum tolerable (or negligible) number of fatalities per shipyear, $f_{upperbound-N}$ (or $f_{lowerbound-N}$) is the maximum tolerable (or negligible) frequency of occurrence of an accident involving N fatalities, $F_{upperbound-1}$ (or $F_{lowerbound-1}$) is the maximum tolerable (or negligible) frequency of accidents involving one or more fatalities, and b denotes the negative of the slope of the FN criteria on log-log scales. N_u is the upper limit of the number of fatalities that may occur in one accident, which is well defined as the maximum number of people on board of a ship.

2.2 Principles for Establishing Risk Criteria

In the literature, various principles can be utilised for establishing appropriate risk criteria in various transport modes. The adopted principles will naturally influence the criteria arrived at. Furthermore, by applying principles, it may be ensured that the risk criteria are based on a sound rationale and that they may easily be justified in a transparent manner[255].

Based on the review provided in European Maritime Safety Agency (2015a)[211], the principles for establishing risk criteria in other transport modes are briefly outlined in Table 2, which may be appropriate to the application of maritime risk criteria.

Although when resources are limited some of the principles discussed in Table 2 seem to be in contrast to each other, they are often used to compliment of each other in risk management and for setting safety goals[206, 211].

Table 2 Application of principles for risk criteria in other transport modes[a]

Transport mode	Principles					
	Justification of activity	Optimization of protection	Equity	Aversion to catastrophes	Proportionality	Continuous improvement
Air traffic management (The European organisation for the safety of air navigation)						√
Road transport (European Union member states)		√				√
Road transport (United States, Norway)		√				
Road transport of dangerous goods (The advisory committee on dangerous substances)	√	√	√	√	√	
Road transport of dangerous goods (Switzerland)		√		√	√	
Road tunnels (Austria)		√		√	√	
Rail transport (The European railway agency)			√			√
Rail transport (United Kingdom)		√	√			√

[a] Note that the names of transport mode and principles in this research are derived from European Maritime Safety Agency (2015a).

2.3 Steps for Risk Criteria Establishment

Based on the literature review, various important points need to be considered when formulating risk criteria[256]. The flowchart presented in Figure 1 schematises the key steps to develop risk criteria for the shipping industry.

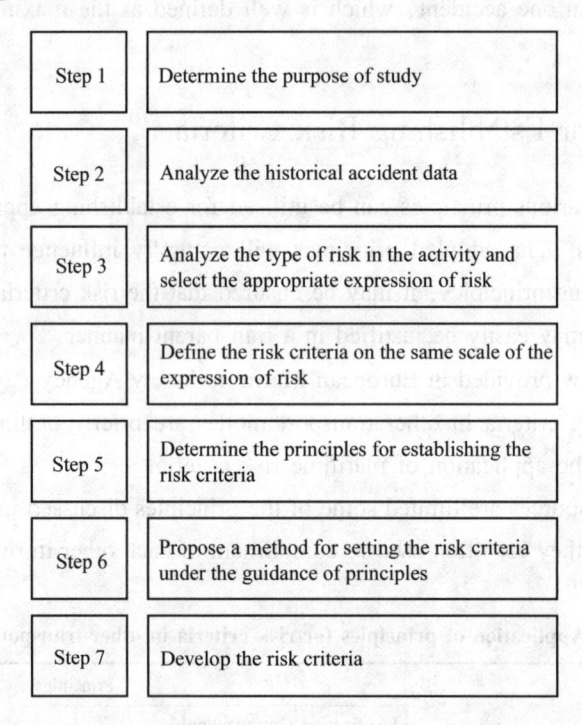

Step 1	Determine the purpose of study
Step 2	Analyze the historical accident data
Step 3	Analyze the type of risk in the activity and select the appropriate expression of risk
Step 4	Define the risk criteria on the same scale of the expression of risk
Step 5	Determine the principles for establishing the risk criteria
Step 6	Propose a method for setting the risk criteria under the guidance of principles
Step 7	Develop the risk criteria

Figure 1 Steps to develop risk criteria for the shipping industry

The seven steps in Figure 1 are described as follows. First, the purpose of study should be presented clearly, which is crucial for the next steps. Second, in order to know what kind of risks are involved, historical accidents need to be analysed. Third, based on the intention of the analysis, the appropriate expression of risk should be selected. For instance, FN diagrams are the better expression of SR than PLL in the context of IMO's SLA. Fourth, risk criteria should be defined on the same scale of the expression of risk. For example, FN criteria are needed for the evaluation of SR expressed by FN curves. Fifth, different principles for setting risk criteria of shipping industry can be found in Section 2.2. According to background demand, principles can be used alone or together. Sixth, under the guidance of selected principles, methods for setting risk criteria should be proposed. Finally, the risk criteria are established.

3 A PRACTICAL METHOD FOR EVALUATING SR

3.1 Setting New FN Criteria

In general, safety goals need to be set based on the current safety level and risk criteria. Following the steps presented in Figure 1, risk criteria will be developed. To set safety goals for people on board, new risk criteria need to be established (step 1). Based on the discussion in the introduction, FN diagrams have been selected as the expression of SR (step 2 to 3), and FN criteria need to be developed, which are on the same scale of the expression of SR (step 4). Because of the implementation of new regulations and constant renewal of fleets, the principle of continuous improvement is chosen to guide the establishment of new FN criteria which can be used in the context of the IMO's SLA (step 5).

The sixth step is to propose a method to establish the new FN criteria. This paper intends to develop the new FN criteria consistent with revised the IR criteria. This idea is based on a simple formula for PLL (Kaneko et al., 2015) as follows:

$$IR_{upperbound} N_u = PLL_{upperbound} = \sum_{N=1}^{N_u} Nf_{upperbound-N}$$
$$IR_{lowerbound} N_u = PLL_{lowerbound} = \sum_{N=1}^{N_u} Nf_{lowerbound-N} \qquad (2)$$

where $IR_{upperbound}$ (or $IR_{lowerbound}$) is the maximum tolerable (or negligible) IR. It must be pointed out that $IR_{upperbound}$ and $IR_{lowerbound}$ are different from the current IR criteria in IMO regulations since they are used to develop the new FN criteria in the context of IMO's SLA. In order to make it possible to do so, the worst IR derived from the annual data is chosen to be the $IR_{upperbound}$ according to the principle of continuous improvement. As 10^{-6} is accepted mostly as the negligible IR criteria[257], the $IR_{lowerbound}$ of all types of ships can be set to 10^{-6} for simplification. Furthermore, to take the uncertainty in the IR calculation into consideration, the worst IR is revised by multiplying by a value of 10. In order to confirm that the worst IR is not over enlarged, the $IR_{upperbound}$ of passengers should not be higher than the maximum tolerable risk for crew, which is 10^{-3} annually. That is, the $IR_{upperbound}$ of passengers should be assigned a value equal to the lower value of the revised worst IR and the maximum tolerable risk for crew. Similarly, the $IR_{upperbound}$ of crew should be assigned a value equal to the lower value of the revised worst IR and 10 times the maximum tolerable risk for crew, which equals 10^{-2} annually. In this paper, new FN criteria are also depicted as straight lines on log-log scales. Therefore, from Equations (1) and (2), Equation (3) can be derived.

$$IR_{\text{upperbound}}N_u = F_{\text{upperbound}-1}\left(\frac{1}{N_u^{b-1}} + \sum_{N=1}^{N_u-1} \frac{(N+1)^b - N^b}{N^{b-1}(N+1)^b}\right)$$

$$IR_{\text{lowerbound}}N_u = F_{\text{lowerbound}-1}\left(\frac{1}{N_u^{b-1}} + \sum_{N=1}^{N_u-1} \frac{(N+1)^b - N^b}{N^{b-1}(N+1)^b}\right)$$

(3)

According to the definition of b, the slope of the FN criteria on log-log scales equals -1 when b is assumed to be 1, which means that FN criteria represent the "accident size neutral" criteria[258]. When b is set to 1, Equation (3) simplifies to:

$$IR_{\text{upperbound}}N_u = F_{\text{upperbound}-1}\sum_{N=1}^{N_u}\frac{1}{N}$$

$$IR_{\text{lowerbound}}N_u = F_{\text{lowerbound}-1}\sum_{N=1}^{N_u}\frac{1}{N}$$

(4)

It is reasonable that the new FN criteria are chosen to have a slope of -1 because dynamic factors are proposed to express risk aversion in the process of measuring the tolerance of SR, which will be discussed in Section 3.2. When N_u of one type of ship is set, $F_{\text{upperbound}-1}$ and $F_{\text{lowerbound}-1}$ can be calculated. Finally, the new upper and lower bound FN criteria can be described as straight lines with a slope of -1 and a certain intercept on log-log scales. It should be noted that when FN curves cross the new upper bound FN criteria, the system should not be regarded as intolerable, but an indication that the tolerance of FN curves may be relatively low.

3.2 Tolerance Measurement

In order to avoid sudden discontinuities, safety goals of SR need to be set based on the current SR and should present continuous improvement. Therefore, a method to compare various FN curves is needed. Based on the new upper bound FN criteria, this paper proposes an approach to measure the tolerance of FN curves, which can be used as a tool to compare FN curves. The idea is to use the equivalent average distance between the FN curve and the new upper bound FN criteria as an indicator of risk tolerance. The equivalent average distance is defined as:

$$T' = \sum_{N=N_{\min}}^{N_{\max}} (F_{\text{upperbound}-N} - F_N) g_N' \quad \text{If } F_{\text{upperbound}-N} > F_N$$

$$T'' = \sum_{N=N_{\min}}^{N_{\max}} (F_N - F_{\text{upperbound}-N}) g_N'' \quad \text{If } F_{\text{upperbound}-N} < F_N$$

$$g_N'' = \frac{1}{g_N'}$$

$$T = \frac{1}{n}(T' - T'')$$

(5)

where T' (or T'') is the sum of distances when $F_{\text{upperbound}-N} > F_N$ (or $F_{\text{upperbound}-N} < F_N$) which means that the FN curve is below (or above) the new upper bound FN criteria, F_N is the frequency of accidents involving N or more fatalities, $F_{upperbound-N}$ is the maximum tolerable frequency of accidents involving N or more fatalities, and T denotes the equivalent average distance between the FN curve and the new upper bound FN criteria. N_{max} (or N_{min}) is the maximum (or minimum) value of N, which is obtained by the risk analysis model, such as the event tree model. n is the total number of possible values of N, which is used for averaging ($T' - T''$). g_N' (or g_N'') is proposed as a dynamic factor to express risk aversion since the actual distances $F_{upperbound-N} - F_N$ (or $F_N - F_{upperbound-N}$) cannot be added directly when N becomes larger. Risk aversion can be descried from two aspects. On one hand, the degree of risk aversion increases as N increases, and on the other hand, it also increases as $F_N - F_{upperbound-N}$ (if $F_{upperbound-N} < F_N$) increases. This idea is to express risk aversion by transforming the actual distances to the equivalent distances when N is N_{min}. It should be noted that two conditions need to be satisfied for the determination of g_N' (or g_N''). First, g_N' (or g_N'') decreases (increases) and decreases (increases) faster when N increases. That is, the degree of risk aversion increases as N increases, and the increase in velocity of the risk aversion increases with the increasing N. Second, $g_{N_{min}}'$ (or $g_{N_{min}}''$) equals 1. It means that the actual distance equals the equivalent distance when N is N_{min}. The initial change rate of g_N' (or g_N'') is set to 0 for the simplification. Furthermore, the authority needs to select an appropriate value $g_{N_{max}}'$ (or $g_{N_{max}}''$) which represents the maximum degree of risk aversion. Based on the above discussion, it is reasonable to set g_N'' to the reciprocal of g_N'. Therefore, the actual distances are all transformed into the equivalent distances when N is N_{min}, which makes it possible to be added up. If the equation of g_N' is parabola, g_N' is defined as follows:

$$(N - h)^2 = 4p(g_N' - k) \qquad (6)$$

where h and k are the coordinates of the vertex (h, k) of the parabola and p is the distance from the vertex to the focus. Equation (6) can be solved by taking in vertex $(N_{min}, 1)$ and point $(N_{max}, g_{N_{max}}')$. When g_N' is obtained, g_N'' is just the reciprocal of g_N'.

In general, the tolerances of FN curves are comparable when they are derived from the same upper bound FN criteria. For FN curves with the same N_{min}, the equivalent average distances can be directly compared, which is the indicator of risk tolerance. But for FN curves with different N_{min}, further processing is required for the comparison of the equivalent average distances. It is noted that the comparison is much easier to make when one FN curve lies wholly below another one. This paper proposes to transform all FN curves to equivalent FN curves. The equivalent FN curves are straight lines which have the same degree of tolerance with the original FN curves and are parallel to each other with the same slope as FN criteria. The idea is to make it possible to compare FN curves with different N_{min} because a spatial relationship between parallel lines is easy to identify. The equivalent FN curves are defined as:

$$\begin{aligned} T &= \frac{1}{n} \sum_{N=N_{min}}^{N_{max}} (F_{upperbound-N} - F_N') g_N' \qquad \text{If } T > 0 \\ T &= \frac{1}{n} \sum_{N=N_{min}}^{N_{max}} (F_{upperbound-N} - F_N') g_N'' \qquad \text{If } T < 0 \end{aligned} \qquad (7)$$

where F_N' denotes the equivalent frequency of accidents involving N or more fatalities. As the slope of the equivalent FN curves equals -1, the right-hand side of Equation (7) can be further simplified according to the following process:

$$\log_{10} F_{upperbound-N_{min}} = -\log_{10} N_{min} + \log_{10} F_{upperbound-1}$$
$$\log_{10} F_{upperbound-N_{max}} = -\log_{10} N_{max} + \log_{10} F_{upperbound-1}$$
$$\log_{10} \frac{F_{upperbound-N_{min}}}{F_{upperbound-N_{max}}} = \log_{10} \frac{N_{max}}{N_{min}}$$
$$F_{upperbound-N_{max}} = \frac{N_{min}}{N_{max}} F_{upperbound-N_{min}} \quad (8)$$

$$Similarly, F_{N_{max}}' = \frac{N_{min}}{N_{max}} F_{N_{min}}'$$

$$F_{upperbound-N_{max}} - F'_{N_{max}} = \frac{N_{min}}{N_{max}} F_{upperbound-N_{min}} - \frac{N_{min}}{N_{max}} F'_{N_{min}} = \frac{N_{min}}{N_{max}} (F_{upperbound-N_{min}} - F_{N_{min}}')$$

where $F_{upperbound-N_{min}}$ (or $F_{upperbound-N_{max}}$) is the maximum tolerable frequency of accidents involving N_{min} or more fatalities (or N_{max} or more fatalities), $F_{N_{min}}'$ (or $F_{N_{max}}'$) is the equivalent frequency of accidents involving N_{min} or more fatalities (or N_{max} or more fatalities). It should be noted that the above process is based on the discussion in Section 2.1 that the FN criteria are depicted as straight lines plotted on log–log scales. Equation (8) indicates that all $F_{upperbound-N} - F_N'$ can be transformed to the format of $F_{upperbound-N_{min}} - F_{N_{min}}'$. Therefore, the equivalent FN curves can be obtained.

4 CASE STUDY

The methods illustrated in Section 3 have been applied to the FSA reports of cruise ships and RoPax ships from European Maritime Safety Agency (2015b) and IMO (2008) (hereafter both of the reports called the FSA report).

4.1 New FN Criteria in the Context of the IMO's SLA

The risk levels of cruise ships and RoPax ships are dominated by collision, grounding and fire/explosion scenarios according to the FSA report. Therefore, the number of fatalities caused by the three types of accidents and the number of ship years are summarised for the period 2000 to 2012, as shown in Tables 3 and 4.

Table 3 Fatalities from the three types of cruise accidents and ship years of cruises between 2000 and 2012

Year	2000	2001	2002	2003	2004	2005	2006	2007	2008	2009	2010	2011	2012
Fatalities	3	7	4	2	3	7	6	11	12	14	10	3	4
ship years	140	157	169	180	193	201	207	215	223	232	244	253	259

Table 4 Fatalities from the three types of RoPax ship accidents and ship years of RoPax ships between 2000 and 2012

Year	2000	2001	2002	2003	2004	2005	2006	2007	2008	2009	2010	2011	2012
Fatalities	6	9	1	11	11	15	12	23	36	19	21	16	20
ship years	285	311	338	361	373	392	410	433	453	468	485	503	515

In the FSA report, 4,000 and 1,700 people are assumed on board of a cruise ship and a RoPax ship during the period 2000 to 2012, respectively. As the number of passengers is considerably larger than the number of crew, when it comes to IR, all people on board are treated as passengers for simplification. From the given fatality data and ship years data in Tables 3 and 4, the number of fatalities per ship year, PLL for cruise ships and RoPax ships can be estimated. Based on the assumed number of people on board a cruise ship and a RoPax ship, IR can be derived by dividing PLL by the number of people on board. By comparing IR for cruise ships calculated from the years 2000 to 2012, the worst IR which is the maximum value of IR can be computed as 1.51×10^{-5}, which corresponds to the IR in 2009. To take the uncertainty in IR calculation into consideration, the worst IR is revised by multiplying by a value of 10, which equals to 1.51×10^{-4}. According to the discussion in Section 3, the $IR_{upperbound}$ of passengers on board should be assigned a value equal to the lower value of revised worst IR and the maximum tolerable risk for crew. Therefore the $IR_{upperbound}$ for passengers on board of cruises is set to 1.51×10^{-4}. From Equation (4), $F_{upperbound-N_{min}}$ of cruise ships equals 6.8×10^{-2}. Similarly, when it comes to RoPax ships, $F_{upperbound-N_{min}}$ is 9.9×10^{-2}. As 10^{-6} is set as the $IR_{lowerbound}$ of all types of ships for simplification, according to Equation (4), $F_{lowerbound-N_{min}}$ of cruise ships and RoPax ships are 4.5×10^{-4} and 2.1×10^{-4}, respectively. The new FN criteria of cruise ships and RoPax ships are shown in Figures 2 and 3, and are compared with the original FN criteria. According to the event tree model in the FSA report, the exact frequencies of N fatalities per accident category for cruise ships and RoPax ships can be found in Tables 5 and 6. In order to plot FN curves, the cumulative frequency of N or more fatalities needs to be derived by adding all the exact frequencies of N or more fatalities. Based on the data in Tables 5 and 6, FN curves of cruise ships and RoPax ships are also plotted in Figures 2 and 3, respectively.

As can be seen in Figure 2, the new lower and upper bound FN criteria are all below the original ones for cruise ships. However, in Figure 3, the new lower and upper bound FN criteria for RoPax ships are below and above the original ones, respectively. The new upper bound FN criteria for cruise ships are relatively low because cruise ships remain at low levels of IR, which is the input for criteria development according to the principle of continuous improvement. FN curves of cruises and RoPax ships cross the corresponding new upper bound FN criteria, which do not mean that current SR are intolerable. It means that the tolerance degree of cruises and RoPax ships could be relatively low.

Table 5 Frequency of N fatalities per accident category for cruise ships

N	Collision	Grounding	Fire/explosion	Total
2			3.61×10^{-4}	3.61×10^{-4}
5			2.39×10^{-4}	2.39×10^{-4}
20			7.78×10^{-5}	7.78×10^{-5}
100			8.75×10^{-5}	8.75×10^{-5}
200	7.99×10^{-5}	6.09×10^{-4}		6.89×10^{-4}
300			1.94×10^{-5}	1.94×10^{-5}
3,200	1.17×10^{-5}	4.61×10^{-5}		5.78×10^{-5}

Table 6 Frequency of N fatalities per accident category for RoPax ships

N	Collision	Grounding	Fire/explosion	Total
12			9.06×10^{-5}	9.06×10^{-5}
85	1.68×10^{-4}	9.51×10^{-4}		1.12×10^{-3}
136			1.74×10^{-4}	1.74×10^{-4}
1,275			9.06×10^{-5}	9.06×10^{-5}
1,360	2.46×10^{-5}	2.17×10^{-4}		2.42×10^{-4}

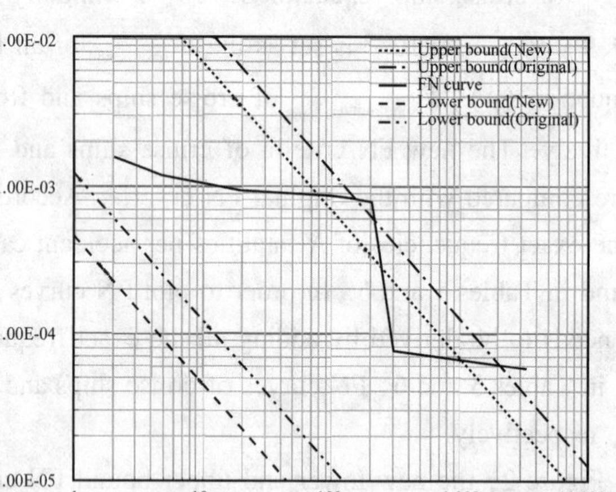

Figure 2 The comparison between original and new FN criteria of cruise ships

4.2 Risk Tolerance Comparison

In order to test the method described in Section 3.2, FN curves of cruise ships and RoPax ships are used as examples, and the tolerance degrees are measured and compared. In order to make it possible to do so, new upper bound FN criteria of RoPax ships is chosen as the reference

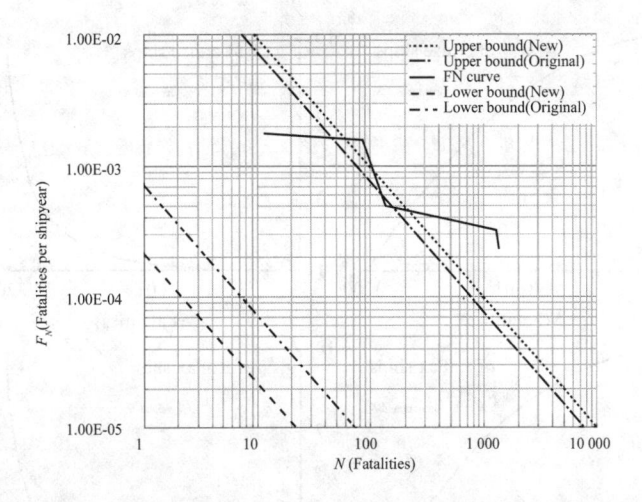

Figure 3 The comparison between original and new FN criteria of RoPax ships

level. As can be seen from Figure 5, the two FN curves have different N_{min} and cross each other, which were previously incomparable to each other. The data of the FN curves and the corresponding values of FN criteria are shown in Tables 7 and 8.

Table 7 The data of the FN curve of cruises and the corresponding value of FN criteria

N	2	5	20	100	200	300	3,200
F_N	1.53×10^{-3}	1.17×10^{-3}	9.31×10^{-4}	8.53×10^{-4}	7.66×10^{-4}	7.72×10^{-5}	5.78×10^{-5}
$F_{upperbound-N}$	4.96×10^{-2}	1.98×10^{-2}	4.96×10^{-3}	9.91×10^{-4}	4.96×10^{-4}	3.31×10^{-4}	3.10×10^{-5}

Table 8 The data of the FN curve of RoPax ships and the corresponding value of FN criteria

N	12	85	136	1,275	1,360
F_N	1.72×10^{-3}	1.63×10^{-3}	5.06×10^{-4}	3.32×10^{-4}	2.42×10^{-4}
$F_{upperbound-N}$	8.33×10^{-3}	1.17×10^{-3}	7.29×10^{-4}	7.78×10^{-5}	7.30×10^{-5}

For simplification, $g_{N_{max}}'$ is set to 0.1. From Equation (6), based on the data in Tables 7 and 8, g_N' and g_N'' can be obtained and are represented in Figure 4.

According to Equations (5), (7) and (8), equivalent FN curves of cruises and RoPax ships can be obtained and are plotted in Figure 5.

As can be seen in Figure 5, the equivalent FN curve of RoPax ships lies wholly above the equivalent FN curve of cruise ships when the new upper bound FN criteria of RoPax ships is chosen as the reference level. It can be concluded that the tolerance degree for cruise ships is higher than RoPax ships. It can be seen from Figure 5 that the FN curve of RoPax ships lies mostly above that for cruise ships, which means the SR of RoPax ships is relatively higher. This is consistent with the above conclusion.

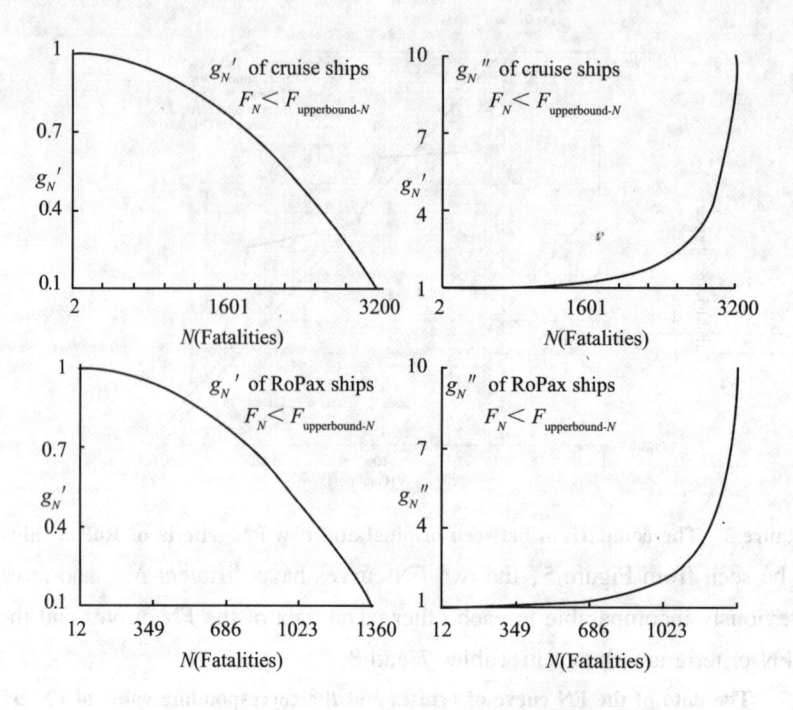

Figure 4 g_N' and g_N'' of cruise ships and RoPax ships

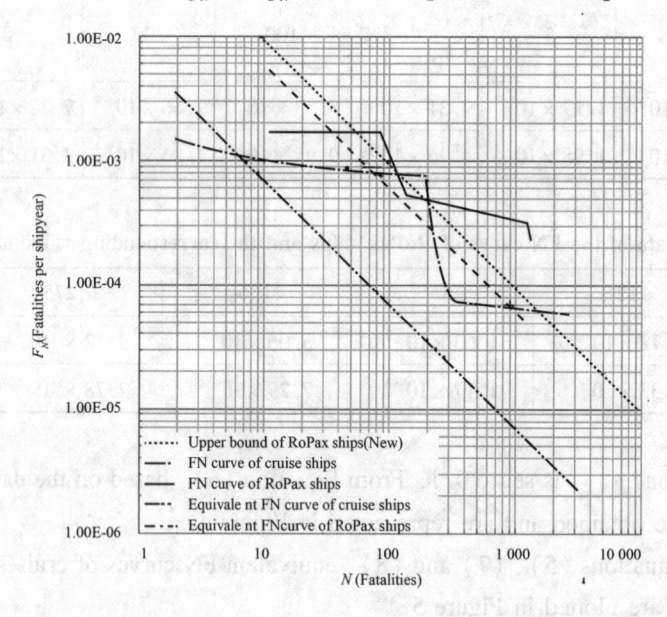

Figure 5 Equivalent FN curves of cruise ships and RoPax ships

5 CONCLUSIONS

This paper has focused on the problem of evaluating SR in the context of the IMO's SLA. Two main difficulties are mentioned. One is the absence of FN criteria which can be used for setting safety goals for people on board, the other is the inability to measure the tolerance of FN curves. To overcome the first difficulty, this paper summarises the steps of developing risk criteria for the shipping industry, and proposes an approach for establishing the FN criteria in the context of the IMO's SLA. In addition, by defining dynamic factors to express risk aversion, a simple method to measure the tolerance of FN curves is proposed for the second difficulty. The proposed approaches seem adequate to remove the inconsistency between IR criteria and SR criteria, and can make it possible to measure and compare the tolerance of crossed FN curves.

The proposed method in this study is essentially an application of risk analysis and risk management theory to maritime safety and it may provide a guide for the IMO to continuously improve maritime safety. However, it is not limited to use in the IMO rule-making process. Considering limited available resources and budgets, the proposed method is also beneficial for government agencies and shipping companies in prioritising safety strategies. Based on the tolerance variation of societal risk before and after the implementation of various safety strategies, efficient strategies can be selected. Lastly, it should be noted that some simplifications are made in the paper. These issues are worth further investigation both from the theoretical and practical points of view.

Uncertainty Analysis Method Based on Fuzzy Random Variables and Time Window Selection*

Abstract: The uncertainty analysis has been conceived as a necessary step in the engineering research in various fields. The purpose of this article is to introduce the uncertainty analysis technique into the process of statistical modelling. Based on the theory of fuzzy random variables, aleatory and epistemic uncertainties in the statistical modelling process can be modeled by fuzzy random variables, which are interpreted as random variables with fuzzy statistical properties. An important aspect of modelling uncertainties lies in the appropriate selection of time window, which is used for the inclusion of data. In order to avoid the arbitrary choice of time window, a simple method for time window selection is proposed by analyzing the uncertainty and the stability of statistic data. Finally, a case study is carried out on the accident statistics. The results show that the proposed methods are effective and can provide more information for decision-making.

1 Introduction

The uncertainty analysis investigates the uncertainty of variables that are used in decision-making problems. In other words, the uncertainty analysis can investigate the robustness of an engineering research when the research includes some form of statistical modelling through the quantification of uncertainties in the relevant variables. In general, uncertainty is considered of two different types: aleatory and epistemic uncertainties. The aleatory uncertainty arises from randomness due to inherent variability, and the epistemic uncertainty refers to imprecision due to lack of knowledge or information[259].

There are several methods that can be used to model uncertainties. When there is sufficient information for statistical analysis, probability distributions are often assigned to model aleatory uncertainties[260]. In terms of modelling epistemic uncertainties, a number of representation frameworks have been proposed. These include the fuzzy set theory, the possibility theory, the interval analysis and the evidence theory[261]. In addition, several approaches have been proposed to model aleatory and epistemic uncertainties simultaneously, such as the theory of fuzzy random variables based approach[262], the possibilistic-Monte Carlo approach[263], the possibilistic-scenario

---

* 本文发表在《IOP Conference Series: Materials Science and Engineering》第382卷,作者孙墨林、郑中义。

based approach[264] and the evidence theory based hybrid approach[265]. Among them, the theory of fuzzy random variables based approach has received growing attention because of its representation power and its relative mathematical simplicity. Since aleatory and epistemic uncertainties are very common in the process of statistical modelling, the theory of fuzzy random variables is selected to model uncertainties in this article.

An important aspect of modelling uncertainty lies in the appropriate selection of time window, which is used for the inclusion of data. Traditional empirical approach can lead to either too precautionary or non-conservative estimates of the magnitude of uncertainties based on the arbitrary choice of the length of time window[266]. Although the time window is an important factor for uncertainties modelling, it has received little empirical study. To reasonably characterize the uncertainty in the engineering research, it is considered necessary to propose a method to select the optimal time window used for the inclusion of data.

2 Uncertainties modelling

The theory of fuzzy random variables was first proposed by Kwakernaak in 1978 [267] and can be used to address aleatory and epistemic uncertainties simultaneously. Fuzzy random variables can thus be interpreted as random variables with fuzzy statistical properties, leading to multiple uncertainties. In other words, when using probability distributions to model aleatory uncertainties, parameters of the selected probability distributions are represented by fuzzy numbers instead of crisp numbers.

The selection of probability distributions is an important aspect of modelling aleatory uncertainties. In the process of statistical modelling, the discrete data obtained from counting the numbers of occurrences of events during specified periods of time are often encountered. Since Poisson distribution is a suitable model for modelling the above type of data[268], it is selected as the probability distribution for modelling aleatory uncertainties in this study. According to the Poisson distribution properties, the confidence interval of the number of times an event occurs can be calculated by[268]:

$$\lambda_U = \frac{\chi^2_{1-\omega/2}(2n+2)}{2}$$
$$\lambda_L = \frac{\chi^2_{\omega/2}(2n)}{2} \qquad (1)$$

where λ_U and λ_L are the upper and lower boundaries for the confidence interval of the mean value of a Poisson distribution; n is the number of occurrences of events during a specified time window; ω is the significance level of the statistics; $\chi^2_{1-\omega/2}(2n+2)$ is the $(1-\omega/2)$ th quantile of the chi-squared distribution with $(2n+2)$ degrees of freedom; $\chi^2_{\omega/2}(2n)$ is the $(\omega/2)$ th quantile of the chi-squared distribution with $(2n)$ degrees of freedom; $\chi^2_{1-\omega/2}(2n+2)$ and $\chi^2_{\omega/2}(2n)$ can be found in the table of chi-squared distribution.

For parameters of the Poisson distribution with epistemic uncertainties, fuzzy numbers are used to model the epistemic uncertainty. According to the interpretation of the uncertainty in these parameters, the range of values of parameters can be estimated roughly by expert judgments. In order to introduce epistemic uncertainties as small as possible, we use directly value ranges rather than select fuzzy distributions to represent epistemic uncertainties. When there are more interpretations of parameters with epistemic uncertainties, the usage of fuzzy distributions is possible.

3　Method for time window selection

Time window can be taken as the time interval for which historical data are collected. It starts from the research date and goes backwards[269]. However, traditional empirical approach can lead to either too precautionary or non-conservative estimates of the magnitude of uncertainties based on the arbitrary choice of the length of time window. To reduce the subjectivity, it is considered necessary to propose a simple method for time window selection. It should be noted that the longer the time window is, the more informative data for statistical analysis, and the more accurate uncertainty modelling is. It means that time window used for the inclusion of data should be as long as possible. There are also indications that more recent statistics represent a more conclusive database than old statistics reflecting recent technical developments or new requirements. To coordinate the contradiction described above, the uncertainty degree and the stability degree of statistic data are used as the two indexes to determine the optimal length of the time window, denoted by S and V. We, thus, have[270]:

$$S = \lambda_U - \lambda_L \qquad (2)$$

$$V = \left[\frac{1}{y} \sum_{i=1}^{y} (n_i - \bar{n})^2 \right]^{1/2} \qquad (3)$$

Where S can be taken as the spread between the uncertainty boundaries $[\lambda_L, \lambda_U]$ from the Poisson distribution under a certain level of confidence; V is defined as the standard deviation; n_i is the i th observed value, $\bar{n}$ is the mean value of the observed values and y is the number of observed values; consistent with the qualitative analysis of the time window selection described above, both S and V should be as low as possible. When S and V may not reach the minimum at the same time, a comprehensive index T which is set as the product of S and V is proposed. Therefore, the length of the time window could be optimal when we get minimum T.

4　Case study

Approaches for uncertainties modelling and time window selection illustrated in Section 2 and 3 have been applied to the accident statistics in the engineering report[211]. Since our goal here is to apply the proposed methods and to verify their effectiveness, the particular selection of the applied engineering field can be changed if needed. In other words, the proposed methods focus on the type of data which is discrete and obtained from counting the numbers of occurrences of events during specified periods of time. According to the engineering report, the accident statistic data for the period 2000 to 2010 are listed in Table 1.

Table 1　The accident statistic data between 2000 and 2010

Year	2000	2001	2002	2003	2004	2005	2006	2007	2008	2009	2010
The number of accidents	10	19	21	30	25	36	25	42	47	43	40

4.1　The process of uncertainties modelling

When the values in table 1 are put into equation (1), the confidence interval of the number of accidents for each year 2000 to 2010 can be calculated under a certain level of confidence. Taking the data in 2010 as an example, the number of accidents is 40 and the corresponding confidence interval can be calculated as [30, 52] for the confidence value 0.9. According to the research[271], a certain percentage of accidents is missing from the records and in order to complete the uncertainty modelling of high quality, it was necessary to complement the available data with additional data. We assume the rate of under-reporting is no more than 50% based on the priori knowledge[272]. Thus the number of accidents in 2010 can be estimated as [40, 60]. When the number of accidents is 60, the confidence interval can be calculated as [48, 74] for the same confidence value. Finally, the confidence interval of the number of accidents is estimated as [30, 74] considering aleatory and epistemic uncertainties simultaneously. The data in other years can repeat the above computation process to obtain the corresponding confidence interval. The accident statistic data and the corresponding confidence interval are represented by short dashes and line segments in Figure 1. For representing the change of the confidence interval more vividly, upper and lower boundaries of the confidence interval are connected with the line, respectively.

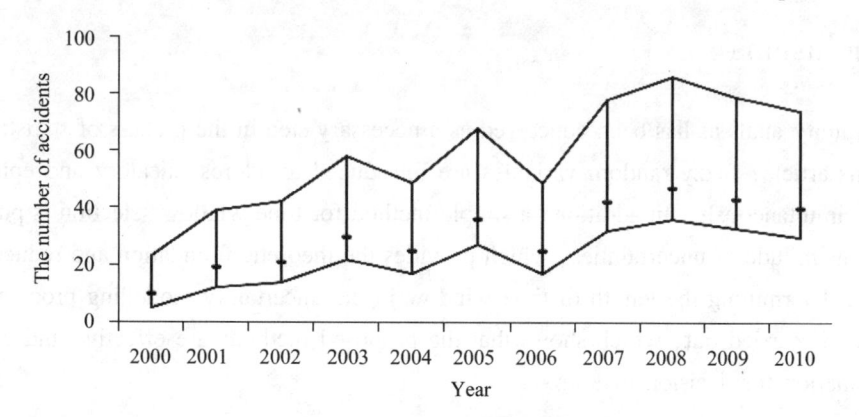

Figure 1　The accident statistic data and the corresponding confidence interval

4.2　Time window selection

In the process of selecting the length of the time window, the sliding window method is used to calculate S and V indexes. Nine time windows will be estimated, from the recent three years

(2008 to 2010), to the recent eleven years (2000 to 2010). The S index can be calculated according to the uncertainty model process in Section 4.1 and equation (2). When the values in Table 1 are put into equation (3), the V index can also be obtained. Table 2 shows the calculation results of S and V indexes.

Table 2 The calculation results of S and V indexes

Time window	3	4	5	6	7	8	9	10	11
S	36	34	30	29	27	26	24	23	22
V	3.5	2.9	8.4	7.7	8.7	8.5	9.4	10.1	11.8

As can be seen in Table 2, S and V may not reach the minimum at the same time. The comprehensive index T, which is the product of S and V, reaches the minimum when the time window is 4. Accident data in recent four years will be used to estimate the magnitude of uncertainties in the process of statistical modelling. Thus the confidence interval of the average number of accidents annually can be calculated as [38, 72] for the confidence value 0.9. In order to verify the effectiveness of the proposed methods, the confidence interval calculated above is compared with another two statistical results, which are estimated by the data from the recent one year and the recent eleven years. According to Section 4.1, the confidence interval of the number of accidents in 2010 is estimated as [30, 74]. It is obvious that the confidence interval calculated by the proposed methods is smaller because there are more informative data for statistical analysis and the uncertainty modelling is more accurate. When it comes to the data from recent eleven years, the confidence interval is calculated as [28, 50]. The statistical result does not take into account that the number of accidents presents rising trend on the whole, which can be seen in Figure 1.

5 Conclusions

Uncertainty analysis has been conceived as a necessary step in the process of statistical modelling. In this article, fuzzy random variables are introduced to address aleatory and epistemic uncertainties simultaneously. In addition, a simple method for time window selection is put up to estimate the magnitude of uncertainties, which provides the theoretic foundation and reduces the subjectivity for determining the length of time window in the uncertainty modelling process. Finally, a case study is carried out, which shows that the proposed methods are effective and can provide more information for decision-making.

Vessel Traffic Risk Assessment Based on Uncertainty Analysis in the Risk Matrix*

Abstract: Uncertainty analysis is considered to be a necessary step in the process of vessel traffic risk assessment. The purpose of this study is to propose the uncertainty analysis algorithm which can be used to investigate the reliability of the risk assessment result. Probability and possibility distributions are used to quantify the two types of uncertainty identified in the risk assessment process. In addition, the algorithm for appropriate time window selection is chosen by considering the uncertainty of vessel traffic accident occurrence and the variation trend of the vessel traffic risk caused by maritime rules becoming operative. Vessel traffic accident data from the United Kingdom's marine accident investigation branch are used for the case study. Based on a comparison with the common method of estimating the vessel traffic risk and the algorithm for uncertainty quantification without considering the time window selection, the availability of the proposed algorithms is verified, which can provide guidance for vessel traffic risk management.

Keywords: Vessel traffic; Risk assessment; Risk matrix; Time window selection; Uncertainty analysis

1 Introduction

Vessel traffic risk management aims to enhance maritime safety, which includes the protection of life, health, the marine environment and property[195]. An important aspect of risk management lies in vessel traffic risk assessment, which can guide the authority's work for improving safety. The risk matrix is widely used for vessel traffic risk assessments[273]. The risk matrix displays the frequency (or probability) of events and their consequence (or severity) using a matrix[274].

The risk matrix provides a mechanism for assigning risk and making risk acceptance decisions using a risk categorization approach. Each cell in the risk matrix corresponds to a specific combination of the frequency and consequence, which indicates a level of risk. In the risk matrix, both the frequency and consequence are measured by a category scale: frequency, reasonable probability, remoteness and extremely remoteness for the frequency measurement; minor, significant, se-

---

* 本文发表在《Algorithms》2018 年第 11 卷,作者孙墨林、郑中义。

vere and catastrophic for the consequence measurement. In addition, each cell in the matrix can be assigned an indication of risk acceptability for decision-making on risk[225, 275].

During the process of vessel traffic risk assessment, there are several methods that can be used to estimate the vessel traffic accident frequency and consequence[208, 276]. The fundamental way to calculate the vessel traffic accident frequency is to divide the number of accidents recorded in a given period by the corresponding exposure for that period[273]. In general, the vessel traffic accident consequence can be measured in different ways, such as economic, environmental and safety consequences[277]. For the purposes of this study, only safety consequences are considered. However, concerns have been raised about the reliability of vessel traffic risk assessment results[225, 278, 279]. In order to investigate the vessel traffic risk assessment reliability, uncertainties in the risk assessmentprocess should be analyzed. In practice, several qualitative frameworks [209, 280] and quantitative methods[281] have been proposed to assess uncertainty in the field of maritime risk analysis.

There are typically two types of uncertainty: randomness resulting from inherent variability and cognitive imprecision resulting from expert opinions. The former type of uncertainty is often referred to as aleatory uncertainty whereas the latter is often referred to as epistemic uncertainty[212]. As vessel traffic accidents are random events, the number of accidents can be considered as a random number generated from a random event[282]. Thus, the vessel traffic accident frequency calculated by the number of accidents is often taken as a variable with aleatory uncertainty due to inherent variability[214]. With regards to the vessel traffic accident consequence, it can be taken as the result of many factors affecting one another through an ambiguous development process. In the field of maritime risk analysis, the number of fatalities is generally far less than the number of vessel traffic accidents. The accident consequence is often considered as a variable with epistemic uncertainty, as the available information is usually scarce and expert judgements are often incorporated in the process of analyzing the accident consequence[211].

Different mathematical methods are required in order to quantify different types of uncertainty. Aleatory uncertainty is often quantified by probability distributions[283]. For the quantification of epistemic uncertainty, a number of methods can be used, such as possibility theory and evidence theory[284]. In this study, possibility theory is selected to quantify epistemic uncertainty due to its mathematical simplicity[285]. It should be noted that the time window used for the inclusion of data has a major effect on the quantification of uncertainty[286]. Without considering the time window selection, uncertainties will be measured too conservatively or too optimistically. Therefore, it is considered necessary to propose an algorithm for time window selection.

When selecting the time window, the aleatory uncertainty of vessel traffic accident occurrences should be taken into account. In addition, it should be noted that the vessel traffic accident frequency changes over time due to maritime rules becoming operative on the vessel traffic being analyzed[287]. In other words, the time series of the accident frequency may reveal certain trends. Due to uncertainties and variation trends of the vessel traffic accident frequency, the time window selection comes down to constructing and splitting the uncertain time series. In this study, the aleatory uncertainty of the vessel traffic accident frequency is quantified by the Poisson distribution[211], so that the confidence intervals of the accident frequency can be obtained each year. When the confidence intervals are arranged in chronological order, the uncertain time series of the accident frequency is built up. Based on the orderliness of time series, the sliding window method[288] is used to split the uncertain time series, which aggregates the relatively concentrative confidence intervals. The latest segmentation is selected as the statistical time window.

The rest of the paper is organized as follows. Section 2 describes the algorithm for the quantification of the two types of uncertainty identified in the risk assessment process. In Section 3, the time window selection algorithm is described. The case study is carried out and comparisons are made to verify the superiority of the proposed algorithms in Section 4. Conclusions are provided in Section 5.

2 Algorithm for Uncertainty Analysis

2.1 The Aleatory Uncertainty Quantification

During the process of quantifying aleatory uncertainties, it is important to choose the suitable probability distribution. The European Maritime Safety Agency assumes that the occurrence of vessel traffic accidents obeys the Poisson distribution according to expert experience, historical statistical data and theoretical analysis[211]. According to the a priori knowledge of the European Maritime Safety Agency, the Poisson distribution is chosen to quantify the aleatory uncertainty of vessel traffic accidents in this study. With a given confidence level, the confidence interval of Poisson-distributed data can be calculated by[289]:

$$\lambda_U = \frac{\chi^2_{1-\alpha/2}(2n+2)}{2}$$
$$\lambda_L = \frac{\chi^2_{\alpha/2}(2n)}{2}$$
(1)

where λ_U and λ_L are defined as the upper and lower limits of the confidence interval of n, which is the number of times an event occurs in a certain time window. α denotes the significance level and $(1-\alpha)$ denotes the confidence level. $\chi^2_{1-\alpha/2}(2n+2)$ is the $(1-\alpha/2)$ th quantile of the chi-squared distribution with $(2n+2)$ degrees of freedom; $\chi^2_{\alpha/2}(2n)$ is the $(\alpha/2)$ th quantile of the chi-squared distribution with $(2n)$ degrees of freedom.

It should be noted that there is epistemic uncertainty when selecting the probability distribution due to referring to the a priori knowledge of the European Maritime Safety Agency. In other words, other probability distributions can also be selected to quantify aleatory uncertainty, such as the Normal distribution, the Log-normal distribution and the Beta distribution. However, the information available in this study is insufficient to model the Normal distribution, the Log-normal distribution and the Beta distribution. In order to make the epistemic uncertainty as small as possible, the Poisson distribution is selected in this study. When there is more information, it is possible to select other probability distributions to quantify the aleatory uncertainty of vessel traffic accidents. For the sake of simplicity, the possible effects of the epistemic uncertainty of selecting the Poisson distribution are not considered in this study, which can be studied further in the future.

2.2 The Epistemic Uncertainty Quantification

As discussed in the introduction section, the possibility theory is selected to quantify the level of epistemic uncertainty. Specifically, λ-cuts of the possibility distribution are calculated as the result of the epistemic uncertainty quantification, which is similar to the confidence interval $[\lambda_L, \lambda_U]$ at the confidence level $(1-\alpha)$ in Section 2.1[97]. According to the possibility theory, the domain of discourse of the variable X is set as U_x and R is set as the fuzzy set contained in U_x, and it is possible to obtain the λ-cut of X from the possibility distribution $\pi(x)$ of X, by[291]:

$$R_\lambda = \{x \mid \pi(x) \geq \lambda, \ x \in R\} \tag{2}$$

where R_λ is defined as the λ-cut of X, λ is taken as the threshold and $\lambda \in [0,1]$.

In addition, the possibility measure $\Pi(R)$ and the necessary measure $N(R)$ can be used to estimate the confidence level of R, denoted by $P\{x \in R\}$. We thus have:

$$\Pi(R) = \max_{x \in R}\{"\pi(x)\}$$
$$N(R) = 1 - \Pi(\bar{R}) \tag{3}$$
$$N(R) \leq P\{x \in R\} \leq \Pi(R)$$

When R is replaced by R_λ, we thus have:

$$\Pi(R_\lambda) = 1$$
$$N(R_\lambda) = 1 - \lambda \tag{4}$$
$$N(R_\lambda) \leq P\{x \in R_\lambda\} \leq \Pi(R_\lambda)$$

By simplifying the Equation (4), we have:

$$P\{x \in R_\lambda\} \geq 1 - \lambda \tag{5}$$

According to Equation (5), R_λ can be regarded as the confidence interval at the confidence level $(1-\lambda)$.

3 Algorithm for Time Window Selection

The vessel traffic accident frequency is chosen as the index in the process of time window selection because accident consequences are generated through a fuzzy development process after accidents occur and are considered as variables with epistemic uncertainty. Based on Equation (1), the limits of the confidence interval for the number of accidents can be calculated. Then the confidence interval for the vessel traffic accident frequency can be measured in the number of accidents per ship year. When the confidence intervals for the accident frequency each year are arranged in chronological order, the uncertain time series is formed[99].

According to the orderliness of time series, the closer the time interval is to the current time, the nearer the vessel traffic accident frequency measured over the time interval approximates to the current accident frequency. In order to reflect the variation trend of the vessel traffic accident frequency due to maritime rules becoming operative on the vessel traffic being analyzed, it is considered necessary to split the uncertain time series of the vessel traffic accident frequency calculated above.

The sliding window approach is applied in the process of splitting the uncertain time series. It regards the first year as the first segmentation and continues to expand until the vessel traffic accident frequency in certain years exceeds the confidence interval of the former segmentation. Then the next segmentation starts with this year. The aforementioned splitting procedure is repeated until the last year in the uncertain time series. It should be noted that whether the accident frequency in certain years exceeds the confidence interval of the former segmentation is used as the criterion for splitting the uncertain time series. The criterion is reasonable because it can aggregate relatively concentrative confidence intervals at a certain level of confidence. When the accident frequency exceeds the confidence interval of the former segmentation, it means that the accident frequency still changes under the influence of outside factors after overcoming the randomness of the accident data. In other words, different segmentations show different levels of the vessel traffic accident frequency. Changes in levels of the vessel traffic accident frequency reflect the effects of technical or operational developments, new requirements, or specific arrangements on the vessel traffic being analyzed. The above developments are often carried out along with maritime rules becoming operative. To represent the splitting process of the uncertain time series more clearly, the flowchart is shown in Figure 1.

After the preliminary segmentation, there is one more step to obtain the final segmentation result. When one segmentation only contains one year and there is no remarkable change between its adjacent segmentations, it means that the large random fluctuation of data from the year leads to the segmentation. In order to avoid excessive segmentation, the segmentation and its adjacent segmentations should be merged. It should be noted that the condition for the segmentation, as can be seen in Figure 1, is used to judge if there is a remarkable change. Finally, the latest segmentation is considered to be the statistical time window.

4 Results

Using the vessel traffic accident data from the United Kingdom's marine accident investigation branch[293], the case study is carried out on the algorithms for uncertainty quantification and time window selection that were illustrated in Sections 2 and 3. The vessel traffic accident data include the number of United Kingdom's vessels, vessel traffic accidents and fatalities caused by the accidents for each year 2000 to 2016, which are shown in Table 1.

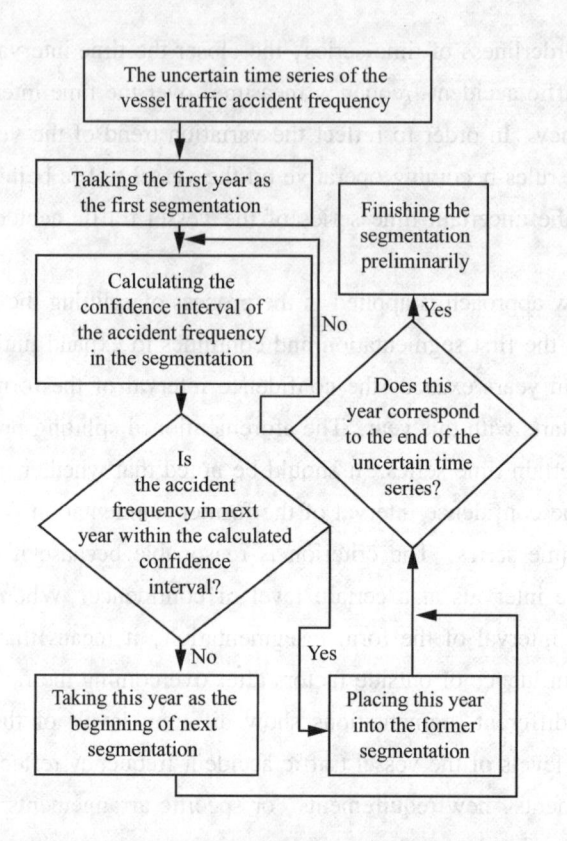

Figure 1   Flowchart for splitting uncertain time series

Table 1   Vessel traffic accident data

Year	2000	2001	2002	2003	2004	2005	2006	2007	2008
Number of vessels	1050	1047	1210	1343	1406	1443	1480	1518	1578
Number of vessel traffic accidents	139	139	129	146	144	197	130	116	131
Number of fatalities	48	47	48	50	49	38	38	46	46
Year	2009	2010	2011	2012	2013	2014	2015	2016	
Number of vessels	1564	1520	1521	1450	1392	1361	1385	1365	
Number of vessel traffic accidents	128	141	115	133	122	120	118	107	
Number of fatalities	38	36	35	26	19	21	23	21	

The vessel traffic accident frequency can be measured in the number of accidents per ship year. A ship year is defined as one ship sailing for one year, which can be understood as the corresponding exposure of the vessel traffic being analyzed. Then the vessel traffic accident frequency for each year between 2000 and 2016 can be calculated by dividing the number of vessel traffic accidents by the number of vessels listed in Table 1. According to Equation (1), the confidence intervals of the vessel traffic accident frequency for each year between 2000 and 2016 can be estimated using a given confidence level. Different confidence values can be set for different research purposes. In this study, the confidence level is set as 0.95 based on the a priori knowledge of the European Maritime Safety Agency[17]. When the confidence intervals are arranged in chronological order, an uncertain time series is formed. The uncertain time series is represented in Figure 2, in which the accident frequency for each year 2000 to 2016 are represented by diamond icons and are connected by a line, the limits of the confidence interval are shown and connected by dotted lines.

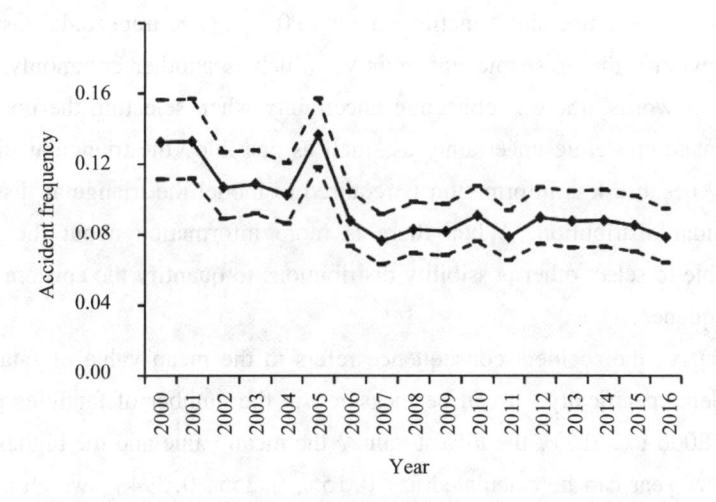

Figure 2 Uncertain time series of the vessel traffic accident frequency

According to Section 3, the uncertain time series in Figure 2 is split by the sliding window approach. The first year (2000) in the uncertain time series is regarded as the first segmentation. As can be seen in Figure 2, the vessel traffic accident frequency and the corresponding confidence interval in the year 2000 are 0.132 and [0.111, 0.156]. Since the vessel traffic accident frequency in the year 2001 is 0.133 and it does not exceed the confidence interval [0.111, 0.156], the year 2001 should be merged into the first segmentation. Then the confidence interval is updated to [0.117, 0.149] based on Equation (1). The vessel traffic accident frequency in the year 2002 is 0.107 and it exceeds the confidence interval [0.117, 0.149]. As a result, the second segmentation starts with the year 2002. The above-mentioned splitting procedure is repeated until the year 2016. Then four segmentations are obtained, which are the years 2000 to 2001, 2002 to 2004, 2005, and 2006 to 2016. The year 2005 fits the required situation that a single segmentation only contains one year. The mean value of the vessel traffic accident frequency during the years 2006 to 2016 can be calculated as 0.084 and it exceeds the confidence interval of the segmentation from the year 2002 to 2004, which is [0.096, 0.116]. This indicates that there is remarkable change between the segmentation from the year 2002 to 2004 and the segmentation from the year 2006 to 2016. As discussed in Section 3, the remarkable change between segmentations reflects the effects of technical or operational developments, new requirements, or specific arrangements on the vessel traffic being analyzed. Thus, the above-mentioned segmentations should not be merged. Finally, four segmentations are determined, which are the years 2000 to 2001, 2002 to 2004, 2005, and 2006 to 2016. The most recent segmentation, 2006 to 2016, is treated as the statistical time window.

Based on the selected time window (2006 to 2016), the aleatory uncertainty of the vessel traffic accident frequency can be quantified as [0.080, 0.089] for the confidence value 0.95. For accident consequences, triangular distributions are used for the epistemic uncertainty quantification. The triangular distribution has three parameters (i,j,k), where j denotes the most likely value when the membership function is 1; i and k respectively denote the lowest and the highest possible values when the membership function equals to $0^{[294]}$. The trapezoidal distribution can also be selected to quantify the epistemic uncertainty, which is another commonly used possibility distribution. In other words, there is epistemic uncertainty when selecting the possibility distribution. In order to make epistemic uncertainty as small as possible, the triangular distribution is selected in this study because less information is required to model the triangular distribution than to model the trapezoidal distribution. When there is more information about the accident consequence, it is possible to select other possibility distributions to quantify the epistemic uncertainty of the accident consequence.

In the risk matrix, the accident consequence refers to the mean value of fatalities from each vessel traffic accident specifically. It can be measured in the number of fatalities per accident. In the time window (2006 to 2016), the lowest value, the mean value and the highest value of fatalities per accident per year can be calculated as [0.155, 0.255, 0.394], which are considered as the three parameters of the triangular distribution. According to Equation (5), the epistemic uncertainty of accident consequence can be quantified as [0.160, 0.387] for the confidence value 0.95. Since the aleatory uncertainty of the vessel traffic frequency and the epistemic uncertainty of the accident consequence are quantified for the same confidence value, they can be represented in one risk matrix, which is shown by the rectangle of solid lines in Figure 3.

In order to verify the availability of the proposed algorithms, two comparisons have been made. The first comparison is between the common method of estimating the vessel traffic risk and the algorithm proposed to quantify uncertainties. The common method [2,5] measures the vessel traffic accident frequency and the accident consequence by averaging the historical accident data in Table 1. Then the accident frequency and consequence are calculated as 0.095 and 0.279, respectively, which are represented by a cross symbol in Figure 3. Using the algorithm proposed to quantify uncertainties, the confidence interval of the vessel traffic accident frequency and consequence can be estimated as [0.092, 0.099] and [0.165, 0.389], which make the dashed rectangle seen in Figure 3. It should be noted that the seventeen most recent years (2000 to 2016) are taken as the time window in the first comparison. As can be seen in Figure 3, the cross symbol is in the dashed rectangle area. It means that the algorithm proposed to quantify uncertainties is effective and can provide more information for vessel traffic risk management.

The second comparison is carried out to verify the availability of the proposed algorithm for time window selection. It is obvious in Figure 3 that the vessel traffic risk considering the time window selection is less than the vessel traffic risk calculated by all the historical accident data in the risk matrix. The reason for this is that the algorithm for time window selection can reflect the

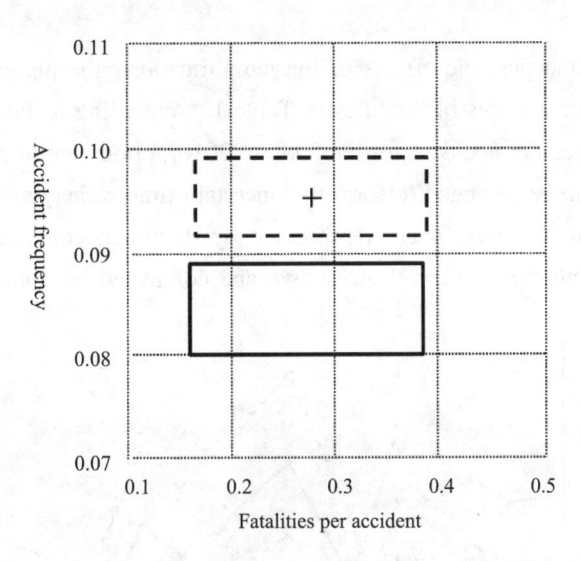

Figure 3 The risk matrix of the vessel traffic risk

effects of technical or operational developments, new requirements, or specific arrangements on the vessel traffic being analyzed. According to Table 1 and Figure 2, the vessel traffic risk declines overall from the year 2000 until 2016. Thus, the vessel traffic risk may be overestimated without considering the time window selection.

5 Discussion

As the time window used for the inclusion of data has a major effect on the uncertainty quantification of the vessel traffic risk, the algorithm for time window selection is proposed, which has several assumptions or simplifications. Thus, the possible effects of selecting the vessel traffic accident frequency as the index, selecting one year of data as a basis and the underreporting of vessel traffic accidents on the time window selection are discussed.

5.1 The Selection of the Vessel Traffic Accident Frequency as the Index

The vessel traffic risk can be measured in two dimensions by the risk matrix, which displays the frequency and the consequence of the vessel traffic accident at the same time. As discussed in the introduction section, the time window selection should be considered in the process of uncertainty analysis of the vessel traffic risk. As accident consequences are generated through a fuzzy development process after accidents occur and are often determined by incorporating expert judgements[211], the vessel traffic accident frequency is selected as the representative index for the time window selection in the uncertainty analysis for simplification. Then the epistemic uncertainty of the accident consequence is quantified based on all the information included in the selected time window. If the vessel traffic risk is measured by a one-dimension value, the algorithm for time window selection should apply to the time series of the product of the accident frequency and the accident consequence.

In order to discuss the possible effects of the simplification, the algorithm for time window selection applies to the time series of fatalities in Table 1. According to Equation (1), the confidence intervals of fatalities per accident for the 2000 to 2016 period can be estimated for the confidence value 0.95 and can be arranged to form the uncertain time series, which is shown in Figure 4. Fatalities per accident in Figure 4 are represented by diamond icons and are connected by a line; the limits of the confidence interval are shown and connected by dotted lines.

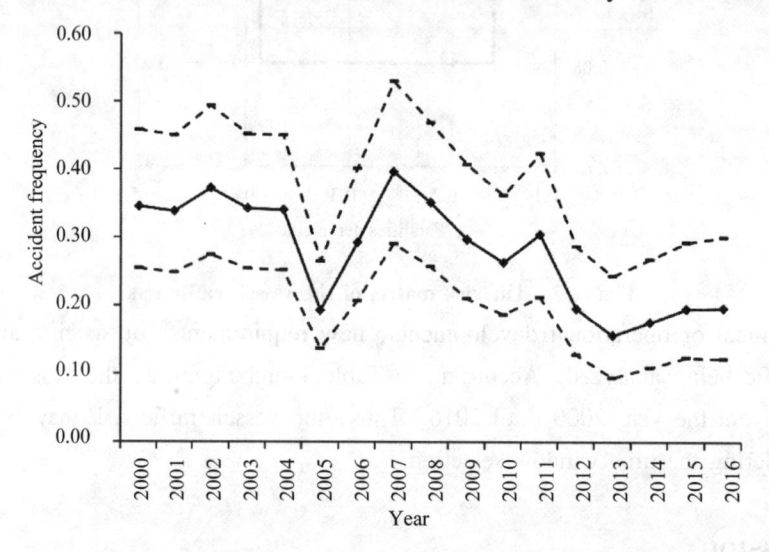

Figure 4 Uncertain time series of fatalities per accident

According to Section 3, the uncertain time series in Figure 4 can be split into four segmentations, which are the year 2000 to 2004, 2005, 2006 to 2011 and 2012 to 2016. By comparison with the segmentation result in Figure 2, we find that accident frequency declines while fatalities per accident remain stable from the year 2000 to 2004. In addition, the accident frequency remains stable while fatalities per accident decline from the year 2006 to 2016. The variation of the accident consequence is not always in accordance with that of the accident frequency and sometimes the volatility of the accident consequence is strong because of one accident with multiple fatalities. In this study, the vessel traffic accident frequency is selected as the representative index for the time window selection in the uncertainty analysis, which is one of the limitations of the work and should be studied further in the future.

5.2 The Epistemic Uncertainty of Selecting One Year of Data as a Basis

In the process of time window selection, one year of vessel traffic accident data is selected as a basis to calculate the confidence interval and to split the uncertainty time series of the vessel traffic accident frequency. As there is no a priori knowledge of selecting one year of data as a basis, this choice will introduce epistemic uncertainties. In order to discuss the possible effects of selecting one year of data as a basis on the time window selection, two years or three years of data are taken as the basis for comparative purposes. According to Equation (1), the confidence intervals of the vessel traffic accident frequency for every two years from the year 2001 to 2016 can be estimated for the confidence value 0.95 and can be arranged to form the uncertain time series, which is shown in Figure 5(a). Similarly, the uncertain time series can be formed based on the confidence intervals calculated by every three years of the accident data from the year 2002 to 2016, which is shown in Figure 5(b). In Figures 5(a) and 5(b) accident frequencies are represented by diamond icons and are connected by a line, while the limits of the confidence interval are shown and connected by dotted lines.

From the comparison of the uncertainty time series in Figures 2 and 5, we can find that the longer the time interval of data selected as the calculation basis, the lower the volatility of the uncertain time series are. According to Section 3, the uncertain time series in Figure 5(a) can be split into two segmentations, which are the years 2001 to 2006 and 2007 to 2016. The latest segmentation, 2007 to 2016, is considered as the statistical time window. Similarly, the uncertain time series in Figure 5(b) can also be split into two segmentations, which are the years 2002 to 2007 and 2008 to 2016. The latest segmentation, 2008 to 2016, is taken as the statistical time window. In Section 4, the segmentation, 2006 to 2016, is taken as the statistical time window when one year of vessel traffic accident data is selected as a basis in the process of time window selection. By comparison, the length of the time window selected by taking one year of data as a basis is longest. This means that more vessel traffic accident data can be included, which are useful for statistical analysis and uncertainty quantification.

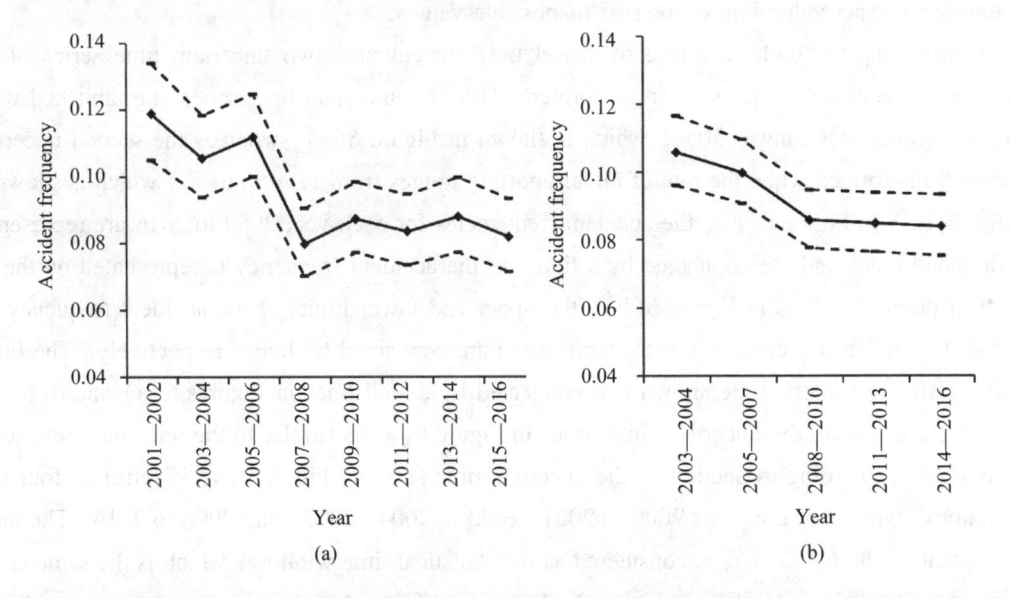

Figure 5 (a) Uncertain time series calculated by every two years of accident data; (b) Uncertain time series calculated by every three years of accident data

5.3 Underreporting of Vessel Traffic Accidents

The level of quality in accident data has an important impact on vessel traffic risk analysis. However, it has been argued that a certain number of vessel traffic accidents may be unreported[295]. Although the underreporting of vessel traffic accidents is an important factor for the quantification of the actual vessel traffic risk level, there are few studies on this issue[103]. The underreporting of vessel traffic accidents is not considered in the process of uncertainty analysis in this study because the assumption of the underreporting rate will introduce epistemic uncertainties. The rate of underreporting can be defined as the ratio of the unreported accidents to the true number of accidents[296]. The possible effects of the underreporting of vessel traffic accidents on the time window selection are discussed below.

According to the research[297], the percentage of accidents, which are missing from the records, varies from database to database and the average number of unreported accidents makes up roughly 50% of all accidents. In addition, the underreporting rate of the United Kingdom's maritime accident databases is estimated at 11% to 61% in the period from 2005 to 2009. Regardless of the degree of underreporting, the available data in this study will be complemented by additional data. When the rate of underreporting is assumed to be 50%, the number of vessel traffic accidents in Table 1 will be doubled. Similarly, the accident data will be complemented when the underreporting rate ranges from 11% to 61%. In such cases, the number of vessel traffic accidents is no longer an exact value but an interval of possible values.

Considering the underreporting of vessel traffic accidents, two uncertain time series of the vessel traffic accident frequency can be formed. The first uncertain time series is established when the rate of underreporting is 50%, which is shown in Figure 6(a), whereas the second uncertain time series is formed when the rate of underreporting ranges from 11% to 61%, which is shown in Figure 6(b). In Figure 6(a), the accident frequencies for each year 2000 to 2016 are represented by diamond icons and are connected by a line. As the accident frequency is represented by the interval of possible values in Figure 6(b), the upper and lower limits of the accident frequency are represented by square icons and circle icons, and are connected by lines, respectively. The limits of the confidence interval are shown and connected by dotted lines in Figures 6(a) and 6(b).

By comparison, the uncertain time series in Figure 6(a) is similar to the uncertain time series in Figure 2. According to Section 3, the uncertain time series in Figure 6(a) is split into four segmentations, which are the years 2000 to 2001, 2002 to 2004, 2005, and 2006 to 2016. The latest segmentation, 2006 to 2016, is considered as the statistical time window, which is the same as the result of time window selection in Figure 2. Thus, no effects of the underreporting of vessel traffic accidents on the time window selection have been found when the underreporting rate is assumed to be an exact value. Using the sliding window approach described in Section 3 to split the uncertain time series in Figure 6(b), we find that there is always an intersection between the interval of the vessel traffic accident frequency in the next year and the confidence interval of the former seg-

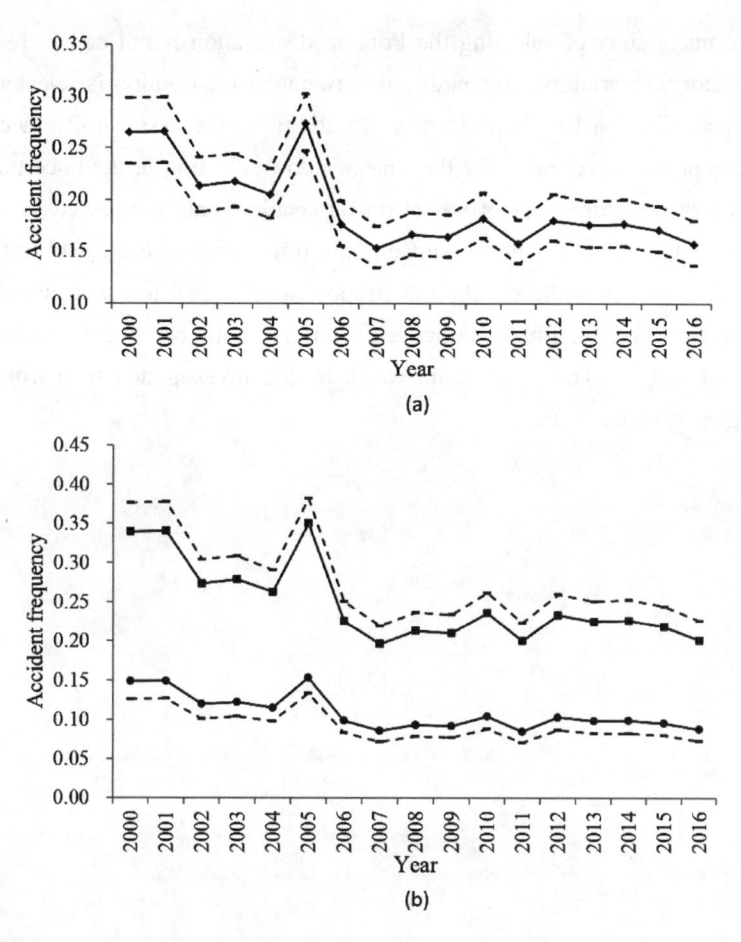

Figure 6 (a) **Uncertain time series when the rate of underreporting is 50%**; (b) **Uncertain time series when the rate of underreporting ranges from 11% to 61%**

mentation. In other words, the algorithm for time window selection proposed in this study may not work well in the case that the rate of underreporting is assumed to be an interval of possible values.

6 Conclusions

Uncertainty analysis is necessary when assessing the vessel traffic risk. It can be used to investigate the reliability of the risk assessment result, which is the basis for vessel traffic risk management. According to the uncertainty classification of the vessel traffic accident frequency and consequence, the Poisson distribution and the triangular distribution are selected for the uncertainty quantification. In addition, the algorithm for appropriate time window selection is used to make reasonable measurements of the uncertainties. The vessel traffic accident data for the years 2000 to 2016 from the United Kingdom's marine accident investigation branch are used for the case study. It is worthy of mention that there are several simplifications and limitations in this study. First of all, the epistemic uncertainty of selecting the Poisson distribution is not considered in the process of quantifying aleatory uncertainty. Secondly, the triangular distribution is selected for the epistemic uncertainty quantification for simplification. In addition, the vessel traffic accident frequency is selected as the representative index for the time window selection in the uncertainty analysis for simplification. Afterwards, one year of vessel traffic accident data is selected as a basis to calculate the confidence interval and to split the uncertainty time series of the vessel traffic accident frequency for simplification. In addition, the underreporting of vessel traffic accidents is not considered. Finally, the algorithm for time window selection may not work well in cases that vessel traffic accident data are scarce. These issues are worth further investigation both from the theoretical and practical points of view.

基于改进粒子群－BP 神经网络算法的 PSC 选船模型

摘要：本文以 2009/16/EC 巴黎备忘录目标船选船机制 NIR 为研究对象，提出基于改进的粒子群－BP 神经网络算法的 PSC 新选船模型。该算法可针对 BP 神经网络算法收敛速度慢、易陷入局部极小值等问题，根据群体早熟收敛度及个体适应值调整惯性权重，更新粒子速度和位置。将改进的粒子群算法训练 BP 网络用于 PSC 选船，实验结果表明，较常规 BP 网络，改进的自适应粒子群优化神经网络算法能够有效改善神经网络的训练效率，提高训练精度。

关键词：粒子群优化（PSO）算法；BP 神经网络；PSC 选船

0 引言

巴黎备忘录目标船选船机制 NIR（New Inspection Regime）中船舶风险等级的评估由包括船型、船龄、船旗国、认可组织及管理公司表现在内的通用参数和基于一定历史时期内在巴黎备忘录地区港口国监督检查缺陷数和滞留次数的历史参数共同确定[298]。国内外对 PSC 选船模型研究主要集中在层次分析法和模糊综合评价方法[164, 299-303]。本文提出一种改进的 PSO 优化算法——动态自适应惯性权重粒子群优化算法（Dynamic Adaptive Particle Swarm Optimization, DAP-SO）。该算法权重系数可根据离散度和迭代次数不同而非线性减少，并用 DAPSO 算法训练 BP 神经网络，提出一种新 PSC 选船模型。

1 改进的粒子群算法

1.1 标准粒子群算法

PSO 算法在可行解空间随机初始化 M 个粒子种群，每个粒子有 N 维，每个粒子都对应优化问题的一个解，由目标函数确定其适应值，然后根据以下公式迭代更新速度和位置：

$$v_{i,j}^{t} = v_{i,j}^{t-1} + C_1 r_1 (P_{\text{best},i,j}^{t-1} - X_{i,j}^{t-1}) + C_2 r_2 (G_{\text{best},i,j}^{t-1} - X_{i,j}^{t-1})$$

$$X_{i,j}^{t} = X_{i,j}^{t-1} + v_{i,j}^{t}$$

其中：$i = 1,2,\cdots,N$ 为粒子维数；$j = 1,2,\cdots,M$ 为粒子数量；$v_{i,j}^{t}$、$v_{i,j}^{t-1}$ 分别为第 j 个在第

---

* 本文发表在《大连海事大学学报》2012 年第 3 期 38 卷，作者孙忠华、郑中义、杨婷婷。

i 维的 t 和 $t-1$ 时刻的速度；$X_{i,j}^t$、$X_{i,j}^{t-1}$ 分别为第 j 个粒子在第 i 维的 t 和 $t-1$ 时刻位置；$P_{\text{best},i,j}^{t-1}$、$G_{\text{best},i,j}^{t-1}$ 分别为第 j 个粒子及全部粒子 $t-1$ 时刻的最优位置；C_1、C_2 为加速学习因子。

1.2 惯性权重改进算法

文献[3-4]提出惯性权重概念调整搜索速度：

$$v_{i,j}^t = \omega^t V_{i,j}^{t-1} + C_1 r_1 (P_{\text{best},i,j}^{t-1} - X_{i,j}^{t-1}) + C_2 r_2 (G_{\text{best},i,j}^{t-1} - X_{i,j}^{t-1})$$

其中：$r^k (k=1,2)$ 为随机数，$r^k \in [0,1]$；ω 为惯性权重因子，用于控制前一次的速度对当前速度的影响，较大的 ω 可以加强局部搜索能力。基本 PSO 可以看作 $\omega=1$，因此在迭代后期缺少局部搜索能力。实验结果表明，$\omega \in [0.8,1.2]$，PSO 有更快的收敛速度。文献[300]中试验了将 ω 设置为从 0.9 到 0.4 的线性下降，使得 PSO 在开始时探索较大区域，较快定位最优解的大致位置；随着 ω 的逐渐减小，粒子飞行速度减慢，开始精细的局部搜索。该方法加快了收敛速度，提高了 PSO 算法的性能。

1.3 压缩因子改进算法

文献[304]证明压缩因子有助于确保 PSO 算法最终收敛，得到高质量的解。其速度更新公式为：

$$v_{i,j}^t = a[v_{i,j}^{t-1} + C_1 r_1 (P_{\text{best},i,j}^{t-1} - X_{i,j}^{t-1}) + C_2 r_2 (G_{\text{best},i,j}^{t-1} - X_{i,j}^{t-1})]$$

$$a = 2/(|2 - C - \sqrt{C^2 - 4C}|)$$

$$C = C_1 + C_2$$

1.4 基于压缩因子及惯性权重的改进算法

将压缩因子及惯性权重改进算法的优点相结合，进一步优化惯性权重和加速学习因子 C_1、C_2。C_1、C_2 决定了粒子之间信息交换程度，可使粒子避免陷入局部最优解。这里 $C=4.2$，$a=0.64$。其算法为：

$$v_{i,j}^t = a[\omega^t v_{i,j}^{t-1} + C_1 r_1 (P_{\text{best},i,j}^{t-1} - X_{i,j}^{t-1}) + C_2 r_2 (G_{\text{best},i,j}^{t-1} - X_{i,j}^{t-1})]$$

1.5 惯性权重 ω 的改进

本文提出一种使 ω 值随粒子群离散度变化而自适应变化的 PSO 优化算法——动态自适应惯性权重粒子群优化算法（DAPSO）。

离散度的概念：引用概率统计学中标准差的概念，定义 σ 表示粒子群的离散程度。

$$\sigma = \sqrt{\frac{1}{N} \sum_{i=1}^{N} ((f_i - \bar{f})/\Delta f)^2}$$

其中：N 为粒子群的规模数；f_i 为粒子在当前迭代次数时的适应值；$\bar{f}$ 为所有粒子当前适应度值的平均值，即 $\bar{f} = \frac{1}{N} \sum_{i=1}^{N} f_i$；$\Delta f = \max_{1 \leq i \leq N} \{f_i - \bar{f}\}$ 表示粒子当前前适应值与平均适应值差值

的最大值。Δf 越小,说明整个群体越趋于早熟收敛。参考文献[305]预先给定 σ 阈值,当 σ 小于该阈值时,就认为该粒子群的离散度低,将存在陷入局部最优的可能,因此应减小 ω 的下降速度,尽量保持 ω 以较大值且粒子以较大幅度进行搜索,可扩大搜索范围跳出局部最优;当 σ 大于该阈值时,就认为该粒子群的离散度高,证明粒子群正保持着多样性且进行着全局搜索,故此时应尽量增大 ω 的下降速度,保证粒子群尽快收敛。

为满足上述两种情况的要求,本文参考文献[305]中 ω 的凹函数递减算法,通过粒子群的离散程度不同,提出自适应调整惯性权重 ω 的改进算法:

$$\begin{cases} \omega^t = \sqrt{\omega_{\min}\left(1-\dfrac{\omega_{\min}}{\omega_{\max}}\right)^{\left(\frac{T_{\max}-t}{T_{\max}}\right)^k}}, \sigma < 0.5 \\ \omega^t = \left[\omega_{\min}\left(1-\dfrac{\omega_{\min}}{\omega_{\max}}\right)^{\left(\frac{T_{\max}-t}{T_{\max}}\right)^k}\right]^2, \sigma \geq 0.5 \end{cases}$$

其中:$\omega_{\max}$ 为惯性权重最大值;$\omega_{\min}$ 为惯性权重最小值;$T_{\max}$ 为粒子群最大迭代次数;t 为当前迭代次数。这里 $k=3, \omega_{\max}=0.9, \omega_{\min}=0.4$。

2 基于改进粒子群-BP神经网络算法的PSC选船模型

2.1 BP神经网络评价模型

本文采用权值训练中使用误差逆向传播方式的反向传播(BP)神经网络。

(1)网络结构:根据Kosmogorov定理,3层BP网络可以逼近任意函数,因此选取3层;采用Sigmoid函数作为传输函数。

(2)输入层神经元个数及样本预编码:根据NIR风险因素,挑取 $n=7$ 个条件属性,且自定义编码为:{TYPE,MARINER,FLAG,CNSM,DEF,DUR,ROUTE}。船型={其他类型,散货船,油船客船及危险品船}={0.82,0.84,0.86}。船员扣分情况={未扣过分,扣分1次,扣分2次,扣分2次以上}={0.72,0.74,0.76,0.78}。船旗国={是否方便旗国家,船旗国的滞留率,船旗国核准公约程度}={0.62,0.64,0.66}。公司NSM体系={A类,B类,C类}={0.52,0.54,0.56}。过去36个月每次检查记录的缺陷数量={前3次安检平均缺陷数≤5,5<前3次安检平均缺陷数≤10,10<前3次安检平均缺陷数≤15,前3次安检平均缺陷数>15}={0.42,0.44,0.46,0.48}。距前滞留时间={0~6个月,7~12个月,13个月+}={0.32,0.34,0.36}。航线={国内航线,国际航线}={0.24,0.26}。

(3)输出层神经元个数:PSC选船评价结果作为网络输出,因此去输出层个数为 $m=1$。

输出层元素编码:自定义风险程度取值区间:极高风险船舶:{0.7,1};高风险船舶:{0.5,0.7};一般风险船舶:{0.3,0.5};低风险船舶:{0,0.3}。

(4)隐含层神经元个数:根据Kosmogorov定理

$$s = \sqrt{0.43nm + 0.12m^2 + 2.54n + 0.77m + 0.35} + 0.51 = 5$$

2.2 训练学习过程选船结果分析

粒子群算法优化 BP 神经网络权值的关键在于:

(1)神经网络学习过程就是权(阈)值更新过程,因此代替梯度下降法训练网络权(阈)值,建立 PSO 粒子的维度空间与神经网络连接权值之间的映射,即神经网络有多少个连接权(阈)值,PSO 算法中的每个粒子就应有多少维度。

(2)使用神经网络的均方误差作为 PSO 的适应度函数,借助 PSO 算法强大的全局搜索能力使适应度函数达到最大,使神经网络均方误差最小。

定义第 k 个粒子适应度函数为指数形式,使误差平方和大的粒子其适应值变小: $\xi_k = 1/\exp(E_k)$

$$E_k = \frac{1}{2m} \sum_{k=1}^{m} \sum_{t=1}^{n} (y_t^k - c_t^k)^2$$

其中: m 为样本个数; n 为网络输出神经元个数; y_t^k 为第 k 个样本第 t 个输出神经元期望输出; c_t^k 为第 k 个样本第 t 个输出神经元实际输出。

改进粒子群算法训练神经网络的流程(见图1):

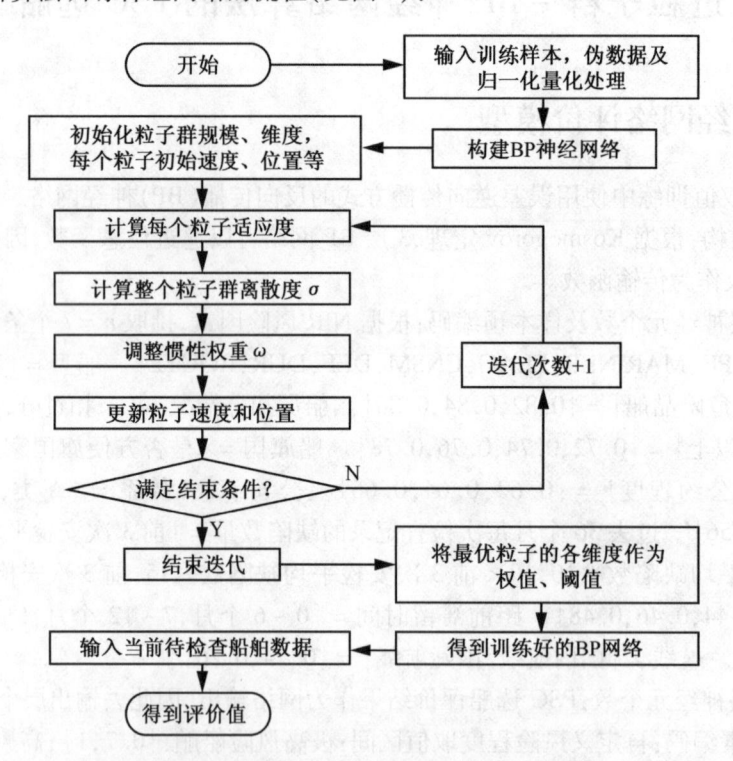

图 1 改进粒子群算法训练神经网络流程图

(1)构建 BP 神经网络结构,定义粒子 $\vec{x_m} = (x_{m1} \quad x_{m2} \quad \cdots \quad x_{mN})$ 分别表示神经元的连接权值和阈值。这里 PSO 粒子群个数 $M = 40$,粒子维度 $N = $ 输入层至隐含层连接权个数 + 隐含层至输出层连接权个数 + 隐含层的阈值个数 + 输出层阈值个数 $= 7 \times 5 + 5 \times 1 + 5 + 1 = 46$;

(2)初始化粒子初始位置、速度、惯性权重、最大迭代次数等参数;

(3)计算每个粒子适应度及粒子群离散度 σ;

(4)计算惯性权重调整值、每个粒子最好位置及全局最优值,根据公式更新粒子位置和速度;

(5)满足精度要求时,搜索结束,输出全局最优位置。

2.3 选船结果分析

使用 Matlab 语言的神经网络工具箱提供的函数和神经网络类,采用 Sigmoid 函数作为传输函数。具体设置如下:自学习的学习率 net. trainParam. lr = 0.02;Marquardt 调整参数 net. trainParam. mu = 0;学习系数下降因子 net. trainParam. mu-dec = 0.9;学习系数上升因子 net. trainParam. mu-inc = 1.05;训练步数 net. trainParam. epochs = 10000;训练目标 net. train-Param. goal1 = 0.01(BP);net. trainParam. goal2 = 0.0001(PSO-BP)。

将训练样本进行数据预处理后,从辽宁海事局 PSC 检查数据库中另选 10 组样本对网络进行测试。本文基本的 BP 神经网络算法精度选取 10^{-2}。如图 2 所示,训练步长为 7 419 时,精度达到要求。改进粒子群 – BP 神经网络算法的精度选取 10^{-4},如图 3 所示,训练步长为 20 时,系统精度即达到要求。表 1 为测试样本。由表 1 可见,改进 PSO-BP 与 BP 算法辨识结果误差非常小,从而证明该网络同样具有可逼近性,满足实际 PSC 工作需要。

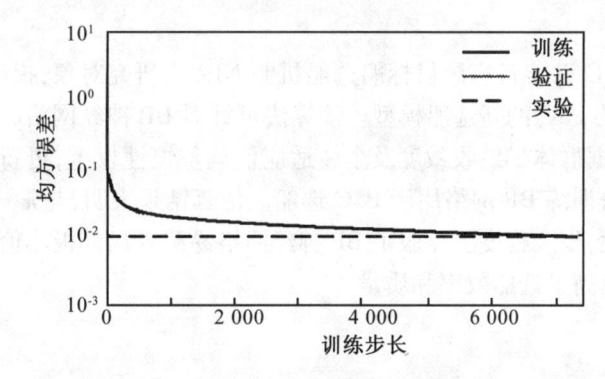

图 2 采用改进粒子群算法训练神经网络算法的均方误差曲线

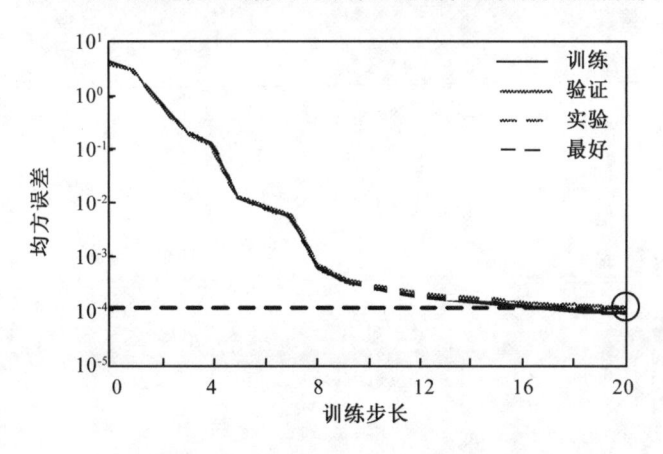

图 3 采用 BP 神经网络算法的均方误差曲线

表1 测试样本

样本	TYPE	MARINE	FLAG	CNSM	DEF	DUR2	ROUTE	BP	PSO-BP	绝对误差
1	0.82	0.72	0.62	0.56	0.46	0.32	0.24	0.436 2	0.451 0	0.014 8
2	0.86	0.74	0.64	0.52	0.42	0.34	0.26	0.703 5	0.714 3	0.010 8
3	0.84	0.76	0.66	0.54	0.44	0.36	0.26	0.816 4	0.821 7	0.015 2
4	0.86	0.72	0.64	0.52	0.48	0.34	0.24	0.712 0	0.734 3	0.005 3
5	0.82	0.74	0.62	0.56	0.42	0.32	0.26	0.528 7	0.540 4	0.011 7
6	0.86	0.78	0.66	0.54	0.42	0.36	0.26	0.904 1	0.912 6	0.008 5
7	0.84	0.76	0.62	0.52	0.44	0.32	0.24	0.671 3	0.684 6	0.013 3
8	0.82	0.74	0.64	0.54	0.46	0.34	0.26	0.736 9	0.751 3	0.014 4
9	0.82	0.72	0.62	0.52	0.42	0.32	0.24	0.138 2	0.150 1	0.014 1
10	0.82	0.76	0.66	0.56	0.44	0.32	0.26	0.782 4	0.796 5	0.014 1

3 结论

本文以2009/16/EC巴黎备忘录目标船选船机制NIR为研究对象,提出基于改进的粒子群-BP神经网络算法的PSC的新选船模型。该算法可针对BP神经网络收敛速度慢、易陷入局部极小值等问题,根据群体早熟收敛度及个体适应值调整惯性权重,更新粒子速度和位置,采用改进的粒子群算法训练BP网络用于PSC选船。仿真结果表明,与常规BP网络相比,该网络同样具有可逼近性,很大程度上克服了BP神经网络易陷入局部极小值、网络收敛速度慢的缺点,迭代次数少,提高了选船效率和质量。

港口国监控选船新模型研究*

摘要:本文针对已有 PSC 选船模型采用层次分析法、模糊综合评价方法和 BP 神经网络等方法存在的诸如不能反映各风险因素之间相关性、专家主观因素带来偏差、样本需求量过大和收敛速度慢等问题,以 2009/16/EC 巴黎备忘录目标船选船机制 NIR 为研究对象,提出一种新的基于支持向量机理论的 PSC 选船模型,并选取巴黎备忘录"THETIS"检船数据库的部分船舶信息进行实证分析。结果表明,使用基于支持向量机理论的 PSC 选船模型测试的船舶样本结果与其公布的船舶实际情况一致,使用该算法可十分有效地在样本少且检查资源有限时对船舶进行快速分类,对 PSC 选船的实际操作具有实用价值。

关键词:水路运输;支持向量机;港口国监控选船;拉格朗日乘子;巴黎备忘录

0 引言

港口国监控(Port State Control,PSC)也称港口国监督,是指港口所在国家根据有关国际公约规定的标准,对进入其港口的外国籍船舶所实施的一种监督与控制。为了对船旗国海事当局的管理进行制约和补充,纠正与消除受检船舶上所存在的不符合标准的缺陷,以确保船舶航行、人身和财产的安全以及保护海洋环境,促进经济贸易的发展和航运经营水平的提高。1991 年 IMO(International Maritime Organization)要求在全球各地区建立 PSC 备忘录组织。

2009/16/EC 法令是欧洲议会及委员会于 2009 年 5 月 28 日颁布的欧盟最新港口国监督法令。该法令核心是为巴黎备忘录组织(Paris-Memorandum of Understanding,P-MOU)成员间通过制定全新的船舶风险评估体系,合理的检查周期安排等建立一个科学的检查程序、滞留处理等,即巴黎备忘录目标船选船机制 NIR(New Inspection Regime)。该机制中船舶风险等级的评估则由包括船型、船龄、船旗国、认可组织及管理公司表现在内的通用参数和基于一定历史时期内在巴黎备忘录地区港口国监督检查缺陷数和滞留次数的历史参数共同确定[298]。但由于该选船方法中的风险因素只提供了一些相对具有代表性的因素,这些因素未考虑各风险因素之间的相关性,只是对风险因素进行打分并通过简单的相加得出船舶风险值,属于线性选船模型,而实际上 PSC 预测选船是一个非线性问题,即各风险因素之间是具有明显的相关性。

PSC 选船模型国内外相关研究主要集中在层次分析法和模糊综合评价方法,这些方法因为引入专家的主观因素,可能产生主观偏差[306]。魏栋等人采用 BP(Back Propagation)神经网络可以很好地逼近非线性性函数的特性,采用 BP 神经网络建立了 PSC 检查选船模型[164]。此方法在参数合适和样本足够多的情况下能够得到比较好的辨别效果,但在实际使用时,参数隐

---

* 本文发表在《中国航海》2012 年第 4 期第 35 卷,作者孙忠华、郑中义、杨婷婷。

层个数和学习率较难确定,而且 BP 神经网络需要大量样本数据对进行训练,收敛速度慢,并易陷入局部最优。

支持向量机(Support Vector Machine,SVM)的原理是根据风险最小化原则,以尽量提高学习机泛化(预测)能力为目的,能够较好地解决小样本、非线性高维数及局部极小点等问题[307]。SVM 基本思想是通过非线性映射,将输入空间映射到高维空间,引入不敏感函数构建最佳超平面,从而将寻找最佳超平面算法归结为求解一个有约束的凸二次规划问题。应用 SVM 理论及其方法用于 PSC 选船模型构建和分析,能够很好地将抽象的关系通过定量分析得到较为精确的评价结果,并可以通过灵活设置参数满足不同领域的研究需求[308],解决了检查资源有限时对船舶进行快速分类的问题。

在应用粗糙集和层次分析法相结合进行属性约简后确定的评价条件属性的基础上(包括船型、船旗国、认可机构、航线、过去36个月每次检查记录的缺陷数量、过去36个月滞留数量、是否存在未纠正缺陷),提出一种基于支持向量机理论的 PSC 选船模型,并对巴黎备忘录公布的 PSC 数据进行实例验证。

1 支持向量机非线性回归原理

采用支持向量机的非线性回归方法,通过构建非线性映射关系将评价参数数据映射到高维 Hilbert 空间,在此空间进行线性回归。

优化过程为:假设训练集为 $\{(x_1,y_1),\cdots,(x_n,y_n)\}$,则 SVM 非线性回归问题就转换为寻找线性函数 $f \in F$,使期望风险达到最小的问题。

$$f(x) = \omega\varphi(x) + b \tag{1}$$

式(1)中 $\varphi(x)$ 为从输入空间到高维空间的非线性映射,ω 为权系数,b 为偏置量。

SVM 回归中,损失函数 L 定义为 ε 不敏感损失函数,ε 是事先确定的可容忍的误差,表示函数 $f(x)$ 与样本观测值最多只有 ε 偏差,则 f 的估计转变为以下约束优化问题[309]:

$$\min \frac{1}{2}\|\omega\|^2 \tag{2}$$

$$\text{s.t.} \begin{cases} y_i - \omega\varphi(x_i) - b \leq \varepsilon \\ -y_i + \omega\varphi(x_i) - b \leq \varepsilon \end{cases} \tag{3}$$

式(3)中:ε 越小,则训练精度越高,但是推广能力比较差[310]。

SVM 算法优化计算过程如下:

(1)训练集 $T = \{(x_i,y_i) | i=1,2,\cdots,n\}$,$x_i$ 和 y_i 分别为船舶评价因素及评价值,i 为船舶样本。

(2)选择适当的 ε 和 c 值,c 为惩罚函数。

(3)选择适当的核函数 $k(x_i,x)$。

(4)构造求解式(3)的优化问题,得到最优解 a_i 和 a_i^*。

(5)构造决策函数:

$$f(x,a_i,a_i^*) = \sum_{i=1}^{n}(a_i^* - a_i)k(x_i \cdot x) + b^* \tag{4}$$

式(4)中:

$$b^* = y_i - \sum_{i=1}^{n}(a_i^* - a_i)k(x_i \cdot x) - \varepsilon \tag{5}$$

当将船舶风险评价输入量输入到该决策函数即可得到船舶风险评价值。

2 基于支持向量机理论的 PSC 选船模型构建

图 1 是基于支持向量机理论的 PSC 选船模型。

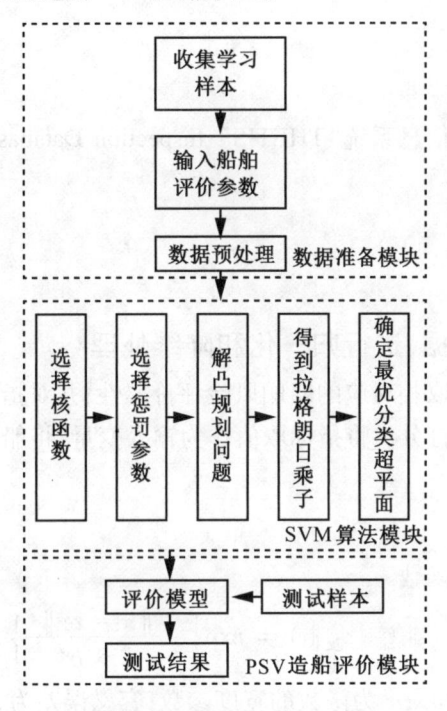

图 1　基于支持向量机理论的 PSC 选船模型

2.1 数据准备模块

(1)收集船舶数据作为学习样本,划分出训练样本用于以构建模型,划分出测样本集用于验证模型有效性。

(2)数据预处理。归一化处理,将评价指标进行线性伸缩至[0,1]区间内以及降维预处理。编制降维预处理,进行样本精简。

2.2 SVM 算法模块

(1)选取学习参数,包括核参数取值、容忍误差取值及惩罚参数取值。

(2)获取 SVM 知识,包括利用训练学习样本,建立目标函数,求解凸二次规划问题,寻找最优分类面,获得训练集中支持向量和对应的参数,从而构建决策函数。

2.3 PSC 选船评价模块

利用求得的参数构建决策函数,然后输入测试样本获得船舶风险评价等级。

3 实例验证

3.1 选取资料

在巴黎备忘录组织的新信息系统"THETIS" Inspection Database 中选取中国籍的 30 条船舶信息。

3.2 评价过程

3.2.1 收集学习样本数据,进行归一化和降维处理

在以上的数据样本中选取相对应的船舶风险评价属性,并对指标进行归一化处理,分别按照 1.0 和 0.2 两个等级进行打分。将指标取值作为输入变量,将船舶风险评价作为输出变量,从而构建出训练集。

3.2.2 选取学习参数

这里选用高斯径向基核函数

$$k(\|x - xc\|) = \exp\left\{-\frac{\|x - xc\|^2}{2 \times \sigma^2}\right\} \tag{6}$$

式(6)中:xc 为核函数中心;σ 为函数的宽度参数;容忍误差为 2×10^{-5}。惩罚参数 c 和核参数 g 采用仿真验证方式。

3.2.3 获得 SVM 知识,测试样本,寻找最佳参数

应用 SVM 重要的一点是寻找惩罚因子 c 和 g 值,采用 MATLAB 软件编制 SVMcg 程序寻找最佳的 c 和 g。采用 LIBSVM 所带的 SVMcg,将数据分为 15 组进行随机检验,在 $[-2 \times 10^{-5}, 2 \times 10^{-5}]$ 中寻找,建立预测模型所用的 c、g,预测结果最好的作为我们采用的 c、g。同时随机选取 10 组数据作为测试集合(5 个 0,5 个 1),使用四个参数指标灵敏度(Sn)、特异性(Sp)、准确率(Acc)和 Matthew 关联系数(MCC)检验所建模型方法评价效果。

各指标定义如下:

灵敏度

$$Sn = \frac{TP}{TP + FN} \tag{7}$$

特异性

$$Sp = \frac{TN}{TN + FP} \tag{8}$$

准确率

$$ACC = \frac{TN + TP}{TP + TN + FP + FN} \tag{9}$$

$$MCC = \frac{TP \times TN - FP \times FN}{\sqrt{(TP + FP)(TP + FN)(TN + FP)(TN + FN)}} \tag{10}$$

式(7)～式(10)中:TP 为真阳性;TN 为真阴性;FP 为假阳性;FN 为假阴性。

图 2 为取数据 1/15 作为测试的结果准确率,这里取得的 c 和 g 的值是预测结果最好的那一点所对应值。由图 2 可见,当 $c=32$,$g=1.4142$ 时,预测结果为 92.22%,达到最好的预测结果。

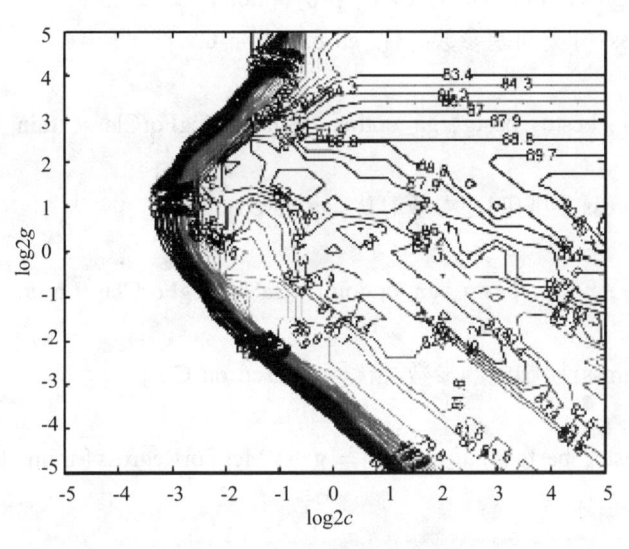

图 2　参数 c 和 g 的关系图

3.3　选船评价模型算法的 Matlab 实现过程

caleForSVM:归一化
函数接口:
[train_scale, test_scale, ps] = scaleForSVM(train_data, test_data, ymin, ymax)
pcaForSVM:pca 降维预处理
函数接口:
[train_pca, test_pca] = pcaForSVM(train, test, threshold)
fasticaForSVM:ica 降维预处理
函数接口:
[train_ica, test_ica] = fasticaForSVM(train, test)
SVMcgForClass:分类问题参数寻优[grid search based on CV]
函数接口:
[bastacc, bestc, bestg] = SVMcgForClass(train_label, train, cmin, cmax, gmin, gmax, v, cstep, gstep, accstep)
SVMcgForRegress:回归问题参数寻优[grid search based on CV]

psoSVMcgForClass:分类问题参数寻优[pso based on CV]

函数接口:

[bestCVaccuracy, bestc, bestg, pso_option] = psoSVMcgForClass(train_label, train, pso_option)

psoSVMcgForRegress:回归问题参数寻优[pso based on CV]

函数接口:

[bestCVmse, bestc, bestg, pso_option]

psoSVMcgForRegress(train_label, train, pso_option)

gaSVMcgForClass:分类问题参数寻优[ga based on CV]

函数接口:

[bestCVaccuracy, bestc, bestg, ga_option] = gaSVMcgForClass(train_label, train, ga_option)

gaSVMcgForRegress:回归问题参数寻优[ga based on CV]

函数接口:

[bestCVaccuracy, bestc, bestg, ga_option] = gaSVMcgForClass(train_label, train, ga_option)

gaSVMcgForRegress:回归问题参数寻优[ga based on CV]

函数接口:

[bestCVmse, bestc, bestg, ga_option] = gaSVMcgForRegress(train_label, train, ga_option)

3.4 实例计算结果分析

表1为测试样本及其测试结果,表1只列出了部分样本数据。将表1中数值除以15进行归一化处理作为测试集。

表1 测试样本数据

U	C 属性								D 属性	辨识结果	精度
	TYPE	MARINER	FLAG	CS	ROUTE	DEF	DEF2	DET	ACC		
1	1	1	1	2	1	2	2	1	0	0	100%
2	1	2	1	1	2	1	1	1	0	0	100%
3	2	1	1	1	2	2	2	2	1	1	100%
4	3	1	2	1	2	1	3	2	1	1	100%
5	2	1	1	2	1	1	1	1	0	0	100%
6	2	3	2	1	1	1	1	2	1	1	100%
7	2	1	1	2	1	1	3	2	1	1	100%
8	2	4	1	2	1	1	4	2	1	1	100%
9	1	2	1	1	1	1	1	2	0	0	100%
10	1	1	2	1	1	1	1	1	0	0	100%

表 1 中对已挑选出的各条件属性指标数值采用离散化赋值,其规则如下:
(1)船型(TYPE)
其中:1 =（其他类型）,2 =（散货船）,3 =（油船客船及危险品船）。
(2)船员扣分情况(MARINER)
其中:1 =（未扣过分）,2 =（扣分 1 次）,3 =（扣分 2 次）,4 =（扣分 2 次以上）。
(3)船旗国(FLAG)
其中:1 =（是否方便旗国家）,2 =（船旗国的滞留率）,3 =（船旗国核准公约程度）。
(4)认可机构船级社(CS)
其中:1 =（是否为 IACS 会员）,2 =（船级社的滞留率）。
(5)航线(ROUTE)
其中:1 =（国内航线）,2 =（国际航线）。
(6)过去 36 个月每次检查记录的缺陷数量。
其中:1 =（前三次安检平均缺陷数小于等于 5 个）,2 =（前三次安检平均缺陷数大于 5 个但小于等于 10 个）,3 =（前三次安检平均缺陷数大于 10 个但小于等于 15 个）,4 =（前三次安检平均缺陷数大于 15 个）。
(7)过去 36 个月滞留数量
其中:1 =（未被滞留）,2 =（被滞留 1 次）,3 =（被滞留 2 次）,4 =（被滞留 2 次以上）。
(8)是否存在未纠正缺陷
其中:1 =（不存在）,2 =（存在）。由此,得到相应的预测结果为:
准确率 $Acc = 100\%$（10/10）(classification)
真阳性 $TP = 5$
真阴性 $TN = 5$
灵敏度 $Sn = 1$
特异性 $Sp = 1$
Matthew 关联系数 $MCC = 1$

从计算结果可见,训练精度达到 100%,明显高于使用层次分析法、模糊综合评价和 BP 神经网络等方法得到的结果。而且基于支持向量机理论的 PSC 选船模型测试船舶样本结果与巴黎备忘录的信息系统"THETIS"公布实际情况一致,表明基于支持向量机理论的 PSC 选船模型更加便于实际工作中对待检船舶进行快速分类。

4 结语

本文提出了基于支持向量机理论的快速 PSC 选船模型,并选取巴黎备忘录"THETIS"检船数据库的部分船舶信息进行实证分析。结果表明,基于支持向量机理论的 PSC 选船模型测试船舶样本结果与其公布的船舶实际情况一致,避免采用 BP 神经网络时,参数隐层个数和学习率确定的难点。该算法特别适用于检查资源有限时对船舶进行快速分类,对 PSC 选船具有一定的实用价值。

基于突变机理的海上交通事故致因研究

摘要：为预防海上交通事故,必须建立海上安全预控机制。首先,定性分析海上交通事故的致因,利用突变理论对海上交通事故进行定义;然后,对海上交通安全系统的突变状态进行研究,进而建立了海上交通安全系统的尖点突变模型。本文基于模型分析了海上交通事故的动态致因机理,最后探讨了突变理论在海上交通风险预控中的应用。

关键词：水路运输;海上交通安全系统;海上交通事故;突变理论;动态致因;风险预控

0 引言

广义的海上交通安全是指人类在航海生产实践过程中,通过不断适应自然界达到减少危险和隐患的目的,进而减少事故或者避免事故的发生[311]。海上交通事故是海上交通安全系统中的一个突变状态,可以用突变理论分析并描述安全系统安全状态与危险状态的转化过程,同时探索事故的形成机理,以达到预控海上交通安全系统风险的目的。

1 海上交通事故致因分析

海上交通安全是一个完整的交通安全系统,涉及的因素众多。不同学科对海上交通安全系统的理解不同:海上交通工程学认为海上交通安全系统由"人""船""环境"[312]三个子系统组成;工程管理学从安全系统工程管理出发,把海上交通安全系统划分为"人""船""环境""管理"[312]四个子系统。尽管划分方式不同,海上交通安全系统都可以概括为由主观因素和客观因素组成的系统。其中,人的不安全行为主要指航行人员和管理人员的失误,属主观因素;物的不安全状态包括船舶因素和环境因素存在的隐患,属客观因素。

2 突变理论在海上交通安全系统中的应用

突变理论主要研究动态系统在连续发展过程中出现的突然变化的现象,进而解释突然变化与连续变化因素之间的关系[314]。其主导思想是,任何一个动态系统的势函数均表示该系统具有某种趋向的能力,可以描述为：

$$V = V(x,c) \tag{1}$$

式(1)中:x 为系统状态变量;c 为系统控制变量。

---

* 本文发表在《中国航海》2013年第3期第36卷,作者齐迹、郑中义、李建民。

当势函数一阶导数为零,其 Hessen 矩阵的行列式 $\det V_{ij} \neq 0$ 时(其中 $V_{ij} = \dfrac{\partial^2 V}{\partial x_i \partial x_j}, i, j = 1, 2, \cdots, n$)的点称为孤立临界点,即系统状态呈连续光滑的变化;当势函数一阶导数及 Hessen 矩阵的行列式 $\det V_{ij} = 0$ 时的点称为非孤立临界点,即系统状态可能发生突变。因此突变理论的关键是寻求非孤立临界点构成的集合,即分叉集,通过研究分叉集的性质对突变现象进行界定。

事故是安全系统中一个连续与突变相统一的复杂发展过程。当系统内部人和物的控制参数连续变化到某临界点时,系统状态将会发生突然质变,这为突变理论解释事故现象提供了理论依据。因此,将突变理论应用于海上交通事故形成机理分析中,建立海上交通安全系统突变模型来解释和描述海上交通事故的形成过程是可行的。

托姆曾经证明,当控制变量不大于4个时,系统最多有7种突变形式[315],其势函数如表1所示。

表1 基本突变模型

突变类型	状态变量数目	控制参量数目	余维数	势函数
折叠	1	1	1	$V(x) = x^3 + ux$
尖点	1	2	2	$V(x) = x^4 + ux^2 + vx$
燕尾	1	3	3	$V(x) = x^5 + ux^3 + vx^2 + wx$
蝴蝶	1	4	4	$V(x) = x^6 + tx^4 + ux^3 + vx^2 + wx$
双曲脐点	2	3	3	$V(x) = x^3 + y^3 + wxy + ux + vy$
椭圆脐点	2	3	3	$V(x) = x^3 - xy^2 + w(x^2 + y^2) + ux + vy$
抛物脐点	2	4	4	$V(x) = y^4 + x^2y + wx^2 + ty^2 + ux + vy$

海上交通安全系统可以通过两个控制变量(人和物的因素)以及一个状态变量(系统的安全状态)来描述。通过对表1中各突变模型的适用情况进行分析,可以选用尖点突变模型对海上交通事故突变现象进行描述。一般的,海上交通安全系统势函数形式可以表达为:

$$V(F) = F^4 + HF^2 + MF \tag{2}$$

式(2)中:V 为海上交通安全系统保持稳定运行趋势的能力;F 为系统安全状态变量,表示系统总体是否安全;H 为人的因素;M 为物的因素。

$V(F)$ 的状态空间是三维的,状态变量为 F,控制变量分别是 H 和 M。它的平衡曲面(系统所有临界点所在的曲面)由方程(3)确定。

$$\frac{\partial V}{\partial F} = 4F^3 + 2HF + M = 0 \tag{3}$$

突变理论认为,当系统处于稳定状态时,安全状态变量 F 的取值是唯一的。当控制变量参数 H、M 在某个范围内变化,即安全状态函数极值不唯一时,系统处于不稳定状态。

令 $V = V(F)$ 的 Hessen 矩阵为零,求出奇点集:

$$\frac{\partial^2 V}{\partial F^2} = 12F^2 + 2H = 0 \tag{4}$$

式(4)表示一般平衡曲面的一个子集。由式(3)和式(4)消去 F,得到一般分叉集方程:
$$\Delta = 8H^3 + 27M^2 = 0 \tag{5}$$
可以看出,分叉点集即平衡曲面的折痕在分叉集平面上的投影。

3 海上交通安全系统建模

由于海上交通安全系统的特殊性,F、H、M 三个变量都有与实际相对应的临界平衡点,因此有必要完善安全系统的一般势函数,建立安全系统标准势函数 $V_0(F)$ 及标准平衡曲面 Z 和标准分叉集 B。海上交通安全系统标准势函数为:
$$V_0(F) = (F - F_0)^4 + (H - H_0)(F - F_0)^2 + (M - M_0)(F - F_0) \tag{6}$$
式(6)中:F_0、H_0、M_0 为系统固有的特征量,在这里分别为系统的安全状态、人的不安全行为、物的不安全状态所对应的临界平衡点。

标准平衡曲面 Z 为:
$$\frac{\partial V_0}{\partial F} = 4(F - F_0)^3 + 2(H - H_0)(F - F_0) + (M - M_0) = 0 \tag{7}$$
标准奇点集 S 为:
$$\frac{\partial^2 V_0}{\partial F^2} = 12(F - F_0)^2 + 2(H - H_0) = 0 \tag{8}$$
联立式(7)与式(8)消去状态变量,得出标准分叉集方程:
$$\Delta = 8(H - H_0)^3 + 27(M - M_0)^2 = 0 \tag{9}$$
为了清晰地表示上述方程的空间关系,需要建立一个空间坐标系,以 F、H、M 为空间坐标轴,O 为空间原点。首先,确定标准平衡曲面 Z,它的方程由式(7)确定,如果把它看成一元三次方程,则参数空间的一个点 (F, H, M) 对应三个互异定态解。进一步分析解的结构时,得到标准奇点集 S[即式(8)],此时若两个定态解合二为一,它们的全体即为非孤立奇点集 S。这样就找到了分析问题的方法,以 H、M 为投影平面坐标轴,做标准奇点集 S 在投影平面 C 上的投影,得到标准分叉集 B,它就是根据 $\Delta = 0$ 确定的由两个半立方抛物线组成的尖点曲线,其尖点突变的折叠线如图1所示。

4 海上交通事故致因突变分析

图1(a)部分,标准平衡曲面 Z 分为上、中、下三叶。上叶(安全状态)和下叶(危险状态)都是系统的稳定状态,中叶(突变状态)是系统的不稳定状态。由于分叉集 B 是曲面中叶部分在底面 C(即控制平面)上的投影,当安全系统两控制变量 H、M 的变化曲线(即系统特征演化曲线的投影)落入分叉集时,系统状态发生突变,即发生事故。

为了分析海上交通事故的致因过程,采用数学方法寻找系统的突变路径。在图1(a)部分中选取 A_1、A_2、A_3、A_4、T_1、T_2、T_3、T_4 共8个不同点,其中 A_1、A_2、T_4 在标准平衡曲面 Z 的上叶,A_3、A_4、T_2 在 Z 的下叶,T_1、T_3 在 Z 的中叶。在控制平面 C 上做 A_1、A_2、A_3、A_4、T_1、T_2、T_3、T_4 的投影 A_1'、A_2'、A_3'、A_4'、T_1'、T_2'、T_3'、T_4',其中 T_1' 与 T_2' 重合,T_3' 与 T_4' 重合。连接相应的点,其连线即表示系统特征演化的路径,据此建立海上交通安全系统尖点突变模型,如图2所示。

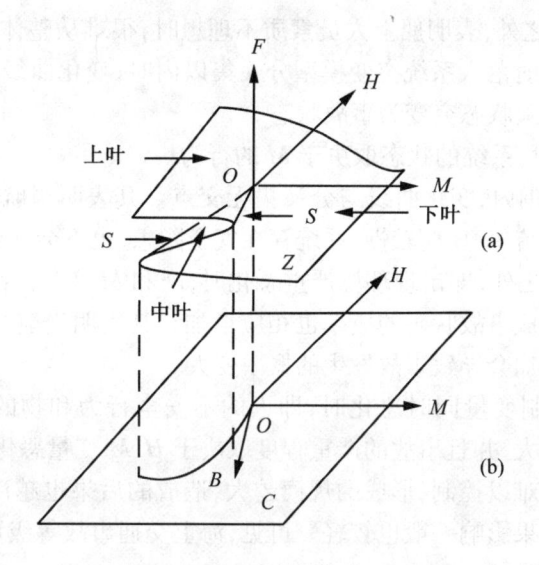

图1 安全系统的尖点突变折叠线

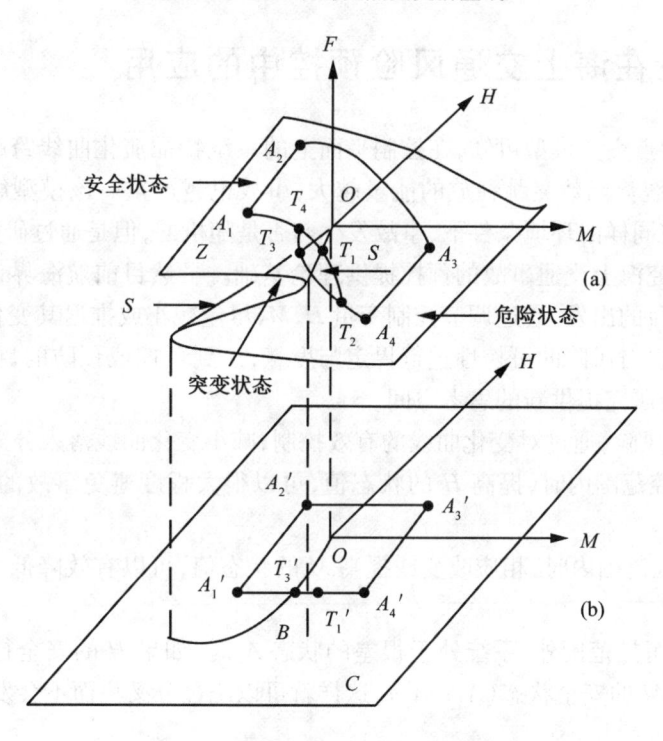

图2 海上交通安全系统尖点突变模型

通过系统特征演化曲线(包括直线)来研究系统功能所处的状态[316-322],分析得出交通事故形成过程有以下几种形式:

(1)当M不断恶化时,系统的状态取决于H的行为。

①如果H在可控范围内,变化曲线与分叉集无交点。其表明人员因素较好时(船员素质高、技能强、管理合理)能在一定程度上克服天气变化、航道条件变差或海上交通环境恶化等因素,安全系统虽然存在安全隐患,但还不至于导致交通事故。

②当 H 在可控范围之外,表明船上人员素质不理想时,很难从整体上把握系统安全状态。而当 H 和 M 变化曲线同时落入系统突变模型分叉集以内时,变化曲线与分叉集相交,表明系统发生突变,即系统由危险状态突变为事故状态。

(2)当 H 不断恶化时,系统的状态取决于 M 的行为。

①如果 M 在可控范围内,变化曲线与分叉集无交点。其表明当航行环境良好、船舶性能可靠时,即使有人员偶尔疏忽、反应较慢,系统存在安全隐患,也不会立刻发生交通事故。

②当 M 在可控范围之外,即出现环境严重恶化时,H 和 M 变化曲线落入分叉集的概率增大,系统由危险状态突变成事故状态的概率也相应增加。其表明当航行环境和船舶性能较差时,人的不安全行为的增加会导致事故发生的概率变大。

(3)当 H 和 M 两控制变量同时恶化时,即人的不安全行为和物的不安全状态同时存在时,事故发生概率明显增大,并且事故的严重程度取决于 H、M 变量恶化的程度。H、M 的恶化程度越大,产生的事故越难以控制,形成的规模越大,造成的后果也越严重;反之,产生的事故容易得到及时的控制,后果影响一般也较轻。可见,海上交通事故等级可以通过系统势函数突跳释放的能量大小来判断。

5 突变理论在海上交通风险预控中的应用

由安全系统尖点突变模型可知,在控制平面上的系统特征演化曲线跨越分叉集程度越大(突跳值越大),系统势函数突跳释放的能量越大,事故也越严重。该模型解释了海上交通事故的突发现象。在同样的环境条件下,事故发生与否是随机的,但是通过研究安全系统的致因突变机理,可为研究海上交通事故的预控提供理论基础。虽然目前航海界认为事故突变不可控,但是从预防的目的出发,通过调节控制变量 H、M,尽量减小或推迟其变化曲线落入分叉集的概率与时间,可以对风险的可控性进行界定与度量,达到预控或预防的目的,这也为海上交通风险分析与预控研究提供新的思考空间。

(1)对于可控风险,通过对变化曲线的有效控制,减小变化曲线落入分叉集的概率。

①当 M 在可控范围内时,提高 H 的状态值,可以很大程度避免事故的发生,消除系统的隐患。

②当 H 在可控范围内时,相应改变或提高 M 的状态值,可以有效降低系统的隐患和事故的发生概率。

③当 H、M 在可控范围外,系统处于很差的状态 A_4 时,如果 H 的安全行为($A_4 \rightarrow A_3$)得以改善,然后再提高 M 的安全状态($A_3 \rightarrow A_2$),这样就可以绕过分叉集而不会发生突跳,避免事故的发生。

(2)对于不可控风险,从突变程度和突变时间两方面做好预防措施。

①通过对变化曲线的有限控制,缩短系统突变的跳跃距离,减少系统的跳跃势能,直接减小事故危害。反映到图2中为在分叉集 B 上趋近于原点 O 的有限控制点处才发生系统突变行为。

②通过推迟变化曲线落入分叉集,拖延系统突变的跳跃时间,减缓事故的发生。

6 结语

安全事故的突变模型不仅可以反映安全系统的风险形成过程,也可帮助人们预测系统发生重大事故的可能性和安全系统与重大事故内在的逻辑关系,对于防止事故尤其是重大事故的发生具有直接的现实意义[323,324]。

基于突变理论的海上交通安全系统演化[*]

摘要：为揭示系统本质，建立海上交通风险预控机制，基于突变理论对安全系统的演化行为进行研究。建立海上交通安全系统尖点突变模型，定义系统的安全、事故、风险状态，通过研究系统的演化原理，分析系统在不同状态间的演化模式，并探讨每种演化模式的实际应用。基于系统演化模式提出广义的海上交通风险预控模型，也是对 FSA 的完善。

关键词：海上交通；安全系统；演化模式；突变理论；风险预控

0 引言

保障海上交通安全一直是各国海事管理机构，尤其是国际海事组织（IMO）所极力追求的目标[325]。其中，最有效的方法就是通过找到事故致因，采取相应的措施，尽可能减少或避免同类事故的发生[326]。通过研究海上交通安全系统状态及演化模式，可以预测系统的未来变化，找出事故演化的突变路径，建立科学有效的海上交通风险预控机制。

1 突变理论在海上交通安全系统应用

海上交通安全系统由"人""船""环境"组成[327]，是一个复杂的动态系统。在深入研究三者各自特性的基础上，有必要从系统的总体特性出发，运用系统论方法，揭示系统演化的本质，从根本上提高系统的安全性。

突变理论用来描述动态系统在演化中出现的突变现象，已在海上安全评价领域得到应用[328]。应用突变理论的重点是寻找适合系统的势函数模型，通过对初等突变结构的选择[317]，建立海上交通安全系统势函数模型：

$$V(F) = F^4 + HF^2 + MF \tag{1}$$

其中：$V(F)$ 表示系统稳定能力；F 为状态变量，表示系统的安全性；H、M 为控制变量，分别表示人的因素（人）、物的因素（船、环境）。

突变势函数以参数（F、H、M）描述海上交通安全系统。假设系统原来处于势函数的一个全局极小点，当参数变化时，势函数的形状会有所变动，原来的全局极小点可能转化为一个局部极小点而不再是全局极小点，也可能消失。因此需要某种约定来研究系统在新突变势函数下所处的位置，以此判断系统的变化情况[317]。

（1）理想延迟约定：系统留在原来的稳定平衡位置上，直至该稳定平衡位置消失，如图 1

---

[*] 本文发表在《大连海事大学学报》2013 年第 4 期第 39 卷，作者齐迹、郑中义、李建民。

所示。

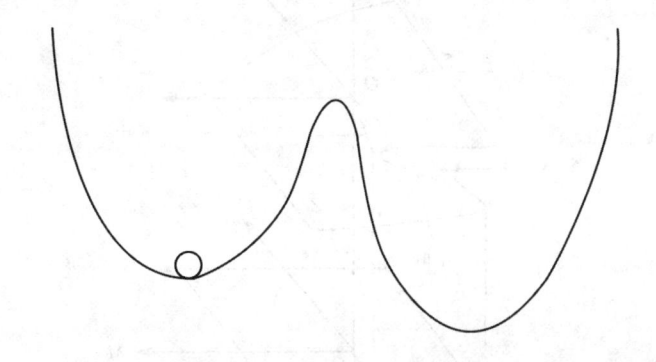

图1　理想延迟约定

(2) 全局约定：系统总是转移到使其势全局极小的稳定平衡位置，如图2所示。

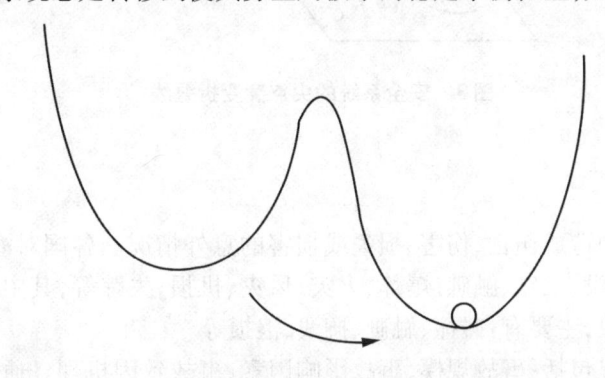

图2　全局约定

从两种约定可以看出，海上交通安全系统受参数影响，系统的稳定状态和安全状态实时改变。如图3所示，在同一空间坐标系中绘制海上交通安全系统的尖点突变折叠线，系统平衡曲面用 Z 表示，临界奇点集用 S 表示，控制平面 C 内分叉集用 B 表示，Z 上不同的点处于不同的状态，这些点随时间的变化形成一条行动轨迹，即系统特征演化曲线 L。当 L 变化时系统会处于不同的演化模式中，并对系统产生不同的影响。

2　海上交通安全系统状态分析

2.1　安全状态

所谓安全，是指在生产实践中，系统不受威胁，没有事故发生，因此安全与危险和事故是紧密相关的。通常用事故状况来表征危险情况，用危险和事故的情况来描述安全。事故多、危险大说明系统的安全状况较差，反之则说明安全状况较好[330]。

海上交通安全取决于政策或标准的量化，达到一定安全阈值就是"安全"。在图3中，Z 上叶部分的点就是系统的安全点，对应系统的安全状态。

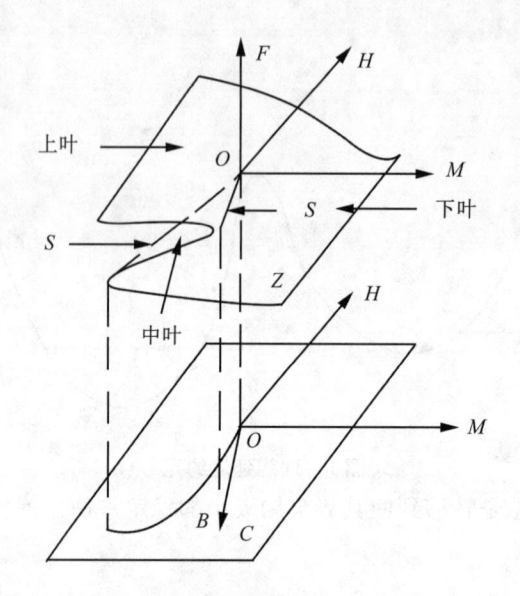

图 3　安全系统的尖点突变折叠线

2.2　事故状态

事故是生产实践中造成伤亡、伤害、损失或损害的意外情况。各国对海事的分类不同,大致分为:碰撞、搁浅、沉没、触碰、触礁、爆炸、火灾、风灾、机损、失踪等,其中与船舶交通有关的海事称为海上交通事故,主要有:碰撞、触礁、搁浅、浪损等[312]。

海上交通事故实况包括:事故规模、事故影响因素、事故致因机理。通过实况分析有利于吸取经验教训,避免类似事故的发生。图 3 中上叶和下叶的点通过 S 时就会发生事故,事故的种类与影响由控制变量的取值和通过 S 时系统突跳所释放的能量决定。

2.3　风险状态

风险是指生产实践中遭到损害的可能性,包括受损可能性的大小和损害程度,此外,还应考虑风险的转化方向,它是区分风险变化趋势的有力工具。

海上交通风险是海上交通安全系统在动态变化过程中出现海上交通事故的可能性。在图 3 中,上叶和下叶的点有通过 S 的趋势时,此时处于风险状态。

FSA 是一套系统的综合安全评估方法,用于提高海上运输安全。IMO 给出了 FSA 的基本步骤,其步骤实施基础是海上交通风险分类和可接受性标准的制定[331]。

(1)风险分类标准

基于不同的评价对象,风险造成的影响不同,导致风险分类具有模糊性。将风险后果用 n 维的空间向量表示,即

$$X = (X_1, X_2, \cdots, X_n) \tag{2}$$

其中: $X_1 = (x_1, 0, \cdots, 0), \cdots; X_n = (0, 0, \cdots, x_n); X_i$ 为待评价对象; x_i 为评价对象的损失。利用向量模型结合专家调查表可以基于船舶损耗、人员伤亡以及环境等视角给出分类标准。

(2) 风险的可接受性标准

根据 IMO 对 FSA 的建议，制定不同船舶种类的风险可接受标准[9]，用风险矩阵表示，如图 4 所示。

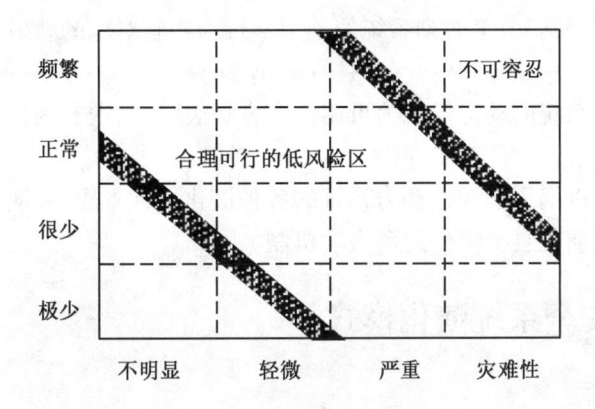

图 4　某类型船舶的风险矩阵

风险矩阵图将风险分为 3 个层次：①不可容忍：该区域风险非常大，是普遍不能接受的风险区域；②低风险区：该区域内采取预防和控制措施，一般不会引发安全问题；③可忽略：即可容忍风险，该区域风险较小，无预防措施也不会构成重大损失。

风险矩阵图能够全面反映事故发生的频率以及事故后果的严重性。

3　海上交通安全系统演化模式

3.1　海上交通安全系统演化原理

根据系统的势函数模型，得到平衡曲面 Z 的表达式：

$$V'(F) = 4F^3 + 2HF + M = 0 \tag{3}$$

式(3)为一元三次方程，按照判别式 $\Delta = 48(8H^3 + 27M^2)$ 的符号，根的形式为：

(1) $\Delta > 0$ 时，方程有 1 个实根；
(2) $\Delta = 0$ 时，方程有 3 个实根，其中 1 个根为两重根；
(3) $\Delta < 0$ 时，方程有 3 个不等实根。

通过判断 Δ 符号，导致方程根不同形式的变量是 H，当 H 从"$-\infty$"向"$+\infty$"变化时，可得到系统整体演化行为：(1) $H \geq 0$ 时，式(3)有唯一实根，系统稳定渐变；(2) $H < 0$ 时，式(3)有 3 个实根，系统不稳定，有突变可能。

通过对 L 变化分析，可以定义海上交通安全系统的演化模式：当 L 处于远离 S 的位置时，系统稳定在安全演化模式；当 L 受系统惯性作用通过 S 时，系统突变为事故演化模式；当 L 有通过 S 的趋势时，系统有发生突变可能，系统进入风险演化模式，即系统在演化过程中，演化模式随参数的变化而发生转换。为提高系统演化时间序列的精准度，采用胞映射理论[332]。对海上交通安全系统(将其视为非线性动力系统)进行全局分析，以"平滑"削弱观测初值的随机性和系统的内在随机性对系统动力学模式的影响。

设 n 维动力系统的非线性动力学方程为：
$$dx_t/dt = f_t(x_1, x_2, \cdots x_n; a_t) \tag{4}$$
其中：x_t 为系统状态变量；a_t 为控制变量。

设 ζ 为胞向量，将 n 到 $n+1$ 时刻系统的动力学行为用胞对胞的映射表示，有
$$\zeta(n+1) = c\zeta(n) \tag{5}$$
对于广义胞映射，系统的动力学行为可用概率方程表示，其中 p 为概率矩阵。
$$\xi(n+1) = p\xi(n) \tag{6}$$
利用上面关系，可以揭示非线性动力系统的各种演化特性本质，并演绎模式之间的相互转化，从整体上反映系统演化直至突变的动力学机制。

3.2 海上交通安全系统演化模式

(1) 安全演化模式

由定义可知，安全是系统不受威胁，没有事故发生的状态，当 L 远离 S，且在 Z 的上叶变化时，将其视为系统的安全演化模式。

基于系统的安全演化模式，可开展海上交通安全状况评价，即对系统的安全状况进行定量和定性评估，其目的是判别系统是否达到规定的安全目标及安全要求，并根据评价结果，制定相应的决策或控制方案。安全是通过风险程度来表述的，因此可通过风险评价间接得到系统的安全等级。

(2) 事故演化模式

事故演化模式分为两种情况：

① $H \geqslant 0$ 时，L 从 Z 的上叶渐变到下叶，由于参数 M 的变化导致机械、载运工具的损耗，最终发生事故。这种属于事故渐变模式，其影响一般不大。

② $H < 0$ 时，L 受系统惯性作用通过 S 发生事故。这种属于事故突变模式，事故的影响取决于 L 越过 S 时系统释放的能量。

(3) 风险演化模式

当 L 有通过 S 的趋势时，视为系统处于风险演化模式。风险演化时既有从上叶向下叶转化的客观过程，也有从下叶向上叶转化的主观行为。建立海上交通风险模型：
$$R = f(R_D, R_B, R_A) \tag{7}$$
其中：R_D 为风险演化方向（设定系统由安转危时，$R_D = +1$；反之，$R_D = -1$）；R_B 为风险突变的可能性；R_A 为风险突变后果。

在交通活动中不可能完全根除一切危害和危险，因此系统风险演化模式是研究系统动力行为的核心。对系统的风险模式进行预测，可以制订相应的海上交通风险预控方案，有效减少事故的发生。

4 基于系统演化海上交通风险预控

相对陆上交通而言，海上交通具有明显的复杂性。通过研究海上交通安全系统的动力学特征，阐述了系统演化的普适性原理。进一步对演化模式深入研究，可以建立科学有效的海上

交通风险预控机制,这也是对 FSA 体系的完善[333]。建立广义的海上交通风险预控模型:
$$R_{P-C} = f(R, P, P_{-C}, C) \tag{8}$$

其中:R 为海上交通风险模型,系统的安全状态取决于风险综合评价结果;P 为海上交通风险预测模型,用于预测宏观交通流、海域的风险等级;P_{-C} 为海上交通风险预测控制模型,包含系统突变点、突变方向、突变时间、风险致因能力、风险致因效率等因素,可为系统控制提供可控性方案;C 为海上交通风险控制模型,根据不同的控制方案用于系统的控制研究,基于此制定针对风险的保护措施,会对相应职能部门履职产生影响。

5 结语

本文基于突变理论对安全系统的演化行为进行研究,这是突变理论在海上交通风险预控领域的开拓性应用。在此基础上深入研究可以建立科学有效的海上交通风险预控机制。

Risk Mutability Analysis and Pre-control of Dynamical System*

Abstract: Based on systematical research on catastrophe theory, system dynamics is a general theory to describe dynamical systems with the goal of achieving structural stability and dynamic stability. In this paper, catastrophe model of dynamic system is established and elements of the system are defined as well. Conditions for system structure mutating are also defined via analysis on dynamism, fuzziness and mutability of system structure. In view of the fact that modes and strength of disturbance or damage to system structural stability are two decisive factors for major accident occurrence and consequences, the course of disturbance or damage can be deemed as the process of quantitative evaluation of major accident risks. Hence, by adopting combination of qualitative and quantitative methods and with the help of simulation technology, decision-makers can do researches on industrial control process to make scientific and effective pre-control.

Keywords: Dynamic system; Structural stability; Catastrophe model; Risk mutability analysis; Risk evaluation; Risk pre-control

0 Introduction

System dynamics (also referred to as dynamic system) is a theory employed to represent general motion system. In general all dynamic differential equation of higher order can be converted into a first order differential equation group to study. The objective of system dynamics research is to achieve stability of dynamic system (i. e. normal state of the system), so regulation or control of various system elements is needed for this purpose[1]. In other words, regulation or control is an approach to force the system to transform in predetermined direction by means of maintaining or changing system conditions until the stability of a dynamical system is achieved. In the dynamic system, both the occurrence of any major accident and its consequences are determined by the modes and strength of disturbance or damage to system structural stability[2]. The course of disturbance or damage can be deemed as a process that incurs accident risk. Since the process can be precisely computed in light of system dynamics approach, it is the quantitative evaluation of major accident risks in essence.

Therefore, it is advisable for decision-makers to adopt principles and methods of system dy-

---

* 本文发表在《大连海事大学学报》2013 年第 4 期第 39 卷,作者 Ji Qi, Zhongyi Zheng, Jianmin Li。

namics to analyze actual system and subsequently establish concept model and quantitative model integrated system dynamics model. By employing qualitative and quantitative combined methods and with the aid of simulation technology, it is impossible for decision-makers to conduct researches on engineering, social and economic systems so as to make scientific and effective pre-control[3].

1 Mutation model of dynamic system

As catastrophe theory is an important component of system theory, which mainly studies the catastrophe phenomenon of dynamic system in the process of evolution[4], any dynamic system can be described by a potential function[5]. We can create a cusp potential function model of dynamic system as following:

$$V(F) = (F - F_s)^4 + (H - H_s)(F - F_s)^2 + (M - M_s)(F - F_s) \quad (1)$$

Where $V(F)$ represents the ability of system to keep current situation, namely the inertia of system; F means overall safety status of system; H is the subdivision factor, which decides the mutation behavior of the system; M is the regular factor, which determines the mutation process of the system; H_s, M_s, F_s are inherent characteristic quantities, respectively represent H, M, F corresponding critical equilibrium point in the system.

The profile of equilibrium Z consists of an infinite number of equilibrium points which meets formula: $\partial V/\partial F = 0$. Then the singularity set S, as well as a subset of Z, is able to be got when $\partial^2 V/\partial F^2 = 0$. Finally the expression of bifurcation set B (2) is able to be obtained from the two formulas above. The curves which cross the bifurcation set would result in catastrophe of system status, which reveals the origin of system traffic accidents occurrence essentially.

$$\Delta = 8(H - H_s)^3 + 27(M - M_s)^2 = 0 \quad (2)$$

If the point (H, M) cross the bifurcation, the value of F will be mutated. This is the criterion of the dynamic system risk mutability.

2 The risk mutability analysis of the dynamic system

The characteristics of dynamic system determine many outstanding uncertainties of system risk[6]:

(1) Dynamics: When the system is unstable in middle layer in Figure 1, it would likely leap to upper layer or to lower layer. This is called "dual-mode" in the process of risk evolution, which shows the dynamic property of system risks.

(2) Fuzziness: Dynamic leads to the fuzziness of risk evolution direction. Fuzziness makes all points on S own various evolution trends. Small variations of S parameters would cause greater difference in system final state.

(3) Mutability: Due to system inertia, when L varies continuously and moves to the singularity set S, it will cause system state change suddenly[7], which means traffic risk evolves into

traffic accident.

In this paper, to study conveniently, the word "catastrophe" is selected as the unified expression to describe mutation.

In order to overcome the effects of system uncertainty, fuzzy catastrophe theory, inspired by idea that apply theory of fuzzy mathematics to catastrophe, is put forward to solve the flaws brought by fuzziness and mutability of risk.

Given that the uncertainty of system potential function is caused by control variable u (suppose $u > 0$), then u is dealt with by fuzzy processing to be $\tilde{u} = E + u$. Formula (1) shows ($H - H_s$) and ($M - M_s$) are original hypothesis for $\tilde{u} = E + u$. If variable E is set as triangular fuzzy structural units, the membership function of $\tilde{u}$ is got as $E(x - u)$, then fuzzy equilibrium surface $\tilde{Z}$ will satisfy $d\bar{V}(x)/dx = R_0$, among them " $= R$" means limiting operation, which makes u_i's support set $Supp\tilde{u}$ satisfy limiting type $u_i = \tilde{u} = E + u$.

Finally the fuzzy singular equation is sorted out and solved, the membership degree $\mu_{E+u}(0)$ of the membership function will be obtained, which means possibility of system catastrophe. Fuzzy bifurcation set is expressed by $\tilde{B}$, and $\tilde{B}(0) \in [0,1]$. With catastrophe theory, it can be concluded unquestionably that system has catastrophe possibility when $\tilde{B}(0) > 0$.

$$\tilde{B}(0) = \mu_{E+u}(0) \tag{3}$$

After control variable is dealt with by fuzzy processing, fuzzy system is expressed as a bunch of potential function $V_i(x)$, $i = 1,2,\cdots,k$. u_i ($i = 1,2,\cdots,k$) is the statistic of item i among system control variable $\tilde{u}$. Then $\tilde{u}$ can be got by mathematical expectation u and standard deviation $d(u)$. Given $\tilde{u} = f(E) = u + \delta E$, the membership function of $\tilde{u}$ is shown as:

$$\tilde{u}(x) = E[f^{-1}(E)] = E[(x - \bar{u})/\delta] \tag{4}$$

When the standard fuzzy bifurcation set of system was expressed as B, the expression is shown as:

$$\bar{B}(0) = \mu_{\delta E+\bar{u}}(0) \tag{5}$$

In order to reduce the error brought by external factors in controlling process, the expression value of control variable is set as u_b. The actual utility value is set as u_s, and expressed by fuzzy number $\tilde{U}$, which is limited by control condition and environment. As the degree of system catastrophe is determined by u_s to $\bar{B}$, the possibility of system catastrophe which is caused by variable u_b is shown as:

$$B = \min[\tilde{U}(u_b = u_s), \bar{B}(0)] \tag{6}$$

Given that E_1 and E_2 respectively represent the triangular fuzzy number of ($\tilde{H}, \delta_1$) and ($\tilde{H}, \delta_2$), following formula can be obtained from formula (1) dealt with fuzzy processing:

$$\tilde{V}(F) = F^4 + \bar{H}F^2 + \bar{M}F \tag{7}$$

When $\bar{B}(0) > 0$, the system catastrophe probability is shown as:

$$\bar{B}(0) = \min[E_1(-\frac{\bar{H}+6F^2}{\delta_1}), E_2(-\frac{\bar{M}-8F^3}{\delta_2})] \tag{8}$$

Taking the error caused by external factors into consideration, the final catastrophe probability of dynamic system is shown as:

$$B = \min[\tilde{U}(u_b = u_s), E_1(-\frac{\bar{H}+6F^2}{\delta_1}), E_2(-\frac{\bar{M}-8F^3}{\delta_2})] \tag{9}$$

3 The risk pre-control decision of the dynamic system

Risk modeling provides basis theoretically for the risk evaluation of dynamic system. Considering the fact that $R + F = 1$, the comprehensive evaluation and decision-making of R can be indirectly achieved by utilizing catastrophe progression method to multi-level decompose the evaluation target.

However, some flaws exist in practical application[8]:

(1) Sorting process of index weight often mixes unbearable subjectivities, which will affect the objectivity of evaluation results.

(2) It is obviously unscientific that defining certain evaluation indexes with fuzziness to accurate values.

Fuzzy catastrophe progression evaluation method is put forward to evaluate risk accordingly, and the key of which is treating fuzzy numbers[9].

The index u_{ij} of evaluation object u_i is observed in column to obtain a digital series $x_1, x_2, \cdots, x_k$, of which mean, variance and standard deviation is represented by $U(u_{ij})$, $Var(u_{ij})$, $\delta(u_{ij})$ respectively.

Known from structured element theory, there is $R = f(E)$ in the interval of $[-1,1]$. The analysis formula f can be obtained from membership function of $E(x)$:

$$f(x) = \delta(u_{ij})x + U(u_{ij}) \tag{10}$$

Given H_E is fuzzy functional in $[-1,1]$ derived from E, considering $\tilde{T}$, $\tilde{W}$ are limited fuzzy numbers, it's easy to know that $g_1 \in H_E^{-1}(\tilde{T})$, $g_2 \in H_E^{-1}(\tilde{W})$. Formula (11) is the structured element ordering formula of fuzzy numbers.

$$d_E(\tilde{T}, \tilde{W}) = \int_{-1}^{1}[g_1(x) - g_2(x)]dx \tag{11}$$

The evaluation indexes can be normalized according to formula (11). Suppose the vector group of fuzzy risk value is $\tilde{R} = (\tilde{R}_1, \tilde{R}_2, \cdots, \tilde{R}_k)$, among which $\tilde{R}_i = f_i(E)$, and $f_{\max}(E)$, $f_{\min}(E)$ are respectively maximum and minimum value of fuzzy array, the fuzzy numbers normalized formula (12), as well as membership function formula (13) can be obtained via formula

(11) combined with same ordering transformation formula $-f(E) = f^{\tau 1}(E)$, $1/f(E) = f^{\tau 2}(E)$ of monotonic bounded function[10].

$$e\tilde{R}_i = [f_i(E) - f_{\max}(E)]/[f_{\max}(E) - f_{\min}(E)] = [(f_i + f_{\min}^1)(f_{\max} + f_{\min}^1)^{\tau 2}]E \quad (12)$$

$$\tilde{R}^{1/k} = [f(E)]^{1/k} = g[f(E)] \quad (13)$$

When the membership function of $\tilde{R}$ satisfies the formula $\mu_{\tilde{R}}(x) = \sup_{x=(x_1+\cdots+x_k)/k} \min[\mu_{\tilde{R}_i}(x_i)]$, the expression of $\tilde{R}$ is shown as:

$$\tilde{R} = (\tilde{R}_1 \oplus \tilde{R}_2 \oplus \cdots \oplus \tilde{R}_k)/k = (f_1 + f_2 + \cdots + f_k)(E)/k \quad (14)$$

Further on given that the object of system evaluation are the safety state F_1 and F_2, and the control variables H and M in formula (1) is multi-level decompose to H (human factor), S (machine factor) and C (environment factor), the comprehensive fuzzy catastrophe evaluation model of dynamic system can be established as following:

$$F_i(x) = [H_i^{1/h}(x) + S_i^{1/j}(x) + C_i^{1/k}(x)]/3 \quad (15)$$

Considering $F_i(x)$ is bounded and monotonically increasing function in $[-1,1]$, the risk pre-control decision of the dynamic system can be described as following:

$$D_{12} = \int_{-1}^{1} |F_1(x) - F_1(x)| dx \quad (16)$$

The ordering relation of fuzzy numbers can be got according to the positive or negative of D_{12} in formula (16), in which we can know that the greater the value of ordering relation, the better F_1 than F_2. The comprehensive evaluation and scientific and reasonable pre-dontrol decision-making is depending on the conclusion above[11].

The equation $f(x) = x^{1/k}$ on interval $[0,1]$ can be pictured by MATLAB (shown in Figure 1). The final decision-making depends on the ordering relation D_{12}. The utilization of risk decision-making model deals with the differences among values effectively[12]. And the ordering relation of system decision-making can be given by accumulating the difference between the two functions. The ordering relation result can be the basis of final pre-control decision-making and fully proves the scientific and rationality of fuzzy catastrophe progression evaluation method. The final pre-dontrol decision-making resulted by comparing the value of ordering relation D_{12} is that F_1 state owns the lowest risky level and is safer than F_1.

Catastrophe progression method has advantage of preserving the fuzzy characteristic of the original parameters by the fuzzy processing. In this way, system safety state F_1 and F_2 can be calculated in the form of safety interval to evaluate the system safety level (or to get the system risk level indirectly) and predict the evolution trend of system state [13].

In the light of dynamics model which based on catastrophe theory and fuzzy mathematics, the risk of dynamic system is to be evaluated, the influence of various elements of the dynamic system is able to be analyzed too[14]. Both of them will contribute to the risk pre-control decision-making and the practice for the dynamical systems.

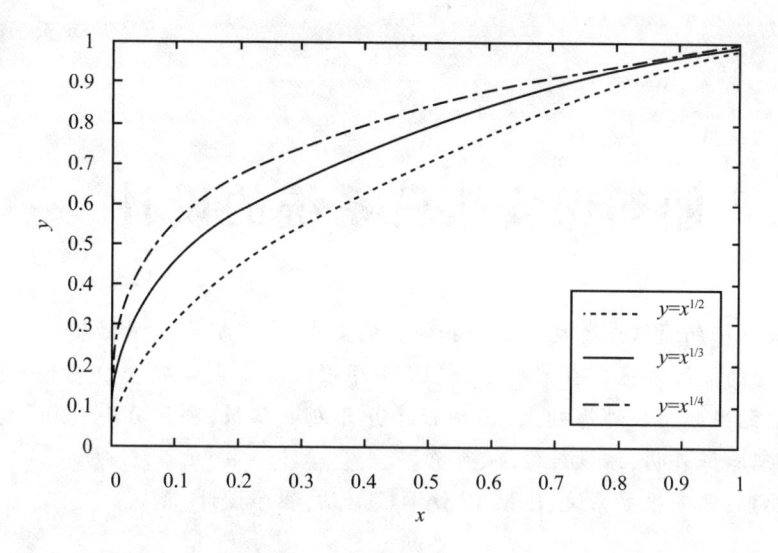

Figure 1 The curve of $x^{1/k}$ ($k = 2, 3, 4$) on $[0,1]$ interval

4 Conclusion

A universal dynamic system based on catastrophe theory was developed in the paper. It is the pioneering application of catastrophe theory in the field of dynamic engineering. Moreover, the flaws that evolution of dynamic system is often interfered with by uncertain factors are solved by putting forward to the fuzzy catastrophe theory. Then by modeling dynamic system risk, a comprehensive fuzzy catastrophe evaluation method was presented to pre-control decision-making and evaluating the system safety state. The implement of the work has directly significant and realistic meaning to industrial technologies, such as materials processing, traffic safety control, and environment protection, etc.

船舶保安报警系统的设计[*]

摘要:为减少船舶通信设备购置和维护保养的支出,本文提出利用船舶已经安装的通信设备完成保安报警的设计方案。在系统分析《1974年国际海上人命安全公约》关于保安报警设备功能要求、船站内部指令的基础上,编制程序并开发电路板,利用TT-3020C终端实现保安报警功能。实船验证表明,该设计经济、可靠。

关键词:船舶;保安报警系统;INMARSAT C 船站;程序设计

0 引言

船舶保安报警系统是旨在加强海上保安,基于一定通信平台,设计、安装于船舶上并用于船舶保安报警的通信系统[334]。

根据《1974年国际海上人命安全公约》(以下简称《公约》)第XI-2章第6条的要求,系统应该隐蔽工作,不允许报警信号被无关台站接收。鉴于通信终端体积小、重量轻、保密性强[335]等优点,目前多采用卫星通信手段实现保安报警,诸如铱星系统、INMARSAT C、Mini C、INMARSAT D + 等[336]。在设计理念上,多数方案要求船舶为实现保安报警功能安装专用的通信设施。但如果能够利用船舶已经安装的、较成熟的通信设备实现报警,无疑是一种经济、可靠的方式。为此,本文针对TT-3020C系列船站设计专用报警器,使一台C船站同时满足《公约》第Ⅳ章和第XI-2章的要求,即同时拥有GMDSS和保安报警两项功能。系统的研究和设计主要包括:系统主流程程序、初始化配置程序、航行数据调用程序、启动测试与报警程序、电文生成与发送程序、电文回执处理程序、E-mail 报警程序[337]等。本文主要研究系统的组成与工作流程、报警电文的形成与发送。

1 保安报警系统设计

1.1 保安报警系统功能

根据《公约》第XI-2章第6条的要求,系统应该具有下述功能:
(1)报警系统启动后向主管机关指定的当局,包括船舶公司发送船对岸形式的保安报警,表明船舶身份、船位、航向及航速等,并指出船舶的保安状况受到威胁。

---

[*] 本文发表在《大连海事大学学报》2010年第1期第36卷,作者李建民、郑中义、李红喜。

(2)除主管机关指定的当局,报警信息不应该被其他任何无关单位接收。

(3)系统应该隐蔽报警,不允许工作时发出任何警示信息。

(4)报警时无须手动调节报警器和通信设备,如调谐信道、选择菜单等。

(5)系统包含至少两个启动点,分别位于驾驶台和其他位置。启动时无须移动铅封或打开盖子、封条就能够让一个无线电通信系统持续运转发送报警。

(6)具有防止误报警的功能。

(7)保安报警系统具有测试功能,一般包括内部链路和无线链路的测试[338]。

另外,《公约》第Ⅺ-2章第6条还规定,船舶可以使用为符合《公约》第Ⅳ章要求安装的无线电设备实现保安报警,但是不允许由于船舶保安报警系统的启动削弱 GMDSS 装置的功能[338]。

1.2　TT-3020C 船站指令

方案设计中调用了大量的 C 船站内部通信指令,其中重要的包括:

(1)"se-u"指令:船站水上移动业务码设置与显示指令。

(2)"se-p"指令:命令 INMARSAT C 船站传送船位信息。

(3)"se-o"指令:请求 INMARSAT C 船站传回预置洋区、目前网络协调站(NCS)代码、名称和卫星同步情况。

(4)"st-t"指令:请求船站传回"发送记录列表",供报警后查询发送状态时使用。

(5)"transfer"指令:在 C 船站存储器中建立一个新文件。

(6)"tx"指令:命令 C 船站发送电文。格式为:tx < filename > < options >。

"option"选项中与本文设计方案相关的主要有:"-a""-c""-e""-h""-l""-n""-s""-v""-t"等[339,340]。

1.3　系统组成框图

保安报警系统利用已经装船的 INMARSAT C 系统通信,但是工作时不应影响船站的正常工作[341]。为此,采取中断服务方式,报警设备与控制计算机并联到 C 终端,具体如图 1 所示。4 个按钮分别提供报警、测试和配置键盘等;RS232 接口芯片实现电平转换;根据按钮的状态和 RS232TX 引脚电平的情况,CPU 发出指令控制模拟多路控制开关状态;模拟多路控制开关决定 C 船站的使用权归属;通过 3 个指示灯的灯质表明系统运行状态。

2　系统初始化配置与主要航行参数的获得

系统接通电源后检测自身配置状态。如果检测发现自身数据配置不完整,将执行相应的配置子程序。对于多数的缺失配置数据,系统启动配置指示灯提醒操作员手动完成配置;少数配置数据,例如水上移动业务码等,系统可以发送指令自动从 C 船站内部获得。

2.1　CPU 初始化

CPU 初始化主要包括:端口初始化;通用异步接收发送设备初始化;实时时钟初始化;定

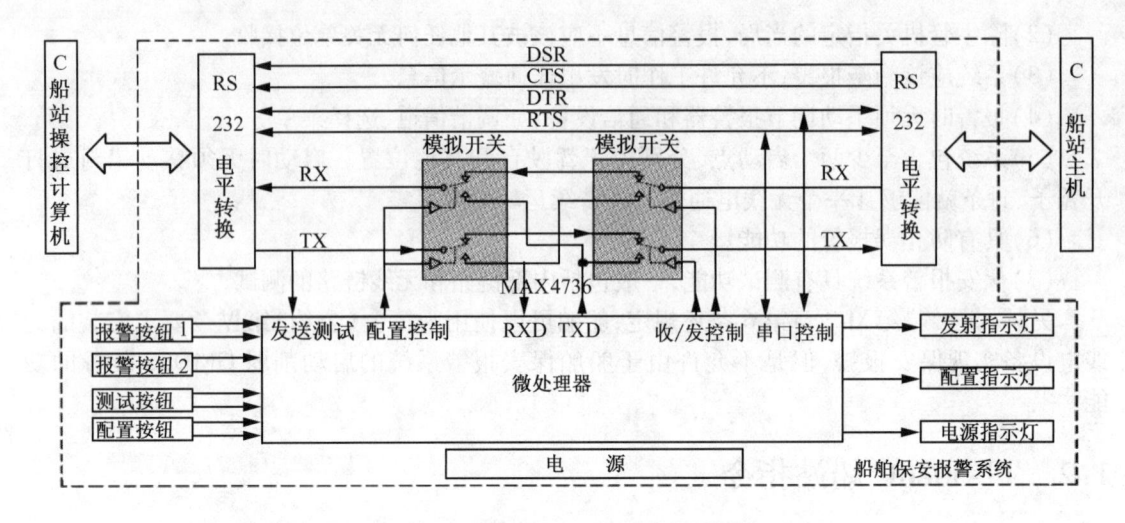

图1 保安报警系统组成方框图

时器初始化；ISP 初始化；键盘中断初始化；"看门狗"初始化等。

2.2 中断服务申请

报警系统通过中断服务的形式完成工作。当报警按钮、测试按钮或者配置按钮被按下时，分别形成不同的键盘中断申请。CPU 获得中断申请后启动相应的中断服务子程序，完成测试、报警、配置等工作。进入中断服务前，CPU 首先核实 C 船站的工作状态。完成相应服务后 CPU 回到主程序或者继续其他中断服务。

2.3 自动配置水上移动业务码

初始化结束后，CPU 检测保安报警系统水上移动业务码配置情况。由于不允许保安报警系统工作时影响 GMDSS 设备的正常功能，保安报警系统首先查询 INMARSAT C "是否空闲"。如果 C 船站处于"空闲"状态，CPU 经过一定延时后，会以同样的方式再次确认。确认无误后，保安报警系统 CPU 将触发开关电路 MAX4736 翻转，"切断"C 船站控制计算机和 IN-MARSAT C 主机的通信链路，同时系统自身和 INMARSAT C 终端连接。连接后报警系统向船站发送"se-u"指令，请求船站发送水上移动业务码。收到应答数据后，报警系统进入接收中断服务子程序，处理存储收到的数据并完成相应的自动配置，最后系统结束该中断服务程序。

2.4 自动获得位置信息

系统运行时 CPU 一直检测实时时钟的计时情况。在本方案中，为不影响船站的 GMDSS 功能，同时尽可能获得"近于实时"的船位，保安报警系统每 10 min 查询一次船位，实时时钟为此提供了计时参数。当条件满足时 MAX4736 发生翻转，系统利用"se-p"指令获得有关航行数据信息。船站的典型应答格式如表 1 所示。

表1　C船站航行数据信息应答格式

```
< enter >
Position：< STX > 56 44 43 N 012 28 61 E < ETX > at 15:52:
          22 UTC < STX > Valid < ETX > < enter >
Course：< STX > 245 < ETX > deg/true north < enter >
Speed：< STX > 00 < ETX > knots;0001 kmph;0000 mph < enter > < enter >
```

回到主程序后,CPU进一步查询报警系统的设置状态,包括密码、报警地址是否被正确设置等,并且通过指示灯显示配置状态。

3　保安报警电文生成与发送

为防止误报警,本文设计如下:

(1)利用"se-o"检测卫星船站工况;

(2)保安报警按钮必须持续按下一定时间(32 s)才开始发送报警报文,该功能可以通过自锁方式实现;

(3)为防止由于按钮机械抖动引起的误触发,发射程序启动前有20 ms的延时;

(4)发射和测试按钮采用自锁式双触点开关,包括一个常开触点(NO)和一个常闭触点(NC),只有以上两个触点的状态同时发生翻转时,系统才启动发射程序,保证系统工作安全、可靠。

系统报警时启动程序并发送"se-o"后启动定时器1。在定时器1中断服务中,系统完成报文的整个发送过程。

定时器1启动后CPU检测接收中断子程序中收到的洋区码情况,如果成功获得洋区码,说明船站和卫星链路正常,可以进行下一步操作,洋区码也是后面调取地面站的依据;同时CPU检测按钮状态,判断报警的虚实。如果不满足报警条件,定时器1停止、32 s和5 min计数值全部清零,并且退出本次报警状态。当条件满足报警要求时,系统开始查询刚才是否已经发送一次报警电文,如果:

(1)刚刚发送过电文,系统进入回执查询程序模块。

(2)没有发送过电文,CPU启动新一轮报警程序。

如果条件如(2)所述,CPU会每20 ms检测一次遇险报警按钮的状态,同时32 s计数值计数,以此核实报警按钮是否持续按下,当:

(1)满足32 s时,CPU判定系统属于正确报警操作,执行以后的流程。

(2)否则,CPU将判定该操作属于误操作,系统复原。经查询,条件满足(1)所述,系统进入回执查询状态,并且20 s计数值和5 min计数值计数。其中,20 s是CPU查询报文回执的周期,5 min计数值是设定的发送周期。在"已经发送过电文"的前提下,如果:

(1)20 s时间没到,程序转到结束状态,即本次循环结束。

(2)如果到了20 s,CPU发出"st-t"指令,询问报文发送状态,也就是查询回执情况。发送查询指令后,20 s计数值归零,表明为期20 s的回执查询过程结束一次。回执的情况会在相关接收中断服务中处理、存储,CPU根据回执情况决定报文是否需要重发。

如果在一个发送周期(5 min)没有收到地面站的有效回执，CPU做出"需要重新发送"的判断。无论是第一次发送保安报警电文，还是经过回执判断后需要重新发送电文，系统均进入"新的发送周期"。

可见，在两种情况下系统启动发射报警程序：经过CPU判断，以前从未发送报警；系统在5 min没有收到有效的回执。报警发送流程如图2所示。

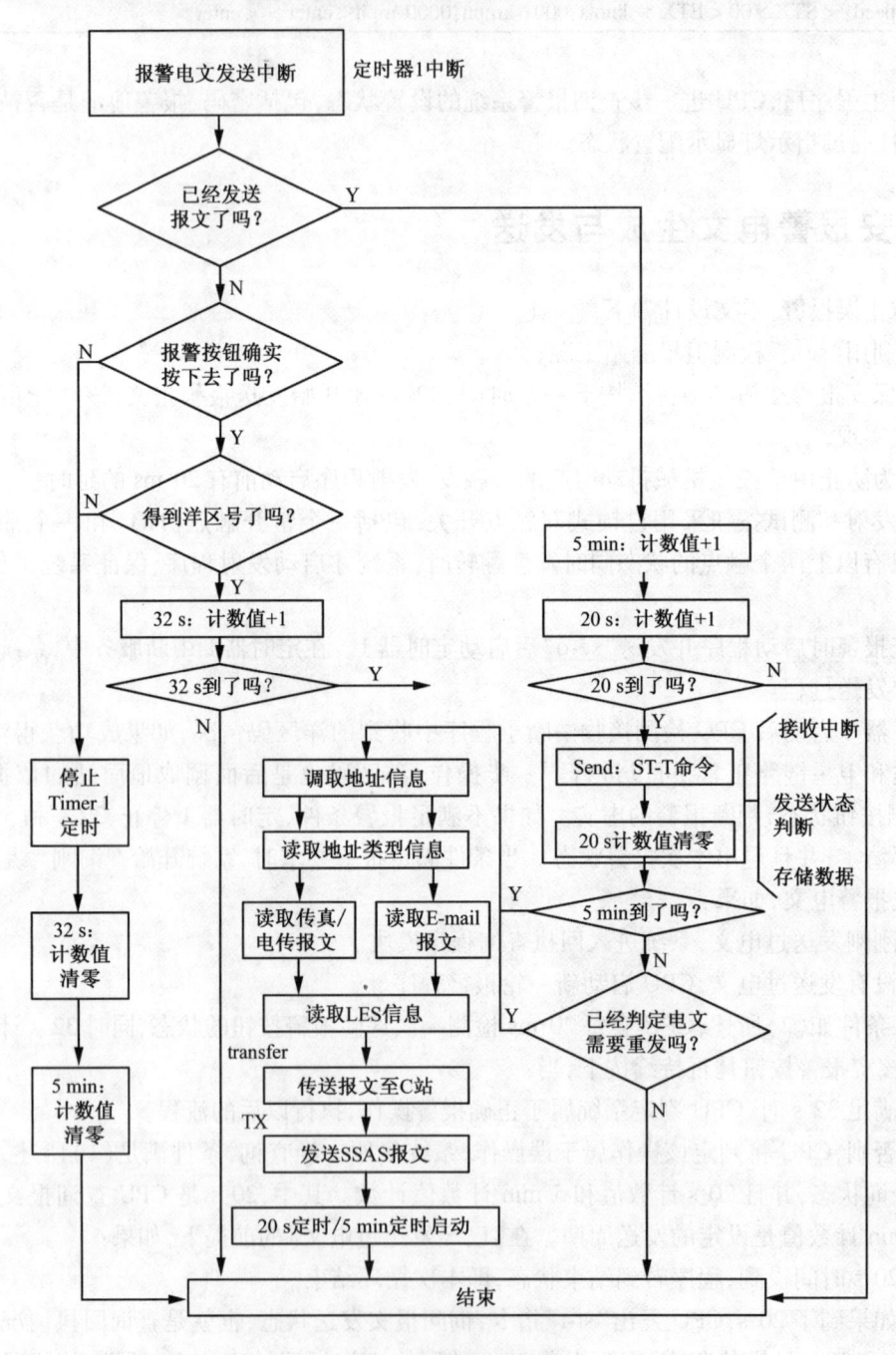

图2 报警发送流程图

保安报警电文生成时,系统:

(1)到 eeprom 中读取配置的收件人地址和地址类型等信息。

(2)根据发送报警的不同地址类型,调取相应格式的报警电文。

(3)读取地面站信息。在读取该信息时,CPU 根据从 INMARSAT C 获得的洋区码信息,到 eeprom 中调用预先配置、适合目前洋区的地面站作为首选;如果首选地面站发送失败,CPU 还可以随机调用其他的地面站。通过上述方法,遇险报文发送的速度和可靠性均可以得到保障。

(4)汇总前面得到的地址信息(Address),同时调取相关航行资料(IMN、Position、Course、Speed、UTC 等)形成报警电文,并且把电文存为文本文件。

(5)调用 INMARSAT C 船站内部指令"transfer < filename > -b"将前面已经编辑好的文本文件发送到船站中。

(6)汇总地面站信息(LES)、地址类型信息(type)、地址类型参数(param)、电文名称(filename)等诸元,形成"tx"内部指令。方案设计时强制 E-mail 信息经由"station12"提交用户,所以选择 E-mail 报警时"param"参数被程序默认为"400",地面站信息默认为"X12",其中"X"表示洋区:"1"、"2"、"3"或者"0"。

(7)为使打印机静默,在内部指令"tx"后面加上选项"-n"。

(8)为以后查询回执,在内部指令"tx"后面加上选项"-v"。

(9)利用完整的"tx"内部指令命令 INMARSAT C 主机发射报警信息。

(10)结束本次中断服务。

INMARSAT C 获得完整的"tx"指令后开始执行发送任务。此时保安报警系统启动 20 s 和 5 min 定时,为查询回执和重复发送信息做准备。

本文开发设计实物图如图 3 所示。

图 3 开发设计实物图

4 结论

本文在设计中充分考虑了《公约》对船舶保安报警系统、GMDSS 系统的要求,在不妨碍船舶正常通信安全的前提下,利用目前航运通信市场上保有量较大的 TT-3020C 实现了保安报警,减少了设备保养及安装支出。实船测试证明该方法是可行的,也是经济、可靠的[342]。

基于熵与耗散理论的海上危险化学品运输系统[*]

摘要：本文充分考虑海上危险化学品运输的复杂性和不确定性，并基于熵与耗散理论，从"人""船""货""环境"四个方面对海上危险化学品运输系统的安全性进行研究，提出系统安全熵概念并建立安全熵模型，用于海上危险化学品运输系统的安全评价。

关键词：海上危险品；运输系统；不确定性；耗散理论；系统安全熵；系统安全评价

0 引言

海上货物运输是一个典型的复杂社会系统，人们一般从"人""船""环境"三个方面对其安全性进行研究。其中的"船"因素，人们研究较多的是船舶本身的性能，货物特性只是影响性能的一个因素。危险化学品具有易燃易爆、急性与慢性毒性作用、与其他物质或者本身反应（或聚合）、生物毒害积聚和沿食物链传导等特性。因此，有必要从"人""船""货""环境"四个方面对海上危险化学品运输系统的安全性进行研究[312, 343]。"货"因素的引入使海上危险化学品运输系统的复杂性明显增强，需要研究新的方法对其安全性进行评价。

1 海上危险化学品运输系统的复杂性

相对于线性系统而言，复杂系统多是非线性的，系统各元素之间既具有相互因果关系，又具有不确定关系。海上危险化学品运输系统是一个典型的复杂系统，具有以下几个特点。

（1）开放性。海上交通安全系统是一个开放系统，时刻与外部环境之间存在物质、能量与信息的交换。危险化学品运输是海上交通安全系统的特例。

（2）动态性。首先，海上危险化学品运输系统本身是动态的，包括航海环境的变化、人员的变更、管理体系的更新等。其次，危险化学品船舶承载的货物具有明显的动态特性，例如货物理化等特性的变化。

（3）不可逆性。当系统状态不可人为地再现时，系统就具有不可逆性。危险化学品运输系统是典型的不可逆系统，一旦货物出现泄漏或者理化反应，系统状态经常是不可逆的。

（4）不确定性。由于海上危险化学品运输中环境因素的随机性和模糊性，其系统风险具有典型的不确定性特征。

（5）突变性。无论是海上危险化学品运输系统控制参数的变化，还是危险化学品货物理化特性的变化，如温度、压力、含水量等，都可能导致海上危险化学品运输系统状态的突变。

---

[*] 本文发表在《大连海事大学学报》2013年第1期第39卷，作者李建民、齐迹、郑中义、李红喜。

2 熵理论及其应用

"熵"主要用来度量系统的无序程度,对复杂系统的研究至关重要。开放系统的熵用 dS 表示,包括熵流和系统内部熵产生两部分,即 $dS = dS_e + dS_i$,其中 dS_e 表示熵流(可以是正数或者负数,也可以为零);dS_i 表示系统内部熵的产生(为非负数),因此,$dS \geq dS_e$。通过分析可知,dS 的变化决定了系统的状态。

(1)若 $dS = 0$,即 $dS_i = -dS_e$,系统处于定态;

(2)若 $dS > 0$,则负熵流不足以抵消系统产生的熵(包含外界供给正熵流的情况),即系统状态不稳定,需要改进甚至重新规划系统路径,降低路径中的潜在能量;

(3)若 $dS < 0$,负熵流充分,安全系统处于良性状态,并且向更加有序的方向发展。

熵概念已在热力学、统计物理学、信息论中得到充分的解释和发展。在熵的概念中,如果随机变量 X 取值 x_k 的可能性为 $P(x_k)$,则一个随机产生的事件所包含的信息本体数量:

$$I(x_k) = \lg \frac{1}{P(x_k)} = -\lg P(x_k) \tag{1}$$
$$k = 1, 2, \cdots, K$$

对所有信息量进行统计评价即可得到整个系统的平均不确定性,即系统的熵。香农进而提出了离散随机变量的信息熵公式:

$$H(X) = H(p_1, p_2, \cdots, p_k) = \sum p_k I(x_k) = -\sum_{k=1}^{K} p_k \lg p(x_k) \tag{2}$$
$$0 \leq p_k \leq 1, \quad \sum_{k=1}^{K} p_k = 1$$

其中:p_k 为危险化学品运输系统中第 k 个危险因素的权重[344,345]。

3 危险化学品运输系统耗散结构特征

耗散理论是布里津对物理-化学系统的动力学试验基础上提出的理论,其动力学系统模型是著名的布鲁塞尔振子[315]:

$$\begin{cases} \dot{x} = a - bx + x^2 y - x \\ \dot{y} = bx - x^2 y \end{cases} \tag{3}$$

结合"熵"概念、开放系统和非线性系统的分析,提出能量转换、远离均衡、涨落、自组织等新概念,给出一套具有普适性的一般系统的能量交换过程描述,揭示系统变化的本质性特征。

该理论认为,一个远离平衡态的开放系统,当外界条件或系统的某个参量变化到一定的临界值时,通过发生突变,就有可能转变为一种时间、空间或功能有序的新状态,并需要不断地与外界交换物质和能量,以形成或维持新的稳定结构,这种需要耗散物质能量的有序结构就称为耗散结构,具有不可逆性[346,347]。耗散理论作为分析处理开放系统的有力工具,已广泛应用于工程、管理和医学等领域。

海上危险化学品运输系统是一个远离平衡态的开放系统,在系统的演化过程中,不但受自身船舶、人员、货物等要素变化的影响,由于其开放性,还会受到外界各种因素突变的影响,如管理体系和法规的变化、外部环境(航海环境、气象条件等)的作用等,使得系统原有的平衡不断被打破,系统始终处于从一种平衡态向新的平衡态迁跃的过程中。因此,海上危险化学品运输系统具有典型的耗散结构特征。

4 海上危险化学品运输系统状态与熵流分析

系统状态是指系统中可以识别、观测到的特征与态势。当特征与态势随时间变化达到稳定状态时,系统即达到平衡态。

从热力学角度看,熵是非可用能的量度。熵增加意味着系统能量的质量变差,可用程度降低,体现了系统能量在质量方面的耗散;熵减过程是熵增过程的逆过程,负熵包含于熵减过程中,是系统与环境交换并吸收利用交换物的结果。如果把环境中的物质、能量和信息分为增熵因子和减熵因子,对维持系统有序、有贡献且可以被系统利用的物质、能量和信息,称为减熵因子;相反,破坏系统有序化的物质、能量和信息,则称为增熵因子[348,349]。

分析可知,海上危险化学品运输系统具有耗散结构特征,结合海上危险化学品运输的特点,建立危险化学品运输耗散系统的熵流图,如图1所示。通过研究耗散系统的熵变化行为,分析系统状态的相应变化,寻找系统最小风险路径,从而最大限度地提高系统安全。

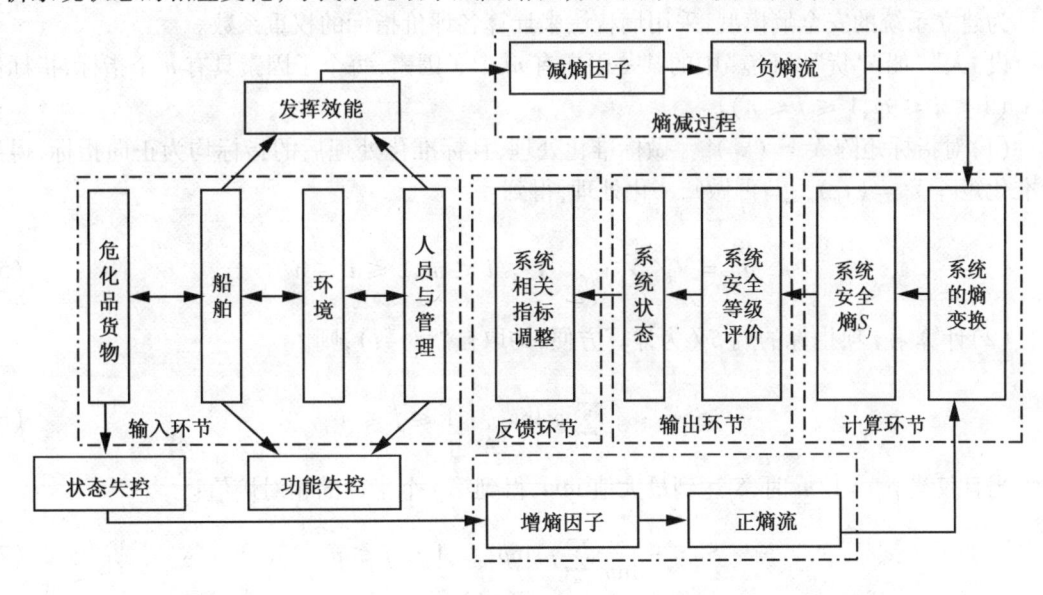

图1 危险化学品运输耗散系统熵流图

如图1所示,为使系统获得最高的安全性,可以采取的措施包括:(1)强化减熵因子,控制增熵因子;(2)引入负熵流,减少系统总熵;(3)维持系统的有序结构,增加系统与外界环境的物质和能量的交换,最大限度地实现物质和能量的耗散。

5 基于不确定信息的海上危险化学品运输系统安全熵及评价方法

影响危险化学品船舶安全的因素很多,为找到适合的危险化学品船舶安全状态度量标准,充分考虑信息的不确定性及量化困难等特点,结合危险化学品系统特点和信息熵原理,从"系统和谐"的角度提出"系统安全熵"概念[350,351],对海上危险化学品运输安全系统进行安全评价和研究。

根据信息熵公式可以得出海上危险化学品运输系统的危险源指标熵公式为:

$$S(X) = -g_i \sum_{i=1}^{n} P(x_i) \lg P(x_i) \tag{4}$$

其中:g_i 为常数,表示系统信息的不确定度,通常情况下取值为 1;$P(x_i)$ 为危险源发生突变的概率;$S(X)$ 为系统的危险源指标熵,用来度量和评价该指标在危险化学品运输系统中的和谐与安全程度:某个指标的熵越小,表明其指标值的信息有序程度越高,即系统可控性越强,在系统风险控制中所起的作用越大,该指标的权重也就越大;反之,某指标的信息熵越大,表明其指标值的变异程度越低,提供的信息量越小,即系统可控性较弱,在评价中所起的作用越小,其权重也就越小[352]。

为建立系统的安全熵模型,采用熵权法来计算各评价指标的权重系数。

设"人""船""货""环境"中的某一因素有 m 个子因素,每个子因素具有 n 个指标,指标值为 $x_{ij}(1 \leq i \leq m, 1 \leq j \leq n)$。

(1) 对指标矩阵 $X = (x_{ij})_{m \times n}$ 做标准化处理,且标准化处理后的指标均为正向指标,得到标准化矩阵 $Y = (y_{ij})_{m \times n}$。再做归一化处理,得到

$$p_{ij} = y_{ij} \Big/ \sum_{i=1}^{m} y_{ij}, \quad 1 \leq i \leq m, 1 \leq i \leq n \tag{5}$$

(2) 计算第 j 项指标的熵 S_j(为计算方便,均取自然对数),则

$$S_j = -g_i \sum_{i=1}^{m} p_{ij} \ln p_{ij}, \quad 1 \leq j \leq n \tag{6}$$

当且仅当 $p_{ij} = 1/m$ 时,S_j 达到最大值 $\ln m$,得到第 j 个指标的相对熵值:

$$S_j = -\frac{g_i}{\ln m} \sum_{i=1}^{m} p_{ij} \ln p_{ij}, \quad 1 \leq j \leq n \tag{7}$$

(3) 定义第 j 项指标的"反向系数" $G_j = 1 - S_j (1 \leq j \leq n)$。对于第 j 项指标,指标值的反向系数越大,对被评价系统的作用越大,熵值越小。反之,差异越小,熵值越大。

(4) 危险化学品运输系统的第 j 项指标权重为:

$$w_j = G_j \Big/ \sum_{i=1}^{m} G_j, \quad 1 \leq j \leq n \tag{8}$$

从而得到系统总的安全熵模型:

$$S_j = \sum_{i=1}^{n} w_i S_{y_i}^j, \quad S_{y_i} = -y_i \ln y_i \tag{9}$$

在式(9)中,若安全熵值计算结果较大,表示海上危险化学品运输系统的安全程度差,系统路径中存在的风险也较大。因此,可以进一步利用上式结果评定系统的安全等级,确定系统的实时安全状态。

安全熵评价方法对信息的利用率高,并且很好地处理了系统不确定性对评价结果的影响,因此,可应用该方法对海上危险化学品运输系统的安全进行评价和预测。

6 结语

对海上危险化学品运输系统的复杂性和不确定性进行研究,证明系统符合耗散结构特征,并绘制了系统状态变化的熵流图,建立了系统的安全熵模型。

海上危化品运输系统安全管理博弈模型*

摘要：海上危化品运输系统是一个典型的复杂社会系统。为保证运输安全,科学、有效的管理水平,首先分析该系统的特点以及博弈论在该领域应用的可行性,针对运输管理活动中的不安全行为建立系统安全博弈管理模型,定义岸基博弈、船基博弈、船岸间博弈等博弈关系,基于事故案例验证安全博弈管理模型,实现海上危化品运输系统的和谐管理。基于博弈论模型开展管理研究对保障海上危化品运输安全具有重要意义。

关键词：水路运输;危化品运输;博弈理论;博弈行为;安全管理

0 引言

伴随航运业分工的细化,海上危险化学品运输活动日益频繁。交通运输部《公路水路交通运输行业发展统计公报》显示,2005年我国拥有万吨级以上液体化工品泊位35个,2012年增加到123个;2011年、2012年全国规模以上港口分别完成液体散装货物运输8.54亿吨、9.06亿吨,分别比2005年上升46.2%和55.1%。研究表明,在过去几十年里发生的3 222起危险货物事故中,有41%的事故发生在运输过程中,且比一般危险货物运输事故造成的经济损失和社会后果更严重。[353]因此,开展海上危化品运输安全管理技术研究意义重大。

1 海上危化品运输系统的特点

"海上危化品运输"一般特指散装危险化学品海上运输。根据《国际散装运输危险化学品船舶构造和设备规则》的定义,"危险化学品"是指那些在温度为37.8 ℃时,蒸气压力不超过0.28 MPa(绝对压力)的液体。这些货物通常具有易燃、易爆、毒害、腐蚀、放射性等性质,在生产、运输、装卸和储存保管等过程中,极易造成人身伤亡和环境灾难,因而需要特别管理。

从海上交通工程学角度看,危化品还具有以下危险特性:

1.1 易流动性

货物的流动性和自由液面容易造成船舶稳性下降,影响航行安全。

---

* 本文发表在《中国航海》2014年第1期第37卷,作者李建民、郑中义、齐迹。

1.2 理化特性

货物的理化特性可能对承载船舶造成损害,包括舱壁涂层侵蚀、泵系和管路凝固阻塞等。

1.3 易于变质

化工产品的高纯度要求,使其在海运条件下易于变质,包括蒸发、吸潮、结晶、氧化、吸附氯离子和杂质等。

1.4 种类复杂性

海上危化品运输系统货物种类繁杂,一个航次可能同时承运多种危险特性各异(例如每种货物有不同的爆炸极限,货物之间的相容性[354]等)的货物,使海上危化品运输系统具有其他任何海上运输系统所无法比拟的复杂性和危险性。

1.5 人员疲劳带来的危险

海上危化品运输系统中船舶承载货物种类更换频繁,经常涉及洗舱、除气、取样、惰化等操作,船员劳动强度大,加班频繁,易因疲惫导致疏忽,造成人员、环境、货物损失。

可见,海上危化品运输系统包括"人""船""环境""货""管理"等五个安全因素,是一个典型的复杂社会系统。其中"人"是主体;"船""环境""货物"是受体;"管理"是"人"联系各因素的媒介;"货物"不仅会对"人""船""环境"造成风险,也易于受到前者的反作用。

2 海上危化品运输系统博弈管理研究

2.1 博弈论在危化品运输系统中应用的可行性

博弈论是研究两人或多人谋略以及决策问题的理论。博弈双方在相互依存、相互制约的状态下展开竞争,以尽可能地提高自己利益所得为原则。[354]博弈论可以划分为合作博弈和非合作博弈,当人们之间的行为相互作用时,当事人会达成一个具有约束力的协议,如果达成协议就是合作博弈,否则就是非合作博弈。目前博弈论在经济、人力资源管理等领域应用较多,在采矿安全[356]、食品安全[356]、信息技术[358]等领域也获得了很好的应用,但在海上危化品运输安全保障领域的应用较少[359]。研究表明,人为因素是海上交通事故的重要致因[312],人的可靠性是衡量管理者产生不安全行为的重要指标[360]。在海上危化品运输系统中,建议管理者基于不同得益,对产生不安全行为的管理者采取不同态度,这将产生博弈行为。可见,基于博弈开展海上危化品运输安全管理技术的研究是可行的和必要的。

2.2 海上危化品运输系统安全博弈管理

2.2.1 海上危化品运输系统博弈组织结构

海上运输管理组织包括国家各级政府、海事主管部门、港航企业、船员等。虽然各级管理组织的社会分工不同,但对海上危化品运输系统的安全管理目标是一致的,为研究方便,统称管理者。各级管理组织之间在管理与被管理时必然产生安全效率与经济效益问题,使组织之间维系不同的协同博弈关系,包括岸基博弈、船基博弈和船岸间博弈等,如图1所示。这就形成了海上运输博弈关系的层次性与复杂性。

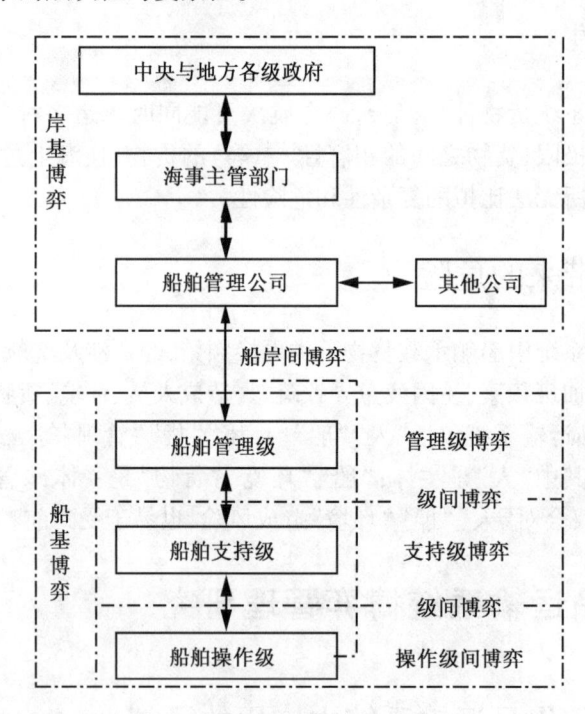

图1 危化品运输博弈组织结构图

(1)岸基博弈一般指岸上港航企业与管理部门、港航企业与其他企业之间的博弈,包括安全效率博弈和效益博弈两种形式;

(2)船基博弈包括本级(管理级、支持级、操作级)船员间的同级博弈和不同级船员间的级间博弈,以安全效率博弈为主要形式,一般不涉及经济效益博弈;

(3)船岸间博弈一般指船员整体与岸基管理组织之间的博弈,但是当个体利益明显受到岸基管理组织影响时,个别船员可能会直接参与到船岸之间的博弈活动,后者以经济效益博弈居多。

2.2.2 管理者与建议管理者间动态博弈假设

(1)风险由管理活动中的不安全行为导致,按管理者的意识分为非故意性不安全行为和故意性不安全行为。

(2)管理者的分类:产生不安全行为的管理者、对前者进行制止的建议管理者。

(3)管理者具备有限理性特征。
(4)管理者的得益分类:经济得益、心理生理得益等。

2.2.3 管理者与建议管理者博弈得益矩阵

管理者从自身利益出发,面对不安全行为有两种决策:制止或不制止(即建议或者不建议)。建立的管理者与建议管理者博弈得益矩阵见表1。

表1 管理者与建议管理者博弈得益矩阵

得益矩阵		不安全行为管理者($1-x$)	
		安全行为	不安全行为
建议管理者(x)	制止	$A, -B$	$-C, 0$
	未制止	$0, D$	$0, 0$

A、B 分别为管理者出现不安全行为并被制止时建议管理者和管理者的得益;C 为管理者未出现不安全行为且被制止时建议管理者的得益;D 为管理者未出现不安全行为且未被制止时管理者的得益。

2.2.4 建议管理者的动态演变机理模型

建议管理者的期望得益由两部分组成,即
(1)建议管理者制止不安全行为的期望为:
$$E(u) = x \cdot A + (1-x) \cdot (-C) = u_1 \quad (1)$$
(2)建议管理者未制止不安全行为的期望为:
$$E(u) = x \cdot 0 + (1-x) \cdot 0 = u_2 = 0 \quad (2)$$
建议管理者制止不安全行为的平均期望为:
$$V(E(u)) = x \cdot [x \cdot A - (1-x) \cdot C] \quad (3)$$
建立建议管理者得益动态演变机理模型,它表征了建议管理者制止行为的得益动态变化速度。
$$f(x) = \frac{dx}{dt} = x \cdot \{u_1 - V[E(u)]\} = (A+C) \cdot x \cdot (1-x) \cdot (x - \frac{C}{A+C}) \quad (4)$$
令 $dx/dt = 0$,得到三个方程解,即
$$x_1 = 0, \; x_2 = 1, \; x_3 = C/(A+C) \quad (5)$$
有 $f'(0) < 0, f'(1) < 0, f'[D/(D+B)] > 0$,故 $x_1 = 0$,$x_2 = 1$ 是本动态博弈模型的进化稳定策略,$x_3 = C/(A+C)$ 不是稳定策略,本模型见图2(a)。

对于某一时刻,当 $dx/dt > 0$ 时,建议管理者的得益比较明显,通过示范和模仿效应逐渐形成良好风气,达到该模型的 Nash 均衡点 $x=1$;反之,$dx/dt < 0$ 时,建议管理者无明显得益,当建议行为演化为负担时,不良风气形成,达到该模型的 Nash 均衡点 $x=0$,此时安全事故发生的可能性变大。

2.2.5 不安全行为管理者的动态演变机理模型

不安全行为管理者的期望得益由两部分组成:
(1)产生不安全行为的期望为:

$$E(u) = x \cdot (-B) + (1-x) \cdot D = u_1 \quad (6)$$

(2)未产生不安全行为的期望为:
$$E(u) = x \cdot 0 + (1-x) \cdot 0 = u_2 = 0 \quad (7)$$

不安全行为管理者的平均期望为:
$$V[E(u)] = x \cdot [x \cdot B - (1-x) \cdot D] \quad (8)$$

建立不安全行为管理者动态演变机理模型,它表征了产生不安全行为的得益动态变化速度。

$$f(x) = \frac{dx}{dt} = x \cdot \{u_1 - V[E(u)]\} = (B+D) \cdot x \cdot (1-x) \cdot (x - \frac{D}{B+D}) \quad (9)$$

令 $dx/dt = 0$,得到三个方程解,即
$$x_1 = 0, x_2 = 1, x_3 = D/(B+D) \quad (10)$$

有 $f'(0) > 0, f'(1) > 0, f'[D/(D+B)] < 0$,故 $x_1 = 0, x_2 = 1$ 是本动态博弈模型的进化稳定策略,$x_3 = D/(B+D)$ 不是稳定策略,本模型如图2(b)所示。

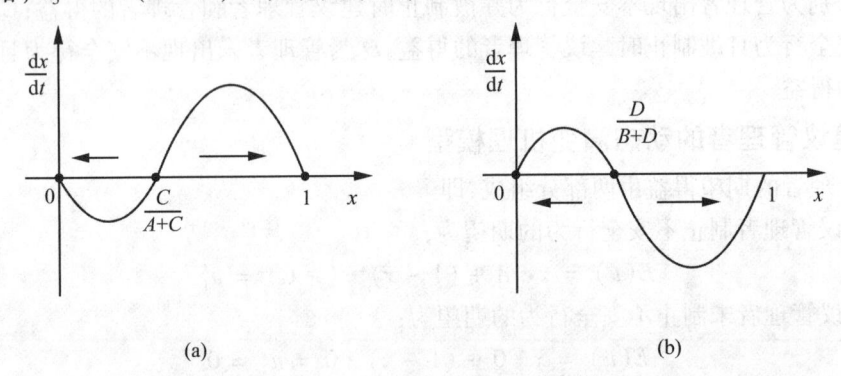

图2 建议管理者与不安全行为管理者得益动态演变机理模型图

对于某一时刻,当 $D > B(dx/dt > 0)$ 时,不安全行为管理者的得益比较明显,不良风气逐渐形成,最终达到该模型的 Nash 均衡点 $x = 1$,此时无法杜绝不安全行为;反之,当 $D < B(dx/dt < 0)$ 时,不安全行为管理者的得益明显下降,不安全行为逐步减少,通过示范和模仿效应逐渐形成良好风气,达到 Nash 均衡点 $x = 0$,此时安全事故发生的可能性变小。

2.3 海上危化品运输系统和谐管理机制

由系统的安全博弈管理模型可知,在人与物互动过程中,使系统互动秩序失调(即发生事故)的根本原因在于理性个人(管理者)为追逐自身利益所形成的强大冲动力,它既是事故形成的主要原因,也是预防和遏制事故的主要手段。对于高风险生产系统,其安全性很大程度上依赖于管理者之间、管理者与系统之间的交互作用,微观行为(不安全行为)常会导致严重的宏观结果,这也体现出系统和谐管理的重要性。

海上危化品运输系统是一个复杂的社会系统,在运输过程中必然存在安全效率与经济效益问题,因此有必要建立海上危险化学品运输系统和谐管理机制,如图3所示。

可以看出,在保证运输系统某一安全标准的前提下,管理者的生理得益与经济效益得益是博弈的主要对象。这表示在经济得益不明显时,管理者转向追求更高的生理得益,这导致劳动

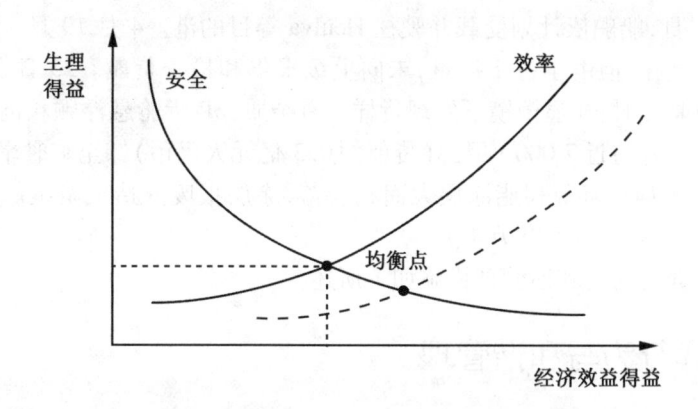

图 3 博弈活动中安全与效益关系模型图

付出减少,安全隐患增加。因此,生理得益的下降是以提升经济得益为手段的。

效率的提升包含时间的缩减(生理得益)、工作量的增加(经济得益)两层含义。提升效率势必以牺牲安全为代价,即只有在保证管理者取得一定经济得益的前提下才能提高系统生产效率。因此,管理者在保证基本生理得益的前提下经济得益才能获得局部最大。

3 海上危化品运输系统博弈模型应用

2010 年 3 月 20 日,巴拿马籍散化船 H6 轮(DWT:35 033 t)接到管理公司指示,计划 3 月 30 日在伊朗 BIK 和 Assaluyeh 港装载甲醇和苯驶往西班牙 Heulva、比利时 Antwerp 和荷兰 Rotterdam,请船舶预配载。公司同时提示,运输合同为包运合同,涉及 9 300 t 苯和 17 500 t 甲醇。据此,大副做出了配载计划(如表 2 所示)并报公司审核,公司审核后一周下达了受载命令。制订配载计划时,船舶大副、船长、船舶管理公司航运部均未注意到 H62P/S 和 4P/S 货舱涂层环氧树脂不具备抗醇性。

表 2 危化品船舶 H6 货舱不知情况及 06W01 航次配载计划

Slop-P=818 m³	7P=2 636 m³	6P=2 296.0 m³	5P=2 765.5 m³	4P=2 295.7 m³	3P=2 768.2 m³	2P=2 231 m³	1P=1 398 m³
甲醇	甲醇	苯	甲醇	甲醇	苯	甲醇	甲醇
98%	98%	98%	98%	98%	91%	98%	98%
无机锌	无机锌	无机锌	无机锌	环氧树脂	无机锌	环氧树脂	无机锌
Suitable	Suitable	Suitable	Suitable	Suitable	Suitable	Suitable	Suitable
626.000	2 017.000	1 953.000	2 116.000	1 757.000	2 177.000	1 707.000	1 070.000
Slop-S=819 m³	7S=2 638 m³	6S=2 295.6 m³	5S=2 768.2 m³	4S=2 294.4 m³	3S=2 768.3 m³	2S=2 234 m³	1S=1 398 m³
甲醇	甲醇	甲醇	甲醇	甲醇	苯	甲醇	苯
98%	98%	98%	98%	98%	91%	98%	91%
无机锌	无机锌	无机锌	无机锌	环氧树脂	无机锌	环氧树脂	无机锌
Suitable	Suitable	Suitable	Suitable	Suitable	Suitable	Suitable	Suitable
626.000	2 019.000	1 953.000	2 118.000	1 756.000	2 177.000	1 709.000	1 094.000

2010年4月1日,船舶依计划受载并驶往Heulva等目的港。4月19日,水手长在甲板闻到4舱附近有异样气味,但由于过于疲惫,未向上级报告和检查货舱。25日,H6轮抵达Rotterdam。30日开舱验货时,在显微镜下发现货样含有杂质,2P货舱悬浮颗粒肉眼可见。H6立即报告公司发生货损并将近7 000 t甲醇(货值约0.3亿元人民币)卸至临时岸槽,除气后验舱发现2P/S、4P/S货舱舱壁环氧树脂涂层大面积脱落,涂层报废并造成货损。H6轮随即空载驶往迪拜维修舱涂层,费用达500万美元。

案例中主要博弈行为与和谐管理措施如下所述。

3.1 船基博弈行为与和谐管理

水手长发现问题后没有上报是出于对自身得益的考虑,即 $V[E(u)] = (1-x)[x(-B) + (1-x)D]$。该船舶没有奖励机制,船员由于劳动强度大而过分关注生理得益(休息时间),因此存在 $D>B$,不安全行为管理者得益模型在 $x=1$ 处形成Nash均衡点,不安全行为使得系统不和谐,最终风险变大。为克服上述不安全因素,公司和船舶管理级应努力使 $D<B$,让不安全行为者的得益(事实得益或感知得益)明显变小,这样模型的均衡点会发生本质上的逆转,在 $x=0$ 处形成Nash均衡点,系统逐渐和谐,风险逐渐变小。具体措施包括减轻船员劳动强度,增大船员生理得益;建立适当的奖励机制,转移船员生理得益关注度等。

采用专家调查表,建立奖励机制并对奖励金额进行划分,利用MATLAB软件对系统安全与效率关系曲线进行仿真见图4。图4中3条效率曲线由左至右分别对应公司对船员无激励机制、每月加班奖励100美元和200美元。由图4可知,当奖励金额设定为100美元时,安全与效率均衡点较无奖励机制时开始向右移动;当励金额设定为200美元时,安全与效率均衡点右移明显。这充分说明奖励机制的设立可以有效促进新博弈行为的产生,即船员克服生理得益去获得经济得益。这种方法对不安全行为的减少起到了关键性的作用。

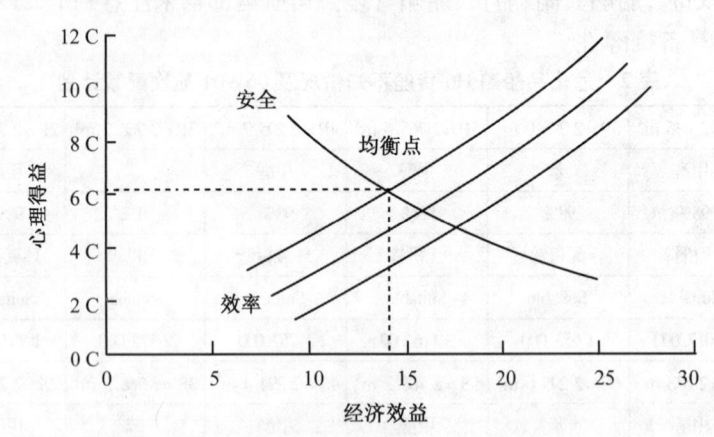

图4 基于奖励机制的安全与效益仿真图

3.2 船岸之间博弈行为与和谐管理

对于管理公司而言,若没有与船舶建立良好的奖惩机制,也会形成与图4类似的船岸间博弈行为,即管理者面对安全与效率问题时,仅从自身利益出发权衡 D 与 B 之间的得益。本案例中,公司航运部、船长都没能及时发现货舱不适货的情况,没有对不安全管理者(本案例中为大副)尽到"建议"义务,这说明需要在航运部和船舶间建立责、权、利明晰的奖惩机制,以转移安全与效率均衡点、转化不同得益类型来提高管理者的安全得益关注度。

4 结语

从系统管理学的角度看,海上危化品运输系统的风险性主要由管理者的不安全行为产生,管理者在面对安全与效率时会出现博弈行为。以博弈论为基础,建立系统安全管理博弈模型,寻找预防危化品运输事故的演变机理,对于保障海上危化品运输系统安全与和谐管理具有重要经济和社会意义。

不确定条件下海上危化品运输安全演变机理*

摘要:为研究不确定因素对运输系统的影响,基于耗散理论提出海上危险化学品运输系统安全演变机理,从能量观点建立系统势能函数模型,在研究系统安全过程中同时考虑系统的熵和能量。利用熵原理推导出系统安全熵变化曲线,并对曲线进行安全等级划分。数值算例验证了熵与能量结合能够定量描述不确定因素对运输系统的影响,有利于系统安全路径的选择。结果表明,熵和能量与海上危化品运输系统安全演变密切相关。

关键词:海上危化品运输系统;耗散机理;系统安全演变;演变机理;势能函数;安全路径选择;不确定

0 引言

海上大宗危化品货物运输是国民经济发展的基础和有力保障。一般研究认为,海上货物运输系统由"人""船""环境"3方面因素组成,是一个典型的复杂社会系统[361]。在系统安全研究中,"人"因素主要研究人为失误对系统安全造成的影响[362];"船"因素主要研究船舶本身的安全性能[363],货物属性只是影响船舶安全性能的一个子因素;"环境"因素主要研究了水文气象条件对航行安全的影响[364]。危化品运输是海上货物运输的一个特例。

但是鉴于海上危化品运输系统具有明显的耗散结构特征,上述研究方法难以揭示系统本质,需要基于自组织与他组织的系统熵流机理开展海上危化品运输系统安全研究。

1 海上危化品运输系统

1.1 海上危化品运输系统特性

与普通货物相比较,危化品具有易燃易爆、生物毒害积聚等特殊危险属性,因此开展危化品运输系统安全研究时必须充分重视"货"因素。这样就形成了以"人""船""环境""货"4方面因素为研究对象的海上危化品运输系统。为了深入研究系统安全演变机理,保障运输安全,以非线性理论为基础,得出海上危化品运输系统以下几个特性。

(1)开放性。开放性体现在与环境的信息、物质和能量交换3个层面上。与普通运输系统相比,海上危化品运输系统能量交换更为复杂,既包括危化品船舶与外环境的能量交换,又

---

* 本文发表在《哈尔滨工程大学学报》2014年第6期第35卷,作者李建民、齐迹、郑中义。

包括危化品货物与内外环境的热交换。

(2)动态性。系统的开放特性决定了其动态性。与普通运输系统相比,海上危化品运输系统动态性多体现在货物因素及与其密切相关诸因素的改变上,包括货物理化属性的改变,及由此引起的其他因素的改变。

(3)不确定性。①货物的理化属性、安全指标等易于受到其他三方面因素扰动的影响,各扰动具有很强的随机性和模糊性;②"货"与"人""船""环境"之间的相互作用具有较强的不确定性。

(4)突变性。受到开放性、动态性、不确定性的影响,海上危化品运输系统随时会从一种安全状态迁跃到另一种安全状态,即发生突变。货物易燃易爆属性的引入,使得系统突变性更强。

(5)不可逆性。海上危化品运输系统的突变现象一般都是不可逆的,包括货物理化属性改变的不可逆性和事故后果的不可逆性。货物理化属性不可逆性包括货物的燃烧、爆炸、凝固、吸湿、聚合、氧化等。

1.2 海上危化品运输系统的耗散结构

耗散理论以熵(dS)为工具,描述了系统具有普适意义的能量交换过程,揭示出系统演变的本质特征[315]。海上危化品运输系统是一个远离均衡态的开放系统,时刻与环境存在着物质、能量与信息的交换。在安全演变过程中,系统不但受自身各安全因素变化的影响,还受到外界各种扰动因素的影响,使系统原有的均衡不断被打破,始终处于向新均衡态迁跃的行为状态,因此海上危化品运输系统具有典型的耗散结构特征。

2 海上危化品运输系统耗散机理

设海上危化品运输系统为 S,它始终与环境保持着能量交换。该系统中,由一定时间里不可人为改变的因素所构成的环境称为外环境,其他为内环境。若分别记外环境流入流出系统的能量为 N_+ 和 N_-,则 S 与内环境之间的实际能量"强加"或"供给"为 n_+ 或者 n_-。当 $N_+ = n_+$,$N_- = n_-$ 时,系统处于均衡状态,并假设这一时刻是系统的初始点。外界新能量进入系统后一部分转化成系统能,该能量对于系统状态一般没有影响;其余未转换为系统能的部分可以称为"自由能",自由能具有"活跃性"和"非稳定性",并将促使系统"远离均衡态"。

为研究方便,忽略转化为系统能的能量,即外环境流入的能量 N_+ 都保持着"活跃性"和"非稳定性"。N_+ 进入系统时通过边界到达系统内部。当外来强加的能量 n_+ 进入系统时,会有个 n_+ 势与系统边界势产生摩擦、碰撞与斗争,并使系统产生相应能量级别的、不同能量层次的振动,即系统的涨落现象。自由能在系统中引起涨落现象并在涨落过程中得到耗散,也就是说当能量输入系统成为自由能时,系统就开始了耗散机制。

自由能进入系统后,系统经过耗散排出剩余能达到新的均衡态,该过程称为系统的"自组织"过程,它强调了系统的自主演变[365],其目标是系统的新均衡态。由于新均衡态不一定是安全状态,因此为了最终达到"最理想安全状态",需要通过系统外力对系统能量进行有序组织,即系统的"他组织"行为。基于"自组织"过程、"他组织"行为的海上危化品运输系统耗散机理图如图 1 所示。

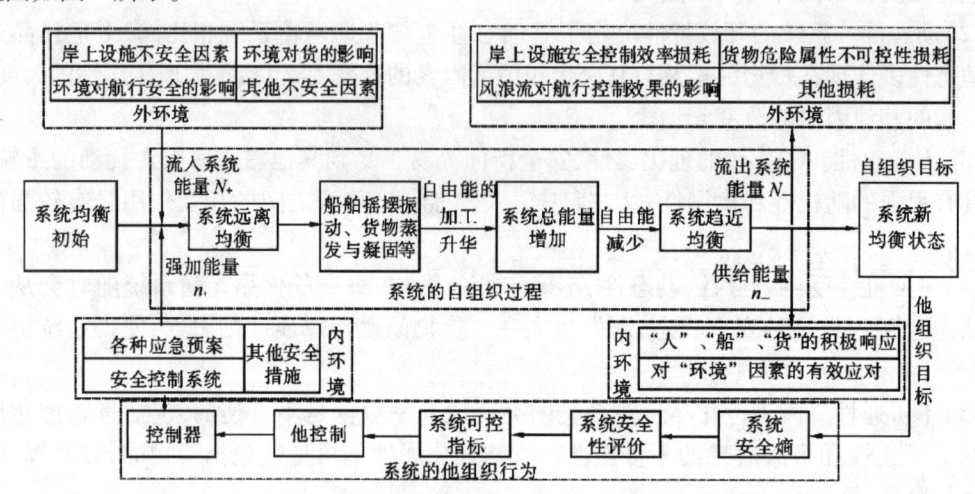

图 1　海上危化品运输系统耗散图

当外部环境变化影响到系统稳定性时，包括对"人""船""货"等各安全因素的影响，即视为流入了 N_+。此时系统开始远离均衡态并产生一定的响应、熵增过程，这表明危化品运输系统稳定性变差。在他组织过程中，通过分析危化品运输系统相关指标，做出相应调整，经他控制器对系统实时控制，即视为引入 n_+。在系统他组织行为中，有些控制能量对系统稳定性形成影响，即视为供给能量 n_-，有些能量没有形成对稳定性的有效控制而流入外环境，即视为 N_-。通过调整他组织行为中 n_+ 供应量，促使系统能逐步定位并排放出剩余的自由能，导致系统熵减少，最终达到新的均衡状态。

3　危化品运输系统安全演变机理

通过研究海上危化品运输系统耗散机理可知，系统稳定性取决于自组织过程中自由能的耗散以及在他组织行为中对自由能的调控。若将系统中导致熵流变化的效用路径称为"系统路径"，那么系统演变可理解为系统路径中所有涨落现象促使系统能持续产生的过程，这就是海上危化品运输系统演变机理，其中的演变因子为系统的自由能，系统的演变模式伴随着能量变化并取决于自由能的耗散程度。

由 Logistic 方程可知，在初始条件一定时，海上危化品运输系统是一个能量有界的增长演变系统，能量增长率在系统发展中期附近最为凸显，之后能量增长率会逐步减速以致趋于零，其能量也达到内在的最大值[366]。可见，海上危化品运输系统具有较大的不确定能量，为了定量描述安全演变机理，从系统能量角度出发进行研究是十分必要的。

海上危化品运输系统总能量由势能和动能两部分组成，而势能根据其作用可以分为正势能和反势能：正势能是指系统维持稳定提高安全性的趋势；反势能是指系统克服正能量对"人""船""货""环境"产生消极影响的趋势；动能是势能释放的结果。系统的能量变化既有势能间的量变，也有势能和动能间的质变。可见，能量决定了系统安全状态，因此能量在系统路径上的作用点可定义为"系统熵流节点"，即多条系统路径的交叉点，它是联系熵与能量的纽带。

若将系统输入能量 n_+ 和 N_+ 之间的权重比 $\alpha:\beta$ 视为一种"势能"的作用[366],当 α 在[0,1]变动时(假设 α 由 $1/n$ 表示,n 为自然数),系统的安全状态不断改变,系统的稳定性也不断变化。

(1)当 $\alpha=0$ 或 1 时(即 $n=\infty$ 或 $n=1$),进入系统的自由能只有一种存在形式(n_+ 或 N_+),系统非常不均衡,即系统很不稳定。

(2)当 $\alpha=1/2$ 时(即 $n=1/2$,此时 $n_+=N_+$),此时系统非稳定势能达到局部最大值,系统均衡状态不能保持,涨落现象明显增大,系统不稳定。由此,在(0,1/2)及(1/2,1)区间内一定存在至少2个对应的 α 值,使得系统均衡稳定。根据上述分析得到系统势能函数变化率曲线 $F'(x)$(视 α 和 β 为自变量"x"),把 $F'(\alpha)=0$ 的 α 点称为系统的均衡点。曲线图如图2所示。

由图中曲线可以得出:

(1)当 $\alpha=1/n(n>4)$ 时,$\alpha>\beta$,系统严重不均衡,系统非常不稳定;

(2)当 $n=4$ 时,$\alpha<\beta$,系统不均衡程度明显,系统不能稳定;

(3)当 $2<n\leq3$ 时,$\alpha\approx\beta$,此时可近似看作系统稳定均衡点。

当海上危化品运输系统能量权重映射到[0,1]后,将以 1/3:2/3 或 2/3:1/3 的最佳比例促使系统均衡稳定,这样的规律被称为"2/3 原理"[367]。系统中能量存在形式的不同将导致系统演变模式的不同,系统的安全演变模式取决于系统势能的耗散。

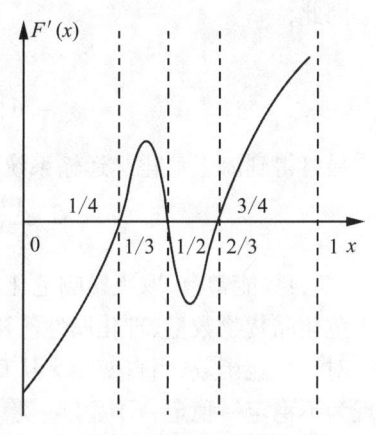

图2 系统势能函数变化率曲线

4 危化品运输系统势能函数模型

通过对危化品运输系统能量权重的分析,可以基于系统势能函数变化率曲线,以能量权重为自变量在[0,1]上建立海上危化品运输系统势能函数,其函数曲线见图3。

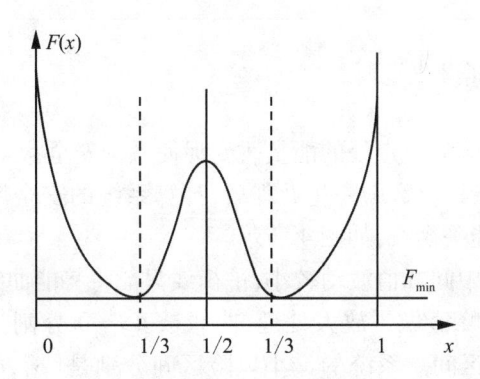

图3 基于权重 α 的[0,1]区间上系统势能函数曲线

图3表明α和β系数间的权重比在"互胀活动"中总是趋向1/3或2/3点。从系统动力学角度来说,0、1/2、1点都是系统均衡点,但它们是不稳定的,权重比的变化趋势是远离0、1/2、1点而指向1/3或2/3点,这2点是系统稳定均衡点。

假设在x,y坐标系下,该势能函数可表示为$y=F(x)$型。$F(x)$在x为1/3、2/3处最低,其变化率在1/3、1/2、2/3这3处为0[即$F'(x)=0$],同时$F(x)$在x取0或1时最大且变化率也最大,0、1及1/2时曲线皆趋向1/3、1/2且急剧下降。设$F(x)$在x取0或1时变化率为无穷大,在1/3、1/2、2/3处变化率为0,则势能函数变化率曲线为:

$$\frac{dy}{dx}=F'_x(x)=A\frac{\left(x-\frac{1}{3}\right)\left(x-\frac{1}{2}\right)\left(x-\frac{2}{3}\right)}{(x-0)(x-1)} \tag{1}$$

因此,

$$y=A\int\frac{\left(x-\frac{1}{3}\right)\left(x-\frac{1}{2}\right)\left(x-\frac{2}{3}\right)}{(x-0)(x-1)}dx \tag{2}$$

最终得到海上危化品运输系统势能函数模型:

$$y=\frac{A}{2}x(1-x)-\frac{A}{9}\ln|x(x-1)|+C \tag{3}$$

式中:C为势能常数,取决影响危化品船舶安全的稳定因素;A为危化品系统势能影响因子,取决于危化品货物数量、理化属性等不稳定因素。

对于势能函数,当自变量x从0→1/3→1/2→2/3→1变化时,海上危化品运输系统稳定性表现为不稳定→稳定→不稳定→稳定→不稳定;$α=1/3$或$α=2/3$时分别表示海上危化品运输系统的两种均衡状态,其他时刻系统涨落现象明显增大,系统处于不断的耗散过程中。熵流节点处能量的变化可理解为正负熵流间的互胀关系的作用。他组织控制策略是通过调节x(即内环境对系统控的制能力)来实现的,通过他组织控制可以促使海上危化品运输系统保持安全稳定状态,也可以认为系统引入了负熵流。势能函数的建立完善了海上危化品运输系统安全演变的数学描述过程。

5 危化品运输系统安全路径选择

5.1 最小风险路径原理

由系统演变机理可知,熵流节点处的能量改变促使系统安全状态不断变化,因此有必要研究系统安全路径。对系统指标参数归一化处理后,计算系统的安全熵,得到系统的稳定程度。将$dS=0$定义为系统的熵能平衡线,如图4所示。

一般情况下,能量曲线中间峰值波动较小,平衡线只能将势能曲线划分为3个区域。为了表述完整,图4将中间波动峰值做了放大处理,曲线被$dS=0$分割为$[0,α_1)$,$[α_1,α_2)$,$[α_2,α_3)$,$[α_3,α_4]$,$[α_4,1]$ 5个区间。系统的最小风险区间分别是$[α_1,α_2)$和$[α_3,α_4)$,此区间内系统非稳定,势能局部最小,利于系统能量的耗散,这就是海上危化品运输系统最小风险路径原理。当$α=1/3$或2/3时,系统势能最小且最稳定。最小风险路径原理为海上危化品运输系

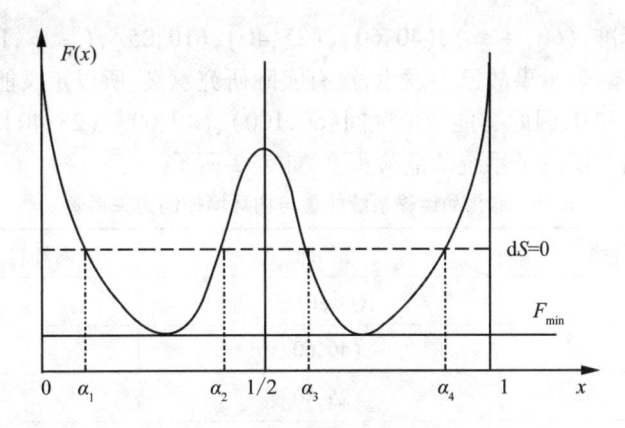

图4 基于熵与能量的安全状态分级

统安全等级的制定提供了依据。

5.2 安全等级

由于一般情况下 dS 为曲线,且有 $dS>0$,这体现了海上危化品运输系统的不可逆性。熵曲线 $S_j = -\omega_i y_i \ln y_i$ [368]在(0,1)上先增再减。它与势能函数曲线最多可以有4个交点,如图5所示,因此得到势能区间分别为 $(0,\alpha_1)$,$[\alpha_1,\alpha_2)$,$[\alpha_2,\alpha_3)$,$[\alpha_3,\alpha_4)$,$[\alpha_4,1)$。

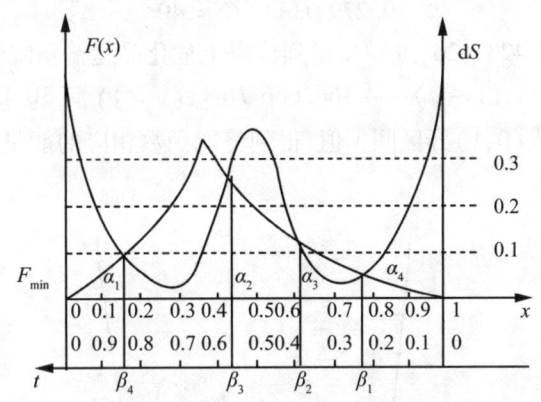

图5 最小风险路径原理图

参照交通运输部"水上交通事故分级标准表",根据专家打分标准制定系统稳定性等级表和系统能量等级表,各指标等级均采用相对值。其中,稳定性分级标准为:Ⅰ级(0,40);Ⅱ级[40,60);Ⅲ级[60,75);Ⅳ级[75,90);Ⅴ级[90,100];通过计算各区间安全熵得到系统稳定区间,见表1。

表1 安全熵与稳定性等级关系表

系统稳定性等级	安全熵	系统稳定性
Ⅰ	(0.366 5, ∞)	最不稳定
Ⅱ	(0.306 5, 0.366 5]	不稳定
Ⅲ	(0.215 8, 0.306 5]	临界
Ⅳ	(0.094 8, 0.215 8]	较稳定
Ⅴ	(0, 0.094 8]	最稳定

制定能量分级标准:$(60,+\infty),(40,60],(25,40],(10,25],(-\infty,10]$。考虑到曲线两侧较陡,能量上升明显,表示事故已经发生,没有实际研究意义,所以定义能量的最大极限和最小极限值分别为100和0,因此有能量值区间$(60,100)、(40,60]、(25,40]、(10,25]、(0,10]$。能量等级在一个侧面上反映了系统的危险程度,如表2所示。

表2 危化品运输系统能量与内环境控制力关系表

系统相对能量等级	能量值	内环境对系统控制能力
很大	(60,100)	很低
较大	(40,60]	较低
一般	(25,40]	一般
较小	(10,25]	较高
很小	(0,10]	很高

在式(3)中,y值是系统势能,取值范围为$(0,100)$。如果对于一个特定的危化品运输系统,按照表2研究临界状态,有$y(1/3)=10$和$y(1/2)=40$(即映射系统的最安全状态和中间临界状态),建立关系方程:

$$\begin{cases} 0.278\ 23A + C = 10 \\ 0.279\ 03A + C = 40 \end{cases} \tag{4}$$

得出$A=37\ 500,C=-10\ 423.625$,进一步得到该海上危化品运输系统势能函数为:

$$y = 18\ 750x(1-x) - 4\ 166.666\ 7\ln|x(x-1)| - 10\ 423.625 \tag{5}$$

利用式(5),通过输入(0,1)开区间x值,得到势能函数相应的能量曲线,如图6所示。当$y \geq 100$时,取极限值100。

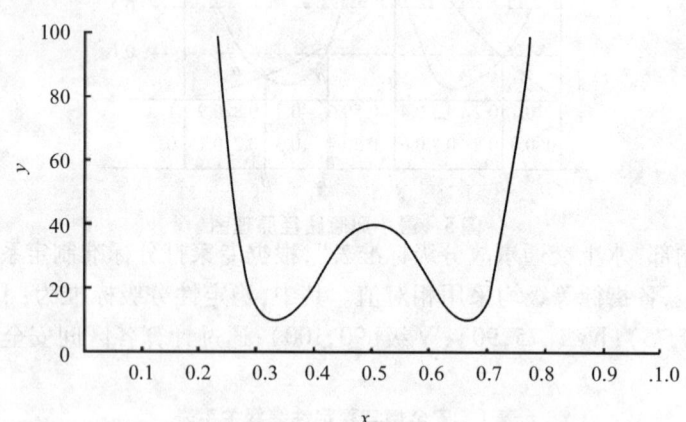

图6 基于事故分级表的危化品运输系统势能曲线

由势能能量值,通过相应的映射关系得出表3中的系统风险路径。

表3 危化品运输系统风险路径

$(0,\alpha_1)$	$[\alpha_1,\alpha_2)$	$[\alpha_2,\alpha_3)$	$[\alpha_3,\alpha_4)$	$[\alpha_4,1)$
0,0.29	0.29,0.4	0.4,0.6	0.6,0.71	0.71,1
最危险	较危险	一般	较安全	安全
稳定	不稳定	临界	稳定	稳定

5.3 验证

根据船舶航次计划，制作专家评价表，对影响危化品船舶安全的稳定因素，包括船舶总吨、船龄、船舶设施、船舶配员情况以及其他影响运输系统安全的因素赋值，得到式(3)的 C 值；对影响危化品船舶安全的不稳定因素，包括货物数量、危险属性、危化品船舶操作环境、气象条件等赋值，得到式(3)的 A 值。

某化学品船舶计划于伊朗阿萨鲁耶港装载苯和甲醇驶往荷兰鹿特丹，专家赋值情况如下：
$$A = 41\,250, C = -11\,462.987\,5$$

代入式(3)，得到实际系统势能函数为
$$y = 41\,250 \cdot [0.5 \cdot x(1-x) - 0.111\,1 \cdot \ln|x(x-1)|] - 11\,462.987\,5 \quad (6)$$

从式(6)得到实际内环境控制力输出与势能变化曲线如图7所示。该图体现出危化品运输系统的开放性与动态性。

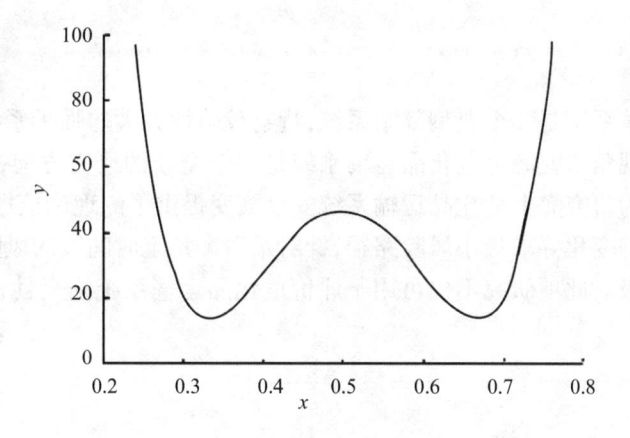

图7 某化学品船舶能量 y 与内环境控制力 x 关系曲线

依照"人""船""环境""货"4个因素，处理评价表中各项指标，得到要素权重表，如表4所示。

表4 某化学品船舶"人""船""环境""货"要素权重表

因素	人	船舶	环境	危化品
权重	0.33	0.21	0.31	0.15
危险值	55	35	90	70

对表4危险值进行归一化并代入安全熵公式,有 $dS = (0.33 \times 0.55 \times \ln 0.55 + \cdots + 0.15 \times 0.70 \times \ln 0.70) = 0.2525$。对照表1得出系统稳定性为Ⅲ级,即临界稳定,此时熵与控制力曲线关系如图8所示。经计算,此时系统熵流节点为0.12和0.69,这体现出运输系统的不确定性。如果控制力在[0.6,0.71],系统是较安全稳定的;如果控制力下降到(0,0.29),系统将面临失控风险,此时安全等级有大幅度迁跃可能,事故发生的概率明显增加。

针对实际的危化品运输系统,首先得到势能函数,再利用专家评价表计算出危化品运输系统安全熵,得到系统安全熵与控制力关系曲线如图8所示,利用该图可求出相应的系统熵流节点。可见,控制力的强弱将导致安全熵值的改变,即熵流节点沿着不同的风险路径影响着系统的安全状态,这也为海上危化品运输系统的安全评价提供了新的思路。

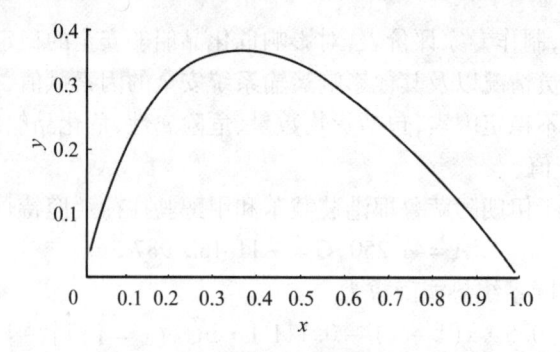

图8 某化学品安全熵与控制力关系曲线

6 结束语

海上危化品运输系统是一个典型复杂系统,货物危险性大大增强了系统风险的不确定性。以熵与能量结合为视角研究海上危化品运输系统是一个全新的研究方向,系统熵流变化机理与势能函数的建立为研究海上危化品运输系统安全演变提供了的理论依据。该方法通过研究系统安全熵与能量的变化寻求最小风险路径,针对某一个特定时间段的风险状态,采取措施最终提升系统安全等级。此项研究不仅可用于评价危化品运输系统安全性,还可用于有效控制运输系统的稳定性。

港口船舶航行环境危险度的灰色评估数学模型*

摘要：本文利用灰色系统理论指标定权聚类方法，通过分析选取了影响港口船舶航行安全的八种环境因素，并对我国沿海十个港口船舶航行环境的危险度进行了评估。该方法的结果可用于我国港口船舶交通管理系统的规划和建设，也可使船员了解其所处的环境危险程度，以达到保证水上交通安全的目的。

0 引言

随着我国改革的深入，沿海主要港口的船舶交通日益繁忙，船舶交通量大幅度增长，同时由于水文、气象和地理等因素的综合作用，使船舶发生事故的可能性增大，据统计，全国1980—1985年发生海损事故18 666起，造成直接经济损失25 586万元。但是，由于各港口的环境因素是不同的，因此船舶在不同的港口航行发生事故的可能性也是不同的。正是基于此，借助灰色系统理论对我国沿海十个港口的危险度进行评估，以给我国沿海航行船舶的船员和进出我国港口船舶的船员提供航行参考，也为水上安全管理提供依据，并采取适当的措施避免事故的发生。

1 港口环境因素分析

本文所指的航行危险度是指船舶所处环境对船舶航行安全的不利影响及造成船舶航行事故的可能性，但不包括船舶发生事故后后果的好坏和损失的大小。

众所周知，水上交通安全系统是由"人""船""环境"组成的，船舶的外部环境是由众多的因素组成的，概括起来大致有：港口水域船舶交通量的大小、风、流、主航道的长度、船舶宽度与航道宽度之比、船舶的长度与航道宽度之比、船舶的最大吃水与航道水深之比、港口能见度情况、航道转向点个数、主航道与次航道交叉点的个数航道距危险物的距离、港口航标的情况、港口船舶的交通密度等。

根据调查和专家咨询，在上述影响港口船舶交通安全的因素中确定了下述主要因素：能见度、大风、港口最大流速、港口主航道长度、主航道与次航道交叉点和转向点的个数、船舶宽度与航道宽度之比、船舶长度与航道宽度之比、船舶吃水与航道深度之比、港口船舶交通量、船舶

---

* 本文发表在《1998年大连国际海事技术交流会论文集(第一卷)》，作者郑中义、吴兆麟。

交通密度十因素。

(1) 能见度

能见度直接影响到船舶交通安全,特别是在低能见度时,船舶发生事故的可能性增大。据统计,交通危险程度与能见度距离成反比。在世界许多港口的港章中,大都有当能见度达到一定程度时,禁止船舶进出港口和禁止船舶靠离码头的规定。因此,港口能见度是船舶航行危险程度的重要反映指标。选取的能见度是指港口近五年的平均低于1 km的能见度年积累天数,单位为天/年。

(2) 大风

大风和台风造成船舶偏航、搁浅以及造成船舶走锚等。港口的年大风天数越多,港口的危险程度也越高。在评价中,大风值是指该港口近五年风力达6级(蒲福风级)及以上的平均年累计发生天数与台风警报发生即预计48 h内可能侵入港口或边缘距离距港口只有500 km至台风警报消除为止的年积累天数之和。

(3) 港口最大流速

港口最大流速是指特定港口最大流的节数。港口的流速也是船舶安全航行的天敌,由于流速的存在使船舶操纵困难。在狭水道,流加速了逆流船舶船侧及船底水流的相对速度,而使船舶发生岸壁效应、船舶之间的相互作用以及船舶体等,使船舶发生碰撞、搁浅等事故。

(4) 港口主航道长度

由于航道的宽度受到限制,船舶转向能力受到限制,由于船舶吃水的限制,极易发生船舶之间的相互作用、岸壁作用与船体下坐,从而发生船舶碰撞和搁浅事故,因此特定港口主航道的长度是其环境危险度的因素之一。在评价中,主航道的长度是指统计的港口年500总吨及以上船舶人工航道的航行海里数值。

(5) 主航道与次航道交叉点和转向点的个数

港口航道交叉点与转向点的个数越多,船舶在该处的会遇次数也越多,越易发生船舶碰撞事故。同时,在航道的交叉与转向点处,船舶密度增加,容易出现紧迫局面而发生碰撞与搁浅事故。评价中采用的与主航道交叉点个数是指主航道与通航水深大于1 m的次航道的交叉角度大于25°的个数。

(6) 船舶宽度与航道宽度之比

船舶宽度与航道宽度之比也是港口船舶航行环境危险程度的重要标志之一。该比值越小,表明船舶航行的水域余量就越小,从而发生船舶间碰撞、岸壁效应及船体下坐的可能性也就越大。评价中采用的船舶宽度是特定港口允许通航船舶宽度的平均值,航道宽度为特定航道最窄处的宽度。

(7) 船舶长度与航道宽度之比

该比值的大小也与港口环境危险程度有关,它主要是在船舶转向和旋回时对船舶安全产生影响。但由于各港口一般都为水域较为宽阔的区域指定了掉头区,因此在评价中该因素没有考虑。

(8) 船舶吃水与航道深度之比

船舶吃水与航道水深之比也是反映船舶航行安全的标志之一,但是由于各港口都有关于船舶港内航行最大吃水的规定,因此该比值在本文中不考虑。

(9) 港口船舶交通量

港口船舶交通量反映了港口的繁忙程度。对于特定港口船舶交通量越大,船舶的会遇率也就越高。许多学者对船舶交通量对航行安全的影响有较为详细的论述。在本文船舶交通量采用加权船舶交通量,以使评价结果具有横向的可比性。船舶加权系数采用藤井弥平(日本)《海上交通工学》中提出的加权系数,如表1所示。

表1 船舶吨位换算系数表

吨位	0~20	20~100	100~500	500~3 000	3 000~20 000	20 000~100 000	100 000 以上
加权系数	1/6	1/4	1/2	1	2	4	6

(10)船舶交通密度

船舶交通密度是影响港口船舶航行安全的重要因素之一。它与船舶碰撞、搁浅等事故有重要关系。

另外,还有港口航标的完好率和航道距危险物的最近距离等也是港口环境危险度的影响因素,但它们相对于上述因素不十分重要,因此在评价时不考虑。

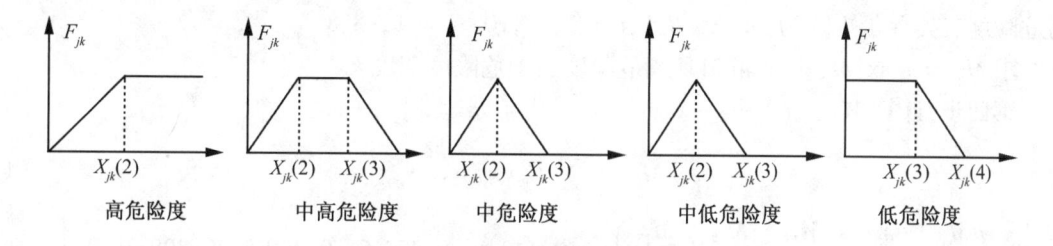

图1 各危险度灰类的白化权函数

2 灰色评估数学模型及评价

对于要评价的港口各因素 B_{ij}(其中 i 为各港口编号,j 为选定出来的八个因素的编号)分成高危险度、中高危险度、中危险度、中低危险度和低危险度五类(k)。根据灰色理论,当(j)各值的量纲不同、意义不同,且在数值上相差较大时,如采取指标变权聚类,其结果的可售程度较低,而先采取初始化算 f 或均值化算子化为无量纲后再评价,又不能反映出不同指标的影响程度,因此本文采用定权估方法。其步骤如下:

第一步:给出选取各因素 B_{ij} 对于所分类(k)的白化权函数 $F_{jk}(*)$,其中:$j=1,\cdots,8;k=1,2,3,4,5$。

在各灰类白化权函数中,最为关键的 $X_{jk}(*)$ 的选取。根据海上的实际及对专家的咨询,高危险度灰类的 $X_{jk}(2) = \max\{B_{ij}\}$、中危险度灰类的 $X_{jk}(2) = \max\{B_{ij}\}/2$、中高危险度灰类的 $X_{jk}(2) = 3\max\{B_{ij}\}/4$、中低危险度灰类的 $X_{jk}(2) = \max\{B_{ij}\}/4$;中高危险度灰类的 $X_{jk}(3) = $ 其相应的 $X_{jk}(2) + 10$,其他依次类推。

第二步:根据两两对比法请专家打分,确定选定各因素的权重 N_j 为:$N_1=0.1, N_2=0.1, N_3=0.1, N_4=0.1, N_5=0.1, N_6=0.1, N_7=0.2, N_8=0.2$。

第三步:选定的各因素列表,如表2所示,并构造矩阵。

表2 评价港口及环境因列表

序号	港口	能见度	大风	最大流	航道长	交叉点	船宽/航道宽	密度	加权交通量
1	大连港	27	40.4	3	9.5	5	0.1	1.5	57.86
2	秦皇岛	11.3	8.6	3	14	2	0.25	1.2	30.74
3	天津港	9.8	80.2	1.5	20.2	1	0.14	1.6	41.2
4	烟台港	24.2	77.4	0.5	4.2	2	0.24	2.1	13.98
5	青岛港	54	94.8	3	7.4	8	0.65	8.1	45.7
6	连云港	16.1	139	2.9	3.6	7	0.36	0.68	14
7	上海港	24.7	51.1	6	85.8	29	0.12	24.3	76.24
8	宁波港	28	21.4	5	13.6	6	0.2	17.6	21.8
9	黄埔港	25	73.3	3.5	63.7	1.3	0.2	2.9	42
10	湛江港	13.3	11.3	3.5	40.8	18	0.1	0.5	32.8

则危险度灰类评价矩阵为:$A = (B_{ij})$, $i = 1,\cdots,10$ $i = 1,\cdots,8$。

求 $M_{jk} = \max\{M_{jk}\}$,则港口环境危险度属于危险度灰度 k。

第四步:计算 M_{jk}

$$M_{jk} = \sum_{j=1}^{8} F_{jk}(x_{jk}) \times N_j \tag{1}$$

$$M_{jk} = \begin{pmatrix} M_{11} & M_{12} & M_{13} & M_{14} & M_{15} \\ M_{21} & M_{22} & M_{23} & M_{24} & M_{25} \\ M_{31} & M_{32} & M_{33} & M_{34} & M_{35} \\ M_{41} & M_{42} & M_{43} & M_{44} & M_{45} \\ M_{51} & M_{52} & M_{53} & M_{54} & M_{55} \\ M_{61} & M_{62} & M_{63} & M_{64} & M_{65} \\ M_{71} & M_{72} & M_{73} & M_{74} & M_{75} \\ M_{81} & M_{82} & M_{83} & M_{84} & M_{85} \\ M_{91} & M_{92} & M_{93} & M_{94} & M_{95} \\ M_{101} & M_{102} & M_{103} & M_{104} & M_{105} \end{pmatrix} = \begin{pmatrix} 0.4484 & 0.4765 & 0.4908 & 0.3980 & 0.4219 \\ 0.2603 & 0.3537 & 0.4453 & 0.4421 & 0.4970 \\ 0.2797 & 0.3935 & 0.5160 & 0.5138 & 0.5004 \\ 0.2442 & 0.3339 & 0.3947 & 0.3753 & 0.7000 \\ 0.4588 & 0.5442 & 0.5670 & 0.4774 & 0.2571 \\ 0.3473 & 0.3435 & 0.2984 & 0.3386 & 0.6000 \\ 0.7826 & 0.5771 & 0.2378 & 0.2592 & 0.0066 \\ 0.4394 & 0.5979 & 0.5352 & 0.4464 & 0.2872 \\ 0.4640 & 0.6022 & 0.7144 & 0.4449 & 0.0200 \\ 0.3165 & 0.4416 & 0.5629 & 0.3823 & 0.3258 \end{pmatrix}$$

则 $M_{jk} = \max\{M_{jk}(k = 1,2,3,4,5)\}$ 为:

$\max M_{1k} = M_{13} = 0.4908$

$\max M_{2k} = M_{25} = 0.4970$

$\max M_{3k} = M_{33} = 0.5160$

$\max M_{4k} = M_{43} = 0.3947$

$\max M_{5k} = M_{53} = 0.5670$

$\max M_{6k} = M_{65} = 0.6000$

$\max M_{7k} = M_{71} = 0.7826$

$\max M_{8k} = M_{82} = 0.5979$

$$\max M_{9k} = M_{93} = 0.7144$$
$$\max M_{10k} = M_{103} = 0.5629$$

属于高危险度的港口有：上海。
属于中高危险度的港口有：宁波。
属于中危险度的港口有：大连、烟台、青岛、黄埔、湛江、天津。
属于低危险度的港口有：秦皇岛、连云港。

3 结论

(1)用灰色系统对港口船舶航行环境危险度进行评价是可行的。得到的结果与交通部科技项目《我国沿海 VTS 等级划分》的结果基本一致，但方法更为简便。

(2)从我国沿海十个港口的评价情况看，上海港环境最危险，这不但与实际相符，而且要求到上海船舶的驾驶员或船长更应谨慎驾驶船舶，以保证航行安全。

(3)从评价结果看，我国目前沿海大多数港口环境危险度属于中等，这反映了地理条件和安全管理综合的均等，如果要降低船舶的航行危险，增进水上安全，主要的工作是加强管理。

(4)从模型看，评价的结果还较为粗略，可通过改进以增加评价的精度。

90年代海上交通定量研究成果的统计分析[*]

摘要:海上交通定量研究是分四个领域进行的,按领域、研究方法与手段、研究者国籍等做了统计分析,这从整体上反映了1990年以来海上交通定量研究的动态,对掌握海上交通工程学科的前沿、了解海上交通工程的理论基础等具有一定的实际指导意义。

关键词:海上交通;定量研究;成果;统计分析

0 引言

海上交通是指定区域内船舶运动的组合与船舶行为的总体[312]。它是船舶、船员、海上交通环境相互作用的反映。近年来,随着海运业的发展,航行于海上的船舶数量、类型和吨位都发生了巨大的变化,大量船舶频繁活动于港口和海上交通要道,使海上通航密度大为增加,重大海上交通事故时有发生。为了改善船舶航行秩序、减少海上事故、保证海上交通安全,国内外许多专家、学者对此进行了深入的研究。海上交通的研究一般可分为定性研究与定量研究,一般意义上的定量研究是指在对问题的论证中采用数学工具,从量上进行的分析研究,从中找出其普遍规律性,揭示其内在联系,抓住其主要矛盾,从而为科学管理提供依据,有助于管理者做出最佳决策。因此,进行海上交通定量研究是十分必要的。

由于我国的海上交通定量研究起步较晚,与日本相比,我国在研究的深度和广度方面都存在着不小的差距。因此需要了解和掌握国内外海上交通定量研究的成果及其发展动态和研究方向。它对于正在从事和即将从事海上交通研究的学者都具有十分重要的指导意义。

1 调查范围

海上交通定量研究的成果主要以专著、刊物或学术会议上发表的论文等多种形式表现。鉴于专著中的精华部分都以论文的形式在刊物上发表,多数学术会议论文在会议之后也都在有关刊物上正式发表,因此从收集资料的可行性出发,主要针对国内外正式出版的有关刊物。国内刊物主要是海运院校学报、航海学会主办的刊物及其他有关反映海上交通的刊物;国外刊物主要是日本航海学会论文集、东京商船大学研究报告、海难与审判(日语)、人与船(日语)、

---

[*] 本文"90年代"指20世纪90年代,发表在《大连海事大学学报》1999年第2期第25卷,作者邵哲平、郑中义、杨丹、吴兆麟。

航海杂志(英)、导航(美国导航学会杂志)、海上航路(英语)、海上安全(英语)等。从1990年至1998年,经过大量查阅与筛选刊物共收集到97篇论文,具体如表1所示。

表1 各刊物的简要情况及有关海上交通定量研究论文数量表

刊物名称	创刊时间/年	刊次	刊登论文的有关领域	论文数/篇
大连海事大学学报	1957	季刊	航海技术、机电、航管、法规等	12
上海海运学院学报	1979	季刊	文理综合版	3
集美航海学院学报	1982	季刊	自然科学、社会科学与高教研究	4
武汉交通科技大学学报	1959	双月	船舶与海洋工程、交通土木等	3
海军大连舰艇学院学报	1978	季刊	航海与海洋测绘及其他领域	3
中国航海	1965	半年	航海技术、轮机管理、法规等	1
航海技术(中)	1981	双月	航海、通信导航、机电、航管等	3
日本航海学会论文集	1949	半年	与海上交通有关的领域	62
航海杂志(英)	1947	季刊	航海技术、导航技术等	6

2 调查结果分析

2.1 海上交通定量研究领域的划分

根据所查得的文献,将海上交通定量研究分为以下四个研究领域:

(1)交通实态与交通流。交通实态主要研究某一水域的船舶密度、船舶密度分布与航迹密度分布情况。船舶密度、船舶密度分布与船舶航迹分布是表示一个水域船舶交通实况的基本量与基本概念,也是建立交通流模型的基础。交通流是从时空上研究某一水域的运动状态,它通常用系统仿真的方法来描述广阔水域中众多船舶的运动状态[369]。

(2)船舶行为。在海上交通定量研究中,关于船舶行为的研究是相当重要的部分。它分别从微观与宏观的角度分析船舶在操纵避碰方面的方式、方法、特征和规律,发现其中存在的问题,以便为进一步研究船舶交通其他内容提供依据[312]。在海上交通定量研究中,船舶行为不是指某一具体船舶的某一具体行为,而是指船舶群体的同类行动的方式与规律。由于船舶是人操纵的,船舶行为在某种意义上是驾驶人员的行为。然而,船舶行为不仅取决于人的意识、思维、决策与操纵,而且受到船舶本身特性和周围环境的影响。

(3)交通事故统计分析。它主要研究交通事故的规模、发生的规律、影响的因素与事故的原因(包括人为过失、船舶及其设备的性能与缺陷、交通环境和条件的不利或妨碍因素三方面的具体问题)。它不是指交通事故的个例分析,而是指其总体的分析[370]。

(4)交通安全评价。海上交通是一个人—船—环境的大系统,因此安全评价就是对这个大系统的安全状况进行定量和定性的估计和评定。因为安全也可通过危险来表述,所以安全评价也可以通过对系统所处的危险状态进行估计和评价。其目的是判别系统是否达到规定的安全目标或是否符合安全要求,并根据评价结果,对系统进行调整或采取某些加强和完善的安全措施[371, 372]。根据上述的研究领域划分,对查得的97篇论文中这四个研究领域的论文情况如图1所示。我国及日本在安全评价和船舶行为两大领域都做了大量的研究工作。在船舶行为研究领域中,我国的论文数量与日本相差无几,但在交通安全评价研究领域日本则占据主导地位。在交通事故统计分析和交通实态与交通流两大领域,我国及日本的研究力度相对较小。这说明了我国及日本在海上交通定量研究方面的主要方向是安全评价和船舶行为这两大领域。

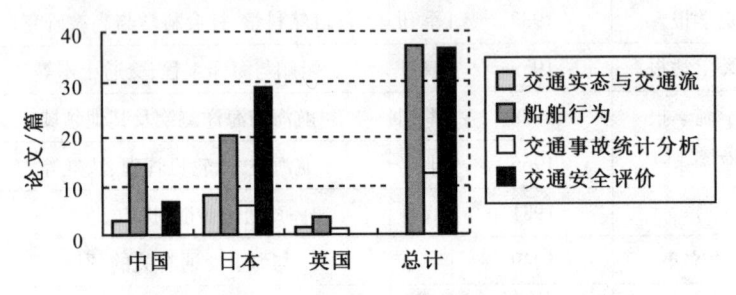

图1 各研究领域论文数量直方图

2.2 按研究方法与手段划分进行比较

20世纪90年代以来,各国从事海上交通定量研究的专家和学者通过应用操船模拟器试验、问卷调查、数据统计分析、模糊分析、计算机模拟和实态调查等多种方式和手段,对海上交通的四大领域进行了深入的研究。在论文中采用这些研究方法的情况如表2所示。

表2 按研究方法划分的统计表

论文中采用的研究方法	应用次数	占百分比
操船模拟器试验	28	29%
问卷调查	20	21%
数据统计分析	17	18%
模糊分析	12	12%
计算机模拟	8	8%
实态调查	2	2%
其他	10	10%

从表2中可以看出在研究方法中很大一部分是利用操船模拟器进行的。它的应用范围主要在船舶行为和安全评价两个研究领域。因为我国在操船模拟器研制方面还没有普及,所以在利用操船模拟器进行船舶行为和安全评价方面未能做深入地研究。

数据的采集主要是通过问卷调查与实态调查的方式进行的。但要获得交通实态调查的数据需要大量的时间,投入相当多的人力、物力和财力,因此要得到交通实态调查数据较为困难。

大量的数据主要是通过问卷调查方式得到,在后续的论文中还要对问卷调查表的形式、内容与编排等做专题研究。

在研究中对采集到的数据主要采用数据统计分析和模糊分析的方法,因此对即将成为海上交通的研究者们必须掌握数理统计和模糊数学等基础科学知识。

2.3 按研究者的国籍划分进行比较

以年度指标来统计各年度论文数量的分布情况如图 2 所示。我国在这些领域的年平均论文数为 4 篇,日本为 7 篇,英国为 0.6 篇。

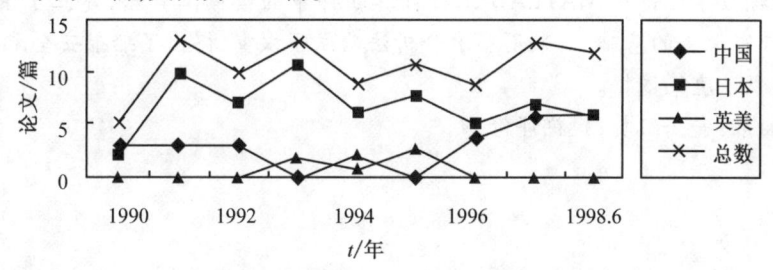

图 2　以年度指标划分的论文数量曲线图

从收集到的 97 篇论文中,英国在 20 世纪 90 年代对海上交通的定量研究较少。我国研究者的论文占 30 篇,日本研究者的论文占 62 篇,英国作者的论文只有 5 篇,按作者国籍划分的论文数量百分比情况见图 3。日本研究者的论文占总数的 64%,从查得的文献中可知其论文作者的单位多数是日本东京商船大学及神户商船大学,这说明在日本进行海上交通定量研究的主要单位是东京商船大学和神户商船大学。中国研究者发表了 30 篇论文,占总数的 30%,其中有 12 篇论文是大连海事大学的研究者发表的,在国内研究者中占的比例最大,这说明在海上交通定量研究领域中,研究的主要力量在大连海事大学。为了进一步增加海上交通定量研究领域的成果,必须通过各种形式加强国际间的学术交流。

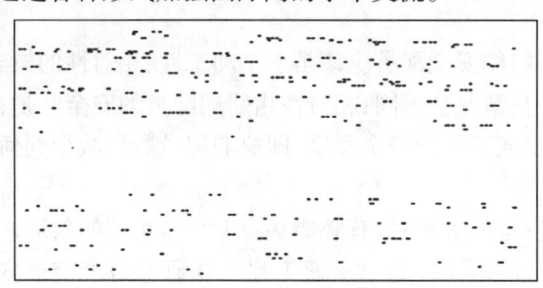

图 3　按研究者国籍划分的论文数量百分图

3　结束语

本文只对 20 世纪 90 年代以来国内外的海上交通定量研究成果总体进行了概括的统计分析,大致反映出海上交通定量研究的趋势,这将为是我们今后在其各领域中进行深入分析打下基础。我们将在此基础上对其各领域做更全面的分析和汇总。

船舶安全配员研究*

摘要：基于安全系统工程理论，采用定性、定量相结合的方法，分析了影响船舶安全配员的因素。利用模糊数学理论及 MATLAB 工程计算软件中的模糊工具箱，建立了主要因素的隶属度函数，在专家调查的基础上，采用层次分析法确立了权重，得出了船舶安全配员指数，为船舶安全配员提供了决策依据。

关键词：船舶；安全配员；模糊评价

0 引言

在船舶自动化技术的进步、世界航运市场竞争的日益激烈、船员综合素质的提高、发达国家船员短缺等多方面因素的综合作用下，在世界范围内船舶配员数量出现减少的趋势，尤其是 20 世纪 80 年代以来，发达国家的船舶配员数量急剧减少，使得航运界开始关注船舶配员减少是否会影响船舶安全的问题。国际海事组织（IMO）已敦促各成员国加强对船舶最低安全配员证书的港口国监督。我国作为一个航运大国，船舶配员也在发生着变化，因此，有必要系统地研究船舶安全配员，从而为海上安全主管机关、航运公司等提供决策依据。

1 船舶配员与安全

从安全的角度来看，船舶安全配员应该是一个动态性、相对性的概念。动态性指随着各种相关条件的改变，船舶配员情况会不同；相对性指船舶配员的安全性是在一定的时空条件下达到的人们所能够普遍接受或认可的安全程度，即船舶配员数量减少到何种程度时，才能保证船舶安全地完成航行任务。

在研究船舶配员与安全的关系时，有必要从海上交通系统的角度来分析海事发生的原因，并深入探求各种潜在的危险因素。海上交通工程学在研究海上交通安全时，将其分为人（船员）、船舶和环境三个部分[312]。而船舶配员的减少所带来的潜在危险性也应从这三个方面分析，如图 1 所示。例如，船舶配员的减少是否会增加船员的疲劳程度，是否会导致船员忽略对船舶基本的维修保养，以及船员的素质与培训状况是否令人满意，等等。从海事统计分析来看，由于船员的疲劳因素、船员的素质和培训情况、船舶维修保养状况所造成的事故占有较大的比例，而船舶配员水平直接影响着这些海事致因，因此，船舶配员水平对船舶航行安全至关重要。

---

* 本文发表在《大连海事大学学报》2000 年第 1 期第 26 卷，作者侯玉强、吴兆麟、郑中义。

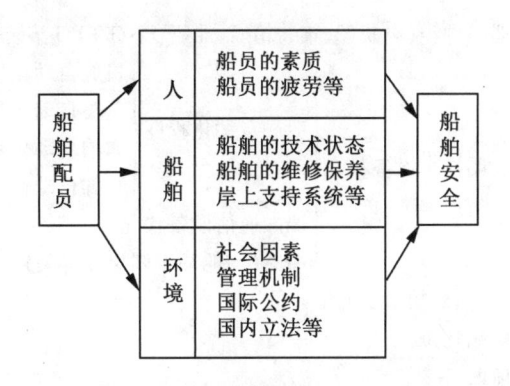

图1 船舶配员与安全的关系

2 我国船舶配员现状及存在的问题

纵观我国船舶配员的改革情况,由于影响船舶安全配员的因素较多,加之我国船队中既有先进的自动化船舶,又有船龄较大、技术水平落后的船舶,在船舶自动化技术水平上呈现多层次的特点,并且对船舶配员缺乏较系统的研究,这样就给船舶配员决策带来一定困难。

目前我国的船舶配员体制改革相对于西方发达国家起步较晚,处于不断探索之中,且因各国的国情、船舶的总体条件、船员的素质和培训、管理体制等因素的差异,决定了我国的船舶配员应该根据我国的具体国情,在继承以前配员的基础上稳步地改革,并且在船舶配员决策中,运用定量化分析方法来研究,以适应各种因素的变化,保证船舶和人命的安全。

3 评价指标体系的建立

为了客观地选取能够真实反映评价对象的综合评判指标,本文在综合分析船舶安全配员所涉及的因素的基础上,通过对航海界专家、港监工作人员、航运公司等多方面的咨询、调查,确立了评价指标体系,如图2所示,这为数学模型的建立奠定了基础。

4 评价模型的建立

4.1 评价指标权重的获取

由于船舶安全配员所涉及的因素较多,在综合评价中,为了突出主要的影响因素,客观、合理地评价船舶配员水平,利用层次分析法(AHP)来计算评价指标的权重,其基本步骤是:(1)层次结构的建立;(2)判断矩阵的建立;(3)依照判断矩阵进行权重计算,即解特征根

$$AW = \lambda_{max} W \tag{1}$$

W 经正规化后为指标 $A_1, A_2, A_3, \cdots$,在准则 C_k 下的排序权重,此法称为排序权向量的特征根法。计算一致性指标 CI:

$$CI = (\lambda_{max} - n)/(n - 1) \tag{2}$$

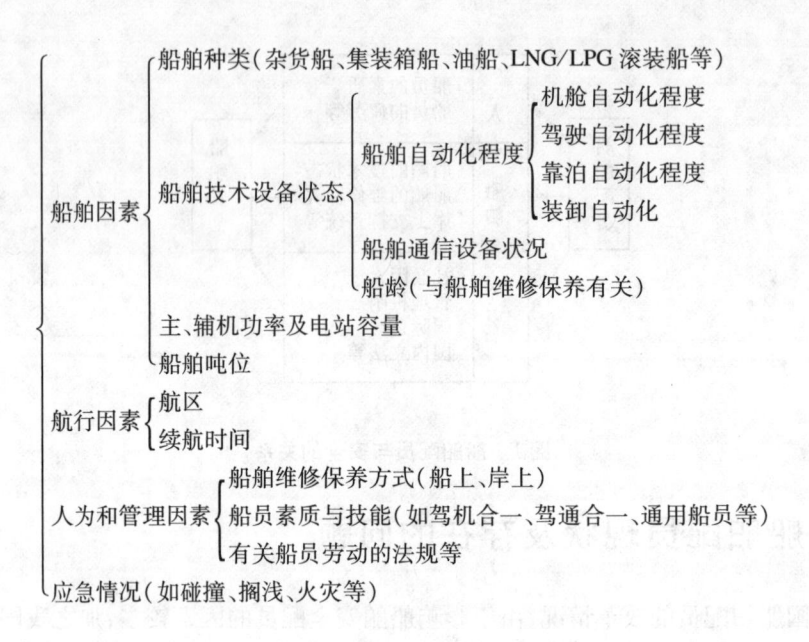

```
                    ┌ 船舶种类(杂货船、集装箱船、油船、LNG/LPG滚装船等)
                    │                          ┌ 机舱自动化程度
         ┌ 船舶因素 │          ┌ 船舶自动化程度 │ 驾驶自动化程度
         │         │ 船舶技术  │                │ 靠泊自动化程度
         │         │ 设备状态  │                └ 装卸自动化
         │         │          │ 船舶通信设备状况
         │         │          └ 船龄(与船舶维修保养有关)
         │          主、辅机功率及电站容量
         │          船舶吨位
         │         ┌ 航区
         │ 航行因素│
         │         └ 续航时间
         │                    ┌ 船舶维修保养方式(船上、岸上)
         │ 人为和管理因素     │ 船员素质与技能(如驾机合一、驾通合一、通用船员等)
         │                    └ 有关船员劳动的法规等
         └ 应急情况(如碰撞、搁浅、火灾等)
```

图 2　船舶安全配员评价指标体系

一般认为，$CI<0.1$ 时，A 的一致性是可以接受的。

利用 MATLAB 工程计算软件，编制层次分析法的计算程序，对收回的调查表进行计算，得到各层次指标的权重：{船舶因素，航行因素，人为和管理因素，应急情况} = {0.448 0, 0.200 5, 0.250 0, 0.101 5}；{船舶种类，船舶技术设备状态，主辅机功率及电站容量，船舶吨位} = {0.053 5, 0.563 4, 0.197 8, 0.185 3}；{船舶自动化程度，船舶通信设备状态，船舶维修保养状态(船龄)} = {0.478 8, 0.120 0, 0.401 2}；{机舱自动化程度，驾驶自动化程度，靠泊自动化程度，装卸自动化程度} = {0.579 2, 0.307 4, 0.062 2, 0.051 2}；{航区，续航时间} = {0.512 0, 0.488 0}。

4.2　隶属函数的确定

隶属函数的确定目前主要依靠经验，从实践效果中进行反馈，不断校正自己的认识以达到预定目标。尽管用各种方法建立的隶属度函数难免会带有人为主观性的影响，但都是对客观现实的一种"逼近"。

将评判等级集 V 定义为 7 个等级的集合，即：

$$V = \{V_1, V_2, V_3, \cdots, V_7\} = \{-3, -2, -1, 0, +1, +2, +3\}$$

其中 $-3, -2, -1, 0, +1, +2, +3$ 为等级高低量度，分别对应的各等级如表 1 所示。

表 1 评价等级

量度	等级
+3	非常大
+2	很大
+1	较大
0	临界
-1	较小
-2	很小
-3	非常小

该评价等级表示:如果减少船舶配员数量,每项指标则表示对船舶安全的影响程度,也就是发生海事的潜在危险程度。

本文在确定各个指标对应于各因素的隶属函数时,根据问卷调查结果以及征求专家的意见,并参考 MATLAB 软件模糊工具箱[373]中提供的隶属函数进行拟合。如采用高斯隶属函数,其公式如下:

$$f(x,a,c) = e^{-\frac{(x-c)^2}{2a^2}} \tag{3}$$

该隶属函数是由 a、c 两个参数决定的,a 的大小决定隶属函数曲线的宽度,当 a 较大时,隶属函数曲线较宽,对论域的覆盖面积大,具有较低的分辨率;当 a 较小时,隶属函数曲线较窄,对论域的覆盖面积小,具有较高的分辨率。这些直接影响到评价的结果。c 的大小决定隶属函数对应于论域的位置,其特点是:曲线为正态型分布,在论域上对应的值比较集中,能够明显地反映出各个因素对应的不同论域。

根据问卷调查表的统计,对船舶技术设备状态隶属度子集表进行隶属函数曲线拟合,如图 3 所示;同理也可求出其他的隶属函数。

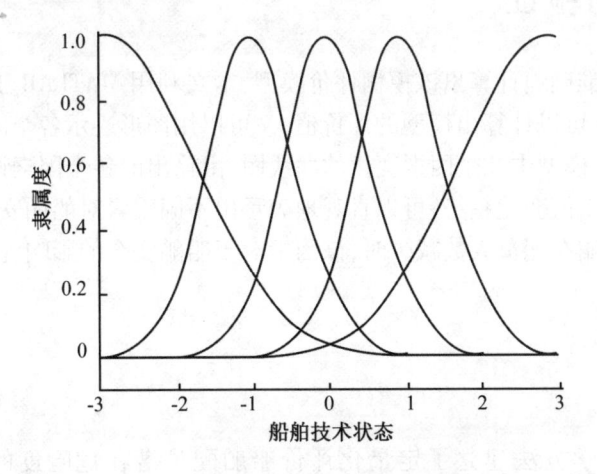

图 3 船舶技术设备状态隶属度

4.3 模型的建立

在确定了评价对象的指标体系、各指标的权重及其隶属函数后,就可以建立模糊评价模型。由于船舶配员涉及因素较多,为了避免一些指标加权后被忽略或评价结果过于笼统,有必要既从微观的角度(即单因素评价模型),又从宏观的角度(即多层次综合评价模型)来全面、系统地分析这些指标。模糊综合评价模型的建立包括以下几个基本步骤:

第一步:将因素集 $U = \{U_1, U_2, \cdots, U_n\}$ 按某些属性分成 n 个子集:

$$U_i = \{U_{i1}, U_{i2}, \cdots, U_{in}\}, i = 1, 2, 3, \cdots, n \tag{4}$$

第二步:对子因素集 U_i,分别做出综合评判,设 $V = \{V_1, V_2, \cdots, V_m\}$ 为评判集,U_i 中各因素相对 V 的权重分配为:$A_i = (a_{i1}\ a_{i2}\ \cdots\ a_{in})$ 其中,$a_{i1} + a_{i2} + \cdots + a_{in} = 1$,若设 R_i 为单因素评判矩阵,则得出一级评判向量:$B_i = A_i \cdot R_i = (b_{i1}\ b_{i2}\ \cdots\ b_{im}), i = 1, 2, \cdots, m$。

第三步:将每个 U_i 视为一个因素,记:$\_ = \{U_1, U_2, \cdots, U_S\}$,于是 $\_$ 又是一个因素集,其单因素评判矩阵为:

$$R = \begin{pmatrix} B_1 \\ B_2 \\ \cdots \\ B_S \end{pmatrix} = \begin{pmatrix} b_{11} & b_{12} & \cdots & b_{1m} \\ b_{21} & b_{22} & \cdots & b_{2m} \\ \vdots & \vdots & & \vdots \\ b_{s1} & b_{s2} & \cdots & b_{sm} \end{pmatrix} \tag{5}$$

每个 U_i 作为 U 的一部分,反映 U 的某种属性,按其重要性得到权重。

$$A = (a_1\ a_2\ \cdots\ a_s) \tag{6}$$

于是得到二级评判向量:

$$B = A \cdot R = (b_1\ b_2\ \cdots\ b_m) \tag{7}$$

根据所得的二级评判向量,利用反模糊化方法,可以得到评价对象所最终对应的等级。

5 评价模型的验证

为了便于快速而准确地计算出该模糊评价模型,本文利用 MATLAB 工程计算软件中的模糊推理系统工具箱,既可以计算出模型的评价值,又可以用图形表示各个因素变化的趋势。例如,图 4 和图 5 选取了模型中几个因素变化的曲线图,由输出的各个因素评价结果随单因素和随任意两个因素的输出值变化趋势,可以直观地表示出不同因素对船舶安全配员的影响程度。该数值的大小表示船舶在配员人数减少时,该因素对于船舶安全的影响程度,即减少船舶配员潜在危险度的大小。

6 结束语

本文借助模糊数学方法建立了定量化评价船舶配员潜在危险度的数学模型,并运用 MATLAB 软件中的模糊工具箱实现模型的计算机化,可以方便而直观地给出评价值的大小及其随各种因素的变化趋势,为海上安全监督机关、航运公司等安全管理决策人员决定船舶安全配员提供了定量化的依据。但是,由于本文是将模糊数学理论应用于船舶配员决策的一个探索,在隶属函数的构造和模糊算子的选取以及模型中人的因素方面有待于进一步完善和研究。

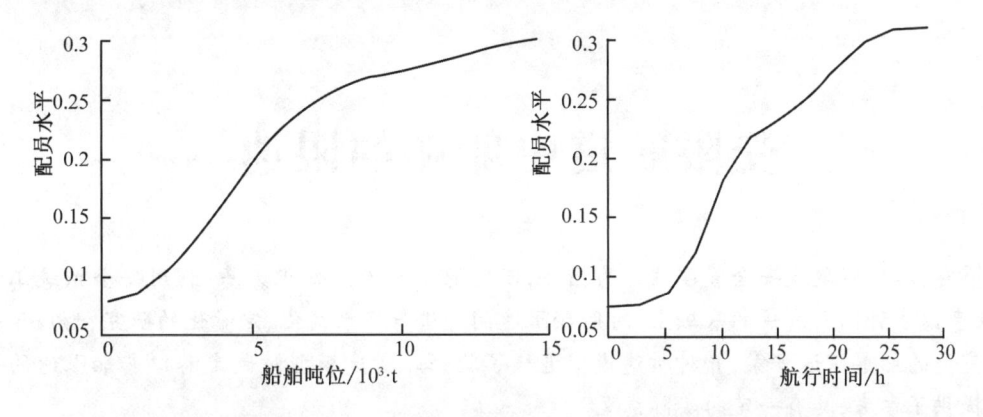

图4 评价结果随单因素变化的曲线图

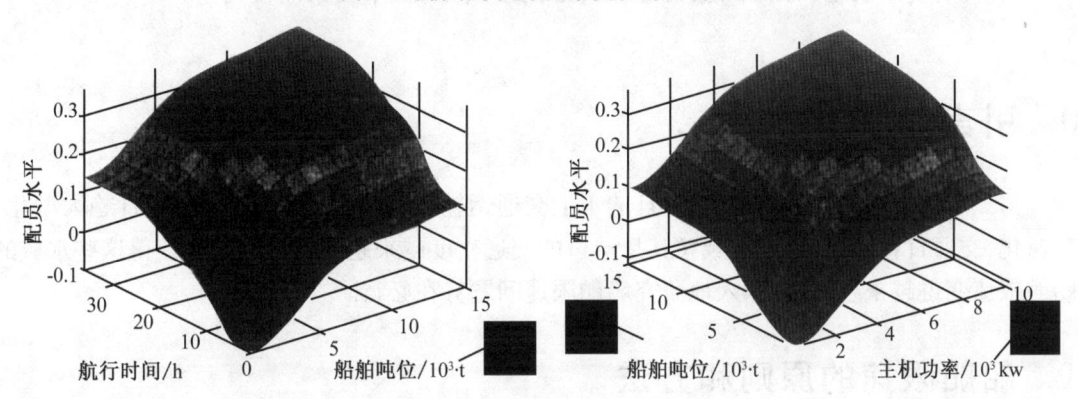

图5 评价结果随双因素变化的曲线图

受限航道中船舶的限速*

摘要:本文以现代安全管理理论为指导,以航海学科专业知识为基础,用安全系统工程方法,在考虑多种因素影响的基础上,对船舶限速问题进行了系统化、定量化的研究,形成了一套比较完整的船舶限速方案,并对所建模型进行了验证。所建模型对制定港口船舶限速的规章制度提供了参考,具有一定的实际意义。

关键词:受限航道;船舶限速;能量释放论;层次分析法;安全乘潮模式

0 引言

与二十世纪七八十年代相比,今日的水上交通运输发生了显著的变化:船舶日趋大型化、高速化,交通日益繁忙,许多水域尤其是港口的交通密度越来越大。这种变化使得这些水域的船舶限速变得越来越重要,深入地研究船舶限速问题势在必行。

1 船舶限速的原则和方法

1.1 船舶限速的原则

与水上交通密切相关的两个方面是安全与效益,综合考虑社会、经济等各方面因素,尤其是考虑到在当前各港口船舶交通量都远未达到其交通容量的情况下,坚持"安全第一"的原则应该说是科学、合理的。因此,港口船舶限速的原则应是:安全为主,兼顾效率,即在安全有保障的前提下尽可能提高限速值。

1.2 船舶限速的方法

第一,船舶限速中应考虑的主要危险。在安全系统设计的初始阶段,一般要对系统进行危险性预先分析,找出系统中存在的所有危险,船舶限速中应考虑的主要危险如下:(1)浪损;(2)碰撞;(3)搁浅;(4)擦底;(5)错过乘潮时机。

第二,船舶限速影响因素系统。为了克服因航速不当带来的危险,船舶限速应考察的因素如下:(1)船舶兴波;(2)船体下沉量;(3)潮高;(4)航道曲度;(5)船舶密度、能见度、风、流、碍

---

* 本文发表在《大连海事大学学报》2002年第2期第28卷,作者徐春、郑中义、吴兆麟。

航物分布、信息服务、航道(包括航标、航道宽度、曲度)等。

第三,限速方案。由前面的分析可知,船舶限速要克服的危险共有以下几类:(1)浪损;(2)错过乘潮时机;(3)擦底;(4)碰撞、触碰和搁浅。前三种危险可以通过限制航速而避免,因为航速是造成这种危险的主导因素。对于船舶碰撞、触碰和搁浅这些危险,仅通过限制航速是无法避免的,因为该危险还与船舶密度、航道条件、信息服务等多种因素有关,航速只不过是其中一个与这些因素处于同等地位的条件而已,所以只能根据既定的各种条件找到一个与之最相适应的最有利的航速,即最佳航速。

由于以上因素都是独立因素,需分别考虑它们与船舶限速的关系,然后结合为克服各种危险对船舶限速的要求,得出合理的限速规定。要克服浪损、擦底,需确定航速的上限值 v_{max},要防止错过乘潮时机须确定航速的下限值 v_{min},它只限制第一个浅水区与最后一个浅水区之间航段的航速。而对于减小避碰、触碰和搁浅危险要求的最佳航速值 v 只限制非浅水和非急弯的一般航段。对于急弯航道也要对其进行专门限速以防止船舶碰撞。

2 数学模型的建立

2.1 效益与限速

这里的效益主要指两个方面:保障安全和提高效率。保障安全主要是避免或减轻碰撞、触碰和搁浅的危险,提高效率是指提高交通效率。结合限速特点及其因素分析,可得到与效益有关的因素:(1)船舶密度;(2)风;(3)流;(4)碍航物情况;(5)信息条件;(6)吃水与可用水深的关系;(7)航道曲度、宽度。

从提高效益角度考虑船舶限速时,涉及因素较多,还需要兼顾安全与效率,这是一个多目标、多因素的决策问题,因此,考虑使用层次分析法[374]。此方法一般有四个步骤:

第一,建立描述系统功能或特征的内部独立的递阶层次结构;

第二,两两比较结构要素,构造出所有的判断矩阵;

第三,解此矩阵,得出特征根和特征向量并检验每个判断矩阵的一致性,若不满足一致性条件,则要修改判断矩阵,直到满足条件为止;

第四,计算各层元素的组合权重。

以效益为目标的船舶限速递阶层次结构如图1所示。

根据递阶层次结构图即可构造判断矩阵。本文选用根法解判断矩阵,步骤如下:

(1)各行元素按行相乘, $u_{ij} = \prod_{i=1}^{n} a_{ij}$;

(2)所得乘积分别开 n 次方, $u_i = \sqrt[n]{u_{ij}}$;

(3)将方根向量正规化,得排序权向量 w。

然后根据方程 $\boldsymbol{Aw} = \lambda \boldsymbol{w}$ 即可求得 λ_{max}。

在求出 λ_{max} 后要进行一致性检验,这是保证结论可靠的必要条件,步骤为:

计算一致性指标 CI

$$CI = (\lambda_{max} - n)/(n - 1)$$

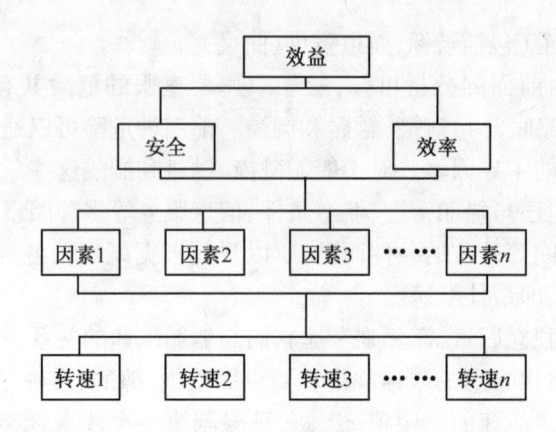

图1 以效益为目的的船舶限速阶梯层次结构图

计算一致性比例

$$CR = CI/RI$$

当 $CR<0.10$ 时,一般认为 A 的一致性是可以接受的。

最后计算组合权重,据权重值对措施或方案进行选择。

2.2 浪损与限速

根据理论上定性分析和实际调查得到:防止浪损的船舶限速值须满足的条件为 $F_{nh} \leqslant 0.57$[375,376]。

2.3 擦底与限速[377,378]

对船体下沉量的计算可使用简化的 Tuck-Taglor 公式

$$s = C \frac{\Delta}{L_{pp}^2} \frac{F_{nh}^2}{\sqrt{1-F_{nh}^2}}$$

考虑到下沉与纵倾双重因素,公式中的系数取值为:杂货船 $C=1.55$;散货船 $C=1.75$;油船 $C=1.91$。

2.4 航道曲度与限速

对有居间障碍物遮蔽的弯曲航道处的避碰要求是:两船的倒车冲程之和不能小于其互见时两船间航道的长度。港口可选出其代表船,设船冲程为 n 倍船长,两船互见时的距离为 S,则限速应满足 $2nL \leqslant S$。

2.5 乘潮与限速

第一,船舶乘潮的影响因素。

船舶乘潮作业必须满足一定的条件,据此条件可得出船舶乘潮的影响因素:(1)海图水深;(2)潮高;(3)船舶吃水;(4)富余水深;(5)船舶数量;(6)船舶间距;(7)浅段长度;(8)可航时段;(9)乘潮通航时段。

第二,安全乘潮模式与最小限速值的求取由任意时潮高公式可得
$$\Delta t = \arccos[1 + 2(H_t + H_h)/\Delta H]T/\pi$$

用一个高潮前后的两个低潮分别求得涨落潮过程中的 Δt,且以 Δt_b 和 Δt_a 表示,于是乘潮的初始值和终了值为
$$T_s = T_h + \Delta t_b; \quad T_e = T_h + \Delta t_a$$

由此得一次高潮期间对应的可航时段
$$\Delta T_{bc} = T_e - T_s$$

单船过浅时段
$$\Delta T_{ss} = L_{sw}/v_c$$

通航时段
$$\Delta T_n = \Delta T_{be} - \Delta T_{ss}$$

每潮船舶通航量
$$N_{st} = INT[\Delta T_n/(D/v_c)] + 1 \quad (D \text{ 为船舶间的距离})$$

平均每潮通航量
$$N_{sa} = \sum_{i=1}^{n} (N_{st})_i/N_{ty} \quad (N_{ty} \text{ 为每年可通航潮数})$$

将平均每潮通航量与实际平均每潮通航量相比较,取平均每潮通航量约大于实际平均每潮通航量条件下的计算航速值为限速值。

3 应用实例

应用该数学模型对我国某港口的船舶限速进行计算。

3.1 基于最佳效益的限速

某港航道以效益为目标求最佳航速的递阶层次结构如图 2 所示。
判断矩阵及计算如下:
安全:效率 = 0.857 1:0.142 9

$$\boldsymbol{B}_1 = \begin{pmatrix} 1 & 1/5 & 5/17 & 17/5 & 1 & 5/33 \\ 5 & 1 & 13/5 & 37/5 & 5 & 5/13 \\ 17/5 & 5/13 & 1 & 29/5 & 17/5 & 5/21 \\ 5/17 & 5/37 & 5/29 & 1 & 5/17 & 1/9 \\ 1 & 1/5 & 5/17 & 17/5 & 1 & 5/33 \\ 33/5 & 13/5 & 21/5 & 9 & 33/5 & 1 \end{pmatrix}$$

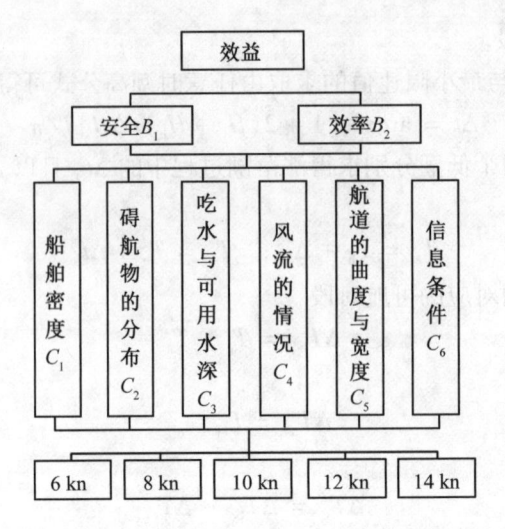

图 2 某港最佳航速阶梯层次结构

$$B_2 = \begin{pmatrix} 1 & 1/8 & 1 & 1/8 & 1/4 & 1/8 \\ 8 & 1 & 8 & 1 & 5 & 1 \\ 1 & 1/8 & 1 & 1/8 & 1/4 & 1/8 \\ 8 & 1 & 8 & 1 & 5 & 1 \\ 4 & 1/5 & 4 & 1/5 & 1 & 1/5 \\ 8 & 1 & 8 & 1 & 5 & 1 \end{pmatrix}$$

$W_i^0 = (0.06\ 0.26\ 0.15\ 0.03\ 0.06\ 0.44)$

$W_i^0 = (0.03\ 0.29\ 0.03\ 0.29\ 0.08\ 0.29)$

$\lambda_{max} = 6.52 \quad CI = 0.11 \quad CR = 0.08$

$\lambda_{max} = 6.39 \quad CI = 0.08 \quad CR = 0.06$

$$C_1 = \begin{pmatrix} 1 & 1/3 & 1/5 & 1/7 & 1/2 \\ 3 & 1 & 1/3 & 1/5 & 1 \\ 5 & 3 & 1 & 1/2 & 1 \\ 5 & 3 & 1 & 1/2 & 2 \\ 7 & 5 & 2 & 1 & 4 \\ 2 & 1 & 1/2 & 1/4 & 1 \end{pmatrix}$$

$$C_2 = \begin{pmatrix} 1 & 1/3 & 3 & 5 & 7 \\ 3 & 1 & 2 & 4 & 9 \\ 1/3 & 1/2 & 1 & 3 & 7 \\ 1/5 & 1/4 & 1/3 & 1 & 5 \\ 1/7 & 1/9 & 1/7 & 1/5 & 1 \end{pmatrix}$$

$W_i^0 = (0.05\ 0.11\ 0.25\ 0.47\ 0.11)$

$W_i^0 = (0.29\ 0.41\ 0.18\ 0.09\ 0.03)$

$\lambda_{max} = 5.01, \quad CI = 0.04, \quad CR = 0.03$

$\lambda_{max} = 5.30, \quad CI = 0.08, \quad CR = 0.07$

$$C_3 = \begin{pmatrix} 1 & 1/3 & 1/5 & 3 & 7 \\ 3 & 1 & 1/2 & 5 & 8 \\ 5 & 2 & 1 & 7 & 9 \\ 1/3 & 1/5 & 1/7 & 1 & 4 \\ 1/7 & 1/8 & 1/9 & 1/4 & 1 \end{pmatrix}$$

$$C_4 = \begin{pmatrix} 1 & 1/3 & 1 & 5 & 8 \\ 3 & 1 & 3 & 5 & 7 \\ 1 & 1/3 & 1 & 3 & 5 \\ 1/5 & 1/5 & 1/3 & 1 & 4 \\ 1/8 & 1/7 & 1/5 & 1/4 & 1 \end{pmatrix}$$

$W_i^0 = (0.14\ 0.29\ 0.47\ 0.07\ 0.03)$

$W_i^0 = (0.24\ 0.45\ 0.20\ 0.08\ 0.04)$

$\lambda_{\max} = 5.45,\quad CI = 0.11,\quad CR = 0.09$

$\lambda_{\max} = 5.37,\quad CI = 0.09,\quad CR = 0.08$

$$C_5 = \begin{pmatrix} 1 & 1/4 & 1/6 & 1/8 & 1/4 \\ 4 & 1 & 1/3 & 1/5 & 1/2 \\ 6 & 3 & 1 & 1/2 & 1 \\ 8 & 5 & 2 & 1 & 3 \\ 4 & 2 & 1 & 1/3 & 1 \end{pmatrix}$$

$$C_6 = \begin{pmatrix} 1 & 2 & 4 & 6 & 9 \\ 1/2 & 1 & 3 & 5 & 8 \\ 1/4 & 1/3 & 1 & 4 & 7 \\ 1/6 & 1/5 & 1/4 & 1 & 5 \\ 1/9 & 1/8 & 1/7 & 1/5 & 1 \end{pmatrix}$$

$W_i^0 = (0.04\ 0.10\ 0.23\ 0.45\ 0.18)$

$W_i^0 = (0.45\ 0.30\ 0.16\ 0.07\ 0.03)$

$\lambda_{\max} = 5.17,\quad CI = 0.04,\quad CR = 0.04$

$\lambda_{\max} = 5.38,\quad CI = 0.09,\quad CR = 0.08$

措施层各要素的组合权重：$W_i^2 = (0.30\ 0.32\ 0.22\ 0.12\ 0.04)$，则该港的最佳航速是 8 kn。

3.2 基于控制浪损的限速

$$F_{nh} = v/\sqrt{gh}$$

对于既定的船舶，兴波的大小主要与航道水深和船舶航速有关，因此，我们主要关注浅水区。该港口进出口航道共有 6 个浅点，经计算，对出港船除第 6 浅点（拦江沙航道）取 7 kn 为最大限速值外，其他各浅点取 8 kn 为其最大限速值。而对于进港船，第 6 浅点仍需限速 7 kn，其他航段限速 10 kn。

3.3 基于安全乘潮的限速

该港口对船舶安全乘潮产生影响的唯一浅段是拦江沙航道。由于该浅段短,进出口船舶数量少,估计对船舶的限速值影响不大,因此只做一简单的估算。由估算的结果可知:若以 7 kn 速度航行,全部船舶能够在平潮时期通过。由此也很容易看出,若用前面的数学模型严格计算,得到的限速值将会很小,这种限速已无实际意义。所以,乘潮对该港的船舶限速值并无影响。

3.4 基于防止擦底的限速

在式

$$s = C \frac{\Delta}{L_{pp}^2} \frac{F_{nh}^2}{\sqrt{1-F_{nh}^2}}$$

中代入各已知数计算可得 $F_{nh} \approx 0.8$。实际上,$F_{nh} \approx 0.8 < 0.57$,这就说明在保持该港章规定的富余水深的条件下,如果没有发生浪损的危险,就不会有擦底的危险。

3.5 弯道处的限速

据调查,进出该港口的船舶基本上是杂货船,能够进出的最大船舶为 5 000 t,因此选 5 000 t 级船舶为代表船。5 000 t 级杂货船的长度为 117 m(保证率为 98%)。从海图上量得永远角处两船的初见距离为 0.5 n mile,取其一半为 0.25 n mile,约 4 倍于 5 000 t 级杂货船的船长,根据船舶航速与冲程的关系和条件 $2nL \leq S$ 可得:航速应控制在 7 kn 以下。

总结以上结果可得出:
(1)以效益为目标的最佳航速为 8 kn;
(2)为防止浪损要求拦江沙航道航速不超过 7 kn,其他航段出港不超过 8 kn;
(3)船舶乘潮对限速值没有影响,即没必要据此进行最低限速;
(4)为防止擦底,限速 8.5 kn;
(5)为防止船舶碰撞,永远角急弯处限速 7 kn。
综合以上各条,得到该港的限速措施为:
(1)江沙航段和永远角急弯处 1.5 n mile 航段限速 7 kn。
(2)其他航段:出港时最大航速不超过 8 kn,进港时不超过 10 kn。对该港口引航员的调查表明,本文得出的限速方案更具有针对性,而且在更有利于安全的情况下提高了交通效率。

4 结束语

本文的研究是针对限制航道的,由于限制航道是相对复杂的水域,所以经简化改造后本模型也可适用于一般水域。必须提出的是,本文虽然试图找到一个普遍适用的方案,但是由于各港口毕竟都有自己的特点,实际应用中可能要对本模型稍加改造。特别需要提到的是本文的不足之处:对具体问题的研究不够深入;调查范围不够;对某些因素欠缺考虑。由于本文的主要目的在于对船舶限速方法的开发,所以容忍了以上缺点。

大风浪船舶安全航行的研究综述*

摘要:大风浪中航行安全是船舶安全航行研究的重要课题。通过对该问题研究方法的分析和所涉及方面的探讨,从整体上反映了当前大风浪船舶航行安全研究的现状,提出了今后研究的方向。

关键词:大风浪;船舶安全航行;船舶稳性;船舶强度

0 引言

大风浪中船舶安全航行的问题一直是航运界所关注的焦点之一。从更严格的意义上讲,该问题可追溯到第二次世界大战时期,当时为了保证军用物资运输,同盟国与轴心国建造了很多大型的、相对较为简易的船舶,其中一些船舶在大风浪中由于断裂而沉没。因此,为了保障船舶和海上设施在海上航行时的人命和财产安全而制定了两个较为重要的公约(《载重线公约》、SOLAS 公约)。在国际上,大型油船及散货船的事故一直是关注的热点,直到 20 世纪 90 年代初期,关于该类事故的原因才基本查清[379],并从统计的角度,指出了影响该类船舶事故的相关原因。近几年来,国际上对大风浪中不断发生的重特大事故的分析和研究,也推动了我国在该方面的研究工作。

本文根据收集到的有关研究论文,对该方面的研究进行综述,以期能够反映在该方面的研究情况,并提出以后的研究方向。

1 研究的基本状况

当前,研究大风浪中船舶安全航行的方法主要有以下几种。

1.1 根据风浪情况,定性分析船舶在大风浪中的安全航行方法

(1)在船舶进入大风浪区前根据波浪预报资料提供的航经海区的平均波高,求取主成分波和有效成分波,再根据临界状态的划分方法,看本船的谐摇波长处在哪个临界状态,进而判断本船的摇摆程度。如横浪中要摆脱临界状态可改为顶浪或顺浪航行,顶浪中为摆脱临界状态可改变航向与降速。这是一种较实用又可行的预报安危的方法[380]。

(2)通过总结被航海实践证明了的船舶战胜大风浪的要领,即:一主动(掌握主动权),二

---

* 本文发表在《大连海事大学学报》2002 年第 4 期第 28 卷,作者王凤武、郑中义、吴兆麟。

避免(避免在波谷中船被打横和横向谐摇),三保持(保持动力、浮力和稳定),提出在顶浪、顺浪、横浪、滞航、漂航和调头时的操纵方法。

(3) 从特殊类型船舶——集装箱船在大风浪中的航行特点出发,提出在航海实践中,应引进日本的横摇衡准,以决定是否为降低横摇幅度而改向或变速;根据 ASRTSSEN 速度衡准,决定为避免船舶剧烈振动、颠簸、冲撞和主机负荷等的界限速度,进而求得主机转速。

(4) 从影响大型散装货船安全的重要因素——横摇、纵摇、垂荡和纵向强度出发,提出了大型散装货船防止大倾角横摇的操船方法:既要保证合适的稳性,又要及时调整船舶的航向和航速,还要避免大舵角旋回或避让或快速回舵的急剧的突然倾斜。保证船舶纵向强度的操船方法是:将船首与波浪的夹角放在 10°~40°,改向直到摇摆最小、上浪最小的航向为止。

(5) 利用相对运动原理和航海学公式,通过在墨卡托海图上作图计算,从而判断台风、危险大风是否对船舶构成威胁。如船舶受到威胁,则采取改向使船舶相对于台风的相对运动线发生变化,在台风、危险大风海区以外通过;或者改变船舶相对于台风的相对运动速度,待台风减弱、消失或转向后,从台风外围的安全海区通过。这一避离方法,为船长决策提供了可靠依据[381]。

1.2 统计分析的方法

该类方法主要是针对船舶在营运过程中出现事故的原因,利用统计分析的方法,得出哪种因素对事故的影响较大。据统计分析得出油船和散货船在商船灭失吨位中占很大的比例。对于散货船来讲,其中船龄、天灾等不可抗力的外在因素,船舶不适航,人为疏忽,货物,船舶结构和船体因素,船舶碰撞,船舶搁浅因素是海难事故的主要原因。

1.3 模糊综合评判的方法

该种方法主要是针对影响船舶大风浪中安全航行的因素,建立指标体系、隶属度函数,并利用模糊推理的理论,对船舶在大风浪中的安全状态进行评价。

(1) 从船舶的物理条件入手,综合考虑多方面因素建立评价指标体系,运用层次分析法计算得到每个评价指标对于船舶安全的重要程度,最后建立船舶安全模糊综合评判模型,并通过具体实例加以验证,这为船舶管理部门了解船舶安全状况提供依据。

(2) 采用模糊数学方法,依据试验结果建立隶属函数,提出综合评估船舶在尾斜浪中航行可能发生倾覆危险模型,并对实船进行模拟评估,得到了与事实基本相符的结论[382]。

1.4 校核的方法

该种研究方法主要是针对特定船舶在发生事故后,根据其开航前的船舶、货物及相关资料等,对该船舶在发生事故前的安全状态进行逐项校核,得出发生海难事故的主要原因是:在风浪中横摇摆幅过大、积载不当、风浪中谐摇引起货物大量移动、对本船的抗风能力估计不足和跨航区航行等。

1.5 事故树及可靠性分析的方法

该种方法将大风浪中发生的船舶事故作为顶上事件,分析产生事故的机理,找出事故原因,对船舶的可靠性和安全性做出定量和定性的研究。可靠性理论和方法的引入,标志着对船舶安全有了科学的评价标准,但目前应用得并不多。

2 研究所涉及的相关理论

2.1 船体及其相关问题

关于船体及其强度问题,是国内外研究的重点之一。尤其对于船龄较大的散装货船,主要集中在:船体结构的应力腐蚀(特殊货物加速腐蚀),装卸过程中造成过大的应力,船壳外板的脱落、破裂,货舱浸水,大舱肋骨、舷侧结构和横舱壁结构的疲劳强度不足,主机等设备自身缺陷,船体局部强度不足等。对于船龄较大的油船,研究的重点主[383]要集中在构件出现裂纹的问题。

2.2 船舶稳性及相关问题

(1)货物移动对船舶稳性的影响

我们知道海船稳性规范提出的稳性衡准要求所基于的前提条件是船舶无初始横倾角,全过程中船上所有固定货物(除谷物外的固体散货、件杂货)重心保持不变,而事实上航行中的船舶其舱内或舱面上固体货物受外力作用发生横向移动后存在初始横倾角,进而使船舶的动稳性急剧下降,从而使一项或几项衡准指标不符合规定的要求,继而为船舶在海上发生倾斜而倾覆提供了条件,货物移动再加上恶劣天气将引起船舶倾斜甚至出现倾覆的危险[384]。

海船稳性事故在小船和装运散货情况中发生较多,而最后导致船舶倾覆的往往是大风浪中发生货物移动、甲板上浪、船体进水、尾斜浪袭击、随浪中的稳性损失又操舵转向不当等因素的连锁反应所造成的复合结果。如船舶装载措施不力、港方装舱不良、航行途中海况恶劣、遇险情时采取的应急措施不力等,均将使船舶面临危险境地[385]。

(2)船舶在随浪航行情况下稳性损失的问题

IMO 对横浪中的稳性标准已在 1968 年的 A167 和 1985 年的 A562 中提出了建议,驾驶人员对横浪造成的倾覆危险以及如何采取措施避开这种危险已有了较全面的了解,而对船舶在随浪中稳性的减少和船舶倾覆的关系方面,及达到现行的横浪衡准的船舶在大的随浪及偏随浪中是否发生倾覆、如何操纵正处在探讨之中,并越来越多地引起航海界的重视。船舶在随浪中倾覆原因有:稳性损失、不稳定和横甩等。船舶在随浪中存在着三种危险:一是船舶骑在波峰上会因纯稳性丧失而引起倾覆;二是当船舶遭遇的波浪频率和船本身的横摇频率接近时(即谐摇)而引起倾覆;三是船舶几乎与波速相同的速度航行,处在波浪的下坡段上将加速而处于冲浪状态,此时极易产生横向急转而导致倾覆。船舶在尾随浪中存在着即使海况并不恶劣或仅属中等,但在某些航行条件下也可能不断地遭到高波群的连续冲击而最终导致倾覆的可能。如何解决在随浪和尾随浪中的操纵问题,海上安全委员会在1995年的第65次会议上通过了附件《在随浪和尾随浪情况下避免危险局面的指南》,提供了一个"船长操纵图",它是综合相对于波浪的船速、航向,以极坐标的简化形式给出了安全与否的忠告(一般界限),但并没有考虑某条船的实际稳性和动态特性[386,387]。

2.3 重大件货物的绑扎问题

各国对海运重大件货物都有其规定的标准,重大件货物的特点决定了其在装运过程中需有特殊要求。在航运生产中,对装载重大件货物问题的研究主要集中在两方面,一是对重大件货物的绑扎系固问题,二是承载重大件货物甲板的局部强度问题。在恶劣海况下,由于不规则波浪的作用将使船舶出现横摇、纵摇、垂荡等,货物对船舶的各个方向都产生了运动加速度。"大舜号"的失事就是由于对滚装货物的绑扎系固工做出现了严重的失误,导致了在大风浪中的货物移动,使车辆在货舱中发生剧烈碰撞,油箱起火,进而蔓延到全船,最终致使动力丧失而倾覆[388]。"盛鲁"船沉没的原因之一也是车辆系固不良导致摇摆而倾斜、移位和碰撞,近而发生火灾,致使舵机失灵、船舶失控,最终沉没。IMO在几年前就已经关注此类事件,并最终制定了《货物积载与系固安全实用规则》,该规则是介于经验法与理论计算法之间的一种方法,既克服了经验法的粗糙,又避免了理论计算法的烦琐,乃为船员所接受的实用方法。

2.4 船舶抗风浪等级

随着航海技术的日趋完善和各种保障航行安全的国际公约的制定,船舶在海上航行的风险已越来越小,但大风浪仍然是航海的主要危害之一。据统计,在1988—1991年的世界全损船舶中,由于气象原因造成的全损船舶数位居榜首,占全损船舶总数的32.8%,而在气象原因中,大风浪是影响船舶安全的主要原因。众所周知,从船舶建造时起,就已确定了船舶的压载抗风能力和满载抗风能力,而船舶在具体的航次中是否具备了建造时所具备的抵御风浪的能力,实际具有多大的抗风浪能力,即确保船舶达到适航标准,仍为人们所重视。一方面,从安全的角度即从船舶稳性、船舶强度及船舶的特殊装载状态出发,确定了船舶抗风浪等级,为船舶优选航线划定了限制条件[388]。另一方面,分析大风浪与船舶航行安全的关系,根据在大风浪中船舶致损事故统计得出了各类船舶的大风浪可航界限等,这为船舶抗风浪等级的研究奠定了基础。

3 存在的问题及今后研究思路

综上所述,有关船舶航行安全的研究集中在:对于中小船舶,主要研究的侧重点在大风浪中的稳性损失、谐摇和操纵问题;对于大型船舶,主要研究的侧重点在大风浪中操纵和航法问题。对于老龄船(如散货船),主要研究的是结构强度、疲劳损伤等问题。

3.1 存在的问题

目前,有关船舶航行安全的研究已由单一事故分析推断船舶安全进入到从系统工程的角度考虑航行安全的失误链导致事故的方面。从上述分析可看出,从方法上看,虽既有统计分析,又有事故发生后的校核综合评判,还有定性的分析船舶在大风浪中安全航行的方法,但都缺乏系统性,尤其是对在恶劣气象条件下,从定性和定量相结合的角度对船舶安全航行问题进行的研究很少。

3.2 研究思路

从安全系统工程的角度,综合考虑船舶特点与状况、气象条件、船舶装载货物情况和船员技术条件等,通过定性与定量分析,在综合有关学者在相关方面的研究成果及意见的基础上,给出评价模型,较全面地评价特定船舶在特定条件下开航的安全性问题,为船长、船舶公司及主管机关的安全管理提供较为科学的参考依据,从而有效地保证水上人命、财产安全,避免由于决策不当给船舶公司所带来经济损失。

4 结束语

船舶航行安全问题一直是航运人员所关心的。本文就大风浪中船舶安全航行所使用的方法、研究所涉及的方面进行了综述,大致反映了船舶航行安全研究的趋势,这将为在该领域的深入分析研究打下基础,我们将在此基础上按照预定思路对在恶劣气象条件下船舶安全航行的安全技术标准进行研究。

Relation Between the Number of Observational Days and the Accuracy on the Estimation of Marine Traffic Volume*

Abstract: The theories of mathematical statistics and probability theory are used to define the ratio between the length of confidence interval and the average estimation of daily traffic volumes as the " relative error ", some conclusions are drawn on relations between the number of observational days and the accuracy on the estimation of traffic volume. These conclusions may be applied to the harbour planning, establishment vessel traffic separation scheme, and the determination of the numbers of exchanger on shore-based radio station.

Keywords: Ships; Marine traffic volume; Observational days; Observation accuracy

1 Introduction

The investigation and observation of traffic volume in a given water way section is important for the planning and management of the water way. For example, the investigation of ship type helps determine the modification of the depth and width of the channel; the investigation of the distribution of the track of traffic flow helps the competent authorities to decide whether to adopt the traffic separation scheme, the observation of traffic volume contribute to determine whether to expand the harbor, and determine the volume of VHF station in given waters. So, the investigation and observation of traffic in the given water is an important scientific basis for the competent authorities to make decision on the planning and construction of the given harbor.

But, due to the fact that the traffic observation involves the proper dealing with the relationships between of manpower, finance and the accuracy of observation of traffic, as far as the underdeveloped countries concerned, it's not possible to pursue the best accuracy of traffic observation regardless the cost of the manpower, finance, as well as materials.

At present, most shipping-developed countries have conducted many observations and investigations on marine traffic. But from all the papers as many as we can consult, we found that the research on the relations between the number of observational days and the accuracy on the estimation of traffic volume is relatively few. Based on the sample theories, through studying the data obtained by the actual observations conducted in the Akashi Kaikyo, Irago suido, Kanmon Kaikyo, the Japanese scholars Kinzo INOUE and Kiyoshi HARA has made some researches on the

---

* 本文发表在《大连海事大学学报》2002 年第 28 卷增刊,作者郑中义、吴兆麟、赵连昌。

mentioned issue above and concluded as followings[390, 391]: First, the annual daily traffic volume is estimated by applying the formula of variation coefficient. In the case of 7-day continuous observations in the Akahsi kaiyo, the maximum standard error is about ±17 %; Second, the maximum daily traffic volume in a year is about equal to the 1.6 – 1.8 times of the annual daily traffic volume obtained by interval estimation; Third, annual standard error, same as the variation of annual daily traffic volume, could be obtained from dividing the difference between the maximum annual daily traffic volume and the annual daily traffic volume by 2.5 – 3.0. Besides, at present the method of conducting continuous 3-day observations is popular.

The preconditions of the conclusions made in references[390, 391] are as following: conducting the observations while the daily traffic volume varies relatively lowly and annul traffic volume that passed the survey section varies relatively lowly too.

In our country the actual conditions of all the water ways vary greatly. For example, there remain phenomena that affect greatly the traffic such as, dry season and mature periods of crops and fruits. So we think as far as our country concerned, it's very necessary to explore, based on foreign research on this field, the better method to traffic observation.

2 Estimation of parameter of ship arrival law

2.1 Law of ship arrival

Generally, law of ship arrival means the probability of the number of ships, which arrive at a given gate line in a given period. The distribution of distant between the sequentially arriving ships would be obtained by calculating the intervals of ships which pass the given gate line.

Ship arrives at the given gate line randomly. Based on traffic flow theory, the probability $p(t)$ of k arriving ships in t time generally obeys the Poisson distribution. This conclusion has been accepted worldwide. The inference of the law of ship's arrival could be found in the reference and will not be mentioned in this paper too.

2.2 Estimation of parameter of Poisson distribution

The thinking of research on traffic flow is, by calculating the mean value of Poisson distribution and through error analysis, the relatively appropriate number of observational days, as to the Poisson distribution of traffic flow which pass a given survey section, is able to be determined, also taking the manpower, materials and cost into account.

Supposed: Poisson distribution of traffic flow which pass a given survey section is

$$p_i(t) = \frac{(\lambda t)^i e^{-\lambda t}}{i!} \quad \text{(where is nonnegative integer)} \tag{1}$$

If the traffic survey continues n days, then we get the number of daily arriving ships: x_1, $x_2, \cdots, x_n$. These data can be regarded as the samples, which are drawn out of the totality of Poisson distribution X. Hence,

$$\bar{x} = \frac{1}{n}(x_1 + x_2 + \cdots + x_n)$$

is a random variable, $x_i (i = 1, 2, \cdots, n)$ where conform to the same Poisson distribution $p(x)$.

Thus we get

$$E(x) = \lambda$$

As Statistics shows, we come to that following

$$Y_n = n\bar{x} = x_1 + x_2 + \cdots + x_n$$

conforms to Poisson distribution $p(nx)$, where mean value and variance both are $n\lambda$. Thus we can obtain the confidence interval $[\underline{\lambda}, \bar{\lambda}]$ with $(1 - \alpha)$ of confidence level, where

$$\underline{\lambda} = \chi^2_{\frac{\alpha}{2}}(2k)/2n$$
$$\bar{\lambda} = \chi^2_{\frac{\alpha}{2}}(2k + 2)/2n \qquad (2)$$

Where k is the observed value of $\sum_{i=1}^{n} x_i = x_1 + x_2 + \cdots + x_n$, $\chi^2_{\frac{\alpha}{2}}(2k)$ is the $\alpha/2$ fractile of χ^2.

When $k \geqslant 20$ and according to central limiting theorem, we know that

$$\frac{Y_n - n\lambda}{\sqrt{n\lambda}} \quad \text{or} \quad \frac{\bar{x} - \lambda}{\sqrt{\lambda/n}}$$

conforms to normal distribution $N(0,1)$, whose mean value is 0 and variance 1. Thus we get the confidence interval $[\underline{\lambda}, \bar{\lambda}]$, where

$$\bar{\lambda} = \bar{x} + \chi^2_{\frac{\alpha}{2}}/2n + \chi_{\frac{\alpha}{2}}\sqrt{\chi^2_{\frac{\alpha}{2}}/(4n^2) + \bar{x}/n}$$
$$\underline{\lambda} = \bar{x} + \chi^2_{\frac{\alpha}{2}}/2n - \chi_{\frac{\alpha}{2}}\sqrt{\chi^2_{\frac{\alpha}{2}}/(4n^2) + \bar{x}/n}$$

2.2.1 The discussion of confidence interval when the ship number which pass the survey section is relatively few.

From

$$\bar{\lambda} - \underline{\lambda} = [\chi^2_{1-\frac{\alpha}{2}}(2k + 2) - \chi^2_{\frac{\alpha}{2}}(2k)]/2n$$

We should pay attention to the estimation of λ_0.

$$\lambda_0 = \frac{\sum_{i=1}^{n} x_i}{n} = \frac{k}{n}$$

From the table of fractile distribution of χ^2, we know that when $f \geqslant 45$, $\chi^2(f)$, should be expressed approximately by the normal distribution

$$\chi^2_\alpha(n) \approx \frac{1}{2}(Z_\alpha + \sqrt{2n - 1})^2$$

in which Z_α is normal distribution and α is fractile. For all $2k+2 \geq 44$ the equation(2) will be adopted to calculate the confidence interval in our discussion.

If $(\bar{\lambda} - \lambda)/\lambda_0$ is defined as the relative error of estimation of the actual λ, the following Table 1 can illustrate the above-mentioned theme.

Table 1   Distribution of relative error varying with number of observational days and the total number of arriving ships

$\frac{k}{n}$	1 ship	5 ship	10 ship	15 ship	20 ship
$n=1$	$\lambda_0 = 1$	$\lambda_0 = 5$	$\lambda_0 = 10$	$\lambda_0 = 15$	$\lambda_0 = 20$
	$[\lambda,\bar{\lambda}] = [0.105, 3.889]$	$[\lambda,\bar{\lambda}] = [2.483, 9.275]$	$[\lambda,\bar{\lambda}] = [6.222, 15.406]$	$[\lambda,\bar{\lambda}] = [10.300, 21.293]$	$[\lambda,\bar{\lambda}] = [14.526, 27.045]$
	$\bar{\lambda} - \lambda = 3.784$	$\bar{\lambda} - \lambda = 6.792$	$\bar{\lambda} - \lambda = 9.185$	$\bar{\lambda} - \lambda = 10.993$	$\bar{\lambda} - \lambda = 12.520$
	$\frac{\bar{\lambda} - \lambda}{\lambda_0} = 3.784$	$\frac{\bar{\lambda} - \lambda}{\lambda_0} = 1.3584$	$\frac{\bar{\lambda} - \lambda}{\lambda_0} = 0.9185$	$\frac{\bar{\lambda} - \lambda}{\lambda_0} = 0.7329$	$\frac{\bar{\lambda} - \lambda}{\lambda_0} = 0.6260$
$n=2$	$\lambda_0 = 0.5$	$\lambda_0 = 2.5$			
	$[\lambda,\bar{\lambda}] = [0.053, 1.156]$	$[\lambda,\bar{\lambda}] = [1.241, 4.637]$	...	...	...
	$\bar{\lambda} - \lambda = 1.099$	$\bar{\lambda} - \lambda = 3.396$			
	$\frac{\bar{\lambda} - \lambda}{\lambda_0} = 2.197$	$\frac{\bar{\lambda} - \lambda}{\lambda_0} = 1.358$			

If supposing $Z = \frac{\bar{\lambda} - \lambda}{\lambda_0}$, then the curve of relative error Z is shown as Figure 1.

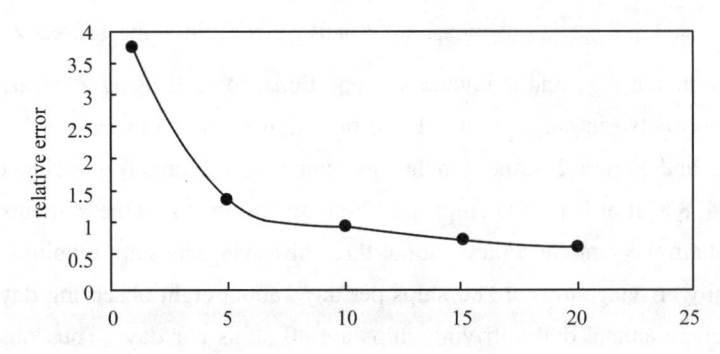

Figure 1   Relations between observed ship number and relative error

We may draw some conclusions from Table 1 and Figure 1 as following:

(1) k is the number of observed ships in total n day observation, when n keeps unchanged,

the bigger k, the more arriving ships and the estimation of arriving ships λ_0.

(2) when n is fixed, both $\bar{\lambda}$ and $\underline{\lambda}$ of confidence interval $[\underline{\lambda},\bar{\lambda}]$ increase in accompanying-with increasing, and so does $[\underline{\lambda},\bar{\lambda}]$.

(3) when k is fixed, and increases, both $\bar{\lambda}$ and $\underline{\lambda}$ of confidence interval $[\underline{\lambda},\bar{\lambda}]$ decrease in accompanying with k increasing, it is inversely proportional to n.

(4) if $Z = \dfrac{\bar{\lambda} - \underline{\lambda}}{\lambda_0}$ is referred to "relative error" in some sense, for all $k \leqslant 0$, Z has nothing to and has something to only k. The bigger k, the smaller "relative error". When $k = 20$, then $Z = 0.626\,0$; when $k = 10$, then $Z = 0.918\,5$; difference between two-said results of above Z is relatively big.

2.2.2 Discussion on confidence interval, when k is relatively big

When $k \geqslant 20$, in fact $\dfrac{\bar{x} - \lambda}{\sqrt{\lambda/n}}$ conforms to normal distribution $N(0,1)$, and a conclusion similar to conclusion (4) with relative small is arrived at too.

Knowing from formula (2):

$$\underline{\lambda},\bar{\lambda} = 2 \cdot u_{\frac{\alpha}{2}}\sqrt{u_{\frac{\alpha}{2}}^2/(4n^2) + \frac{\bar{x}}{n}} = \frac{1}{n}u_{\frac{\alpha}{2}}\sqrt{u_{\frac{\alpha}{2}}^2 + 4n\bar{x}}$$

When $\dfrac{\alpha}{2} = 0.10$, being said to confidence level $1 - \alpha = 0.80$, $u_{\frac{\alpha}{2}} = 1.282$

$$\underline{\lambda},\bar{\lambda} = \frac{1}{n} \cdot 1.282\sqrt{1.282^2 + 4k}$$

$$\frac{\bar{\lambda} - \underline{\lambda}}{\lambda_0} = \frac{1.282}{k}\sqrt{1.282^2 + 4k} \approx \frac{2.564}{\sqrt{k}}$$

It's thus clear that for all $k \geqslant 20$:

When using $Z = (\bar{\lambda} - \underline{\lambda})/\lambda_0$ to measure "relative error" in some sense, Z decreases in accompanying with k increasing, and is inversely proportional to k. If using Z to measure relative error, thus the relation between ships acquired and precision is shown as Figure 2.

From Table 2 and Figure 2 some conclusions could be reasonably concluded: relative error can be less than 14.8% if at least 300 ships are observed and its correctness attains about 80% (or so). In order to attain the same accuracy, about three observing days are required if the number of average annual daily arriving ships are 80 ships per day, about eight observing days are required if the number of average annual daily arriving ships are 40 ships per day. Thus observing days decrease in congested water or waterway; while more observing days relatively are demanded in relatively non-congested water or waterway, the "relative error" can be roughly the same.

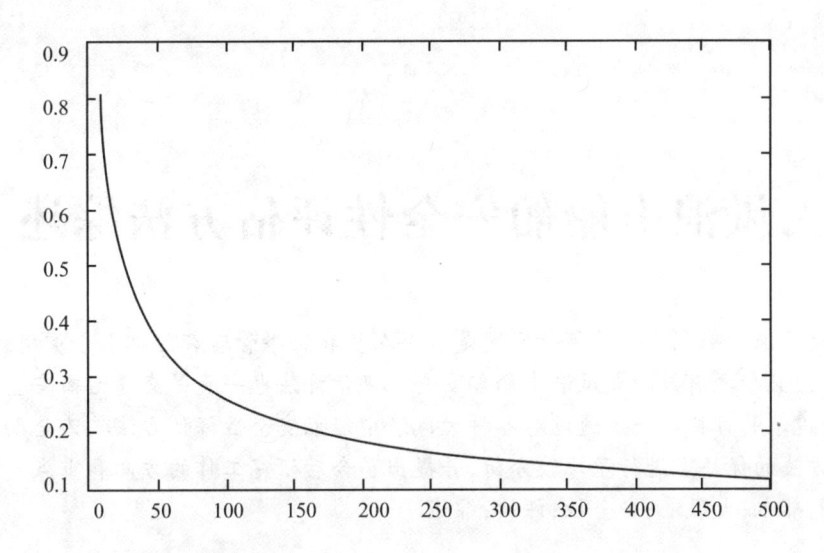

Figure 2 Figure of relation between ships observed and observational precision under big sample

Table 2 Table of relation between ships observed and observational precision

Observational Ships	100	150	200	250	300	350	400
Relative Error	0.2563	0.2093	0.1812	0.1621	0.1480	0.1370	0.1208

3 Conclusion

Law of ship arrival conforms to Poisson distribution since that traffic flow is random, confidence interval of mean value to ship arrival is studied when number of ship arrival is about less than 45 arriving ships per day; and relations between ships number observed and observational precision is studied when the ratio between length of confidence interval and arrival mean value is defined as "relative error" in some sense; we can draw a conclusion as following:

First, observing time may be relatively shorten and relatively high accuracy can be reached if the more number of ship is observed in time unit if distribution of ship arriving at a given observing section keep roughly stable; the more observational time is needed to get the high observational precision if the number of observational ships in time unit is relatively less.

Second, simultaneously, because observational precision is in inversely proportional to square root of the number of observed ships, continuous observation cannot improve observational precision greatly when specific ship number is observed. The cost of observation and other conditions determine whether the observation is continued or not.

In accordance with features of Poisson distribution of law of ship arrival, the relation between observational time and observational precision is studied and some conclusions are drawn. Any comments and criticism on this above-discussed matter from specialists from homeland and abroad are welcome.

大风浪中船舶安全性评估方法综述

摘要：大风浪中船舶安全性评估问题是航海人员和海事管理部门都十分重视的研究课题。寻找使用方便且行之有效的大风浪中船舶安全性评估方法也一直是交通运输安全保障方向的研究人员所追求的目标之一。通过对各种大风浪中船舶安全性评估方法较为全面的介绍和总结，对各种方法的优缺点进行了比较分析，并提出了今后研究工作的方向和重点。

关键词：船舶；大风浪；安全性；评估；综述

0 引言

大风浪对船舶安全的影响历来受到航海者的重视，当海上的水文气象条件非常恶劣时，由于风浪对船舶的作用力加大，不但使船舶的适居性和使用性会受到很大影响，而且可能给船舶造成致命的危险。因此，对大风浪中船舶安全性评估问题的研究由来已久，使用的方法也是多种多样。这些方法可谓各有千秋，但是也各有其局限性。了解以往研究所用的各种评估方法及其研究成果，分析比较各种评估方法的优缺点，对于进一步完善大风浪中船舶安全性的评估手段，找到更加方便、合理、准确的评估方法，减少船舶在大风浪中发生危险的可能性，无疑有着重大的意义。为此，本文力图对以前的研究进行较为全面的归纳和分析，对各种评估方法及其研究成果和各种评估方法的优缺点给予介绍，并提出了大风浪中船舶安全性评估问题今后研究工作的方向和重点。

1 各种大风浪中船舶安全性评估方法

1.1 通过单项重要指标评估船舶的安全性

1.1.1 根据海浪情况结合船舶状态来评估船舶安全性的方法

文献[380]提出根据海浪情况结合船舶状态来评估船舶安全性的方法，根据不规则波的理论，横摇主成分波的波长大致在 $30H_{1/3}$ 与 $50H_{1/3}$ 之间；纵摇和垂荡主成分波的波长大致在船长与最大能量波（$40H_{1/3}$）之间。当船舶的谐摇波长位于主成分波长区间内时，船舶就会处于所谓临界状态，这时，船舶将出现谐摇，即船舶的横摇、纵摇和垂荡都会非常严重，甚至出现严重的砰击和上浪。因此，可根据船舶进入大风浪区之前所收到的海浪预报资料，分别求出对船

---

* 本文发表在《交通运输工程学报》2003 年第 1 期第 3 卷，作者刘大刚、郑中义、吴兆麟。

舶横摇、纵摇和垂荡起主要作用的主成分波的波长,再根据船舶的载态求出自身相应的谐摇波长,并由此来评估船舶的航行是否有危险。

1.1.2 船舶抗风等级和抗浪等级

文献[389]提出船舶抗风等级和抗浪等级的公式为:

$$V_{10} = 77 \left(\frac{10}{Z_f}\right)^{0.125} \overline{l_q D/KA_f Z_f} \tag{1}$$

$$h = 2(M_0/g + K_1 DL_{w1} - K_2 W_0 L_{w1} - \frac{1}{2}\sum P_i X_i)/K_3 BL_{w1}^2 \tag{2}$$

式中:V_{10} 为船舶在该装载状态下可安全航行的最大风速;Z_f 为风力作用力臂;l_q 为最小倾覆力臂;D 为船舶排水量;K 为稳性衡准系数;A_f 为船舶受风面积;h 为船舶船体强度所能承受的最大浪高;M_0 为船舶的船中弯矩;g 为重力加速度;K_1 为平水排水量力矩系数;L_{w1} 为船舶水线长;K_2 为空船重量力矩系数;W_0 为空船重量;$\sum P_i X_i$ 为所有载荷对船中的力矩;K_3 为波形排水量力矩修正系数;B 为船宽。

1.1.3 其他方法

其他类似的仅考虑某个单项指标来对船舶航行的安全性进行评估的方法还有:通过预测船舶甲板淹湿的状况来评估船舶的安全性[392];通过水槽试验和一系列计算得到船首船桥船在3种不同的不规则波中,发生船桥玻璃被浪击碎的一般条件及判断。基准以此作为在实际航行中避免发生危险的依据[393,394]。

1.2 从船舶耐波性的角度来评估大风浪中船舶的安全性

1.2.1 船舶耐波性的标准

由于船舶的耐波性诸方面的性质不尽相同,对不同船型、吨位、载态和任务的船舶,其具体要求也各不相同,因此,船舶耐波性标准,诸如对船舶安全影响较大的横摇、纵摇、升沉、船首加速度、砰击、甲板淹湿、失速率、偏转、稳性、纵向波浪弯矩和飞车次数等因素的临界状态值,也各不相同。表1为部分研究确定的船舶耐波性标准,表中资料为各因素的最大允许值和允许概率。

1.2.2 船舶耐波性评估方程

从船舶耐波性的角度来评估船舶安全性,其总的思路是,在考虑了耐波性的诸方面后,确定出每一个因素的临界状态值,并确定出每一临界状态值的允许出现概率。然后,提出船舶安全性的评估公式,以此来评估船舶在风浪中的安全性。文献[396]提出的评估公式如下:

$$R_x = k_1[P(\theta_{横}) - 0.05] + k_2[P(j_{纵}) - 0.05] + k_3[P(Z_{升}) - 0.05] + k_4[P(a_{首}) - 0.05] +$$
$$k_5[M(F_{砰})_{20} - 2.64T_{平}] + k_6[M(Y_{湿})_{20} < 2.64H_{首}] + k_7[P(\theta_{偏}) - 0.05] + k_8[P(M_{弯}) - 0.01]$$

若 $0.8M_{横} \geq M_{倾}$,则 $R_x = \infty$,且

$$V_{允} \leq V_{静}[1 - (m/L + N)] \tag{3}$$

式中:R_x 为当时航向、航速组合下船舶耐波性指数的评估值,R_x 越小越安全,R_x 越大越危险;$P(\theta_{横})$、$M(F_{砰})_{20}$、……为根据数学模型模拟船舶在当时风浪中的运动算出的船舶在风浪中各运动参数的临界状态值出现的概率或最大振幅平均值;$k_1, k_2, \cdots, k_n$ 是系数,根据船舶的

性能、使命、任务等而定。

表1 部分船舶耐波性标准

项目	来源		
	参考文献[6]	参考文献[7]	参考文献[8]
横摇	<15°,0.05	≤20°	≤15°
纵摇	<5°,0.05	≤10°	<3.6°,0.05
升沉	<2 m,0.05	≤2.5 m	<3 m,0.05
船首加速度	≤0.69 g,0.05	≤0.64 m/s²	≤0.81 g,0.05
砰击	$M(F_{砰})_{20}<2.64\ T_{平}$	0.05	1次/分,0.05
甲板淹湿	$M(Y_{淹})_{20}<2.64\ H_{首}$	≤30 次/h	$M(Y_{淹})_{20}<L/10,0.05$
允许航速	$V\leqslant V_{静}[1-(m/L+N)]$	$\Delta V/V_0<0.2$	
偏转	<15,0.05		
稳性	$M_{倾}\geqslant 0.8M_{横},h_{稳}\geqslant 0$		
纵向波浪弯矩	$M_{弯}<M_0,0.01$		0.01

注:未考虑直升机起降,文献[395]参考对象为渔船。

1.3 用航行记录仪记录船舶在风浪中的实际运动状态

为了解船舶在实际风浪中的运动响应状态,日本东京商船大学与日本邮船株式会社进行了合作。从1990年开始,通过在一艘日本—北美—东南亚航线的集装箱船上安装航行资料自动记录系统,得到了船舶在不同载态、不同航行状态下、不同的风、浪条件作用下,大量的船舶运动特征量响应值的实际资料[281-284]。

所获取的资料包括:时间、船位、航向、航速、波高、升沉、横摇角、纵摇角、船首上下加速度、纵荡加速度、垂荡加速度的平均值、最大值和平均周期,以及相对风向、风速的平均值和绝对风向、风速的平均值,共计26项内容。所有资料均为每小时记录10 min,在记录资料的10 min内,记录每组资料的时间间隔为0.5 s。

通过对这些实际风浪中船舶运动特征量的分析,得到了许多真实且重要的结论,如各船舶运动特征量的平均值与最大值的相互关系(见表2)、$H_{1/3}$与H_{max}的关系、波高与航速的关系、波高与航速及各船舶运动特征量的相关系数、波高与各船舶运动特征量的相关系数(见表3)、$H_{1/3}$与纵摇角的关系、$H_{1/3}$与横摇角的关系等。

表2 船舶运动特征量的平均值与最大值的相互关系

	波高	风速	横摇角	纵摇角	垂荡	纵荡
相关系数	0.967	0.910	0.964	0.929	0.981	0.802
比(平均)	1.58	1.34	2.64	3.45	3.29	3.54

表3 波高与船舶运动特征量的相关系数

	波高	船首上下动	横摇角	纵摇角	艏摇角速度	纵荡加速度	垂荡加速度	横荡加速度
波高	1	0.864	0.587	0.842	0.747	0.626	0.609	0.594
船首上下动		1	0.411	0.562	0.494	0.427	0.475	0.454
横摇角			1	0.617	0.736	0.381	0.578	0.854
纵摇角				1	0.805	0.769	0.734	0.688
艏摇角速度					1	0.713	0.617	0.751
纵荡加速度						1	0.726	0.571
垂荡加速度							1	0.841
横荡加速度								1

1.4 利用船舶主要参数来表达耐波性指数进而评估船舶的安全性

由于通过各种模拟计算得到的船舶耐波性特征值有一定误差,而通过实验方法获得船舶耐波性特征值所耗费的人力、物力和财力过于巨大,一些学者试图寻找船舶主要参数与耐波性的关系。这其中较著名的是贝尔斯通过对驱逐舰船型和耐波性特征量之间关系所做的深入研究,把反映耐波性能优劣的"耐波性品级"与船型的几何特征用简明的数学关系式直接联系起来[401,402]。

贝尔斯认为,船舶耐波性指数 R 与以下 8 种耐波性特征量相联系:纵摇、垂荡、在 0 站处和 20 站处的相对运动、3 站处的砰击、0 站处的垂向绝对加速度和垂荡加速度、20 站处的垂向绝对运动。在经过深入分析后,贝尔斯认为,最有影响的水下参数有 6 个:船中前、后水线面积系数 C_{wf}、C_{wa},吃水与船长比 d/L,截至比 C/L,船中前、后棱形系数 C_{vpf}、C_{vpa};船舶耐波性指数 R 与上述逐个参数间存在简单的线性关系。经过对 20 艘有代表性的舰船的计算分析,通过多元回归法得到下式:

$$R = 8.422 + 45.104C_{wf} + 10.078C_{wa} - 378.465d/L + 1.273C/L - 23.501C_{vpf} - 15.8875C_{vpa} \tag{4}$$

1.5 大风浪中操船环境危险度的模糊评价方法

模糊评价方法是基于控制理论和模糊数学的思想方法,将船舶航行系统认为是由人—船—环境组成的多因素复杂的大环境,其中气象海况条件是操船环境的一个因素[403]。在实际进行评估时,不去考虑风浪等因素对船舶具体的影响机制,而是通过模糊推理的方法,得出一个明确的、与操船者实际在船上操船时的感觉相符的操船环境危险度的量值。

这里以参考文献[404,405]的研究为例予以说明。这种评价船舶在大风浪中安全性的方法,是建立一个基于模糊推理系统上的,在能见度、风、流等因素影响下的操船环境危险度的评价模型。在实际使用时,将能见度、风、流等因素作为输入变量,应用模糊推理方法,对操船环境的危险度进行评价,在得到评价的模糊集后,用反模糊化方法,得出一个清晰的评价值和输入因素与输出评价值的映像。

模糊推理系统由三个基本部分组成,包括含有可供选择的模糊规则的规则库(规则库由一系列 If-then 语句构成)、定义了用于模糊规则的隶属函数的数据库和可在规则和给定值的基础上执行推理程序来产生一个合理输出的推理机[406]。

操船环境危险度指由于能见度、风、流等因素对操船环境所造成的影响,使操船者从主观感觉上对操船环境感到的危险程度的一种量度。操船环境危险度的定义如图1所示。

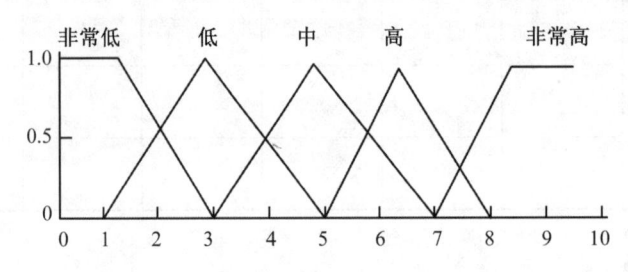

图1 操船环境危险度隶属函数曲线

2 各种大风浪中船舶安全性评估方法比较分析

归纳起来,大风浪中船舶安全性的评估方法主要有以下几种。

(1)直接对风浪等一些重要的单项指标进行分析,考察船舶是否存在危险。

(2)建立船舶操纵运动数学模型,模拟船舶在风浪中的运动,计算出船舶在风浪中各运动参数的响应值,然后在考虑了船舶耐波性的基础上,通过建立船舶耐波性评估方程,对船舶的安全性从理论上进行计算和分析。

(3)通过在实船上安装风浪及船舶运动要素的自动测记仪器,记录实际船舶在风浪中的运动响应情况,然后再加以分析,找出最优的安全航行方案。

(4)利用船舶的主要参数来表达船舶的耐波性,进而评估船舶的安全性。

(5)运用现代数学手段,如模糊推理等方法,从一些主要的影响要素出发,对操船环境的危险度进行评价。

通过对重要单项指标,诸如海浪高度、波长、周期、风级和甲板淹湿等,来评估船舶安全性的方法有较高的实用价值。但是,考虑到船舶安全性的标准是诸多方面的,故此方法在考虑影响航海安全的因素方面似乎有些不够全面。

使用船舶耐波性指标分析的方法,显然较仅仅通过某些单项指标来评估船舶在大风浪中的安全性更为全面。但是,要得到这些耐波性指标,必须首先得到各耐波性特征量值,而到目前为止,这些耐波性特征量值基本上都是通过建立船舶操纵运动数学模型后,模拟船舶在风浪中的运动而得到的。由于船舶在风浪中的响应运动非常复杂,以至于各种模拟计算都无法确切真实地反映船舶的实际运动状态。如目前较为广泛使用的切片理论,虽然在用于计算垂荡和纵摇问题时误差不大,但在计算斜波中船舶的横摇、横荡和首摇时,误差仍很大。因此,所得到的各耐波性因素的响应值或出现概率也就有或大或小的误差。

实船测记资料的分析和应用,对描述船舶在风浪中的实际运动状态有着重大的意义。但是,获得这种实际资料的成本实在太大,到目前为止,也只有日本在一艘集装箱船上实施过。若要获得各种不同船型的实际资料实在过于困难。

利用船舶的主要参数来表达船舶耐波性的方法,能较好地表达船舶耐波性品级与船型参数间的关系,而且成本低廉,使用简便。然而,该方法仅是计算方法的实现,对船舶耐波性指数的确定等,并无实质性帮助。

经实际计算表明,利用模糊推理方法得到的能见度、风、流等因素对操船环境危险度的对应值与操船者实际在船上操船时的感觉相符,因而认为此方法是可行的。但该方法存在的问题是,隶属度函数的建立和各指标权重的获取都基于经验和大量的调查工作,而且,目前见到的方法所用指标也不够全面。因此,欲使此方法真正能够得以推广使用,尚有一些更为细致的工作要做。综合以上分析可以将各种方法的特点列于表4中。

表4　各种大风浪中船舶安全性评估方法

方法	优点	缺点	使用范围
单项指标评估	简便易行,使用价值高	分析不全面	船上人员估算使用
耐波性指数评估	理论依据充分,因素分析全面,过程清晰	船舶运动模拟计算误差较大,准确性不高	理论分析使用
实际运动状况记录	资料真实可靠,准确性高	成本过高,推广难度大	个别实验研究使用
船舶参数表达耐波性	经济,使用简便	过程不清晰	理论估计分析使用
危险度模糊评价	方便,实用性强	目前研究对影响因素分析不够全面,过程不够清晰	进一步开发后,可在船上使用

3　结语

通过对到目前为止所见到的各种关于大风浪中船舶安全性评估研究的综合考察可以看出,较适于航行船舶上使用的还是风浪等单项要素指标评估和危险度模糊评价方法,但要使这些方法更为完善,则还需要做一些细致的工作。

对风浪等单项要素指标评估法,可采用船舶安全状态校核的方法,即对大风浪引起的海难事故,根据当时的风浪条件和船舶状态,推算出不同状态的,可以将各船舶可以承受的风浪及作用时间的极限值,使该方法的评估标准更为准确和客观。

对危险度模糊评价方法,应对影响船舶安全的诸方面指标进行更全面、细致地分析,使分析工作更为客观具体,过程更为清晰,理论依据更为充分。耐波性指数评估方法理论依据充分,因素分析全面、过程清晰,是进行理论分析的重要手段,但由于受船舶运动模拟计算数学模型的限制,准确率有待提高。除了可进一步加强对数学模型的开发研究外,应深入研究实船运动状况纪录资料。实船运动状况纪录资料的可信性和真实性是模拟计算所无法替代的,因此,这两方面的综合研究有望得到理论依据充分、因素分析全面、过程清晰,而且准确性高的分析手段和结果。

安全管理体系运行有效性的评价[*]

摘要：在总结归纳国际安全管理规则对船舶航运公司安全管理体系运行有关要求的基础上，通过广泛征求安全管理体系审核员、船舶航运公司管理人员和有关专家学者的意见，建立了安全管理体系运行有效性评价指标体系；运用模糊理论建立了安全管理体系运行有效性定量评价数学模型；通过建立的数学模型对安全管理体系运行有效性进行具体的分析和评价，对进一步加强船舶航运公司安全管理及主管机关的管理决策都有一定的参考价值。

关键词：船舶营运；安全管理体系；模糊综合评判；数字模型

0 引言

我国于1995年3月正式开始实施《国际安全管理规则》(International Safety Management Code，以下简称 ISM 规则)[161,407]，即要求船舶航运公司建立《安全管理体系》(Safety Management System，SMS)，经我国主管机关——交通部海事局授权中国船级社对船舶航运公司的 SMS 运行有效性进行评价和审核[408]，并于1998年和2000年完成第一批和第二批船公司及船舶的审核发证工作。在审核发证工作中，我国审核员依据 ISM 规则和我国的相关法律法规，凭个人经验和学识进行判断，对船舶航运公司的 SMS 体系运行有效性进行评价。这种方法有较大的随意性和主观性，因而需要一种科学合理并具有可操作性的评价方法以满足工作需要。鉴于以上情况，本文在国内外有关研究非常少的情况下，集中大多数审核员、船舶航运公司专家和学者的经验和观点，从定量的角度，确立了船舶航运公司的 SMS 运行有效性评价指标体系和定量的数学评价模型。据此可对航运公司所建立的 SMS 运行的有效性进行较为科学客观的判断。

1 船舶航运公司 SMS 运行有效性指标体系的建立

1.1 概述

评价指标体系的建立对有效地评价船舶航运公司 SMS 运行的有效性是十分重要的，也是最关键的一步[409,410]。本文采取以下原则建立航运公司 SMS 运行有效性指标体系：

（1）考虑国际和国内相关法律法规的要求并征求专家学者的意见；

---

[*] 本文发表在《大连海事大学学报》2003年第4期第29卷，作者郑中义、潘家财、吴兆麟。

(2) 具有科学性、客观性、合理性和可操作性;
(3) 分析研究在船舶航运公司及船舶的审核发证中积累的经验和数据。

1.2 确定评价指标体系

根据 ISM 规则的要求,在征求专家意见的基础上,设计了"船舶航运公司 SMS 运行有效性指标调查表"(以下简称"调查表")。为了保证能够较为全面地反映水上交通安全主管机关及航运公司的观点和看法,调查表的发放比例为专家学者和主管机关 50%,船舶航运公司 50%。本次调查总共收回调查表 131 份,其中有效 127 份。在调查表统计结果的基础上,经过参加会议的专家的认真讨论,最后形成共识,确立了船舶航运公司 SMS 运行有效性评价指标体系,如表 1 所示。

表 1 船舶航运公司 SMS 运行有效性评价指标

序号	评价指标名称
指标一	被查船舶的平均单船缺陷数(船舶 FSC 和 PSC 检查的缺陷数与被查船舶总数之比)
指标二	被查船舶平均滞留率(船舶 FSC 和 PSC 检查的滞留总次数与被查船舶总数之比)
指标三	平均单船事故率(船舶发生事故总件数与体系内船舶总数之比)
指标四	SMC 失效率(体系内船舶 SMC 失效数与体系内船舶总数之比)
指标五	内审发现的不符合规定数与外审中发现的缺陷数之比
指标六	一般不符合规定数与被查岗位数之比
指标七	同类问题重复发生次数

各位专家认为,严重或重大不符合规定[161,407,408]情况出现,已说明了航运公司 SMS 运行出现严重问题,应立即进行整顿、整改,而不存在 SMS 运行有效性评判问题,因而把这两种情况列为"一票否决"指标,如表 2 所示。

表 2 航运公司 SMS 运行有效性评价"一票否决"指标

序号	一票否决指标
1	外审中发现的严重不符合规定数
2	外审中发现的重大不符合规定数

2 评价模型的建立

2.1 SMS 运行有效性评价模型的建立

船舶公司 SMS 体系运行有效性具有模糊性[408-410],涉及的模糊概念多,同时涉及的评价因素也多,因此利用模糊综合评判较为理想,它具有系统性和模糊性的特点,为 SMS 运行有效性评价提供了一种理想途径。由于 SMS 运行有效性评价指标体系的层次只有一层,因此只用一级模糊综合评判即可。模糊综合评判模型建立的基本步骤[5]包括以下几个环节。

第一步,将因素集 $U = \{U_1, U_2, \cdots, U_n\}$ 按某些属性分成 s 个子集:$U_i = \{U_{i1}, U_{i2}, U_{i3}, \cdots, U_{in}\}, i = 1, 2, \cdots, s$。它们满足条件:$n_1 + n_2 + \cdots + n_s = n$;$U_1 \cup U_2 \cup \cdots \cup U_s = U; U_i \cap U_j = \emptyset, i \neq j$。

第二步,对子因素集 U_i,分别做出综合评判,设 $V = \{V_1, V_2, \cdots, V_m\}$ 为评判集,U_i 中各因素相对 V 的权重分配为:

$$A_i = (a_{i1}\ a_{i2}\ \cdots\ a_{in}) \tag{1}$$

其中 $a_{i1} + a_{i2} + a_{i3} + \cdots + a_{in} = 1$。若设 R_i 为单因素评判矩阵,则得出一级评判向量:

$$B_i = A_i \circ R_i = (b_{i1}\ b_{i2}\ \cdots\ b_{im}), i = 1, 2, \cdots, s \tag{2}$$

根据所得的评判向量,利用反模糊化方法,可以得到评价对象所最终对应的等级。

(1)模糊算子

常见的模糊算子有主因素决定型、主因素突出型和加权平均型等。结合本文模糊评价模型的特点和各类模糊算子的特性,选用了主因素突出型的加法合成法(加权线性和法)算子。其基本公式为:

$$y^j = \sum_{i=1}^{n} w_i x_i^j \tag{3}$$

其中:y^j 表示综合评价向量;w_i 表示第 i 个指标权重;x_i^j 表示第 i 个指标对应于第 j 等级隶属度。

(2)反模糊化

模糊综合评价的结果是一模糊向量,确定评价对象的等级时需要对该向量进行精确化,或称为反模糊化。反模糊化的方法有多种[5]。根据 SMS 有效性评价模型的特点,本文采用重心法来确定模糊量中能反映出整个模糊量信息的精确值,这个过程类同于概率论中的求数学期望过程。

$$u^* = \left[\sum_i \mu(u_i) \times u_i\right] / \left[\sum_i \mu(u_i)\right] \tag{4}$$

加权系数不同,则所得精确值就会不同,这样显然会影响系统的输出结果。在重心法中,选取 $\mu(u_i)$ 为加权系数是恰当的。为了加强隶属度大指标的作用,加权系数还可以取为 $[\mu(u_i)]^2$,这样就可以加强隶属度大的元素的作用。

2.2 指标权重的获得

本文采用层次分析法[6]确定评价指标的权重。步骤如下:

(1)判断矩阵的建立

判断矩阵是层次分析法的基本信息,也是进行各要素优先级权重计算的重要依据。建立判断矩阵的目的是各个要素进行两两比较,以确定矩阵的元素值。

(2)依照判断矩阵进行权重计算

对于每一准则 C_k 下的判断矩阵 $A(a_{ij})$,$A = (a_{ij})_{n \times n}$。判断矩阵有如下性质:$a_{ij} > 0$,$a_{ii} = 1, a_{ij} = 1/a_{ji}, i = 1, 2, 3, \cdots, n$。据此计算各指标的排序权重,而且进行一致性检验。

(3)计算指标的权重

利用编制的层次分析法的计算程序,对收回的 127 份调查表进行计算,得出表 3 结果。

表3 SMS运行有效性评价指标权重表

指标	指标一	指标二	指标三	指标四	指标五	指标六	指标七
权重	0.070 8	0.181 3	0.193 2	0.252 7	0.062 5	0.083 9	0.156 0

从表3中,我们可以进一步得出各评价指标的影响大小。

2.3 隶属函数的确定

在模糊评判中,隶属函数的确定[410],无论是从理论上还是实践上都是模糊集合及其应用的基本而关键的问题。目前确定隶属函数的方法多数还处于研究阶段,远没有达到像确定概率分布那样成熟的阶段。在参考其他领域的有关模糊评判模型的基础上,借鉴专家确定法、模糊统计法和对比排序法的优点,本文采用主观经验和概率分布规律确定隶属函数。

(1)建立指标集和评价集

根据本文的研究对象及主管机关的要求,将评判等级集 V 定义为7个等级的集合,即:

$$V = \{V_1, V_2, V_3, \cdots, V_7\} = \{-3, -2, -1, 0, +1, +2, +3\}$$

其中的 $-3, -2, -1, 0, +1, +2, +3$ 为等级高低的度量,分别对应各等级|非常差,很差,较差,临界,较好,很好,非常好|。

(2)确定隶属函数曲线

根据问卷调查结果以及征求专家的意见和收集到的统计数据,以指标"被检查船舶的平均单船缺陷数"为例,说明指标隶属度曲线的确定方法及过程,限于篇幅,其余略。

根据收集到的资料经计算可知,2001年我国对船舶安全检查的情况:内河平均单船缺陷数为0.52个,沿海船舶平均单船缺陷数为5.87个;2001年亚太地区备忘录港口国管理中的平均单船缺陷数为2.83个;而在巴黎备忘录港口国管理中的平均单船缺陷数为5.88个(其他指标也是依据国内外相关数据确定的)。

根据这些数据,可认为若船舶的平均单船缺陷数为5.88个,则可认为船舶航运公司所建立的SMS的运行有效性属于平均状态,即SMS运行有效性属于临界状态的隶属函数值为1。而在5.88~0个缺陷之间采用"三分法"所获得的值依次作为隶属于较好、很好和非常好为1的参数值,即当船舶平均缺陷数为1.96个时隶属于"很好"的隶属度函数为1;而当单船平均缺陷数为3.92个时,隶属于"较好"的隶属度函数为1;而当单船平均缺陷数为0个时,隶属于"非常好"的隶属函数为1。同样从平均单船缺陷数5.88个以后,以1.96相同的步长,每增加1.96个缺陷,则分别隶属于"较差""很差""非常差"的隶属度函数值分别为1。船舶平均缺陷数的隶属度函数曲线如图1所示,而其相应的代数式略去。

3 评判模型的应用与验证

利用上述建立的航运公司SMS运行的有效性评价模型,我们可以对船舶航运公司SMS运行有效性进行评价。根据本评价模型的特点,依清晰化的评价结果,船舶航运公司SMS运行情况分为如表4的7个等级。

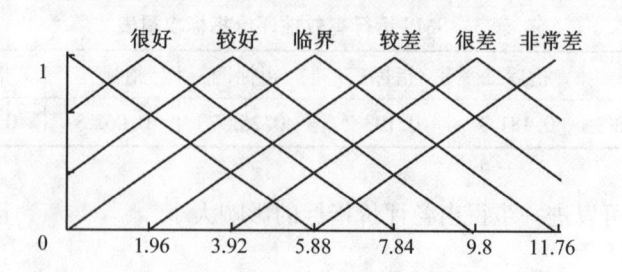

图1 船舶平均缺陷数与隶属于各种状态的隶属度曲线图

表4 航运公司 SMS 运行情况评价等级表

评价结果	等级	运行情况	评价结果	等级	运行情况
$0 \leq R_e \leq 0.959$	3	非常好	$3.50 < R_e \leq 4.375$	−1	较差
$0.959 < R_e \leq 1.625$	2	很好	$4.375 < R_e \leq 5.04$	−2	很差
$1.625 < R_e < 2.50$	1	较好	$5.04 < R_e$	−3	非常差
$2.50 < R_e \leq 3.50$	0	临界状态			

注:在利用上述的评价模型进行评价时,若某一航运公司的 7 个指标均为"非常好"时,所得到的评价值为 0.667;若指标值均为"很好"时,评价值为 1.250。这样取两者的中值为 0.959,因此有表 4 的结果。

为了更好地验证本评价模型,向已经建立并运行 SMS 体系的航运公司发放了调查表,经过整理,获得 8 个有效验证样本。为此设计了计算机程序,验算结果如表 5 所示。

表5 4个航运公司 SMS 运行状况表

船舶公司	1999 年	评价等级	2000 年	评价等级	2001 年	评价等级
船舶公司一			1.860	2	1.288	1
船舶公司二					1.387	1
船舶公司三			1.387	1	1.853	2
船舶公司四	1.142	1	0.856 4	0	1.338	1

从表 5 可以看出:

第一,横向比较。以上 4 家航运公司 SMS 运行有效性指标一"被查船舶的平均缺陷数"的数值普遍比较大,这说明了这些公司船舶状况大多不理想,存在较多的缺陷,这与我国大部分船舶船龄较大有很大的关系。

第二,纵向比较。船舶公司 4 个 SMS 体系建设与管理比较理想,但不是很稳定。特别是 SMS 运行有效性指标一、指标六和指标七数值一直降不下来,公司管理层应加强这三方面的管理与监督。

4 结束语

通过本文的评价结果可见,应用该模型对船舶航运公司 SMS 运行有效性的评价符合客观实际,评价结果具有应用价值;且该模型有很强的可操作性,经计算机程序实现后,可以直接应用于实际工作中。我国在1998年才通过第一批船舶航运公司及其船舶的SMS审核发证,取得的样本数据有限,因此该模型还有待进一步验证。

大风浪中航行船舶风险体系分析[*]

摘要:介绍了风险分析理论与综合安全评估,以及开展大风浪中航行船舶风险分析的意义,引入了有关大风浪中航行船舶风险分析的概念,初步建立了相应的风险体系框架,并提出了大风浪中航行船舶风险分析的主要任务。

关键词:交通安全;风险分析理论;综合安全评估;大风浪;航行船舶;风险体系

0 引言

尽管当今的造船技术和航海技术不断发展,风浪预报水平也不断提高,但海上复杂多变的天气条件和难以预测的大风浪威胁着航行的船舶,由于水文气象条件恶劣造成的海上重大人身伤亡事故和重大财产损失事故时有发生[410]。因此,十分有必要对大风浪中航行船舶的风险状况进行定量评估,以便对大风浪中船舶开航或航行方案的选定有一个便于执行的评估手段及技术标准,为决策者科学决策提供参考,达到既能减小风险,又能保证船公司和货主利益的双重目标。风险分析理论和风险分析方法是近年来在工业领域首先发展并应用的一项新技术,主要用于较大风险领域的安全管理,如核工业、海上石油生产和金融投资等[290,412]。目前为止,尚未见到利用风险分析理论和技术对大风浪中航行船舶进行系统的风险分析。为了充分利用风险分析理论和技术在其他领域已取得的研究成果和经验,有效地进行大风浪中航行船舶的风险分析,本文试图引入有关概念,建立相关的风险体系,并对有关今后研究的主要任务做了初步分析。

1 风险分析理论与综合安全评估

海事界和航运界已将在其他工业领域取得成功经验的风险分析方法引入到航运管理中,形成以风险分析技术为核心的综合安全评估(FSA)方法。从1993年起,世界各国及国际海事组织逐步开展了多项FSA的研究和应用,并于1997年通过了《IMO制定安全规则过程中应用FSA暂行指南》。综合安全评估(FSA)方法是一种关于工程技术与工程运行管理中用于制定合理的规则和提供风险控制的综合性、结构化和系统性的分析方法[413,414]。在航运安全管理中应用综合安全评估技术,可以通过风险评估和费用、收益评估,尽可能全面、合理地在航运管理中有效地提高海上船舶航行的安全性。依照国际海事组织通过的《IMO制定安全规则过程中应用FSA暂行指南》,综合安全评估由5个步骤组成,即风险识别、风险评估、降低风险的措

---

[*] 本文发表在《交通运输工程学报》2004年第2期第4卷,作者刘大刚、郑中义、吴兆麟。

施、降低风险措施的费用效益评估、提出降低风险措施的决策建议,具体流程如图1所示。

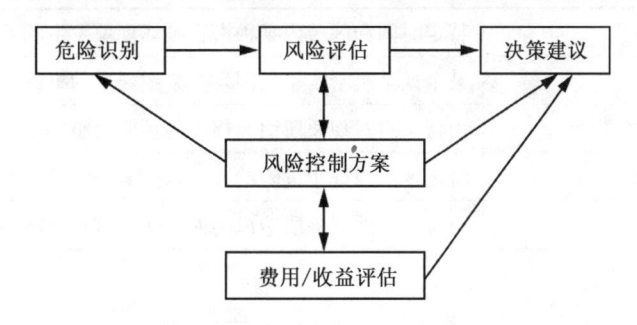

图1 综合安全评估流程

可以看出,这其中的风险识别和风险评估部分均属于风险分析技术的范畴,它们是进行综合安全评估的基础和核心部分。用风险分析理论和技术对大风浪中航行的船舶进行风险分析,可以使船舶驾驶人员和航运管理部门能够对在大风浪中航行船舶的安全性有一个全面、准确的掌握,以便在选择大风浪中航行方案时,能够做出更为合理的决策,从而进一步提高大风浪中船舶航行的安全性。

2 风险分析理论

2.1 风险的概念

风险是决策的结果达不到目标的概率,用数学公式表示为:

$$R = f(D,S) \tag{1}$$

式中:f 为风险函数;D 为人们的决策;S 为客观的状态集合[413,414]。

2.2 风险体系的组成

风险体系由风险源、风险要素、风险事件、风险决策和风险后果组成。灾害的发生是由孕灾环境、致灾因子和承灾体之间的相互作用形成的,灾害的轻重取决于孕灾环境的稳定性、致灾因子的风险性及承灾体的脆弱性[290]。

2.3 风险分析的内容

风险分析主要包括风险辨识、风险估算和风险评价。风险辨识主要是要描述可能发生的各种风险事件、引发风险事件的原因及风险事件可能引起的后果和严重程度;风险估算是在风险辨识的基础上,给出各风险事件发生的概率及其后果;风险评价是评价已确定的风险因素或致险因子对可能受影响的承灾体的重要性,为决策者进行决策提供可供权衡的风险指数或指标。灾害和风险的有关定义如表1所示。

表1 灾害和风险的有关定义

自然灾害	特定时间和区域内某种潜在破坏现象发生的可能性
脆弱性	某个或某组给定单元因发生一定规模的事件而产生损失的程度
具体风险	由特定自然现象所引起损失的预期大小
风险单元	特定区域内处于危险的人口、财产、经济活动等
总风险	由特定自然现象所造成的人员伤亡、财产或经济损失的预期值

3 大风浪中航行船舶的风险体系

3.1 风险分析

船舶航行对水文气象条件有着较大的依赖性,在大风浪条件下,若海况过于恶劣,则可能给船舶带来危险。但是,随着当代造船技术的发展,以及船舶驾驶人员素质的提高,船舶抗风能力和大风浪中操船的技能也在不断提高。因此,从风险的角度来看,在大风浪中航行的船舶所面临的风险程度的高低与三大因素有关:环境条件,主要是大风浪的强度和作用时间等;船舶条件,包括船型、船龄、装载情况、船舶性能、船舶强度和货物装载情况等;决策,主要指决策人对航行方案的选择。大风浪中船舶的风险指具体某一船舶在大风浪区航行时,由于航行方案决策和船舶自身条件与大风浪条件变化的不确定性而可能引起的具有危险性的后果,用数学公式可表达为:

$$R_N = f(D_N, C_N, S_N) \tag{2}$$

即大风浪中船舶的风险 R_N 是决策 D_N、环境条件 C_N 和船舶条件 S_N 的函数。

3.2 风险体系构成

风险体系应包括风险源、风险要素、风险事件、风险决策和风险后果等,可做如下表述。

(1) 风险源或孕灾环境:主要指造成大风浪的天气系统,如热带气旋、强温带气旋和强寒潮冷锋等。

(2) 风险要素或致灾因子:主要包括大风的风向、风速,大浪的浪高、浪向、周期及作用时间等。

(3) 承灾体(船舶)的脆弱性:主要指船舶自身的缺陷,如船体过于老化、船舶的结构强度不足,以及稳性、绑扎、水密、排水设施有缺陷等。

(4) 风险事件:船舶在大风浪中航行本身就是风险事件的主体。

(5) 风险单元:船舶、所载货物和船上人员。

(6) 风险决策:指大风浪中航行方案的选择。

(7) 风险后果或总风险:指与不同的航行方案相对应的,从开始进入受大风浪威胁的海区,直到这种威胁消失的整个过程中,大风浪对船舶造成的各种损坏乃至失事的总称。

可以认为,对大风浪中航行的船舶来说,风险是人为因素、船舶条件和环境条件三者共同作用的结果。即,当按人们所确定的航行方案在大风浪中航行时,大风浪等致灾因子作用于作为承灾体的船舶,而船舶又存在着不同程度的脆弱性,如果所遇到的风浪超出船舶所能承受的限度时,风险就会发生。图2为大风浪中航行船舶的风险体系结构。

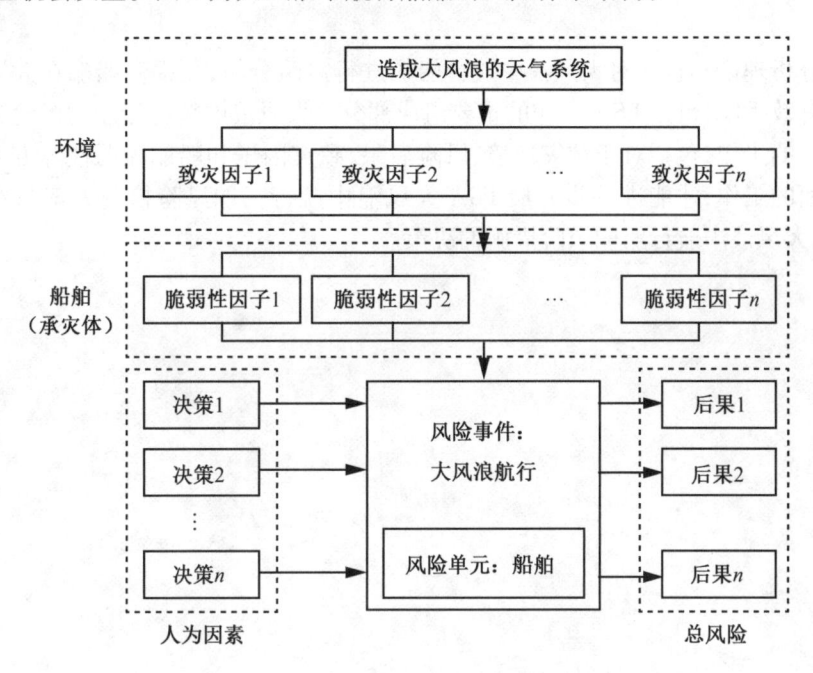

图 2 大风浪中航行船舶的风险体系结构

4 风险分析的主要任务

4.1 风险辨识

（1）孕灾环境:采用统计方法,针对产生大风浪的各种天气系统和天气过程,对负责发布不同海区船舶气象报告的主要气象台的预报结果进行统计,得到其预报的准确率,作为进行风险分析的依据。

（2）风险后果:可采用较为科学、合理的方法,并结合实际生产部门的具体标准或规定,对大风浪中航行船舶可能发生的风险后果进行分级,为进行相关的分析工作提供必要的标准。

4.2 风险评估

（1）致灾因子:选定直接造成船舶发生风险事故的致灾因子,建立对大风浪中航行船舶进行风险估算的模型,分析各致灾因子的强度与不同的船型在不同的载态、航行状态下,发生不同等级的风险事故之间的相关性。

（2）船舶的脆弱性:针对特定的船型,考虑到不同的船龄、结构强度、稳性及绑扎、水密、排水设施等因素,确定其对相同的船型,在一定的致灾因子的作用下对发生不同等级风险事故的影响程度。

5 结语

用风险分析理论和技术对大风浪中航行船舶进行风险分析,是提高船舶在大风浪中航行安全水平的有效手段,也是 FSA 工作的重要组成部分。大风浪中航行船舶的风险分析工作有许多亟待研究的工作,包括对于孕灾环境、风险后果、致灾因子和船舶脆弱性等方面。只有完成了这些方面的工作,才能进一步开展 FSA 大风浪中航行船舶风险控制方案与费用效益评估,提出降低大风浪中航行船舶风险措施的决策。

恶劣天气条件下船舶开航安全性评估方法[*]

摘要:从安全系统工程角度,利用层次分析法(AHP),研究了船舶在恶劣天气条件下开航安全性影响因素,建立了安全性评估指标体系和评估模型,确定了各评价指标对船舶开航安全的影响程度,运用模糊数学的综合评判方法,对恶劣天气条件下船舶开航安全性进行了评估。结果表明该评估方法能给出清晰的安全定量指标,是可行的。

关键词:交通安全;航行安全保障;开航;层次分析法;模糊数学;综合评判;恶劣天气

0 引言

船舶综合安全性评估是一种结构化的系统方法,其目的在于提高船舶海上航行的安全性。船舶开航安全性评估是船舶综合安全性评估最重要的一个环节,进行该项评估的意义在于确定船舶在开航时所涉及的安全因素,借助于数学方法,从定性与定量相结合的角度研究船舶在恶劣天气条件下船舶开航的安全性,以期为船长、船舶管理公司及海事监督部门的安全管理提供科学的参考依据,最大限度地减少船舶在恶劣天气条件下发生海难事故。

1 评估指标体系

船舶的开航安全性,应该放在船舶营运大系统中研究。从静态角度应考虑船舶开航时的状态要素,即人、船舶和管理要素;从动态的角度应考虑航行中的状态要素,即环境要素。在这个大系统中,应全面反映各个因素对安全的影响作用。根据各个因素的相互关联及作用情况,不难发现船舶开航安全性评估系统可以由船舶、船员和环境三个子系统组成。这三个子系统本身便构成对船舶安全性全方位的评估,因此是船舶开航安全性评估系统的直接因素[416,417]。由于船舶开航安全性是个复杂的系统性问题,在进行综合评估时,需要考虑的因素很多,因此需要将各因素按不同的层次分属为不同的类别,每一类别中都包含下一级因素;每一类为上一级的组成因素,每一次的评估仅在同一类同一层次的因素间进行。本文综合专家学者的研究成果、专家调查的情况和海难事故调查的结论,对人、船、环境三个子系统所涉及的要素进行必要的筛选,合理归纳选取那些对船舶开航安全有直接影响的要素,按照多层次分析原理,最终得到如图1所示的船舶开航安全性评估指标体系[418,419]。

---

[*] 本文发表在《交通运输工程学报》2004年第3期第4卷,作者王凤武、吴兆麟、郑中义。

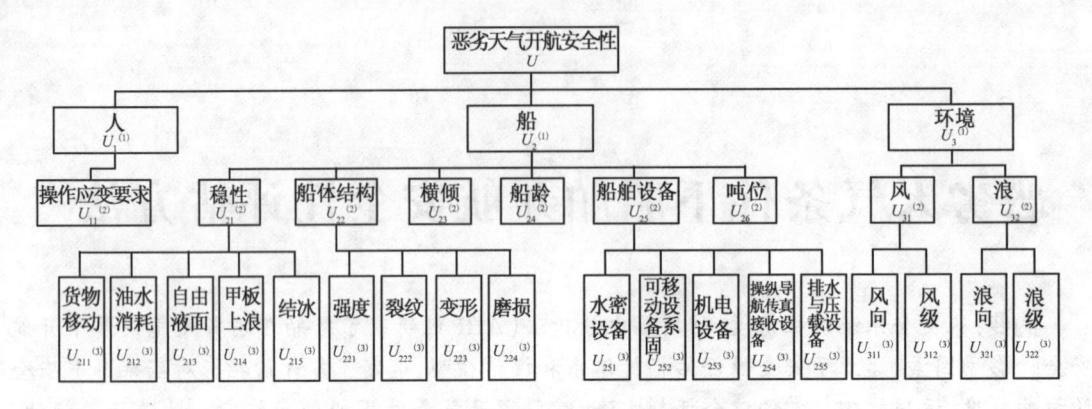

图1 船舶开航安全性能评估指标体系

2 评估方法

本文采用模糊综合评判方法对船舶开航安全性进行评估[420]。模糊综合评判是对给定对象综合考虑多种因素进行评估和判决的方法。模糊综合评判方法涉及因素集、评价集和单因素评判。

由于船舶营运系统是由船舶、船员、环境和管理组成的综合系统,船舶开航安全性不仅由船舶本身状况、在船船员的组合情况及船舶所处位置的自然情况所决定,而且还与他们之间的交互作用相关联。在进行开航安全性评估中,以船舶、船员和环境作为最基本的组成因素入手,再分别考虑其中各个因素内对开航安全发生作用的单一个体。这是符合多层次的模糊综合评判要求的,只有这样,才能避免考虑因素权数分配过小和被"淹没"问题。

2.1 模糊综合评判原理

2.1.1 建立因素集

因素集 U 是影响评判对象的各个因素所组成的集合,表示为:

$$U = \{U_1, U_2, U_3, \cdots, U_n\}$$

2.1.2 建立权重集

上述所建立的因素集 U 中的诸因素在评判中具有不同的重要程度,区分各因素的重要程度有助于突出主要因素的作用,并提高评估结果的准确性,因此必须对 U_i 按重要程度给出不同的权重值 A_{U_i}。权重集 A 是因素集 U 上的模糊子集,表示为:

$$A = \{A_{U_1}, A_{U_2}, A_{U_3}, \cdots, A_{U_n}\}$$

式中:$A_{U_i}(i=1,2,\cdots,n)$ 是因素 U_i 对 U 的权重值,应满足归一性和非负性标准,即

$$\sum_{i=1}^{n} A_{U_i} = 1$$

$$A_{U_i} \geq 0$$

2.1.3 建立评价集评价集

评价集是由对评判对象可能做出的评判结果所组成的集合,表示为:

$$V = \{v_1, v_2, v_3, \cdots, v_m\}$$

式中：$v_j(j = 1,2,\cdots,m)$ 是若干可能做出的评判结果。模糊综合评判的目的在于通过对评判对象综合考虑所影响因素，能够从评价集中获得一个最佳的评判结果。

2.1.4 模糊评判

单因素评判是指从一个因素出发，以确定评判对象对评价集因素的隶属程度。设评判对象按因素集中的第 i 个因素 U_i 进行评判，对评判集中的第 j 个因素 v_j 的隶属度为 r_{ij}，则按第 i 个因素 U_i 评判的结果可表示为：

$$R_i = \{r_{i1}, r_{i2}, r_{i3}, \cdots, r_{im}\}$$

式中：R_i 为单因素评判集。由因素集、评判集和单因素评判集可得到一级模糊综合评判模型为：

$$B^{(1)} = A^{(1)} R^{(1)} = (b_1, b_2, \cdots, b_m)$$
$$R^{(2)} = (B_1^{(1)}\ B_2^{(1)}\ B_3^{(1)}\ \cdots\ B_k^{(1)})^T$$

依此可以得到 $B_i^{(1)}$，用 $B_i^{(1)}$ 作单因素评判集可构成评判矩阵，于是可得第二级综合评判

$$B^{(2)} = A^{(2)} \circ R^{(2)}$$

因此应对图 1 的评估指标体系进行分层后，做多层次的评判[421]。

2.1.5 评价指标的处理

以最上层模糊综合评判向量 b_j 为权数，对评判集 v_j 进行加权平均得到最终的评判结果为：

$$v = \frac{\sum_{j=1}^{m} b_j v_j}{\sum_{j=1}^{m} b_j}$$

2.2 综合评估

2.2.1 因素集

在对恶劣天气条件下船舶开航安全性评估时，应从船舶营运系统的整体和全局出发，将影响船舶开航安全性的因素分为人、船舶和环境 3 大类，分别用 $U_1^{(1)}$、$U_2^{(1)}$ 和 $U_3^{(1)}$ 表示，即

$$U = \{U_1^{(1)}, U_2^{(1)}, U_3^{(1)}\}$$
$$U_1^{(1)} = \{U_{11}^{(2)}\}$$
$$U_2^{(1)} = \{U_{21}^{(2)}, U_{22}^{(2)}, U_{23}^{(2)}, U_{24}^{(2)}, U_{25}^{(2)}, U_{26}^{(2)}\}$$
$$U_3^{(1)} = \{U_{31}^{(2)}, U_{32}^{(2)}\}$$
$$U_{21}^{(2)} = \{U_{211}^{(3)}, U_{212}^{(3)}, U_{213}^{(3)}, U_{214}^{(3)}, U_{215}^{(3)}\}$$
$$U_{22}^{(2)} = \{U_{221}^{(3)}, U_{222}^{(3)}, U_{223}^{(3)}, U_{224}^{(3)}\}$$
$$U_{25}^{(2)} = \{U_{251}^{(3)}, U_{252}^{(3)}, U_{253}^{(3)}, U_{254}^{(3)}, U_{255}^{(3)}\}$$
$$U_{31}^{(2)} = \{U_{311}^{(3)}, U_{312}^{(3)}\}$$
$$U_{32}^{(2)} = \{U_{321}^{(3)}, U_{322}^{(3)}\}$$

2.2.2 权重向量

为了较准确地获得各指标的权重,本文采用层次分析法(AHP法)[422],并结合59位专家(船长、大副)的咨询调查获得指标的权重。将专家调查的数据经过几何平均法处理,则得到判断矩阵,再根据一致性指标进行检验,其判别公式为:

$$C_R = \frac{C_I}{R_I} < 0.1$$

$$C_I = \frac{\lambda_{max} - n}{n - 1}$$

$$\lambda_{max} = \sum_{i=1}^{n} \frac{(AW)_i}{nW_i}$$

当 $C_R < 0.1$ 时,认为判断矩阵具有满意的一致性,否则应需要调整判断矩阵,并使之具有满意的一致性。经过计算得出7组权重数值。

第一层3大类的权重集模糊向量为:

$W^{(1)}$ = (人权重 船舶权重 环境权重) = (0.443 105 0.293 275 0.263 620)

第二层各方面的权重模糊向量如下。

船舶方面

$W^{(2)}$ = (稳性权重 船体结构权重 横倾权重 船龄权重 船舶设备权重 吨位权重)
= (0.317 556 0.212 176 0.204 089 0.093 850 0.121 478 0.050 857)

环境方面

$W^{(3)}$ = (风权重 浪权重) = (0.335 969 0.664 031)

第三层各方面的权重模糊向量为:

$W_{21}^{(1)}$ = (货物移动权重 油水消耗权重 自由液面权重 甲板上浪权重 结冰权重)
= (0.443 852 0.076 574 0.152 510 0.184 079 014 985)

$W_{22}^{(3)}$ = (强度权重 裂纹权重 变形权重 磨损权重)
= (0.356 468 0.398 040 0.166 584 0.078 908)

$W_{25}^{(3)}$ = (水密设别权重 可移动设备系固权重 机电设备权重 操纵导航传真接收机设备权重 排水与压载设备权重)
= (0.228 655 0.171 546 0.274 913 0.195 127 0.129 759)

$W_{31}^{(3)}$ = (风向权重 风级权重) = (0.634 678 0.365 322)

$W_{32}^{(3)}$ = (浪向权重 浪级权重) = (0.458 487 0.541 513)

2.2.3 评价集

参考国内外学者、专家常用的评判等级划分方法,本文将评判等级集定义为5个等级,即

$$V = \{v_1, v_2, v_3, v_4, v_5\} = \{-2, -1, 0, 1, 2\}$$

可描述为 V = {低危险,较低危险,一般危险,较高危险,高危险},以表示船舶在恶劣天气条件下开航安全性评价等级,其中 -2、-1、0、1、2 是模糊数,用来表示一些模糊概念,目的是对评语进行量化处理。

2.2.4 评价指标隶属度的确定

本文采用发放打分调查表的方法让有经验的专家对每一具体评价指标进行认定,汇总并

经归一化处理后,即可得到各个因素对应于等级的隶属度,进而得到单因素评判矩阵。表1、表2为操纵应变要求、水密设备的隶属度模糊子集。

表1 操作应变要求的隶属度模糊子集

	低危险	较低危险	一般危险	较高危险	高危险
熟悉操作应变要求	0.511	0.489	0.000	0.000	0.000
对操作应变要求掌握一般	0.021	0.075	0.820	0.084	0.000
对操作应变要求不熟悉	0.000	0.000	0.021	0.617	0.362

表2 水密设备的隶属度模糊子集

	低危险	较低危险	一般危险	较高危险	高危险
水密设备好	0.936	0.043	0.021	0.000	0.000
水密设备较好	0.085	0.788	0.106	0.021	0.000
水密设备一般	0.000	0.064	0.808	0.128	0.000
水密设备较差	0.000	0.000	0.043	0.532	0.425

3 模型验证

为了检验评估方法的有效性,本文根据WINTEC轮的调查情况(2003年8月20日查验船舶保养记录和其他船舶资料),验证本文提出的评估方法的准确性。评价要素如下:船员对操纵应变要求掌握一般;吨位为36 623 MT属于30 000 ~ 50 000 MT;船龄14 a,在10 ~ 14 a之间;强度的拱垂值为0.168,在$L_{bp}/1\ 200 \sim L_{bp}/800$;磨损率为6%,在5% ~ 10%之间;有轻微变形;裂纹损伤频度较低;水密设备较好;机电设备较好;操纵、导航与气象接收设备较好;排水与压载设备较好;可移动设备系固效果较好;无横倾;货物系固效果一般;油水消耗合理;无自由液面;甲板上浪较小;无结冰;顶风7 ~ 8级;顶浪中浪。

将上述指标进行相应的计算便可得到评估结果,即$v = -0.401\ 383$,结论为一般危险和较低危险之间。说明开航前应对影响船舶安全的3大类因素进行很好的检查,消除隐患,确保船舶在开航前处于安全适航状态。

4 结语

本文首次利用模糊综合评判方法对恶劣天气条件下开航安全性进行评估,其目的是使船长在开航前对船舶的适航情况做到心中有数,有清晰的定量指标概念,为船长开航前的检查和开航后的操船决策提供了科学的依据,同时也为海事监督人员和公司管理人员提供参考。由于安全因素涉及的方面很多,本文在确定评价指标的隶属度还显得粗糙,待以后研究中进一步构造其隶属函数,更趋完善。

通航水域危险度评价模型*

摘要：本文在确定通航水域危险度评价指标体系的基础上，运用灰色关联分析和因子分析方法，分析了通航水域环境各因素与通航水域船舶交通事故关系。基于模糊综合评价理论，建立了通航水域危险度评价模型。在模型中，利用灰色关联分析和因子分析所得结果，确定了各个评价指标的权重。这种方法可以避免由人的主观因素所引起的偏差，也避免了由于单一方法所带来的缺陷，并且各评价指标的权重随一定时期内船舶交通事故的变化而变化，更为客观地反映现实情况。通过该模型可对特定通航水域危险度进行评价，所得结果可为海上安全主管机关确定重点管理水域提供科学参考。

关键词：通航水域；危险度；灰色系统理论；因子分析；模糊评价

0 引言

关于通航水域危险度的研究所涉及的论文较多，总结这些研究成果，可归纳为如下几个方面：碰撞危险度研究、搁浅危险度研究、水域危险度研究等。在总结和分析这些研究成果的基础上，认为对通航水域危险度的研究应做到：(1)加强基础数据的收集和研究。只有保证基础数据的全面和准确，才能保证定量化研究的实际意义。(2)掌握好定性与定量的界限。只进行定性分析不足以解决问题，而过度地追求评价中量化的比重，有时反而会造成使用评价方法的困难。(3)单一的评价方法往往针对某一特定方面，难以揭示整个系统的问题。采用多种方法综合评价，可以做到互相补充。

为此，本文提出了一种综合评价模型。该模型运用的是模糊综合评价理论，但在确定权重时，创新性地采用了以灰色关联分析和因子分析结果来综合确定权重的方法。这样各指标的权重就是根据各因素与事故的关系而取得，使得这些权重更能反映客观情况，也更科学；并且，由于运用了灰色关联分析和因子分析两种方法相结合，避免了由单一方法所带来的缺陷。

模糊综合评价的基本方法和步骤为：(1)建立指标集；(2)建立权重集；(3)建立评价集（备选集）；(4)单因素模糊评判；(5)模糊综合评判；(6)评判指标的处理。

1 建立指标集

影响港口船舶交通事故的要素是比较多的，通过定性分析和专家咨询得到事故的要素序列，它们是：能见度（X_1：指通航水域近5年平均低于1 km的年累计天数，单位：天/年）、大风

---

* 本文发表在《第四届亚太可持续发展交通与环境技术大会论文集》，作者郑中义、陈新、黄忠国。

(X_2:指通航水域近 5 年风力达 6 级(蒲福风级)及以上的平均年累计发生天数与台风警报发生(即预计 48 h 内可以侵入通航水域或边缘距离通航水域只有 500 km)至台风警报消除为止的年累计天数之和,单位:天/年)、最大流(X_3:指被评价相应通航水域的最大流速值,单位:n mile/h)、主航道长度(X_4:航道长度,单位:n mile)、交叉点和转向点数(X_5:指主航道与通航水深大于 1 m 的次航道的交叉角大于 25°的个数)、船宽/航道宽度(X_6:船舶宽度是指特定通航水域允许通航船舶宽度的平均值,航道宽度为特定航道最窄处的宽度,单位:n mile)、船舶交通密度(X_7:指单位时间每平方海里的船舶数,单位:艘/n mile^2·h)、船舶加权交通量(X_8:采用藤井弥平提出的加权系数将每天通航船舶艘数换算为标准船艘数,单位:艘/天)、VTS 管理程度(X_9:专家评分)、分道通航程度(X_{10}:专家评分)和助航标志(X_{11}:航标正常率)。建立如图 1 的评价指标体系。

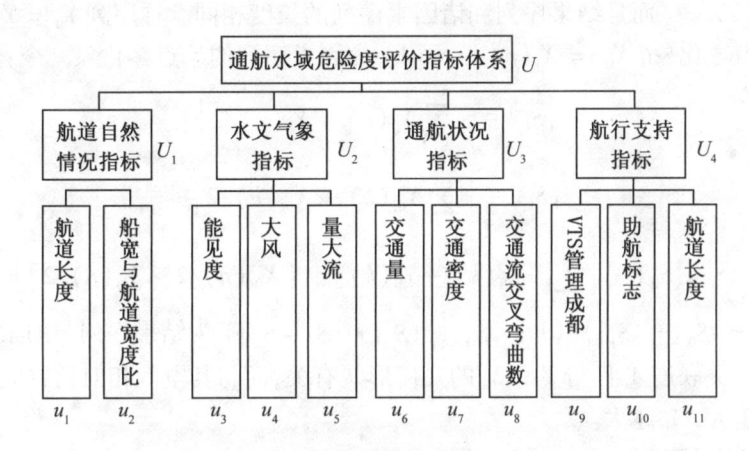

图 1 通航水域危险评价指标体系层次结构图

根据上面建立的综合评判指标体系,设评价指标集:
$$U = \{U_1, U_2, U_3, U_4\}$$
并且有:
$$U_1 = \{u_1, u_2\}, U_2 = \{u_3, u_4, u_5\}$$
$$U_3 = \{u_6, u_7, u_8\}, U_4 = \{u_9, u_{10}, u_{11}\}$$

2 建立权重集

一般说来,指标集 U 中的各个指标在评判中具有的重要程度不同,因而必须对各个指标 u_i 按其重要程度给出不同的权数 a_i;由各权数组成的指标权重集 A 是指标集 U 上的模糊子集,可表示为
$$A = (a_1, a_2, \cdots, a_n)$$
其中元素 $a_i(i = 1, 2, \cdots, n)$ 是指标 u_i 对 A 的隶属度,反映了各个指标在综合评价中所具有的重要程度,通常应满足归一性和非负性条件:
$$\sum_{i=1}^{n} a_i = 1, a_i \geq 0 \tag{1}$$
这里先分别运用灰色关联分析和因子分析方法来确定各指标的权重,再将这两种分析结

果综合,获得最后的权重结果。

2.1 灰色关联分析方法

2.1.1 灰色关联分析原理

本文采用灰色综合关联度,由于它不但反映了因素序列与结果序列几何形状的相似程度,而且也反映了因素序列与结果序列相对于始点的变化率,更能反映出因素对结果的影响程度。

(1)灰色绝对关联度

设:结果序列Y和因素序列X_i,分别为:

$$Y = (Y(1), Y(2), \cdots, Y(n)); X_i = (X_i(1), X_i(2), \cdots, X_i(n))$$

其中$n = 1, 2, \cdots$。而且结果序列和诸因素序列的长度相同。称序列$Y_0 = Y(n) - Y(1)$为结果序列的始点零化象,$X_{0i} = X_i(n) - X_1(1)$为因素序列的始点零化象。令:

$$|S_0| = \left| \sum_{k=1}^{n-1} Y_0(k) + Y_0(n)/2 \right| \tag{2}$$

$$|S_i| = \left| \sum_{k=1}^{n-1} X_{0i}(k) + X_{0i}(n)/2 \right| \tag{3}$$

$$|S_i - S_0| = \left| \sum_{k=1}^{n-1} [X_{0i}(k) - Y_0(k)] + [X_{0i}(n)/2 - Y_0(n)/2] \right| \tag{4}$$

则称:$A_i = (1 + |S_0| + |S_i|)/(1 + |S_0| + |S_i| + |S_i - S_0|)$为结果序列与因素序列的灰色绝对关联度。绝对关联度$A_i$只与$Y$和$X_i$的几何形状有关,而与其空间相对位置无关。$Y$与$X_i$几何上相似程度越大,$A_i$越大。

(2)灰色相对关联度

若结果序列Y与因素序列X_i的长度相同,且初值都异于零,称序列$Y_z = Y/Y(1)$和$X_{zi} = X_i/X(1)$为结果和因素序列的初值象,称Y_z与X_{zi}的灰色绝对关联度为Y与X_i的灰色相对关联度,记为R_i。灰色相对关联度R_i仅与序列Y, X_i相对于始点的变化速率有关;当Y与X_i相对于始点的变化速率越趋于一致时,R_i越大。

(3)灰色综合关联度A_i和R_i分别为Y, X_i的灰色绝对关联度和灰色相对关联度,有

$$P_i = K \times A_i + (1 - K) \times R_i \tag{5}$$

其中:$0 < K < 1$,则P_i为Y, X_i的灰色综合关联度。

2.1.2 灰色关联分析模型的应用

(1)各港口诸因素、船舶事故次数(Y)。综合我国部分港口的统计数据如表1所示。

表1 部分港口的统计数据

	港口1	港口2	港口3	港口4	港口5	港口6	港口7	港口8	港口9
Y	29.2	3.2	4.8	6.4	39.0	23.0	3.0	37.0	40.0
X_1	27.0	11.3	9.8	24.2	54.0	16.1	28.0	25.0	13.3
X_2	40.4	8.6	80.2	77.4	94.8	139.0	21.4	73.3	11.3
X_3	3.0	3.0	1.5	5	3.0	2.9	5.0	3.5	3.5

续表

	港口1	港口2	港口3	港口4	港口5	港口6	港口7	港口8	港口9
X_4	9.5	14.0	20.2	4.2	7.4	3.6	13.6	63.7	40.8
X_5	5.0	2.0	1.0	2.0	8.0	7.0	6.0	13.0	18.0
X_6	0.1	0.25	0.14	0.24	0.065	0.36	0.2	0.2	0.1
X_7	1.5	1.2	1.6	2.1	8.1	0.68	17.6	2.9	0.5
X_8	57.86	30.74	41.20	13.980	45.70	14.00	21.80	42.00	32.80
X_9	5.0	4.7	5.0	4.5	4.9	4.8	5.0	5.0	4.6
X_{10}	5.0	4.18	4.55	4.06	4.44	4.5	4.21	5.0	4.11
X_{11}	99.98	99.98	99.98	99.98	99.92	99.92	99.92	99.90	99.90

(2)计算港口船舶事故与其因素的灰色综合关联度。利用表1数据,通过前面所述的计算过程,分别得出A_i和$R_i (i = 1,2,\cdots,11)$。

进而利用式(6),取$K = 0.5$,得到:

$P_1 = 0.7773, P_2 = 0.6116, P_3 = 0.6860, P_4 = 0.5916, P_5 = 0.6403, P_6 = 0.5947$
$P_7 = 0.5643, P_8 = 0.8185, P_9 = 0.6819, P_{10} = 0.7055, P_{11} = 0.6739$

由$P_8 > P_1 > P_{10} > P_3 > P_9 > P_{11} > P_5 > P_2 > P_6 > P_4 > P_7$得到如下结论:

从上面的结果看,港口交叉点是港口船舶交通量的主要致因,其次是港口能见度情况。

2.1.3 灰色关联分析方法确定指标权重

(1)一级评价指标权重的确定。

$$A_1' = (\frac{P_4}{P_4 + P_6} \quad \frac{P_6}{P_4 + P_6})$$

即:$A_1' = (0.4987 \quad 0.5013)$

同理可得:

$$A_2' = (0.3746 \quad 0.2948 \quad 0.3306)$$
$$A_3' = (0.4046 \quad 0.2789 \quad 0.3165)$$
$$A_4' = (0.3310 \quad 0.3418 \quad 0.3271)$$

(2)二级评价指标权重的确定。

$$A' = (\frac{P_4 + P_6}{\sum_{k=1}^{11} P_k} \quad \frac{P_1 + P_2 + P_3}{\sum_{k=1}^{11} P_k} \quad \frac{P_5 + P_7 + P_8}{\sum_{k=1}^{11} P_k} \quad \frac{P_9 + P_{10} + P_{11}}{\sum_{k=1}^{11} P_k}) \tag{6}$$

即:$A' = (0.1615 \quad 0.2825 \quad 0.2754 \quad 0.2806)$。

2.2 因子分析方法

2.2.1 因子分析的数学模型和相关概念

因子分析的出发点是用较少的互相独立的因子变量来替代原有变量的绝大部分信息,可以将这一思想用一个数学模型来表示。假设原有变量有 P 个,分别用 $x_1,x_2,\cdots,x_P$ 来表示,其中 $x_i(i=1,2,\cdots,P)$ 是均值为零、标准差为1的标准化变量,$F_1,F_2,\cdots,F_m$ 分别表示 m 个因子变量,m 应小于 P。于是有:

$$\begin{aligned} x_1 &= a_{11}F_1 + a_{12}F_2 + \cdots + a_{1m}F_m + a_1\varepsilon_1 \\ x_2 &= a_{21}F_1 + a_{22}F_2 + \cdots + a_{2m}F_m + a_2\varepsilon_2 \\ &\vdots \\ x_p &= a_{P1}F_1 + a_{P2}F_2 + \cdots + a_{Pm}F_m + a_P\varepsilon_P \end{aligned} \tag{7}$$

也可用矩阵的形式表示为: $X = AF + a\varepsilon$。

在这个数学模型中,F 为因子变量或公共因子,可以把它们理解为在高维空间中的互相垂直的 m 个坐标轴;A 为因子载荷矩阵,a_{ij} 称为因子载荷,是第 i 个原有变量在第 j 个因子变量上的负荷。如果把变量 x_i 看成 m 维因子空间中的一个向量,则 a_{ij} 表示 x_i 在坐标轴 F_j 上的投影,相当于多元回归分析模型中的标准回归系数;ε 为特殊因子,表示了原有变量不能被公共因子所解释的部分,相当于多元回归分析模型中的残差项。

2.2.2 因子分析模型应用

根据表1的数据,运用 Spss 统计软件的因子分析功能,得出各影响因素与事故数(Y)之间的关系如下:

$$\begin{aligned} Y = &20.622 + 3.15zx_1 + 2zx_2 + 1.53zx_3 + 0.79zx_4 + 0.83zx_5 - 1.43zx_6 + \\ &1.34zx_7 + 1.6zx_8 + 2.3zx_9 + 2.19zx_{10} - 2.67zx_{11} \end{aligned} \tag{8}$$

由上述方程系数可知各个因素的影响程度:

$$X_1 > X_{11} > X_9 > X_{10} > X_2 > X_8 > X_3 > X_6 > X_7 > X_5 > X_4$$

权重的获取:对系数取绝对值,而后归一化可得各个因素的相对权重。计算式如下:

$$Q_i = \frac{|M_i|}{\sum_{k=1}^{11} M_k}$$

得出:

$Q_1 = 0.1589; Q_2 = 0.1009; Q_3 = 0.0772; Q_4 = 0.0398; Q_5 = 0.0419; Q_6 = 0.0721;$
$Q_7 = 0.0676; Q_8 = 0.0807; Q_9 = 0.1160; Q_{10} = 0.1104; Q_{11} = 0.1346$。

通过分析我国9个港口11个因素同船舶事故数之间的关系,能见度和助航标志状况对船舶安全的影响较大,航道长度和航道交叉点影响较小。

2.2.3 因子分析方法确定各影响指标权重

(1)一级评价指标权重的确定。

$$A'' = \left(\frac{Q_4}{Q_4 + Q_6} \quad \frac{Q_6}{Q_4 + Q_6} \right) \tag{9}$$

同理得出:

$$A_2'' = (0.4716 \quad 0.2994 \quad 0.2290)$$
$$A_3'' = (0.4224 \quad 0.3554 \quad 0.2202)$$
$$A_4'' = (0.3212 \quad 0.3059 \quad 0.3729)$$

(2)二级评价指标权重的确定。
$$A'' = (Q_4 + Q_6 \quad Q_1 + Q_2 + Q_3 \quad Q_5 + Q_7 + Q_8 \quad Q_9 + Q_{10} + Q_{11})$$
$$= (0.1120 \quad 0.3369 \quad 0.1901 \quad 0.3611)$$

即:$A_1'' = (0.3559 \ 0.6441)$。

2.3 评价指标权重的确定

综合灰色关联分析和因子分析得出的权重可算得各评价指标的权重。具体方法如下:
$$A_1 = (A_1' + A_1'')/2 \tag{10}$$

即:$A_1 = (\dfrac{a_{11}' + a_{11}''}{2} \quad \dfrac{a_{12}' + a_{12}''}{2}) = (0.4273 \quad 0.5727)$。

同理可得:
$$A_2 = (0.4231 \quad 0.2971 \quad 0.2798)$$
$$A_3 = (0.4145 \quad 0.3172 \quad 0.2683)$$
$$A_4 = (0.3261 \quad 0.3239 \quad 0.3500)$$
$$A = (0.1368 \quad 0.3097 \quad 0.2327 \quad 0.3208)$$

3 建立评价集

评价集又称备择集,是由对评判对象可能做出的评判结果所组成的集合,可表示为:
$$V = \{v_1, v_2, \cdots, v_m\}$$

其中,元素 $v_j(j = 1,2,\cdots,m)$ 是若干可能做出的评判结果。模糊综合评判的目的就在于,通过对评判对象综合考虑所影响因素,能够从评价集 V 中获得一个最佳的评判结果。在确定通航水域模糊综合评判的评价集时,应适当确定评价种类;如果评价集内的评价种类太多,且当评判对象又不是太多时,则所得出的评判结果借鉴的意义不大,并且也浪费了资源。在通航水域危险度的评价中,拟将评价集划分为五个级别。设评价集为 V,指标集为 U 则有:

评价集 $V = \{$低危险度,较低危险度,中等危险度,较高危险度,高危险度$\}$

4 单因素模糊综合评判

单独从一个因素出发进行评判,以确定评判对象对评价集元素的隶属程度,称为单因素模糊评判。设评判对象按因素集中第 i 个因素 u_i 进行评判,对评价集中第 j 个元素 v_j 的隶属程度为 r_{ij} 则按第 i 个因素 u_i;评判的结果可表示为:
$$\underset{\sim i}{R} = (r_{i1}, r_{i2}, \cdots, r_{im})$$

$\underset{\sim i}{R}$ 称为单因素评判集,它是评价集 V 上的模糊子集。

根据表1所列的部分港口的统计数据,对照评价集 V,将各个评价指标的隶属度评价标准确定如表2所示。

表2　各评价指标的隶属度评价标准

危险度	低危险度	较低危险度	中等危险度	较高危险度	高危险度
能见度	~12.3	12.3~20.5	20.5~28.7	28.7~36.9	36.9~
大风	~38.4	38.4~64	64~89.6	89.6~115.2	115.2~
最大流	~1.5	1.5~2.5	2.5~3.5	3.5~4.5	4.5~
主航道长	~10.05	10.05~16.75	16.75~23.45	23.45~30.15	30.15~
交叉点和转向点	~3	3~5	5~7	7~9	9~
船宽/航道宽度	~0.105	0.105~0.175	0.175~0.245	0.245~0.315	0.315~
船舶交通密度	~1.5	1.5~2.5	2.5~3.5	3.5~4.5	4.5~
船舶加权交通量	~16.5	16.5~27.5	27.5~38.5	38.5~49.5	49.5~
VTS 管理	4.5~	3.5~4.5	2.5~3.5	1.5~2.5	~1.5
分道通航	4.5~	3.5~4.5	2.5~3.5	1.5~2.5	~1.5
助航标志不正常率	~0.6	0.6~1.0	1.0~1.4	1.4~1.8	1.8~

5　模糊综合评判

单因素评判集构成多因素综合评判($\underset{\sim}{R_i}$评判矩阵)的基础,即

$$\underset{\sim}{R} = \begin{pmatrix} \underset{\sim}{R_1} \\ \underset{\sim}{R_2} \\ \vdots \\ \underset{\sim}{R_n} \end{pmatrix} = \begin{pmatrix} r_{11} & r_{12} & \cdots & r_{1m} \\ r_{21} & r_{22} & \cdots & r_{2m} \\ \vdots & \vdots & \ddots & \vdots \\ r_{m1} & r_{m2} & \cdots & r_{mm} \end{pmatrix}$$

其中元素 $r_{ij} = u_R(u_i, v_j) \, 0 \leq r_{ij} \leq 1$,表示对评判对象在考虑 u_i 时做出评判结果 v_j 的程度。

当因素权重集 $\underset{\sim}{A}$ 和评判矩阵 $\underset{\sim}{R}$ 已知时,按照模糊矩阵的乘法运算,便得到模糊综合评判集 $\underset{\sim}{B}$,即

$$\underset{\sim}{B} = \underset{\sim}{A} \circ \underset{\sim}{R} = (a_1 \, a_2 \, \cdots \, a_n) \circ \begin{pmatrix} r_{11} & r_{12} & \cdots & r_{1m} \\ r_{21} & r_{22} & \cdots & r_{2m} \\ \vdots & \vdots & \ddots & \vdots \\ r_{m1} & r_{m2} & \cdots & r_{mm} \end{pmatrix} = (b_1 \, b_2 \, \cdots \, b_m) \qquad (11)$$

b_j 称为模糊综合评判指标,其含义是:在综合考虑所有影响因素的情况下,评判对象对评价集 V 中第 j 个元素的隶属度。显然,模糊综合评判集 B 是评价集 V 上的模糊子集。

6 评判指标的处理

求出评判指标 b_j 后,可采用最大隶属度法确定最终的评判结果,即把与最大的评判指标 $\max b_j$ 相对应的评价集 v_j 取为评判结果。

7 评价模型验证

在前述几个部分中,已经建立了通航水域的评价模型,现在根据所掌握的各通航水域的指标数值,对模型进行验证。在验证的基础上,对模型进行综合分析与评价,在进一步完善评价模型的同时,优化我国水通航水域的评价方法。

在此验证的数据采用表 1 所列的港口统计数据。得出结果如下:
港口 1:该港水域属低危险。
港口 2:该港水域属低危险。
港口 3:该港水域属低危险。
港口 4:该港水域属中等危险。
港口 5:该港水域属高危险。
港口 6:该港水域属较低危险。
港口 7:该港水域属低危险。
港口 8:该港水域属中等危险。
港口 9:该港水域属低危险。

8 结论

根据前面的模型验证的情况来看,所得的结果基本符合这些港口水域的实际情况,证明该模型具有实用价值;而且,模型中应用的数学工具都是综合评判中运用较多发展完善的数学理论,使得模型具有科学性。

另外,相对原有的通航水域评价模型,本文所建的模型还具有以下创新点:

(1)确定的指标体系,应以海事主管机关实用为前提,并能够反映近几年通航水域在管理手段等方面所发生的变化,反映我国所建立的 VTS 系统、船舶定线制系统以及助航标志等方面对船舶航行安全的影响。

(2)在确定各指标的权重时,采用了以灰色系统理论关联分析及系统工程因子分析结果综合确定权重。这既避免了由于人的主观因素所引起的偏差,也避免了由单一方法所带来的缺陷,使得各评价指标的权重随船舶事故的变化而变化,更为客观地反映现实情况,从而使评价结果更为客观,进而保证了评价方法的科学性。

Maritime Compulsory Salvage in China*

Abstract: This paper cites a real salvage case as an example, and introduces the concept of maritime compulsory salvage, distinguishs its characters from the traditional salvage concepts and pointed out its constitute requirements. The paper emphasizes the necessities of maritime compulsory salvage in the modern ad-ministration for the country and gives some short-term and long-term suggestions both in theory and in practice.

Keywords: Salvage at sea; Maritime compulsory salvage; Legal issues; Administrative coercive measure

1 Introduction of YP case

The salvage case of YP was regarded as one of most serious maritime casualties in the Chinese salvage history. The competent authorities had to deal with an incident of a Gas Carrier, which was in execrable condition with the hull immersed in water and a lot of LPG leaking out from the broken pipe. There were few documentary records covering such kinds of casualties even in the history of the international salvage.

1.1 The occurrence of YP accident

LPG Carrier YP, loaded with 520 MT cargo of LPG, was sailing to a nearby oil pier after heaving up from Shekou dangerous anchorage at 0643 May 31, 2006. Unfortunately, it collided with a cargo vessel about ten minutes later. Both the hull and cargo pipe of YP were broken, which led to the hull flooded with seawater and the cargo leaked out from the broken pipe. The captain of YP, in accordance with the ship's casualty handling manual, reported the incident to local Sub-Rescue Center (SRC) immediately.

1.2 Experience of the salvage operation

1.2.1 Successful saving the lives from the sea

After receiving the accident report, the duty officer of local SRC suggested the vessel proceed

---

* 本文发表在《大连海事大学学报》2007 年第 2 期第 33 卷,作者谭振宏、郑中义。

to a shallow water area, which was about 2 nautical miles from the site of collision and near the recommended route for the High Speed Crafts. Almost at the same time, the SRC launched the Contingency Plan and carried out rescue action.

With the help of the SRC, the seafarers piled the vessel in the shallow water area and strove for self-help but failed. They could not stop the leakage efficiently after over two hours. With the consideration of the situations, it would be too dangerous for the crews to keep on board. Under the suggestion of the On Scene Commander of the salvage operation, the captain expressed his abandon intention to the ship owner and asked for instructions, whereas, the petition was denied by the ship owner. Owing to the endangered human lives on board, the captain declared abandon. Both the captain and crews were shifted to the patrol boat of the local Maritime Safety Administration (MSA) safely.

1.2.2 Plug up the gas leak triumphantly

According Chinese Contingency Planning Procedures, the SRC reported the incident to the local Emergency Command Center (ECC) and Chinese Maritime Search and Rescue Cooperation Center (MRCC). Chinese MRCC delegated the SRC to organize the salvage operation. Endowed with the delegation, the SRC notified local Fire Department, local Administration of Work Safety, local Salvage Bureau, local Environmental Protection Administration, Hong Kong MRCC and other relevant units to cooperate the action.

In order to avoid deuterogenic incidents and facilitate the salvage operation, the SRC set up a temporary forbidden area within radius 1.5 kilometers from the vessel and a double range as a control area. They asked the local Vessel Traffic Service to warn relevant vessels not to break into the area, and required the HSC suspend using the recommended routes immediately.

At about 1100, the vessel listed dramatically with a maximum angle about forty degrees, which increasing the difficulties for the salvage forces to work on board. The SRC had to consider all kinds of risks and did all it could. Luckily, one hour later, the vessel restored to a status with five degrees list angle. It created opportunities for salvage forces to execute the salvage operation.

Worrying about that the vessel might lead to further danger and damage the public safeties once it explodes, the SRC decided to enlarge the alert scope. At about 1330, the SRC requested all vessels anchoring at Shekou dangerous anchorage area should heave up and sail far away immediately, and notified relevant harbor operators and ships suspend operations and prepare for departure.

Almost all vessels followed the instruction and acted orderly except one. Tanker SZY, anchored at the dangerous anchorage area with full load of gasoline, was maintaining its main engine at that time. The SRC suggested its owner to hire a tugboat for assistance. The ship owner arranged another ship of his to tow the tanker because he could not reach an agreement with any tug companies in such an emergency. However, it would take several hours for the ship to arrive at the spot. The SRC denied his arrangement and ordered a tugboat to tow the tanker.

With the coordination of local ECC, some experts, who do not belong to the expert teams of the Search and Rescue (SAR), were invited to the scene and assisted the salvage operation. Following the requirement of the SRC, local Salvage Bureau sent a salvage team and two rescue vessels to participate the salvage operation.

The leakage was blocked with all salvors' efforts at 0048 June 1. Next step was to re-trim and re-float YP. The ship owner suggested to recovery the power of the vessel to drain, but his suggestion was denied by the SRC. At last local Salvage Bureau carried out the task of repairing the hole and draining. It took another day for the vessel to trim again after the block of the leakage.

At 0900 June 2, the ship owner notified the local Salvage Bureau that the salvage operation was completed because the ship could be afloat and it was not in danger anymore. However, the Salvage Bureau kept on their salvage operation without getting further instruction from the SRC.

1.2.3 Release the vessel from shallow water

Under the requirement of the SRC, the ship owner had to apply for survey before the vessel was removed by external forces from the shallow water area, but the Classification Society (CS) believed that because the vessel was under salvage operation, instead of giving a direct survey report, they would assess the salvage operation planning afforded by the competent authorities

In the afternoon of June 2, the SRC required the ship owner to ask the captain and crews go back to the vessel and maneu-ver it. Almost at the same time, the local ECC delegated the local Administration of Work Safety as the supervisor to command and monitor the discharge operation. The SRC questioned the delegation as it would cause confusion about command authorities. After a careful review, the local ECC withdrew the delegation and declared that the SRC should be in charge the whole salvage operation.

In the morning of June 3, under the cooperation and supervision of the SRC, the vessel was re-floated and sailed to the pier for discharge. In the afternoon, the SRC declared that the salvage operation was completed after all the cargo was discharged.

1.3 Claim for salvage payments

All the salvors, including both administrations and enterprises, delegated the SRC as the representative to claim for the payments from the salved party. As the representative of the salvors, the SRC negotiated with the ship owner. It took them about one month to reach the compensation agreements.

2 Survey of maritime compulsory salvage

2.1 The concept of maritime compulsory salvage

There is no uniform interpretation about the concept of maritime compulsory salvage until now though it has been mentioned in different scenes. In this thesis it means the coastal States or its competent authorities to take compulsory salvage measures for the existing maritime disasters or casualties with the aim to protect the public safeties and interests within their dominative water areas through performing the public powers, no matter relevant captain, ship owners or possessors agree or not. The salved party shall compensate the expenses of these measures no matter the salvage operation has useful result or not.

2.2 Legal characters or maritime compulsory salvage

2.2.1 Distinguish from contract salvage and employed salvage

Compared with contract salvage and employed salvage, five characters of maritime compulsory salvage are quite obvious. First of all, maritime compulsory salvage is one kind of administrative coercive measure implemented by competent authorities according to public law. Secondly, voluntary principle is not applied to the salvage operation under maritime compulsory salvage. Thirdly, the competent authorities could carry out mari-time compulsory salvage directly and indirectly. Fourthly, the purposes of salvage must be related to human lives, public safeties or public interests. Finally, the competent authorities own the right of discretion during the operation of maritime compulsory salvage.

2.2.2 Different from the administrative coercive enforcement

To better understand the characters of maritime compulsory salvage and master them properly, two vital points have to be emphasized. On the one hand, maritime compulsory salvage is one kind of administrative coercive measure, which is different from administrative coercive enforcement. First of all, it is depended on whether the behavior of administrative counterpart would endanger the public safeties and interests or human lives. Next, it aims to keep the surroundings and social orders retain in normal conditions through preventing, deterring or controlling the behavior which endanger the society occur or spread. Finally, the cause for administrative coercive measure could be behaviors, or incidents or status. On the other hand, maritime compulsory salvage also is one kind of direct coercion. Generally, the situations of salvage at sea are too urgency to use indirect coercion.

2.3 Constitutive requirements or maritime compulsory salvage

The discussion above is useful for the competent authorities to understand maritime compulsory salvage perfectly. In order to carry out the salvage operation correctly, the constitutive requirements of maritime compulsory salvage should also be introduced, from both the administrative nomology and the practice of salvage. First, the legal subject of maritime compulsory salvage must be the competent authorities endowed by the laws. Secondly, the competent authorities implementing maritime compulsory salvage operation is one kind of action of legal authorities, it must be legal both in entities and processes. Thirdly, the maritime casualty must have been happened or happen immediately and the aims for salvage are to save human lives, safeguard public safeties or protect public interests. Finally, the competent authorities must express the salvage nature and behavioral, agent to the salved clearly when implementing maritime compulsory salvage.

3 Necessities of maritime compulsory salvage

Four necessities of maritime compulsory salvage are list as follows.

First is the requirement of modem nomocracy. The principle of modem nomocracy requires the administrative subjects not only performing their administrative behaviors legally, but also adopting relevant measures positively. Owing to the legal systems are still under completion and perfection in China at present, appropriate compulsory authorities for the administrations to solve issues flexibly and decidedly are necessary.

Next are the safeguards of the shipping industries. To comply with the development of present society, larger vessels are built and more dangerous cargos are shipped. Thus, some dangers are not limited on themselves as traditional shipping risks, and some risks are beyond their control. Under such conditions, only the administrations could help them to maneuver and harmonize all social resources to eliminate the dangers at a lower cost in a short time.

Thirdly, protecting public safeties and interests, safeguarding social orders and public rights are important functions of the administration of State. With the development of shipping industries, the danger of shipping are not limited in ship's itself. The governments and the competent authorities may be anxious to ensure that salvage operations are performed in such a way as to ensure that the protection of the public interest is paramount.

Last is the need for sustainable development. The more diversification of utilizing the ocean, the more outstanding of the issues about environment and resources would be. The conflicts among different sectors and industries could not be avoided when they use the oceans. The authorities have to be act as peacemakers and harmonize the development.

4 Analyzing legal issues of YP case

Owing to unsound legal framework and the authorities' overlaps, the characters of the salvage operation were still under delimitation in the YP Case. Follows are evident.

4.1 The competent authorities are unclear

Because the mixture of Chinese SAR regime and the MSA in their authorities and the existing governmental regime about accidents and emergencies, the competent authorities are still unclear when an accident or emergency appears, no matter it regulates that the MSA should be the competent authority according to the Maritime Traffic Safety Law of the People's of China 1983 (MTSL). The competent authorities would be puzzled when different direct instructions came from various authorities are conflicted. In YP Case, Chinese MRCC had delegated that the local

SRC as the commander to organize and cooperate the salvage operation at the beginning of the accident, but the local ECC tried to assign the local administration of Work Safety as the supervisor to monitor the discharging operation later. Though discharging operation was only small part of the salvage operation, it could also cause command power overlap and lead to unnecessary trouble.

4.2 The character of behavior is undefined

The character of the salvage operation is hard to be identified in YP Case. If the salvage operation was based on the humanitarianism or responsibilities in the beginning, the rescue action should be finished after the shift of the seafarers from the vessel in distress. Similarly, it could not be an employed salvage because there were not employed agreements between the salvors and the salved party.

If the salvage operation was deemed to be contract salvage, voluntariness should be one of the vital principles, and relevant rights and obligations should be complied with. However, there was no agreement between the salvors and the salved party. Further, the salvage operation did not be suspended when the salved party rejected the salvage operation.

Owing to the undefined character and unpredictable conse-quence of the YP accident, the local CS tried to avoid the risk of involving into the lawsuit and did not give a formal survey report. What is more, the action of towing the tanker SZY was argumentative. They did not reach an agreement about the behavior of the towing. These doubts were existed for the application of voluntariness in the case.

The analysis and evidences above led the salvage operation prefer to maritime compulsory salvage more than others. In fact, most of the behaviors were acted as maritime compulsory salvage during the salvage operation in the YP Case, but no authorities claimed or confirmed that, which leads to an absence of the constitute requirements of maritime compulsory salvage. As presented at 2.3, the competent authorities must express the salvage nature and behavioral agent to the salved party clearly when implementing compulsory salvage operation. The absence of this statement led to constitute requirements of maritime com-pulsory salvage in this case incomplete.

4.3 The rights and obligations are indistinct

Because the illegibility of the competent authorities and characters of the salvage operation in the YP Case, Both their rights and obligations of the salvors and the salved party are hard to be identified.

The competent authorities have the power to control both parties as well as relevant vessels in maritime compulsory salvage. In the YP Case, because the salvage operation was performed and controlled by the competent authorities, both the salvors and the salved party were under the command of the competent authorities. As a result, they are not voluntary in the salvage operation. Instead of reaching salvage agreements with the salved party, the salvors only followed the competent authorities' instructions. Furthermore, as their aims are more on public safeties and public interests than in the vessel or the private properties, they should entitle the rights to obtain compensation in such kind of salvage even there was not beneficial result. In fact, most behaviors were followed the characters of maritime compulsory salvage in YP Case, but the necessary de-clared procedure was absent.

Similarly, the legal status of the captain and crews was indistinct in domestic laws after the declaration of abandon this case. After the declaration of the captain to abandon the ship, the relationships between ship owner and captain are various as well as crews in different maritime states. In Anglo-American law system, once the ship disappears legally, the obligation of the captain and crews for salvaging the ship would not exist anymore. The captain and crews should be regarded as one of the salvors after the abandon.

However, their behaviors are not definite in Chinese laws. Though all units concerned and vessels or installations in the vicinity of the scene must act under the orders of the competent authority in the salvage operation, the captain and the crews had far away the scene when they were asked the maneuver the vessel again in the YP Case, whether this condition could be regulated by above provisions was unsure.

4.4 The compensations are confused

The legal basis for the competent authorities to ask compensations is based on the Article 192 of the Maritime Law of the People's Republic of China (ML). It states that "with respect to the salvage operations performed or controlled by the relevant competent authorities of the State, the salvors shall be entitled to avail themselves of the rights and remedies provided for in this Chapter in respect of salvage operations".

However, there are different interpretations about this article in practice. Both the salvors and the salved party are confused when they negotiate the compensation. It would be a stiff journey for them to reach a compensation agreement. In the YP Case, all the salvors, both the public services and enterprises, delegated the SRC as the representative to negotiate with the salved party, which facilitated the process of negotiation and make it simple, but it still took over one month for them to reach the agreement. Their divarications were focused on the amount of the compensation because the economic loss would be the first care for the salved party. However, several doubts could not be avoided from the legal view. The first is about the character of the compensations. Next is the compensation was paid by the ship owner in this case. The third is the relationship between the competent authorities and the salvors during the salvage operation. Last is that the SRC negotiated the compensation with the salved party as the representative of the salvors. These doubts are quite outstanding.

5 Conclusion and suggestions for maritime compulsory salvage

No matter how the YP Case was solved perfectly in practice, there are still so much disputations in law. Because it is not a sole case, in order to deal with similar cases legally, smoothly and efficiently, several suggestions are given for maritime compulsory salvage both in practice and in legislations.

5.1 Establish or modify relevant regulations

At present, owing to the unsound Chinese legal framework at sea, it would be better for China through legislations to fix on the course, policy principle and active criterion, nail down the administrant authorities for different organizations and divide the work, provide the measures and procedures for various contingencies.

As for shipping industries, it is necessary through legislation to enhance the administration of maritime compulsory salvage, confirm the legal status of the competent authorities and responsibilities as well as rights and obligations of relevant parties.

There are several suggestions for maritime compulsory salvage. One view prefers to modify Article 192 of ML to solve the argument of the salvors and the salved party under maritime compulsory salvage operation. Personally, I prefer to set up a new regulation than modify existing regulation for it based on following three reasons. First of all, they belong to different categories in law systems. The ML is a special rule of civil law, whereas, the regulations of maritime compulsory salvage should be administrative laws. Next, Article 192 of the ML does not provide the obligations of the salvor because it should be regulated by the administrative law. However, there are not existing relevant regulations at that time. This regulation is a compromise to protect the interests of the salvor in order to encourage the salvage operation. Last but not least, Article 31 of the MTSL regulated clearly the competent authorities has the power to carry out compulsory measures under certain situation, but no further rules or relevant provisions to support this article owing to the absence of legislation. Following principles had better be complied with when such kind of regulation is established.

First, the purpose of the regulations should be to protect human lives in distress, public safeties and public interests, which are the most important principles for maritime compulsory salvage. Further, the regulation should belong to public law, which would not be intervene with the private law.

Secondly, the application of the regulation should be limited into the coastal water area, which complied with the MTSL.

Thirdly, the competent authorities should be the MSA, which would comply with MTSL also. Furthermore, it is defined by its authorities and responsibilities.

Fourthly, the procedure for declaring maritime compulsory salvage should be simple and direct.

Fifthly, the responsibilities and obligations should be defined clearly among the competent authorities, the salvors and the salved party as well as their relationships.

Sixthly, to encourage the salvage, the payment for the salvage operation should not lower than the actual expenditure of the salvors.

Seventhly, to avoid abusing the measures by the salved party, the authority should have the right of discretion to decide whether it would be a maritime compulsory salvage or not.

Finally, to prevent abuse the power of maritime compulso-ry salvage, remedial measures should be set up clearly.

5.2 Pay attention to the status when carrying out compulsory salvage operation

Instead of setting up a new regulation for maritime compulsory salvage operation in long views, it is easier for the competent authorities to pay attention to their status in different kinds of salvage operations in the near future. If the aim of the salvage operation is to save human lives at sea, then all salvors are under the organization and cooperation of the SAR Regime. They have to follow relevant provisions to carry out their responsibilities and obligations. If the purpose of the salvage operation is to salvage the vessels or relevant properties, it could be regulated by pure salvage, contract salvage or employed salvage. Once the focus has been shifted to public safeties and public interests, the competent authorities should consider launching maritime compulsory salvage process.

Under maritime compulsory salvage operation, it is the basis of other relationships to clear the competent authorities. It would be easier to identify the authorities and responsibilities, rights and obligations once the competent authority is clear. According to the MTSL, the MSA should be the competent authority of compulsory salvage operation.

Article 31 of the MTSL endowed the competent authorities to take compulsory measures. Furthermore, Article 38 of the MTSL offers legal basis not only provides the responsibilities of the competent authorities, but also regulates the relationship between the competent authorities and the salvors or relevant parties. In addition, Article 3 of the MTSL emphasizes that the MSA should be the competent authority in China owing to its authorities and responsibilities.

These articles clear provide that the MSA should be the competent authority when carry out maritime compulsory salvage. Though the staffs have double positions as the MSA officers and behalf of the MRCC officers, they had better clear their representative when carrying out salvage operations.

干散货船在大风浪中的安全评价*

摘要:为定量评价大风浪中干散货船的航行安全,对干散货船事故、船舶适航性的要求及PSC检查重点项目等方面进行研究分析,获得模糊综合评判指标。运用系统工程学原理和层次分析法(AHP),确定各评价指标对干散货船航行安全影响的重要程度,建立多级模糊综合评判数学模型并应用于实践进行模型验证。结果表明该模型有效、可靠。

关键词:干散货船;大风浪;安全评价;模糊综合评判;层次分析法(AHP)

0 引言

近年来,大量散货船全损海难案件不断发生,损失吨位居所有船舶海难损失载重吨位中的第一位,造成严重的人命和财产损失。据相关资料统计[423],1992年1月—2002年5月,全球共发生109起散装船全损海难案件,占全球全损海难案件的12.49%。其中,损失的载重吨位占所有全损案件的38%,位居所有船舶全损海难损失载重吨位之最。在这109起散货船全损海难案件中,天气因素引起35艘散货船全损,占总数的32.1%,损失的载重吨占散货船全损损失载重吨的38.4%。散装船一系列的事故引起国内外航运界的极大关注[424]。除了从散装船的设计缺陷寻找原因外,加强对散货船安全状况的评价,及时发现并消除存在的安全隐患,做好事故预防等措施尤为重要[424]。本文着重对大风浪中干散货船的船体断裂、倾覆、进水沉没风险进行定量的综合评价,获得模糊综合评判指标,建立多级模糊综合评判数学模型,为预防事故的发生提供参考。

1 评价方法的选取

影响船舶安全的因素众多,大部分指标概念模糊,而且难以进行精确的定量分析与评价。模糊综合评判方法为解决该类问题提供了一种有效的数学工具,由此得出的评价值与实际值相符[426]。本文采用模糊综合评判方法建立评判大风浪中载货干散货船安全的数学模型。

2 评价指标体系的确立

鉴于船舶系统评价的复杂性,在确定评价船舶安全指标时,需考虑以下5个方面:①船舶安全航行条件;②船舶适航性要求;③PSC检查的重点项目及在检查中船舶存在的主要缺陷统

---

* 本文发表于《大连海事大学学报》2010年第2期,作者郑中义、李红喜、赵京军。

计;④与船舶相关的海事统计分析资料;⑤征求专家、船员、港口官员的意见。根据上述五个方面,初步拟定评价大风浪中载货干散货船安全的评价指标体系,然后发放调查表,征求专家的修改意见。关于人的因素方面,只考虑一票否决制指标;关于环境因素方面,仅考虑自然环境中风和浪的影响,最终确立模糊综合评判指标体系[427],如表1所示。

表1 大风浪中干散货船安全模糊评判指标体系

人	船									环境	
	船龄	船舶吨位	船体结构			船舶设备			稳性		风	浪
			蚀耗	变形	裂纹	机电设备	操纵设备	排水与压载设备	水密设备	初始横倾角	初稳性高度	货物平舱固定	风级	风舷角	浪级	浪舷角

3 评价模型的建立

3.1 模糊综合评判概述

模糊综合评判的基本思想是利用模糊线性变换原理和最大隶属度原则,考虑与被评价事物相关的各因素,对其做出合理的综合评价[428]。模糊综合评判模型有3个基本要素:

(1)因素集:建立的模糊评判指标体系。

(2)评价集:将评价集 V 定义为7个等级,即 $V = \{v_1, v_2, v_3, \cdots, v_7\}$ = {非常危险,很危险,较危险,一般,较安全,很安全,非常安全}。

(3)单因素评判:求取各指标对评价集中评语的隶属度。

3.2 隶属度的求取

为适应散货船安全评价的需要,综合考虑统计和非统计的观点和处理方法,确定隶属度函数。根据各因素对大风浪中载货干散货船安全的影响关系,建立安全度与因素值之间的函数关系,如图1所示,并将安全度转化为对应各评价等级的隶属度。

(1)船龄隶属度

据统计表明,发生海事最多的散货船船龄为20~25 a,船龄与事故的发生率成正比例关系,不同船龄散货船的灭失率资料(表2)说明了这一点[426]。

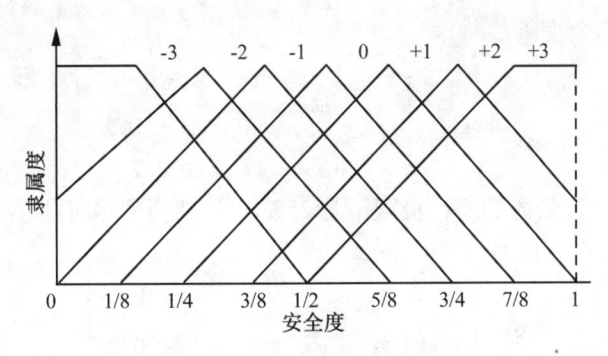

图 1 安全度与隶属度转换关系

表 2 散货船灭失率与船龄的关系

船龄/a	灭失率
0~4	0.12%
5~9	0.17%
10~14	0.29%
15~19	0.86%
20~24	0.19%
≥25	0.42%

散货船的灭失率与船龄的关系曲线贴近函数 $y = kx^2$ 曲线,即散货船灭失率与船龄的平方成正比(图2)。以 25a 为基准(即船龄为 25 时的安全度为 0),建立船龄与安全度的函数

$$S(x) = \begin{cases} 1 - \left(\dfrac{x}{25}\right)^2 & x < 25 \\ 0 & x \geqslant 25 \end{cases}$$

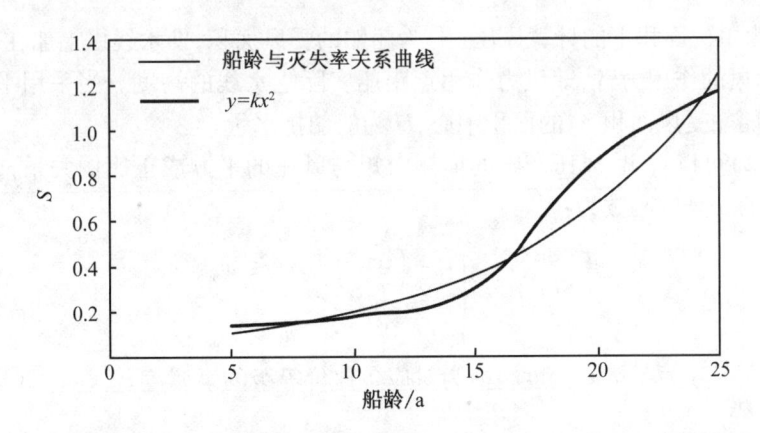

图 2 船龄与灭失率关系曲线

然后,通过图 1 中的函数关系将安全度转换为对应各评价等级的隶属度。

(2) 船体蚀耗大小隶属度

当船长 $L \geqslant 90$ m 时,船体的磨损极限值为 20%[429],期望值尽可能小。根据模糊分布中的

戎下型,得出蚀耗与安全度函数

$$S(x) = \begin{cases} 1 & x = 0 \\ 1 - e^{\frac{-(0.2-x)}{x}} & 0 < x < 0.2 \\ 0 & x \geq 0.2 \end{cases}$$

当船长 $L < 90$ m 时,船体的磨损极限值为 25%[429],期望值尽可能小。根据模糊分布中的戎下型,得出蚀耗与安全度函数

$$S(x) = \begin{cases} 1 & x = 0 \\ 1 - e^{\frac{-(0.25-x)}{x}} & 0 < x < 0.25 \\ 0 & x \geq 0.25 \end{cases}$$

很明显,船体无磨损时,安全度为 1;达到磨损极限时,安全度为 0。通过图 1 中的函数关系将安全度转换为对应各评价等级的隶属度。

(3)风级隶属度

船受到来自正横方向风压产生的横倾力矩 M_f 或力臂 l_f 为[430, 431]:

$$M_f = 0.001 p_a A_f z$$
$$l_f = \frac{M_f}{D} \tag{1}$$

风舷角 α 为风速方向与船的纵中剖面之间的夹角。如果船速不大,考虑空气绕流的影响,侧横风压倾侧力矩 M_f^α 或力臂 l_f^α 为[430, 431]:

$$M_f^\alpha = 0.001 p_a A_f z \sin\left(\frac{9\alpha}{7}\right)$$
$$l_f^\alpha = \frac{M_f^\alpha}{D} \tag{2}$$
$$p_a = \frac{V^2}{16}$$

其中:p_a 为单位面积上的计算风压;A_f 为船舶的受风面积,即水线以上船在中线面上的投影侧面积;z 为风的作用力臂,即风力作用点距船实际吃水线的高度。当采用平均风压强时,风力作用点为船舶受风面积 A_f 的面积中心;D 为船舶排水量。

从式(1)(2)可以看出,风压产生的横倾力矩与风速的平方成正比例关系,即风级与船舶在风浪中航行的安全度函数为:

$$S(w) = \begin{cases} 1 - \left(\dfrac{w}{w_{\max}}\right)^2 & w \leq w_{\max} \\ 0 & w > w_{\max} \end{cases}$$

通过图 1 中函数关系将安全度转换为对应各评价等级的隶属度。

3.3 权重求取

采用 AHP 求取各指标权重。发放 80 份专家调查表,收回 58 份,2 份无效。对 56 份有效调查表按照下列步骤进行筛选:

(1)将各专家给出的各指标相对重要程度表转换为判断矩阵,进行一致性检验:当 $CR \leq$

0.1时,通过一致性检验,表明相对重要程度表有效;当 $CR > 0.1$ 时,无法通过一致性检验,表明相对重要程度表无效,无法采用。

(2)将有效的各指标相对重要程度表进行统计,采用重心法,选出各指标合适的相对重要程度值,重新组成新的相对重要程度表。

(3)将新各指标相对重要程度表转化为判断矩阵,计算判断矩阵的最大特征值 λ_{max} 及 λ_{max} 对应的特征向量,对得到的各指标对应的权重向量进行归一化。

经计算,各指标权重值如表3所示。

表3 各因素权重值

因素集	因素/权重	
船舶系统 0.5	船龄/0.134	
	船舶吨位/0.074	
	船体强度/0.218	蚀耗/0.435
		变形/0.078
		裂纹/0.487
	船舶设备/0.219	机电设备/0.227
		操纵设备/0.227
		排水与压载设备/0.122
		水密设备/0.424
	稳性/0.355	初始横倾角/0.210
		初稳性高度/0.550
		货物平舱固定情况/0.240
环境系统 0.5	风/0.25	风级/0.667
		风舷角/0.333
	浪/0.75	浪级/0.667
		浪舷角/0.333

3.4 模型建立

采用"加权平均型"模糊算子建立评价大风浪中载货干散货船安全评价模型。从最低级开始逐级向上评判,最终获得干散货船安全的综合评价值。

4 模型验证

以浙江省舟山市普陀永和海运有限公司所属的"顺达2号"京唐—上海航次为例加以检验。"顺达2号"本航次的基本资料为[10]:散货船、船龄25 a、总吨9 330 t、船长144 m、型宽

21.35 m、船舶装载后平均吃水 9.08 m。检查缺陷数 18 个,船体蚀耗率 17%,装载煤炭,无横倾,平舱合格,船体水密性较差。所经海区水文环境为:东北风 11 级,东北浪 7 级(狂浪)。

将"顺达 2 号"实船数据代入模型中,经计算获得各层因素的评判结果。

(1)船舶系统评判结果

$u_1 = (0.366\ 6, 0.357\ 3, 0.367\ 6, 0.470\ 4, 0.361\ 4, 0.268\ 4, 0.163\ 0)$

(2)环境系统评判结果

$u_2 = (0.838\ 7, 0.766\ 8, 0.433\ 5, 0.161\ 3, 0, 0, 0)$

"顺达 2 号"整体最终评判结果:

$U = (0.602\ 6, 0.562\ 1, 0.400\ 6, 0.315\ 9, 0.180\ 7, 0.134\ 2, 0.081\ 5)$

根据最大隶属度原则,各部分的评价结果为:船舶系统一般,环境系统非常危险。"顺达 2 号"最终评判结果:非常危险。

"顺达 2 号"本航次在 38°37.1′N,119°29.7′E 处在风浪中沉没,各因素的评判结果与事故调查报告中反映的情况基本一致。

5 结语

本文在参考大量相关文献和大量统计干散货船事故的基础上,经征求专家意见,建立了模糊综合评判指标体系及评价大风浪中干散货船安全的模糊综合评判数学模型,重点评价干散货船在大风浪作用下船体断裂、倾覆和进水沉没危险等事故,使得船员有清晰的定量指标概念,为船舶大风浪天气开航前检查和开航后操船决策提供科学依据,同时为海事监督人员和航运公司管理人员提供参考。

基于粗糙集的港口通航环境对航行安全的影响*

摘要:为定量分析港口水域通航环境对船舶航行安全的影响,提出基于粗糙集理论的属性重要度方法。采用海事部门港口安全调查数据,建立决策表,利用属性约简算法,计算属性在可分辨矩阵中的出现频率,得出各因素的重要度和对航行安全的影响程度。属性重要度方法克服了主观影响,提高了评价结果的客观性和准确性。

关键词:港口水域;航行安全;粗糙集;可分辨矩阵;属性约简

0 引言

港口通航环境因素种类繁多,对航行安全的影响方式及程度各异[361]。传统分析方法受主观因素影响,难以成为海事管理的依据[317]。粗糙集方法作为智能化的数据处理工具,无须任何先验知识,可从样本数据中提取简明、直接、易于理解的决策规则,计算各属性对决策的重要度[433-435]。本文将粗糙集方法应用于港口通航环境因素对航行安全影响的分析,建立决策表,从而获知影响航行安全的主要因素及其重要度。

1 粗糙集理论及其相关知识

(1)决策表

一个决策表是一个信息表达系统,记作 $S = (U, A, V, f)$。其中,U 为论域,是对象的集合;$A = C \cup D$ 为属性的非空有限集合,C 为条件属性,D 为决策属性;$V = \bigcup_{a \in A} V_a$,$V_a$ 为属性 a 的值域;$f : U \times A$ 是一个信息函数,为每个对象的每个属性赋予一个信息值[433]。

(2)约简与核

令 R 为一等价关系,且 $r \in R$,若 $\mathrm{ind}(R) = \mathrm{ind}(R - r)$,则称 r 为 R 中可省略关系的集合;否则,称 r 为 R 中所有不可省略关系的集合,称为 R 的核,记作 $\mathrm{core}(R)$,即 $\mathrm{core}(R) = \cap \mathrm{red}(R)$,其中 $\mathrm{red}(R)$ 是 R 的所有简化族。

(3)可分辨矩阵

设全集 U 按决策属性 D 被分成不相交的类族,即 $D = \{X_1, X_2, \cdots, X_m\}$,则 U 中 C 的区分

---

* 本文发表于《大连海事大学学报》2012 年第 2 期,作者李红喜、郑中义、齐迹。

矩阵记作 $M(C) = \{m_{i,j}\}_{n\times n}$。

(4)属性重要度

判断属性重要性的方法：一个属性在可分辨矩阵中出现频率越高,其在决策表中的重要性越大。在计算属性的出现频率时,根据属性出现分辨矩阵的长度加权。属性 c_i 的重要性计算公式为

$$\gamma_{c_i}(D) = \sum_{i=1}^{n}\sum_{j=1}^{n}\frac{\gamma_{ij}}{\text{card}(m_{i,j})} \tag{1}$$

其中,$\text{card}(m_{i,j})$ 为 m_{ij} 包含属性的个数。

(5)属性权重

定义 w_i 为指标权重,利用属性重要度计算指标权重

$$w_i = \gamma_{ci}/\sum_{i=1}^{n}\gamma_{ci} \tag{2}$$

2 影响港口水域船舶安全航行因素

本文通过分析港口水域的事故案例及海事部门调查报告,提取影响航行安全的主要因素,并对各指标值对影响航行风险进行分级[4-6],如表1所示。

表1 影响港口水域安全航行的因素

影响因素	因素描述	影响航行风险等级				
		危险	较危险	一般	较安全	安全
能见度	年均能见度不良的天数/天	<15	15~25	25~40	40~50	>50
风	年均标准大风的天数/天	<30	30~60	60~100	100~150	>150
流	航道平均流速/kn	<0.25	0.25~0.75	0.75~1.25	1.25~2.00	>2.0
航道宽度	最大船宽/航道宽度	<0.05	0.05~0.10	0.1~0.3	0.3~0.5	>0.5
航道水深	航道水深/船舶吃水	>4.0	2.0~4.0	1.5~2.0	1.3~1.5	<1.3
航道弯曲度	航道最大弯曲角度	<15°	15°~30°	30°~45°	45°~60°	>60°
航道交叉	最大交叉角度	<20°	20°~45°	45°~60°	60°~70°	>70°
碍航物	与航道最近距离/m	>200	200~100	100~50	50~20	<20
船舶交通量	加权船舶交通量/艘	<10	10~15	15~25	25~60	>60
VTS	VTS管理等级	5	4	3	2	1
助航标志	标志完善率	95%~100%	90%~95%	80%~90%	70%~80%	<70%

注:①年均能见度不良天数指能见距在2 km以内的天数;②年平均标准风天数=(6~7级)年平均风的天数+1.5×(8级以上)年平均风的天数。

3 影响港口水域航行安全因素重要性分析

运用粗糙集方法对影响港口水域航行安全因素的重要性进行分析。首先,将所要分析的问题转化为信息表达系统,挖掘知识,生成决策表,计算条件属性重要度[437]。

3.1 数据收集

采用国家海事部门 2010 年港口安全评估收集的数据,提取影响港口航行安全的主要指标。选取 33 个港口数据进行分析,指标值如表 2 所示。

表 2 港口水域影响因素数值

指标 港口	能见度/天	风/天	流/kn	航道宽度	航道深度	航道弯曲度	航道交叉	碍航物/m	交通量/艘	VTS	助航标志	危险等级
1	25	107	5.8	0.31	2.18	71°	71°	148	19	4.6	88%	较安全
2	13	31	2.4	0.22	2.6	3.5°	0°	200	43	4.8	92%	较危险
3	36	107.5	3.2	0.24	1.42	46°	72°	246	36	4.3	85%	较危险
4	24.2	77.4	0.5	0.24	4.2	23°	26°	140	13.98	4	98%	危险
5	54	94.8	3	0.065	3.4	38°	56°	50	45.7	5	92%	危险
…	…	…	…	…	…	…	…	…	…	…	…	…

依据粗糙集的基本知识,建立决策表 T,记作 $T = (U,A)$。其中 $U = \{P_1,P_2,P_3,\cdots,P_{33}\}$ 为港口集合,$A = C \cup D$,定义 C = {Visi, Wind, Curr, Wid, Dep, Bend, Cross, Obst, Traffic, VTS, Aid} = {能见度,风,流,航道宽度,航道深度,航道弯曲度,航道交叉,碍航物距离,交通量,VTS,助航标志}为条件属性;$D = \{d\}$ = {风险等级}为决策属性。对决策属性值,分为 5 级量化:{危险,较危险,一般,较安全,安全};其中,危险置为 5,依次类推,安全置为 1。

3.2 数据离散化及决策表生成

依据表 1,对表 2 属性值进行离散化处理,形成港口水域航行安全影响决策表。应用 RS-ES[8] 生成港口水域航行安全评价决策表,如图 1 所示。

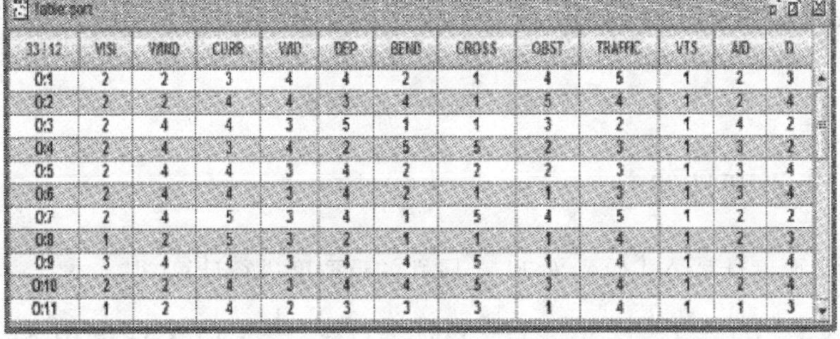

33 12	VISI	WIND	CURR	WID	DEP	BEND	CROSS	OBST	TRAFFIC	VTS	AID	D
0:1	2	2	3	4	4	2	1	4	5	1	2	3
0:2	2	2	4	4	3	4	1	5	4	1	2	4
0:3	2	4	4	3	5	1	1	3	2	1	4	2
0:4	2	4	3	4	2	5	5	2	3	1	3	2
0:5	2	4	4	3	4	2	2	2	3	1	3	4
0:6	2	4	4	3	4	2	1	1	3	1	3	4
0:7	2	4	5	3	4	1	5	4	5	1	2	2
0:8	1	2	5	3	2	1	1	1	4	1	2	3
0:9	3	4	4	3	4	4	5	1	4	1	3	4
0:10	2	2	4	3	4	4	5	3	4	1	2	4
0:11	1	2	4	2	3	3	3	1	4	1	1	3

图 1 影响港口水域安全航行决策表

3.3 约简

应用优化约简算法——穷举算法对决策表约简[438-440],结果如图2所示。

图2 基于穷举算法的约简集

图2表明,通过穷举算法约简共产生94个约简集,各自包含不同的属性,所有约简集的属性长度也不完全相同,所有约简集的稳定系数均为1,正域也均为1。其中,各属性的出现频度如图3所示。

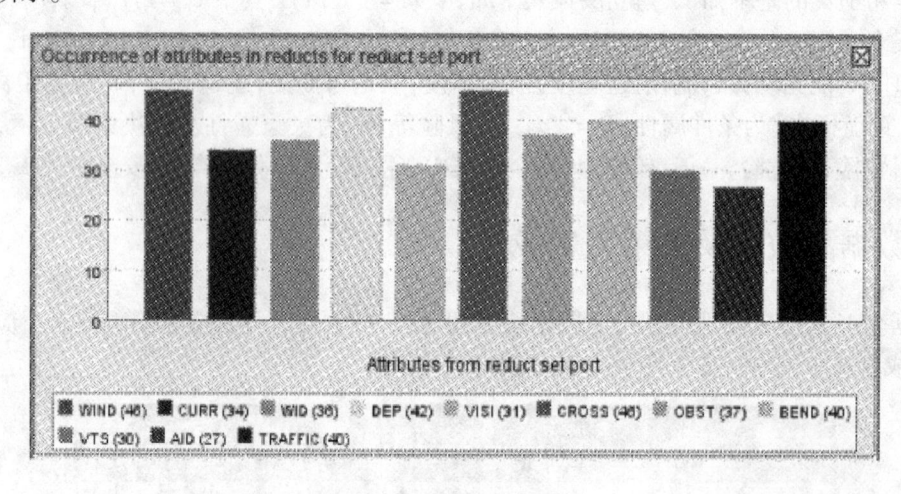

图3 属性的出现频度

3.4 属性重要度计算

根据属性重要度计算公式(1),对11个属性的重要度进行计算,得

$$\gamma_{\text{Wind}}(D) = (\frac{1}{6} \times 1) + (\frac{1}{5} \times 1) \times 11 + (\frac{1}{4} \times 1) \times 34 \approx 10.87$$

其余的条件属性同理计算,得

$\gamma_{\text{Visi}}(D) = 6.85, \gamma_{\text{Curr}}(D) = 8.09$

$\gamma_{\text{Wid}}(D) = 8.12, \gamma_{\text{Dep}}(D) = 10.15$

$\gamma_{\text{Bend}}(D) = 9.33, \gamma_{\text{Cross}}(D) = 11.07$

$\gamma_{\text{Obst}}(D) = 8.85, \gamma_{\text{Traffic}}(D) = 9.07$

$\gamma_{\text{VTS}}(D) = 6.3, \gamma_{\text{Aid}}(D) = 5.9$

3.5 属性权重

应用式(2)计算各指标权重,结果如图4所示。从图4可以看出,助航标志和VTS权重最小,对安全航行影响最小;航道交叉和大风权重最大,是影响安全航行的最主要因素。

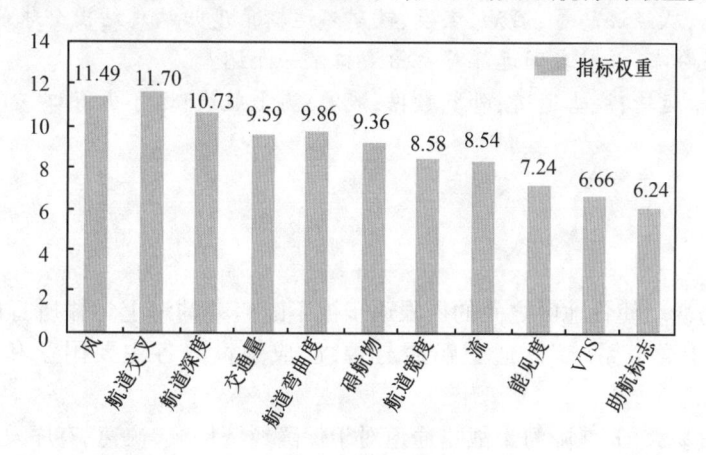

图4 各指标权重

4 结语

本文应用RSES粗糙集数据处理系统,对港口通航环境因素组成的通航安全决策表进行约简处理和规则提取,计算属性重要度和各因素对船舶航行安全的影响权重。分析认为,大风和航道交叉是影响船舶安全航行的主要因素。基于粗糙集的港口通航环境对航行安全影响的量化分析,减少了主观因素的影响,结果更具有客观性、普遍性和适应性。

我国海上战略通道数量及分布*

摘要：作为贸易大国及能源进口大国，我国的经济发展与世界紧密相连。我国的货物运输广泛依赖于海洋通道，一旦通道不畅，将影响我国的国家安全和经济建设。因此，研究与我国利益紧密相关的海上战略通道具有重大意义。探讨战略通道内涵及外延，通过统计分析我国对外贸易的数据，从经济总量、石油、煤炭、铁矿石运输角度归纳总结出全球范围内我国海上战略通道的数量及分布，并对我国远洋贸易出海口做一介绍。

关键词：水路运输；战略通道；外贸数据；能源；海上航线；远洋出海口

0 引言

全球性贸易活动使各地区之间的界限逐步被不断繁荣的海上运输所打破，并形成了融合世界资源的"海上通道系统"。通道畅通与否，已成为世界各主要国家和地区经济发展的关键。

我国作为贸易大国，保障海上战略通道对于保障经济持续、快速、有序发展，维护国家切身利益都具有举足轻重的作用。因此，必须明确我国的战略通道数量及分布，以确保我国经济、政治、军事利益不受侵害。

1 战略通道

2009年，英国运输部发表了 *Eddington Transport Study*。该研究确立了14条国家战略通道，主要目的是识别对国家经济重要的运输通道，体现中心城市经济地位，判别交通流的战略重要性[441]。确立战略通道时，写明战略通道是在交通网络中用于连接2个或2个以上的战略目的地。除此以外，也包括基础设施或提供的服务，当不满足上述标准，若其是唯一进入战备要地的国际通道时，也是战备通道。由此从英国的情况看，战备通道强调的是通道上运送货物对国际经济的重要影响，即强调通道服务于大量货、客流。

按澳大利亚新南威尔士州立法规《客运法1990》的定义，强调"战略通道"时应体现通道的连接性、整合性、便捷性[442]。美国南卡罗来纳州在道路规划中，把战略通道网络解释为能够满足城市在中长期内稳定快速发展需求的通道网，这样的发展包含人流增长、商业规模扩大及物流量的增加，且是高效、可靠、安全的运输通道[443]。

综上所述，战略通道应满足：

---

* 本文发表在《中国航海》2012年第2期第35卷，作者郑中义、张俊桢、董文峰。

(1) 该运输通道客货流量大,对城市、区域或国家的经济影响大。

在复杂通道系统里的通道要升格为战略通道,其先决条件是该通道上须承载大量客货流,使得该通道连接的起始地和目的地紧密关联。一旦这种承担大运输量的通道受到不可抗力因素影响被迫中断或改变,将对原来这一通道的相关各方产生重大的影响。比如19世纪开通的苏伊士运河,改变了原西欧和远东地区海运贸易单纯依赖于绕行好望角的局面,大幅度促进了世界贸易。

(2) 通过该通道运输的货物特殊性,对城市、区域或国家经济发展起到了决定性作用。比如我国海上石油运输通道。

(3) 与国家地区安危有重大关联,具有很强的政治意义。在更广阔的国际长距离通道系统中,特别是一些涉及国际贸易的大通道,除了要承担大量民用运输任务、促进各国家地区的发展繁荣之外,也不可避免地要面对各国之间的贸易摩擦和政治对抗。一旦发生战事或区域冲突,这些通道将被用于运输军事和战略物资,并且会对战争进程、大国之间关系甚至是格局演变起到决定性作用[444]。

2 我国经济与海上通道

改革开放以来,我国进出口贸易飞速发展,为我国经济建设做出了重要贡献。2010年货物进出口总额达到创纪录的29 728亿美元,同比增长34.7%[445]。外贸依存度不断提高,2010年达到49.4%。

巨额的进出口贸易量及对外贸易高的依存度说明我国经济发展与世界紧密相连。在此基础上,海运作为货物运输的主要形式,业务量不断扩大。因此要保证经济快速稳定的发展,就必须维护海上运输通道畅通。

在双边贸易中,从我国进出口贸易总额(见表1)可以看出:欧盟、美国、日本及东盟为我国四大贸易伙伴,对应的欧洲、北美、东北亚及东南亚四个区域的贸易量占到了我国年对外贸易总量的80%以上,可见同这些区域的贸易运输通道在我国对外经济领域中占据重要地位。

表1 我国对外贸易主要国家及地区

国家或地区	总值(亿美元)	2008年	2009年	2010年
欧盟	12 694	4 256	3 641	4 797
美国	10 172	3 337	2 982	3 853
日本	7 934	2 668	2 288	2 978
东盟	7 387	2 311	2 130	2 946
韩国	5 497	1 862	1 563	2 072
俄罗斯	1 510	568	388	554
印度	2 227	518	434	617

2.1 我国的主要海上贸易战略通道

(1) 以欧盟国家为主的中—欧海上通道:中国大陆—台湾海峡—中国南海—马六甲海峡(望加锡、巽他海峡)—印度洋—曼德海峡—红海—苏伊士运河—地中海(抵达地中海沿岸国家)—直布罗陀海峡—欧洲。

(2)美加为主的中—北美海上通道:中国大陆—中国东海(对马海峡—日本海—津轻海峡)—太平洋—北美西海岸;中国大陆—太平洋—巴拿马运河—北美东岸;中国大陆—台湾海峡—中国南海—印度洋—曼德海峡—红海—苏伊士运河—地中海—直布罗陀海峡—北大西洋—北美东岸。

(3)日韩及俄罗斯为主的东北亚方向:中国大陆—中国黄海(抵达韩国西岸)—朝鲜海峡(抵达韩国东岸及日本西岸各港口)—大隅、对马、津轻海峡(抵达日本西岸各港口)—日本海(宗谷海峡)—俄罗斯鄂霍次克海沿岸港口。

(4)与东盟的贸易往来,我国主要依赖于陆路交通,在海运方面的运输通道则使用南海通道。

2.2 我国在全球范围内的重要远洋通道

(1)中—新澳通道:中国大陆—马来群岛、太平洋西南部岛群(巽他、龙目、望加锡和布干维尔海峡)澳、新。

(2)中—南美通道:中国大陆太平洋—南美西岸各国;中国大陆—太平洋—麦哲伦海峡—南美东岸各国;中国大陆—台湾海峡—中国南海—龙目、巽他、望加锡海峡—印度洋—好望角—大西洋—南美东岸各国。

(3)中—印通道:中国大陆—台湾海峡—中国南海—马六甲海峡—印度。

3 能源领域

能源是经济发展的驱动力,包括石油、煤炭、水能、天然气、核能在内对经济安全影响尤为重要。20世纪70年代,两次石油危机都严重冲击了西方经济;1991年海湾战争、2003年伊拉克战争,也是为控制中东石油资源而采取的战略行动。由此可见,石油安全是关系国民经济发展和国家安全的重大战略问题。

自1994年我国成为石油净进口国以来,石油消费量不断上升,2010年创下2.393亿吨的新纪录,比2009年增长了17.4%。石油对外依存度超过50%。

从我国原油进口的主要地区来看,中东、非洲以及中亚为我国原油进口的主要地区,其分别占到原油进口量的47.8%、30.0%、11.1%。从具体国别来看(见图1),十大石油来源国依次是:沙特(4 464.68万吨)、安哥拉(3 938.12万吨)、伊朗(2 131.74万吨)、阿曼(1 567.62万吨)、俄罗斯(1 534.07万吨)、苏丹(1 259.89万吨)、伊拉克(1 123.75万吨)、哈萨克斯坦(1 005.38万吨)、科威特(983.06万吨)、利比亚(737.4万吨)。

除中亚及俄罗斯可通过陆路及管道运输外,其他地区的原油运输大都靠海运。

海湾及非洲地区石油进口主要依靠3条海上线路:

(1)波斯湾—霍尔木兹海峡—马六甲海峡(或者望加锡海峡)—台湾海峡—中国。

(2)北非—地中海—直布罗陀海峡—好望角—马六甲海峡—台湾海峡—中国。

(3)西非—好望角—马六甲海峡—台湾海峡—中国。

随着我国进一步拓宽原油进口渠道,来自南美的石油进口量也逐年上升。因此,南美东海岸—墨西哥湾—巴拿马运河—琉球群岛—中国大陆;南美东海岸—麦哲伦海峡—太平洋—中

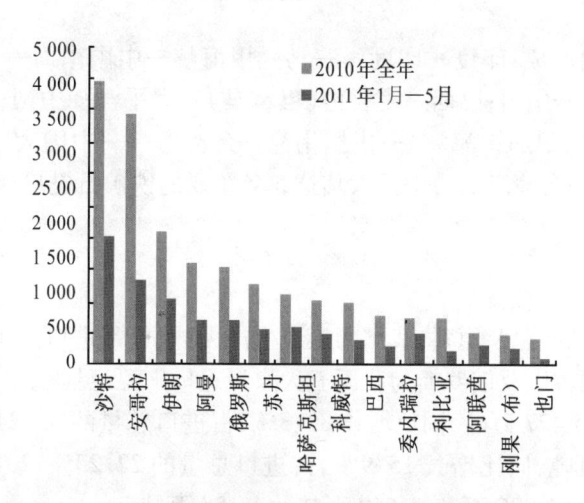

图 1　我国原油进口主要渠道(万吨)

国大陆的南美航线也是原油通道的重要航线。

4　铁矿石及煤炭领域

2010年在我国进口的主要物品中铁矿石及其精矿、煤、原油三类能源产品占到进口量总吨数的86.13%，其份额分别为52.11%、13.9%、20.2%。

4.1　铁矿石

在铁矿石方面，我国进口主要来自澳大利亚、巴西、印度和南非等国(见表2)，近年来，我国从这些国家进口的铁矿石量占进口总量的近90%。其中，澳大利亚由于地理位置上的优势，成为我国最大的铁矿石来源国。巴西凭借其铁矿石资源丰富已成为目前世界上铁矿石开采成本最低的国家。印度也是我国铁矿石主要来源国家之一，其铁矿石最大优势为价格低，是我国进口铁矿中价格最低的，但品质一般，而且其西岸受季风影响，一年中有半年时间船舶不能靠泊装卸。南非铁矿石具有含铁高、料级好等突出优点，但其矿石的高碱度和远运距又限制了其在我国市场的销售[446]。国际上的铁矿石物流航线相对稳定，出口国主要为巴西、澳大利亚、印度、南非，进口国主要为中国、日本、韩国和欧洲国家。

表 2　我国铁矿石进口主要来源(万吨)

年份	澳大利亚		巴西		印度		南非		合计
	进口量/万吨	比例	进口量/万吨	比例	进口量/万吨	比例	进口量/万吨	比例	
2008	18 341	41.3%	10 063	22.8%	9 098	20.5%	1 452	3.3%	87.9%
2009	26 187	41.6%	14 214	22.6%	10 724	17.1%	3 346	5.3%	86.6%
2010	26 528	42.9%	13 083	21.1%	9 654	15.6%	2 954	4.8%	84.4%
2011年1月—5月	11 129	39.3%	6 059	21.4%	4 229	14.9%	1 443	5.1%	80.7%

这样,中国方向就形成:印度—印度洋—马六甲海峡—中国南海—台湾海峡—北方各港口;澳大利亚—太平洋—中国;巴西—麦哲伦(巴拿马)—太平洋—中国;巴西—好望角—印度洋—马六甲海峡(巽他、望加锡海峡)—中国南海—台湾海峡—中国大陆;南非—印度洋—马六甲海峡—中国南海—台湾海峡—中国大陆这5条主要的铁矿石进口通道。

4.2 煤炭

煤炭是重要的基础能源及原料,我国为煤炭生产大国,也是进口大国。2010年,印度尼西亚、澳大利亚、越南、蒙古以及俄罗斯为我国五大煤炭进口来源(见表3)。其中,来自印度尼西亚的煤炭进口量达到5 477万吨,同比增长80.3%,占进口总量的33.24%;来自澳大利亚的煤炭进口量为3 697万吨,同比增长15.9%,占进口总量的22.23%;2010年来自越南、蒙古、俄罗斯的进口量分别为1 805万吨、1 659万吨及1 158万吨。

表3 国煤炭进口主要来源构成

国家	2010年/万吨	占比	同比增长/%	2011年1月—5/万吨	占比/%
印度尼西亚	5 477	33.24%	80.3%	1 791	31.49%
澳大利亚	3 697	22.23%	−15.9%	827	14.54%
越南	1 805	10.95%	−25.1%	825	14.54%
蒙古	1 659	10.06%	176.4%	622	10.93%
俄罗斯	1 158	7.03%	−1.7%	382	6.70%
南非	700	4.31%	857.2%	153	2.90%
加拿大	520	3.16%	27.2%	171	3.01%
美国	478	2.90%	492.6%	247	4.34%
朝鲜	463	2.80%	28.9%	391	6.87%

2010年,来自前5个国家的煤炭进口总量达到13 796万吨,占总量的83.8%。随着进口渠道有所增加,煤源进一步分散,来自南非、美国、朝鲜、哥伦比亚等国的煤炭进口急剧增加,2010年从上述国家进口总量达到2 539万吨,并且从2011年前5个月数据来看,来自这些国家的进口比重均大幅提高。

因此在航线上,有印尼—马六甲—中国南海—中国大陆;澳大利亚—太平洋(琉球群岛)—中国南海—中国大陆;越南—琼州海峡—台湾海峡—北方各港口为主要的通道,同时来自北美非洲的煤运量激增也促使北美—中国大陆航线、南非—好望角—马六甲海峡(巽他、望加锡海峡)—中国南海—中国大陆这两条航线在煤炭运输领域地发挥日渐突出的作用。

5 战略通道划分

综合我国一般性贸易、石油、铁矿石、煤矿等物资的进出口渠道及所在的水域类型做如下划分:

5.1 海峡战略通道

(1) 台湾海峡。
(2) 新加坡与马六甲海峡(望加锡、巽他海峡)。
(3) 曼德海峡。
(4) 直布罗陀海峡。
(5) 琼州海峡。
(6) 对马海峡。
(7) 津轻海峡。
(8) 朝鲜海峡。
(9) 宗谷海峡。
(10) 英吉利海峡。
(11) 白令海峡。

5.2 大洋战略通道

(1) 马六甲海峡西口到曼德海峡的印度洋通道。
(2) 马六甲海峡西口到好望角的印度洋通道。
(3) 中国东海到北美的太平洋通道。
(4) 中国南海到澳大利亚的太平洋通道。
(5) 中国东海经日本海和宗谷海峡到白令海峡的太平洋通道。
(6) 北冰洋东北航路。
(7) 北冰洋西北航路。

5.3 海上运河战略通道

(1) 苏伊士运河。
(2) 巴拿马运河。
(3) 红海战略通道。

5.4 沿海战略通道

(1) 我国海上出海口。
(2) 我国南海战备通道。
(3) 我国沿海南北战略通道(含台湾海峡、琼州海峡)。

6 我国远洋贸易出海口

从地理上看,中国处于封闭或半封闭的海域,无论是东出太平洋,还是南下大洋洲和印度洋,都必须穿过许多战略通道,这些战略通道对我国的军事、经济安全都有重要的影响。

(1)渤海海峡,位于辽东半岛老铁山西角至山东半岛蓬莱之间黄海与渤海交界处,是进出渤海的咽喉要道,北京和天津的门户。

(2)台湾海峡,位于台湾地区和福建省之间。台湾海峡位于太平洋和印度洋的航线上,是保卫我国东南沿海地区的战略要地。

(3)琼州海峡,位于雷州半岛和海南岛之间。其是大陆和海南岛联系通道,是广东和广西沿海港口联系的便捷通道。

(4)朝鲜海峡,广义为朝鲜半岛南岸和日本九州岛北岸之间的海峡。东北通日本海,西南接东海,两岸多良港、小湾[447]。

(5)琉球诸通道。东出太平洋,我国主要利用的是琉球诸通道,其位于日本九州至台湾地区之间的海岛之间长约 600 n mile 的水域内,是太平洋东岸及大洋洲各国出入东海和黄海的重要航道。

(6)马六甲海峡。西向印度洋或南下大洋洲,我国需要穿越马六甲海峡、翼他海峡、龙目海峡等。马六甲海峡对中国相当重要,中国的运油船大多是 10 万吨级油船,主要走马六甲海峡。

(7)卡里马塔海峡,位于印度尼西亚加里曼丹与勿里洞岛之间,海峡宽约 115 n mile,水深 18~37 m。卡里马塔海峡是南海通往爪哇海和印度洋的重要通道,也是中南半岛至澳大利亚的常用通道[448]。

(8)巴士诸海峡,位于台湾地区南端与菲律宾之间,南北宽约 210 n mile,是连接南海与菲律宾海的重要通道。

港口船舶事故致因的灰色关联分析模型[*]

摘要:运用灰色系统理论中的灰色关联分析方法,建立了港口因素对港口水域船舶事故主要致因的关联分析模型。该模型既可为我国水上安全宏观管理提供依据,也可为特定港口的安全管理提供依据,对于避免和减少港口事故的巨大经济损失具有一定的意义。

关键词:灰色系统理论;关联度;港口船舶事故

1 灰色关联分析的原理

本文采用综合关联度,由于它不但反映了因素序列与结果序列几何形状的相似程度,而且也反映了因素序列与结果序列相对于始点的变化率,更能反映出因素对结果的影响程度。

1.1 灰色绝对关联度

设:结果序列 $Y = (Y(1), Y(2), \cdots, Y(n))$ $n = 1, 2, \cdots$

因素序列 $X_i = (X_i(1), X_i(2), \cdots, X_i(n))$ $n = 1, 2, \cdots$

结果序列和诸因素序列的长度相同,称序列 $Y_0 = Y(n) - Y(1)$ 为结果序列的始点零化象,$X_{0i} = X_i(k) - X_i(1)$ 为因素序列的始点零化象。

令:
$$S_0 = \int_1^n [Y(n) - Y(1)] dt \qquad |S_0| = \left| \sum_{k=1}^{n-1} Y_0(k) + Y_0(n)/2 \right|$$

$$S_i = \int_1^n [X_i(n) - X_i(1)] dt \qquad |S_i| = \left| \sum_{k=1}^{n-1} X_{0i}(k) + X_{0i}(n)/2 \right|$$

$$S_i - S_0 = \int_1^n (X_{0i} - Y_0) dt$$

$$|S_i - S_0| = \left| \sum_{k=1}^{n-1} [X_{0i}(k) - Y_0(k)] + [X_{0i}(n) - Y_0(n)]/2 \right|$$

则称
$$A_i = (1 + |S_0| + |S_i|)/(1 + |S_0| + |S_i| + |S_i - S_0|)$$

为结果序列与因素序列的灰色绝对关联度。绝对关联度 A_i 只与 Y 和 X_i 的几何形状有关,而与其空间相对位置无关。Y 与 X_i 几何上相似程度越大,A_i 越大。

---

[*] 本文发表于《大连海事大学学报》1997年第2期,作者郑中义、吴兆麟、杨丹。

1.2 灰色相对关联度

若结果序列 Y 与因素序列 X_i 的长度相同,且初值都异于零,Y_z,X_{zi} 分别为 Y,X_i 的初值象,则称 Y_z 与 X_{zi} 的灰色绝对关联度为 Y 与 X_i 的灰色相对关联度,记为 R_i。

定义 $Y_z = Y/Y(1) = (Y(1)/Y(1),Y(2)/Y(1),\cdots,Y(n)/Y(1))$

$$X_{zi} = X_i/X(1) = (X(1)/X(1),X(2)/X(1),\cdots,X(n)/X(1))$$

为 Y,X_i 的初值象。R_i 仅与序列 Y,X_i 相对于始点的变化速率有关,而与各观测点数据大小无关;当 Y,X_i 相对于始点的变化速率越趋于一致时,R_i 越大。

1.3 灰色综合关联度

设序列 Y,X_i 长度相同,且初值都不为零,A_i 和 R_i 分别为 Y,X_i 的灰色绝对关联度和灰色相对关联度,若 $0 < K < 1$,称

$$P_i = K \times A_i + (1 - K) \times R_i$$

为 Y,X_i 的灰色综合关联度。综合关联度既体现了 Y 与 X_i 的相似程度,又可反映出 Y 与 X_i 相对于始点的变化速率,是较为全面地表征序列之间联系是否紧密的一个数量指标。

利用上述原理,求得各港口船舶事故数序列与各港口诸因素序列之间的灰色综合关联度,则 P_i 值最大的因素就是影响港口事故的主要因素。

2 灰色关联分析模型的应用

进行国内全部港口船舶事故的灰色关联分析。

2.1 各港口诸因素、船舶事故次数(Y)

影响港口事故的因素非常多,通过定性分析并通过专家咨询得到因素序列集 X_i,它们是:能见度(X_1)、大风(X_2)、最大流(X_3)、主航道长(X_4)、交叉点和转向点(X_5)、船舶交通密度(X_6)和船舶加权交通量(X_7)。为了较为准确地反映港口诸因素与船舶事故之间的关系,各因素的数值取各港口 1983—1987 年 5 年的平均值。

(1)能见度是指港口近 5 年低于 1 km 能见度的年平均积累天数(天/年)。

(2)大风指港口风力达蒲福 6 级及以上的年平均积累天数(天/年)。

(3)最大流速特定港口最大流的节数(kn)。

(4)港口主航道长度统计港口年 500 总吨以上船舶人工航道总的航行海里数值(n mile)。

(5)航道交叉和转向点的个数主航道与通航水深大于 1 m 的次航道的交叉点数与两直航道的航线交叉角度大于 25°的转向点的个数之和(个)。

(6)船舶密度是指单位时间每平方海里的船舶数(艘/平方海里·小时)。

(7)加权船舶交通量计算 500 总吨以上船舶的日平均船长加权交通量。

总吨	500~3 000	~20 000	~10 万	10 万以上
权系数	1	2	4	6

船舶事故次数(Y),亦取年平均值。

1983—1987年船舶交通事故资料统计的年平均船舶交通事故数量如表1所示。

表1 港口名称、诸因素和船舶事故表

	大连	秦皇岛	天津	烟台	青岛	连云港	南通	镇江	宁波1	宁波2	福州	黄埔	湛江
Y	29.2	3.2	4.8	6.4	39	23	51	25	3	46	30	37	46
X_1	27	11.3	9.8	24.2	54	16.1	11.3	17	28	28	25.7	25	13.3
X_2	40.4	8.6	80.2	77.4	94.8	138.6	36	32.3	21.4	21.4	22.9	73.3	11.3
X_3	3	3	1.5	0.5	3	2.9	3.2	3.8	4.5	5	7	3.5	3.5
X_4	9.5	14	20.2	4.2	7.4	3.6	1.0	1.7	30	13.6	25.6	63.5	40.8
X_5	5	2	1	2	8	7	6	10	7	6	15	13	18
X_6	1.5	1.2	1.6	2.1	8.1	0.68	5.5	13	1.29	17.6	4.63	2.9	0.5
X_7	57.9	30.7	41.2	14	45.7	14	60	72	9.09	21.8	8.92	42	32.8

2.2 计算港口船舶事故与其因素的绝对关联度

得到：$A_1 = 0.8968$ $A_2 = 0.5013$ $A_3 = 0.5050$ $A_4 = 0.5018$

$A_5 = 0.5034$

$A_6 = 0.5029$ $A_7 = 0.5777$

由 $A_1 > A_7 > A_3 > A_5 > A_6 > A_4 > A_2$ 得到：港口能见度曲线与港口事故曲线的相似程度最大，其次是港口交通量，也即港口的能见度是影响船舶事故的主要因素，其次是港口船舶交通量。

2.3 计算港口船舶事故与其因素的相对关联度

得到：$R_1 = 0.8318$ $R_2 = 0.5152$ $R_3 = 0.7229$ $R_4 = 0.5079$

$R_5 = 0.5091$ $R_6 = 0.5034$ $R_7 = 0.7738$

由 $R_1 > R_7 > R_3 > R_2 > R_5 > R_4 > R_6$ 说明：从各因素相对于始点变化速率的角度上讲，港口能见度的变化速率与港口船舶事故的变化速率最相近，其次是港口船舶交通量。

2.4 计算港口船舶事故与其因素的灰色综合关联度

利用 $P_i = K \times A_i + (1-K) R_i$ 取 $K = 0.5$

得到：$P_1 = 0.8643$ $P_2 = 0.5082$ $P_3 = 0.6139$ $P_4 = 0.5048$ $P_5 = 0.5062$

$P_6 = 0.5031$ $P_7 = 0.6757$

由 $P_1 > P_7 > P_3 > P_2 > P_5 > P_4 > P_6$ 得到如下结论：从我国沿海13个港口的整体情况看，港口船舶事故与港口七种因素中，能见度的综合灰色关联度最大，其次是港口的船舶交通量，即港口能见度是港口船舶事故的主要致因，再次是港口的船舶交通量的大小。从国家宏观管理的角度,主要是加强在港口能见度不良时对船舶的监督管理。制定严格的在能见度不良时船舶的行为规则,以实现有效的管理,减少和避免船舶事故发生和船舶事故造成的巨大损失。从13个港口的灰色关联分析中也说明:船舶交通量的增长并非导致船舶事故的主要因素。

但是在进行关联分析时,不能忽视了因素之间对事故的综合作用。近几年,由于港口船舶交通量增大,又增大了在能见度不良时船舶发生事故的可能性,实际上也如此。例如我国山东成山头附近,该区域是我国沿海有名的能见度不良多发区,也是船舶交通较为繁忙的区域,船舶的交通事故也较多。因此我们不能将影响船舶港口事故的各个因素割裂开来,应在对各不良影响因素改善的同时,抓住主要矛盾。

3 具体港口船舶事故的灰色关联分析

上述关联分析的数学模型不但可以对我国所有的港口船舶事故进行分析,找到导致事故的主要因素,还可以对单个港口船舶事故的主要导致因素进行分析,找到具体港口导致船舶事故的主要因素,为特定港口的安全管理提供依据。

仍利用上述的序列,设事故序列 Y 和因素序列 X_i 为等时距序列,即结果序列和因素序列的取值为相同时间间隔内的数值。需说明的是对于特定的港口,港口的某些因素可能不随时间的变化而改变,因此,在具体港口关联分析时可将其省略,如主航道长度、交叉点和转向点的个数、最大流速等。

下面仅以甲港口的能见度、大风、交通量与港口船舶事故的关联度对甲港口事故致因进行灰色关联分析(各因素的单位同上)。

      1982 1983 1984 1985 1986 1987 1988 1989 1990 1991

甲港口事故序列 $Y = ($ 24 32 64 130 66 120 80 96 110 88 $)$

因素序列(能见度) $X_1 = ($ 25 28 34 39 18 23 31 29 27 16 $)$

(大风) $X_2 = ($ 30 27 60 38 46 53 39 49 35 56 $)$

(交通量) $X_3 = ($ 31 33 42 53 58 74 75 83 84 87 $)$

计算灰色绝对关联度得到: $A_1 = 0.5232; A_2 = 0.6119; A_3 = 0.7623$

计算灰色相对关联度得到: $R_1 = 0.5337; R_2 = 0.5982; R_3 = 0.7094$

计算灰色综合关联度得到: $P_1 = 0.5285; P_2 = 0.6051; P_3 = 0.7359$

由于 $P_3 > P_2 > P_1$,所以在能见度、大风和船舶港口交通量三因素中,交通量是甲港口船舶事故的主要致因,大风其次,能见度再次。因此,在甲港口的安全管理中,除了在港口能见度不良时加强管理外,更主要是应加强船舶交通的管理,如果条件许可可实施分道通航制或制定严格的限速的规章等。

4 结束语

用灰色系统理论分析港口诸因素对港口船舶事故影响,这一方法在我国资料不全、资金有限的情况下,能为管理提供科学的依据;有助于抓住主要矛盾,提高水上安全管理的水平,从而减少船舶事故所造成的巨大经济损失。

船舶交通事故等级模糊划分的数学模型*

摘要:针对目前《船舶交通事故统计规则》在实践中存在的问题和国外在这方面的做法指出我国海事分级方法的不足之处,并利用模糊数学的模糊聚类和模糊评判方法,建立模型对船舶交通事故进行分级。

关键词:交通事故;等级划分;聚类分析;模糊评价

0 引言

我国的《船舶交通事故统计规则》根据发生事故的船舶吨位大小、死亡人数和造成的直接经济损失,对船舶交通事故进行等级划分。但是,在实践中存在着一些问题。为此,我们在对事故等级划分进行研究的基础上,提出了事故等级模糊划分的数学模型。

1 现行船舶交通事故等级划分中存在的不合理之处

1.1 现行的等级划分方法

我国的《船舶交通事故统计规则》(下面简称"规则")规定:事故船舶按其总吨位或主机额定功率(拖船)分为11级。如果事故导致人员伤亡,则事故的分级和船舶等级大小无关,即不论事故船舶的大小,凡事故造成死亡3人及以上,属重大事故;死亡1~2人,属大事故;人员有重伤,属一般事故;依此类推,事故只造成人员轻伤,属小事故。如果船舶沉没、全损或无修复价值,不论船舶大小,一律算作重大事故。如果事故未造成人员伤亡或船舶灭失而只带来直接经济损失的,则按照船舶大小的11个级别分别确定等级。对于特别重大事故,《特别重大事故调查程序暂行规定》另外规定:造成特别重大人身伤亡或巨大经济损失以及性质严重、产生重大影响的事故属特别重大事故。劳动部解释:水运事故造成一次死亡50人及其以上,或一次造成直接经济损失一千万元以上的即为特别重大事故。因而,实际上存在小事故、一般事故、大事故、重大事故和特别重大事故5个等级。

1.2 规则等级划分方法存在的问题

我国海事分级的方法注重人命损失,偏重于相对经济损失,对于同样大小的船舶来说具有

---

* 本文发表于《大连海事大学学报》1997年第4期23卷,作者黄燕品、郑中义、吴兆麟。

一定的横向可比性和合理性。但是,对于不同吨位的船舶,在划分等级中存在着不少问题。从国家实施海上交通安全管理的角度来看,我国海上安全方面的有关专家也认为规则具有很大的不合理性。我们认为至少存在以下几个问题:(1)等级划分缺乏模糊性。比如,对于直接经济损失为3万元的交通事故,如果事故船舶的吨位为200总吨及以上,那么该事故应属于大事故。如果船舶吨位为200总吨以下,哪怕是199总吨,也应划分为重大事故。划分等级过于绝对造成等级划分的不合理。(2)规则中有关人命伤亡的规定也不合理。规则指出,只要发生了人员伤亡,在划分等级时,就不考虑吨位的大小,死亡3人或以上属重大事故;死亡1~2人属大事故;人员只受重伤属一般事故;人员受轻伤为小事故。我们认为,既然死亡3人属重大事故,那么很难说将死亡2人同时伴有上百人乃至数百人重伤的事故划分为大事故是合理的。(3)将全损事故一律划分为重大事故也存在着不合理性。设想一条50万吨的超级大船的灭失和一条仅为数十吨的小船全损,二者的严重程度显然不可同日而语,根据规则它们同属重大事故是不切实际的。(4)规则注重人命的原则可能导致等级划分矛盾。假如一条1 200总吨的船舶发生事故导致50多万元的经济损失和2人死亡,根据规则注重人命的原则,在有人命伤亡的情况下,由2人死亡应当将其划分为大事故。然而同样的船舶如果只带来50多万元的损失,却应当根据船舶吨位等级划分为重大事故。这样就存在着因划分的指标不同而导致划分结果之间的相互矛盾。

1.3 由国际上的做法看现行方法的不合理性

国际海事组织在1986年海安会第433号通函中规定各国应该向IMO报告的"重大海损事故"中指出:(1)1 600总吨或1 600总吨以上的船舶,因发生海事而造成全损(含推定全损);(2)500总吨及以上船舶,因发生海事而致人命损失的事故。苏联《海上船舶事故调查程序》规定凡发生事故造成船舶破损导致丧失海上通航能力需48 h以上修理的;或船舶碰损岸边建筑设施致使设施停用48 h以上;货船搁浅48 h或48 h以上、客船搁浅12 h或以上(无论破损与否)均为事故,否则只视为事故性情况。美国海事法也类似规定了应向海岸警卫队报告并接受其调查的海事等级标准和应由运输部进行调查的"重大海损事故"等级标准。利比里亚也在《关于海事调查和听证的规定》中对要求报告的海事标准做出了类似规定。总之,就国际上的做法来看,在考虑事故的严重性时,都综合考虑经济损失、人命伤亡和事故引起的耽搁时间。

2 船舶交通事故等级的模糊划分模型

2.1 利用模糊方法的依据

船舶在发生海上交通事故时,不仅船舶的吨位、造成的直接经济损失不同,而且发生人命伤亡情况、造成设施的损坏程度也不同,应当利用多种因素综合衡量事故等级大小,用某单一指标(如人命伤亡数、全损与否)决定性地来划分事故的等级容易造成等级划分的不合理性。利用模糊数学对事故的不同指标综合分析可以弥补这样的不足。

2.2 模糊分析方法

根据实践中发现的问题,并参照专家对现行事故等级划分方法的意见(主张用事故损失的绝对数字进行等级划分),模糊划分方法如下:

2.2.1 指标的选定

在确定事故等级划分的指标时,我们认为应当选取以下三个指标:(1)船舶交通事故造成的人员伤亡数;(2)事故带来的直接经济损失(含船舶修理费、检查费、施救费、事故处理费、赔偿费,赔偿费含一次性赔偿费、货损赔偿费、抚恤费等);(3)事故带来的间接经济损失。可以利用事故造成的设施或船舶不能马上投入正常运作所必需的延滞时间来衡量,因为上述两个指标不足以反映事故造成的真正损失的大小。

2.2.2 定量化划分过程

首先,确定事故等级集{小事故,一般事故,大事故,重大事故}。其次,选定一定数量而且具有代表性的船舶交通事故实例,选取指标{人命伤亡,直接财产损失,延滞时间损失},利用模糊综合评判方法进行综合评判,得到事故等级综合评价向量矩阵。再次,利用模糊聚类方法借助 C 语言编制的程序对上述矩阵进行聚类分析,得到事故聚类。然后,根据第二步所得事故等级综合评价向量,得到每一件事故的事故等级综合评价值和每一类事故的平均综合评价值,按照平均综合评价值的大小顺序将事故类别和事故等级相对应。最后,可以得出每一级事故相对应的各指标推荐标准值,对于实践中发生的每一起事故,均可以依据其对应的 3 个指标值利用模糊评判法并借助于编定的计算机程序进行综合评判,从而可以很方便地进行事故等级划分。

2.3 应用

2.3.1 根据交通事故的危害和可能造成的损失,确定描述具体事故的指标

建立指标集 D:{人命伤亡,事故经济损失,延时损失}。

2.3.2 无量纲化

消除各因素量纲不同的影响。第 i 起事故的第 j 个指标值 X_{ij} 由下式确定:

$$X_{ij} = \begin{cases} 1 & X_{ij}' > X_{j\max} \\ \dfrac{X_{ij}' - X_{j\min}}{X_{ij} - X_{j\min}} & X_{j\min} < X_{ij}' < X_{j\max} \\ 0 & X_{ij}' < X_{j\min} \end{cases}$$

X_{ij}' 为第 i 事故第 j 个指标的原始值;$X_{j\min}$ 为第 j 指标下限值;$X_{j\max}$ 为第 j 指标上限值。

2.3.3 对单因素的初始评价

根据无量纲化后每一个 X_{ij} 值,由表 1 得到每一个事故的 3 个指标值各对应的 7 个影响度值,经综合评制得到每一事故的评判向量 C_i(见表 2)。

$$R^i = (r_{11}^i, r_{12}^i, r_{13}^i, \cdots, r_{17}^i)$$

表 1 模糊子集表

Y/隶属度/影响程度	极端重要 1	非常重要 0.8	比较重要 0.65	重要 0.5	稍微重要 0.35	较不重要 0.2	不重要 0
1~0.8	0.67	0.33	0	0	0	0	0
0.8~0.7	0.25	0.5	0.25	0	0	0	0
0.7~0.6	0	0.25	0.5	0.25	0	0	0
0.6~0.4	0	0	0.25	0.5	0.25	0	0
0.4~0.3	0	0	0	0.25	0.5	0.25	0
0.3~0.2	0	0	0	0	0.25	0.5	0.25
0.2~0	0	0	0	0	0	0.33	0.67

2.3.4 最终评判

对于每一个事故的评判向量 C_i 进行综合评定,依据 $M = C^i \cdot N^T$,得到事故等级综合评价值 M(见表2),其中 $N = (1, 0.8, 0.65, 0.5, 0.35, 0.2, 0)$。

表 2 事故评判向量表

事故	评判向量							综合评价值 M
A_1	0.67	0.33	0	0	0	0	0	0.934
A_2	0	0.055	0.305	0.445	0.195	0	0	0.533
A_3	0	0	0	0	0.09	0.391	0.519	0.110
A_4	0	0	0	0	0.105	0.401	0.494	0.133
⋮								
A_{16}	0.241	0.224	0.265	0.215	0.055	0	0	0.719
A_{17}	0	0	0	0	0	0.33	0.67	0.066
A_{18}	0	0	0.055	0.11	0.055	0.257	0.523	0.161
A_{19}	0	0.105	0.30	0.285	0.09	0.073	0.147	0.467
A_{20}	0	0	0	0	0.105	0.401	0.494	0.117

2.3.5 聚类分析

(1)首先将所得的数据标准化。本文采用绝对值减数法,即:

$$r_{ij} = \begin{cases} 1 & i = j \\ 1 - C \sum_{k=1}^{m} |x_{ik} - x_{jk}| & i \neq j \end{cases}$$

r_{ij} 为事故 A_i 与事故 A_j 的相似程度,系数 C 取 0.4。
(2)建立相似关系矩阵。
(3)求取最小传递闭包,得到等价矩阵。

(4)取截取系数 h,进行聚类分析。编制模糊聚类 C 语言程序把上述步骤程序化,截取系数 h 取 0.75,聚类结果:$\{A_1, A_5, A_7, A_9\}$;$\{A_{13}, A_{15}, A_{16}\}$;$\{A_2, A_{19}\}$;$\{A_3, A_4, A_6, A_8, A_{10}, A_{11}, A_{12}, A_{14}, A_{17}, A_{18}, A_{20}\}$。

2.3.6 等级划分

根据所求得的每一类事故平均综合评价值大小得到事故等级划分表3。

表3 事故等级划分结果

事故等级	事故序号
重大事故	A_1, A_5, A_7, A_9
大事故	A_{13}, A_{15}, A_{16}
一般事故	A_2, A_{19}
小事故	$A_3, A_4, A_6, A_8, A_{10}, A_{11}, A_{12}, A_{14}, A_{17}, A_{18}, A_{20}$

2.4 聚类结果的进一步应用

2.4.1 推荐标准值

交通事故推荐标准值如表4所示。

表4 交通事故推荐标准值

事故等级/标准	人员伤亡数(人)	财产损失(万元)	延滞时间(天)
重大事故	4	200	20
大事故	2	100	15
一般事故	1	50	10
小事故	0	10	3

2.4.2 推荐标准的应用

事故的指标集 $E = \{e_1, e_2, e_3\} = \{$人命伤亡,经济损失,延滞时间$\}$ 和事故的等级集 $Y = \{y_1, y_2, y_3, y_4\} = \{$重大事故,大事故,一般事故,小事故$\}$ 各指标对第 K 等级隶属度函数为:
$$\_(x_{ij}) = (x_{k+1}) - (x_{ij})/(x_{k+1}) - (x_k) \quad (i = 1, 2, 3; j = 1, 2, 3, 4; k = 1, 2, 3)$$

由此可以建立各指标对事故等级的单因素评价向量 $\boldsymbol{r} = (r_1, r_2, r_3, r_4)$,从而得到了事故样本的各因素特征值和事故等级之间的模糊变换关系 $R: R^i = (r_1^i, r_2^i, \cdots, r_4^i)$。根据各因素在等级划分中的重要性,取权重 $A = \{0.42, 0.36, 0.22\}$。由模糊转换:$A \rightarrow R \rightarrow B$ 得到:$B = A \cdot R = (b_1, b_2, \cdots, b_4)$。根据最大原则,选取最大的 b 所对应的等级即为该事故的事故等级。鉴于特别重大事故的特殊意义,其仍适用暂行规定。

2.4.3 模型的合理性

上述综合评判模型对交通事故等级进行综合评定的合理性在于:(1)等级推荐值来自所收集到的事故资料并经筛选后在模糊聚类和评判的基础上得到,因而具有一定的典型性和代表性。(2)模糊评判方法综合考虑了事故的各个特征值,从3个方面进行综合评估,能够避免上文所述的现行划分方法所存在的不合理性,而且能够避免因不同指标的使用而可能造成的矛盾,从而有效地避免了1.2中所述的缺陷。

3　结语

模糊分析方法的使用能够消除现行事故等级划分的方法在实践中暴露出的问题且有利于国家主管机关宏观掌握海上交通事故真实情况。用模糊数学的有关方法对事故等级进行多指标的评定具有一定的可行性和合理性。推荐标准的进一步改善还有待于进行深入研究。

大风浪海损事故的灰色关联分析*

摘要：针对大风浪天气发生的海损事故，运用灰色系统理论中的关联分析方法，建立了大风浪海损事故与其致因间的关联矩阵，进行了事故原因的灰色关联分析，从定量的角度得出造成海损事故的主因是船舶不适航和人为因素，不仅有助于船长在大风浪天气开航前，根据船舶的航次特点，有针对性地做好防止海损事故发生的预防措施，提高船舶的适航性和大风浪中的操船水平，也为大风浪天气中的安全评估的评估体系的确定提供了科学的理论依据，具有实际意义和应用价值。

关键词：大风浪；海损事故；灰色系统理论；关联度；安全评估

0 引言

根据 LIOYD 资料统计，1961—1993 年的 32 年间共造成全损船舶 9 838 艘，其中沉没（主要是大风浪天气中）的船舶为 3 520 艘，占 35.8%。根据日本海上保安厅的资料统计，1997—2001 年的 5 年间，造成搁浅、触礁、主机故障、倾覆、推进器损坏、火灾、进水等 11 类海损事故的共有 9 502 宗，其中倾覆（主要是大风浪天气中）事故有 892 宗，占 9.4%，居海损事故的第 4 位。根据我国交通部的海事资料统计，1979—1999 年的 20 年间，造成碰撞、搁浅、触礁、触损、浪损、火灾和风灾等 8 类海损事故共有 59 759 宗，其中风灾（主要是大风）有 1 894 宗，占 3.2%，居海损事故的第 6 位[449]。可见，大风浪天气导致的海损事故占有很大的比例。

1 灰色系统关联分析的基本原理

灰色系统理论[450]应用于海损事故原因的分析，是因为船舶在大风浪中出现的海损事故系统就是一个灰色系统，因其构成事故的原因诸如水密系统不水密、跨航区航行、船员不适任、超载（结冰）、货物系固绑扎不牢等在相互关系、作用程度、数据收集方面均符合灰色系统的概念。因此说这种分析方法是分析海损事故的重要补充，为防止海损事故的发生提供了定量依据[451]。

本文就船舶在大风浪天气中出现的海损事故的产生机理，利用灰色系统理论对事故的原因进行关联分析，以期在定量上加以研究。

进行关联分析的步骤是：确定比较数列与参考数列，求关联系数，求关联度和将关联度按大小排序。

---

* 本文发表于《大连海事大学学报》2003 年第 4 期，作者王凤武、吴兆麟、郑中义。

设参考(母)序列为 $x_0(k)$ ($k=1,2,3,\cdots,m$)，比较(子)序列为 $x_i(k)$ ($k=1,2,3,\cdots,m$, $i=1,2,\cdots,n$)，则 $x_i(k)$ 与 $x_0(k)$ 的关联系数为：

$$\xi_i(k) = \frac{\min_i \min_k |x_0(k) - x_i(k)| + \rho \max_i \max_k |x_0(k) - x_i(k)|}{|x_0(k) - x_i(k)| + \rho \max_i \max_k |x_0(k) - x_i(k)|}$$

记 $\Delta_i(k) = |x_0(k) - x_i(k)|$ 则

$$\xi_i(k) = \frac{\min_i \min_k \Delta_i(k) + \rho \max_i \max_k \Delta_i(k)}{\Delta_i(k) + \rho \max_i \max_k \Delta_i(k)}$$

这里，ρ 称为分辨系数，一般 $\rho \in [0,1]$，$\rho = 0.5$，$\min_i \min_k \Delta_i(k)$ 为两级最小差，其中 $\min_k \Delta_i(k)$ 为第一级最小差，$\min_i \min_k \Delta_i(k)$ 表示在找出的 $\min_k \Delta_i(k)$（即第一级最小差）基础上，挑选出最小差。$\max_i \max_k \Delta_i(k)$ 为两级最大差，意义与两级最小差相似。据此，可以求出 $x_i(k)$ 与对应 $x_0(k)$ 的关联度，即

$$r_i = \frac{1}{m} \sum_{k=1}^{m} \xi_i(k)$$

比较 r_i 与 r_j，若 $r_i > r_j$，则表明第 i 个因素对结果的影响比第 j 个因素大。

2 大风浪海损事故的灰色关联分析

本文根据多年的海损事故报告进行了统计，得出 90 艘海损事故船舶的总吨位、种类、船长及船龄的分布情况，如表 1 所示。从统计数据可知，大风浪中发生海损事故主要有沉没、触礁、机损、倾斜[451]；就海损事故的船舶种类而言，有货船、客船、工作船和渔船等。虽然大风浪是最重要的外因，但船舶本身(包括船员)是造成事故的主要原因，这些原因可分为水密系统不水密、跨航区航行(如Ⅲ航区船舶航行到沿海作业)、船员不适任、未配备新版海图、设备故障、结构缺陷、航行计划不符合要求、超载(结冰)、货物系固绑扎不牢、航行中操纵不当、锚泊操纵不当等，而水密系统不水密、跨航区航行、船员不适任、未配备新版海图、超载可归属于船舶不适航；结构缺陷、航行计划不符合要求、货物系固绑扎不牢和设备故障等均与航行前未实行良好的检查有关，严格上讲也应属于船舶不适航；航行与锚泊中的操纵不当所造成的海损事故虽与自然条件有关，但主要还是操船者业务能力的问题，属人为因素所致。大风浪天气中海损事故及主要原因统计如表 2 所示。

表 1 大风浪天气海损事故分类统计

总吨位/t	船数/艘	船舶种类	船数/艘	船长/m	船数/艘	船龄/年	船数/艘
<100	21	货船	62	<100	29	<10	15
100~5 000	38	客船	5	>100	26	10~20	23
>5 000	13	工作船	9			>20	17
不详	18	渔船	14	不详	35	不详	35

表2　大风浪天气海损事故及主要原因统计

事故原因	货船	客船	工作船	渔船	沉没	触礁	机损	倾斜	其他
水密系统不水密	6	0	0	1	7	0	0	0	0
跨航区航行	6	4	3	9	22	0	0	0	0
船员不适任	2	0	1	0	3	0	0	0	0
未配备新版海图	0	0	1	0	0	1	0	0	0
设备故障	4	0	1	0	2	0	3	0	0
超载	3	0	0	3	6	0	0	0	0
结构缺陷	6	0	0	0	6	0	0	0	0
航行计划不符合要求	2	0	0	0	2	0	0	0	0
货物系固绑扎不牢	16	1	0	0	14	0	0	3	0
航行中操纵不当	2	0	0	0	1	1	0	0	0
锚泊操纵不当	14	0	0	1	6	9	0	0	0
其他原因	1	0	3	0	2	0	0	0	2
总计	62	5	9	14	69	13	3	3	2

(1)设事故总数为母序列 $x_0(k)$，大风浪导致海损事故的主要原因构成了子序列 $x_i(k)$ ($i=1,2,\cdots,12$)。

$$\begin{pmatrix} x_0(k) \\ x_1(k) \\ x_2(k) \\ x_3(k) \\ x_4(k) \\ x_5(k) \\ x_6(k) \\ x_7(k) \\ x_8(k) \\ x_9(k) \\ x_{10}(k) \\ x_{11}(k) \\ x_{12}(k) \end{pmatrix} = \begin{pmatrix} 事故总数 \\ 水密系统不水密 \\ 跨航区航行 \\ 船员不适任 \\ 未配备新版海图 \\ 设备故障 \\ 超载 \\ 结构缺陷 \\ 航行计划不符合要求 \\ 货物系固绑扎不牢 \\ 航行中操纵不当 \\ 锚泊操纵不当 \\ 其他原因 \end{pmatrix} = \begin{bmatrix} 62 & 5 & 9 & 14 \\ 6 & 0 & 0 & 1 \\ 6 & 4 & 3 & 9 \\ 2 & 0 & 1 & 0 \\ 0 & 0 & 1 & 0 \\ 4 & 0 & 1 & 0 \\ 3 & 0 & 0 & 3 \\ 6 & 0 & 0 & 0 \\ 2 & 0 & 0 & 0 \\ 16 & 1 & 0 & 0 \\ 2 & 0 & 0 & 0 \\ 14 & 0 & 0 & 1 \\ 1 & 0 & 3 & 0 \end{bmatrix}$$

$$\begin{pmatrix} x_0(k) \\ x_1(k) \\ x_2(k) \\ x_3(k) \\ x_4(k) \\ x_5(k) \\ x_6(k) \\ x_7(k) \\ x_8(k) \\ x_9(k) \\ x_{10}(k) \\ x_{11}(k) \\ x_{12}(k) \end{pmatrix} = \begin{pmatrix} 事故总数 \\ 水密系统不水密 \\ 跨航区航行 \\ 船员不适任 \\ 未配备新版海图 \\ 设备故障 \\ 超载 \\ 结构缺陷 \\ 航行计划不符合要求 \\ 货物系固绑扎不牢 \\ 航行中操纵不当 \\ 锚泊操纵不当 \\ 其他原因 \end{pmatrix} = \begin{pmatrix} 69 & 13 & 3 & 3 & 2 \\ 7 & 0 & 0 & 0 & 0 \\ 22 & 0 & 0 & 0 & 0 \\ 3 & 0 & 0 & 0 & 0 \\ 0 & 1 & 0 & 0 & 0 \\ 2 & 0 & 3 & 0 & 0 \\ 6 & 0 & 0 & 0 & 0 \\ 6 & 0 & 0 & 0 & 0 \\ 0 & 2 & 0 & 0 & 0 \\ 14 & 0 & 0 & 3 & 0 \\ 1 & 1 & 0 & 0 & 0 \\ 6 & 9 & 0 & 0 & 0 \\ 2 & 0 & 0 & 0 & 2 \end{pmatrix}$$

(2) 以母序列 $x_0(k)$ 为参考序列，以子序列 $x_i(k)(i=1,2,\cdots,12)$ 为比较序列，求 $\Delta_i(k)$，如表3所示。

表3 最小差

	货船	客船	工作船	渔船	最小差	最大差	沉没	触礁	机损	倾斜	其他	两级最小差	两级最大差
$\Delta_1(k)$	56	5	9	13	5	56	62	13	3	3	2	2	62
$\Delta_2(k)$	56	1	6	5	1	56	47	13	3	3	2	2	47
$\Delta_3(k)$	60	5	8	14	5	60	66	13	3	3	2	2	66
……													
$\Delta_{12}(k)$	61	5	6	14	5	61	67	13	3	3	0	0	67

(3) 求关联系数序列 ξ_i 及关联度 γ_i。其目的是比较与造成海损事故的各原因间的关联关系。

从计算的关联度可得出如下结论：

(1) 从大风浪天气中海损事故的原因与事故船舶种类的关联性可知，其排列顺序为跨航区航行>货物系固绑扎不牢>锚泊操纵不当>其他原因>超载>水密系统不水密>设备故障>船员不适任>结构缺陷>未配备新版海图>航行计划不符合要求=航行中操纵不当。可见，造成大风浪中各类船舶海损事故的主要原因是船舶跨航区航行、货物系固绑扎不牢和锚泊操纵不当。

(2) 从大风浪天气中海损事故的原因与事故种类的关联性可知，其排列顺序为跨航区航行>货物系固绑扎不牢>锚泊操纵不当>设备故障>其他原因>航行计划不符合要求>水密系统不水密>超载=结构缺陷>航行中操纵不当>未配备新版海图>船员不适任。可见，造成大风浪中海损事故的主要原因是船舶跨航区航行、货物系固绑扎不牢和锚泊操纵不当。

$$\begin{pmatrix} \xi_1 \\ \xi_2 \\ \vdots \\ \xi_{10} \\ \xi_{11} \\ \xi_{12} \end{pmatrix} = \begin{pmatrix} 0.367\,82 & 0.888\,89 & 0.8 & 0.727\,27 \\ 0.367\,82 & 1 & 0.864\,86 & 0.888\,89 \\ \cdots & \cdots & \cdots & \cdots \\ 0.351\,65 & 0.888\,89 & 0.8 & 0.711\,11 \\ 0.405\,06 & 0.888\,89 & 0.8 & 0.727\,27 \\ 0.347\,83 & 0.888\,89 & 0.864\,86 & 0.711\,11 \end{pmatrix}$$

$$\begin{pmatrix} \gamma_1 \\ \gamma_2 \\ \gamma_3 \\ \gamma_4 \\ \gamma_5 \\ \gamma_6 \\ \gamma_7 \\ \gamma_8 \\ \gamma_9 \\ \gamma_{10} \\ \gamma_{11} \\ \gamma_{12} \end{pmatrix} = \begin{pmatrix} 0.696\,00 \\ 0.780\,39 \\ 0.693\,04 \\ 0.691\,15 \\ 0.695\,02 \\ 0.701\,59 \\ 0.691\,96 \\ 0.687\,91 \\ 0.710\,25 \\ 0.687\,91 \\ 0.705\,30 \\ 0.703\,17 \end{pmatrix} \begin{pmatrix} 水密系统不水密 \\ 跨航区航行 \\ 船员不适任 \\ 未配备新版海图 \\ 设备故障 \\ 超载 \\ 结构缺陷 \\ 航行计划不符合要求 \\ 货物系固绑扎不牢 \\ 航行中操纵不当 \\ 锚泊操纵不当 \\ 其他原因 \end{pmatrix}$$

$$\begin{pmatrix} \xi_1 \\ \xi_2 \\ \vdots \\ \xi_{10} \\ \xi_{11} \\ \xi_{12} \end{pmatrix} = \begin{pmatrix} 0.357\,51 & 0.726\,32 & 0.92 & 0.92 & 0.945\,21 \\ 0.423\,31 & 0.726\,32 & 0.92 & 0.92 & 0.945\,21 \\ \cdots & \cdots & \cdots & \cdots & \cdots \\ 0.336\,59 & 0.741\,93 & 0.92 & 0.92 & 0.945\,21 \\ 0.353\,85 & 0.896\,10 & 0.92 & 0.92 & 0.945\,21 \\ 0.339\,90 & 0.726\,32 & 0.92 & 0.92 & 1.357\,51 \end{pmatrix}$$

$$\begin{pmatrix} \gamma_1 \\ \gamma_2 \\ \gamma_3 \\ \gamma_4 \\ \gamma_5 \\ \gamma_6 \\ \gamma_7 \\ \gamma_8 \\ \gamma_9 \\ \gamma_{10} \\ \gamma_{11} \\ \gamma_{12} \end{pmatrix} = \begin{pmatrix} 0.773\,81 \\ 0.786\,97 \\ 0.770\,96 \\ 0.772\,09 \\ 0.786\,29 \\ 0.773\,08 \\ 0.773\,08 \\ 0.775\,36 \\ 0.786\,82 \\ 0.772\,75 \\ 0.786\,54 \\ 0.781\,24 \end{pmatrix} \begin{pmatrix} 水密系统不水密 \\ 跨航区航行 \\ 船员不适任 \\ 未配备新版海图 \\ 设备故障 \\ 超载 \\ 结构缺陷 \\ 航行计划不符合要求 \\ 货物系固绑扎不牢 \\ 航行中操纵不当 \\ 锚泊操纵不当 \\ 其他原因 \end{pmatrix}$$

本文从不同角度分析了造成大风浪天气中海损事故的原因与事故船舶及事故种类的关联性。可以看出,船舶跨航区航行、货物系固绑扎不牢与锚泊操纵不当是导致海损事故的主要原因,而船舶跨航区航行、货物系固绑扎不牢是属于船舶不适航,锚泊操纵不当是属于人为因素。

因此,为了从源头上杜绝或减少海损事故的发生,就应从产生事故的主要原因入手,重点解决船舶不适航及人为因素造成的操纵不当问题,这也是大风浪中安全评估所要考虑的主要因素。

3 结语

用灰色系统理论分析大风浪天气中诸因素对海损事故影响,这一方法在我国海损事故资料不全的情况下,能为海事部门和船务公司的管理提供科学定量的分析依据,有助于船长在大风浪天气开航前,根据船舶的航次特点,有针对性地做好防止海损事故发生的预防措施,提高船舶的适航性和大风浪中的操船水平,同时,也为大风浪中的船舶安全评估的评估体系的确定提供了科学的理论依据。

通航水域航行安全评价的研究*

摘要：为了对通航水域船舶航行安全性进行定量的评价，应用模糊综合评判方法建立我国主要港口通航水域的安全评价模型。根据当前影响通航水域船舶航行安全的11类主要因素建立综合评价集，应用灰色关联分析法和因子分析法确定评价指标的权重系数。利用此模型对我国10个主要港口水域的安全性进行了评价。

关键词：水路运输；海上交通安全；模糊综合评判；灰色关联分析；评价模型

0 引言

近几年来，关于通航水域航行的安全性分析，专家学者们从不同的角度、采用多种方法，对通航水域的危险程度或安全性进行了分析及评价，其结果大多是定性的，它们主要是根据经验和直观判断来对水域的航行安全进行分析。本文利用模糊综合评判方法对通航水域的安全性进行定量的计算，利用建立的评价模型对各港口的安全性进行评价。根据当前通航水域的实际情况，影响水域船舶航行安全的11类主要因素：航道长度、平均船宽与航道宽度之比、能见度、流、风、船舶交通量、交通密度、转向点及交叉点的数量、VTS管理程度、分道通航和助航标志[361]，利用模糊综合评判方法建立我国通航水域的船舶航行安全评价的隶属度函数，在文献[361]研究的基础上，应用灰色关联分析法和因子分析法确定评价指标的权重系数，建立不仅能够反映通航水域的特点，而且能够反映水域在应用VTS系统及实施船舶定线制后的通航水域安全性的评价模型，利用此模型对我国通航水域的航行安全性进行评价。

1 模糊综合评判方法

通航水域交通究竟存在多大的危险性，人们可接受的安全指标究竟有多大，需要采取哪些对策或措施才能使系统的危险程度降到安全的指标内，这些都有赖于安全评价。在多因素对系统影响的评价中，特别是各因素对系统影响的信息不充足或不明确的情况下，采用模糊综合评价理论进行研究是较好的方法。通航水域及附近水域船舶交通安全的本身就是模糊概念，而且影响评价对象的因素众多，具有很强的模糊性。

综合评判是对给定对象综合考虑多种因素进行评价和判决的问题。模糊综合评判涉及3个要素：因素集、评价集、单因素评判。在单因素评判的基础上，进行多因素的模糊综合评判。其基本方法和步骤如下：

---

* 本文发表于《中国航海》2008年第2期，作者郑中义、李红喜。

(1) 建立因素集；
(2) 建立判断集(评价集)；
(3) 单因素模糊评判；
(4) 建立权重集；
(5) 模糊综合评判[453]。

2 评价指标隶属度函数

2.1 模糊综合评判的评价集

在确定通航水域模糊综合评判的评价集时，将评价集划分为5个级别。设评价集为V，指标集为U，则有：评价集$V=\{$低危险度，较低危险度，中等危险度，较高危险度，高危险度$\}$ = $\{Ⅰ,Ⅱ,Ⅲ,Ⅳ,Ⅴ\}$。根据影响通航水域船舶航行安全的11类主要因素建立综合评判集，将评价指标集U定义为$U=\{$航道状况U_1，水文气象因素U_2，交通状况U_3，航行支持$U_4\}$，并且有：$U_1=\{$航道长度u_1，平均船宽与航道宽度之比$u_2\}$；$U_2=\{$能见度u_3，大风u_4，最大流速$u_5\}$；$U_3=\{$交通量u_6，交通密度u_7，交通流交叉及弯曲数量$u_8\}$；$U_4=\{$VTS管理程度u_9，分道通航u_{10}，助航标志状况$u_{11}\}$。

2.2 隶属度函数的建立

船舶碰撞危险度评价的关键在于如何衡量各因素对碰撞危险度的影响，对碰撞危险度的评价应当从各因素对其影响程度入手，即确定隶属度。先做出模糊综合评判的隶属度函数曲线，当确知某一指标的隶属度函数分布时，则采用确定的曲线分布；如果不知道或不确切地知道，则采用较为简单的直线分布。

(1) 航道状况(U_1)的隶属度函数

影响航道状况的因素很多，选取航道长度u_1、航道宽度与通航船舶平均宽度之比u_2两个主要因素为评价指标，对通航水域船舶的安全性进行评价。

①航道长度u_1

根据我国各通航水域的资料，当前国内的各港口中，航道最长的为上海，其人工航道长度为86 n mile[454]。为此，航道长度属于各航行危险度的隶属度函数分布如图1所示。

②平均船宽与航道宽度之比u_2

评价中采用的船舶宽度是指特定通航水域允许通航船舶宽度的平均值，航道宽度为特定航道最窄处的宽度。为了合理确定船舶宽度与航道宽度之比指标的隶属度函数，根据我国沿海港口的实际情况来看，船舶宽度与航道宽度之比最大的港口为连云港，其比值为0.36。该比值最小的为青岛港口，其比值为0.065。由此可知，船舶宽度与航道宽度属于评语集5个危险度的隶属度函数。

(2) 其他指标的隶属度函数

与前面的推理一样，可得出水文气象指标(U_2)的能见度u_3、风u_4、流u_5，交通状况(U_3)的

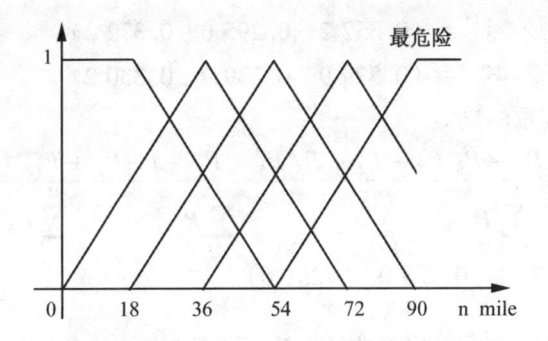

图 1 航道长度的隶属度函数分布

船舶交通量 u_6、交通密度 u_7 及交通流交叉及弯曲 u_8 以及航行支持状况（U_4）的通航水域 VTS 的管理程度 u_9、船舶定线制的实施情况 u_{10} 以及助航标志情况 u_{11} 的隶属度函数。

3 权重的确定

3.1 灰色关联分析法确定各因素权重系数

利用灰色关联分析法原理，求得各港口船舶事故数序与各港口诸因素序列之间的灰色综合关联度，P_i 值最大的因素就是影响港口事故的主要因素。综合我国部分港口的统计数据得出港口船舶事故与其因素的灰色综合关联度：$P_1 = 0.594\ 1$；$P_2 = 0.655\ 0$；$P_3 = 0.538\ 5$；$P_4 = 0.598\ 9$；$P_5 = 0.696\ 5$；$P_6 = 0.604\ 9$；$P_7 = 0.553\ 3$；$P_8 = 0.621\ 7$；$P_9 = 0.539\ 5$；$P_{10} = 0.555\ 8$；$P_{11} = 0.539\ 9$[455]。

3.2 确定各因素权重系数

(1) 对各因素的综合关联度值进行归一化处理

由公式：$a_i = \dfrac{P_i}{\sum_{k=1}^{11} P_k}$ 可计算出：$a_1 = 0.091\ 4$；$a_2 = 0.100\ 8$；$a_3 = 0.082\ 9$；$a_4 = 0.092\ 3$；$a_5 = 0.107\ 2$；$a_6 = 0.093\ 1$；$a_7 = 0.085\ 1$；$a_8 = 0.095\ 7$；$a_9 = 0.083\ 0$；$a_{10} = 0.085\ 5$；$a_{11} = 0.083\ 1$ 为各因素的权重系数。

(2) 一级评价指标权重的确定

$$A_1' = \left(\frac{P_4}{P_4 + P_6}\ \frac{P_6}{P_4 + P_6} \right)$$

即：$A_1' = (0.497\ 5\quad 0.502\ 5)$

$$A_2' = \left(\frac{P_1}{P_1 + P_2 + P_3}\ \frac{P_2}{P_1 + P_2 + P_3}\ \frac{P_3}{P_1 + P_2 + P_3} \right)$$

即：$A_2' = (0.332\ 4\quad 0.366\ 4\quad 0.301\ 2)$

同理：

$$A_3' = (0.3322 \quad 0.2956 \quad 0.3722)$$
$$A_4' = (0.3299 \quad 0.3399 \quad 0.3302)$$

(3) 二级评价指标权重的确定

$$A' = \left(\frac{P_4 + P_6}{\sum_{k=1}^{11} P_k} \quad \frac{P_1 + P_2 + P_3}{\sum_{k=1}^{11} P_k} \quad \frac{P_5 + P_7 + P_8}{\sum_{k=1}^{11} P_k} \quad \frac{P_9 + P_{10} + P_{11}}{\sum_{k=1}^{11} P_k} \right)$$

即:$A' = (0.1854 \quad 0.2751 \quad 0.2880 \quad 0.2516)$

3.3 因子分析方法确定各因素权重系数

根据文献 1 中因子分析方法得到的各因素与事故数之间的关系,得出 11 个主要因素权重为:$Q_1 = 0.2110$;$Q_2 = 0.1413$;$Q_3 = 0.0885$;$Q_4 = 0.0473$;$Q_5 = 0.0697$;$Q_6 = 0$;$Q_7 = 0.0782$;$Q_8 = 0.0952$;$Q_9 = 0.1304$;$Q_{10} = 0.1383$;$Q_{11} = 0$。

(1) 一级评价指标权重

$A_1'' = (1 \quad 0)$;

$A_2'' = (0.4787 \quad 0.3205 \quad 0.2008)$;

$A_3'' = (0.3916 \quad 0.3217 \quad 0.2867)$;

$A_4'' = (0.4853 \quad 0.5147 \quad 0)$。

(2) 二级评价指标权重 $A'' = (0.0473 \quad 0.4408 \quad 0.2431 \quad 0.2687)$。

3.4 通航水域安全性评价的隶属度函数的各因素权重系数

综合灰色关联分析和因子分析得出的权重可算得各评价指标的权重,$A_i = (A_i' + A_i'')/2$ 可得一级评价指标权重为:

$A_1 = (0.7488 \quad 0.2512)$;

$A_2 = (0.4056 \quad 0.3434 \quad 0.2510)$;

$A_3 = (0.3619 \quad 0.3087 \quad 0.3294)$;

$A_4 = (0.4076 \quad 0.4273 \quad 0.1651)$。

二级评价指标权重为:

$A = (0.1164 \quad 0.3579 \quad 0.2655 \quad 0.2602)$。

4 模型的验证

根据本文建立的通航水域的评价隶属度函数和各因素的权重系数,组建水域安全评价模型,利用所掌握的各通航水域的指标数值,对模型进行验证。在此基础上,进行综合分析与评价,在进一步完善评价模型的同时,完善我国通航水域的评价方法。本文研究中所使用的数据是 2006 年在进行港口 VTS 论证时所收集的数据,并在此基础上,收集了验证评价模型的其他指标数据,如表 1 所示。

表 1　港口水域指标体系数值表

序号	水域	航道长	船宽/航道宽	能见度	大风	最大流	加权交通量	密度	交叉点	VTS管理	分道通航	助航标志
1	港口1	9.5	0.1	27	40.4	3	57.86	1.5	5	5	5	99.98
2	港口2	14	0.25	11.3	8.6	3	30.74	1.2	2	4.7	2.78	99.98
3	港口3	20.2	0.14	9.8	80.2	1.5	41.2	1.6	1	5	3.55	99.98
4	港口4	4.2	0.24	24.2	77.4	0.5	13.98	2.1	2	4.5	2.56	99.98
5	港口5	7.4	0.065	54	94.8	3	45.7	8.1	8	4.9	3.44	99.92
6	港口6	3.6	0.36	16.1	139	2.9	14	0.68	7	4.8	3.5	99.92
7	港口7	85.8	0.12	24.7	51.1	6	76.24	24.3	29	5	5	99.92
8	港口8	13.6	0.2	28	21.4	5	21.8	17.6	6	5	3.21	99.92
9	港口9	63.7	0.2	25	73.3	3.5	42	2.9	1.3	5	5	99.90
10	港口10	40.8	0.1	13.3	11.3	3.5	32.8	0.5	18	4.6	3.11	99.90

4.1　港口 1 的评价

港口 1 的因素集为：$U_1 = \{9.5\ \ 0.1\}$；$U_2 = \{27\ \ 40.4\ \ 3\}$；$U_3 = \{57.86\ \ 1.5\ \ 5\}$；$U_4 = \{5\ 5\ \ 99.98\}$。评价集为：$V = \{低(1); 较低(2); 中等(3); 较高(4); 高(5)\}$。先进行第一级的评价。港口 1 的各因素属于各评价集的隶属度函数为：

$$R_1 = \begin{pmatrix} 1 & 0.2639 & 0 & 0 & 0 \\ 0.875 & 0.625 & 0.125 & 0 & 0 \end{pmatrix}$$

$$R_2 = \begin{pmatrix} 0.2727 & 0.7727 & 0.7273 & 0.2273 & 0 \\ 0.7786 & 0.7214 & 0.2214 & 0 & 0 \\ 0.25 & 0.75 & 0.75 & 0.25 & 0 \\ 0.875 & 0.625 & 0.125 & 0 & 0 \end{pmatrix}$$

$$R_3 = \begin{pmatrix} 0 & 0.1214 & 0.6214 & 0.878 & 0.378 \\ 1 & 0.15 & 0 & 0 & 0 \\ 1 & 0.4167 & 0 & 0 & 0 \end{pmatrix}$$

$$R_4 = \begin{pmatrix} 1 & 0.5 & 0.3333 & 0.25 & 0.2 \\ 1 & 0.5 & 0.3333 & 0.25 & 0.2 \\ 1 & 0.025 & 0 & 0 & 0 \end{pmatrix}$$

根据上一节中得出的通航水域安全性评价的隶属度函数的各因素权重系数，进行第一级的评价 $B = A \circ R$，评价结果为：$B_1 = (0.9686\ \ 0.3546\ \ 0.0314\ \ 0\ \ 0)$；$B_2 = (0.4407\ \ 0.7494\ \ 0.5593\ \ 0.1549\ \ 0)$；$B_3 = (0.6381\ \ 0.2275\ \ 0.2249\ \ 0.3180\ \ 0.1370)$；$B_4 = (1\ \ 0.4216\ \ 0.2783\ \ 0.2087\ \ 0.1670)$。由第二级中各指标的权重为 $A = (0.1164\ \ 0.3579\ \ 0.2655\ \ 0.2602)$，得二级评价结果为：$B = A \circ R = (0.7001\ \ 0.4796\ \ 0.3359\ \ 0.1942\ \ 0.0798)$，利用加权平均法进行反模糊化过程如下：以 b_j 为权数，对评价集 v_j 进行加

权平均得到的值取为评判结果,即:

$$v = \sum_{j=1}^{m} b_j v_j / \sum_{j=1}^{m} b_j = 2.1473$$

根据评价集:$V = \{低(1),较低(2),中等(3),较高(4),高(5)\}$,建立如表2所示的评判结果与危险程度的对应关系:

对照表2,因$1.5 \leq V = 2.1473 < 2.5$,所以港口1水域属较低危险。

表2 评判结果与危险程度的对应关系

V的取值	$0 \leq V < 1.5$	$1.5 \leq V < 2.5$	$2.5 \leq V < 3.5$	$3.5 \leq V < 4.5$	$4.5 \leq V$
危险程度	低危险	较低危险	中等危险	较高危险	高危险

4.2 对所有港口进行评价

其他港口的评价和港口1的评价类似,综合上述评价结果,得出我国主要港口的评价结果,如表3所示。

表3 我国主要港口评价结果表

序号	水域	评价值V	评价结果(等级)
1	港口1	2.1473	较低
2	港口2	2.0759	较低
3	港口3	2.1031	较低
4	港口4	2.1861	较低
5	港口5	2.7197	中等
6	港口6	2.3196	较低
7	港口7	3.0261	中等
8	港口8	2.4170	较低
9	港口9	2.3769	较低
10	港口10	2.2694	较低

5 结语

根据在进行港口VTS论证时所收集的数据,得出如下结论:本文中所建立的模糊综合评判模型评价结果与实际港口的危险度基本相符,模型在综合VTS、助航设施等因素的基础上,能够对港口水域的航行及搁浅危险进行评价,可操作性很强,避免了在其他模糊综合评价中由于人为因素对通航水域安全性评价带来的偏差。

港口交通事故与其环境要素关系研究*

摘要:因子分析方法提取的主因子反映了大部分的原始信息,并且各个主因子之间彼此是不相关的。在应用因子分析方法分析全国九个港口环境要素数据的基础上,对各港口的综合因子得分与港口事故数进行线性回归分析,得到回归方程,通过回归方程中各要素系数确定各环境要素对港口交通事故的影响程度,结果表明:能见度、助航标志、VTS 管理程度和分道通航程度对交通安全影响较大,航道长度和交叉点数影响较小,基本上反映了各环境要素对港口交通事故的影响。这种分析方法可定量确定各环境要素对交通安全的影响,用于港口交通事故的原因分析、评价等。

关键词:因子分析方法;主因子;综合因子;港口环境要素;港口交通事故

港口安全系统的人、船、环境三子系统又各自包括许多要素,如环境子系统包括港口水文气象条件、航道的长度、转向点数、航道的宽度、船舶交通量、船舶交通密度、VTS 管理程度、分道通航程度、助航标志等。在目前的分析方法中,由于变量的个数太多,并且彼此之间存在着一定的相关性,分析所得的结果中信息有重复。而且要素太多,在管理中很难做到有的放矢,所以必须找出几个主因子来代表原来为数众多的要素,同时这些主因子应尽可能反映原要素的信息且彼此之间不相关。基于以上考虑,本文将因子分析方法应用于港口环境要素分析中,在反映原有资料大部分信息的前提下,提取几个主因子,减少了数据的相关性。在应用因子分析方法分析全国九个港口环境要素数据的基础上,对各港口的综合因子得分与港口事故数进行线性回归分析,得到回归方程,通过回归方程中各要素系数确定各环境要素对港口交通事故的影响程度。

1 因子分析的数学模型

设有一组相关变量,其原始数据为:

$$X_0 = \begin{pmatrix} x_{11} & x_{12} & \cdots & x_{1n} \\ x_{21} & x_{22} & \cdots & x_{2n} \\ \vdots & \vdots & \ddots & \vdots \\ x_{p1} & x_{p2} & \cdots & x_{pn} \end{pmatrix}$$

p 设为变量数,n 为样本数。

将原始数据经过标准化变换(变换方法如主成分分析方法所述),变换后的变量 x_{ij} 的均值

---

* 本文发表在 2005 年中国公路学会《第四届亚太可持续发展交通与环境技术大会论文集》。

为0,方差为1,这样相关矩阵 R 与协方差矩阵 S 就完全一样了。相关矩阵为 $R = XX^T$。其中 $X = \|x_{ij}\|$。

求解 R 矩阵的特征方程 $|R - \lambda I| = 0$,得出特征值 $\lambda_1 > \lambda_2 > \cdots > \lambda \geq 0$,令特征向量矩阵为:

$$U = \begin{pmatrix} u_{11} & u_{12} & \cdots & u_{1p} \\ u_{21} & u_{22} & \cdots & u_{2p} \\ \vdots & \vdots & \ddots & \vdots \\ u_{p1} & u_{p2} & \cdots & u_{pp} \end{pmatrix}$$

因而,$R = U \begin{pmatrix} \lambda_1 & & & 0 \\ & \lambda_2 & & \\ & & 0 & \\ 0 & & & \lambda_p \end{pmatrix} U$ 为正交阵,满足:$U^T U = UU^T = I$,即

$$XX^T = U \begin{pmatrix} \lambda_1 & & & 0 \\ & \lambda_2 & & \\ & & 0 & \\ 0 & & & \lambda_p \end{pmatrix} U^T$$

上式两边左乘以 U^T,右乘以 U,并令 $F = U^T X$,则 $FF' = \begin{pmatrix} \lambda_1 & & & 0 \\ & \lambda_2 & & \\ & & 0 & \\ 0 & & & \lambda_p \end{pmatrix}$,$F$ 就是主因子阵。

在因子分析中,一般只选 $m(m < P)$ 个主因子使所含信息量基本保持原有信息,例如使 $(\lambda_1 + \lambda_2 \Lambda + \lambda_m) / \sum\limits_{i=1}^{p} \lambda_i \geq 80\%$,因而 U 阵可剖成 $U = (\underset{p \times m}{U_{(1)}} \ \underset{p \times (p-m)}{U_{(2)}})$。将式 $F = U^T X$ 两端左乘 U 得出:

$$X = UF = (U_{(1)} \ U_{(2)}) \begin{pmatrix} F_{(1)} \\ F_{(2)} \end{pmatrix} = \underset{p \times m}{U_{(1)}} \underset{p \times m}{F_{(1)}} + \underset{p \times (p-m)}{U_{(2)}} \underset{p \times (p-m)}{F_{(2)}} = U_{(1)} F_{(1)} + \varepsilon$$

上式即因子模型,它可以用求出的主因子 $F_{(1)}$ 表达 X_0,ε 为残余部分。上式展开(忽略残余部分)为:

$$x_1 = u_{11} F_1 + u_{12} F_2 + \cdots + u_{1m} F_m$$
$$x_2 = u_{21} F_1 + u_{22} F_2 + \cdots + u_{2m} F_m$$
$$\vdots$$
$$x_p = u_{p1} F_1 + u_{p2} F_2 + \cdots + u_{pm} F_m$$

便是具体的表达式,它比主成分分析进了一步,可以得到 X 的表达式,这样更容易从经济或技术意义上进行解释。

特征向量通常须进行规格化处理

$$a_{ij} = u_{ij} \sqrt{\lambda_j}$$

$$A = \begin{pmatrix} a_{11} & a_{12} & \cdots & a_{1m} \\ a_{21} & a_{22} & \cdots & a_{2m} \\ \vdots & \vdots & \ddots & \vdots \\ a_{p1} & a_{p2} & \ddots & a_{pm} \end{pmatrix} = \begin{pmatrix} u_{11}\sqrt{\lambda_1} & u_{12}\sqrt{\lambda_2} & \cdots & u_{1m}\sqrt{\lambda_m} \\ u_{21}\sqrt{\lambda_1} & u_{22}\sqrt{\lambda_2} & \cdots & u_{2m}\sqrt{\lambda_m} \\ \vdots & \vdots & \ddots & \vdots \\ u_{p1}\sqrt{\lambda_1} & u_{p2}\sqrt{\lambda_1} & \cdots & u_{pm}\sqrt{\lambda_m} \end{pmatrix}$$

这样因子模型变成为：

$$x_1 = a_{11}F_1 + a_{12}F_2 + \cdots + a_{1m}F_m$$
$$x_2 = a_{21}F_1 + a_{22}F_2 + \cdots + a_{2m}F_m$$
$$\vdots$$
$$x_p = a_{p1}F_1 + a_{p2}F_2 + \cdots + a_{pm}F_m$$

$F_1, F_2, \cdots, F_m$ 叫主因子，a_{ij} 叫因子载荷，它是第 i 个变量在第 j 个主因子上的负荷，反映了第 i 个变量在第 j 个主因子上的相对重要性。A 叫作因子载矩阵，因此，a_{ij} 绝对值越大，则主因子和原有变量 j 的关系越强。对因子载荷矩阵进行回归分析可以计算出各个主因子得分函数：

$$\begin{cases} F_1 = b_{11}zx_1 + b_{12}zx_2 + \cdots + b_{1p}zx_p \\ F_2 = b_{21}zx_1 + b_{22}zx_2 + \cdots + b_{2p}zx_p \\ \vdots \\ F_m = b_{m1}zx_1 + b_{m2}zx_2 + \cdots + b_{mp}zx_p \end{cases}$$

其中，zx_i 为标准化得到的数据。

利用综合因子得分公式：$F = \sum_{i=1}^{m}[\lambda_i/(\lambda_1 + \lambda_2 + \cdots + \lambda_m)]F_i$，计算得出综合因子得分[2]。

2 港口船舶交通事故主致要素的因子分析

影响港口船舶交通事故的环境要素是比较多的，通过定性分析和专家咨询得到影响事故的环境要素序列，它们是：能见度（X_1：指通航水域近 5 年平均低于 1 km 的年累计天数，单位：天/年）、大风[X_2：指通航水域近 5 年风力达 6 级（蒲福风级）及以上的平均年累计发生天数与台风警报发生（即预计 48 h 内可以侵入通航水域或边缘距离通航水域只有 500 km 至台风警报消除为止，单位：天/年]、最大流（X_3：指被评价相应通航水域的最大流速值，单位：n mile/h）、主航道长度（X_4：指航道长度，单位：n mile）、交叉点和转向点数（X_5：指主航道与通航水深大于 1 m 的次航道的交叉角大于 25°的个数）、船舶宽度/航道宽度（X_6：船舶宽度是指特定通航水域允许通航船舶宽度的平均值，航道宽度为特定航道最窄处的宽度，单位：n mile）、船舶交通密度（X_7：指单位时间每平方海里的船舶数，单位：艘/n mile^2·h），船舶加权交通量（X_8：采用藤井弥平提出的加权系数将每天通航船舶艘数换算为标准船艘数，单位：艘/天）、VTS 管理程度（X_9：专家评分）、分道通航程度（X_{10}：专家评分）和助航标志（X_{10}：航标正常率）。原始数据如表 1 所示。

表1 评价通航水域及环境要素列表

水域	能见度 X_1	大风 X_2	最大流 X_3	航道长 X_4	交叉点 X_5	船宽/航道宽 X_6	密度 X_7	加权交通量 X_8	VIS管理 X_9	分道通航 X_{10}	助航标志 X_{11}	事故数 Y
港口1	27	40.4	3	9.5	5	0.1	1.5	57.86	5	5	99.98	29.2
港口2	11.3	8.6	3	14	2	0.25	1.2	30.74	4.7	4.18	99.98	3.2
港口3	9.8	80.2		20.2	1	0.14	1.6	41.2		4.55	99.8	4.8
港口4	24.2	77.4	0.5	4.2	2	0.24	2.1	13.98	4.5	4.06	99.98	6.4
港口5	54	94.8	3	7.4	8	0.065	8.1	45.7	4.9	4.44	99.92	39
港口6	16.1	139	2.9	3.6	7	0.36	0.68	14	4.8	4.50	99.92	23
港口7	28	21.4	5	13.6	6	0.2	17.6	21.8	5	4.21	99.92	3
港口8	25	73.3	3.5	63.7	1.3	0.2	2.9	42	5	5	99.90	37
港口9	13.3	11.3	3.5	40.8	18	0.1	0.5	32.8	4.6	4.11	99.90	40

使用SPSS统计软件SPSS 11.5正确输入原始数据,对原始数据($X_1 - X_{11}$)进行因子分析。对主成分法提取的初等因子载荷矩阵进行方差最大化正交旋转,旋转后的因子贡献及贡献率如表2所示,旋转后的因子载荷矩阵如表3所示。

表2 旋转后因子贡献及贡献率

	1	2	3	4	5
特征值	2.434 3	2.151 0	2.054 2	2.027 3	1.483 6
贡献率	22.129 7	19.554 3	18.674 6	18.430 0	13.487 7
累计贡献率	22.129 7	41.684 0	60.358 6	78.788 6	92.276 3

表3 旋转后因子载荷矩阵

	X_1	X_2	X_3	X_4	X_5	X_6	X_7	X_8	X_9	X_{10}	X_{11}
1	0.032 2	0.181 9	0.196 8	0.399 2	-0.541 3	-0.072 5	-0.013 0	0.591 3	0.847 8	0.913 9	0.008 3
2	0.031 0	-0.030 9	0.583 5	0.680 8	0.666 1	-0.079 5	0.040 6	-0.012 1	0.023 6	0.089 8	-0.940 6
3	0.528 2	-0.274 8	0.009 5	0.035 4	0.349 4	-0.955 6	0.011 5	0.776 5	0.151 7	0.187 4	0.042 1
4	0.522 5	-0.176 3	0.652 3	-0.265 7	0.008 9	-0.071 6	0.971 0	-0.103 1	0.421 5	-0.153 4	-0.259 4
5	0.576 7	0.909 2	-0.318 5	-0.336 3	-0.058 6	0.136 0	-0.026 1	-0.122 9	0.034 8	0.180 5	-0.195 9

通过表2提取了5个主因子,它们反映了原始数据的大部分信息(92.28%)。表3表明了各个主因子同原始变量的相关性:第一个主因子基本上反映了VTS管理程度(X_9)、分道通航程度(X_{10});第二个主因子反映了主航道长度(X_4)、交叉点和转向点数(X_5)、助航标志(X_{11});第三个主因子反映了最大流(X_3)和船舶交通密度(X_7);第四个主因子反映了能见度(X_1)、船宽/航道宽度(X_6)和船舶加权交通量(X_8);第五个主因子反映了大风(X_2)。

根据因子得分矩阵(如表4所示),计算各个主因子的得分,因子得分如表5所示,最后得出各个港口的综合因子得分,结果如表6所示。

表4 因子得分矩阵

	X_1	X_2	X_3	X_4	X_5	X_6	X_7	X_8	X_9	X_{10}	X_{11}
1	-0.0952	0.0696	0.0968	0.1901	-0.2942	0.0935	-0.0123	0.1660	0.3558	0.3752	0.0181
2	-0.0230	0.1026	0.1889	0.3468	0.3220	0.0315	-0.1009	-0.0507	-0.0510	0.0645	-0.4726
3	0.2897	-0.0999	-0.1229	-0.0759	0.2294	-0.5022	-0.0668	0.3491	-0.0631	-0.0037	0.0772
4	0.2130	-0.1123	0.2917	-0.2165	-0.0964	0.0355	0.5180	-0.1098	0.2061	-0.1208	-0.0189
5	0.4217	0.6167	-0.2102	-0.1829	0.0750	0.0290	-0.0561	-0.0626	-0.0297	0.1035	-0.2110

表5 因子得分

	港口1	港口2	港口3	港口4	港口5	港口6	港口7	港口8	港口9
F_1	0.9841	-0.3129	0.7573	-1.2702	-0.2928	-0.1044	-0.1145	1.6891	-1.3356
F_2	-0.7454	-0.8174	-0.9149	-1.1512	0.0900	0.4966	0.1336	1.2189	1.6899
F_3	1.2062	-0.5387	0.0765	-0.4229	1.5350	-1.6121	-0.5900	-0.4216	0.7675
F_4	-0.2123	-0.1860	-0.6755	-0.5987	0.8437	-0.3020	2.3430	-0.4078	-0.8043
F_5	-0.2908	-1.3422	-0.2198	0.5910	1.5542	1.3655	-0.7462	0.0257	-0.9374

表6 综合因子得分

	港口1	港口2	港口3	港口4	港口5	港口6	港口7	港口8	港口9
综合因子得分 F	0.2373	-0.5906	-0.1638	-0.6673	0.6552	-0.1068	0.2403	0.5004	-0.1046
事故数 Y	29.2	3.2	4.8	6.4	39	23	3	37	40

根据表6列出的九个港口的综合因子得分,利用SPSS 11.5 中的 Bivariate 过程分析港口综合得分与港口事故数之间的关系。在显著水平为0.05的情况下,测得综合因子得分 F 与事故数 Y 之间的相关系数为0.646,表明两者之间存在中度相关关系。

以港口综合得分 F 为目变量,港口事故数 Y 为因变量,调用 SPSS 11.5 中的线性回归(Linear Regression)分析过程对两者进行线性回归分析,回归方程为:

$$Y = 20.622 + 23.291F$$

将单因子得分函数和综合因子得分公式代入回归方程得到标准化后变量与事故数之间的关系式:

$$Y = 20.622 + 3.15zx_1 + 2zx_2 + 1.53zx_3 + 0.79zx_4 + 0.83zx_5 - 1.43zx_6$$
$$+ 1.34zx_7 + 1.6zx_8 + 2.3zx_9 + 2.19zx_{10} - 2.67zx_{11}$$

由以上求得方程因素系数绝对值可知各个因素对事故的影响程度:

$$X_1 > X_{11} > X_9 > X_{10} > X_2 > X_8 > X_3 > X_6 > X_7 > X_5 > X_4$$

通过分析我国9个港口11个环境要素同船舶事故数之间的关系,能见度、助航标志、VTS管理程度和分道通航程度对事故影响较大,航道长度和交叉点数的影响较小。由此可见,助航标志正常率、VTS 管理程度和分道通航程度等环境要素在避免交通事故过程中起到了很大的作用,今后应进一步加强管理的作用。同时,能见度不良对港口交通事故的发生有很大影响,在以后工作中,应加强能见度不良情况下的安全管理。本方法的分析结果对主管部门的近期、中长期规划也可以起到指导作用：及时获取上一年度和近五年的环境要素数据，可以有针对性地制定下一年度和未来五年的工作重点。

3 结语

本文引入了一种基于因子分析方法确定水域环境要素对事故影响程度的方法，这种方法在反映大部分原始数据的前提下，避免了各个要素之间的相关性，为科学合理地确定各个要素对事故的影响程度提供了一种新的方法。由于选取的港口数量有限，综合因子得分与事故数之间的相关性不是很强，如果选取的样本数量增多，结果会更加合理。

港口交通事故与环境要素关系[*]

摘要：为了评价港口交通环境的安全性,合理确定各环境要素的权重,在应用因子分析方法分析全国9个港口环境要素数据的基础上,对各港口的综合因子得分与港口事故数进行线性回归,得到回归方程,通过回归方程中各要素系数确定各环境要素对港口交通事故的影响程度。分析结果表明:能见度、助航标志、VTS管理程度和分道通航程度对交通安全的影响较大,航道长度和交叉点数的影响较小,基本上反映了各环境要素对港口交通事故的影响程度,可见因子分析方法可定量确定各环境要素对交通安全的影响,可用于港口交通事故的原因分析与评价。

关键词：海上交通安全；港口交通事故；港口环境要素；因子分析方法；主因子

0 引言

港口安全系统的人、船、环境三个子系统又各自包括许多要素,如环境子系统包括:港口水文气象条件、航道长度、转向点数、航道的宽度、船舶交通量、船舶交通密度、VTS管理程度、分道通航程度、助航标志等[456]。在目前的分析方法中,由于变量的个数太多,并且彼此之间存在着一定的相关性,分析所得的结果中信息有重复,而且要素太多,在管理中很难做到有的放矢,所以必须找出几个主因子来代表原来为数众多的要素,主因子应尽可能反映原要素的信息而彼此之间不相关。基于以上考虑,本文将因子分析方法应用于港口环境要素分析中,在反映原有资料大部分信息的前提下,提取几个主因子,减少了数据的相关性[457]。在应用因子分析方法分析全国9个港口环境要素数据的基础上,对各港口的综合因子得分与港口事故数进行线性回归分析,得到回归方程,通过回归方程中各要素系数确定各环境要素对港口交通事故的影响程度。

1 因子分析数学模型

设有一组相关变量,其原始数据为:

$$X_0 = \begin{pmatrix} x_{11} & x_{12} & \cdots & x_{1n} \\ x_{21} & x_{22} & \cdots & x_{2n} \\ \vdots & \vdots & \ddots & \vdots \\ x_{p1} & x_{p2} & \cdots & x_{pn} \end{pmatrix}$$

---

[*] 本文发表在《交通运输工程学报》2006年第1卷,作者郑中义、黄忠国、吴兆麟。

p 设为变量数,n 为样本数。

将原始数据经过标准化变换(变换方法如主成分分析方法所述),变换后的变量 x_{ij} 的均值为 0,方差为 1,这样相关矩阵 R 与协方差矩阵 S 就完全一样了。相关矩阵为:

$$R = XX^T$$

式中:X 为原始数据经过标准变化后的变量所组成的矩阵。求解 R 矩阵的特征方程

$$|R - \lambda I| = 0$$

得出特征值 $\lambda_1 > \lambda_2 > \cdots > \lambda_p \geq 0$,令特征向量矩阵为:

$$U = \begin{pmatrix} u_{11} & u_{12} & \cdots & u_{1p} \\ u_{21} & u_{22} & \cdots & u_{2p} \\ \vdots & \vdots & \ddots & \vdots \\ u_{p1} & u_{p2} & \cdots & u_{pp} \end{pmatrix}$$

因而,$R = U \begin{pmatrix} \lambda_1 & & & 0 \\ & \lambda_2 & & \\ & & \ddots & \\ 0 & & & \lambda_p \end{pmatrix} U^T$ 为正交阵,满足:$U^T U = U U^T = I$,即

$$XX^T = U \begin{pmatrix} \lambda_1 & & & 0 \\ & \lambda_2 & & \\ & & \ddots & \\ 0 & & & \lambda_p \end{pmatrix} U^T$$

上式两边左乘以 U^T,右乘以 U,并令 $F = U^T X$ 则:

$$FF' = \begin{pmatrix} \lambda_1 & & & 0 \\ & \lambda_2 & & \\ & & \ddots & \\ 0 & & & \lambda_p \end{pmatrix}$$

F 就是主因子阵。

在因子分析中,一般只选 $m (m < P)$ 个主因子使所含信息量基本保持原有信息,例如使

$$(\lambda_1 + \lambda_2 \Lambda + \lambda_m) / \sum_{i=1}^{p} \lambda_i \geq 80\%$$

因而 U 阵可剖成 $U = [U^1_{p \times m} \quad U^2_{p \times (p-m)}]$。

将 $F = U^T X$ 两端左乘 U 得出

$$X = UF = (U^1 \quad U^2) \begin{pmatrix} F^a \\ F^b \end{pmatrix} = U^1_{p \times m} F^a_{p \times m} +$$

$$U^2_{p \times (p-m)} F^b_{p \times (p-m)} = U^1 F^a + \varepsilon$$

上式即因子模型,它可以用求出的主因子得分矩阵 F^a 表达 X,ε 为残余部分。上式展开(忽略残余部分)为:

$$x_1 = u_{i1} F_1 + u_{i2} F_2 + \cdots + u_{im} F_m (i = 1, 2, \cdots, p)$$

便是具体的表达式,它比主成分分析进了一步,可以得到 X 的表达式,这样更容易从经济或技

术意义上进行解释。

特征向量通常须进行规格化处理

$$a_{ij} = u_{ij}\sqrt{\lambda_j}$$

$$A = \begin{pmatrix} a_{11} & a_{12} & \cdots & a_{1m} \\ a_{21} & a_{22} & \cdots & a_{2m} \\ \vdots & \vdots & \ddots & \vdots \\ a_{p1} & a_{p2} & \cdots & a_{pm} \end{pmatrix} = \begin{pmatrix} u_{11}\sqrt{\lambda_1} & u_{12}\sqrt{\lambda_2} & \cdots & u_{1m}\sqrt{\lambda_m} \\ u_{21}\sqrt{\lambda_1} & u_{22}\sqrt{\lambda_2} & \cdots & u_{2m}\sqrt{\lambda_m} \\ \vdots & \vdots & \ddots & \vdots \\ u_{p1}\sqrt{\lambda_1} & u_{p2}\sqrt{\lambda_1} & \cdots & u_{pm}\sqrt{\lambda_m} \end{pmatrix}$$

这样因子模型变成为:

$$x_i = u_{i1}F_1 + u_{i2}F_2 + \cdots + u_{im}F_m (i = 1,2,\cdots,p)$$

$F_1, F_2, \cdots, F_m$ 叫主因子,a_{ij} 叫因子载荷,它是第 i 个变量在第 j 个主因子上的负荷,反映了第 i 个变量在第 j 个主因子上的相对重要性。A 叫作因子载矩阵,因此,a_{ij} 绝对值越大,则主因子凡和原有变量 j 的关系越强。对因子载荷矩阵进行回归分析可以计算出各个主因子得分函数:

$$F_i = b_{i1}zx_1 + b_{i2}zx_2 + \cdots + b_{ip}zx_p (i = 1,2,\cdots m)$$

式中:zx_i 为标准化后的数据。综合因子得分为[458-461]:

$$F = \sum_{i=1}^{m} [\lambda_i/(\lambda_1 + \lambda_2 + \cdots + \lambda_m)]F_i$$

2 港口船舶交通事故主致要素分析

通过定性分析和专家咨询得到影响事故的环境要素序列:能见度 x_1:指通航水域近 5 年平均低于 1 km 的年累计天数/($d \cdot a^{-1}$),大风 x_2:指通航水域近 5 年风力达 6 级(蒲福风级)及以上的平均年累计发生天数与台风警报发生,即预计 48 h 内可以侵入通航水域或边缘距离通航水域只有 500 km 至台风警报消除为止)的年累计天数之和/($d \cdot a^{-1}$);最大流 x_3:指被评价相应通航水域的最大流速值/n mile $\cdot h^{-1}$;主航道长度 x_4/(n mile);交叉点和转向点数 x_5:指主航道与通航水深大于 1 m 的次航道的交叉角大于 25°的个数;船宽/航道宽度 x_6:船舶宽度是指特定通航水域允许通航船舶宽度的平均值,航道宽度为特定航道最窄处的宽度;船舶交通密度 x_7:指单位时间每平方海里的船舶数/[ship $\cdot$ (n mile^{2}h)]$^{-1}$;船舶加权交通量 x_8:采用藤井弥平提出的加权系数[458-461]将每天通航船舶艘数换算为标准船艘数/(ship $\cdot d^{-1}$);VTS 管理程度 x_9:由专家评分得出;分道通航程度 x_{10}:由专家评分得出;助航标志正常率 x_{11}。要素原始数据如表 1 所示[452]。

使用 SPSS 统计软件 SPSS 11.5 正确输入原始数据,对原始数据($x_1 - x_{11}$)进行因子分析。对主成分法提取的初等因子载荷矩阵进行方差最大化正交旋转,旋转后的因子贡献及贡献率见表 2,旋转后的因子载荷矩阵见表 3。

表 1　原始数据

港口序号	x_1	x_2	x_3	x_4	x_5	x_6	x_7	x_8	x_9	x_{10}	x_{11}	Y
1	27.00	40.40	3.00	9.50	5.00	0.10	1.50	57.86	5.00	5.00	99.98	29.20
2	11.30	8.60	3.00	14.00	2.00	0.25	1.20	30.74	4.70	4.18	99.98	3.20
3	9.80	80.20	1.50	20.00	1.00	0.14	1.60	41.20	5.00	4.55	99.98	4.80
4	24.20	77.40	0.50	4.20	2.00	0.24	2.10	13.98	4.50	4.06	99.98	6.40
5	54.00	94.80	3.00	7.40	8.00	0.07	8.10	45.70	4.90	4.44	99.92	39.00
6	16.10	139.00	2.90	3.60	7.00	0.36	0.68	14.00	4.80	4.50	99.92	23.00
7	28.00	21.40	5.00	13.60	6.00	0.20	17.60	21.80	5.00	4.21	99.92	3.00
8	25.00	73.30	3.50	63.70	1.30	0.20	2.90	42.00	5.00	5.00	99.90	37.00
9	13.30	11.30	3.50	40.80	18.00	0.10	0.50	32.80	4.60	4.11	99.90	40.00

表 2　旋转后因子贡献及贡献率

	1	2	3	4	5
特征值	2.434 3	2.151 0	2.054 2	2.027 3	1.483 6
贡献率	22.129 7	19.554 3	18.674 6	18.430 0	13.487 7
累计贡献率	22.129 7	41.684 0	60.358 6	78.788 6	92.276 3

表 3　因子载荷矩阵

	x_1	x_2	x_3	x_4	x_5	x_6	x_7	x_8	x_9	x_{10}	x_{11}
1	0.032 2	0.181 9	0.196 8	0.399 2	-0.541 3	-0.072 5	-0.013 0	0.591 3	0.847 8	0.913 9	0.008 3
2	0.031 0	-0.030 9	0.583 5	0.680 8	0.666 1	-0.079 5	0.040 6	-0.012 1	0.023 6	0.089 8	-0.940 6
3	0.528 2	-0.274 8	0.009 5	0.035 4	0.349 4	-0.955 6	0.011 5	0.776 5	0.151 7	0.187 4	0.042 1
4	0.522 5	-0.176 3	0.652 3	-0.265 7	0.008 9	-0.071 6	0.971 0	-0.103 1	0.421 5	-0.153 4	-0.259 4
5	0.576 7	0.909 2	-0.318 5	-0.336 3	-0.058 6	0.136 0	-0.026 1	-0.122 9	0.034 6	0.180 5	-0.195 9

通过表 2 提取 5 个主因子，它们反映了原始数据的大部分信息(92.28%)。表 3 表明了各个主因子同原始变量的相关性：第 1 个主因子基本上反映了 VTS 管理程度(x_9)、分道通航程度(x_{10})；第 2 个主因子反映了主航道长度(x_4)、交叉点和转向点数(x_5)、助航标志(x_{11})；第 3 个主因子反映了能见度(x_1)、船宽/航道宽度(x_6)和船舶加权交通量(x_8)；第 4 个主因子反映了最大流(x_3)和船舶交通密度(x_7)；第 5 个主因子反映了大风(x_2)。

根据因子得分矩阵(如表 4 所示)，计算各个主因子的得分，因子得分如表 5 所示，最后得出各个港口的综合因子得分，结果如表 6 所示。

表4　因子得分矩阵

	x_1	x_2	x_3	x_4	x_5	x_6	x_7	x_8	x_9	x_{10}	x_{11}
1	-0.0952	0.0696	0.0968	0.1901	-0.2942	0.0935	-0.0123	0.1660	0.3558	0.3752	0.0181
2	-0.0230	0.1026	0.1889	0.3468	0.3220	0.0315	-0.1009	-0.0507	-0.0510	0.0645	-0.4726
3	0.2897	-0.0999	-0.1229	-0.0759	0.2294	-0.5022	-0.0668	0.3491	-0.0631	-0.0037	0.0772
4	0.2130	-0.1123	0.2917	-0.2165	-0.0964	0.0355	0.5180	-0.1090	0.2061	-0.1208	-0.0189
5	0.4217	0.6167	-0.2102	-0.1829	0.0750	0.0290	-0.0561	-0.0626	-0.0297	0.1035	-0.2110

表5　因子得分

港口序号	1	2	3	4	5	6	7	8	9
F_1	0.9841	-0.3129	0.7573	-1.2702	-0.2928	-0.1044	-0.1145	1.6891	-1.3356
F_2	-0.7454	-0.8174	-0.9149	-1.1512	0.0900	0.4966	0.1336	1.2189	1.6899
F_3	1.2062	-0.5387	0.0765	-0.4229	1.5350	-1.6121	-0.5900	-0.4216	0.7675
F_4	-0.2123	-0.1860	-0.6755	-0.5987	0.8437	-0.3020	2.3430	-0.4078	-0.8043
F_5	-0.2908	-1.3422	-0.2198	0.5910	1.5542	1.3655	-0.7462	0.0257	-0.9374

表6　综合因子得分

	港口1	港口2	港口3	港口4	港口5	港口6	港口7	港口8	港口9
综合因子得分 F	0.2373	-0.5906	-0.1638	-0.6673	0.6552	-0.1068	0.2403	0.5004	-0.1046
事故数 Y	29.20	3.20	4.80	6.40	39.00	23.00	3.00	37.00	40.00

根据因子得分矩阵(如表4所示),计算各个主因子的得分,因子得分如表5所示,最后得出各个港口的综合因子得分,根据表6列出的9个港口的综合因子得分,利用SPSS 11.5中的Bivariate过程分析港口综合得分与港口事故数之间的关系。在显著水平为0.05的情况下,测得综合因子得分F与事故数Y之间的相关系数为0.646,表明两者之间存在中度相关关系。以港口综合得分F为目变量,港口事故数Y为因变量,调用SPSS 11.5中的线性回归(Linear Regression)分析过程对两者进行线性回归分析,回归方程为

$$Y = 20.622 + 23.291F$$

将单因子得分函数和综合因子得分公式代入回归方程得到标准化后变量与事故数之间的关系式:

$$Y = 20.622 + 3.15zx_1 + 2zx_2 + 1.53zx_3 + 0.79zx_4 + 0.83zx_5 - 1.43zx_6$$
$$+ 1.34zx_7 + 1.6zx_8 + 2.3zx_9 + 2.19zx_{10} + -2.67x_{11}$$

由以上求得方程因素系数绝对值可知各个因素对事故的影响程度:

$$x_1 > x_{11} > x_9 > x_{10} > x_2 > x_8 > x_3 > x_6 > x_7 > x_5 > x_4$$

通过分析我国9个港口11个环境要素同船舶事故数之间的关系,能见度、助航标志、VTS管理程度和分道通航程度对事故影响较大,航道长度和交叉点数影响较小。由此可见,助航标志正常率、VTS管理程度和分道通航程度等环境要素在避免交通事故过程中起到了很大的作

用,今后应进一步加强管理发挥更大的作用。同时,能见度不良对港口交通事故的发生有很大影响,在以后工作中,应加强能见度不良情况下的安全管理。本方法的分析结果对主管部门的近期、中长期规划也可以起到指导作用:及时获取上一年度和近5年的环境要素数据,可以有针对性地制定下一年度和未来5年的工作重点。

3 结语

本文引入了一种基于因子分析方法确定水域环境要素对事故影响程度的方法,这种方法在反映大部分原始数据的前提下,避免了各个要素之间的相关性,为科学合理地确定各个要素对事故的影响程度提供了一种新的方法。由于选取的港口数量有限,综合因子得分与事故数之间的相关性不是很强,如果选取的数量增大,结果会更加合理。

客滚船船龄与船舶事故关系研究*

摘要：为对中韩客货班轮运输安全管理中船龄进行控制，本文研究了客滚船船龄与船舶事故之间的关系，对我国、英国 MAIB-UK、加拿大 TSB 及日本 NKSMC 统计的客滚船事故报告中当时船龄进行了调查和统计。得出为更好地减少客滚船事故，船龄超过 25 年的客滚船应尽量改做其他用途的船，客滚船船龄应控制在 25 年左右的结论。

关键词：船龄；老旧运输船舶；MAIB；TSB

0 引言

自 1990 年 9 月 15 日威海威东航运有限公司率先以中韩合资经营的方式开通了第一条中韩客货班轮航线以来，中韩两国之间的经济交流日益频繁，双边经贸合作迅猛发展，两国的货物进出口量也随之快速增长，中韩海运市场上至今经营集装箱班轮航线的中国公司有 17 家，船舶 37 艘，经营客货班轮的公司有 14 家，船舶 15 艘。当前 14 家中韩客货班轮公司的管理水平参差不齐，船舶状况也不容乐观，渐趋老化，有的船舶船龄已达 27 年之久。为保证客滚船安全营运，中韩海运协会会谈多次，对客滚船船龄进行了探讨。本研究是对中韩客货班轮运输市场的船舶安全管理现状进行调研，在此基础上，提出客滚船运输安全管理中船龄的控制。

1 我国关于老旧运输船舶的相关规定

船龄，是指船舶自建造完工之日起至现今的年限。自 2006 年 8 月 1 日起施行的《老旧运输船舶管理规定》对船舶购置、光租、改建管理、船舶营运管理、监督和处罚做了明确规定。该规定还对购置、光租外国籍船舶的船龄、特别定期检验船龄、强制报废船龄做了明确规定，具体规定如表 1 所示。其中，第四条对老旧客滚船有以下规定：船龄在 10 年以上的客滚船、客货船、客渡船、客货渡船（包括旅客列车轮渡）、旅游船、客船，为二类老旧海船。

---

* 本文发表在《2008 年船舶安全管理理论文集》，作者李红喜、郑中义、李猛。

表1 老旧运输船舶定理规定

船舶类别	购置、光租外国籍船舶船龄	特别定期检验船龄	强制报废船龄
一类船舶	10年以下	18年以上	25年以上
二类船舶	10年以下	24年以上	30年以上
三类船舶	12年以下	26年以上	31年以上
四类船舶	18年以下	28年以上	33年以上
五类船舶	20年以下	29年以上	34年以上

按此规定客滚船属于二类老旧海船,应该强制报废船龄为30年。根据《老旧运输船舶管理规定》,达到规定的老旧运输船舶船龄的运输船舶,应申请特别定期检验。完成特别定期检验,一律换发船舶检验证书,并注明下一次特别定期检验的日期,有效期均为一年。

2 客滚船船龄与事故之间的关系

为研究客滚船船龄与事故之间的关系,对英国MAIB-UK、加拿大TSB、日本海岸警备队报告统计发生事故的客滚船船龄进行了分析研究。

2.1 英国 MAIB-UK 客滚船船龄与事故关系

MAIB(Marine Accident Investigation Branch)-UK 英国船舶事故调查局,MAIB的管理目标是增进海上安全。调查事故,找出事故发生的原因和环境条件;提出安全管理建议,减少同类事故的发生等。MAIB对2000年至2006年roro(roll-on/roll-off ship)客滚船事故进行了调查,根据这些报告统计了英国近15年来的客滚船船龄与事故之间的关系如表2所示[463]。

表2 MAIB 客滚船事故与当时船龄

船龄(年)	0~4	5~9	10~14	15~19	20~24	25~30
事故数(件)	4	4	3	1	5	7

根据 MAIB 中自2000年到2006年的24起客滚船事故,对船龄进行了分时间段统计如表3所示,它们之间的关系如图1所示。

从图1可以看出,船龄在20年以上的客滚船发生事故的概率呈明显上升的趋势,30年以上的客滚船发生事故的概率最大。

2.2 加拿大 TSB 客滚船船龄与事故关系

TSB(The Transportation Safety Board)加拿大运输安全委员会,是在1990年3月29日,由《加拿大运输事故调查和安全委员会法案》成立。该委员会的任务是对海上、管道、铁道和航空4种形式的运输事故进行独立的调查或公开听证会。本文对TSB自1990年到2005年公布的客滚船事故进行了统计与分析,如表3所示。

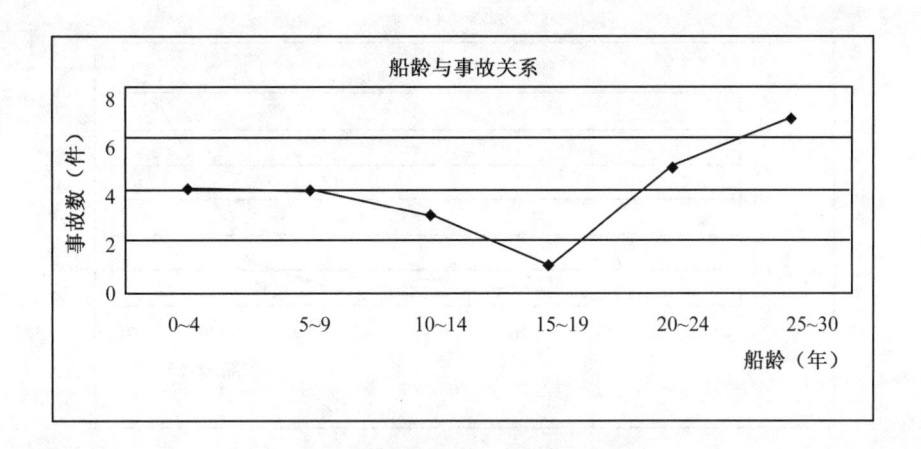

图1 客滚船船龄与事故关系

表3 1990年到2005年加拿大客滚船船龄与事故统计

年份	0~4年	5~9年	10~14年	15~19年	20~24年	25~29年	30+年	未知船龄
1990	1	0	4	1	1	2	3	3
1991	0	0	0	1	0	3	6	0
1992	0	0	0	0	1	0	3	1
1993	0	0	1	0	0	2	4	2
1994	0	0	1	0	0	2	3	2
1995	0	0	0	0	0	1	5	1
1996	0	0	0	0	0	1	6	0
1997	0	0	0	1	0	0	6	0
1998	0	1	0	0	0	2	5	0
1999	1	0	0	0	1	0	2	1
2000	0	0	0	0	1	0	3	0
2001	1	1	0	0	1	0	4	0
2002	1	0	0	0	0	0	3	4
2003	0	0	0	0	0	0	2	2
2004	0	0	0	0	0	0	1	0
2005	0	0	0	0	0	0	1	1
总计	4	2	6	3	5	13	57	17

加拿大TSB统计的客滚船事故报告中船龄与事故数之间的关系如图2所示：

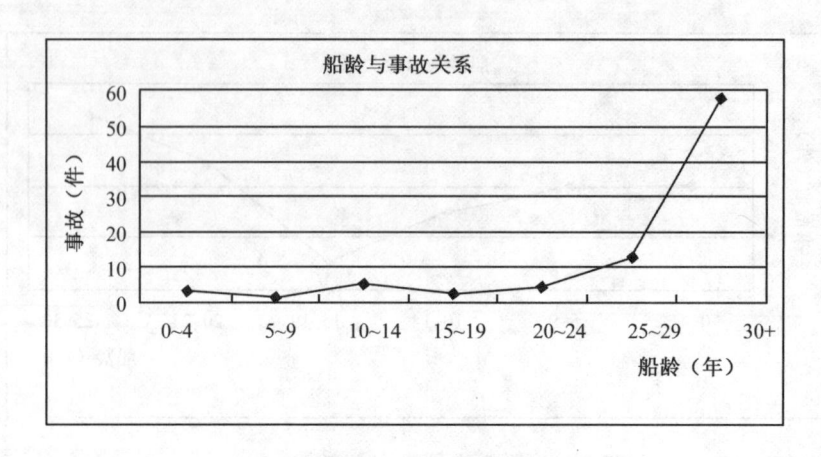

图2 客滚船船龄与事故关系

从图2可以看出,船龄在20年以上的客滚船发生事故的概率呈明显上升的趋势,30年以上的客滚船发生事故的概率最大。

2.3 日本船舶处分率与船龄关系

从1999年到2002年,NKSMC船受到ISM处分的艘数和处分率,按船龄分布如表4及图3所示。

表4 1999年至2002年NKSMC处分的船舶艘数与船龄统计

船龄	ISM处分艘数				NKSMC处分艘数			
	1999年	2000年	2001年	2002年	1999年	2000年	2001年	2002年
0~4	4	7	10	27	739	779	848	959
5~9年	7	9	19	29	544	609	690	952
10~14年	14	8	5	15	394	378	342	471
15~19年	17	17	22	49	427	442	486	510
20~24年	16	15	13	21	313	306	315	369
25年以上	2	3	6	10	124	150	121	186

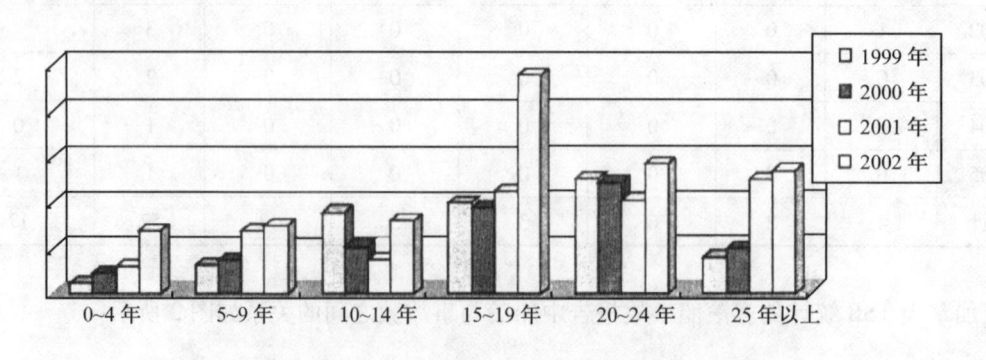

图3 1999年至2002年NKSMC处分的船舶艘数与船龄统训

整体上来看,随着船龄的增加处分率也增加,这种情况每年都是相同的,整体上的处分率在这4年期间呈增长趋势。

3 结论

从以上分析可得出,船龄在20年以下的客滚船发生事故的概率没有明显变化。20~24年以上船龄的客滚船,事故数呈明显上升的趋势;25~29年以上船龄的客滚船事故发生概率最大,随着船龄的增加,事故数上升的趋势也最快。为保证旅客生命安全和财产免受损失,我国《老旧运输船舶管理规定》对客滚船强制报废船龄为30年是正确的。从以上发生事故的船舶船龄分析,为更好地减少客滚船事故,船龄超过25年的客滚船应尽量改做其他用途的船,客滚船船龄应控制在25年左右。中韩海运在第三次和第四次的会谈中双方约定新投入中韩航线营运的客货船的船龄原则上应不超过20年,对超过此船龄的船舶需经双方协商同意后方可投入营运,为保证旅客和货物安全,这项规定是很有必要的。本文研究得出,中韩航线上营运的客滚船最大船龄不应超过25年。

海上搜救模拟中的可视化灾难再现模型研究*

摘要:为进一步提高海上搜救模拟系统的模拟搜救效果,本文采用了系统建模的手段建立航空器的灾难再现模型。在模拟系统的开发中,采用外部因素和内部因素相结合的方法分析航空器遇难原因,生成模型,并根据真实情况设定其发生概率。同时在模拟系统中还进行了通信系统模型的研究,采用Socket通信技术、音视频编码技术、音视频数据的网络传输技术建立通信系统模型,实现了系统间的文字及语音信息的基本传输,使得该系统从整体上语音结合,效果逼真,为真实的海上搜救提供了宝贵的数据。

关键词:海上搜救;智能;模拟;信息通信

0 引言

随着我国经济、贸易的发展和海洋开发战略的实施,远洋运输、捕捞、海上石油勘探等活动日益频繁,发生水上险情和事故的频率也在不断增大,引起了国家和社会对海上交通安全的广泛关注。目前,我国已经建立了中国海上搜救中心、各省级搜救中心以及分中心的三级海上应急救援体系和海上险情应急反应预案,并举行了多次海上搜救演习。但由于实战训练周期长、消耗大,并且可能发生状态失控,造成不必要的人员伤亡,因此,采用计算机模拟进行海上搜救的训练模式则成了提高海上搜救能力的重要训练途径。今年,政府尤其提出从实战演练方式向计算机模拟救援训练转化,向数字化救援训练转化。为此,国家有关海上安全部门与大连海事大学多学科联合攻关,试图解决海上搜救数字化模拟中的关键技术。本文主要以随机模拟的理论为基础,对海上航空器的模拟飞行以及模拟遇难的建模过程进行了分析及研究,同时探讨模拟系统中的通信理论与方法,增强了模拟的逼真效果,实现了灾难再现建模方法中的若干关键技术的突破。

1 航空器灾难发生模型

1.1 航空器灾难发生过程

航空器遇难模拟模型以航空器飞行模拟模型的状态输出作为本模型的状态输入,根据本模型计算后,产生模型的状态输出到航空器待救模型中[464]。灾难发生模型采取先发生灾难,

---

* 本文发表在《郑州大学学报》(理学版)2008年第3期第40卷,作者林国顺、马红、郑中义、郭栋。

后寻找原因的方法,即先根据一定的概率使灾难发生,然后再根据各种情况概率的大小来判断原因。可以将这个过程分为两个阶段:灾难发生阶段和灾难原因产生阶段。同时航空器的各个模块的状态根据灾难的影响发生变化,产生事故情况描述。

(1)灾难发生阶段

这一阶段主要解决的问题是航空器的灾难是如何产生的。根据航空器灾难发生模型产生灾难,决定航空器灾难的等级。

(2)灾难原因产生阶段

这一阶段主要解决的问题是航空器灾难的原因是什么。根据航空器灾难原因产生模型判断灾难的原因,并根据原因判断航空器的损坏情况,为以后的航空器待救模型提供状态输入。

1.2 航空器灾难原因产生模型

引发空难的原因是多种多样的,任何小的故障和疏忽都有可能造成灾难的发生。根据多年来的数据统计发现,引发空难的原因主要有三种:机械故障、天气原因和人为因素。因为任何一起空难的发生都是由多种原因共同作用的结果,本文考虑到将全部原因加入系统中并不现实,因此在海上航空器遇难模型中将航空器灾难发生因子简化为内部因素和外部因素,内部因素主要考虑机械故障与人为因素的影响,外部因素主要考虑天气原因的影响,灾难的发生是内部因素与外部因素共同作用的结果。

1.2.1 航空器遇难的外部因素

航空器遇难的外部因素,主要考虑天气状况的影响。天气是空难发生的一个重要因素,风、雨、雪、雾等天气状况都可能引起航空器灾难的发生。

在灾难发生模型中,天气因素主要考虑大风、雷雨、多雾、晴这四种情况构成一个集合空间 $W(wind, storm, fog, fine)$,其中 wind 代表大风因素,storm 代表雷雨因素,fog 代表多雾因素,fine 代表晴因素。假设天气状况只可能是规定的因素。

定义外部因素的集合空间 $w \in W(wind, storm, fog, fine)$,其中 w 代表当前的天气类型,它是属于集合空间 $W(wind, storm, fog, fine)$ 的一个元素[465]。

1.2.2 航空器遇难的内部因素

航空器遇难的内部因素,主要考虑航空器内部的一些系统原因以及人为原因。其中制动系统故障、油料系统故障、引擎故障是航空器机械故障中比较常见的原因[466]。取制动系统故障、油料系统故障、引擎故障、人为原因以及正常情况[467],建立内部因素集合空间 $I(brake, oil, engine, driver, fine)$,其中 brake 代表制动系统故障,oil 代表油料系统故障,engine 代表引擎故障,driver 代表人为原因,fine 代表一切运转正常。

定义内部因素集合空间 $i \in I(brake, oil, engine, driver, fine)$,$i$ 表示当前的系统状况,它只可能在空间 $I(brake, oil, engine, driver, fine)$ 中取值。

1.3 航空器灾难发生模型

灾难的发生在时间上和地域上是随机的,也就是说,在任一时刻,航空器都有可能发生灾难。灾难概率的大小可以取决于模拟者的意愿[465]。作为本系统来说,由于重点训练航空器遇难后的模拟救援状况,所以航空器发生灾难的概率可以适当变大,甚至每次飞行都发生灾难。

建立数学模型[468] $R = R(t)$, $t = now - start$, now 表示当前的时间, $start$ 表示航空器飞行的开始时间, R 表示航空器发生灾难的事件, $R = 0,1$。也就是说,航空器发生灾难的事件是航空器开始飞行时间与当前时间的函数。函数 R 是一个随机函数,它将参数 $start$ 与 now 的时间差 t 划分为若干个小的时间段 Δt,每个 Δt 内发生灾难的概率为 p,则 $p = [R(t) = 1] = (1 - p)^{t-1} p$。

灾难的等级将决定航空器待救模型的设备可用性情况。定义灾难的等级 $g(g = 0,1,\cdots,4)$。定义函数 $g = g(R)$。当 $R = 0$ 时,$g = 0$。当 $R = 1$ 时,g 随机产生一个1到4之间的整数。

在模型中,灾难发生的概率 p 是可调的,当整个模拟进行时,如果航空器长时间飞行而没发生灾难,显然不利于整个搜救模拟的进行,因此可以适当调整 p 的大小来确保灾难发生。

2 航空器通信系统模型的建立

在海上航空器遇难模拟系统中,不仅需要实时的文字信息交互,而且电话通信以及视频通信也是必要的[468],文字信息传送与语音、视频信息的传送有所不同,具体体现在语音、视频信息需要输入输出设备,并需要编码与解码。

2.1 功能分析

根据航空器通信的具体功能不同,航空器通信系统模块主要分为三个部分,如图1所示。

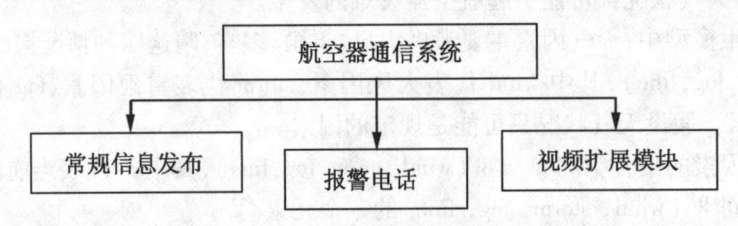

图1 航空器通信系统功能模块

(1)常规信息发布

主要向空管部门发送航空器飞行的常规信息,包括航空器的位置、天气信息、航空器各个系统运行的信息等。主要通过文字形式向空管部门的模拟主机发送,也可直接调用语音传输模块与其他部门进行语音通信。

(2)报警电话

当航空器发生事故时,在航空器通信系统正常的情况下,航空器可以向搜救中心以及其他部门报警。

(3)视频扩展模块

作为该系统的一个扩展模块,视频信息的交互使系统的功能在文字音频信息交互的基础上,增进图像信息的交互。

2.2 语音传输模块

音频通信比文字通信要复杂得多,主要就是发送端将语音信息采集后,编码成为可以在网络上传输的信息再发送到接收端,接收端将编码信息解码后使用音频输出设备输出还原后的信息。音频通信的主要流程有:发送端完成音频采集、压缩编码、码流发送等;接收端主要是码流接收、解码恢复、音频回放等。

语音传输发送端的主要流程如图2所示。语音传输接收端的主要流程如图3所示。

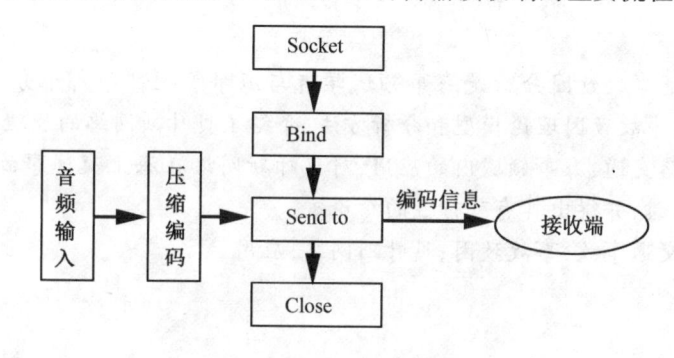

图2 语音通信发送端的主要流程

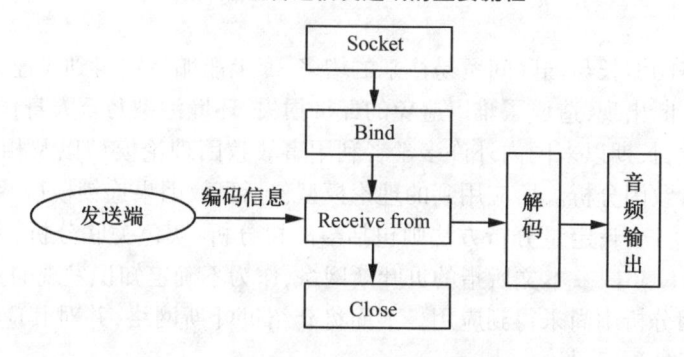

图3 语音通信接收端的主要流程

3 结论

通过以上分析与设计,利用系统建模的思想建立海上航空器遇难模型,考虑灾难产生的内外因素,加入实时通信模型,更增加其协调性使航空器灾难发生模型更加逼真。航空器灾难发生模型的研究是整个海上搜救系统模型的重要环节,模型不正确会导致整个研究失去意义。只有通过正确模拟海上航空器的灾难发生,该模型系统才能准确、及时地为整个海上搜救力量提供决策支持,实行有效的海上搜救。随着我国经济、贸易的发展和海洋开发战略的实施、海上、空中运输航线的大量开通,海上搜救模型的研究及其优化必将具有更广阔的前景。

浅议贝叶斯网络应用于海上交通事故致因分析的可行性*

摘要：海上交通事故致因分析是海事领域学者与海事管理部门都十分重视的研究课题。通过回顾海上交通事故致因理论模型和分析方法，介绍了贝叶斯网络的原理与特征，以及其在事故致因分析、道路交通、海事领域内的应用，对贝叶斯网络在海上交通事故致因分析中应用的可行性进行了探讨，并得出具有可行性的结论。

关键词：海上交通事故；事故致因；贝叶斯网络；应用

0 引言

随着世界经济的增长与国际间贸易往来的增多，海上船舶运输得到飞速发展，随之产生的海上交通事故也不断出现，造成了难以避免的经济损失、环境污染乃至人身伤害。为了减少海上交通事故的发生，长期以来国内外许多学者利用事故致因理论模型以及相关的定量方法对海上交通事故进行致因分析。所应用到的理论模型包括事故因果连锁模型、系统工程理论等，如参考文献[469][470]；定量分析方法则包括事故树分析、灰色关联分析、因子分析等，如参考文献[471][452][361]。本文所指的贝叶斯网络，作为不确定知识发现的重要方法之一，在海上交通事故致因分析中尚未得到应用。下面将介绍贝叶斯网络，并对其应用于海上交通事故致因分析的可行性进行讨论。

1 贝叶斯网络简介——贝叶斯网络的基本原理

贝叶斯网络是一种有向无环的网络拓扑结构，由节点和节点之间的有向边两个要素构成，每个节点代表一个状态变量，有向边则表示变量之间的依赖关系[472]。网络拓扑结构是贝叶斯网络的定性部分，而定量部分则是条件概率表（Conditional Probability Table，CPT）。

条件概率是指子节点与其父节点之间的关联关系。通过条件概率可以描述变量之间的关联强度或者置信度。下面以一个典型的草地淋湿网络为实例，介绍贝叶斯网络模型的构成，如图 1 所示[473]。

在草地淋湿贝叶斯网络模型中包含 4 个变量：阴天（Cloudy, C）、下雨（Rain, R）、洒水器（Sprinkle, S）、草地淋湿（Wet Grass, W）。每个变量分别具有两种取值：T(True) 和 F(False)，

---

* 本文发表在《交通建设与管理》2009 年第 5 卷，作者李东宁、尚云龙、郑中义。

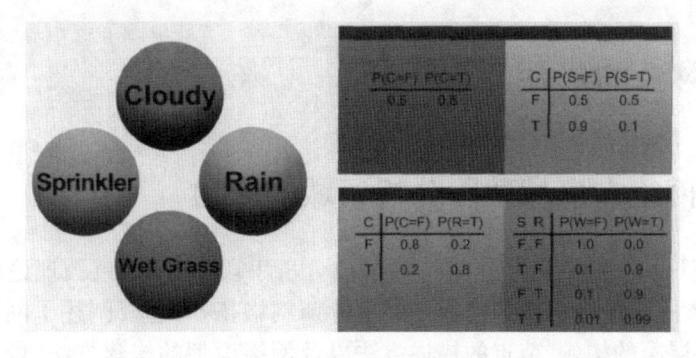

图 1　草地淋湿贝叶斯网络

分别代表是和否两种状态。这四个变量及其之间的关系用 4 个节点、4 条有向边和 4 个条件概率表进行表示。网络模型中蕴涵着因果关系和概率语义,例如草地淋湿(W)可能是由于下雨(R)或者洒水器(S)的原因;而阴天(C)又与下雨(R)或者洒水器(S)之间具有因果关系。在条件概率表中,父节点和子节点之间的条件概率分别一一对应给出。例如,在变量 $C=T$ 的条件下,$p(R=T)$ 为 0.8,在变量 $S=T, R=T$ 的条件下,$p(W=T)$ 为 0.99,$p(W=F)$ 为 0.01。

贝叶斯网络是一种概率推理技术,其推理原理基于贝叶斯概率理论,比较严格[474]。在网络模型中,网络节点具有自身的状态取值,在确定某一证据节点的状态取值之后,可以推理出其他节点的后验概率。贝叶斯网络的推理形式包括三类。其一是因果推理,目的是由原因推导出结果,使用贝叶斯网络的推理计算求出结果发生的概率;其二是诊断推理,目的是在已知结果时找出成因,推理计算得到造成该结果发生的原因和概率;第三是支持推理,旨在对原因间的相互影响进行分析。其中以因果推理和诊断推理较为常用。

随着数据库规模的不断扩大,贝叶斯网络开始逐渐应用于大规模数据库的数据挖掘中[475,476]。20 世纪末,出现了大量的贝叶斯网络学习算法,通过网络学习可以从大量数据中构造出贝叶斯网络模型。同时,利用贝叶斯网络所具有的推理功能,如诊断推理、因果推理等,推理得出节点发生的后验概率。因此,贝叶斯网络综合了数据挖掘和不确定性知识推理两个领域,成为不确定性知识发现的有效方法。利用贝叶斯网络进行不确定性知识发现的过程框架如图 2 所示[362]。

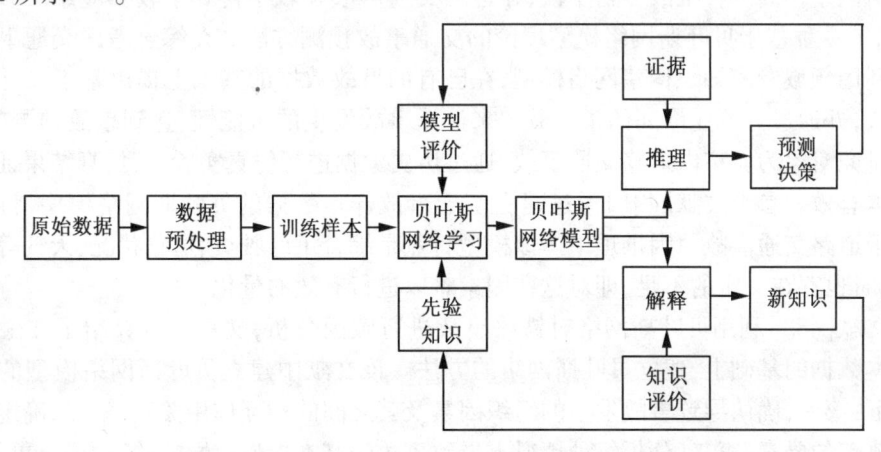

图 2　应用贝叶斯网络模型图

2 贝叶斯网络的应用现状

2.1 贝叶斯网络在事故致因分析领域的应用

参考文献[478]将贝叶斯网络作为一种事故分析手段,在事故致因理论的基础上提出了一种基于危险因素—事故—事故危害的三层贝叶斯网络拓扑模型,阐述了网络模型层次间的因果关联关系、各层次的构成、节点的描述方法以及网络模型的构建方法,最后通过一个天然气球罐的分析案例验证了该模型分析方法的可行性和有效性。该文献基于以往的事故原因分析模型,更加全面地分析事故的致因因素以及其可能导致的各种后果。在进行致因因素分析时,全面考虑人—物—环境作为事故不同类型的诱发因素所涵盖的内容,同时实现对事故类型和事故后果的预测。

参考文献[478]基于贝叶斯网络模型,综合运用诊断推理和支持推理形式,分析致灾因素的因果关系,揭示了人、机、环境与管理因素相互作用的内在规律。该文献首次将高斯贝叶斯网络应用于航空灾害致灾因素的因果关系分析,发现隐含因素从不确定性状态向确定性状态的演变过程和隐含因素程度的变化,以及各表层因素与隐含因素的关系。计算和分析结果表明,利用贝叶斯网络可以挖掘系统中隐含的内部因素对系统的影响程度,有助于表层因素与隐含因素的相关分析。从事故致因分析的角度而言,该文献所应用的高斯贝叶斯网络侧重于对系统内隐含因素的挖掘,对事故致因因素进行了更深入的挖掘,有助于及时发现系统中潜在的事故隐患。

参考文献[363]和[479]表明,贝叶斯网络可以从定量的角度对事故进行致因分析,其自身具有的推理功能可以成为致因分析的有效工具。

2.2 贝叶斯网络在道路交通事故领域中的应用

贝叶斯网络作为一种事故分析手段,在道路交通事故领域中得到了较早应用。参考文献[480]提出了一种基于贝叶斯网络模型理论的交通事故预测方法。在综合考虑交通事故成因的基础上利用领域专家知识构建网络模型,在已有的事故数据的基础上提出基于贝叶斯法则的学习算法,并通过计算变量间的条件概率来计算事故发生的可能性,达到事故预测的目的。该文献的研究对象为城市内道路交通事故,通过历史数据进行仿真实验,其仿真结果证明了预测模型基本有效。参考文献[481]通过建立基于事故样本数据的贝叶斯网络模型,将贝叶斯网络应用于道路交通事故原因推理中。该模型特点是综合了驾驶员、道路状况、天气等多方面因素,但同时也存在一定的不足,即对这些因素难以进行有效的量化。

参考文献[482]利用贝叶斯网络对铁路事故进行致因分析,文章重点介绍了在融合领域知识和样本数据的基础上,建立贝叶斯网络的方法。该文献中建立贝叶斯网络模型的步骤可以总结如下:第一,确认导致事故发生的组织因素及其之间的相互作用关系;第二,确定因果模型中作为节点的要素;第三,分析每种情况下导致事故的基本事件及影响关系,得出事故链条;第四,综合各种情况,融合每条事故链及各个致因要素,节点之间的概率关系由专家给出。

由于交通事故的影响因素复杂,具有较强的主观性,因此在应用贝叶斯网络进行交通事故分析和预测时,重要的工作是要科学合理地确定出网络节点变量。同时,人为因素是影响交通事故的主要因素。因此,如何对网络节点变量进行合理的量化就成为使用贝叶斯网络的关键。

2.3 贝叶斯网络在海上交通安全系统中的应用

在海上交通安全系统中,国内的贝叶斯网络应用较少,国外的许多研究则已经将贝叶斯网络用于海事风险分析。

参考文献[483]结合人为组织因素(HOF),应用贝叶斯网络进行风险分析。在总结前人对高速船舶进行风险分析的基础上,建立起海上运输系统(MTS)的贝叶斯网络模型,利用贝叶斯网络的推理能力,对海上运输系统内的人为组织因素,包括船公司、港口管理、规章制度等,进行风险分析。参考文献[484]基于前人所建的网络结构,进一步确定了船舶碰撞的致因因素,并确定出贝叶斯网络结构,利用 HUGIN 软件,对船舶碰撞事故的发生概率进行了预测分析。

挪威船级社(DNV)在2003年提交给 IMO 的关于综合安全评价(FSA)的报告中,提出将贝叶斯网络用于 FSA 的第二步风险分析中[485]。在该报告中,通过专家组建立起关于高速邮轮的碰撞和搁浅的贝叶斯网络模型,并由专家组给出条件概率表,进而利用 HUGIN 软件对高速邮轮发生碰撞和搁浅事故进行风险分析。分析结果表明,贝叶斯网络的不确定性推理能力十分适合在风险分析中应用。

日本在2006年 MSC 第81届会议上,提交了关于在 FSA 第三步的风险控制中应用贝叶斯网络进行分析的报告[486]。报告的结论表明,贝叶斯网络是对各个因素对碰撞和搁浅风险的影响进行评估的有效工具。同时,贝叶斯网络也适用于对风险控制手段的作用进行预测和评估。报告指出,在海事领域应用贝叶斯网络进行风险分析的劣势在于样本数据的不足,所以不可避免地要应用专家的判断来确定条件概率和网络结构。

3 贝叶斯网络应用于海上交通事故致因分析的讨论

3.1 贝叶斯网络用于海上交通事故致因分析的优势

贝叶斯网络作为目前不确定知识发现的有效工具之一,可以从不确定的知识或信息中做出推理,其应用于海上交通事故致因分析的优势主要体现在以下两个方面。

3.1.1 贝叶斯网络可以表示不确定性关系

事故致因分析是以危险辨识、分析和控制为特征的安全系统工程的重要内容,是安全分析与评价在事故致因机理和风险估计层面的有力补充,为风险降低措施和受益分析决策提供支持。事故本身往往具有突发性、因果性和偶然性的特点,因此事故致因分析必然带有不确定性[12]。海上交通事故系统本身即是一个不确定性的系统。该系统既有人们已知的确定信息(船舶性能状况、气象海况等),也存在一些诸如环境突发因素和操作人员失误等这些未知的不确定信息。

贝叶斯网络可以用节点变量来表示事故致因因素,节点变量可以通过状态信息来表示致因因素的不确定性状态。而节点间的条件概率则可以很好地表示致因因素之间的相互关系。其中,父节点与子节点之间不是简单的二态关系(发生与不发生),而是通过相应的条件概率来表现其间的不确定关系,这一点也是贝叶斯网络比事故树分析法更具有优势之处。

3.1.2 贝叶斯网络可以再现事故的形成过程

贝叶斯网络本身为一种有向无环图,各个节点之间由有向弧相连,可以建立出相应的网络结构。在事故致因分析中,可以通过确定节点及节点间的关系,建立出基于贝叶斯网络的事故致因模型,选择多种推理算法进行诊断推理,可以确定节点变量的后验概率,从而再现事故的形成过程。从这一角度来看,贝叶斯网络要比灰色关联分析或因子分析法具有优势。该两种方法侧重于找出影响因素与事故发生之间的关联度,而难以反映出因素之间的关系。从时间与空间的角度而言,该两种方法侧重于从空间的角度对事故致因进行分析,而贝叶斯网络可以从时间与空间两方面再现事故的形成过程。

3.1.3 贝叶斯网络已在海上交通安全系统领域得到初步应用

贝叶斯网络在事故致因分析、道路交通领域的应用较为广泛,在海上交通安全系统领域中已得到了初步的应用。前面提到的挪威、日本向 IMO 提交的关于 FSA 的报告已经将贝叶斯网络应用于风险分析的步骤。通过专家知识确定出贝叶斯网络结构及其参数,构建出基于贝叶斯网络的事故模型,进而对事故发生进行风险分析。

3.2 贝叶斯网络用于海上交通事故致因分析的不足

贝叶斯网络本身的特性以及目前海上交通事故的存在现状决定了贝叶斯网络存在应用上的不足。

3.2.1 贝叶斯网络节点的选取容易造成网络过于复杂

由于贝叶斯网络需要利用节点间的条件概率进行推理运算,所以节点的数量以及每个节点的状态取值都决定了网络及推理运算的复杂程度。在海上交通安全系统中,导致事故发生的影响因素种类多,状态复杂。从人、船、环境、管理的角度而言,人为因素是导致事故发生的主要因素。而人为因素的内容又十分复杂,难以进行细致的量化。因此,在选取网络节点的过程中,既要考虑到节点的有效性,使其能够充分恰当的反映实际情况;又要考虑到节点的科学性,避免使网络系统过于复杂。

3.2.2 海上交通事故样本数据规模有限

贝叶斯网络的应用需要以充足的样本数量为前提。目前,海上交通事故样本统计工作还处于起步发展阶段,难以提供大量的事故样本数据。国外海事管理部门的官方网站已经能够对外公布一定数量的事故样本,而国内在这方面仍处于起步阶段,仍需得到改善提高。随着相关部门对海上交通事故数据统计的日益重视,进而形成海上交通事故数据库,则可以为贝叶斯网络的应用提供更有利的条件。

4 结论

贝叶斯网络作为不确定性知识发现领域内的流行方法之一,在许多领域都得到了应用。

目前,虽然贝叶斯网络在海上交通事故致因分析领域内的应用较少,但综合比较其中的优势与不足,可以发现贝叶斯网络应用于海上交通事故致因分析具有一定的可行性。针对其中存在的不足,笔者提出以下建议:第一,要遵循科学有效的原则,合理确定出网络节点及结构。第二,要加强事故样本数据支持,尽可能搜集到足够的样本,确保模型应用的准确性。第三,国外已经有相关的研究机构开发出关于贝叶斯网络的软件,可以利用相关的软件进行网络模型运算。

船舶搁浅致因分析研究

碰撞和搁浅是构成船舶海事中最主要的两大类事故,从多年的海事统计资料中可以看出:搁浅事故的发生率和所引起的经济损失几乎与碰撞事故相当。随着船舶大型化、高速化发展和船舶周转量的增加,尤其是大型油船的大量投入使用,船舶搁浅事故的性质发生了显著变化,人们对于船舶搁浅事故的关注和研究程度日益加大。

0 船舶搁浅的概念

船舶搁浅由于研究角度和方式的不同,其外延和内涵也有所差别。

日本和加拿大等国在进行海事调查统计时,往往将船舶搁浅和船舶触礁事故归为一类。日本海难审判厅出版的《海难审判的现状》一书中将其定义为"船舶搁置在或触碰水下岩礁等,造成船舶损伤";而我国由国家海事局编写的《水上安全监督手册》一书中认为:"船舶搁浅是船舶搁置在浅滩上并造成停航或损坏的事故。"由此可见,对于船舶搁浅事故外延的确定争论的焦点在于是否将船舶搁浅和船舶触礁事故归为一类。从基本性质上讲,搁浅和触礁属于同一种事故,即船舶与水下固定物触碰。为了保证研究结果的统一性和完整性,本文采用国际海事组织在1986年海上安全委员会第433号通函所付的海事报告标准格式中对于海难事故的分类,即将船舶搁浅和船舶触礁事故归为一类。

船舶搁浅事故在内涵的确定上有广义与狭义之分。广义概念上的船舶搁浅是指船舶搁置在碍航物上,造成停航或损坏的事故;狭义概念上的船舶搁浅则是指船舶搁置在浅滩上并造成停航或损坏的事故。从上述定义可知,广义概念上的船舶搁浅和狭义概念上的船舶搁浅具有一个相同的要件,即造成船舶停航或经济损失或船体、机具等的损坏,而不同之处在于搁浅的底质——狭义概念上的搁浅底质仅限浅滩,而广义概念上的搁浅底质则包括浅滩、礁石以及沉船、沉物等一切有碍航行的水下物体。为了使研究成果的应用范围更为广泛,应取船舶搁浅事故的内涵为广义概念上的船舶搁浅。

1 船舶搁浅事故致因分析的主要研究内容

探究事故发生原因和形成机理的研究称为事故致因分析。事故致因分析在近百年的发展过程中形成了一系列较为完整的理论体系,如事故因果连锁理论、事故突变理论、能量转移理论等。海事致因分析作为事故致因分析体系的一个分支,由于研究起步较晚且研究对象存在

---

* 本文发表在《交通世界》2009年11期,作者李东宁、朱怀伟、郑中义。

诸多不确定性,与工业领域相比,在研究的深度和广度上都有不小的差距。就船舶搁浅事故的致因分析研究而言,目前的研究主要集中在确定船舶搁浅因素、评价船舶搁浅风险和搁浅事故过程分析三个方面。

2　船舶搁浅因素的确定

为了说明的方便,本文将导致船舶发生搁浅的原因因素称为船舶搁浅因素。船舶搁浅事故并不是自然发生的,而是在具备一定发生条件的情况下,通过各船舶搁浅因素间的相互作用影响而引发的。在通常情况下,海事(包括搁浅事故)的发生往往与六个方面的条件因素有密切的关系,即自然条件、航路条件、交通条件、本船条件、资料条件和人员条件。在某些特定的情况下,海事可以由上述某一单一条件引起,但大量的海事是几个条件相互影响作用的结果。与其他海事一样,在研究船舶搁浅事故发生原因时往往可以发现,人员条件是其中最重要、最活跃的因素,甚至可以说,与其他海事相比,人员因素对于事故的影响程度显得尤为突出。

确定船舶搁浅因素的研究由来已久,主要的研究方法包括事故统计法、专家调查法等。苏联的尤道维奇详细分析了船舶碰撞、搁浅、触碰等事故中船员所犯的具有代表性的错误和违章行为,他分析的各类搁浅案例的原因有:船位监测不佳;船位迷失;观测瞭望不合要求;观测瞭望组织不佳;过分信任引航员操船;在引航水域未用引航员自航;让船时的错误行动;操舵错误和恢复原航向过迟;船速过高;在风暴条件下的错误操船;对遇浪和在浅水中会增大吃水估计不足;过分信任当班驾驶员操船;以及其他"人的因素"和客观的原因。日本海难审判厅将导致海事发生的原因划分为29类,笔者对其发布的2000—2006年事故统计资料进行筛选,发现其中与搁浅事故相关的原因因素有21类(见表1)。上海海运学院的张则谅对国内外的190起搁浅事故进行归纳分析,总结了船员日常具体工作中导致搁浅的诸方面失误共8大类20小项。

从上述分析可以看出,研究的角度不同、分类的方法不一样,得到的船舶搁浅因素也有所差异,但无论是哪个国家、采用何种方法进行分析,都是基于对大量事故样本的统计处理。船舶搁浅因素的提取和量化是分析事故成因机理的基础,这些因素相互影响,有些并不独立,且种类繁多,很多是异量纲的,因而统计分析方法的选择成为能否准确描述事故成因过程的关键。由于海事安全领域内的某些指标只能采用顺序指标进行描述(即只能用语言变量优良中差等进行描述),而不能给出确切的数值,因此有学者引入了模糊数学等人工智能方法,用于对这类指标因素的描述与评价。

表1 2000—2006年船舶搁浅原因统计表（日本）

编号	事故原因	年份							总计
		2000	2001	2002	2003	2004	2005	2006	
1	船舶营运管理不当		3	1	2	4	1	3	14
2	开航准备不充分		3	1	1	1		4	10
3	航路调查不充分	22	38	27	18	17	28	20	170
4	航向选向和保持不当	21	18	29	21	14	17	20	140
5	船舶操纵不当	4	18	29	21	14	17	20	42
6	船位不确定	40	5	6	9	6	5	7	297
7	瞭望不当	2	35	52	38	36	52	44	17
8	打瞌睡	50	66	53	53	45	59	53	379
9	操舵及航行设备不良					1			1
10	天气、海况考虑不周	5	11	8	5	6	4	5	44
11	锚泊、系留不当	9	7	3	4	6	6	3	38
12	应对恶劣天气措施不当		2	1	1		3	6	13
13	未使用安全航速	2	1	1		2	3	2	11
14	不遵守避碰规则		1				3		3
15	辅机维修检查和管理不当			1					1
16	燃油、润滑油等维持、检查或处理不当				1				1
17	电气设备维持、检查或处理不当				1				1
18	甲板货物作业不当					2			2
19	对值班工作指导和监督不当	17	14	22	13	9	17	17	109
20	报告接班不当	16	7	6	6	6	3	5	49
21	其他		1		1	1	1	3	7
	合计	189	212	211	176	160	205	196	1 349
	搁浅事故	154	182	177	153	137	177	162	1 142
	事故涉及船舶数	167	197	187	163	142	185	167	1 208
	导致海难发生的船舶数	154	182	177	153	137	178	162	1 143

3 船舶搁浅概率的计算

对于船舶搁浅因素的分析需要解决两方面的关键问题，即就船员而言，究竟是工作中的哪些失误、又在多大程度上将导致搁浅事故的发生。船舶搁浅因素的确定，解决的是船员日常工作中的哪些失误可能导致搁浅事故发生的问题，而要了解这些具体的搁浅因素究竟在多大程度上影响着事故,还需解决进一步的定性分析和定量计算问题。

在海事领域,对于这一问题的研究主要是通过计算船舶的搁浅概率及进行人因可靠性分析的方法进行。20世纪70年代初期,日本学者藤井及其合作者首次提出了船舶搁浅的风险模型,并在随后的工作中,根据对日本四个海峡的船舶航迹分布研究建立了搁浅模型。杉崎将搁浅事故发生的原因归于航线选定、航迹推算误差和定位误差,并计算了船舶以特定速度在某一长度的航路上发生搁浅的概率;井上欣二根据对大量实测观测数据统计,证明了一般直航路上船舶航迹服从正态分布,故直航路上发生搁浅的船舶仅限于航迹位于特定区域的船舶,其潜在搁浅概率计算方法如式(1)所示,其中 W 表示航路宽度,$p(x)$ 为船舶航迹的概率分布。

$$p = \int_{0.5W}^{+\infty} p(x) \, \mathrm{d}x \tag{1}$$

事故树分析法(FTA)也是用于船舶搁浅概率计算的一种有效方法,一般来说,主要有两种建树为一法:先验性建树和后验性建树。Bea 对 Exxon Valdez 事故建立了详细的事故树,即属于后验性建树。但由于海事领域尚未建立较为完善的人因失效数据库,所以在大多数研究中主要是借鉴其他研究领域中类似动作的统计数据,如 Amrozowicz 在研究船舶搁浅的人为失误时采用了 Swain 提供的核电厂的人为失误率。为解决这一问题,海军大连舰艇学院的杨波等人尝试性地将造成船舶搁浅的原因分为确定性概率事件和非确定性概率事件,采用不同的模糊数对其进行量化,并求解船舶搁浅概率。该方法在一定程度上解决了某些人因基本事件难以量化的问题,但在非确定性概率事件发生概率的确定上多采用专家评判的为一法,受主观性影响较大。

此外,近年来兴起的数据挖掘技术也在船舶搁浅风险评估领域得到应用。Kite-Powell 提出了船舶搁浅的风险分析的贝叶斯模型,确定了不同风险因素对船舶发生搁浅事故的贡献。挪威船级社在2003年提交给 IMO 的关于船舶综合安全评估(FSA)提案中,建立了高速邮轮碰撞和搁浅的贝叶斯网络模型,并利用该模型对高速邮轮发生碰撞和搁浅事故的可能性进行了定量计算。数据挖掘技术的最大特点在于,通过分析大量数据揭示有意义的新的关系、趋势和模式,分析结果基于对样本的学习和训练获得,因而大幅度地减小了分析过程中人为因素的干扰,但在应用于海事致因分析领域时遇到的最大困难在于相关数据样本的匮乏。由于各国的海事统计数据存在明显的不规范、不完整的现象,且相关事故数据缺少必要的现场动态安全信息,导致数据样本在数量上和质量上都难以满足数据挖掘分析的要求。

4 船舶搁浅事故过程的分析

由于海上交通系统存在巨大的复杂性和不确定性,船舶搁浅事故的发生不仅与诸多搁浅因素有关,各因素间的相互作用关系更是错综复杂,因而早期对于船舶搁浅事故的研究多集中在对单一或若干搁浅因素的分析上。随着研究的不断深入,人们开始将研究的重点从因素分析转向事故成因机理分析,即对各搁浅因素间的相互影响关系及事故形成过程的分析和再现,但研究的深度和广度都十分有限。根据研究对象的不同,对船舶搁浅事故的过程分析可以分为以下两方面的内容。

5 单起事故过程的分析

要制定防止海事的措施,首先应该从对已发生的海事进行科学的调查分析开始,既要从量的方面对事故进行统计分析,又要选择一些具有代表性的事故案例从质的方面进行深入的剖析。对于搁浅事故过程分析的研究,以对单起事故发展过程的调查研究居多。这种分析方法能够较为详细完整地再现事故的起因、经过和结果,易于发现整个过程中的失效事件,从而有针对性地提出相应的改善措施。但不足之处在于,所发现的原因和采取的对策仅是针对单起船舶搁浅事故,不具有普遍性和代表性,难以发现引发船舶搁浅事故致因的一般性规律,因而在推广应用上受到限制。

6 整类事故过程的分析

就认识船舶搁浅事故的成因机理而言,更为直接和有意义的方法是实现对整类船舶搁浅事故的一般致因过程分析。而要实现这一目标,核心问题在于建立适当的分析模型。为此,相关学者引入了安全系统工程领域的一些模型方法,其中应用最为广泛的是事件树分析法。事件树分析法既可用于定性分析事故发生的整个变化过程,又可用于定量计算事故各个状态的发生概率,因而适于进行船舶搁浅事故的过程分析。但经典的事件树分析法在基本事件发生概率的确定上存在较大的主观性,因而在定量分析方面还不成熟。针对这一问题,相关领域研究人员对事件树分析法进行了改进,即应用改进的模糊事件树模型对船舶搁浅事故中航次计划失误的致因过程进行分析:针对基本事件发生概率难以确定的问题,引入了模糊失误率及模糊失误概率的概念,以模糊失误率表示人为失误为主的节点事件的发生概率,以模糊概率表示非人为失误为主的节点事件的失效概率,采用混合事件树算法计算事故发生或不发生的概率,为运用事件树进行海事致因分析提供了一种新的思路。

7 研究工作展望

目前,所进行的研究工作表明,为了阐述船舶搁浅事故的相关风险,仍有不少课题有待进一步深入探讨,重点应解决以下两个方面的问题。

第一,船舶搁浅因素的量化问题。建议按照主客观条件的不同将船舶搁浅因素分为确定性因素与非确定性因素分别研究。对确定性因素(如车舵故障、导航设备故障等)的失效概率可参照工业领域的研究成果,采用试验的方法加以确定;对非确定性因素(主要是人为因素)的研究可应用模糊数学、灰色理论、数据挖掘技术等解决不确定性问题的工具,并在此基础上探索新的更为有效的人因可靠性分析方法。

第二,建立船舶搁浅事故的过程分析模型。目前,在船舶搁浅的致因过程分析领域,还没有一种统一高效的模型方法,这对于发现搁浅事故的成因机理和制定预防措施是十分不利的。近年来,国际民航组织(ICAO)防止事故手册上提出了事故致因链的概念,在工业领域和道路交通系统事故致因分析领域已有学者成功构造了某类事故的事故致因链并进行事故致因过程分析,我们认为可为海事领域的事故致因过程分析提供参考。安全系统工程学和数据挖掘技术中的一些模型方法——事故树、事变树、贝叶斯网络等,都可用于事故致因链的构造,但在海事领域的具体应用还有待进一步的检验和探讨。

参考文献

[1] MJOSBORNE, JPEPPER. Creating Marine Spatial Data Infrastructure for the UK[C]. Berlin: Springer Netherlands, 2010. 51-55.

[2] WAHYU S, PRAMONO G H, PURNAWAN B. Establishment of Marine and Coastal Spatial Data Infrastructure in Indonesia[C]. Berlin: Springer Netherlands, 2010. 97-103.

[3] PEPPER J. Unlocking the Marine Data Treasure Chest[C]. Berlin: Springer Netherlands, 2010. 57-64.

[4] CHEN F, REN H. Comparison of Vector Data Compression Algorithms in Mobile GIS[C]. IEEE, 2010:613-617.

[5] HUIFENG J, YIHE W. The Research on the Compression Algorithms for Vector Data[C]. IEEE, 2010:1-4.

[6] K. Chen X Z J X. Fast Corner Detection Algorithm with Sub-Pixel Accuracy Imitating Hessian-Laplace[J]. Application Research of Computers. 2014, 31(7): 2195-2200.

[7] M.S. VERKEENKO. Development of an Algorithm for Fast Corner Points Detection[J]. Journal of Computer AND SYSTEM SCIENCES. 2014, 43(4): 392-401.

[8] 孙波,檀结庆. 改进的曲率尺度空间角点检测[J]. 计算机工程与应用. 2014(19): 161-164.

[9] 刘文进,张蕾,孙劲光. 基于AP聚类图像分块的角点检测改进方法[J]. 计算机工程. 2015(04): 217-221.

[10] 王春芳. 随机Hough变换实现角点检测[J]. 计算机工程与设计. 2015(03): 716-720.

[11] ZHANG X, WANG H, SMITH A W B, et al. Corner Detection Based on Gradient Correlation Matrices of Planar Curves[J]. Pattern Recognition. 2010, 43(4): 1207-1223.

[12] 王浩,周祚峰,曹剑中,等. 基于边缘轮廓上多尺度自相关矩阵的角点检测算法[J]. 系统工程与电子技术. 2014(06): 1220-1224.

[13] WANG F, ZHANG W, ZHOU Z, et al. Corner Detection Using Gabor filters[J]. IET Image Processing. 2014, 8(11): 639-646.

[14] AWRANGJEB M, LU G, FRASER C S. Performance Comparisons of Contour-Based Corner Detectors[J]. IEEE Transactions on Image Processing. 2012, 21(9): 4167-4179.

[15] PINHEIRO A M G, GHANBARI M. Piecewise Approximation of Contours Through Scale-Space Selection of Dominant Points[J]. IEEE Transactions on Image Processing. 2010, 19(6): 1442-1450.

[16] 王蒙,戴亚平. 基于FAST角点检测的局部鲁棒特征[J]. 北京理工大学学报. 2013

(10): 1045-1050.

[17] 王慧勇. 一种快速自适应的 Harris 角点检测方法研究[J]. 电视技术. 2013(19): 208-212.

[18] Y XIE. Information Technology in Multi-object Tracking Based on Bilateral Structure Tensor Corner Detection for Mutual Occlusion[J]. Advanced Materials Research. 2014, 977: 502-506.

[19] A ROSENFELD. An Improved Method of Angle Detection on Digital Curves[J]. IEEE Transactions on computers. 1975, 24(9): 940-941.

[20] PEDROSA G V, BARCELOS C A Z. Anisotropic Diffusion for Effective Shape Corner Point Detection[J]. Pattern Recognition Letters. 2010, 31(12): 1658-1664.

[21] MASOOD A, SARFRAZ M. Corner Detection by Sliding Rectangles Along Planar Curves [J]. Computers & Graphics. 2007, 31(3): 440-448.

[22] ZHANG X, WANG H, HONG M, et al. Robust Image Corner Detection Based on Scale Evolution Difference of Planar Curves[J]. Pattern Recognition Letters. 2009, 30(4): 449-455.

[23] 支晨蛟, 唐慧明. 基于视频角点特征匹配的车速检测方法[J]. 计算机工程. 2013 (12): 176-180.

[24] MOKHTARIAN F, MOHANNA F. Performance Evaluation of Corner Detectors Using Consistency and Accuracy Measures[J]. Computer Vision and Image Understanding. 2006, 102(1): 81-94.

[25] S IZCHAK, S ASSAF, K DANIEL. A Geometric Approach to Monitoring Threshold Functions Over Distributed Data Streams[C]. Berlin: Springer Berlin Heidelberg, 2010. 163-186.

[26] RAY C, GORALSKI R, CLARAMUNT C, et al. Real-Time 3D Monitoring of Marine Navigation[M]. Berlin, Heidelberg: Springer Berlin Heidelberg, 2011: 5, 161-175.

[27] HADZAGIC M. Bayesian Approaches to Trajectory Estimation in Maritime Surveillance [D]. Montreal: McGill University, 2010.

[28] PERERA L P, OLIVEIRA P, GUEDES SOARES C. Maritime Traffic Monitoring Based on Vessel Detection, Tracking, State Estimation, and Trajectory Prediction[J]. IEEE Transactions on Intelligent Transportation Systems. 2012, 13(3): 1188-1200.

[29] PERERA L P, SOARES C G. Ocean Vessel Trajectory Estimation and Prediction Based on Extended Kalman Filter[C]The Second International Conference on Adaptive and self _Adaptive Systems and Applications, 2010:14-20.

[30] LIN L, LU Y, PAN Y, et al. Integrating Graph Partitioning and Matching for Trajectory Analysis in Video Surveillance[J]. IEEE Transactions on Image Processing. 2012, 21 (12): 4844-4857.

[31] ROH G, ROH J, HWANG S, et al. Supporting Pattern-Matching Queries over Trajectories on Road Networks[J]. IEEE Transactions on Knowledge and Data Engineering. 2011, 23(11): 1753-1758.

［32］HU H,ZHOU J. Trajectory Matching from Unsynchronized Videos［C］IEEE Conference on Computer Vision and Pattern Recognition, 2010:1347-1354.

［33］ZDENEK K,MIKOLAJCZYK K,Matas J. Tracking-Learning-Detection［J］. IEEE Transactions on Pattern Analysis and Machine Intellgence. 2012, 34(7): 1409-1422.

［34］YANG D,ZHANG T,LI J, et al. Synthetic Fuzzy Evaluation Method of Trajectory Similarity in Map-Matching［J］. Journal of Intelligent Transportation Systems. 2011, 15(4): 193-204.

［35］DODGE S,LAUBE P,WEIBEL R. Movement Similarity Assessment Using Symbolic Representation of Trajectories［J］. International Journal of Geographical Information Science. 2012, 26(9): 1563-1588.

［36］EVANS M,OLIVER D,SHEKHAR S, et al. Summarizing Trajectories Into K-Primary Corridors: A Summary of Results［C］ACM, 2012:454-457.

［37］SU H,ZHENG K,ZENG K, et al. Making Sense of Trajectory Data: A Partition-And-SumMarization Approach［C］IEEE, 2015:963-974.

［38］BUCHIN M,DODGE S,SPECKMAN B. Context-aware similarity of trajectories［J］. Geographic information science. 2012: 43-56.

［39］GUDMUNDSSON J, LAUBE P, WOLLE T. Computational movement analysis［J］. Springer Handbook of Grographic Information. 2012: 423-438.

［40］谢萍,马小勇,张宪民,等. 一种快速的复杂多边形匹配算法［J］. 计算机工程. 2003 (16): 177-178.

［41］TABIA H,DAOUDI M,VANDEBORRE J, et al. A new 3D-matching method of non-rigid and partially similar models using curve analysis［J］. IEEE Transactions on Pattern Analysis and Machine Intelligence. 2011, 33(4): 852-858.

［42］TIAN Y,YANG X,YI C, et al. Toward a computer vision-based wayfinding aid for blind persons to access unfamiliar indoor environments［J］. Machine Vision and Applications. 2013, 24(3): 521-535.

［43］DANDOIS J P,ELLIS E C. Remote Sensing of Vegetation Structure Using Computer Vision［J］. Remote Sensing. 2010, 2(4): 1157-1176.

［44］AANæS H,DAHL A L,STEENSTRUP PEDERSEN K. Interesting Interest Points［J］. International Journal of Computer Vision. 2012, 97(1): 18-35.

［45］SOLMAZ B,ASSARI S M,SHAH M. Classifying web videos using a global video descriptor［J］. Machine Vision and Applications. 2013, 24(7): 1473-1485.

［46］RAO R S,ALI S T. A Computer Vision Technique to Detect Phishing Attacks［C］IEEE, 2015:596-601.

［47］XUAN Y, COIFMAN B. Identifying Lane-Change Maneuvers with Probe Vehicle Data and an Observed Asymmetry in Driver Accommodation［J］. Journal of Transportation Engineering. 2012, 138(8): 1051-1061.

［48］AVILA S,THOME N,CORD M, et al. Pooling in image representation: The visual codeword point of view［J］. Computer Vision and Image Understanding. 2013, 117(5):

453-465.

[49] CHEN J, TAKAGI N. A Method to Extract Character Strings from Scene Images by Eliminating Non-Character Strings: Towards Development of a Visual Assistance System for People with Visually Impairments[C]. 2013 International Conference on Signal-Image Technology & Internet-Based Systems, 2013:848-853.

[50] LIU F, DUAN H, DENG Y. A chaotic quantum-behaved particle swarm optimization based on lateral inhibition for image matching[J]. Optik. 2012, 123(21): 1955-1960.

[51] KUMAR K, YADAV A, RANI H, et al. 2-Dimensional Wavelet pre-processing to extract IC-Pin information for disarrangement analysis[J]. IOSR Journal of Electronics and Communication Engineering. 2013, 7(6): 36-38.

[52] MIKULKA J, GESCHEIDTOVA E, BARTUSEK K. Soft-tissues Image Processing: Comparison of Traditional Segmentation Methods with 2D active Contour Methods[J]. Measurement Science Review. 2012, 12(4).

[53] YUEN A, ZHANG K, ALTINTAS Y. Smooth trajectory generation for five-axis machine tools[J]. International Journal of Machine Tools and Manufacture. 2013, 71: 11-19.

[54] ZHANG L, GAO H, CHEN Z, et al. Multi-objective global optimal parafoil homing trajectory optimization via Gauss pseudospectral method[J]. Nonlinear Dynamics. 2013, 72(1-2): 1-8.

[55] ORZAN A, BOUSSEAU A, BARLA P. Diffusion Curves: A Vector Representation for Smooth-Shaded Images[J]. Communications of the ACM. 2013, 56(7): 101-108.

[56] LAWONN K, GASTEIGER R, RöSSL C, et al. Adaptive and robust curve smoothing on surface meshes[J]. Computers & Graphics. 2014, 40: 22-35.

[57] FU H, TIAN Z, RAN M, et al. Novel affine-invariant curve descriptor for curve matching and occluded object recognition[J]. IET Computer Vision. 2013, 7(4): 279-292.

[58] OSOWSKI S, NGHIA D D. Fourier and wavelet descriptors for shape recognition using neural networks: a comparative study[J]. Pattern Recognition. 2002, 35(9): 1949-1957.

[59] ZHAO D, CHEN J. Affine curve moment invariants for shape recognition[J]. Pattern Recognition. 1997, 30(6): 895-901.

[60] MOKHTARIAN F, ABBASI S. Shape similarity retrieval under affine transforms[J]. Pattern Recognition. 2002, 35(1): 31-41.

[61] LING H, JACOBS D W. Shape classification using the inner-distance[J]. IEEE Trans Pattern Anal Mach Intell. 2007, 29(2): 286-299.

[62] ALAJLAN N, KAMEL M S, FREEMAN G H. Geometry-Based Image Retrieval in Binary Image Databases[J]. IEEE Transactions on Pattern Analysis and Machine Intelligence. 2008, 30(6): 1003-1013.

[63] FREJLICHOWSKI D. Analysis of Four Polar Shape Descriptors Properties in an Exemplary Application[M]. Berlin, Heidelberg: Springer Berlin Heidelberg, 2010: 6374, 376-383.

[64] CUI M, FEMIANI J, HU J, et al. Curve matching for open 2D curves[J]. Pattern Recognition Letters. 2009, 30(1): 1-10.

[65] TRAN C, TRIVEDI M M. 3-D Posture and Gesture Recognition for Interactivity in Smart Spaces[J]. IEEE Transactions on Industrial Informatics. 2012, 8(1): 178-187.

[66] SUN Z, CHEN Z, HU H, et al. Ship interaction in narrow water channels: A two-lane cellular automata approach[J]. Physica A: Statistical Mechanics and its Applications. 2015, 431: 46-51.

[67] ZHANG L, WANG H, MENG Q. Big Data-Based Estimation for Ship Safety Distance Distribution in Port Waters[J]. Transportation Research Record: Journal of the Transportation Research Board. 2015, 2479(1): 16-24.

[68] MENG Q, WENG J, LI S. Analysis with Automatic Identification System Data of Vessel Traffic Characteristics in the Singapore Strait[J]. Transportation Research Record: Journal of the Transportation Research Board. 2018, 2426(1): 33-43.

[69] S WOLFRAM. Cellular automata as models of complexity[J]. Nature. 1984, 311(5985): 419-424.

[70] SZABÓG, FÁTH G. Evolutionary games on graphs[J]. Physics Reports. 2007, 446(4): 97-216.

[71] S WOLFRAM. Statistical mechanics of cellular automata[J]. Modern Phys. 1983, 55(3): 601-644.

[72] WOLFRAM S. Universality and complexity in cellular automata[J]. Physica D: Nonlinear Phenomena. 1984, 10(1): 1-35.

[73] M TAKAYASU, TAKAYASU H. 1/f noise in a traffic model[J]. Fractals. 1993, 1(4): 860-866.

[74] K NAGEL, M SCHRECKENBERG. A cellular automaton model for freeway traffic[J]. Phy. I. 1992, 2(12): 2221-2229.

[75] BIHAM O, MIDDLETON A A, LEVINE D. Self Organization and a Dynamical Transition in Traffic Flow Models[J]. 1992.

[76] B S KERNER, S L KLENOW, D E WOLF. Cellular automata approach to three-phase traffic theory[J]. Phys. Rev. A: Math. Gen. 2002, 35(47): 9971-10013.

[77] HELBING D. Traffic and related self-driven many-particle systems[J]. Reviews of Modern Physics. 2001, 73(4): 1067-1141.

[78] CHOWDHURY D, SANTEN L, SCHADSCHNEIDER A. Statistical physics of vehicular traffic and some related systems[J]. Physics Reports. 2000, 329(4): 199-329.

[79] Q CHEN, Y WANG. Cellular automata(CA) simulation of the interaction of vehicle flows and pedestrian crossings on urban low-grade uncontrolled roads[J]. Physica A. 2015, 432: 43-57.

[80] LI X, LI X, XIAO Y, et al. Modeling mechanical restriction differences between car and heavy truck in two-lane cellular automata traffic flow model[J]. Physica A: Statistical Mechanics and its Applications. 2016, 451: 49-62.

[81] C MALIKARJUNA, K R RAO. Cellular automata model for heterogeneous traffic[J]. J. Adv. Trans. 2009, 43(3): 321-345.

[82] TANG T, HUANG H, SHANG H. A DYNAMIC MODEL FOR THE HETEROGENEOUS TRAFFIC FLOW CONSISTING OF CAR, BICYCLE AND PEDESTRIAN[J]. International Journal of Modern Physics C. 2010, 21(02): 159-176.

[83] CHEN Q, WANG Y. A cellular automata (CA) model for motorized vehicle flows influenced by bicycles along the roadside[J]. Journal of Advanced Transportation. 2016, 50(6): 949-966.

[84] LIU J, ZHOU F, WANG M. Simulation of Waterway Traffic Flow at Harbor Based on the Ship Behavior and Cellular Automata[C]. IEEE, 2010:542-546.

[85] FENG H. Cellular automata ship traffic flow model considering integrated bridge system [J]. Sci. Technol. 2013, 6(6): 111-120.

[86] QU X, MENG Q. Development and applications of a simulation model for vessels in the Singapore Straits[J]. Expert Systems With Applications. 2012, 39(9): 8430-8438.

[87] BURSTEDDE C, KLAUCK K, SCHADSCHNEIDER A, et al. Simulation of pedestrian dynamics using a 2-dimensional cellular automaton[J]. 2001.

[88] FUJII Y, TANAKA K. Traffic Capacity[J]. Journal of Navigation. 1971, 24(04): 543-552.

[89] PIETRZYKOWSKI Z, URIASZ J. The Ship Domain-A Criterion of Navigational Safety Assessment in an Open Sea Area[J]. Journal of Navigation. 2009, 62(01): 93.

[90] TOYODA S, FUJII Y. Marine Traffic Engineering[J]. Journal of Navigation. 1971, 24(01): 24-34.

[91] LIU J, ZHOU F, LI Z, et al. Dynamic Ship Domain Models for Capacity Analysis of Restricted Water Channels[J]. Journal of Navigation. 2016, 69(03): 481-503.

[92] WANG Y, CHIN H. An Empirically-Calibrated Ship Domain as a Safety Criterion for Navigation in Confined Waters[J]. Journal of Navigation. 2016, 69(02): 257-276.

[93] WANG N. A Novel Analytical Framework for Dynamic Quaternion Ship Domains[J]. Journal of Navigation. 2013, 66(02): 265-281.

[94] MA J, SONG W, ZHANG J, et al. -Nearest-Neighbor interaction induced self-organized pedestrian counter flow[J]. Physica A: Statistical Mechanics and its Applications. 2010, 389(10): 2101-2117.

[95] SCHADSCHNEIDER A, SCHRECKENBERG M. Car-oriented mean-field theory for traffic flow models[J]. Journal of Physics A: Mathematical and General. 1997, 30(4): L69-L75.

[96] JIANG H, ZHANG Z, HUANG Q, et al. Research of vehicle flow based on cellular automaton in different safety parameters[J]. Safety Science. 2016, 82: 182-189.

[97] K P LI, Z Y GAO, B NING. Modeling the railway traffic using cellular automata model [J]. Modern Phys. C. 2005, 16(6): 921-932.

[98] RAHMAN M, CHOWDHURY M, XIE Y, et al. Review of Microscopic Lane-Changing

Models and Future Research Opportunities[J]. IEEE Transactions on Intelligent Transportation Systems. 2013, 14(4): 1942-1956.

[99] PENG J, GUO Y, FU R, et al. Multi-parameter prediction of drivers' lane-changing behaviour with neural network model[J]. Applied Ergonomics. 2015, 50: 207-217.

[100] LAVAL J A, LECLERCQ L. Microscopic modeling of the relaxation phenomenon using a macroscopic lane-changing model[J]. Transportation Research Part B: Methodological. 2008, 42(6): 511-522.

[101] LV W, SONG W, LIU X, et al. A microscopic lane changing process model for multi-lane traffic[J]. Physica A: Statistical Mechanics and its Applications. 2013, 392(5): 1142-1152.

[102] D V KTITAREV, CHOWDHURY D, WOLF D E. Stochastic traffic model with random deceleration probabilities: Queueing and power-law gap distribution[J]. Phys. A: Math. Gen. 1997, 30(8): 221-227.

[103] CHEN Q, WANG Y. A Cellular Automata (CA) Model for Two-Way Vehicle Flows on Low-Grade Roads Without Hard Separation[J]. IEEE Intelligent Transportation Systems Magazine. 2016, 8(4): 43-53.

[104] LI Q, WONG S C, MIN J, et al. A cellular automata traffic flow model considering the heterogeneity of acceleration and delay probability[J]. Physica A: Statistical Mechanics and its Applications. 2016, 456: 128-134.

[105] JIANG R, WU Q. A stopped time dependent randomization cellular automata model for traffic flow controlled by traffic light[J]. Physica A: Statistical Mechanics and its Applications. 2006, 364: 493-496.

[106] MENG Q, WENG J. An improved cellular automata model for heterogeneous work zone traffic[J]. Transportation Research Part C: Emerging Technologies. 2011, 19(6): 1263-1275.

[107] CHEN Q, WANG Y. Cellular automata (CA) simulation of the interaction of vehicle flows and pedestrian crossings on urban low-grade uncontrolled roads[J]. Physica A: Statistical Mechanics and its Applications. 2015, 432: 43-57.

[108] XIANG Z, LI Y, CHEN Y, et al. Simulating synchronized traffic flow and wide moving jam based on the brake light rule[J]. Physica A: Statistical Mechanics and its Applications. 2013, 392(21): 5399-5413.

[109] YANG X, ZHANG W, QIU K, et al. The relations of "go and stop" wave to car accidents in a cellular automaton with velocity-dependent randomization[J]. Physica A: Statistical Mechanics and its Applications. 2007, 384(2): 589-599.

[110] BIJLSMA S J. A Computational Method in Ship Routing Using the Concept of Limited Manoeuvrability[J]. Journal of Navigation. 1999, 57(3): 357-369.

[111] BENTIN M, ZASTRAU D, SCHLAAK M, et al. A New Routing Optimization Tool-influence of Wind and Waves on Fuel Consumption of Ships with and without Wind Assisted Ship Propulsion Systems[J]. Transportation Research Procedia. 2016, 14: 153-162.

[112] MERRICK J R W, VAN DORP J R, BLACKFORD J P, et al. A traffic density analysis of proposed ferry service expansion in San Francisco Bay using a maritime simulation model[J]. Reliability Engineering and System Safety. 2003, 81(2): 119-132.

[113] KUJALA P, HäNNINEN M, AROLA T, et al. Analysis of the marine traffic safety in the Gulf of Finland[J]. Reliability Engineering & System Safety. 2009, 94(8): 1349-1357.

[114] SARIöZ K, NARLI E. Assessment of manoeuvring performance of large tankers in restricted waterways: a real-time simulation approach[J]. Ocean Engineering. 2003, 30(12): 1535-1551.

[115] BREITHAUPT S A, COPPING A, TAGESTAD J, et al. Maritime Route Delineation using AIS Data from the Atlantic Coast of the US[J]. Journal of Navigation. 2017, 70(02): 379-394.

[116] WALTHER L, RIZVANOLLI A, WENDEBOURG M, et al. Modeling and Optimization Algorithms in Ship Weather Routing[J]. International Journal of e-Navigation and Maritime Economy. 2016, 4: 31-45.

[117] FANG M, LIN Y. The optimization of ship weather-routing algorithm based on the composite influence of multi-dynamic elements (II): Optimized routings[J]. Applied Ocean Research. 2015, 50: 130-140.

[118] YUNTAO L, HONG H, BONI S. An integrated model study on the analysis of the influence of heavy rainfall on traffic congestion[C]. IEEE, 2013:1-4.

[119] SORIA I, ELEFTERIADOU L, KONDYLI A. Assessment of car-following models by driver type and under different traffic, weather conditions using data from an instrumented vehicle[J]. Simulation Modelling Practice and Theory. 2014, 40: 208-220.

[120] XU C, WANG W, LIU P. Identifying crash-prone traffic conditions under different weather on freeways[J]. Journal of Safety Research. 2013, 46: 135-144.

[121] AKIN D, SISIOPIKU V P, SKABARDONIS A. Impacts of Weather on Traffic Flow Characteristics of Urban Freeways in Istanbul[J]. Procedia-Social and Behavioral Sciences. 2011, 16: 89-99.

[122] HESHAM RAKHA P P E, ARAFEH M, PARK S. Modeling Inclement Weather Impacts on Traffic Stream Behavior[J]. International Journal of Transportation Science and Technology. 2012, 1(1): 25-47.

[123] KEAY K, SIMMONDS I. The association of rainfall and other weather variables with road traffic volume in Melbourne, Australia[J]. Accident Analysis & Prevention. 2005, 37(1): 109-124.

[124] WU L, XU Y, WANG Q, et al. Mapping Global Shipping Density from AIS Data[J]. Journal of Navigation. 2017, 70(01): 67-81.

[125] ISENOR A W, ST-HILAIRE M, WEBB S, et al. MSARI: A Database for Large Volume Storage and Utilisation of Maritime Data[J]. Journal of Navigation. 2017, 70(2): 276-290.

[126] S L MARPLE. Digital Spectral Analysis:With Applications[M]. USA:Prentice-Hall,1986.

[127] PILZ M,PAROLAI S. On the use of the autocorrelation function: the constraint of using frequency band-limited signals for monitoring relative velocity changes[J]. Journal of Seismology. 2016, 20(3): 921-934.

[128] MENG-LONG Y,YI-GUANG L,ZHI-SHENG Y. A New Cellular Automata Model Considering Finite Deceleration and Braking Distance[J]. Chinese Physics Letters. 2007, 24(10): 2910-2913.

[129] JIA B,LI X,CHEN T, et al. Cellular automaton model with time gap dependent randomisation under Kerner's three-phase traffic theory[J]. Transportmetrica. 2011, 7(2): 127-140.

[130] NAITO Y,NAGATANI T. Effect of headway and velocity on safety-collision transition induced by lane changing in traffic flow[J]. Physica A: Statistical Mechanics and its Applications. 2012, 391(4): 1626-1635.

[131] J WANG,DING Q,R D KHNE. Lane-changing behavior and its effect on energy dissipation using full velocity difference model[J]. 2015.

[132] NAITO Y,NAGATANI T. Safety-collision transition induced by lane changing in traffic flow[J]. Physics Letters A. 2011, 375(10): 1319-1322.

[133] LV W,SONG W,FANG Z. Three-lane changing behaviour simulation using a modified optimal velocity model[J]. Physica A: Statistical Mechanics and its Applications. 2011, 390(12): 2303-2314.

[134] 郑滨,陈锦标,夏少生,等. 基于数据挖掘的海上交通流数据特征分析[J]. 中国航海. 2009(01): 60-63.

[135] 潘家财,邵哲平,姜青山. 数据挖掘在海上交通特征分析中的应用研究[J]. 中国航海. 2010, 32(2): 60-64.

[136] PALLOTTA G,VESPE M,BRYAN K. Vessel Pattern Knowledge Discovery from AIS Data: A Framework for Anomaly Detection and Route Prediction[J]. Entropy. 2013, 15(12): 2218-2245.

[137] 肖潇,邵哲平,潘家财,等. 基于AIS信息的船舶轨迹聚类模型及应用[J]. 中国航海. 2015(02): 82-86.

[138] CHEN J,LU F,PENG G. A quantitative approach for delineating principal fairways of ship passages through a strait[J]. Ocean Engineering. 2015, 103: 188-197.

[139] 周丹,郑中义. 基于AIS数据的船舶领域影响因素分析[J]. 上海海事大学学报. 2016(02): 7-11.

[140] 甄荣,邵哲平,潘家财,等. 基于AIS信息的航道内船舶速度分布统计分析[J]. 集美大学学报(自然科学版). 2014(04): 274-278.

[141] 潘家财,姜青山,邵哲平. 船舶会遇的时空数据挖掘算法及应用[J]. 中国航海. 2010(04): 57-60.

[142] 孟范立. 利用AIS数据挖掘建立船舶到达规律模型[J]. 舰船科学技术. 2016

(10): 28-30.

[143] LIU B, DE SOUZA E N, HILLIARD C, et al. Ship movement anomaly detection using specialized distance measures[C]. ISIF, 2015:1113-1120.

[144] LIU B, DE SOUZA E N, MATWIN S, et al. Knowledge-based clustering of ship trajectories using density-based approach[C]. IEEE, 2014:603-608.

[145] YAO X, MOU J, CHEN P, et al. Ship Emission Inventories in Estuary of the Yangtze River Using Terrestrial AIS Data[J]. TransNav, the International Journal on Marine Navigation and Safety of Sea Transportation. 2016, 10(4): 633-640.

[146] 刘轶华,肖英杰,关克平. 基于AIS海上交通调查的船舶定线制设计[J]. 南通航运职业技术学院学报. 2013(04): 37-41.

[147] 胡菠,王智. 水上移动业务标识码资源的管理[J]. 中国海事. 2009, 3: 50-53.

[148] PALLOTTA G, VESPE M, BRYAN K. Vessel pattern knowledge discovery from AIS data a framework for anomaly detection and route prediction[J]. Entroy. 2013, 15(6): 2218-2245.

[149] 唐存宝,邵哲平,唐强荣,等. 基于AIS的船舶航迹分布算法[J]. 集美大学学报(自然科学版). 2012(02): 109-112.

[150] 宁建强,黄涛,刁博宇,等. 一种基于海量船舶轨迹数据的细粒度网格海上交通密度计算方法[J]. 计算机工程与科学. 2015(12): 2242-2249.

[151] 刘涛,胡勤友,杨春. 水上交通拥挤区域的聚类分析与识别[J]. 中国航海. 2010(04): 75-78.

[152] 丁兆颖,姚迪,吴琳,等. 一种基于改进的DBSCAN的面向海量船舶位置数据码头挖掘算法[J]. 计算机工程与科学. 2015(11): 2061-2067.

[153] 魏照坤,周康,魏明,等. 基于AIS数据的船舶运动模式识别与应用[J]. 上海海事大学学报. 2016(02): 17-22.

[154] 唐建波,邓敏,刘启亮. 时空事件聚类分析方法研究[J]. 地理信息世界. 2013(01): 38-45.

[155] ESTER M, KRIEGEL H P, SANDER J. A Density-Based Algorithm for Discovering Clusters in Large Spatial Databases with Noise[C]. Proceedings of 2nd International Conference on Knowledge Discovery and Data Mining, Portland: Oregon: AAAI, 1996.

[156] 张丽杰. 具有稳定饱和度的DBSCAN算法[J]. 计算机应用研究. 2014(07): 1972-1975.

[157] SANDER J, ESTER M, KRIEGEL H, et al. Density-Based Clustering in Spatial Databases: The Algorithm GDBSCAN and Its Applications[J]. Data Mining and Knowledge Discovery. 1998, 2(2): 169-194.

[158] BIRANT D, KUT A. ST-DBSCAN: An algorithm for clustering spatial-temporal data[J]. Data & Knowledge Engineering. 2007, 60(1): 208-221.

[159] OLIVEIRA R, SANTOS M Y, MOURA PIRES J. 4D+SNN: A Spatio-Temporal Density-ty-Based Clustering Approach with 4D Similarity[C]. IEEE, 2013:1045-1052.

[160] 张敏,常鹏. 试论AIS在海上交通安全管理中的应用及前景[J]. 珠江水运. 2012

(23):73-75.

[161] 张宝晨. ISM 规则与实施[M]. 北京：人民交通出版社，1999.

[162] 李正莲. 港口国监督选船系统研究[D]. 大连：大连海事大学，2008.

[163] CHI Z, JUN S. Automatically optimized and self-evolutional Ship Targeting system for Port State Control[C]IEEE, 2010:791-795.

[164] 魏栋,陈露玲,曾青山,等. 基于神经网络的 FSC 检查选船模型研究[J]. 中国海事. 2010(08):43-46.

[165] XU R, LU Q, LI W, et al. A Risk Assessment System for Improving Port State Control Inspection[C]. IEEE, 2007:818-823.

[166] TOKYO-MOU. MEMORANDUM OF UNDERSTANDING ON PORT STATE CONTROL IN THE ASIA-PACIFIC REGION2013/日期[2013-10-28]. url.

[167] CHANG CHIH-CHUNG, LIN CHIH-JEN. LIBSVM：A Library for Support Vector Machines[J]. ACM Transactions on Intelligent Systems and Technology. 2011, 2: 27-53.

[168] 孙忠华,郑中义,杨婷婷. 港口国监控选船新模型研究[J]. 中国航海. 2012, 35(4):71-75.

[169] IMO. Assessment of the impact and effectiveness of implementation of the ISM Code 2005.

[170] 陈伟炯. 船舶航行安全的可持续改善途径[J]. 交通运输工程学报. 2002(03):115-119.

[171] 徐红明. ISM 规则对船舶海上航行安全的影响[J]. 水运管理. 2006(09):23-26.

[172] 联合国海洋法公约[Z]. 2014.

[173] 张海平. 主管机关授权船级社进行法定检验发证原因探究[J]. 中国水运. 2011(07):12-13.

[174] 交通运输部. 国际船舶安全营运和防止污染管理规则（ISM 规则）2010[S]. 2010.

[175] 郑中义,潘家财,吴兆麟. 安全管理体系运行有效性的评价[J]. 大连海事大学学报. 2003(04):5-8.

[176] 孙书钢. 船舶碰撞事故致因链分析[D]. 大连：大连海事大学，2010.

[177] 张建霞,许乐平,何建海. 从几起案例谈危险品水运事故原因及对策[J]. 航海技术. 2013(05):27-29.

[178] 交通运输部. 交通运输部事故调查报告[R]., 2013.

[179] IMO. MSC 82/5/1：Report of the Correspondence Group on the Safety Level Approach Submitted by Germany and Sweden[R]. London, 2006.

[180] IMO. MSC 83/5/3：Report of the Correspondence Group on Safety Level Approach Submitted by Germany[R]. London, 2007.

[181] IMO. MSC 83/5/10：Level Approach-Safety Levels Submitted by Germany[R]. London, 2007.

[182] IMO. MSC 82/5/7：Comments on the Report of the Correspondence Group on the Safety Level Approach Submitted by the Republic of Korea[R]. London, 2006.

[183] IMO. MSC 83/5/9：Comments on the Report of the Correspondence Group on Safety

Level Approach Submitted by Japan[R]. London, 2007.

[184] IMO. MSC 83/5/16: Comments on the Report of the Correspondence Group on Safety Level Approach Submitted by the Republic of Korea[R]. London, 2007.

[185] IMO. MSC 81/6/3: Safety Level Approach Submitted by Japan[R]. London, 2006.

[186] IMO. MSC 81/6/16: GBS and the RiskSafety Level Approach Submitted by Greece[R]. London, 2006.

[187] IMO. MSC 72/16: Decision Parameters Including Risk Acceptance Criteria Submitted by Norway[R]. London, 2000.

[188] IMO. MSC 81/6/14: Safety Level Approach-Worked Example Submitted by Germany[R]. London, 2007.

[189] IMO. DE57/7/2: Goal-based Standards Safety-level Approach- Exercise Submitted by Germany[R]. London, 2013.

[190] IMO. SSE1/INF5: GBS-SLA: Exercise on Life-saving Appliances Submitted by Germany[R]. London, 2014.

[191] IMO. SSE1/8/2: Goal-based Standards Safety-level Approach-Exercise Submitted by Germany[R]. London, 2014.

[192] IMO. MSC 94/5/2: Future Safety-level Based Standards Submitted by Germany[R]. London, 2014.

[193] IMO. MSC 85/5/3: Definition of SLA and Concept of its Introduction into GBS Submitted by Japan[R]. London, 2008.

[194] IMO. MSC 90/INF8: Consideration on Ship Structural Design Based on the Safety Level Approach Submitted by the Republic of Korea[R]. 2012.

[195] IMO. Revised Guidelines for Formal Safety Assessment (FSA) for Use in the IMO Rule-making Process[S]. 2013.

[196] CIOCA L, IVASCU L. Risk Indicators and Road Accident Analysis for the Period 2012—2016[J]. Sustainability. 2017, 9(9): 1530.

[197] MINEO S, PAPPALARDO G, D URSO A, et al. Event tree analysis for rockfall risk assessment along a strategic mountainous transportation route[J]. Environmental Earth Sciences. 2017, 76(17).

[198] LANDQUIST H, ROSéN L, LINDHE A, et al. Bayesian updating in a fault tree model for shipwreck risk assessment[J]. Science of The Total Environment. 2017, 590-591: 80-91.

[199] ROSSI G, LOMBARDI M, DI MASCIO P. Consistency and stability of risk indicators: The case of road infrastructures[M]. Eng: Int. J. Saf. Secur, 2018.

[200] MORETTI L, CANTISANI G, CARO S. Airport Veer-Off Risk Assessment: An Italian Case Study[R]. 2017.

[201] LEITNER B. A General Model for Railway Systems Risk Assessment with the Use of Railway Accident Scenarios Analysis[J]. Procedia Engineering. 2017, 187: 150-159.

[202] DISTEFANO N, LEONARDI S. RISK ASSESSMENT PROCEDURE FOR CIVIL AIR-

PORT[J]. INTERNATIONAL JOURNAL FOR TRAFFIC AND TRANSPORT ENGINEERING. 2014, 4(1): 62-75.

[203] ZHANG D, YAN X P, YANG Z L, et al. Incorporation of formal safety assessment and Bayesian network in navigational risk estimation of the Yangtze River[J]. Reliability Engineering & System Safety. 2013, 118: 93-105.

[204] IMO. Formal Safety Assessment: FSA-Crude Oil Tankers[S]. 2008.

[205] IMO. General Cargo Ship Safety IACS FSA Study[S]. 2010.

[206] SKJONG R, VANEM E, ENDRESEN. Risk Evaluation Criteria[Z]. 2007.

[207] YANG Z L, WANG J, LI K X. Maritime Safety Analysis in Retrospect[J]. Maritime Policy and Management. 2013, 40(3): 261-277.

[208] GOERLANDT F, MONTEWKA J. Maritime transportation risk analysis: Review and analysis in light of some foundational issues[J]. Reliability Engineering & System Safety. 2015, 138: 115-134.

[209] MONTEWKA J, GOERLANDT F, KUJALA P. On a systematic perspective on risk for formal safety assessment (FSA)[J]. Reliability Engineering & System Safety. 2014, 127: 77-85.

[210] IMO. Introduction to IMO[S]. 2017.

[211] EMSA E M S A. Risk Acceptance Criteria and Risk Based Damage Stability, Final Report, Part 2: Formal Safety Assessment[R]. 2015.

[212] BARALDI P, ZIO E. A Combined Monte Carlo and Possibilistic Approach to Uncertainty Propagation in Event Tree Analysis[J]. Risk Analysis. 2008, 28(5): 1309-1326.

[213] PEDRONI N, ZIO E, FERRARIO E, et al. Hierarchical propagation of probabilistic and non-probabilistic uncertainty in the parameters of a risk model[J]. Computers and Structures. 2013, 126: 199-213.

[214] IMO. Formal Safety Assessment: FSA-Cruise Ships[S]. 2008.

[215] ORGNIZATION I M. Formal Safety Assessment: FSA-Liquefied Natural Gas (LNG) Carriers[S]. 2007.

[216] ZIO E. RISK-INFORMED REGULATION: HANDLING UNCERTAINTY FOR A RATIONAL MANAGEMENT OF SAFETY[J]. Nucl Eng. Technol. 2008, 40: 327-348.

[217] KOMAL. Fuzzy fault tree analysis for patient safety risk modeling in healthcare under uncertainty[J]. Applied Soft Computing. 2015, 37: 942-951.

[218] FLAGE R, BARALDI P, ZIO E, et al. Probability and possibility-based representations of uncertainty in fault tree analysis[J]. Risk Anal. 2013, 33(1): 121-133.

[219] DEOLIVEIRA L W, SETA F D S, DEOLIVEIRA E J. Optimal reconfiguration of distribution systems with representation of uncertainties through interval analysis[J]. International Journal of Electrical Power & Energy Systems. 2016, 83: 382-391.

[220] CURCURù G, GALANTE G M, LAFATA C M. Epistemic uncertainty in fault tree analysis approached by the evidence theory[J]. Journal of Loss Prevention in the Process Industries. 2012, 25(4): 667-676.

[221] KIM Y, M C. Fuzzy Monte Carlo Simulation for Uncertainty and Global Sensitivity Analysis[J]. Sustainability. 2017, 9(4): 539.

[222] SOROUDI A. Possibilistic-Scenario Model for DG Impact Assessment on Distribution Networks in an Uncertain Environment[J]. IEEE Transactions on Power Systems. 2012, 27(3): 1283-1293.

[223] CLAVREUL J, GUYONNET D, TONINI D, et al. Stochastic and epistemic uncertainty propagation in LCA[J]. The International Journal of Life Cycle Assessment. 2013, 18(7): 1393-1403.

[224] RIPAMONTI G, LONATI G, BARALDI P, et al. Uncertainty propagation in a model for the estimation of the ground level concentration of dioxin/furans emitted from a waste gasification plant[J]. Reliability Engineering and System Safety. 2013, 120: 98-105.

[225] GOERLANDT F, RENIERS G. On the assessment of uncertainty in risk diagrams[J]. Safety Science. 2016, 84: 67-77.

[226] FRANTZICH H. Risk analysis and fire safety engineering[J]. Fire Safety Journal. 1998, 31(4): 313-329.

[227] FLAGE R, AVEN T, ZIO E, et al. Concerns, Challenges, and Directions of Development for the Issue of Representing Uncertainty in Risk Assessment[J]. Risk Analysis. 2014, 34(7): 1196-1207.

[228] HU S, FANG Q, XIA H, et al. Formal safety assessment based on relative risks model in ship navigation[J]. Reliability Engineering & System Safety. 2007, 92(3): 369-377.

[229] HSU W, LIAN S, HUANG S. Risk Assessment of Operational Safety for Oil Tankers—A Revised Risk Matrix[J]. Journal of Navigation. 2017, 70(04): 775-788.

[230] HUANG D, CHEN T, WANG M J. A fuzzy set approach for event tree analysis[J]. Fuzzy Sets and Systems. 2001, 118(1): 153-165.

[231] PSARAFTIS H N. Formal Safety Assessment: an updated review[J]. Journal of Marine Science and Technology. 2012, 17(3): 390-402.

[232] IMO. Formal Safety Assessment: FSA-Container Vessels[S]. 2007.

[233] MENG Q, QU X. Uncertainty Propagation in Quantitative Risk Assessment Modeling for Fire in Road Tunnels[J]. IEEE Transactions on Systems, Man, and Cybernetics, Part C (Applications and Reviews). 2012, 42(6): 1454-1464.

[234] MARZOCCHI W, SANDRI L, GASPARINI P, et al. Quantifying probabilities of volcanic events: The example of volcanic hazard at Mount Vesuvius[J]. Journal of Geophysical Research: Solid Earth. 2004, 109(B11).

[235] JOHNSON N L, KEMP A W, KOTZ S. Univariate Discrete Distributions[M]. Hoboken, NJ, USA: John Wiley & Sons, Inc., 2005.

[236] CORPORATION P. @RISK[Z].

[237] VAKILI S, SOBELL L C, SOBELL M B, et al. Using the Timeline Followback to determine time windows representative of annual alcohol consumption with problem drinkers

[J]. Addictive Behaviors. 2008, 33(9): 1123-1130.
[238] BAUDRIT C, DUBOIS D, GUYONNET D. Joint Propagation and Exploitation of Probabilistic and Possibilistic Information in Risk Assessment[J]. IEEE Transactions on Fuzzy Systems. 2006, 14(5): 593-608.
[239] DUBOIS D, BAUDRIT C, GUYONNET D. Postprocessing the Hybrid Method for Addressing Uncertainty in Risk Assessments[J]. Journal of Environmental Engineering. 2005, 131(12): 1750-1754.
[240] IMO. MSC 96/WP.8. Report of the GBS Working Group[S]. 2016.
[241] PRUGH R W. Improved F/N graph presentation and criteria[J]. Journal of Loss Prevention in the Process Industries. 1992, 5(4): 239-247.
[242] COX D C, BAYBUTT P. Limit lines for risk[J]. Nuclear Technology. 1982, 57(3): 320-330.
[243] VRIJLING J K, VANHENGEL W, HOUBEN R J. A framework for risk evaluation[J]. Journal of Hazardous Materials. 1995, 43(3): 245-261.
[244] HORN M E, FULTON N, WESTCOTT M. Measures of societal risk and their potential use in civil aviation[J]. Risk Analysis. 2008, 28(6): 1711-1726.
[245] HIRST I L. Risk assessment A note on F-N curves, expected numbers of fatalities, and weighted indicators of risk[J]. Journal of Hazardous Materials. 1998, 57(1): 169-175.
[246] JONKMAN S N, VRIJLING J K, VANGELDER P H A J. A generalized approach for risk quantification and the relationship between individual and societal risk[C]Proceedings of the ESREL 2006, Estoril, Portugal: 2006:1051-1059.
[247] SCHOFIELD S L. A Framework for Offshore Risk Criteria[J]. Safety and Reliability. 1993, 13(2): 5-18.
[248] MONA K R. Global Risk Assessment of Natural Disasters: new perspectives[R]. 2014.
[249] KANEKO F, ARIMA T, YOSHIDA K, et al. On a novel method for approximation of FN diagram and setting ALARP borders[J]. Journal of Marine Science and Technology. 2015, 20(1): 14-36.
[250] ZHANG Y, LUO Y, PEI J, et al. The establishment of gas accident risk tolerability criteria based on F-N curve in China[J]. Natural Hazards. 2015, 79(1): 263-276.
[251] QU X, YANG Y, LIU Z, et al. Potential crash risks of expressway on-ramps and off-ramps: A case study in Beijing, China[J]. Safety Science. 2014, 70: 58-62.
[252] TRBOJEVIC V M. Risk Criteria for the Shipping Industry[J]. Quality and Reliability Engineering International. 2006, 22(1): 31-40.
[253] SKJONG R, EKNES M L. Societal risk and societal benefits[J]. Risk Decision and Policy. 2002, 7(1): 57-67.
[254] IMO. MSC 72/16. Formal Safety Assessment-Decision parameters including risk acceptance criteria[S]. 2000.

[255] VANEM E. Ethics and fundamental principles of risk acceptance criteria[J]. Safety Science. 2012, 50(4): 958-967.

[256] RODRIGUES M A, AREZES P M, LEãO C P. Defining risk acceptance criteria in occupational settings: A case study in the furniture industrial sector[J]. Safety Science. 2015, 80: 288-295.

[257] CHAKRABARTI U K, PARIKH J K. Risk-based route evaluation against country-specific criteria of risk tolerability for hazmat transportation through Indian State Highways [J]. Journal of Loss Prevention in the Process Industries. 2013, 26(4): 723-736.

[258] EXECUTIVE H A S. Transport fatal accidents and FN-curves: 1967-2001[R]. 2003.

[259] N P, E Z, E F, et al. Comput. Struct[R]. 2013.

[260] K V, K H, K M, et al. Prog. Nucl. Energ[R]. 2014.

[261] P B, E Z. Risk Anal[R], 2008.

[262] S W, H H G, W B B, et al. J. Hydrol[R], 2015.

[263] I B, S S R. Comput. Method[R], 2014.

[264] A S. IEEE T. Power Syst[R], 2012.

[265] J C, D G, D T, et al. Life Cycle Ass[R], 2013.

[266] M B, D P D V. Expert Syst[R], 2012.

[267] H K. Inform. Sciences[R], 1978.

[268] L J N, W K A, S K. Univariate Discrete distributions[R], 2005.

[269] S V, C S L, B S M, et al. Addict. Behav[R], 2008.

[270] J Z, J L. Transport. Plan[J]. Techn. 2016, 39: 1-13.

[271] G P, R S, S E M. Accident Anal. Prev[R], 2010.

[272] M H, E A B, P H L. Accident Anal. Prev[R], 2011.

[273] ENDRINA N, RASERO J C, KONOVESSIS D. Risk analysis for RoPax vessels: A case of study for the Strait of Gibraltar[J]. Ocean Engineering. 2018, 151: 141-151.

[274] DUIJM N J. Recommendations on the use and design of risk matrices[J]. Safety Science. 2015, 76: 21-31.

[275] AVEN T. Improving risk characterisations in practical situations by highlighting knowledge aspects, with applications to risk matrices[J]. Reliability Engineering & System Safety. 2017, 167: 42-48.

[276] LI S, MENG Q, QU X. An Overview of Maritime Waterway Quantitative Risk Assessment Models[J]. Risk Analysis. 2012, 32(3): 496-512.

[277] FERNANDES R, BRAUNSCHWEIG F, LOURENçO F, et al. Combining operational models and data into a dynamic vessel risk assessment tool for coastal regions[J]. Ocean Science Discussions. 2015, 12(4): 1327-1388.

[278] GOERLANDT F, KUJALA P. On the reliability and validity of ship-ship collision risk analysis in light of different perspectives on risk[J]. Safety Science. 2014, 62: 348-365.

[279] DONG Y, FRANGOPOL D M. Probabilistic ship collision risk and sustainability assess-

ment considering risk attitudes[J]. Structural Safety. 2015, 53: 75-84.

[280] HASSEL M, ASBJøRNSLETT B E, HOLE L P. Uncertainty in maritime risk analysis: Extended case study on chemical tanker collisions[J]. Accid. Anal. Prev. 2011, 43: 2053-2063.

[281] MERRICK J R W, VANDORP R. Speaking the Truth in Maritime Risk Assessment[J]. Risk Analysis. 2006, 26(1): 223-237.

[282] ZHAO J, LV J. Comparing prediction methods for maritime accidents[J]. Transportation Planning and Technology. 2016, 39(8): 813-825.

[283] SANKARARAMAN S, MAHADEVAN S. Separating the contributions of variability and parameter uncertainty in probability distributions[J]. Reliability Engineering & System Safety. 2013, 112: 187-199.

[284] TALAVERA A, AGUASCA R, GALVáN B, et al. Application of Dempster-Shafer theory for the quantification and propagation of the uncertainty caused by the use of AIS data [J]. Reliability Engineering & System Safety. 2013, 111: 95-105.

[285] ROHMER J, BAUDRIT C. The use of the possibility theory to investigate the epistemic uncertainties within scenario-based earthquake risk assessments[J]. Natural Hazards. 2011, 56(3): 613-632.

[286] FANG T, LAHDELMA R. Optimization of combined heat and power production with heat storage based on sliding time window method[J]. Applied Energy. 2016, 162: 723-732.

[287] HAAPASAARI P, HELLE I, LEHIKOINEN A, et al. A proactive approach for maritime safety policy making for the Gulf of Finland: Seeking best practices[J]. Marine Policy. 2015, 60: 107-118.

[288] YU Y, ZHU Y, LI S, et al. Time Series Outlier Detection Based on Sliding Window Prediction[J]. Mathematical Problems in Engineering. 2014, 2014: 1-14.

[289] KRISHNAMOORTHY K, PENG J, ZHANG D. Modified large sample confidence intervals for Poisson distributions: Ratio, weighted average, and product of means[J]. Communications in Statistics - Theory and Methods. 2016, 45(1): 83-97.

[290] VINCENT T C, KAZUHIKO K. A Comparison of approaches to enviromental risk management in Japan and The United States[J]. Risk Analysis. 1988, 8(3): 247-260.

[291] ANDRé J C S, LOPES D R. On the use of possibility theory in uncertainty analysis of life cycle inventory[J]. The International Journal of Life Cycle Assessment. 2012, 17 (3): 350-361.

[292] WANG W, LIU G, LIU D. Chebyshev Similarity Match between Uncertain Time Series [J]. Mathematical Problems in Engineering. 2015, 2015: 1-13.

[293] MAIB M A I B. MAIB Annual Report 2016[R]. 2016.

[294] WANG S, HUANG G H, BAETZ B W, et al. Probabilistic Inference Coupled with Possibilistic Reasoning for Robust Estimation of Hydrologic Parameters and Piecewise Characterization of Interactive Uncertainties[J]. Journal of Hydrometeorology. 2016, 17

(4):1243-1260.

[295] SORMUNEN O V, HÄNNINEN M, KUJALA P. Marine traffic, accidents, and underreporting in the Baltic Sea[J]. Sci. J. -Marit. Univ. Szczec. 2016, 46:163-177.

[296] PSARROS G, SKJONG R, EIDE M S. Under-reporting of maritime accidents[J]. Accident Analysis & Prevention. 2010, 42(2):619-625.

[297] HASSEL M, ASBJøRNSLETT B E, HOLE L P. Underreporting of maritime accidents to vessel accident databases[J]. Accident Analysis & Prevention. 2011, 43(6):2053-2063.

[298] YI XIN. NIR:A new weapen of Paris-MOU[J]. The Waterborne Safety. 2009, 8(6):29-32.

[299] EBERHART, SHI Y. Particle swarm optimization: developments, applications and resources[C]. IEEE, 2001:81-86.

[300] EBERHART, SHI Y. Empirical study of particle swam optimization[C]. IEEE International Conference on Evolutionary Computation, Piscataway, USA: IEEE Service Center, 1999:81-86.

[301] 张艳琼. 改进的云自适应粒子群优化算法[J]. 计算机应用研究. 2010(09):3250-3252.

[302] 张文静. 协同粒子群算法及其在多车场路径优化问题中的应用[D]. 上海:华东师范大学, 2010.

[303] 王洪涛,任燕. 基于改进惯性权重的粒子群优化算法[J]. 计算机应用与软件. 2011, 28(10):271-274.

[304] EBERHART, SHI Y. Fuzzy Adaptive Particle Swarm Optimization[C]. Proceedings of the Congress on Evolutionary Computation Seoul, 2001.

[305] 高丙坤,李阳,许明子. 优化粒子群算法在组合供热负荷预测中的应用[J]. 信息与电子工程. 2011(05):655-659.

[306] 楼红飞. 我国港口国监督检查选船机制的研究及实际应用[D]. 大连:大连海事大学, 2008.

[307] 甘旭升,端木京顺,丛伟,等. 基于支持向量机的飞行安全隐患危险性评价[J]. 中国安全生产科学技术. 2010(03):206-210.

[308] 常征,吕靖. 支持向量机在无水港投资风险评价中的应用[J]. 大连海事大学学报. 2012(02):48-50.

[309] SHEVADE S K, KEERTHI S S, BHATTACHARYYA C, et al. Improvements to the SMO algorithm for SVM regression[J]. IEEE Transactions on Neural Networks. 2000, 11(5):1188-1193.

[310] LI Y, VUCETIC B, ZHOU Z, et al. Distributed Adaptive Power Allocation for Wireless Relay Networks[J]. IEEE Transactions on Wireless Communications. 2007, 6(3):948-958.

[311] 吴兆麟. 科学的水上交通安全观之探讨[M]. 大连:大连海事大学出版社, 2006.

[312] 吴兆麟,朱军. 海上交通工程[M]. 大连:大连海事大学出版社, 2004.

[313] 黄曙路. 海上交通安全评价法的选择[J]. 中国水运. 2008(01): 30-31.

[314] Ò内·托姆. 突变论:思想和应用[Z]. 周仲良译. 上海:上海译文出版社, 1989.

[315] 李士勇. 非线性科学与复杂性科学[M]. 哈尔滨:哈尔滨工业大学出版社, 2006.

[316] 湛孔星, 陈国华. 城域突发事故灾害发生机理探索[J]. 中国安全科学学报. 2010 (06): 3-8.

[317] MAO C, DING C G, LEE H. Post-SARS tourist arrival recovery patterns: An analysis based on a catastrophe theory[J]. Tourism Management. 2010, 31(6): 855-861.

[318] PAN YU, ZHANG YONG, WANG ZHI QIANG. Study on Catastrophe Theory of the Starting Process of Coal and Gas Outburst[J]. Chinese Journal of Rock Mechanics and Engineering. 2009, 30(3): 595-612.

[319] XU QIAN. Study on Sustainable Development Based on Catastrophe Theory[J]. Journal of Gansu Lianhe University:Natural Science Edition. 2008, 22(5): 38-40.

[320] SWARUP K S. Artificial neural network using pattern recognition for security assessment and analysis[J]. Neurocomputing. 2008, 71(4-6): 983-998.

[321] ROSSER J B. The rise and fall of catastrophe theory applications in economics: Was the baby thrown out with the bathwater? [J]. Journal of Economic Dynamics and Control. 2007, 31(10): 3255-3280.

[322] 沈斐敏. 交通事故致因分析的突变模型[J]. 福建工程学院学报. 2006(06): 751-754.

[323] 戚杰. 突变理论在环境建模中的应用研究[D]. 武汉:华中科技大学, 2005.

[324] 佘廉, 王超. 水运交通灾害预警管理[M]. 石家庄:河北科学技术出版社, 2004.

[325] 邵哲平, 吴兆麟, 方祥麟. 海上交通系统安全定量评价方法[J]. 大连海事大学学报. 2002(01): 9-12.

[326] 吴兆麟. 水上交通安全观念创新之探讨[J]. 珠江水运. 2006(06): 11-14.

[327] 李红喜, 郑中义, 齐迹. 基于粗糙集的港口通航环境对航行安全的影响[J]. 大连海事大学学报. 2012(02): 8-10.

[328] 刘文远, 陶娟. 基于突变理论的近海船舶航行安全评价[J]. 中国安全科学学报. 1010, 20(10): 113-118.

[329] THOM R. Stuctural stability and morphogenesis[M]. Boulder: Colorado westview press, 1994.

[330] 刘君, 孙立, 吴烽. 海上交通环境安全评价综述[J]. 世界海运. 2005(04): 11-13.

[331] 马文耀, 毕修颖, 曾青山. 海上事故风险评估模型的新方法[J]. 船海工程. 2009 (02): 152-155.

[332] HSU C S, CUTTALU R S. An Unravelling Algorithm for Global Analysis of Dynamical Systems: An Application of Cell-to-Cell Mappings[J]. AEME, J Appl Mech. 1980, 47: 940-948.

[333] 楼永进, 李朝军. 海上交通风险管理对策[J]. 水运管理. 2007(03): 28-30.

[334] 王志明. 船舶保安体系的实施和探讨[J]. 中国航海. 2005(04): 19-22.

[335] MORSE D C, GRIEP K, DEININGER R. Next generation Fans over INMARSAT broad-

band global area network (BGAN)[C]. 23rd DASC Conference, Salt Lake City, UT: IEEE Inc, 2004:11-14.

[336] 陈放. GMDSS 通信设备与业务[M]. 大连：大连海事大学出版社, 2008.

[337] 张国琪. 基于 INMARSAT-C 站的船舶保安报警系统主控单元的研制[J]. 航海技术. 2004(04): 35-38.

[338] IMO. The 2002 Amendments to the International Convention for the Safety of Life at Sea. 1974[S]. London, UK, 2004.

[339] 李建民. 船舶保安报警系统的设计与实现[D]. 大连：大连海事大学, 2006.

[340] THRANE T. TT-3020C, TT-3022C and TT-3022D capsat transceiver software interface reference manual[Z]. Soeborg, Denmark: Thrane & Thrane A S, 199736-89.

[341] 吴军, 李鹤鸣. 船舶保安警报系统的设计研究[J]. 船海工程. 2006, 35(6): 110-112.

[342] 陈秋妹. 论船舶安全与船舶保安的关系[J]. 中国航海. 2004(01): 40-42.

[343] 吴兆麟. 船舶避碰与海上安全研究[M]. 大连：大连海事大学出版社, 2006.

[344] 张连明, 陈志刚, 邓晓衡. 一种基于信息熵的 Internet 宏观行为模型研究[J]. 计算机工程与应用. 2004(19): 33-37.

[345] SHANNON C E, WEAVER W. The Mathematical Theory of Communication[M]. Carbondale: University of Illinois Press, 1963.

[346] 刘兴国. 企业耗散结构模型分析[J]. 工业工程与管理. 2001, 6(3): 33-36.

[347] MASSOTTE. New Concepts and Approaches for the Management of Complex Production System[M]. Mons: FUCAM Press, 1993.

[348] 李晓争. 基于解释结构模型的铁路智能运输系统体系结构研究[D]. 北京：北京交通大学, 2007.

[349] SZWAST Z, SIENIUTYCZ S, SHINER J S. Complexity principle of extremality in evolution of living organisms by information-theoretic entropy[J]. Chaos, Solitons and Fractals. 2002, 13(9): 1871-1888.

[350] 席酉民, 肖宏文, 王洪涛. 和谐管理理论的提出及其原理的新发展[J]. 管理学报. 2005(01): 23-32.

[351] 孙振武, 张自慧. 耗散结构理论视域下和谐社会的特征与理念[J]. 南昌大学学报（人文社会科学版）. 2010(01): 43-47.

[352] WANG LI, TIAN SHUI-CHENG, WANG XIAO-NING. Application of connection entropy in coal mine safety evaluation[C] Progress in Safety Science and Technology: The Proceedings of the 2006 International Symposium on Safety Science and Technology, Beijing: Chemical Industry Press, 2006:102-105.

[353] XUPING W, HONGYAN S, XIAODONG L. Research into Assessment for Emergency Capability of Hazardous Materials Transportation Based on Fuzzy Mathematics[J]. International Journal of Innovative Computing, Information and Control. 2008, 4(10): 2689-2696.

[354] PROCEDURES G F H E. Third Edition by Center for Chemical Process Safety[M].

American Institute of Chemical Engineers, Inc, 2008.
[355] L 丁·奥斯本,里尔·鲁宾斯坦. 博弈论教程[M]. 北京:北京社会科学出版社,2000.
[356] 李爽,宋学锋. 我国煤矿企业安全监管的内外部博弈分析[J]. 中国矿业大学学报. 2010(04):610-616.
[357] 杨青,施亚能. 基于演化博弈的食品安全监管分析[J]. 武汉理工大学学报(信息与管理工程版). 2011(04):670-672.
[358] 陈亚睿,田立勤,杨扬. 云计算环境下基于动态博弈论的用户行为模型与分析[J]. 电子学报. 2011(08):1818-1823.
[359] RENIERS G, DULLAERT W, KAREL S. Domino effects within a chemical cluster: A game-theoretical modeling approach by using Nash-equilibrium[J]. Journal of Hazardous Materials. 2009, 167(1-3):289-293.
[360] 王永刚,王燕. 人为因素的多维事故原因分析模型[J]. 交通运输工程学报. 2008(02):96-100.
[361] 郑中义,黄忠国,吴兆麟. 港口交通事故与环境要素关系[J]. 交通运输工程学报. 2006, 6(1):119-126.
[362] 薛一东. 人为失误与船舶引航事故的预防[J]. 中国航海. 2005, 3:28-32.
[363] SUN L, WANG D. A new rational-based optimal design strategy of ship structure based on multi-level analysis and super-element modeling method[J]. Journal of Marine Science and Application. 2011, 10(3):272-280.
[364] 胡开业,丁勇,王宏伟,等. 船舶在随机横浪中的全局稳定性[J]. 哈尔滨工程大学学报. 2011(06):719-723.
[365] 尼科利斯 G,普利高津 L. 非平衡系统的自组织[M]. 北京:科学出版社,1986.
[366] 高隆昌. 系统学原理[M]. 北京:科学出版社,2010.
[367] 李伟,高隆昌. 二象对偶论及其对偶分析图[J]. 数学的实践与认识. 2009(19):174-179.
[368] 李建民,齐迹,郑中义,等. 基于熵与耗散理论的海上危险化学品运输系统[J]. 大连海事大学学报. 2013(01):85-88.
[369] 桐谷伸夫. 航行シミユレーシヨンにおける交通流モデルと辐辏度[C]. 日本航海学会论文集,87号. 东京:日本航海学会,1992:131-137.
[370] 吴兆麟,王逢辰,赵劲松. 海损事故统计分析与船舶安全综合评判[J]. 大连海运学院学报. 1991(03):240-246.
[371] 井上欣三. 危险の切近に对して操船者が感じる危险感の定量化モデル[C] 日本航海学会论文集,98号. 东京:日本航海学会,1998:235-245.
[372] 方祥麟,王逢辰,吴兆麟. 船舶交通安全评价方法:安全指数法[J]. 大连海运学院学报. 1992(04):337-341.
[373] 施阳. MATLAB 语言工具箱:TOOLBOX 实用指南[M]. 西北工业大学出版社,1998.
[374] 姜次平. 船舶阻力[M]. 上海:上海交通大学出版社,1985.

[375] GOODWIN E M, KEMP J F. The Optimal Speed of Ships[J]. Journal of Navigation. 1979, 32(03): 291-308.

[376] 洪碧光,王逢辰,古文贤,等. 安全航速与航速风险性分析[Z]. 19959.

[377] HOOFT J P. The Behaviour of a Ship in Head Waves at Restricted Water Depths[R]. 1974.

[378] 贵岛滕郎. Squatの简易推定法にについて[J]. 西部造船会会报. 1990, 80.

[379] JACKISBESTER. Bulk Carriers-A Changing World[J]. Seaways. 1996, 9: 45-49.

[380] 王逢辰. 船舶在大风浪区航行中安危的估计[C]. 1995—1997 中国航海学会海洋船舶驾驶委员会海浪与船舶航行安全及防台风经验研讨会论文集, 1997:169-174.

[381] 赵怀森. 台风危险大风海区的避离[C]. 中国航海学会海洋船舶驾驶专业委员会海浪与船舶航行安全及防台经验研讨会论文集, 1998:169-174.

[382] 沈华,邹开其,黄鼎良. 尾斜浪中操船危险性综合评估[J]. 大连海事大学学报. 1997(04): 13-16.

[383] FOXWELL D. Structure Question[J]. Safety at Sea. 1996, 1.

[384] KEITH D. Improving Tanker and Bulker Safety[J]. Safety at Sea. 1993, 8: 20-22.

[385] 乌志强. 由于货物导致的船损事故分析[J]. 青海远洋船员学院学报. 1996, 3: 17-20.

[386] 潘一航. 对船舶在大风浪中避免谐摇的探讨:图表和计算机程序的应用[J]. 上海海运学院学报. 1988(Z1): 21-36.

[387] 曹振海. 随浪稳性的核算方法[J]. 舰船性能研究. 1993, 3: 29-35.

[388] 李文虎. "大舜"轮悲剧给船长们的启示[J]. 世界海运. 2000(03): 17-19.

[389] 王凤武,贾传荥. 船舶抗风浪等级的研究[J]. 大连海事大学学报. 1998(01): 62-64.

[390] KINZO INOUE, KIYOSHI HARA. Relations between the Number of Observational Days and the Estimation of Averag e Annual Daily Traffic Volume[J]. The Journal of Japan Institute of Navigation. 1973: 50.

[391] KINZO INOUE, KIYOSHI HARA. Relations between the Number of Observational Days and the Estimation of Average Annual Daily Traffic Volume[J]. The Journal of Japan Institute of Navigation. 1975, 46: 92-96.

[392] SHUNTAOWAN, AKIJ SHINKAI. Statistical prediction of deck wetness on an ocean-going ship[J]. The Journal of Japan Institute of Shipbuilding. 1996, 180: 151-158.

[393] Hiroyuki SADAKANE. A study on the criterion for the safety navigation of a fore-bridge-ship in rough sea[J]. The Journal of Japan Institute of Navigation. 2001, 104: 121-133.

[394] CHOL-SEONG KIM. A study on the criterion for the safety navigation of fore-bridge-ship in rough sea based on a breakage avoidance of the wheelhouse front glass in irregular head waves[J]. The Journal of Japan Institute of Navigation. 2001, 105: 1-9.

[395] 王云天. 大风浪中渔船的安全性评估与决策[D]. 大连:大连海事大学, 1995.

[396] 杨保璋,石爱国. 大风浪中多因素优化航向航速选择[J]. 中国航海. 1991, 38

(1): 30-40.

[397] SUSUMU KUW ASHIMA. The actual state of ship encounter wave and ship's motions - (Ⅱ)- successive measurement at a container ship in North Pacific Ocean[J]. The Journal of Japan Institute of Navigation. 1994, 92: 167-175.

[398] SUSUMU KUW ASHIMA. The actual state of ship encounter wave and ship's motions-(Ⅲ)- fluctuation of engine output and propeller revolution[J]. The Journal of Japan Institute of Navigation. 1996, 96: 157-165.

[399] 陶尧森. 船舶耐波性[M]. 上海: 上海交通大学出版社, 1985.

[400] SUSUMU KUW ASHIM A. The actual state of ship encounter wave and ship's motions——a trial assemble of voyage recorder[J]. The Journal of Japan Institute of Navigation. 1991, 86: 153-160.

[401] 彭应生. 船舶耐波性基础[M]. 北京: 国防工业出版社, 1989.

[402] 姚杰, 王云天, 古文贤. 舰船耐波性指数的神经网络模糊评价方法[J]. 航海技术. 1999, 20(1): 20-23.

[403] KINZO INOUE. Assessment of the correlation of safety between ship handling and environment[J]. The Journal of Japan Institute of Navigation. 1996, 95: 147-153.

[404] 邵哲平, 李连亭, 吕江海, 等. 南半球西风带操船环境危险度的安全评价[J]. 中国航海. 2000(02): 3-7.

[405] 邵哲平, 吴兆麟, 方祥麟, 等. 基于模糊推理系统的操船环境危险度的评价方法[J]. 大连海事大学学报. 1999(04): 16-20.

[406] JANG J S R. Neuro-fuzzy and soft computing[M]. USA. International Edition, 1997.

[407] 李建明. ISM 规则应用教程[M]. 北京: 人民交通出版社, 1999: 51-116.

[408] 李育平, 张宝晨. 如何建立安全管理体系[M]. 大连: 大连海事大学出版社, 1995.

[409] 北方交通大学. 运输安全保障及信息系统的研究报告[R]. 1995.

[410] 郑中义, 吴兆麟. 船舶避碰的模糊决策[J]. 大连海事大学学报. 1996, 22(2): 5-8.

[411] 郭其顺. 世界海运事故的现状与原因分析[J]. 中国船检. 2000, 2(2): 43-45.

[412] ROBERT W R, JAMES L R, THOMAS D. Incorporating Risk Assessment and Benefit-Cost Analysis[J]. Risk Analysis. 1988, 8(3): 415-420.

[413] 向阳, 朱永峨, 陈国权, 等. FSA 方法在未来船舶工程和航运安全管理中的应用前景[J]. 中国船检. 2000(01): 39-42.

[414] 向阳, 朱永峨, 陈国权, 等. 风险分析与综合安全评估(FSA)[J]. 中国船检. 1999(01): 35-36.

[415] 杜鹏, 李世奎. 中国农业灾害风险评价与对策[M]. 北京: 气象出版社, 1984.

[416] CAPTAINPAULCANTER. Formal safety assessment[J]. CBE. 1997, 35(9): 15-19.

[417] 王凤武, 郑中义, 吴兆麟. 大风浪船舶安全航行的研究综述[J]. 大连海事大学学报. 2002(04): 60-63.

[418] 王凤武, 吴兆麟, 郑中义. 大风浪海损事故的灰色关联分析[J]. 大连海事大学学报. 2003(04): 31-34.

[419] 黄志. 对船舶安全状况的评价及研究[D]. 大连:大连海事大学,2000.

[420] 李洪兴,汪群,段钦治. 工程模糊数学方法及应用[M]. 天津:天津科学技术出版社,1993.

[421] 刘大刚,郑中义,吴兆麟. 大风浪中船舶安全性评估方法综述[J]. 交通运输工程学报. 2003(01):114-118.

[422] 谭跃进. 系统工程原理[M]. 长沙:国防科技大学出版社,1999.

[423] 张道余. 散货船防范大风浪事故探讨[Z]. 200627.

[424] OZGUC O,DAS P K,BARLTROP N. A comparative study on the structural integrity of single and double side skin bulk carriers under collision damage[J]. Marine Structures. 2005,18(7):511-547.

[425] 王运龙,纪卓尚,林焰. 散货船现状及其发展趋势[J]. 船舶工程. 2006(01):58-61.

[426] 刘大刚,徐东华,吴兆麟. 大风浪中航行船舶的危险度估算模型[J]. 交通运输工程学报. 2005(03):83-86.

[427] 赵京军. 大风浪中载货干散货船安全评价研究[D]. 大连:大连海事大学,2008.

[428] M M G,R K R,张伏中,等. 模糊集理论及其应用评述[J]. 系统工程与电子技术. 1981(10):13-22.

[429] 郭振邦,张晋峰,胡云昌. 现役散货船纵向构件蚀耗率的概率估算[J]. 船舶工程. 2001(03):16-20.

[430] SADKANE H,KIM C-S,TAKAKI T. A study on the criterion for the safety navigation of a fore-bridge-ship in rough sea. Based on a breakage condition of the wheelhouse front glass due to the shipped water[J]. Journal of Japan Institute of Navigation. 2001,104:125-131.

[431] 沈华. 船舶稳性与强度计算[M]. 大连:大连海事大学出版社,2001.

[432] 吴坚,梁昌勇,李文年. 基于主观与客观集成的属性权重求解方法[J]. 系统工程与电子技术. 2007(03):383-387.

[433] 张文修,吴伟志,梁吉业. 粗糙集理论与方法[M]. 北京:科学出版社,2001.

[434] 王国胤,姚一豫,于洪. 粗糙集理论与应用研究综述[J]. 计算机学报. 2009,32(7):1229-1246.

[435] 刘斌,陈钉均. 基于粗糙集和遗传算法的道路交通事故分析[J]. 兰州交通大学学报. 2010(01):69-71.

[436] 李焱,郑宝友,陈汉宝. 港口通航环境对船舶航行安全的影响分析及评价[J]. 水道港口. 2007(05):342-347.

[437] 叶先锋. 港口环境对船舶安全航行的影响及安全评价[J]. 中国水运(下半月). 2009(05):57-58.

[438] 徐东华,吴兆麟. 基于粗糙集数据约简的海事事故致因研究[J]. 大连海事大学学报. 2009(03):37-39.

[439] XU DONGHUA,WUZHAOLIN. Rough set based study of the competency for chinese seafarers[C]. Proceedings of the 2008 International Conferece on Intelligent Computa-

tion Technology and Automation, Washington DC: IEEE Computer Society, 2008:806-810.

[440] PAWLAK Z, SKOWRON A. Rudiments of rough sets[J]. Information Sciences. 2007, 177(1):3-27.

[441] UK D F T O. Promoting Connectivity between the Capital Cities of the UK[2010-09-10].

[442] NEWSOUTHWALES A. Passenger Transport Act 1990 No.39.

[443] TRANSPORTATION N C D O. SouthCarolina Strategic Corridor System Plan 2010.

[444] 陆卓明. 世界经济地理结构[M]. 北京:中国物价出版社, 1995.

[445] 国家统计局. 2010年中国统计公报(国家统计局).

[446] 陈世光,赵小燕. 我国进口铁矿石市场分析及对策[J]. 水运管理. 2009(03):13-16.

[447] 李杰. 全球战略海峡通道纵览[J]. 决策与信息. 2010(11):73-76.

[448] 李兵. 国际战略通道问题研究[M]. 北京:当代世界出版社, 2009.

[449] 中华人民共和国交通部交通委员会. 水上交通安全20年[M]. 北京:人民交通出版社, 2001.

[450] 傅立. 灰色系统理论及其应用[M]. 北京:科学技术文献出版社, 1992.

[451] 吴兆麟. 海事调查与分析[M]. 大连:大连海运学院出版社, 1993.

[452] 郑中义,吴兆麟,杨丹. 港口船舶事故致因的灰色关联分析模型[J]. 大连海事大学学报. 1997(02):62-65.

[453] 谢季坚,刘承平. 模糊数学方法及其应用[M]. 武汉:华中科技大学出版社, 2004.

[454] 郑中义. 船舶自动避碰决策系统的研究[D]. 大连:大连海事大学, 2000.

[455] 吴兆麟,郑中义. 时间碰撞危险度及模型[J]. 大连海事大学学报. 2001(02):1-5.

[456] 何晖光,吴兆麟,方祥麟. 海上交通环境的综合评价方法[J]. 大连海事大学学报. 1997(03):37-42.

[457] 王芳. 主成分分析与因子分析的异同比较及应用[J]. 统计教育. 2003, 5(5):14-17.

[458] 于建英,何旭宏. 数据统计分析与Spss应用[M]. 北京:人民邮政出版社, 2004.

[459] 任中奇. 多元统计分析在多指标综合评价问题中的应用[J]. 辽宁大学学报:自然科学版. 1994, 13(1):97-100.

[460] 岑况. 因子分析中变量和样品空间的统一[J]. 地质科技情报. 1994, 13(4):93-97.

[461] 郑士源. 国际干散货航运市场的评价[J]. 交通运输工程学报. 2004, 4(4):89-92.

[462] 藤井弥平. 海上交通工学[M]. 东京:海文堂, 1981.

[463] BRANCH M A I. MAIB Annual Report[R]. 2007.

[464] 彭传圣. 港口计算机模拟技术应用与模拟语言的发展[J]. 港工技术. 1998, 35(3):39-42.

[465] 冯蕴雯,宣建林,国志刚. 飞行器多因素突发性灾难事故的预防及其算法[J]. 航空学报. 2007,28(1):146-150.

[466] 王行仁. 飞行实时仿真系统及技术[M]. 北京:北京航空航天大学出版社,1998.

[467] 翟玉强. 基于三自由度飞行器模型的控制方法研究[D]. 南京:南京理工大学,2007.

[468] 王静瑞. 军用虚拟现实模拟显示器[J]. 现代显示. 1997,12(3):223-225.

[469] 郝勇,童飞. 水上交通事故致因理论探讨[J]. 船海工程. 2006(02):83-86.

[470] 夏良云,魏智勇. 水上交通事故系统要素分析法探讨[J]. 船海工程(S1). 2001:22-26.

[471] 李国定,江海学. 事故树分析法在海事分析中的应用[J]. 集美大学学报(自然科学版). 2005(03):270-274.

[472] HECKERMAN D. A Tutorial onLEARNING WITH BAYESIAN NETWORKS[J]. Technical Report MSR-TR-95-06. 1995.

[473] 张连文,郭海鹏. 贝叶斯网引论[M]. 北京:科学出版社,2006.

[474] 胡玉胜,涂序彦,崔晓瑜,等. 基于贝叶斯网络的不确定性知识的推理方法[J]. 计算机集成制造系统-CIMS. 2001(12):65-68.

[475] DAVIDHECKERMAN. Bayesian Networks for Data Mining[J]. Data Mining and KNOWLEDGE DISCOVERY. 1997,1:79-119.

[476] 林士敏,田凤占,陆玉昌. 贝叶斯网络的建造及其在数据采掘中的应用[J]. 清华大学学报(自然科学版). 2001(01):49-52.

[477] 张少中. 基于贝叶斯网络的知识发现与决策应用研究[D]. 大连:大连理工大学,2003.

[478] 俞娉婷,刘振元,陈学广. 基于贝叶斯网络的一种事故分析模型[J]. 中国安全生产科学技术. 2006(04):45-50.

[479] 罗帆,陈小佳,顾必冲. 基于贝叶斯网络的航空灾害成因机理探析[J]. 北京航空航天大学学报. 2005(08):934-938.

[480] 秦小虎,刘利,张颖. 一种基于贝叶斯网络模型的交通事故预测方法[J]. 计算机仿真. 2005(11):230-232.

[481] 王发智. 基于贝叶斯网络的交通突发事件态势评估技术[D]. 大连:大连理工大学,2006.

[482] MARSH W,BEARFIELD G. Using Bayesian Networks to Model Accident Causation in the UK Railway Industry:International Conference on Probabilistic Safety Assessment[Z]. Berlin:2004.

[483] P TRUCCO,E CARGO,F RUGGERI,et al. A Bayesian Belief Network modeling of organizational factors in risk analysis A case study in maritime transportation Reliability. Engineering and System Safety[J]. Engineering and system Safety. 2008,93:823-834.

[484] PETER FRIES,BOCERUP SIMONSON. GRACAT:software for grounding and collision risk analysis[J]. Marine Structures. 2008,15:383-401.

[485] FSA MIAN TECHNICAL REPORT of DNV Report 2003-0277[R].
[486] Consideration on utilization of Bayesian network at step 3 of FSA Evaluation of the effect of ECDIS, ENC and Track control by using Bayesian network Submitted by Japan. [J]. Maritime Safety Committee 81st session Agenda item 18. 2006.